WESTFIELD MEDIEVAL STUDIES

Volume 3

John Gower, Trilingual Poet
Language, Translation, and Tradition

John Gower wrote in three languages – Latin, French, and English – and their considerable and sometimes competing significance in fourteenth-century England underlies his trilingualism. The essays collected in this volume start from Gower as trilingual poet, exploring Gower's negotiations between them – his adaptation of French sources into his Latin poetry, for example – as well as the work of medieval translators who made Gower's French poetry available in English. 'Translation' is also considered more broadly, as a 'carrying over' (its etymological sense) between genres, registers, and contexts, with essays exploring Gower's acts of translation between the idioms of varied literary and non-literary forms; and further essays investigate Gower's writings from literary, historical, linguistic and codicological perspectives. Overall, the volume bears witness to Gower's literary merit and his importance to English literary history, and increases our understanding of French and Latin literature composed in England.

WESTFIELD MEDIEVAL STUDIES

ISSN 1752–5659

Editorial Board

R.S. Allen (General Editor)
Julia Boffey
Virginia Davis
† Alan Deyermond
Alfred Hiatt
Peter Orton
Mr Brian Place
Silvia Ranawake
Miri Rubin
Rosa Vidal Doval

Westfield Medieval Studies is an interdisciplinary series, publishing scholarly monographs, editions, and collections of broad comparative interest on the culture of Europe (and other areas in exceptional cases) from the early Middle Ages to the late fifteenth century.

Proposals or queries should be sent in the first instance to the editor at the address given below; all submissions will receive prompt and informed consideration.

Rosamund Allen, School of English and Drama, Queen Mary, University of London, Mile End Road, London, E1 4NS

Previously Published
1 *The York Mystery Cycle and the Worship of the City,* Pamela M. King
2 *The N-Town Play: Drama and Liturgy in Medieval East Anglia,* Penny Granger

John Gower, Trilingual Poet
Language, Translation, and Tradition

Edited by
ELISABETH DUTTON
WITH JOHN HINES AND R. F. YEAGER

D. S. BREWER

© Contributors 2010

All Rights Reserved. Except as permitted under current legislation no part of this work may be photocopied, stored in a retrieval system, published, performed in public, adapted, broadcast, transmitted, recorded or reproduced in any form or by any means, without the prior permission of the copyright owner

First published 2010
D. S. Brewer, Cambridge

ISBN 978 1 84384 250 7

D. S. Brewer is an imprint of Boydell & Brewer Ltd
PO Box 9, Woodbridge, Suffolk IP12 3DF, UK
and of Boydell & Brewer Inc.
668 Mt Hope Avenue, Rochester, NY 14620, USA
website: www.boydellandbrewer.com

A CIP catalogue record for this book is available
from the British Library

The publisher has no responsibility for the continued existence or accuracy of URLs for external or third-party internet websites referred to in this book, and does not guarantee that any content on such websites is, or will remain, accurate or appropriate.

This publication is printed on acid-free paper

Printed in Great Britain by
CPI Antony Rowe, Chippenham and Eastbourne

Contents

Editorial Note	viii
Acknowledgements	ix
Abbreviations	xi
Introduction Elisabeth Dutton	1

Gower at Source

1. Southwark Gower: Augustinian Agencies in Gower's Manuscripts and Texts – Some Prolegomena
   Jean-Pascal Pouzet — 11

Gower Looking East

2. The Place of Egypt in Gower's *Confessio Amantis*
   Ethan Knapp — 26
3. Topical and Tropological Gower: Invoking Armenia in the *Confessio Amantis*
   Carolyn P. Collette — 35

Politics, Prophecy and Apocalypse

4. Saving History: Gower's Apocalyptic and the New Arion
   Elliot Kendall — 46
5. Gower's Poetics of the Literal
   Robert R. Edwards — 59
6. Romance, Popular Style and the *Confessio Amantis*: Conflict or Evasion?
   George Shuffelton — 74
7. John Gower: Prophet or Turncoat?
   Nigel Saul — 85
8. The Parliamentary Source of Gower's *Cronica Tripertita* and Incommensurable Styles
   David R. Carlson — 98

Science, Law and Economy

9. John Gower's Legal Advocacy and 'In Praise of Peace'
   Candace Barrington — 112
10. Se-duction and Sovereign Power in Gower's *Confessio Amantis* Book V
    Andreea Boboc — 126

11.	The Fifteen Stars, Stones and Herbs: Book VII of the *Confessio Amantis* and its Afterlife Tamara F. O'Callaghan	139
12.	'Of the parfite medicine': *Merita Perpetuata* in Gower's Vernacular Alchemy Stephanie L. Batkie	157
13.	Inside Out in Gower's Republic of Letters Karla Taylor	169
14.	Gower's Business: Artistic Production of Cultural Capital and the Tale of Florent Brian Gastle	182

Sin, Love, Sex and Gender

15.	Genius and Sensual Reading in the *Vox Clamantis* Matthew Irvin	196
16.	Irony v. Paradox in the *Confessio Amantis* Peter Nicholson	206
17.	Sinning Against Love in *Confessio Amantis* J. A. Burrow	217
18.	The Woman's Response in John Gower's *Cinkante Balades* Holly Barbaccia	230
19.	Rich Words: Gower's *Rime Riche* in Dramatic Action Kim Zarins	239
20.	Florent's *Mariage sous la potence* Richard F. Green	254
21.	Why did Gower Write the *Traitié*? Cathy Hume	263

Gower 'Translated'

22.	Rival Poets: Gower's *Confessio* and Chaucer's *Legend of Good Women* John M. Bowers	276
23.	Reassessing Gower's Dream-Visions Andrew Galloway	288
24.	John Gower's French and His Readers R. F. Yeager	304
25.	Conjuring Gower in *Pericles* Martha Driver	315

Bibliography	327
Index	353

To the memory of Alan Deyermond

Editorial Note

Unless otherwise specified, citations from Gower are taken from G. C. Macaulay, ed., *The Complete Works of John Gower*, 4 vols (London, 1899–1902)
Vol. I *The French Works*
Vols II and III *The English Works*
Vol. IV *The Latin Works*

Translations from *Mirour de l'Omme* are taken from John Gower, *Mirour de l'Omme (The Mirror of Mankind)*, trans. William Burton Wilson, rev. Nancy Wilson Van Baak (East Lansing, MI, 1992).

Translations from *Vox Clamantis* are taken from *The Major Latin Works of John Gower*, trans. Eric Stockton (Seattle, WA, 1962).

Translations from Latin works other than *Vox Clamantis* are taken from *John Gower. The Minor Latin Works*, ed. and trans. R.F. Yeager *(with* 'In Praise of Peace', edited by M. Livingston) (Kalamazoo, MI, 2005).

Unless otherwise specified, citations from Chaucer are taken from *The Riverside Chaucer*, gen. ed. Larry D. Benson (Boston, MA, 3rd edn., 1987).

Acknowledgements

The conference which inspired this volume, '1408–2008: The Age of Gower', was jointly organised by the John Gower Society, Cardiff University Centre for the Study of Medieval Society and Culture, and the Department of English at Queen Mary, University of London. It was hosted by QMUL in July 2008.

The editors acknowledge the support of the Department of English, Queen Mary, University of London, in securing a subvention for the publication of the volume.

Abbreviations

AND	*Anglo-Norman Dictionary*
BL	British Library
Companion	Siân Echard, ed., *A Companion to Gower* (Cambridge, 2004).
CR	*Chaucer Review*
EETS	Early English Text Society
EHR	*English Historical Review*
ELH	*English Literary History*
es	extra series
ES	*English Studies*
ESTC	*English Short Title Catalogue*
JEGP	*Journal of English and German Philology*
JGN	*John Gower Newsletter*
JMEMS	*Journal of Medieval and Early Modern Studies*
JMH	*Journal of Medieval History*
Ker	N. R. Ker, *Medieval Libraries of Great Britain*, 2nd edn (London, 1964).
Ker Suppl.	A. G. Watson, *Medieval Libraries of Great Britain. Supplement to the Second Edition* (London, 1987).
LALME	A. McIntosh, M. L. Samuels and M. Benskin, *A Linguistic Atlas of Late Medieval English*, 4 vols (Aberdeen: Aberdeen University Press, 1986).
LSE	*Leeds Studies in English*
MÆ	*Medium Ævum*
Macaulay	G. C. Macaulay, ed., *The Complete Works of John Gower*, 4 vols (London, 1899–1902)
MED	*Middle English Dictionary*
MLN	*Modern Language Notes*
MLR	*Modern Language Review*
MP	*Modern Philology*
MSt	*Medieval Studies*
NML	*New Medieval Literatures*
ODNB	*Oxford Dictionary of National Biography*
Peck	John Gower, *Confessio Amantis*, ed. Russell A. Peck with Latin translations by Andrew Galloway, 3 vols (Kalamazoo, 2000–2004)
PL	*Patrologiae: Cursus Completus Series Latina*, ed. J. P. Migne (Paris, 1844–73)
PMLA	*Proceedings of the Modern Language Association of America*
PQ	*Philological Quarterly*
RES	*Review of English Studies*
SAC	*Studies in the Age of Chaucer*

ABBREVIATIONS

SC	F. Madan, H. H. E. Craster and N. Denholm-Young, *A Summary Catalogue of Western Manuscripts in the Bodleian Library at Oxford*, 7 vols (Oxford, 1895–1937).
SP	*Studies in Philology*
SQ	*Shakespeare Quarterly*
TLS	*Times Literary Supplement*
TRHS	*Transactions of the Royal Historical Society*
YAJ	*Yorkshire Archaeological Journal*
YoES	*Yearbook of English Studies*

Introduction

ELISABETH DUTTON

2008 marked the 600th anniversary of the death of the poet John Gower, the author of major works in French, Latin and English, and highly respected, on a level with Chaucer, in the centuries following his death. Since the late seventeenth century, and particularly for academic literary critics of the twentieth century, however, Chaucer's pre-eminence has been invidious to the study of Gower. It is only recently that a body of scholarship has begun to recognize the individual character and importance of Gower's literary influence and to re-establish his reputation. Gower has more often been discussed only for purposes of comparison by Chaucerians, or as a contextual figure in studies of Ricardian literature. It has consequently been difficult both to understand and to appreciate the shape and significance of Gower's literary achievement and influence fully.

This volume draws together essays by established medievalists and up-and-coming medieval scholars which, through their collective focus on Gower, provide a thorough exploration of the voices of this significant poet and the discourses in which he participated. This has long been needed. Inspiration for the volume comes from the hugely successful conference, *1408–2008: The Age of Gower*, which was held at Queen Mary University of London, in July 2008: the conference was the first international congress devoted exclusively to Gower and attracted a large group of leading scholars from around the world, testifying to the dynamic interest in rigorous and constructive Gower research. A number of these scholars have been invited to contribute to the present volume.

Most of the essays contained in this volume are primarily literary in focus, but there are also a number of specialized studies involving translation theory, palaeography and bibliography. Gower's French and Latin works, as well as his English, are generously covered: the book is ordered in such a way as to avoid the ghettoization of Gower's French and Latin works, and to encourage comparison between them and the *Confessio Amantis*, which is generally more familiar to English-speaking Gower scholars.

The considerable and sometimes competing significance of French, Latin and English in fourteenth-century England underlies Gower's trilingual output, and essays in the volume consider Gower's negotiations between them – his adaptation of French sources into his Latin poetry, for example – as well as the work of medieval translators who made Gower's French poetry available in English. 'Translation' can also be considered more broadly, as a 'carrying over' (its etymological sense) between genres, registers, contexts. Kurt Olsson writes that

Gower's doctrine is 'translated' not merely out of French *dits* written in his own century, but out of such works as were more certainly familiar to English courtly audiences: the Bible, the *Roman de la Rose*, political treatises such as Aegidius Romanus' *De regimine principum*, books of vices and virtues, encyclopedias *de proprietatibus rerum*, occasional 'tretes amoireux & moralitez & de caroll', as well as collections of tales and 'histories' written by authors ranging from Ovid to Godfrey of Viterbo.[1]

Olssen argues that Gower's selection and re-contextualization of the richly varied sources of his works constitutes an act of translation by which Gower 'redefined his culture'. Essays in this volume will consider Gower's acts of translation between English, French and Latin and between the idioms of varied literary and non-literary forms: the volume as a whole will demonstrate the cultural re-definitions which Gower's trilingual translations of literary traditions and languages achieved.

*

The precise year of Gower's birth is unknown, but he seems to have been born after the accession of Edward III in 1327.[2] Though 'Gower' is not an uncommon name in fourteenth-century England, John Gower can be connected to a Sir Robert Gower who died in 1349 and was buried in Brabourne, south-east Kent, and to a Gower family in Langbargh, North Yorkshire: the same coat of arms which adorns the poet's tomb is to be found on the tombs of these other Gowers. Records associated with these Gowers indicate that the poet was from a family which was itself gentry, but which had high connections, and which was advanced through military service to significant noblemen such as the Earl of Athol, who granted Sir Robert Gower property in Suffolk.

John Gower held property in East Anglia and Kent, and invested in further property as a source of security and income: his profession appears to have been the law. It is possible that he retired from this profession rather early and dedicated himself to writing; it has been suggested that he withdrew to the priory of St Mary Overey, Southwark, to write.[3] But whatever the date and nature of his association with the priory, Gower's works reveal an ongoing and direct engagement with the national politics of his day: his revisions to his English *Confessio Amantis*, for example, show him shifting his allegiance from Richard II, who had been his patron, to Henry, Earl of Derby, the future King Henry IV.

Gower married Agnes Groundolf in 1398, when he was in his sixties, and does not appear to have left any children. Agnes tended to him for the last ten years of his life, and was one of the six executors of his will, in

---

[1] Kurt Olsson, *John Gower and the Structures of Conversion: A Reading of the 'Confessio Amantis'* (Cambridge, 1992), p. 3.

[2] A fuller account of the biographical evidence here summarised may be found in John Hines, Nathalie Cohen and Simon Roffey, '*Iohannes Gower, Armiger, Poeta*: records and memorials of his life and death', in *Companion*, pp. 23–42.

[3] John H. Fisher, *John Gower: Moral Philosopher and Friend of Chaucer* (New York, 1964; London, 1965) pp. 58–60.

which she received an income and material possessions. The will provides the most extensive evidence which survives concerning Gower's personal circumstances, and in particular highlights Gower's association with St Mary Overey, which church, now Southwark Cathedral, houses his tomb. Gower chose to be laid to rest in the St John the Baptist chapel, and made bequests for vestments and a chalice, and a missal and a martyrlogium, for that chapel: he also left money for funeral prayers to be said at St Mary Overey and in the other parish churches of Southwark; he made further bequests to Southwark's hospitals and leper houses on the understanding that there, too, prayers would be offered for his soul.

Gower's tomb remains a striking feature of Southwark Cathedral, a brightly coloured three-arched recess housing a tomb-chest on which an effigy of the poet lies with his hands clasped in prayer. An epitaph records that a 'most famous English poet, and benefactor to this sacred building, lies here'.[4] The effigy's head is pillowed by Gower's three great works: the Latin *Vox Clamantis*, the French *Speculum Meditantis* (elsewhere known as *Mirour de l'Omme*) and the English *Confessio Amantis*; the titles are now painted in this order, with the Latin work on top, but earlier descriptions of the tomb indicate that the books were originally labelled differently, with the French work first – *Speculum Meditantis*, then *Vox Clamantis* and *Confessio Amantis*. This is the order of their composition: it may also have reflected Gower's sense of the importance of his French work,[5] though he perhaps perceived his books more as a trilogy of equal parts.[6] The re-ordering of the books makes a suggestive symbol of the historical shifts in the status of the languages in which each was written; the difficulty in interpreting the re-ordering, which may or may not indicate a change in the priority given to each of Gower's works, parallels the difficulty of interpreting those shifts.

It has long been known that England was, in the Middle Ages, a nation of three languages, but whereas earlier accounts of the language emphasized the separate roles played by different languages – French the language of the law courts and the nobility, Latin the language of the church, English the language of the masses – a growing body of scholarship has, in the last ten years, complicated the picture of the relationships between languages in this trilingual nation.[7] In late medieval England differences in language use

---

[4] 'Hic iacet I. Gower Arm. Angl. Poeta celeberrimus ac huic sacro edificio benefac.'
[5] See R. F. Yeager, 'John Gower's French', in *Companion*, pp. 137–51 (p. 137). The changed order is described in Hines, 'Iohannes Gower', pp. 39–40.
[6] A. G. Rigg and Edward S. Moore make this suggestion, noting that in the colophons to the manuscripts of the *Vox* and the *Confessio*, Gower gives equal weight to each of the three major works and identifies them all as written to educate. See A. G. Rigg and Edward S. Moore, 'The Latin works: politics, lament and praise', in *Companion*, pp. 153–64 (p. 153, n. 1).
[7] See Jocelyn Wogan-Browne *et al.*, eds, *Language and Culture in Medieval Britain: The French of England c.1100–c.1500* (York, 2009); Wogan-Browne with Nicholas Watson, 'The French of England: the *Compileison*, *Ancrene Wisse*, and the idea of Anglo-Norman', in *Cultural Traffic in the Medieval Romance World*, eds Simon Gaunt and Julian Weiss, *Journal of Romance Studies*, 4, 3 (Winter 2004), pp. 35–58; D. A. Trotter, ed., *Multilingualism in Later Medieval Britain* (Cambridge, 2000); L. C. Wright, 'Trade between England and the Low Countries: evidence from historical linguistics', in *England and the Low Countries in the Late Middle Ages*, eds Caroline Barron and Nigel Saul (Stroud, 1995), pp. 169–79.

could relate to class, gender, education and social status as well as to region or country of birth – but languages did not function discretely even within more subtly defined cultural groups. In the fourteenth century, French and Latin were the languages in which law was laid down, but the English vernacular had some influence; business was a strikingly polyglot arena, and was transacted in a rich mixture of English, Latin and French words and phrases, with a Latin grammar.[8]

In the literary realm, the situation was even more complex. For various reasons, some of them political – the Hundred Years War with France – and others less clear, the status of English writing in fourteenth-century England improved, and literary English texts increase hugely in number. English writers 'tried both to articulate their growing consciousness of the distinctiveness and coherent nature of English language and culture and to give the language a status closer to that of French or Latin'.[9] Nicholas Watson has pointed out that many English vernacular texts themselves draw attention to the language in which they are written and give reasons for writing in English: these include efforts to form a separate ethnic identity for the English, distinct from the French oppressors. Such accounts are themselves often politically driven and therefore not to be taken as reliable indicators of the historical circumstances of English, but the ideologies they reveal, however, are themselves of interest to an understanding of England's trilingualism.[10] Other texts employ the vernacular in an effort to increase access to church teaching: as their English necessarily proclaims its dependence on Latin, the status of the vernacular remains subordinate. The virtues of English as a *literary* language were not self-consciously advanced by English writers until the last years of the fourteenth century, fifty years after Dante had made such claims for the Italian vernacular:

> Writing in a Germanic language that was less closely related to Latin than Italian and had long been subordinated to Anglo-Norman, these writers adopted a less aggressive and more varied approach than Dante's.[11]

Gower is enlisted as one of the Middle English poets who contributed to an effort to 'assimilate and displace Latin [and] French hegemony'.[12] Assimilation is clear from the fact that Gower's English is crammed with rich French vocabulary, for example: it is, importantly, not the power of French and Latin which Gower challenges, but rather any exclusion of English from sharing that power. Rita Copeland writes helpfully of *Confessio Amantis* as a 'secondary translation', which thematizes the displacement of its classical

---

[8] See W. Rothwell, 'The trilingual England of Geoffrey Chaucer', *SAC*, 16 (1994), 45–67.
[9] Nicholas Watson, 'The politics of Middle English writing', in *The Idea of the Vernacular: An Anthology of Middle English Literary Theory 1280–1520*, eds Jocelyn Wogan-Browne et al. (Exeter, 1999), pp. 331–52 (p. 333).
[10] Ibid., pp. 334–5.
[11] Ruth Evans, Andrew Taylor, Nicholas Watson and Jocelyn Wogan-Browne, 'The notion of vernacular theory', in *The Idea of the Vernacular: An Anthology of Middle English Literary Theory 1280–1520*, eds Jocelyn Wogan-Browne et al. (Exeter, 1999), pp. 314–30 (p. 319).
[12] Ibid.

sources and implicitly claims equal status with them.[13] Though his English *Confessio Amantis* sets a strong example of the achievements of the English vernacular, the fact that Gower wrote equally ambitious works in French and in Latin seems to indicate an ambition more to create a triumvirate than to topple a dictator.

*

This collection of essays begins with a consideration of a localized Gower, Jean-Pascal Pouzet's 'Southwark Gower: Augustinian Agencies in Gower's Manuscripts and Texts'. Central to this essay are themes of source and transmission: the sources which fed Gower's 'redefinitions of culture' were available to him in the library of the Augustinian priory of St Mary Overey at Southwark. The essay describes the 'flagrant presence' of several texts which are sources for Gower's work in all three languages. Gower's texts were also disseminated along Augustinian channels, as Pouzet discusses in particular relation to the Latin works. Pouzet's essay engages the scholarly debate around the 'Gower *scriptorium*', and argues that challenges to it need not challenge the image of 'Southwark Gower'.

This careful localization of the poet is then juxtaposed with remote locations in his poetry, as two essays consider 'Gower Looking East' – his translation of exotic location into his English *Confessio Amantis*. Ethan Knapp's essay on 'The Place of Egypt' indicates that Gower's use of Egyptian characters and motifs in the *Confessio* is much more specifically grounded than has sometimes been assumed: it is motivated by a very specific sense of Egypt's historical and doctrinal particularity, and Gower is particularly concerned with the Egyptian worship of animals. Animal-worship, as a historical error of religious belief, allows Gower to stage theological questions concerning the limitations of human knowledge and agency. In the process of his discussion, Knapp also draws attention to aspects of Gower's discussion of gold and economic exchange, and of the influence of astronomy – themes which are developed in later essays by Tamara F. O'Callaghan, Stephanie Batkie, Karla Taylor and Brian Gastle.

Carolyn P. Collette, in 'Topical and Tropological Gower: Invoking Armenia in the *Confessio Amantis*', argues that Gower's invocations of Armenia draw on the nation's history and myth to create verbal play but also to encode a serious, topical message about kingship and the politics of international Crusade. Armenia's fascination lay in its attempt to remain Christian and yet independent of Rome: it was also a staging point for crusaders. It represents that which is at once familiar and yet 'other' – the exotic which is yet not entirely alien, and which has therefore great potential as the site of commentary on the poet's immediate milieu.

Gower's reflections on contemporary politics and society are the focus of the next group of essays, on 'Politics, Prophecy and Apocalypse'. Essays by Elliott Kendall ('Saving History: Gower's Apocalyptic and the New Arion')

---

[13] Rita Copeland, *Rhetoric, Hermeneutics, and Translation in the Middle Ages* (Cambridge, 1991), chap. 7.

and Robert R. Edwards ('Gower's Poetics of the Literal) explore Gower's use of the language of prophecy and apocalypse. Kendall considers the *Vox Clamantis* and the prologue to the *Confessio Amantis* in relation to diverging traditions of medieval apocalyptic, and argues for Gower's inflection of apocalyptic language with a commitment to human agency in contemporary history. Edwards' essays demonstrates that, as Gower draws on the various forms of prophecy that inform Christian and medieval traditions, his literalism shows the pressure of history on structures of belief that seemingly stand outside time. These essays together make a strong case for Gower as a poet who, like Chaucer and Langland, has a capacity for radical social and political critique.

George Shuffelton and Nigel Saul also draw observations about Gower's political purposes from considerations of his adaptation of source material. Shuffleton, in 'Romance, Popular Style, and the *Confessio Amantis*: Conflict or Evasion?', argues that the *Confessio Amantis* is not, as has often been thought, elitist high art, but rather a more democratic work which, in its use of folktales and popular lyric, erodes the differences between formal registers and genres: this Shuffelton attributes to Gower's political idealism, rather than elitism. By contrast, Saul's essay, 'John Gower: Prophet or Turncoat?', stresses Gower's authoritarian political tone in relation to his views of kingship: Gower's emphasis on ethical self-government and common profit – ideas he derived from Giles of Rome's *De regimine principum* – leads him to stress the king's ascendancy, but also causes his alienation from Richard II, whom he sees as failing to govern himself appropriately.

David R. Carlson's 'The Parliamentary Source of Gower's *Cronica Tripertita* and Incommensurable Styles' demonstrates that Gower's *Cronica Tripertita* was based on the parliamentary record of the deposition of Richard II, a Latin prose text which he adapted to verbally ornate verse. The translation from prose to verse occasions, strikingly, ubiquitous lexical change, even though Gower is not shifting his source from Latin: Carlson argues that lexical change is necessitated by the extreme stylistic difference between source text and Gower's poem. Gower creates an 'official verse panegyric of the Lancastrian advent', and enters the pay of the Lancastrian regime.

Gower displays his support of Henry IV further in his English poem 'In Praise of Peace', which is addressed to the king. In the first of a group of essays considering 'Science, Law and Economy' in Gower, Candace Barrington's 'Gower's Legal Advocacy and "In Praise of Peace"' argues that the poem draws on a repertoire of linguistic and structural gestures associated with the legal profession, and that Gower chose this as an appropriate language in which to discuss the king's business. With striking difference, as Andreea Boboc argues, Gower also uses legal language to discuss seduction, more usually considered a moral offence: Gower connects seduction to legal offences including perjury, breach of contract and treason. In 'Se-duction and Sovereign Power in Gower's *Confessio Amantis* book V' Boboc, like Barrington, connects Gower's legal language with the crown, since seduction is rendered criminal by Gower because of its disastrous and wide-ranging effect on kingship.

Three essays consider Gower's literary deployment of the language of science. Tamara F. O'Callaghan, in 'The Fifteen Stars, Stones and Herbs: book VII of the *Confessio* and its Afterlife', makes a case for the importance of Gower's discussion of astronomy in the seventh book of *Confessio Amantis*: she demonstrates that, though modern scholars have paid little attention to it, Gower's presentation of astronomy provides a theoretical and philosophical framework for the rest of the poem. She shows, further, that these passages are often cited by readers from the fifteenth to the eighteenth centuries, for whom the *Confessio Amantis* seems to have been a source of occult knowledge more than a story collection (the essay thus also contributes to discussion of Gower's afterlives in the final section of this volume, 'Gower translated'). As Stephanie Batkie and Karla Taylor discuss, Gower also deploys the language of alchemy, another occult pseudo-science and one reviled by many of Gower's contemporary writers. Batkie, in '"Of the parfite medicine": *Merita Perpetuata* in Gower's Vernacular Alchemy', notes that, whereas Latin alchemical texts are in cryptic and often impenetrable language, Gower translates this into a plain style by a 'vernacular alchemy': she argues that alchemy becomes an image of idealized textual practice in which vernacular reading transforms the reader through interpretive effort. Taylor's 'Inside Out in Gower's Republic of Letters' provides a complementary argument – that Gower's 'plain' alchemical language is used as an imaginative model to reconcile sacramentalism with change into the vernacular, while avoiding increasingly divisive theological polemics which aligned the vernacular with heresy.

Brian Gastle's essay, 'Gower's Business: Artistic Production of Cultural Capital and the Tale of Florent', argues that there is a significant intrusion of fiscal language into the Tale of Florent which complicates its status as knightly romance *exemplum*. Gower's knight learns from the economic realities of marriage, which were shifting in the economic and social landscape of the fourteenth century. In introducing the theme of marriage as well as economics, Gastle's essay leads into discussion of love and sex in the following section, on 'Sin, Love, Sex and Gender', which also contains an essay on the Tale of Florent by Richard F. Green, treating the misogyny of its view of marriage.

Essays by Matthew Irvin, Peter Nicholson and John Burrow consider Gower's exploration of love and sin through the figure of Genius, the confessor and also the priest of Venus. Irvin's 'Genius and Sensual Reading in the *Vox Clamantis*' focuses on Gower's Latin work, in which Genius appears as confessor in a convent and encourages nuns to sexual licence through a sensual reading practice: he suggests continuities with the portrait of Genius in the English *Confessio Amantis*, which Nicholson argues depends for its power not on irony but on paradox. Nicholson, in 'Irony v. Paradox in the *Confessio Amantis*', argues that the *Confessio*'s more fully developed Genius is not, as is often thought, an inadequate confessor, but rather one who is aware of the bewildering complexity of moral and amatory experience. Burrow agrees that the *Confessio Amantis* finds a harmony, rather than an opposition, between divine ethics and love. His 'Sinning against Love in

Confessio Amantis' points out that Gower is the first poet to apply the priestly scheme of Seven Deadly Sins to a systematic exploration of love, and argues that the scheme facilitates an analytical, rather than narrative or chronological, tone which proves appropriate to the portrait of Amans' predicament.

Holly Barbaccia's essay, 'The Woman's Response in John Gower's *Cinkante Balades'*, focuses on love as a gendered discourse in Gower's French ballads. Barbaccia discusses the five-ballad woman's reply which completes the narrative of the *Balades*, and shows that it is in the woman's voice that Gower most strongly echoes his French contemporary poets. Gower's rhetorical deployment of the female voice is also explored in Kim Zarins' essay focusing on the authority given to the voices of women and peasants when, in *Confessio Amantis*, they speak in *rime riche*. Whereas Barbaccia concludes that Gower is using the woman's voice in the *Balades* to make a renewed claim for his own mastery of the French lyric tradition, for Zarins, in 'Rich Words: Gower's *Rime Riche* in Dramatic Action', the fictionally framed women within the *Confessio*'s tales challenge the containment of the *rime riche* form as they use it to clarify their experience of abuse by powerful men.

Essays by Richard F. Green and Cathy Hume consider non-literary influences on Gower's French and English works. Green's 'Florent's *Mariage sous la potence'* shows Gower making capital out of a folk custom rather than a narrative device – the practice of *mariage sous la potence*, by which a man could be saved from the death sentence if there were a woman willing to marry him. The custom spawned a misogynistic folktale in which a young man was so appalled at the ugliness of the woman who offered to save his life that he chose to die instead: Green's essay discusses the connections between this tale and the 'loathly lady' tradition, and argues that Gower seeks to mitigate the misogyny of the tradition.

Hume's essay, 'Why did Gower Write the *Traitié?'*, relates Gower's treatment of love and sex to the political realities of his time. Hume argues that Gower's French *Traitié pour essampler les amantz marietz* is not, as has sometimes been thought, a translation and abridgement from his English *Confessio Amantis*, but that it has much in common with Gower's *Mirour de l'Omme* and was written, like the *Mirour*, in criticism of Edward III's affair with Alice Perrers. Gower later translated his *Traitié* in a new context, as appendix to his English *Confessio*, re-addressing it to the whole world.

This example of Gower 'translating' his own work, shifting it from French to English and from specific to generalized context, leads into the final section of the book, 'Gower "Translated"', in which are considered various aspects of the afterlives of Gower and his poetry. This section on the transmission of Gower and his influence begins with John Bowers' 'Rival Poets: Gower's *Confessio* and Chaucer's *The Legend of Good Women'*, on the immediate impact of the *Confessio Amantis* on Chaucer's *Legend of Good Women*. Following Kathryn Lynch's re-assessment of the chronology of the Chaucer canon, Bowers makes a case for Gower's influence on Chaucer's depiction of the classical figures Cleopatra, Medea and Queen Alceste. Bowers also suggests that the Man of Law of Chaucer's *Canterbury Tales*, with his detailed knowledge of the *Legend*, is a figure of Gower himself, who had acted as Chaucer's attorney: Gower as a figure appearing in literature is discussed further by Martha Driver in the final essay of this volume.

Andrew Galloway's 'Reassessing Gower's Dream-Visions' considers that passages in the *Mirour*, the *Vox Clamantis* and the *Confessio Amantis* show a development in his treatment of the genre, from a disenchantment with transcendent authority to a focus on human need and appetite. Gower helped to demolish the traditional kinds of authority in dream visions, and as a consequence writers of the fifteenth century have great difficulty with the genre: Galloway argues that Samuel Daniel's sonnet 'Care-Charmer Sleep' is an heir to Gower's achievement, and shares his vision of the dangerous power of appetite.

R. F. Yeager's essay, 'John Gower's French and His Readers', considers the eighteen French balades of Gower's *Traitié pour essampler les amantz marietz* and their translation into English by a fifteenth-century Yorkshireman who signed himself 'Quixley'. Yeager's close examination of the manuscript – London, British Library MS Stowe 951 – in which Quixley's translations appear, leads him, on literary, historical and palaeographical grounds, to identify the translator as a prior of Nostell Abbey, sister house to St Mary Overey in Southwark. Yeager's essay shows Gower's work being translated by others soon after his death, and provides an Augustinian context for Gower in the fifteenth century which echoes the Augustinian context for Gower's writing defended by Pouzet in the opening essay of this volume.

Finally, Martha Driver's 'Conjuring Gower in *Pericles*' discusses the 'translations' of Gower himself, as the poet who, according to Skelton, 'first garnished our English rude'. Gower appears as an emblem of the great poet in works by Greene, Jonson, Webster and, of course, Shakespeare, for whom he represents, according to Helen Cooper, 'the native English traditions of poetry'. Driver discusses this assertion in her exploration of Shakespeare's representation of Gower in *Pericles*, and goes on to examine the ways in which modern stagings of *Pericles* highlight, suppress or misunderstand Gower as poet, story-teller and figure of the medieval English tradition.

Chapter 1

Southwark Gower: Augustinian Agencies in Gower's Manuscripts and Texts – Some Prolegomena*

JEAN-PASCAL POUZET

John Gower's long-standing association with the community of Augustinian canons at the priory of St Mary 'Over(e)y' in Southwark is variously documented,[1] but the influence of this singular relationship has not always been fully considered in studies of the poet's literary activities. In terms of internal textual evidence, for instance, G. C. Macaulay signalled the technical use of *corrodium* in book IV (line 215) of the *Vox Clamantis* as a possible reflection of the poet's allowance of a corrody by the priory for his sustenance – probably in return for an endowment to the community.[2] More significantly, while arguments put forward by Macaulay and John Fisher in favour of Gower's reliance on the library and a possible scriptorium at the priory maximized the forms of this association, M. B. Parkes and A. I. Doyle have challenged these views and foregrounded other factors explaining patterns of revision and scribal collaboration in Gower manuscripts.[3] But the arguments of Parkes and Doyle are centred on manuscript production and revision *per se*, and their case against the idea of a 'Gower scriptorium'

---

* I thank N. G. Morgan, D. Wakelin, D. Wallace, J. Willoughby and R. F. Yeager for their support, R. Hanna for constructive criticism (not fully attended to for reasons of space) and E. Dutton for some stylistic ministrations.

[1] R. S. Allen, 'John Gower and Southwark: the paradox of the social self', in *London and Europe in the Later Middle Ages*, eds J. Boffey and P. King (London, 1995), pp. 111–47; J. Hines, Nathalie Cohen and Simon Roffey, '*Iohannes Gower, Armiger, Poeta*: records and memorials of his life and death', in *Companion*, pp. 23–41; and R. Epstein, 'London, Southwark, Westminster: Gower's urban contexts', in *Companion*, pp. 43–60.

[2] Macaulay, iv, p. 390, n. to line 215. See also the discussion by R. F. Yeager, 'Gower's French audience: the *Mirour de l'Omme*', *CR*, 41, 2 (2006), 111–37 (pp. 118–19 and nn. 44–8).

[3] Macaulay, ii, pp. cxxx–cxxxi; J. H. Fisher, *John Gower: Moral Philosopher and Friend of Chaucer* (London, 1965), notably pp. 66, 93, 101, 117 (more prudent statements), 124–7, 303–6; M. B. Parkes and A. I. Doyle, 'The production of copies of the *Canterbury Tales* and the *Confessio Amantis* in the early fifteenth century', in *Medieval Scribes, Manuscripts and Libraries: Essays Presented to N. R. Ker*, eds M. B. Parkes and A. G. Watson (London, 1978), pp. 163–210 (p. 200, n. 98); M. B. Parkes, 'Patterns of scribal activity and revisions of the text in early copies of works by John Gower', in *New Science out of Old Books: Studies in Manuscripts and Early Printed Books in Honour of A. I. Doyle*, eds R. Beadle and A. J. Piper (Aldershot and Brookfield, 1995), pp. 81–121 (pp. 81–2).

at the priory does not invalidate the notion that Gower may have made the most of books at Southwark – a theory which has been floated before – nor that Augustinian canons from St Mary and elsewhere may have been instrumental in the dissemination of the poet's works. In his memorial lecture for the great Gower scholar Jeremy Griffiths, Ralph Hanna pointed out that some palpable Augustinian connections 'seem nonetheless worth pursuing':[4] certainly such connections extend beyond the missal bequeathed by Gower for use at the altar of the chapel of St John Baptist in the priory, which once stood adjacent to the north transept of the priory church and which was erected on the funds of the poet who saw to his spiritual needs by founding a chantry therein.[5] This essay – in more than one sense only a critical overview – addresses the need for a fresh consideration of a 'Southwark, or Augustinian, Gower' through an examination of the manuscript evidence – evidence which interweaves two essential strands of thought.

The first strand is signalled by new evidence and suggestions concerning the relationship between aspects of Gower's œuvre and works transmitted by Augustinian channels and/or produced through Augustinian agency. This strand starts with an exploration of the possible influence on the poet's writings of the volumes plausibly found in the late-fourteenth and early-fifteenth century book-holding (if not library, strictly speaking) of the Priory of St Mary. I offer a list (Appendix 1, below), drawn from the identifications of N. R. Ker and A. G. Watson, which presents known records from St Mary, plausibly thought to have been held in the priory (essentially in what must have been a common *armarium*; yet **no. 4** may well have been an altar book) in Gower's time. The reasoning behind this list requires some explanation. Whereas the exclusion of early printed books is self-evident, the evolving resources of a monastic library and the nature of the association with the priory of twenty known manuscripts (in total, so far) impose a measure of caution on the reconstruction of the shape of its manuscript holdings in the time of Gower's long residence. There has been, as yet, no concerted attempt to sketch the history of the book resources at St Mary. Ker had customarily based the identification of surviving Southwark books on the tangible evidence of provenance, which, save in two cases, are *ex libris* inscriptions; he had noted that their usual form is 'Liber beate Marie Overey'. A new examination of most manuscripts, in consultation with the 'Ker Index' held in Duke Humfrey's Library, Oxford, confirms that this *ex libris* inscription is the more attested form of two, is found in twelve manuscripts, and that the possibly two (or three) different hands which wrote them can be dated s. xv *ex*, or s. xvi *in* to s. xvi *med*. These bibliographical gestures may betray relatively late policies of census or ownership identification – some being

---

[4] R. Hanna, 'Augustinian canons and Middle English literature', in *The English Medieval Book: Studies in Memory of Jeremy Griffiths*, eds A. S. G. Edwards *et al.* (London, 2000), pp. 27–42 (p. 34).

[5] The fact that London, BL, MS Additional 59855 may really be the 'large new missal' itself is moot, on account of the dating of the manuscript, thought to be *c*.1410–20 by A. G. Watson, *Medieval Libraries of Great Britain. Supplement to the Second Edition* (London, 1987), p. 63 and n. 1.

perhaps as late as immediately pre- or post-Dissolution – and as such do little to secure the presence of a pre-fifteenth-century book or booklet in the priory in Gower's days. Problematically, such presence should not be formally ruled out for some manuscripts, at least among those dated *s.* xii, *s.* xiii and *s.* xiv: on the one hand, some early booklets or books might have been acquired by the priory at a date later than Gower's time; but on the other hand, a late *ex libris* inscription in an early book (which might have been, unsurprisingly, without an early *ex libris*) might be retroactive. Naturally, the probability of presence is seriously diminished for manuscripts datable as *s.* xv: only manuscripts dated or datable *ante* 1408, such as **no. 7**, might have been available to Gower. That a late *ex libris* inscription does not preclude a strong possibility of earlier Southwark ownership – coeval with the poet in residence – is shown, however, by the conjunction of the (probably) *s.* xv *ex* inscription with variants of the much earlier formula (*s.* xiii), the standard redaction of which is 'Liber sancte Marie de Suwerk(e)', in two *s.* xiii manuscripts, London, British Library, MSS Cotton Faustina A. viii and Egerton 272. My rather prudent list thus reflects an attempt to take account of all these parameters, as it marks in **bold type** the earlier discernible stratum of St Mary books while maintaining a penumbra of manuscripts with potential earlier presence (books dated *s.* xii, *s.* xiii or *s.* xiv, with *ex libris* inscriptions of s. xv *ex* to s. xvi *med*).[6]

Southwark Priory's now vestigial holdings are indeed an important cultural and textual indicator for serious and more systematic study than was possible for Fisher. He based his list solely on Dugdale's *Monasticon* (only three known extant manuscripts), and did not take the matter any further than a short, although thought-provoking, discussion of the relevance of the miscellaneous contents of MS Cotton Faustina A. viii **(no. 5)** essentially to the thematic orientations of the *Mirour de l'Omme*.[7] The contents of those extant manuscripts with a very high (nos 5, 6, 10, 12, 14) or tolerable (nos 1–4, 7–9, 11, 13) probability of presence at Southwark in Gower's time tend to confirm the impression that a once significant canonical, quasi-metropolitan

---

[6] This list is adapted principally from the following sources: the 27 entries (20 manuscripts and 7 early printed books) for 'Southwark, St Mary Overy Priory (Surrey)' in the 'Ker Index' in Duke Humfrey's Library; N. R. Ker, *Medieval Libraries of Great Britain*, 2nd edn (London, 1964), pp. 180–81; Watson, *Supplement*, p. 63; and N. G. Morgan's work-in-progress *List of liturgical texts of English Augustinian canons* (I did not use the 'Handlist of English Augustinian Liturgical Manuscripts' proposed by T. M. Morris, 'The Augustinian use of Oseney Abbey: a study of the Oseney Ordinal, Processional and Tonal' (unpublished doctoral thesis, University of Oxford, 1999), pp. 136–42, on which see now the comments of R. W. Pfaff, *The Liturgy in Medieval England* (Cambridge, 2009), p. 274, n. 8). The proposed dating of *ex libris* inscriptions is mine, on the strength of the opinions of Ker and Watson whenever possible (Ker did not always express an opinion as to dating, even in the fiches in the 'Ker Index'). Further bibliographical information and technical description of these manuscripts will be found in my forthcoming project, provisionally entitled 'Augustinian Canons and the Making of English Culture, *c*.1180–*c*.1540'.

[7] Fisher, *John Gower*, pp. 93 and 347 (n. 50); but he seemed to assume that the first booklet (fols 4r–39v) of MS Cotton Faustina A. viii, containing the penitential materials, was held at Southwark, which was not the case. Allen, 'John Gower and Southwark', likewise only briefly touched on the subject (p. 120, n. 17); her count of books potentially available to Gower coincides in number with my larger list of fourteen books.

institution may have constituted a reservoir of creative lore for a tenant-*cum*-poet-in-residence. Rather unsurprisingly in an Augustinian community, readership at St Mary, predominantly but not exclusively in Latin (at least from the fourteenth century onwards) seems to have been vibrant, with various strands of subject matter and discourse. The number and diversity of books might have inspired Gowerian curiosity, versatility and erudition, which are expressed in the form of borrowing, metrical re-employment and *cento* writing;[8] and at least some of the works these extant books preserve may underlie the pointed political, historical, scientific, exegetical, theological, even ethical actuality of some of the issues broached by the poet. Thus, for instance, the presumed presence at Southwark of a copy of John Wyclif's *De veritate sacrae Scripturae* **(no. 11)** just in time for Gower to have known it within these precincts might make the circumstances of the two versions of his *Carmen Super Multiplici Viciorum Pestilencia*, as well as his sympathies with Arundel in the *Vox Clamantis* and the *Cronica Tripertita*, more biographically palpable.[9]

The clear presence of several texts which are sources throughout his works in all three languages thus invites sustainable reconstructions of Gower's possible contact with at least some Southwark books. In Cambridge, St John's College, MS N. 11 (524) **(no. 1)** Gower would have had access to a good copy of the Vulgate Bible; remarkably, this carefully transcribed Bible has some marginal *notae* suggesting pen-in-hand consultation, and few words added with *caret* signs; but one of these, 'hebes', added in the Hieronimian prologue to the book of Genesis (fol. 3^v, right margin), naturally cannot escape – eye-catching as it is – a tempting comparison with the famous choice of 'ebes sensus' in the first line of Latin verse at the very start of the *Confessio Amantis*. Between the glossed Genesis and Exodus of Paris, Bibliothèque de la Sorbonne, BS MS 153 **(no. 14)**, the comprehensive literal exposition of the four Gospels by Peter Comestor in MS Egerton 272 **(no. 6)** and, possibly, the fine twelfth-century copy of Isidore's commentary on the Heptateuch represented by Oxford, Trinity College MS 31 **(no. 13)**, Gower would have been equipped with authoritative guides to essential narrative and interpretative materials for several books of the Bible. In addition to the *Historia Evangelica*, MS Egerton 272 also communicates in its second booklet (fols 34ra–84rb) many of Comestor's popular sermons addressing secular and regular clerics: 'Incipiunt Sermones Magistri Petri manduc*atoris*. primo ad Sacerdotes. dein*de* ad Regu*lares et* ad Scolares' (fol. 34ra) – a concern famously vented by 'moral Gower' in book IV of the *Vox Clamantis* and again in the *Mirour de l'Omme*. In one of the sermons *ad scolares* there is a marginal notifi-

---

[8] On *cento* writing, see R. F. Yeager, 'Did Gower Write *Cento*?', in *John Gower: Recent Readings*, ed. R. F. Yeager (Kalamazoo, MI, 1989), pp. 113–32, with the contextualising remarks of D. R. Carlson, 'Gower's early Latin poetry: text-genetic hypotheses of an *Epistola ad regem* (ca. 1377–80) from the evidence of John Bale', *MSt*, 65 (2003), 293–317 (p. 308, n. 29).

[9] Contacts between Gower and Arundel are plausibly speculated by Allen, 'John Gower and Southwark', p. 123 – but, *pace* Allen, All Souls College, MS 98 could only be, at most, the draft of a presentation copy to Arundel: see A. G. Watson, *A Descriptive Catalogue of the Medieval Manuscripts of All Souls College Oxford* (Oxford, 1997), p. 202.

cation of a passage on idolatry and images (at fol. 70va); and at the beginning of another such sermon on the Assumption of the Virgin ('De Assu*m*ptione beate Marie Virginis', fols 74vb–76va) are to be found a marginal *manicula* (fol. 74vb, right margin) and a *Nota* in the lower margin (fol. 74vb, under col. b): it is tempting to associate these with a reader's particular hermeneutic or devotional preoccupations in a house dedicated to the Virgin Mary – and one may recall Gower's long final, now atelous, lyrical Marian envoy and dedication in the *Mirour de l'Omme*. But, of course, much more palaeographical and textual comparative work, of the magnitude of that undertaken by Macaulay, would be needed for such rapprochements to materialize as a concerted argument.

If we like to imagine Gower yielding to the temptation of serendipity, it is fruitful to focus briefly on Oxford, Bodleian Library, MS Ashmole 1285 **(no. 10)**, a fantastically accretive library *in parvo* consisting of no fewer than fourteen booklets of patristic snippets and philosophical, constitutional, theological, medical, astronomical and homiletic texts almost undoubtedly brought together at the priory (some of them probably having been copied there); it is one of those books in which the scientific, meditative and pastoral traditions of Augustinian canons are exemplified. Booklet 4 (fols 50^r–89^r) communicates a quality copy of Boethius's *Consolation of Philosophy*, so immensely influential in totality and in many textual details to Gower's works, as shown by Macaulay and Winthrop Wetherbee.[10] This copy is uniquely prefixed (fol. 50^r, top margin) with a five-line annotation on old age and its physiology (blood, flesh, skin), in a hand which is responsible for other annotations in this booklet and elsewhere. Looking at the second booklet, which consists of an essentially patristic *florilegium* (fols 8^r–19^v), Table 1 in Appendix 2 offers two suggestions (among several other possible examples) as to how Gower, through imaginative expansion, may have been inspired to rework citations on hypocrisy and on idleness in the Latin verses about these vices in books I and IV of the *Confessio Amantis*, and (in the second case) perhaps again in English later in the same book. Moreover, the principal of possibly two annotating hands in informal Anglicana, which occurs repeatedly in the upper margins of this second booklet (fols 8^{rv}, 9^{rv}, 10^{rv}, 11^{rv}, 12^{rv}, 13^{rv}, 14^{rv}, 15^{rv}, 16^{rv}, 17^r, 18^v, 19^r) and also twice in the preceding first booklet (fol. 5^{rv}), looks intriguingly close in ink (very pale brown-greyish) and duct to the 'informal Anglicana' of Parkes's Scribe 5, who entered a direction for revision on fol. 184^v of Oxford, Bodleian Library, MS Fairfax 3 (though such a small sample is obviously hard to compare decisively).[11]

---

[10] W. Wetherbee, 'Latin structure and vernacular space: Gower, Chaucer and the Boethian tradition', in *Chaucer and Gower: Difference, Mutuality, Exchange*, ed. R. F. Yeager (Victoria, B.C., 1991), pp. 7–35, and 'Classical and Boethian tradition in the *Confessio Amantis*', in *Companion*, pp. 181–96.

[11] This page is reproduced and discussed by Parkes, 'Patterns of scribal activity', pp. 91 and 112–13 (Plate 15).

Table 2 presents evidence for a conceivable exploitation by Gower in book VI of yet another portion of MS Ashmole 1285. Its fourteenth booklet consists of a series of homilies connected through their common exploration of the branches of gluttony ('gula') based on several of the minor Prophets (Joel, Hosea, Amos and Jonah); the collection begins with drunkenness, from which it takes its title and a sense of ramification: *'De ebrietate multiplici'*. The binary division into *'Ebrietas'* and *'Delicacia'* in Gower's Latin marginalia is reflected to some extent (though with greater sophistication) in the structure of the homiletic collection in MS Ashmole 1285. Once more, the use might be more creative than strictly textual – often the lure, yet the limit, of reconstructive source studies.

Gower's œuvre also reflects various forms of engagement with works of Augustinian authorship or transmission attested in Augustinian libraries whose presence at Southwark cannot, however, be demonstrated. Other possible Augustinian routes by which the poet could have had access to a range of influential texts beyond the priory of St Mary must thus be considered. One brief example must suffice here: as long ago as 1955, Paul Beichner showed Gower's use of the Continental Augustinian canon Peter Riga's *Aurora* in *Vox Clamantis*, where Riga is famously named in book III (lines 1853–4).[12] Several copies of Riga's versified rewriting circulated under Augustinian auspices in England. Among reported manuscripts, one was at Llanthony Secunda in the fourteenth century and two others were listed by William Charyte in his late-fifteenth-century catalogue of books at the abbey of St Mary-in-the-Meadows in Leicester.[13] Beichner also demonstrated that the manuscript of the *Aurora* principally chosen by Macaulay to point out extensive borrowing spread over thousands of lines (Oxford, Bodleian Library, MS Bodley 822) does not reflect the greatest textual proximity with Gower's exemplar. As R. F. Yeager most recently reminds us in his discussion of London, British Library, MS Stowe 951, inter-house circulation of books is likely, for instance at the convocation of the triennial chapters of the Augustinians after 1215.[14] It is therefore relevant that a representative of the actual form of text used by Gower (among a group of other textually eligible manuscripts) is shown by Beichner to be a very good copy of the 'unexpanded' redaction preserved in Oxford, Merton College, MS 325, which has an *ex libris* inscription (s. xiv *in*) of the Augustinian priory of Bridlington (East Yorkshire). Whether or not the Augustinian affiliation of the author of the *Aurora* may have meant anything to Gower, Riga's exceptional

---

[12] P. E. Beichner, 'Gower's use of *Aurora* in *Vox clamantis*', *Speculum*, 30 (1955), 582–95, and the updated list of borrowings (with revised line numbers to match the unexpanded redaction of the *Aurora* from which Gower drew): Peter Riga, *Aurora. Petri Rigae Biblia Versificata. A Verse Commentary on the Bible*, ed. Peter E. Beichner, 2 vols (Notre Dame, 1965), II, Appendix, pp. 62–4.

[13] T. Webber and A. G. Watson, eds, *The Libraries of the Augustinian Canons* (London, 1998), respectively p. 38 (Llanthony Secunda, item A 16.6, described as 'liber mediocris') and p. 123 (Leicester, items A 20.20 and A 20.21a).

[14] See note 35 below, and R. F. Yeager's essay in this volume. Yeager (n. 31) makes judicious implications concerning opportunities of Augustinian inter-house book circulation from evidence in *Chapters of the Augustinian Canons*, ed. H. E. Salter (London, 1922).

creative condensation of the Bible (a magisterial illustration of the discursive subtleties of *abbreviatio*), and the subsequent density of his idiom, must have particularly appealed to Gower, both as a mine for borrowing and as a model of creative *exercitatio* and 'imitative embodiment' in writing Latin verse – in addition, for instance, to Ovid's poetry, and to the *De vita monachorum* of Alexander Nequam, another Augustinian luminary.[15]

A second thread of Augustinian implication can be seen to run through the history of Gower manuscripts, texts and excerpts, and the other works preserved in their company. In line with the spirit animating the *Descriptive Catalogue of the Manuscripts of the Works of John Gower*, this thread promises a significant array of reconsiderations and discoveries of Augustinian contexts. Kate Harris has paved the way with her examination of the content of the textually puzzling *collage* of materials forming a sort of universal history which is now Oxford, Trinity College, MS D 29: this late-fifteenth-century manuscript in the hand of one scribe with some interesting corrections perhaps by another, its late provenance the Augustinian priory of Bisham Montague (in a part of Berkshire not far from Surrey), includes four distinct excerpts of the *Confessio Amantis*.[16] In the later fifteenth century the well-endowed library at Leicester Abbey (already mentioned above) is known to have held one copy of Gower's *Cronica Tripertita*;[17] additionally, some carefully chosen tales, perhaps excerpted as exemplary narratives from the *Confessio Amantis* in London, British Library, MS Harley 7333 (at the beginning of the fourth booklet, fols 120^r–129^r) are thought to have been within the walls of the abbey, not inconceivably worked on (if not positively assembled, or in part written) there between 1485 and 1500. For some reason, none of the works in this famously atypical anthology seem to have been reported by Charyte in his inclusive census, though his own hand might be identifiable as that of one of the (perhaps) eight scribes. Some booklets, including the works by Chaucer and Hoccleve, and the Gower excerpts, are thought to have been derived from exemplars copied at some removes by John Shirley (d. 1456), who was associated with St Bartholomew's Hospital in London, an institution also under Augustinian rule.[18] Inter-house procurement of Gower texts both within a (quasi-) metropolitan context – from Southwark to St Bartholomew's – and then out to Leicester, may once more be presumed.

---

[15] The felicitous phrase 'imitative embodiment' is used by Carlson, 'Gower's early Latin poetry', p. 309.

[16] Kate Harris, 'John Gower's *Confessio Amantis*: the virtues of bad texts', in *Manuscripts and Readers in Fifteenth-Century England: The Literary Implications of Manuscript Study*, ed. Derek Pearsall (Cambridge, 1983), pp. 27–40, and 'Unnoticed extracts from Chaucer and Hoccleve: Huntington MS HM 144, Trinity College, Oxford MS D 29 and *The Canterbury Tales*', SAC, 20 (1998), 167–99.

[17] Webber and Watson, *Libraries*, p. 238 (item A 20.649); see the discussion below.

[18] On Shirley, see M. Connolly, *John Shirley: Book Production and the Noble Household in Fifteenth-Century England* (Aldershot, 1998). On MS Harley 7333, see recently L. R. Mooney, 'John Shirley's heirs', YoES, 33 (2003), 182–98 (pp. 190–94 and 198); M. Gullick and T. Webber, 'Summary catalogue of surviving manuscripts from Leicester Abbey', in *Leicester Abbey: Medieval History, Archaeology and Manuscript Studies*, eds J. Story *et al.* (Leicester, 2006), pp. 173–92 (pp. 189–90); and Alexandra Gillespie, *Print Culture and the Medieval Author: Chaucer, Lydgate, and their Books 1473–1557* (Oxford, 2006), p. 59 (and n. 108).

One manuscript of the first recension 'intermediate', London, Society of Antiquaries, MS 134 (s. xv med), was owned until the Dissolution by the Abbey of the Blessed Virgin Mary and St John the Evangelist at Halesowen, Worcestershire. Its copy of the *Confessio Amantis* (fols 30–249) is flanked by Lydgate's *Life of Our Lady* (acephalous, fols 1–30), Hoccleve's *Regement of Princes* (fols 250–283), and a fragment (fols 283ᵛ–297) of the English verse translation of Boethius's *Consolation of Philosophy* by John Walton, the famous Augustinian canon of Osney, all copied by one scribe.[19] This rather well-endowed abbey was Premonstratensian, thus a member of a regular order following a permeable variant of the rule of St Augustine under which Augustinian canons lived.[20]

Furthermore, issues related, directly or indirectly, to the layout and content of Augustinian books raise new questions about intricate features of Gowerian transmission. One remarkable example of this may also serve to substantiate the first strand of thought. In London, British Library, MS Harley 3490, the 'Rede/Boarstall' Gower fully described twice by Derek Pearsall (as a forerunner of the *Descriptive Catalogue*), the *Confessio Amantis* (first recension, but not consistently 'intermediate' in Macaulay's pedigree) is preceded by a booklet (fols 1ʳ–6ᵛ) containing a copy of Edmund of Abingdon's *Speculum Religiosorum* written in the same hand as that of the Gower text: the scribe may not have been working commercially, and it is conceivable that the copy of the Latin article was commissioned by Sir Edmund Rede himself for devotional purposes.[21] The latter assumption is lent support by the fact that Helen Forshaw, the editor of the Archbishop of Canterbury's Latin theological and devotional treatise, noticed that the 'best copy' of both the *Speculum Religiosorum* and its Latin reflex, the *Speculum Ecclesie*, belonged to Augustinian priories.[22] Originally composed in the second half of the thirteenth century, the *Speculum Ecclesie* is the resulting re-Latinisation of the *Speculum Religiosorum* via the intermediary Insular French *Mirour de*

---

[19] John Gower, *The English Works of John Gower*, ed. G. C. Macaulay, 2 vols, EETS e.s. 81–82 (London, 1900–1901; rpt 1979), I, pp. cxliii–cxliv; John Lydgate, *A Critical Edition of John Lydgate's 'Life of Our Lady'*, eds. R. A. Klinefelter and V. F. Gallagher (Louvain, 1961), pp. 45–6.

[20] Thus Halesowen even came to absorb the small poor Augustinian priory of St Mary at Dodford in two stages, 1332 and 1446; see D. Knowles and R. N. Hadcock, *Medieval Religious Houses: England and Wales*, 2nd edn (London, 1971), p. 156.

[21] Derek Pearsall, 'The Rede (Boarstall) Gower: British Library, MS Harley 3490', in *The English Medieval Book: Studies in Memory of Jeremy Griffiths*, eds A. S. G. Edwards et al. (London, 2000), pp. 87–99, and his revised description in *JGN*, 28, 1 (2009), 20–34. In the latter description, Pearsall deems (p. 20) the *Speculum Religiosorum* to be 'an unexpected companion for the *Confessio*', and suggests (p. 25) that the scribe of MS Harley 3490 was William Salamon (originally from the diocese of León in Spain, but established in Catte Street, Oxford) whose work is documented in a multi-volume series of works of Hugh of St Cher commissioned between 1451 and 1465 by Roger Keyes, Archdeacon of Barnstaple (now MSS Oxford, Exeter College 51–68); but this is unlikely. Salamon is evoked as an example of a commercial scribe by M. B. Parkes, *Their Hands Before Our Eyes: A Closer Look at Scribes* (Aldershot, 2008), p. 47 (and n. 95).

[22] Edmund of Abingdon, *'Speculum Religiosorum' and 'Speculum Ecclesie'*, ed. H. P. Forshaw (London, 1973), pp. 1–2, notes that the Augustinian priory of St Thomas at Baswich, near Stafford, owned Oxford, Bodleian Library, MS Hatton 26, deemed the 'best copy' of the *Speculum Religiosorum* (fols 183ᵛ–204ᵛ).

Seinte Eglise, the latter vernacular text having been itself translated from a copy of the original Latin tract, and most probably itself caught within a network of Augustinian dissemination (if not authorship as well). MS Harley 3490, though not deemed a 'best copy' of the *Speculum Religiosorum*, has a text not so far removed from it; while – as seen above – the 'best copy' of the *Speculum Ecclesie* was precisely a Southwark manuscript, MS Royal 7. A. I (fols 12ʳ–22ᵛ), copied around 1400 according to Forshaw – a manuscript possibly at St Mary at an acceptably early date in the fifteenth century, though not necessarily before Gower's death. Both Latin redactions were sometimes textually interdependent, and are apt to have been circulated in bespoke booklets, not necessarily or simply on a commercial basis, and possibly – in part at least – through Augustinian industry.[23]

The *Vox Clamantis* and the *Cronica Tripertita* may have circulated even more extensively under Augustinian auspices. There are five known copies of the *Cronica Tripertita*, in four of which it is transmitted – as might be expected – with the *Vox Clamantis*. Hanna suggests that the *Cronica Tripertita* once at St-Mary-in-the-Meadows in Leicester, identified in Charyte's catalogue as 'Cronica I. Gower in quaternis', reflects 'a case of transmission by ordinal channels.'[24] Additionally, one may speculate that it may owe its presence to late-fourteenth-century local interest in chronicles, probably fostered by the famous canon chronicler Henry Knighton (d. 1396), a man of Gower's generation whose own house production, the famous *Chronicle*, has one reported copy in the catalogue which still exists (London, British Library, MS Cotton Tiberius C. vii, *s.* xiv *ex*).[25] In his catalogue Charyte very often systematically recorded the whole contents of each manuscript containing more than one text; if the apparently self-standing *Cronica Tripertita* had had the company of the *Vox Clamantis* this might not have gone unnoticed.

Charyte's careful entry suggests, significantly, that the Leicester copy of Gower's *Cronica Tripertita* was in quires ('in quaternis') when it was catalogued – since Charyte does not often specify whether some items were in 'ligatis' or 'non ligatis' quires, it is not impossible that these specific quires may already have acquired the substance of a self-contained unit, a booklet, possibly in limp covers (the more specific sense that 'in quaternis' also had).[26] Although none of the five known extant manuscripts of Gower's chronicle can be proven to match the entry describing the copy at Leicester

---

[23] Some of the ideas in this paragraph are also broached in my 'Augustinian canons and their insular French books in medieval England: towards an assessment', in *Language and Culture in Medieval Britain: The French of England c.1100–c.1500*, eds J. Wogan-Browne *et al.* (York, 2009), pp. 266–77 (pp. 275–6).

[24] Hanna, 'Augustinian canons and Middle English literature', pp. 34–5.

[25] Webber and Watson, *Libraries*, p. 236 (item A 20.636). On Knighton, see recently G. H. Martin, 'Henry Knighton's *Chronicle* and Leicester Abbey', in *Leicester Abbey: Medieval History, Archaeology and Manuscript Studies*, eds J. Story *et al.*, pp. 119–25.

[26] For important considerations on Leicester bindings (the source of my brief remarks on the plausible codicology of Gower's *Cronica Tripertita* at Leicester Abbey), see M. Gullick and T. Webber, 'The binding descriptions in the library catalogue from Leicester Abbey', in *Leicester Abbey: Medieval History, Archaeology and Manuscript Studies*, eds J. Story *et al.* (Leicester, 2006), pp. 147–72.

(its *secundo folio* being 'quo bona'), in matters of format the closest candidate for comparison is Oxford, Bodleian Library, MS Hatton 92 (*SC* 4073).[27] On several grounds this generally intriguing manuscript, dated from the first half of the fifteenth century (perhaps in its second quarter), has an apparent claim to Augustinian provenance. It preserves a number of idiosyncratic works, including, in its first booklet (fols 4–38), the later and more complete copy of the tract *Contra Salomitos* attributed to one Maurice, supposed to have been prior of the Augustinian priory at Kirkham, probably *ante* 1188; the second booklet (fols 40–103) contains a rare assemblage made of two consecutive texts (fols 40^r–70^r and 70^v–100^v) combining prose and verse paraphrase and commentary on Ovid's *Metamorphoses*, with portions attributed respectively to Arnulf of Orléans, John of Garland and, more tellingly, the London schoolmaster John Seward (1364–1435).[28] The *Cronica* is written in distinctive italic-influenced secretary by one scribe on fols 104^r–123^v, and constitutes the first and longest text in the third booklet of the manuscript (fols 104–131). Though there is no sign that this copy of the *Cronica*, possibly displaying the text in a very early version,[29] was ever transmitted with the *Vox Clamantis*, its self-standing nature has been somewhat mitigated by three palaeographical and textual factors: the later addition of a fabricated 'preface' on fol. 103^v (originally blank), a purpose-built filler devising some sort of continuity from booklet 1 to booklet 2; the immediate presence, at the end of the *Cronica*, of some of Gower's 'minor' poems (fols 123^v–125^r; in the same booklet and in the same fine hand); and an allusion to the *Vox* as a temporal and discursive predecessor in the form of a 'prohemium' to the *Cronica* which appears to be unique to this manuscript (fol. 104^r). Such a configuration suggests a well-informed scribe who might have had access to a copy of the *Vox*, insofar as he was cognizant of the cluster of short Latin poems, four of which he copied in this order: 'H. aquile pullus' (fol. 123^v), 'O Recolende' (fols 123^v–124^r), 'Rex celi Deus' (fols 124^r–125^r) and 'Quicquid homo scribat' (fol. 125^r). It must be noted that this last piece – famously a problem poem – seems to be a unique short redaction, possibly a fourth, earlier version, combining a few segments, not all verbatim, found at the end of the prose note of the 'Cotton, Harleian, Glasgow version' with four

---

[27] F. Madan, H. H. E. Craster and N. Denholm-Young, *A Summary Catalogue of Western Manuscripts in the Bodleian Library at Oxford*, vol. II, pt II (Oxford, 1937), pp. 828–9.

[28] The tract *Contra Salomitos* is thought to have been composed 1169–77; still no decisive records can be found for Maurice's priorate: see D. Knowles *et al.*, eds, *The Heads of Religious Houses: England and Wales, I. 940–1216*, 2nd edn (Cambridge, 2001), pp. 168 and 281. The Ovidian materials are listed in F. T. Coulson and B. Roy, *Incipitarium Ovidianum. A Finding Guide for Texts in Latin Related to the Study of Ovid in the Middle Ages and Renaissance* (Turnhout, 2000), nos 257 (pp. 83–4), 333 (pp. 101–2) and 346 (p. 105); on Seward, see V. H. Galbraith, 'John Seward and his circle', *Mediaeval and Renaissance Studies*, 1 (1941–3), 85–104, A. G. Rigg, *A History of Anglo-Latin Literature 1066–1422* (Cambridge, 1992), p. 302, and Richard Sharpe, *A Handlist of the Latin Writers of Great Britain and Ireland before 1540* (Turnhout, 1997), no. 883 (pp. 313–14).

[29] This is argued by D. R. Carlson, 'Gower on Henry IV's rule: the endings of the *Cronica Tripertita* and its texts', *Traditio*, 62 (2007), 207–36 (p. 221); I disagree with the judgment that MS Hatton 92 is 'carelessly written' (p. 219). See also P. Nicholson's review, 'David Carlson, "Gower on Henry IV's rule"', in *JGN* 28, 1 (2009), 7–8.

lines of verse corresponding to only three lines (9–10 and 14) of its verse part – or, more consistently, with the last four lines of the all-verse 'Trentham version'.[30]

The *Vox Clamantis* may have appealed to an Augustinian readership on account of its erudite, hortatory and 'self-sacrificial' nature. In his reflection on the sense of place in Gower's poem, Kurt Olsson has pointed out the comparative relevance of *sermones ad status* to books III–VI in particular; Eve Salisbury has recently commented on the strategic presentation of apotropaic sacrificial violence performed within communities and the extreme control of overt and implied meanings of recast sources, especially through *cento*.[31] All this may be congruent with the regulars' concern for *cura animarum* and good relations with local communities, including those in Southwark;[32] with Augustinian traditions of erudition; and, more topically, with the proven presence of homilies at St Mary, notably those in MS Ashmole 1285, most of which have a theme drawn from the minor Prophets or the Gospels. But there is also biographical and scribal evidence of Augustinian agency more than once in the course of the textual tradition or ownership of the *Vox Clamantis* in the later fifteenth century; for reasons of space, only one case will be briefly illustrated here. Oxford, Bodleian Library, MS Digby 138, a fine codex in regular formal secretary heavily influenced by italic features, is one among seven manuscripts known to have been transcribed by the prolific scribe Roger Walle (documented 1436–1488), whose 'versatility' and some of whose scribal traits Parkes has characterized.[33] The somewhat restless career of Walle, from the diocese of Coventry and Lichfield, found him at one point at least, though briefly, in an Augustinian position: from December 1449 to March 1451 he was in the vicarage of Maxstoke, Warwickshire, the advowson of which had been the property of the adjacent Augustinian priory of Maxstoke since its foundation in 1336–7.[34] In MS Digby 138 Walle signed his name on fol. 98^r (top right margin), and inscribed his *ex libris* with a *rebus* of his name on fol. 145^r (also top right margin): 'Claudatur

---

[30] Compare with *John Gower. The Minor Latin Works (with 'In Praise of Peace' Edited by M. Livingston)*, ed. and trans. R. F. Yeager (Kalamazoo, MI, 2005), pp. 46–9 (I follow Yeager's description of versions), and the note p. 79; for a discussion of the three versions, see also Parkes, 'Patterns of scribal activity', p. 85.

[31] K. Olsson, 'John Gower's *Vox Clamantis* and the medieval idea of place', *SP*, 84 (1987), 134–58; E. Salisbury, 'Violence and the sacrificial poet: Gower, The *Vox*, and the critics', in *On John Gower. Essays at the Millenium*, ed. R. F. Yeager (Kalamazoo, MI, 2007), pp. 124–43. Significantly, Olsson begins his rich contextualisation with the spiritual dimension of place in Hugh of St Victor's *De sacramentis ecclesiasticis*, a copy of which would have been available to Gower in an unambiguously early St Mary book, MS Egerton 272 (**no. 6** in Appendix 1).

[32] M. Carlin, *Medieval Southwark* (London and Rio Grande, 1996), p. 74.

[33] A. B. Emden, *A Biographical Register of the University of Oxford to A. D. 1500*, vol. III (Oxford, 1957, rpt 1989), p. 1966, and Sharpe, *Handlist*, no. 1594 (pp. 597–8); M. B. Parkes, *English Cursive Book Hands 1250–1500*, 2nd edn (London, 1979), p. 22 and facing plates 22 (i) and 22 (ii); and *Their Hands Before Our Eyes*, p. 110, n. 41 and Plate 34; Jean-Pascal Pouzet, 'Book production outside commercial contexts', in *The Production of Books in England 1350–1530*, eds. A. Gillespie and D. Wakelin (Cambridge, forthcoming).

[34] Knowles and Hadcock, *Medieval Religious Houses*, p. 166.

muro constat Liber iste Rogero'. It is perhaps both significant and ironic that he copied the *Vox* in which, in book IV, the *claustrales* and importance of life within the walls of the cloister are emphasized. It may be suggested, finally, that Roger Walle would cut a likely figure for the informed scribe who copied works by Gower in MS Hatton 92, the more so as the italic-influenced secretary script he uses in several of his manuscripts – including the totality of MS Digby 138 – is in all particulars extremely close, if not identical, to the script employed to write the Gower texts in MS Hatton 92. Both manuscripts are not inconsistent with a dating around the middle of the fifteenth century.

In sum: manuscript and textual evidence contributes to a canvas on which are traced the remarkable codicological and textual associations central or immediately adjacent to the production of Gower's œuvre, and the circulation of Gower manuscripts and texts, in the late fourteenth and fifteenth centuries. It is hoped that, thanks to these prolegomena, a realistic 'Southwark Gower' may start to emerge, a complex figure silhouetted against this canvas. There is a density of evidence which may be found significant and awaits further exploration. Such considerations may also be taken to chime with (my) current attempts to map out the larger pattern of Augustinian implication in the production and dissemination of texts important to the religious and literary culture of medieval England.[35]

---

[35] In this respect, further to R. F. Yeager's essay in this volume (referred to in my note 14 above), evidence for Augustinian influence in the making of the *Mirour de l'Omme* and the circulation of the *Traitié pour essampler les amantz marietz* is discussed by him in 'Gower's French audience: the *Mirour de l'Omme*' and 'John Gower's French and his Readers', in *Language and Culture in Medieval Britain: The French of England c.1100–c.1500*, pp. 135–45. Inferentially, the meditative strand in the *Mirour*, examined by T. H. Bestul, 'Gower's *Mirour de l'Omme* and the Meditative Tradition', *Mediaevalia*, 16 (1993), 307–28, may be seen as congruent with Augustinian *ethos*. Such an adequacy may be fruitfully contectualised also in the light of the sociolinguistic approach offered by T. W. Machan, 'Medieval Multilingualism and Gower's Literary Practice', *SP*, 103 (2006), 1–25 and which Yeager's essays also consider.

Appendix 1: Volumes held by the Priory of St Mary in Gower's time

Bold type indicates volumes known definitively to have been held at St Mary's in Gower's lifetime: items not in bold are plausible, but not certain, holdings contemporary with Gower.

1. Cambridge, St John's College, MS N. 11 (524): Bible (fols 1–553^r) + alphabetical *Interpretationes* (fols 553^v–594) (s. xiii *med*; *ex libris* inscription s. xv *ex*).

2. Cambridge, Trinity College, MS O. 2. 30 (1134) (fols 1–128; not inconceivably the whole book): devotional and theological anthology in booklets of various dates, including extracts of Isidore's *Etymologiae*; Augustine's *De trinitate*; *Vita sancti Dunstani*; *Regula Sancti Benedicti* (s. ix, s. xi / xii, s. xii; *ex libris* inscription s. xvi *in*, perhaps 2nd quarter).

3. Canterbury Cathedral, Dean and Chapter Library, MS Lit. E. 10 (101): theological anthology (*Testamenta XII Patriarcharum*; *Suidas*; *Meditationes beati Bernardi*) (s. xiii *ex*).[1]

4. London, British Library, MS Additional 63592: Psalter (s. xiii *ex*, but Morgan '*c*.1250'; *Dedicacio* of St Mary 'ouery' added at 11 July, in hand s. xv *ex*).

5. London, British Library, MS Cotton Faustina A. viii, fols 40–178: booklets including theological and administrative *miscellanea*; a Calendar; Ralph de Diceto's historical works; prophecies from Geoffrey of Monmouth's *Historia regum Britanniae*; the Southwark Chronicle (AD 1–1240); a Southwark register (mostly s. xiii *in* to s. xiv *in*; Calendar dated *c*.1205–7 for its main part by Morgan; *ex libris* inscriptions s. xiii *ex*, s. xv *ex* and s. xvi *in* or *med*).

6. London, British Library, MS Egerton 272: 3 booklets containing respectively Peter Comestor's *Historia Evangelica* (fols 2ra–33vb); Comestor's *Sermons* (fols 34ra–84rb); Hugh of St Victor's *Tractatus de Sacramentis Ecclesiasticis* (fols 86ra–99vb) (s. xiii; *ex libris* inscriptions s. xiii *ex* and s. xv *ex*).

7. London, British Library, MS Royal 7. A. I: theological and devotional anthology, including two anonymous gospel homilies; an 'excellent copy' of the *Speculum Ecclesie* (fols 12^r–22^v); meditations and prayers of St Anselm; Bonaventure's *Meditationes Vitae Christi*; Pseudo-Augustine's *Visitacio Infir-*

---

[1] C. E. Woodruff, *Catalogue of the Manuscript Books in the Library of Christ Church, Canterbury* (Canterbury, 1911), p. 52; N. R. Ker, *Medieval Manuscripts in British Libraries* (Oxford, 1969–92), vol. II, p. 284. This manuscript is treated as 'borderline', because there is no Southwark *ex libris* inscription *per se*, its evidence of provenance being apparently found in a post-medieval *ex dono* inscription to Canterbury (by William Kingsley, 1667); in somes cases Ker treated notes of gift on a par with *ex libris* inscriptions (both subsumed under his criterion 'e').

morum; Dindimus's letter to Alexander; *Stimulus amoris* (s. xiv/s. xv, Forshaw 'c.1400'; *ex libris* inscriptions s. xv *ex*).[2]

8. London, British Library, MS Royal 7. A. IX, fols 1–65 according to Ker, but more probably the whole book (*ex libris* inscriptions at fol. 6ʳ *and* fol. 117ᵛ): theological anthology, including some works by Robert Grosseteste (mostly s. xiii; *ex libris* inscriptions s. xv *ex*).

9. London, British Library, MS Royal 10. B. VII: Richard Fishacre's Commentary on Peter Lombard's *Sentences* (s. xiii; inscription s. xiv *in*, and *ex libris* inscription s. xv *ex*, probably 2nd quarter).

10. Oxford, Bodleian Library, MS Ashmole 1285: fourteen booklets including patristic *florilegium*; **a Customary (glossed Hymnary); Boethius's** *De Consolatione Philosophie*; **computistica; astronomica; medica; one Augustinian chapter; devotional/theological texts; one French song; homilies (s. xii *ex* to s. xiv *in*; Customary dated 'c.1275–1300' by Morgan;** *ex libris* **inscriptions s. xiv *in*).**

11. Oxford, Bodleian Library, MS Bodley 924: J. Wyclif's *De Veritate Sacrae Scripturae* (s. xiv / s. xv; *ex libris* inscription s. xv *in*).

12. Oxford, Bodleian Library, MS Rawlinson B. 177: historical compilation (in 2 booklets) communicating principally Roger of Wendover's *Flores historiarum* **(s. xiv *in*; *ex libris* inscription s. xiv *in*).**

13. Oxford, Trinity College, MS 31: Isidore's Commentary on the Heptateuch (s. xii; *ex libris* inscriptions s. xvi *in*).

14. Paris, Bibliothèque de la Sorbonne, MS 153: Genesis and Exodus glossed (s. xiii).

---

[2] Edmund of Abingdon, *'Speculum Religiosorum' and 'Speculum Ecclesie'*, ed. Forshaw, p. 7 and passim; she chose London, BL, Royal 7. A. I as her base text for the *Speculum Ecclesie*.

Appendix 2: Gower's possible inspiration from Oxford, Bodleian Library, MS Ashmole 1285

Table 1

	Confessio Amantis		MS Oxford, BodL. Ashmole 1285
I.v (verse)	Laruando faciem ficto pallore subornat Fraudibus Ypocrisis mellea verba suis. Sicque pios animos quamsepe ruit muliebres Ex humili verbo sub latitante dolo.	Bklet 2 (fol. 14ᵛ)	§ annotation (s. xiv *ex*?) in upper margin (under the authority of 'Augustinus'): 'ypocrit*us et* dol*um* et laudar*e* dom*inum* Aliud loq*ui* aliud intellig*ere*'
IV.v (verse)	Absque labore vagus vir inutilis ocia plectens, Nescio quid presens vita valebit ei. Non amor in tali misero viget, immo valoris Qui faciunt opera clamat habere suos. (see also *Confessio* IV, lines 1757–60 on the oxymoron 'besinesse' / 'ydelnesse')[1]	Bklet 2 (fol. 10ᵛ)	§ annotation (s. xiv *ex*?) in upper margin: 'mens ociosa' § 'Gregori*us*. Ociose menti maligni spir*itus* pr*a*uas cogit*ationes* initiunt. ut *et* si quiescit ab op*er*e no*n* quiescat malorum op*er*um delect*ation*e'

Table 2

	Confessio Amantis		MS Oxford, BodL. Ashmole 1285
VI.i (verse)	Est gula que nostrum maculauit prima parentem Ex vetito pomo, quo dolet omnis homo. Hec agit vt corpus anime contraria spirat, Quo caro fit crassa, spiritus atque macer. Intus et exterius si que virtutis habentur, Potibus ebrietas conuiciata ruit. Mersa sopore, labris, que Bachus inebriat hospes, Indignata Venus oscula raro premit.	Bklet 14 (fol. 334ʳ)	fols 334ʳ–375ʳ 'De ebrietate multiplici' = series of homilies on the branches of that topic, based on minor Prophets (Joel, Hosea, Amos, Jonah) [Incipit] <Experg[esc]imini ebrii et flete etc. Joel 1. Duo dicenda sunt. primo quot modis sumatur ebrietas ...>
VI.i marg.	Hic in sexto libro tractare intendit de illo capitali vicio quod Gula dicitur, nec non et de eiusdem duabus solummodo speciebus, videlicet Ebrietate et Delicacia, ex quibus humane concupiscencie oblectamentum habundancius augmentatur.		(Joel 1. 5: expergescimini ebrii et flete et ululate omnes qui bibitis vinum in dulcedine quoniam periit ab ore vestro)

---

[1] On this oxymoron, see John Gower, *The Latin Verses in the 'Confessio Amantis': An Annotated Translation*, eds Sîan Echard and Claire Fanger, with A. G. Rigg (East Lansing, MI, 1991), p. 50, n. 75.

Chapter 2

The Place of Egypt in Gower's *Confessio Amantis*

ETHAN KNAPP

When we think about the inheritance of a classical past, we tend to think towards Greece and towards Rome. Of course, as medievalists, there are very many good reasons to do so. The dominance of ecclesiastical Latinity, its works disseminated through the network of the Roman church, tied the most significant intellectual trends of the era to a culture that was palpably rooted in the shared inheritance of this Greco-Roman past. And in the world of vernacular literature the varied romance traditions laboured mightily to tell the story of the descent of contemporary aristocratic cultures from their progenitors in Rome, in Thebes and in Troy. The twin pillars of *'translatio studii'* and *'translatio imperii'* frame the *'longue durée'* that organizes much of our work, helping us feel history as, say, a Chaucer or Gower certainly would have done.

In more recent years there has been a great deal of re-examination of these narratives, often under the rubric of locally adapted post-colonial studies. Work by scholars such as Christine Chism, Jeffrey Jerome Cohen, Geraldine Heng and David Wallace has called into question the westward drift of medieval culture, asking many vital questions about the impact of non-European cultures on writers whom we had often read within a relatively hermetic European tradition.[1] Inspired in part by Edward Said's brilliant work on the formation of Orientalism, such scholars, and many others, have drawn our gaze Eastward, asking us to re-examine the medieval thirst for marvels of the East and the impact of both mercantile networks and Crusading campaigns on the literature produced on the fourteenth-century home front. But in the present essay I want to look neither West nor East, but South, and ask about the place of Egypt in the medieval imagination, specifically the place of Egypt in Gower's work.[2] And even to call it South is something of a misdirection here, as I will want to argue that, even more

---

[1] See, for example, Christine Chism, *Alliterative Revivals* (Philadelphia, 2002); Jeffrey Jerome Cohen, ed., *The Postcolonial Middle Ages* (New York, 2000); Geraldine Heng, *Empire of Magic: Medieval Romance and the Politics of Cultural Fantasy* (New York, 2003); and David Wallace, *Premodern Places: Calais to Surinam, Chaucer to Aphra Behn* (Oxford, 2004).

[2] For another essay that suggests the importance of setting aside the East–West binary and looking South, see Suzanne Conklin Akbari, 'Alexander in the Orient: bodies and boundaries', in *Postcolonial Approaches to the European Middle Ages*, eds Ananya Jahanara Kabir and Deanne Williams (Cambridge, 2005), pp. 105–26.

than the mutually fashioning dialectic of East and West, Egypt appeared to Gower as a historical problem in that it was both utterly alien and yet utterly intrinsic to the crucial theological and political inheritances of the classical Mediterranean world. Egypt, as Said, among others, reminds us, has long served as an almost totemic rebuke to dreams of a Europe with clearly identifiable disjunctions – whether historical or spatial – between itself and the rest of the world. In the period Said analyzed, the heyday of Empire, this irresistible conjunction was figured in the persistence of colonialist metaphors of Egypt as a fickle lover – would Egypt stay with Britain, her stolid spouse, or succumb to the allures of a flashy but untrustworthy France?[3] Gower, of course, would never have thought of the problem in just these terms, but I want to argue here that Gower too thought of Egypt as a problem, and as a problem in terms of the difficulty of disentangling it from the space and history of the West.

There are a number of scattered references to Egypt in the *Confessio Amantis*, but it is dealt with at length at two moments in the poem – the excursus on the history of religious belief at the beginning of book V and the story of Nectanabus in book VI. The story of Nectanabus is one of the most remarkable set pieces in the work, and it has attracted considerable attention.[4] However, the treatment of Nectanabus has never been considered in connection with the description of Egyptian beliefs in the earlier excursus. Doing so reveals a significant common thread running through Gower's thoughts about Egypt. Egypt, for Gower, stands for the temptation to believe, in ways that would have been unacceptable to either Christian or pagan Greek, that the human being is only one of many objects in the world, that the human has no spiritual or hermeneutic precedence over other beings. This is a temptation that Gower will argue against, but never, I think, fully set aside.

Gower's first extended treatment of Egyptian thought occurs in his description of the history of religious error at the beginning of book V, his book on Avarice. His chief criticisms of the Egyptians are that they worshipped animals rather than God and that their gods were themselves immoral, being guilty of incestuous relations with each other. I will consider these objections in detail below, but an accurate reading of the stakes involved requires a sense of their contextualization within Gower's complex theory of Avarice. In particular, his analysis of religious error needs to be contextualized within two other discussions that precede the excursus itself – first, the broad historical framework that Gower draws around the vice of Avarice; and, second, the pivotal, and *alchemical*, role of *The Tale of Midas*.

---

[3] Edward Said, *Orientalism* (London, 1978), pp. 211–13.
[4] For other readings of the Nectanabus story, see Patrick J. Gallacher, *Love, the Word, and Mercury: A Reading of John Gower's 'Confessio Amantis'* (Albuquerque, NM, 1975), pp. 40–43; Peter Nicholson, *Love and Ethics in Gower's 'Confessio Amantis'* (Ann Arbor, MI, 2005), pp. 330–33; Russell A. Peck, *Kingship and Common Profit in Gower's Confessio Amantis* (Carbondale, IL, 1978), pp. 134–8; Larry Scanlon, *Narrative, Authority, and Power: The Medieval Exemplum and the Chaucerian Tradition* (Cambridge, 1994), pp. 275–82; and Diane Watt, *Amoral Gower: Language, Sex and Politics* (Minneapolis, MN, 2003), pp. 100–3.

The whole of book V is steeped in Ovid, and Gower begins the book with an account of the historical devolution from a Golden Age.[5] In the beginning of creation there was no division of the world into property. Property and war arrive only with Avarice, and only with the introduction of Avarice's chief tool – money. With the introduction of money into the world, by which Gower means here specifically coinage based on valuable metals, humanity begins to dig ditches and build walls. But, in a fascinating metaphorical reversal, Gower does not say that these walls and ditches are built to keep out those who would steal one's gold; rather, the walls are built to *contain* the gold, as though the very presence of coinage now meant that the form of economic pressure derived not from competition over scarce valuables but rather from some aspect of gold that threatens to burst beyond any suitable constraints.

> And in this wise it cam to londe,
> Werof men maden dyches depe
> And hyhe walles for to kepe
> The gold which Avarice enclosed. (*Confessio* V, lines 18–21)[6]

Under the pressure of gold, Avarice becomes itself a wall, an object that stabilizes division rather than being a motive force for acquisition. The significance of this metaphoric transformation lies in the fact that Avarice forces a perverse transformation in the relation between agents and objects, a transformation that begins to colour the sphere of human agency. As Gower says, the desire for acquisition leads all who fall under its spell to be mesmerized by their own possessions, to lock gold away in coffers just to gaze at it and to be, in essence, mastered by the goods of which they think themselves masters.

> To seie hou such a man hath good,
> Who so that reson understod,
> It is impropreliche seid,
> For good hath him and halt him teid,
> That he ne gladeth noght withal,
> Bot is unto his good a thral ... (*Confessio* V, lines 49–54)

In other words, the first point to be made about Avarice is that Gower diagnoses Avarice as a specific dysfunction in the relationship between humans and objects. Where we should seek out and acquire goods only because they offer us some true value, the fact of Avarice, seemingly unavoidable in this fallen age, suggests that we are now governed by the objects to which we have chosen to impute value.

The following story, *The Tale of Midas*, furthers this analysis through an examination of the unique and almost mystical power of gold to wreak havoc within systems of value. Following his source in the *Metamorphoses*, Gower's Midas releases one of Bacchus's priests from captivity and is offered

---

[5] Here Gower is drawing on Ovid, *Metamorphoses*, I, lines 89–150.
[6] *Confessio* citations in this article will be drawn from Peck.

a reward.[7] What follows is easily read as a parable of value, as the foolish Midas asks for the power to transform all he touches into gold and is chastened to discover that this means he cannot eat or drink, forcing him to ask Bacchus to take away the dangerous gift. In Ovid's version, the central irony of the story is heightened by stripping away the complexities of an economic system and reducing it to two commodities – gold and food. The contrast is then a clear one, between the basic necessity of sustenance and the allure of wealth – and Midas is just as clearly a fool to choose wealth over necessity. Gower, however, amends this narrative in two ways, his alterations complicating both the economic structure and the danger posed by Midas's choice.

First, before Midas asks Bacchus for the ability to turn all objects into gold, Gower adds a moment of introspection, not present in Ovid's original, in which Midas considers and then rejects three other possible gifts (delight, honour and profit), before settling on gold as his reward. The passage is loosely based on Boethius's consideration of the '*summum bonum*' in book III of the *De consolatione philosophiae*, and its effect is similar, positing a world in which value (the nature of the 'good') is apportioned into a single, and hierarchical, structure. For Boethius, and implicitly for Midas in this moment of introspection, all values are connected, and all are determined by their relation to one key value. Indeed, the core of ethical thought in this mode is the need to determine the one value that can serve as a fixed post around which other values might shift and pivot. Setting aside the possibilities of delight, honour and profit, Gower's Midas settles on a choice that would have appalled Boethius, namely gold. The reasons that lead him to this choice are crucial and are worth quoting at length:

> The gold, he seith, may lede an host
> To make werre agein a king;
> The gold put under alle thing,
> And set it whan him list above;
> The gold can make of hate love
> And werre of pes and ryht of wrong,
> And long to schort and schort to long;
> Withoute gold mai be no feste,
> Gold is the lord of man and beste,
> And mai hem both beie and sell;
> So that a man mai sothly tell
> That al the world to gold obeieth. (*Confessio* V, lines 234–45)

There are two points being made here about gold. First, as should not surprise us, gold is imagined not as an object but as an agent, a sort of political power, and the source of all action in the world. Midas is explicit in calling gold a 'lord' and he emphasizes its independent agency by giving gold the grammatical subject position throughout the passage. (Gold 'leads the host', 'makes war' and 'destroys all things' – 'Man', by way of contrast, performs only the action of recognizing that the world obeys gold.) Moreover, the power of gold is imagined as a power of *transformation*, an ability

---

[7] Gower's source here is Ovid, *Metamorphoses* I, lines 85–145.

to change one thing into another (to change 'hate to love' 'war to peace' or 'short to long'). In short, gold here is not just the symbolized wealth of Ovid's story, but is specifically gold as coin, as money. As Marx, among others, has commented, it is money that acquires the magical power of transformation in a complex economy, allowing humans to exchange goods by making them the same, or, at least, measurable by the same unit. Money, or gold, sits at the summit of, and organizes, the scale of values because it is the one object that can make all other objects (including humans in their labour) fungible.[8]

And if we draw our focal point back, this analysis of gold resonates through multiple structures in the *Confessio*. If we consider, for a moment, the Ovidian heritage of the *Confessio*, the story of Midas can take its place as a meditation on transformation, on metamorphosis, but with a twist. Where Ovid offered the story as an ironic meditation on the foolishness of humanity when offered the divine power to transform the physical universe, Gower seems to be pointing to the fact that it is not so much Midas who gains the power of transformation as it is gold, or the magic of money, that has such a power waiting only to be unleashed by foolish humanity. Furthermore, in addition to this question of metamorphosis, this tale should also clearly now appear as the very literalization of Gower's earlier study of alchemy in book IV. Midas *becomes* alchemy, he *becomes* the capacity to transform the other elements into gold.

But, viewed in this light, the danger is a very different one from that anatomized by Ovid (the foolish preference for wealth over necessity), and this new danger will explain, in turn, Gower's second significant alteration to the Ovidian narrative.[9] The danger in Gower's version is not just that humanity will forget to assign proper value to the necessities of basic sustenance, but rather that value itself will be destroyed. It is a fundamental fact of any economic system that value is based on differential relations between objects. We can only speak of value, in ethics or economics, if we value one thing more than another. The nightmare of Gower's Midas is a world in which the potential for such value has vanished, a world in which there is no end to gold and there is nothing but gold. It is this nightmare that leads to Gower's second addition to Ovid – namely that once Midas has his gift taken away by washing in a stream he returns home to *make laws*, to set limits and boundaries, among others the stipulation that his people should 'seche non encress | Of gold' (lines 331–2). In other words, there is a certain disenchantment in Gower's conclusion to the Midas story. Where his initial historical framework had postulated the walled division of the world as a tragic outcome of greed and the reification of the human, Gower's version

---

[8] As Joel Kaye has argued, the growing monetization of society in the thirteenth and fourteenth centuries led to an increasing interest in Aristotelian models of mathematically equalized exchange in both economic and natural sciences. Kaye, *Economy and Nature in the Fourteenth Century: Money, Market Exchange, and the Emergence of Scientific Thought* (Cambridge, 1998).

[9] Here I depart from Peter Nicholson's very astute reading of the Midas story, wanting to emphasize Gower's modification of Ovid's original ethical lesson. Nicholson, *Love and Ethics*, pp. 258–60.

of the Midas story suggests that there is no going back to a world without such divisions, and that the experience of unbounded value is such as to recommend a return to law and an identification of agency with the act of lawmaking, with a setting of limits and boundaries.

Turning now to the excursus on the history of religion itself, we can see that the ground has been prepared by this careful consideration of the dangerous allure of fetishized objects, by their ability to overwhelm human agency itself. Gower offers a history of false belief understood as a succession of improper object choices: the Chaldeans worship planets and elements; the Egyptians proceed to animals; and the Greeks worship humanity itself, and thus vice embodied. It is only with the discovery of Jewish monotheism and then Christianity that the interpretative object is correctly chosen. Gower's sources here are multiple, but the most important is the story of *Barlaam and Josaphat*, a Christianized version of the life of the Buddha. However, as R. F. Yeager has pointed out, Gower makes one significant change to his source in the treatment of the first three false religions, and, as with his treatment of Ovid, this alteration provides a key to the meaning of his historical survey.[10] In the original narrative, the ascetic Barlaam condemns the Chaldeans, Greeks and Egyptians as idolaters, and he does so in that order, significantly, so as to insist that the Egyptians were the worst of the lot, because they made gods out of animals, and even out of plants (his list, unlike Gower's, extends from animals to the gods 'onion' and 'garlic'). The point in *Barlaam* is clearly that, though the Chaldeans and Egyptians both worshipped objects as idols, the Chaldeans had the virtue of at least choosing objects of some dignity (the planets themselves, for example) and then abstracting these objects by painting images, thus worshipping the thing, but in a partially idealized, or mediated, form. Thus, in *Barlaam*, the hierarchy hinges on the way the worshipper relates to an object: whether the veneration can have some pseudo-Platonic role in using an object as a mediated approach towards something greater than itself (a form of veneration that can be seen in the Chaldean practice, but not in the Egyptian). Gower's point, however, is a different one, as has been pointed out by Yeager and others, namely to array the false and true beliefs along the ascending scale of the hierarchy of being, moving the Egyptian to the position after the Chaldeans so that the progression towards Christ can move through inanimate objects to animals to humans and thence to divinity and divinity embodied.[11] In other words, for Gower it is not about the approach to the object, but about what object is chosen.

But the puzzle in Gower's account comes with his insistence on repeating *Barlaam*'s assertion that the Egyptians' error is the worst in the lot. If the principle involved is one of the chain of being, why are the Chaldeans, the worshippers of simple objects, not guilty of a worse error than the

---

[10] Yeager's insights about Gower's desire to set aside an 'undesirable paganism' in some way as to still retain the 'classical apparatus of his poem' are also very interesting. See R. F. Yeager, ed., *John Gower's Poetic: The Search for a New Arion* (Cambridge, 1990), p. 176.

[11] See Yeager, *John Gower's Poetic*, pp. 170–78.

Egyptians, who at least worship animate objects? I would suggest that in Gower's mind the Chaldeans were to be preferred because, although they worship the elements, as Gower says, 'th'elementz ben servicable | To man' (*Confessio* V, lines 762–3). Properly, such elements should not be worshipped because they are beneath man, yet, if we think back to the dangerous objects we have already examined, the Chaldeans may at least be credited with maintaining a separation between the human and the object-thing. Objects may be beneath them, or they may be superior, but they are always ontologically distinct from the human. The Egyptians, on the other hand, in taking animals as their deities, project the animal as the type of created being towards which the human should aspire, or with which it is already, in some sense, identical. This sense of dangerous identification is reinforced by the anthropomorphic Egyptian gods' delight in incest (a sin Gower associates elsewhere with the descent of the human into an animalistic state), and by the specific deed that inaugurates the worship of Isis as the goddess of childbirth, her production of the first cultivated grains (a metonymic slippage from natural fertility to human birth).[12]

This point may seem rather abstract, but it is given a concrete instantiation in Gower's story of Nectanabus. As the history of religious error in book V serves to tie Egypt to the full immersion of human beings in the world of nature, so the story of Nectanabus in book VI continues to put pressure on the spiritual place of the human in the world. I will conclude by looking at this narrative, and by focusing on the significance of three elements of the story: astrology; Nectanabus's physical transformations; and his paternity of Alexander.

The story of Nectanabus is drawn from the Alexander legends that were so popular throughout the Middle Ages and, in particular, from the version of the Alexander legend derived from the Greek Alexander Romance written by pseudo-Callisthenes at some point before the third century CE, probably in Alexandria. It was this version of Alexander's life that first offered the remarkable claim that Alexander's real father was not Philip of Macedon but Nectanebo II, the last native-born ruler of Egypt, who had (with Greek assistance) resisted Persian control of Egypt but had been overcome and fled in about 343 BC. In the legend, Nectanabus flees to Greece and then Macedonia, where he meets Alexander's mother Olympia, seduces her through his magic, and fathers Alexander. In the version that came down to Gower, Nectanabus meets his end in a moment of great dramatic irony. Nectanabus takes the young Alexander to see the stars and learn the secrets of astrology, and Alexander challenges Nectanabus to predict the form of his own death. When Nectanabus says that he will be killed by his own son, Alexander, the budding sceptic, pushes him over the edge of a tower to prove him wrong. (Thus, ironically, proving Nectanabus correct, if a bit unfortunate.)

Historically, of course, the claim of Nectanabus's paternity is utterly impossible, as the historical Alexander was born in 356 BC, and so was

---

[12] On incest and animalistic behavior, see Kurt Olsson, *John Gower and the Structures of Conversion: A Reading of the 'Confessio Amantis'* (Cambridge, 1992), p. 216.

already seventeen by the time of Nectanabus's deposition. Nevertheless, the legend had great appeal, partly because it suggested that the Hellenistic Egyptian state established by Alexander's conquest was actually linked through a secret genealogical link to the last of the native Pharaohs. And, as Ben Perry has suggested, the pseudo-Callisthenes, although a romance, was very much a document of its time and place in its interest in making the local patriotic case that the Alexandrine conquests were not just Greek conquests, but, in truth, Graeco-Egyptian conquests, leading to the foundation of Alexandria as a city part Greek and part Egyptian.[13] Although these materials had been transmitted to Gower through many subsequent intermediary sources (most immediately, the Anglo-Norman Alexander written by Thomas of Kent), the original importance of Nectanabus's Egyptianness is still palpable in Gower's version.

This Egyptianness is encoded into both of the two major elements of Nectanabus's magic: his powerful astrology and his shape-shifting. Egypt had long been credited as the birthplace of astrological science, and its epistemological contours reinforce Nectanabus's exoticism – marking him with what many commentators have noticed as a strange mixture of absolute foreknowledge linked to an absolute lack of self-knowledge. As Alastair Minnis has observed, both Vincent of Beauvais and Ranulf Higden describe Nectanabus, and other astrologically minded pagans, as, in his words, 'fatalists who cannot escape their fate'.[14] In repeating this judgment of Nectanabus through the irony of his death at the hands of his own son, Gower is dismissing the claims of astrology to any final true understanding, and doing so in exactly the terms familiar to other fourteenth-century writers on predestination, such as Holcot, for whom the claims of astrology were offensive because they would seem to abrogate God's unlimited power. Nevertheless, we should note that the irony in Nectanabus's death cuts both ways. He cannot foresee his own death, but he is, nevertheless, absolutely accurate in its prediction, as he is, for that matter, in every other prediction that he makes. Echoing Minnis, we might say that Nectanabus's fatalism is true for Nectanabus. Within the closed circuit of astrology, the world does indeed proceed as a purely mechanical process, with the human positioned as simply another object pushed and pulled by celestial causation. And this fatalism, I would argue, is to be read as a specifically Egyptian temptation, as the surrender of the self into a world of natural mechanisms.

Nectanabus's shape-shifting, the magic that allows him to trick and seduce Alexander's mother, is, similarly, a form of sorcery that resonates with the model of Egyptian existence that we have been tracking. Like the Egyptian deities castigated in book V, Nectanabus takes on the shape of a series of animals. He appears as an eagle, sends a sea fowl to do his bidding, and

---

[13] On the genesis of this version, see Ben Edwin Perry, *The Ancient Romances: A Literary–Historical Account of Their Origins* (Berkeley, CA, 1967) pp. 34–43. On the Egyptian backgrounds to the medieval Alexander romances, see also Betty Hill, 'Alexanderromance: the Egyptian connection,' *LSE*, n.s. 12 (1981), 185–94.

[14] A. J. Minnis, *Chaucer and Pagan Antiquity* (Cambridge, 1982), p. 63.

comes to Olympia in the shape of a dragon – one of the animals specified in *Barlaam and Josaphat* as an object of Egyptian worship. Moreover, this shiftiness and this affinity with the world of nature seem to be transferred over to Alexander at his birth. Alexander's birth is marked by strange portents, such as an earthquake and storms, a transformation of the sun's light into steely grey darkness and a change of all things from their true nature. As Gower evocatively describes it: 'The see his propre kinde changeth, | And all the world his forme strangeth' (*Confessio* VI, lines 2265–6). The killing of Nectanabus is meant to serve, at a certain level, as a transition to book VII, the pedagogical treatise based largely on Brunetto Latini's Aristotelian *Le Livre du Trésor*. As such, it gestures both through narrative and philosophical content towards a rejection of Nectanabus's shape-shifting sorcery in favour of the inheritance of the proper fathers, Philip and Aristotle, and their science of governance.

But to what extent does the death of Nectanabus expunge the sorcery and astrology of the Egyptians? In the supersessionary logic of the history of religious errors of book V, Gower establishes a clear historical trajectory leading from Chaldeans to Egyptians to Greeks to Jews and then to Christianity as the final, and correct, form of religious veneration. The Nectanabus story, however, suggests that Egypt is not so easily left behind. Both the troubling accuracy of Nectanabus's astrology and the portents surrounding Alexander's birth indicate that this inheritance, this Egyptian strand of the family tree, is not so easily expunged. Egypt remains, with Alexander's dual heritage signifying its continued presence within the trajectories of both Aristotelian science and Western empire.

Chapter 3

Topical and Tropological Gower: Invoking Armenia in the *Confessio Amantis*

CAROLYN P. COLLETTE

Gower's *Confessio Amantis* is famous for its semiotic and narrative complexity: it is a text that deploys familiar exemplary narratives redirected to unexpected or puzzling moral lessons. The question of 'how the poem means' has posed a continual challenge to modern scholars, many of whom have explicated the text within the broad paradigm of reader-response criticism, identifying the reader's mind as the site where meaning is created in response to the various elements of the text.[1] In its mixture of didacticism and indeterminacy, in its implicit focus on how meaning can be implied and inferred, the text reflects aspects of late medieval literary practice described by Virginie Minet-Mahy in *Esthétique et pouvoir de l'oeuvre allegorique a l'époque de Charles VI* where she argues that the late medieval didactic text is a site of semiotic play,[2] in which 'la seule citation du nom suffit souvent a faire emerger à la conscience du lecteur un univers de representation'.[3] Exemplary narratives and allegories are designed more to raise questions than to provide answers; in doing so, they offer a web of potential meaning and possible interpretation to which various readers respond in various ways, but whose general tropological purpose is ethical, to awaken self-knowledge that leads to self-control and ultimately to the harmonious creation of common profit, 'le bien publique'. At the same time, a text that sustains semiotic play is itself already a reading.

---

[1] See, for example, Joyce Coleman, 'Lay readers and hard Latin: how Gower may have intended the *Confessio Amantis* to be read', *SAC*, 24 (2002), 209–35, where she argues that Gower's ideal reader may be an illusion, and that the text was probably received in a variety of modes – aural or silent, publicly or privately – by nobles, clerks and monarchs. Discussing whether the 'plenitude and indeterminacy' of the text 'are actually at odds with the sort of ethical and poetical work Gower has undertaken', J. Allan Mitchell has termed the work 'comprehensive without being coherent' ('Gower for example: *Confessio Amantis* and the ethics of exemplarity', *Exemplaria*, 16 (2004), 203–34 (p. 205), a provocative poem designed to stir the reader to interpretive response to various ethical problems presented serially. Russell Peck, in the introduction to his edition of the poem, has written 'It is a poem best understood as a sequence of queries rather than an anthology of answers' (Peck, p. 18). Subsequent references to *Confessio Amantis* throughout this article are to this edition.

[2] The *play* of a text refers to the variety of interpretations it can generate and sustain; the *play* of a text is therefore not directive or limited.

[3] Virginie Minet-Mahy, *Esthétique et pouvoir de l'oeuvre allégorique à l'époque de Charles VI: Imaginaires et discours* (Paris, 2005), p. 37. ('the single citation of a name often suffices to inspire a universe of representation in a reader's consciousness.')

Authors drawing on sources and shared culture interpret their reading by the way they create their texts. Distilling the result of their own reading, they produce open texts that provide sites of semiotic play for others and latent guides to interpretation at the same time.[4] Authorial intention may not control tropological meaning in reception, for individual circumstances and experience must be central in such moral constructions, but the shaping power of the author's imagination as the primary reader and interpreter of texts appears in structures larger than the collocation of individual signs; it appears in the meta-topical themes whose significance is established outside the text by cultural contexts such as literary convention, common knowledge and shared sociolects: 'Le baggage culturel et littéraire qu'il a à sa disposition constitute un laboratoire d'analyse et d'outils heuristiques dans la recherche de sens articulée sur le "moi" et sur le monde'.[5]

Minet-Mahy's exposition of the fluid semiotics of instructive courtly literature offers insight into Gower's artistry and a way to reconcile Chaucer's admiring apostrophe to 'moral Gower' at the end of the *Troilus* with the current axis of Gower criticism which stresses the indeterminacy of textual signs brought to life in individual receptions of his texts. In his original dedication to Richard II Gower promises that the *Confessio* will bring 'wisdom to the wise | And pley to hem that lust to pleye' (Prol., lines 84–5 of Oxford, Bodley MS 294), hinting at his own expectation of varied receptions of his work as well as suggesting embedded value for those wise enough to find it.[6] Like his French counterparts,[7] he envisages his text invoking multiple informed understandings while assuming an inner circle of those wise enough to read his implied meanings. Gower's several invocations of Armenia in the *Confessio* provide specific and clear sites where he creates the kind of polysemous text that Minet-Mahy describes, sites of semiotic play that make the *Confessio* radically unstable – a site of multiple tropological values – and a source of *wisdom* inscribed within a particular horizon of expectation selected and created by the author. In the pages that follow I outline an exemplary case of how Gower's references to Armenia – the

---

[4] Often written for a specific ideal *lecteur*, a prince who draws on an extensive 'univers de representation', rich in theology and politics, in which he has been educated as a person and a ruler, the late medieval allegorical text is both open and defined: open in respect to moral lessons, more narrowly directive and defined in regard to topical references. The indeterminacy of literary texts ensures an extensive process of interpretation and reflection that defeats absolutist tendencies: 'L'oeuvre allégorique évite ainsi les écueils d'un dogmatisme qui, au lieu de susciter l'interrrogation et d'engager la progression du senses, impose au sujet l'orgueil d'une vérité qui s'expose au risque de la tyrannie' (Minet-Mahy, *Esthétique et pouvoir de l'oeuvre allégorique à l'époque de Charles VI*, p. 148). ('The allegorical work thus evades the dangers of a dogmatism, which, in place of arousing questioning and engaging the advance of the senses, imposes on the subject the conceit that there is a single truth, which exposes him to the risk of tyranny [becoming a tyrant].')

[5] Minet-Mahy, *Esthétique et pouvoir de l'oeuvre allégorique à l'époque de Charles VI*, p. 153. ('The cultural and literary baggage which he has at his disposition constitutes a laboratory and a set of heuristic tools in the search for meaning in regard to the self and the world.')

[6] Milton's assertion that he writes *Paradise Lost* for a 'fit audience though few' among all his potential readers provides a later, parallel paradigm for reception.

[7] Minet-Mahy focuses her attention on how Deschamps, Gerson, and Chartier construct texts broadly available to readers and simultaneously focused on an ideal reader.

allusions he makes, the stories he chooses to tell and the texts he selects to accompany these Armenian stories – to explore how he adapts a series of contemporary topoi associated with that nation, its history and myth, to create verbal play as well as to encode a serious topical message.

From our modern perspective Armenia may seem a distant and minor subject, a slender reed on which to base an argument about the dynamics of this complicated text; yet, as Christopher Tyerman, J. N. N. Palmer and many others have shown, Armenia was a central element in fourteenth-century English geo-politics, particularly important in imagining a new Crusade, an undertaking, although never begun, that was proposed and envisaged throughout the fourteenth century. Armenia's complicated history of resistance to various Islamic powers, its attempts to ally with Mongols to oppose Muslims and its ongoing resistance to accepting the Roman Pope as the head of its church made it a land both distant from and important to Europe.[8] In the seventh book of the *Confessio*, dedicated to the education of the king, Gower includes a description of the twelve signs of the Zodiac associated with four geographical quarters of the earth. *Armenie* and the Occident are linked together, governed by Capricorn, Pisces and Aquarius, signs largely moist and cold, associated with the malevolent Saturn, and with Janus, whose two faces symbolize the distinction as well as the connection between past and present (*Confessio*, VII, lines 1240–70).

Familiar, yet not fully known, Armenia was also a popular setting and *topos* in late medieval English and French literature. English romances like the *King of Tars* and *Beues of Hamtoun*, both found in the Auchinleck MS, tell stories based in the first instance on Armenian history chronicled in the West, and in the second on fictions of English knights finding success in the East through alliance with Armenian royalty. *Mandeville's Travels* recounts the story of the Sparrowhawk and the king of Armenia, whose foolish choice dooms his kingdom, a narrative interwoven into and developed in Jean d'Arras's *Melusine* (1393) and La Couldrette's *Le Roman de Mélusine, ou, Histoire de Lusignan* (1401), translated into English in the early years of the fifteenth century as the *Romans of Partenay or of Lusignen*. Philippe de Mézières narrates the imprisonment of Levon V/VI, the last king of Armenia, at some length in his *Livre de la vertu du sacrament de marriage*, describing the king's unfailing devotion to the Virgin and the death of his wife and children in prison.[9] Several English chronicles tell of Levon's visit to Richard II in the

---

[8] On the place of Armenia in medieval European geo-politics, especially in relation to Crusades see: J. N. N. Palmer, *England, France and Christendom 1377–99* (Chapel Hill, NC, 1972); Christopher Tyerman, *England and the Crusades 1095–1588* (Chicago, LI, 1988); James D. Ryan, 'Toleration denied: Armenia between east and west in the era of the crusades', in *Tolerance and Intolerance: Social Conflict in the Age of the Crusades*, eds. Michael Gervers and James M. Powell (Syracuse, NY, 2001), pp. 55–64; Carolyn P. Collette and Vincent DiMarco, 'The matter of Armenia in the age of Chaucer', *SAC*, 23 (2001), 317–58.

[9] Philippe de Mézières, *Le livre de la vertu du sacrament de marriage*, ed. Joan B. Williamson (Washington DC, 1993), pp. 384–5.

early months of 1386, his royal reception, and the rich support the English king unwisely offered to the deposed Armenian king.[10]

Just why Armenia captured Western European imaginations is a question to which the first answer must be that its well-known history of failed attempts to remain both Christian and independent enlisted Western sympathy while simultaneously raising Western anxiety about whether a similar fate could befall other Christian nations. A second ready answer lies in the fact that Christian Armenia had historically been a staging point for Crusades for centuries and was proposed as such a staging place during fourteenth-century discussions of a possible crusade to liberate the Holy Land. As Christopher Tyerman shows in 'Crusades in "Hethenesse" 1337–1410', the tenth chapter of *England and the Crusades 1095–1588*, English people of all ranks and in all kinds of secular and lay institutions supported crusading on both the eastern frontiers of Europe and in the Middle East. Edward I and Edward II both took the Cross; Edward III was invited to do so on many occasions, but refused to join an Anglo-French alliance to liberate the Holy Land. Members of late-fourteenth-century English chivalry engaged in a variety of battles against pagans in Eastern Europe and the Middle East. Chaucer's Knight in *The Canterbury Tales* fought in a number of crusade sites as well as at the 1347 siege of the Armenian city of Ayas – Chaucer's *Lyas* – a crucial defeat for Armenia and the West. Philippe de Mézières sponsored Levon V/VI in France and England, hoping to use the loss of Armenia and the deposition of her king as leverage for a Crusade to the Holy Land, for which he prepared by creating the *Order of the Passion*. The Armenian prince Hetoum's chronicle of Armenian history, *La Fleur des histoires de la terre d'orient* (c.1307), was well known in France, a country whose nobility had inter-married with Armenian princesses for centuries, and popular enough in England to be printed in the early sixteenth century by Richard Pynson (c.1520).[11]

Given its decline and defeats over the course of the fourteenth century, it is not a surprise that literary invocations of Armenia convey anxiety about loss expressed in terms of infertility, failure and displacement. The plot of *Beues of Hamtoun*[12] turns on successive attempts at failed marriages, on lost wives and children, stolen inheritances. The marriage between the Armenian princess Josian and Beues is forestalled and postponed, but finally fertile; at

---

[10] See *The Westminster Chronicle, 1381–1394*, eds L. C. Hector and Barbara F. Harvey (Oxford, 1982), p. 155; Thomas Walsingham, *Historia Anglicana*, ed. Henry Thomas Riley, 2 vols (London, 1869), I, 276; and *Chronicon Angliae*, ed. Edward Maunde Thompson (London, 1874), pp. 367–8.

[11] Hetoum's work exists in multiple Latin versions, as well as French, and an early modern English printed translation. See *Hetoum: A Lytell Cronycle: Richard Pynson's Translation (c.1520) of 'La Fleur des histories de la terre d'Orient' (c.1307)*, ed. Glenn Burger (Toronto, 1988). Both J. N. N. Palmer and Christopher Tyerman document decades of European entanglement with the slowly and steadily declining fortunes of Armenia during the later thirteenth and fourteenth centuries – see Palmer, *England, France and Christendom*; Tyerman, *England and the Crusades*.

[12] For contemporary criticism of this romance, see Jennifer Fellows and Ivana Djordjević, eds, *Sir Bevis of Hampton in Literary Tradition* (Woodbridge, UK, 2008).

one point lost in the woods, their children eventually gain both English and Armenian thrones. But at the end of the romance Beues, Josian and Beues' marvellous horse, Arondel – Josian's gift that enables her husband's success both at her side and in separate adventures – all die together, without any sense of joy in their union or their ultimate success.[13] In the romance *King of Tars*, a fictionalized narrative that reflects historical Armenian attempts to ally with Mongols against Muslims, the daughter of a Middle Eastern Christian king sacrifices herself to marriage with a Saracen king to prevent more bloodshed.[14] Their marriage, interwoven with conversion narratives, produces a child born as a lump of flesh, only redeemed into human form when its Saracen father converts to Christianity. Often read as a sign meant to represent the sterility of Saracen faith and the vitality of Christianity to its medieval audience, the child may also symbolize the futility of attempts at negotiation and alliance outside the community of Christian nations as well as the failure of Armenian strategies for independence.

A recurrent anxiety about failing bloodlines and loss of land expressed through a theme of sloth is a central element of *Partenay*, a family history tale of the Lusignans, a French noble family that inter-married with Armenian nobility.[15] In the Melusine/Lusignan romance the story of the Sparrowhawk is the story of the valiant king of Armenia's achievement in watching the Sparrowhawk for three days and nights where others have failed, and of how the entire line of Armenian kingship is doomed when he insists that his reward be the Lady of the Sparrowhawk – the one wish he is told cannot be granted him. This scene, which appears in *Mandeville's Travels*, is extended and intensified in the *Romans of Partenay*, where lust is linked to moral sloth. The Partenay/Melusine version includes a painted chamber full of images of the knights who had attempted the challenge of watching the Sparrowhawk for three days and nights without sleeping; those who failed were depicted and shamed for sloth: 'Where the scripture said right in thys manere: | In such A yere such on here gan to wake, | But he slepte and in sompnolence was take' (*Partenay*, lines 5484–6). Their punishment is to remain in stasis: those who attempted and failed remained in the castle 'unto the day of Iugement' (*Partenay*, line 5490). The three kings who succeeded were termed 'full uaillant and wurthy' for their alertness: 'Which noght

---

[13] On *Beues* as a romance in which 'the other' is employed to construct English identity, see Siobhain Bly Calkin, *Saracens and the Making of English Identity: the Auchinleck Manuscript* (New York, 2005). A partial and oblique comprehension of Armenia's complicated politics and its ancient national Church is reflected in some of the confusion of plot and theme in this romance, which designates the king of Armenia as a Saracen. Armenia's continual refusal to accept the spiritual and temporal overlordship of the Roman Church into the fourteenth century may have contributed to a sense of the heterodoxy of the Armenian Orthodox Church, accounting for the description of Josian as a Saracen princess in *Beues*. The Middle English term *Saracen/Sarasine* was used broadly to designate a variety of people who were not Roman Christians: heathens, pagans, infidels, Danes and Jews; see *MED*.

[14] On the identification of Tars with Armenia see Lillian Herlands Hornstein, 'The historical background of *The King of Tars*', *Speculum*, 16 (1941), 404–14; and *The King of Tars*, ed. Judith Perryman (Heidelberg, 1980), p. 47.

[15] *The Romans of Partenay or of Lusignen: Otherwise Known as The Tale of Melusine*, ed. Rev. W. W. Skeat, EETS o.s. 22 (London, 1866).

ne went to sompnolent sleping' (*Partenay*, lines 5507–8). In the Melusine/ Partenay version, a king of Armenia descended from Melusine and Count Raymond of Poitiers succeeds in his attempt to watch wakefully, and asks as his reward the lady Melior's person. When she explains the enchantments that forbid granting his request, the king of Armenia persists, at which point Melior calls him a 'foltish muserde' (*Partenay*, line 5559) – that is, a fool and an 'idler' – and curses all his line so that by him 'may come full huge ill and pine | To you and to all youres of your line' (*Partenay*, lines 5620–21) who will lose their land. The last king of Armenia, she says, will bear the name of a beast (*Partenay*, lines 5622–8). All this will happen because of the seeker king's 'unthriftinesse' (*Partenay*, line 5633); where he could have had profit, he now must endure the consequences of loss. The poem goes on to record how nine successive kings of Armenia became ever worse until, 'Thay lost ther lande and all ther hauour | Inclynyng and coming vnto mischaunce' (*Partenay*, lines 5685–6). The last of these, who was the king Philippe de Mézières sponsored and who travelled to Richard II's court, did indeed bear the name of a beast, for he was called Levon, Armenian for Leon or Leo; dispossessed of his title and land, he fled to France, where he became a dependant of the king of France, and died in Paris, being buried at the Convent of the Celestines.[16]

Gower evokes this web of politics, sterility, and sloth – all central late medieval topics that convey the symbolic as well as the historical significance of Armenia. In the story of Rosiphelee, one of the tales of sloth that comprise the fourth book of the *Confessio*, Gower names Rosiphelee as the daughter of the king of Armenia in the first line of the tale, thus invoking a defined horizon of expectation for his readers, centred in the familiar context of loss and decline that characterizes Armenian narratives in Anglo-French culture. Rosiphelee is introduced as both a princess and heir to her father's kingdom; her refusal to love thus represents more than personal choice:

> Of armenye, I rede thus,
> Ther was a king, which Herupus
> Was hote, and he a lusti maide
> To dowhter hadde and, as men saide,
> Hire name was Rosiphelee,
> Which tho was of gret renomee,
> For sche was bothe wys and fair
> And scholde ben hire fader hair.
> Bot sche hadde o defalte of Slowthe
> Towardes love, and that was rowthe   (*Confessio*, IV, lines 1245–54)

The exemplary value of the story of Rosiphelee is readily apprehensible within the tropological values of book IV, but its topicality alludes to a large number of literary and historical texts that suggest that its exemplary function extends far beyond its function of representing a particular kind of sloth in not being willing to love. Generally regarded as one of Gower's best

---

[16] At the time of the French Revolution his tomb, along with French royal tombs, was moved to St Denis, where it remains to this day.

narratives, the story is a highly wrought idyll in which the daughter of the king of Armenia, previously resistant to loving and therefore slothful in the service of Venus and nature, witnesses a cavalcade of beautifully dressed women riding elegantly caparisoned snow-white steeds through an early May landscape. One of the women is, and is not, part of this company; she follows at a distance, dressed in black, riding a black horse that suffers from galls but is equipped with a jewelled bridle: 'And natheles ther was with that | A riche bridel for the nones | Of gold and preciouse stones' (*Confessio*, IV, lines 1352–4). More puzzlingly, she wears a number of halters 'aboute hir middel' (*Confessio*, IV, line 1356). When Rosiphelee asks her to explain the meaning of the cavalcade and her appearance, she says that the women are true lovers now rewarded for their fidelity and that she, only yielding to the pleasures of love in what became the last two weeks of her life, is part of the company by virtue of her loving, yet not fully so because of her sloth in joining the universal celebration of Venus. Hearing this story, Rosiphelee vows to mend her ways:

> 'I schal amende it, if I may'.
> And thus homward this lady wente,
> And changede al hire ferste entente,
> Withinne hire herte and gan to swere
> That sche none halters wolde bere' (*Confessio*, IV, lines 1442–6)

The tale is full of significant elements that invite various interpretations: the May landscape; the horses, signs of will and passion; the jewelled bridle of the reluctant lover's horse, a gleaming sign of her entry into the world of love, and of willing submission to it; the multiple halters that so frighten Rosiphelee. One might be tempted to read it in isolation. It is, after all, a very richly indeterminate text whose moral messages are various and worth pondering.

The story's topicality emerges in a thread that Gower lays out in the next tale, that of Jephthah's daughter, and in the subsequent discussion between Amans and the Confessor about the value of deeds of arms done for love, at home and away. This larger frame shows how Gower's shaping imagination creates a horizon of expectation for his reader. After the story of Rosiphelee the Confessor shifts the centre of attention from love to fertility as he explicates the benefits of 'love wel at ese | Which set is upon mariage' (*Confessio* IV, lines 1476–7), and of children, and then introduces the exemplary story of Jephthah's daughter, a story of wasted fertility. After the tale of Jephthah's disastrous bargain for victory the focus shifts once more, when Amans asks about men who are slothful in the service of nature and love, thereby introducing a discussion of love and deeds of arms performed in Prussia and Outremer, specifically 'Sometime in Tartarie', a reference to the land through which the fate of greater Armenia was decided among Mongols, Mamluks and Tartars who strove for dominance over that Christian nation and over one another. Love shades into fertility and fertility into futility as Amans invokes the East in questioning the value of deeds of arms in love, 'What scholde I winne over the se | If mi ladi loste at hom?' (*Confessio*, IV, lines

1664–5). Sloth lies not just in failing to act, failing to love, but in not realizing where true gain may lie. Just as the king of Armenia in the Sparrowhawk quest mistook the ability to stay wakeful as his central task and so was unwary of the threat of moral sloth, knights who go abroad to fight may lose the hope of love – that is, profit and good – at home. Gower's marked resistance to crusading ventures shadows this discussion, which is seemingly about chivalric codes such as those Geoffroi de Charny explicated so fully in the mid fourteenth century,[17] but is also a political discussion centred in the value of turning attention from 'home' to the East. Mistaken expectations and misplaced values mark each of these separate episodes: the lady in *Rosiphelee*, slow to love when she was 'able for to lere', figures a sterile separation from the larger community symbolized by participation in loving; Jephthah's rash vow to sacrifice the first thing he sees on his return if God will grant him victory in battle invites thought about the value of victory; the discussion of whether deeds of arms can be or ought to be sufficient basis for love opposes fertility to violence. Taken together and in the context of late medieval Anglo-French semiotics of Armenia, the narratives and exchanges of book IV direct a reader toward a topical as well as a tropological understanding. Armenia, known in history and romance as an example of loss and decline, represents a cautionary tale for Western Europe of the failure of arms and of profit.

In the seventh book, of advice to a prince, Gower turns once more to an Armenian reference – the story of Pompey's generosity to Tigranes, captured king of Armenia and enemy of Rome – to introduce another topical subtheme. Ostensibly a narrative of good kingship and of magnanimous mercy, the story also subtly evokes narratives of betrayal and deposition linked to Armenia in Chaucer's *Anelida and Arcite* and in contemporary accounts of the adventures of Levon V/VI the last king of Armenia. The classical story of Tigranes, which exists in the writing of both Maximus Valerius and Cicero, illustrates the nobility Pompey shows as a merciful ruler. Cicero says that when Pompey 'saw him [Tigranes] as an abject suppliant in his own camp, he made him rise, and he set back on his head the emblem of kingship that Tigranes had cast off; after giving him certain specific injunctions, he bade him rule, judging that being seen to set a king upon his throne brought no less glory to himself and our dominion than holding him in bondage.'[18] Valerius Maximus tells the story this way:

> Tigranes, king of Armenia, had waged major wars against the Roman people on his own and protected with his power a sworn enemy of our city, Mithradates, when he was driven out of Pontus. Pompey did not let him lie before his eyes in supplication for long, but revived him with kindly words, told him to put the diadem, which he had discarded, back on his head, and

---

[17] See Geoffroi de Charny, *A Knight's Own Book of Chivalry*, intro. Richard Kaeuper, trans. Elspeth Kennedy (Philadelphia, PA, 2005).
[18] Marcus Publius Cicero, *Speech on Behalf of Publius Sestius*, trans. Robert A. Kaster (Oxford, 2006), p. 67.

after giving orders on certain points, restored him to his former state of fortune. He thought it equally fine to conquer kings and to make them.[19]

Gower, however, redirects his source in respect to detail and moral: the tropological value of the story lies in the way it exemplifies pity and mercy. But this tropological value is to some extent displaced by the way Gower chooses to dwell on the description on Tigranes' captivity, redirecting focus to the victim, both as challenger and sufferer: Pompey was waging a war which stood in

> ... jeupartie
> Agein the king of Ermenie,
> Which of long time him hadded grieved.
> Bot ate laste it was achieved
> That he this king desconfit hadde,
> And forth with him to Rome ladde
> As prisoner, wher many a day
> In sori plit and povere he lay,
> The corone of his heved deposed,
> Withinne walles faste enclosed;
> And with ful gret humilité
> He soffreth his adversité.
> Pompeie sih his pacience
> And tok pité with conscience,
> So that upon his hihe deis
> Tofore al Rome in his paleis,
> As he that wolde upon him rewe,
> Let give him his corone newe
> And his astat al full and plein
> Restoreth of his regne agein,
> And seide it was more goodly thing
> To make than undon a king ... (*Confessio*, VII, lines 3217–38)

While this passage bears a striking similarity to the way that Philippe de Mézières disseminated the story about the defeat and imprisonment of Levon on the island of Rosetta in Egypt, stressing the sorrows of imprisonment:

> Et tant tint par grant vaillance sa dicte cite de Sys que finablement par force de batailles, de long siege et de famine, il convint render la cite au soldan. Et fu menéz prisonnier le roy, la royne, s'espouse et .v. peti[t]s enfans au Caire en Babilone en la prison du soldan...Et par deffaulte d'ayde le dit roy Lyon d'Armenye fu en la prison du souldan .vij. ans entiers. Et tant y ot de doulours et de meschiés, que en la dicte prison la royne sa compaigne et tous ses enfans morurent de povreté et de mischief et demoura tout seul a grant dolour, povreté et de melencolie.
> (*Livre de la vertu du sacrement* ..., p. 385)

> (And he held the same city of Sis by great valor until finally by force of battle, of a long siege and of famine, he was forced to surrender the city to the sultan. And he, the queen his wife, and five little children were taken prisoner to the Sultan of Babilon in prison in Cairo ... and through lack of

---

[19] Valerius Maximus, *Memorable Doings and Sayings*, ed. and trans. D. R. Shackleton Bailey (Cambridge, MA, 2000), p. 451.

aid [from Europe] the said king Leon of Armenia was in the sultan's prison for seven whole years. And he suffered many sadnesses and afflictions, for in that same prison the queen his companion and all his children died of poverty and misfortune and he remained all alone in great sorrow, poverty and melancholy ...) (my translation).

In both stories the emphasis is on the imprisoned monarch who suffers steadfastly.[20] Just as pity moves Pompey, Philippe tells us that God 'mist au cuer au tres devot Jehan roy d'Espaigne la deliverance du dit roy d'Armenye' (p. 385). In the classical story the ruler of Rome restores the king's crown; Philippe hoped for a similar happy end to his medieval story, and worked assiduously to get Richard II and Charles VI to restore Levon's crown by undertaking a crusade to liberate Armenia and from there the Holy Land, but to no avail. Interestingly, Gower conveniently sanitizes the classical stories of Tigranes's complicated relationship with his son, who betrayed him, and whose children the elder Tigranes murdered. This theme of betrayal in the antecedent of Tigranes aligns Gower's narrative and Chaucer's narrative of Anelida and the brooch of Ermony within the walls of Thebes as part of the larger topos of betrayal evoked by the idea of Armenia and its history of broken alliances.

While no one medieval reader would have responded either to Gower's narratives or to the idea of Armenia with precisely the interpretants I have raised here, many would have recognized the horizon of expectation – the topicality – inherent in the tropological examples discussed here. Many would have known the stories Mandeville and the romances tell about Armenia. Among these, some would surely have been in the king's affinity and would have known of Levon, possibly even known Levon in his 1386 trip to Richard II's court. A work of its time and literary culture, Gower's 'bok for Engelondes sake' raises moral questions and relies on its readers to fashion its meanings. But its author shows himself a master of polysemy as he writes an ethical text which is also a labyrinthine semiotic text that infuses ancient and fictional narratives with current topicality. In late-fourteenth-century Anglo-French court culture Armenia was the other and the familiar, the liminal site of projected anxieties about Christianity, conquest and security. Recognizing the artistry and complex literary strategy inherent in the way that he invokes Armenia, we recognize the brilliance of Gower's open text written in the vernacular for common profit. *Confessio Amantis* is an instructive text that works on multiple levels and in multiple ways for various members of its audience. The reader in Yorkshire, the reader in London, the gentry reader, the court reader will all learn, but each will read a slightly different text. The wise reader who reads for wisdom, the ideal *lecteur* Minet-Mahy identifies with the prince, will read the text most broadly and most profitably, because the text is written for him in terms

---

[20] It is very unlikely that Gower would have read de Mézières's account, but not unlikely that he would have heard of Levon's misadventures and lengthy imprisonment during which time he lost most of his family. On this see Collette and DiMarco, 'The matter of Armenia', pp. 349–50, n. 60.

most readily apprehensible by him. Gower, like Chaucer, says that all that is written is written for 'oure doctrine', and each constructs a literature in which 'doctrine' is not just a function of reader reception, but part of a shared cultural matrix. Gower's genius lies in how deftly and surely he invokes that matrix and reveals its lessons.

4

Saving History:
Gower's Apocalyptic and the New Arion

ELLIOT KENDALL

In the Prologue to *Confessio Amantis*, apocalyptic is the vehicle for a far-reaching statement about the shape of history and about good political order. This is political theology of a different order from the noon-day demon and animal Armageddon fireworks of *Vox Clamantis*.[1] The thoroughness of the poem's apocalyptic indicates how full and theorized is the *Confessio*'s idea of earthly politics. The Prologue's apocalyptic history is mirrored in the lover's personal, penitential apocalypse at the end of the poem. This implies a fulcrum between the political and the personal, and this fulcrum bears a special, politically positive load in Gower's idiosyncratic inflection of apocalyptic with a wished-for new Arion.

Apocalyptic and apocalypse are overlapping but not coterminous categories. Bernard McGinn sets out the distinctions: 'The word *apocalypse* means "revelation", the unveiling of a divine secret.' Apocalypse in this sense might not be apocalyptic in the sense of 'linking the succession of time and its end'. Apocalyptic or apocalypticism is 'a species of the genus eschatology' distinguished by the urgency of its concern for 'the structure and End of history'. It might not be presented in the form of an apocalypse.[2]

The apocalyptic in the *Confessio* is more coherent than that of the *Vox*, but, focusing on the figure of a new Arion, it also introduces a level of contingency untypical of apocalyptic writing in general. Helen Cooper has observed that apocalyptic writing 'in the Middle Ages, and later', uses 'the idea of the non-negotiable judgments of God to take political and moral discourse out of the realm of debate and replace it with a religious absolute'.[3] God's sense of right and wrong functions in such a way in the *Confessio*, but the new Arion passage posits that the timing of Judgment is contingent, and depends on human disunity or social reform. This gives the poem's apocalyptic theory a very significant pro-history twist, imagining for lay poetry and politics independent (if divinely monitored) power on the threshold of the religious

---

[1] See *Vox*, I, lines 737–46 for the 'demon meridianus'.
[2] Bernard McGinn, *Visions of the End: Apocalyptic Traditions in the Middle Ages*, rev. edn (New York, 1998), pp. xvi–xviii, xx, 2–4, quotations at pp. 2, 3, xvi.
[3] Helen Cooper, 'The four last things in Dante and Chaucer: Ugolino in the House of Rumour', *NML* 3 (1999), 39–66 (p. 40).

absolute. In line with the poem's broad sense of politics, this power does not belong to princes, much less the Church. The march of history, for the *Confessio*, is beyond a prince's control, but can be directed by the less choate force of multitudes of (poetically) reformed consciences.

Gower's apocalyptic in the *Confessio* Prologue starts with the book of Daniel and the composite statue of Nebuchadnezzar's dream, updating Daniel's exposition at length to trace a world history of *translatio imperii* and decline from the golden Babylonian head to the fragile mixed feet of the Holy Roman Empire (Daniel 2. 31–45; *Confessio*, Prol., lines 585–880). As in Daniel, the stone of the End time smashes the statue of world history (*Confessio*, Prol., lines 618–24, 651–62).[4] Gower goes on to blend Daniel into gospel apocalyptic, echoing the Synoptic Gospels on signs of the End and on Judgment (*Confessio*, Prol., lines 957–61, 1032–50; Matthew 24. 7–13, 29–35, 25. 31–46; Luke 21. 10–11, 25–36). Then, late in the Prologue, comes a curious, non-deterministic and non-supernatural annex. It ponders what would happen if somebody like the ancient harper Arion intervened and held off Judgment Day for a time (*Confessio*, Prol., lines 1053–83). As it moves to the final moments of Nebuchadnezzar's statue of history, the Prologue takes Arion's successor as its surprising final focus or fulcrum; surprising because, as the End looms, Gower suddenly throws out a drag line to remain on this side of the divide between this world and the next. Surprising also because this brake jolts us from pessimistic world chronicle of empire into a vision of perfected and politically uncentralized society.

Medieval apocalyptic sheds light on Gower's highly individual combination of the End-times and Arion, and underlines the significance in the *Confessio* of the relationship between apocalyptic and penance discussed below. The apocalyptic conspectus in the Prologue sets up a model of history for the whole poem. Appropriately, therefore, the statue of Daniel 2 is one of two main themes in the ordinary illustrative programmes of *Confessio* manuscripts, and Jeremy Griffiths suggests that it was 'the one constant illustration to the text'.[5] In some early manuscripts the statue picture is large and occupies a position conventional for author or presentation pictures, which speak of a text as a whole. This illustrative scheme suggests the importance of apocalyptic to some medieval readings of the *Confessio*.[6] The statue illus-

---

[4] Cf. the exposition of Daniel 2 of Otto of Freising, *The Two Cities: A Chronicle of Universal History to the Year 1146 A.D.*, trans. C. C. Mierow (New York, 1928), 6.36; excerpted in McGinn, *Visions*, pp. 98–9. See also R. W. Southern, 'Aspects of the European tradition of historical writing 2: Hugh of St Victor and the idea of historical development', *TRHS*, 5th ser. 21 (1971), 159–79 (pp. 176–7).

[5] Jeremy Griffiths, '*Confessio Amantis*: the poem and its pictures', in *Gower's Confessio Amantis: Responses and Reassessments*, ed. A. J. Minnis (Cambridge, 1983), pp. 163–78 (p. 171). For the type and location of miniatures in illustrated *Confessio* MSS, see Richard K. Emmerson, 'Reading Gower in a manuscript culture: Latin and English in illustrated manuscripts of the *Confessio Amantis*', *SAC*, 21 (1999), 143–86 (pp. 167–70 and his table of MSS, pp. 184–6). Cf. a similar table in Griffiths, 'The poem and its pictures', pp. 176–7. The other main theme is the kneeling penitent, and only two extant MSS include major miniature cycles: New York, Pierpont Morgan Lib. MS M 126 and the much defaced Oxford, New College MS 266.

[6] Oxford, Bodleian Lib. MS Fairfax 3, San Marino, Huntington Lib. MS Ellesmere 26 A 17 and Princeton, Princeton Univ. Lib. MS 5 have the miniature in frontispiece position. On the (in)

trations (particularly those that depict the fatal stone) signal the urgency in the poem's sense of history ('Al sodeinly the Ston schal falle'; *Confessio*, Prol., line 1038), but they do not include the peculiarly hopeful and provisional turn that the new Arion passage gives to Gower's apocalyptic. Only one extant manuscript illustrates a harper in the Prologue.[7]

Apocalypticism, neatly characterized by McGinn, is a way of thinking about history in which 'history has meaning because it is directed toward an imminent end'. McGinn also proposes that apocalypticism's essential 'sense of the imminence, or nearness' of the end – the urgency that sets it apart from other eschatology – can be psychological as much as chronologically exact, a sense of living in the shadow of the End and being driven by the final events.[8] (These final events might themselves last a long and unspecified time.) In this light, the *Confessio* Prologue's apocalyptic appears much more complex and coherent than the doom-mongering of Gower's earlier Latin complaint, *Vox Clamantis*. The differences between the poems are considerable. Where the *Vox* is visionary, vatic-voiced, and laments an End-like crisis, the *Confessio* is exegetical, heavily theorized, and extends a conspectus of the past into the imagination of a future solution.[9] In *Vox* books I and VII there is an unmistakable sense of crisis; but a properly apocalyptic, End-

---

significance of illustrations to the meanings of late medieval texts, see Elizabeth Salter and Derek Pearsall, 'Pictorial illustration of late medieval poetic texts: the role of the frontispiece or prefatory picture', in *Medieval Iconography and Narrative: A Symposium*, eds Flemming G. Andersen *et al.* (Odense, 1980), esp. pp. 100–106; Patricia Eberle, 'Miniatures as evidence of reading in a manuscript of the *Confessio Amantis* (Pierpont Morgan MS M 126)', in *John Gower: Recent Readings*, ed. R. F. Yeager (Kalamazoo, MI, 1989), pp. 311–17, 344–6. Cf. on 'codicological aesthetics', Ralph Hanna III, *Pursuing History: Middle English Manuscripts and their Texts* (Stanford, CA, 1996), p. 81.

[7] This is New York, Pierpont MS M 126, fol. 7ᵛ (before *Confessio*, Prol. line 1053). The harper plays to a scene of concord, two men clasping hands, prey and predators gathered nose to unthreatening nose. (The statue picture in this MS does not include a boulder.) Oxford, New College MS 266, extensively illustrated like Pierpont MS M 126, pictures no harper, but is missing a folio (fol. 7) where he might have appeared.

[8] McGinn, *Visions*, pp. xx, xvii. Cf. Frank Kermode, *The Sense of an Ending: Studies in the Theory of Fiction* (New York, 1967), p. 5 on the shadow of the End.

[9] Exegesis is a common mode for medieval apocalyptic. On the exegesis and inspired exegesis of the Spanish monk Beatus of Liébana (*c.*750–798), the Calabrian abbot Joachim of Fiore (*c.*1135–1202) and the Franciscan John of Rupescissa (*c.*1310–*c.*1365), see chapters in McGinn, *Visions*; see also Marjorie Reeves, 'The development of apocalyptic thought: medieval attitudes', in *The Apocalypse in English Renaissance Thought and Literature*, ed. C. A. Patrides and Joseph Wittreich (Manchester, 1984), p. 44 (Beatus); Marjorie Reeves, *The Influence of Prophecy in the Later Middle Ages: A Study in Joachimism* (Oxford, 1969), esp. pp. 21–5; Robert E. Lerner, *The Powers of Prophecy: The Cedars of Lebanon Vision from the Mongol Onslaught to the Dawn of the Enlightenment* (Berkeley, CA, 1983), p. 137 (Rupescissa). Cf. the eschatological vision of the New Jerusalem in *Pearl*, which cites and (almost) matches Scripture, and seems to owe inspiration to Apocalypse manuscript illumination: *Pearl*, in *Poems of the Pearl Manuscript: Pearl, Cleanness, Patience, Sir Gawain and the Green Knight*, eds Malcolm Andrew and Ronald Waldron, 5th edn (Exeter, 2007), lines 977–1152; Barbara Nolan, *The Gothic Visionary Perspective* (Princeton, NJ, 1977), pp. 54–83; Muriel A. Whitaker, '*Pearl* and some illustrated apocalypse manuscripts', *Viator*, 12 (1981), 183–96; Rosalind Field, 'The heavenly Jerusalem in *Pearl*', *MLR*, 81 (1986), 7–17; Sarah Stanbury, *Seeing the Gawain-poet: Description and the Act of Perception* (Philadelphia, PA, 1991), pp. 21–35. On the prophetic elements of the *Vox*, see A. J. Minnis, *Medieval Theory of Authorship: Scholastic Literary Attitudes in the Later Middle Ages*, 2nd edn (Aldershot, 1988), pp. 168–77.

moulded sense of history is implicit and faltering at most. For one thing, the narrator has survived and is looking *back* on the beast-rebel onslaught which he has associated with the End time. Gower's use of Daniel 2 provides a direct point of comparison between his poems. In the *Vox*, the historical burden of Nebuchadnezzar's statue is muted and obscured because Gower uses the statue to visualize a dichotomy of glorious past and enfeebled present (rather than a more developed apocalyptic progression; *Vox*, VII, lines 5–8) or even to symbolize synchronous social strata, eliding diachrony altogether (*Vox*, VII, lines 1378–80).[10] The *Vox* sporadically erupts into alarm about divine retribution, but its transformations of apocalyptic iconography might be termed Augustinian because they do not cogently signal imminent and final change.[11] The *Confessio* Prologue, by contrast, is more conversant with apocalyptic. It exhibits a developed sense of historical progression and, specifically, a fully apocalyptic take on history as past, present, and future all directed towards an *imminent* End.

Chiliasm and the *Katechōn*

Gower's apocalyptic theology in the *Confessio* is most innovative at the end of the Prologue, when a wished-for reincarnation of the harper Arion acts (in the subjunctive) in a socially restorative manner:

> Bot wolde god that now were on
> An other such as Arion,
> Which hadde an harpe of such temprure,
> And thereto of so good mesure
> He song, that he the bestes wilde
> Made of his note tame and milde,
> The Hinde in pes with the Leoun,
> ...
> He broghte hem alle in good acord;
> So that the comun with the lord,
> And lord with the comun also,
> He sette in love bothe tuo
> And putte awey malencolie.
> ...
> He [a new Arion] myhte availe in many a stede
> To make pes wher now is hate;
> ...

---

[10] See also Russell A. Peck, 'John Gower and the Book of Daniel', in *John Gower: Recent Readings*, ed. R. F. Yeager (Kalamazoo, MI, 1989), pp. 159–87, which is less concerned to differentiate Gower's use of Daniel in *Vox* and *Confessio*.

[11] On the 'rudimentary' view of historical development that the Middle Ages drew from Augustine of Hippo, see McGinn, *Visions*, pp. 26–7; Southern, 'Idea of historical development', pp. 160–63 (p. 160). In Augustine's eschatology, the present is mired somewhere in the world's sixth and final age, its end unknowable under the authority of Acts 1. 7, 'It is not for you to know the times or moments': Augustine of Hippo, *De civitate dei*, ed. B. Dombart and A. Kalb, 2 vols (Turnhout, 1955), and *The City of God Against the Pagans*, trans. R. W. Dyson (Cambridge, 1998), 18.52–3, 22.30.

> For [rage] bringth in the comun drede,
> Which stant at every mannes Dore.
> (*Confessio*, Prol., lines 1053–83; cf. Isaiah 11. 6; Matthew 24. 33)

Gower's immediate source for Arion seems to be Ovid's *Fasti*, where Arion enchants only non-human nature.[12] Gower makes Arion's political potency explicit, so that he brings lords and commons 'in good acord'. By an equal virtue, a *new* Arion would forestall Judgment Day. That is, his vibe of peace would retard the process of outrage and discord which leads, echoing the gospels again, to the 'comun drede | Which stant at every mannes Dore' (cf. Matthew 24. 33). This is nothing less than the end of the world.

Four aspects of the new Arion passage seem to me especially useful in locating it and its politics in relation to medieval apocalyptic traditions. First, the wish for a new Arion envisages a state of radical social improvement or regeneration on earth. Secondly, this state is one of quasi-feudal political order in which the Church is inconspicuous if not absent. Thirdly, this state, and the appearance of Arion's successor, is wholly contingent and not apparently supernaturally prompted. Finally, the period in which the influence of Arion's successor would be felt is prior to the predetermined events of the End time (not an element of them) and the new Arion would forestall these events.

These four aspects place the passage somewhere between the worldly optimism of millenarianism or chiliasm and the cautious preservative quality of the so-called *Katechōn*. The first aspect – hope for radical social improvement – points towards chiliasm. As distinct from other apocalyptic, chiliasm predicted 'imminent, supernaturally inspired, radical betterment *on earth* before the Last Judgment'.[13] Most orthodox and especially patristic eschatology was anti-apocalyptic and certainly anti-chiliastic; but late medieval apocalyptic was predominantly chiliastic.[14] The other bearing to which the new Arion points, the *Katechōn*, is the force restraining the Antichrist in II Thessalonians: 'For the mystery of iniquity already works; only that he who now holds, do hold, until he be taken out of the way' (II Thess. 2. 7). The *Katechōn* seems to have enjoyed a minor revival in late-fourteenth-century apocalyptic.

Robert Lerner has argued persuasively for the gestation of chiliasm in ideas about the time after Antichrist. Authorities such as Jerome (*c*.345–420), Bede (*c*.673–735), Alcuin (*c*.740–804) and Haymo of Auxerre (d. *c*.860) attempted to deal with enigmatic scriptural pronouncements about this portion of the End times without exciting great temporal hopes. Nonethe-

---

[12] Ovid, *Fasti*, ed. and tr. James G. Frazer, 2nd edn (Cambridge, MA, 1989), II. 83–90. Cf. Herodotus, *The Persian Wars*, tr. A. D. Godley, 4 vols (Cambridge, MA, 1920–25), I. 24; Plato, *Republic*, tr. Paul Shorey, 2 vols (Cambridge, MA, 1930–35), V. 453.d. See also R. F. Yeager, *John Gower's Poetic: The Search for a New Arion* (Cambridge, 1990), pp. 238–9.

[13] Robert E. Lerner, 'The Black Death and Western European eschatological mentalities', *American Historical Review*, 86 (1981), 533–52 (p. 537, emphasis added).

[14] McGinn, *Visions*, pp. 146–8; Reeves, 'Development of apocalyptic thought' and *Influence of Prophecy*; Lerner, 'Black Death'; on England: Kathryn Kerby-Fulton, *Reformist Apocalypticism and Piers Plowman* (Cambridge, 1990), pp. 21–5, 197–200.

less, their work fed into imaginings of this period as one of radical earthly peace.[15] Lerner also observes more generally that a period of respite, purification or exaltation forms part of the basic pattern or 'deep structure' of high and late medieval short prophecies of the End.[16] The chiliasm of Joachim of Fiore (c.1135–1202) or his appropriators is generally seen to be seminal for the decisively optimistic treatments of the end of history typical of apocalyptic, short or elaborate, after the twelfth century.[17]

Joachim envisaged a newly profound regeneration of society in a long peace time after Antichrist, or the bulk of Antichrist's upheavals – a wonderful dispensation of the Holy Spirit and an essentially monastic third 'status' and 'novus ordo', or new people of God. His *Book of Figures* includes the following sequence:

> After the destruction of this [the seventh] Antichrist there will be justice on earth and an abundance of peace ... Men will turn their swords into ploughshares, their spears into sickles. One nation will not lift up the sword against another; there will be no more war (Isaiah 2. 4). The Jews and the many unbelieving nations will be converted to the Lord, and the whole people will rejoice in the beauty of peace because the heads of the great dragon will be crushed. ... [At a time known only to God] Satan again will be released from his prison ...[18]

The mood of agrarian tranquility is similar in the *Confessio* Prologue: 'The Hinde in pes with the Leoun, | The Wolf in pes with the Moltoun', lord and shepherd 'in good acord' (*Confessio*, Prol., lines 1057–65); where Isaiah resonates as strongly as Ovid: 'the calf and the lion, and the sheep shall abide together' (Isaiah 11. 6). Most importantly for a comparison between Joachim and Gower, both scenarios of uncompromised renewal before the End are collective and earthly, where patristic and other anti-apocalyptic exegesis of Isaiah and the Psalms tends to defuse the material's chiliastic potential by ascribing it to the first advent of Christ, or interpreting it as allegory of the present life of the Church or division within individual souls, or assigning it to the next world.[19]

Pre-Antichrist chiliastic schemes are sometimes grouped under the heading of the Last World Emperor myth. The trope of a good Christian

---

[15] Robert E. Lerner, 'Refreshment of the saints: the time after Antichrist as a station for earthly progress in medieval thought', *Traditio*, 32 (1976), 97–144.

[16] Lerner, *Powers of Prophecy*, esp. pp. 190–95.

[17] On Joachim and the question of his influence, see the work of Marjorie Reeves, esp. 'History and prophecy in medieval thought', *Medievalia et Humanistica*, n.s. 5 (1974), 51–75; *Influence of Prophecy*; *Joachim of Fiore and the Prophetic Future* (London, 1976); 'The originality and influence of Joachim of Fiore', *Traditio*, 36 (1980), 269–316. See also Bernard McGinn, 'The abbot and the doctors: scholastic reactions to the radical eschatology of Joachim of Fiore', *Church History*, 40 (1971), 30–47; 'Apocalypticism in the Middle Ages: an historiographical sketch', *MSt*, 37 (1975), 252–86; *The Calabrian Abbot: Joachim of Fiore in the History of Western Thought* (New York, 1985).

[18] Joachim of Fiore, *Il Libro delle Figure*, ed. Leone Tondelli, Marjorie Reeves and Beatrice Hirsch-Reich, 2 vols (Turin, 1953), plate xiv, trans. McGinn, *Visions*, p. 138.

[19] For example, Jerome, *Commentariorum in Isaiam prophetam libri duodeviginti*, in *PL*, 24, col. 0147–9; Augustine, *De civitate dei*, 20.7–9, 19.

conqueror who would lead the faith to universal triumph and inaugurate a wondrous age of peace before the advent of Antichrist went back to the seventh-century Pseudo-Methodius if not earlier. The Emperor's dominion could be a period of material prosperity and spiritual enervation akin to the time before the Flood, but Last World Emperor discourse mixed with optimistic, Joachite ideas in the late Middle Ages.[20] Survivals of one especially positive example, the so-called 'Tripoli' prophecy, include five manuscripts from late-fourteenth-century England. The prophecy tells of a ruler who will restore Jerusalem and initiate an era of peace amounting to the best time in all history.[21] Various short political prophecies approximate the Last World Emperor pattern but, like Gower, do not invoke Antichrist at all. A representative version of the 'Toledo Letter', possibly the most popular short medieval prose prophecy, speaks from astrological authority of calamities, a war leader, a great war and 'the change of kingdoms, the pre-eminence [*excellentiam*] of the Franks, the destruction of the Saracen nation, greater charity and the greatest exaltation of the law of Christ, and a longer life for those who will be born afterward'.[22] The plain social tranquillity, the Christian peace and charity envisaged resemble the new Arion's age of 'good acord' and 'love'.

Another short prophecy, a sonnet by Petrarch from 1347, provides a classically inflected chiliastic parallel to Gower's new Arion passage. It is directed against the Avignonese papacy, which in the fourteenth century inspired a great deal of apocalyptic writing, unfavourable and favourable. The sonnet accuses Babylon (Avignon) of making its gods 'Not Jove and Pallas, but Venus and Bacchus'. The poet awaits a new ruler who will unite the Church in 'One See ... in Baghdad'. This ruler will act as a scourge in advance of a new golden age:

> Anime belle et di virtute amiche
> terrano il mondo, et poi vedrem lui farsi
> aureo tutto et pien de l'opre antiche.
>
> Fair souls and friends of virtue
> Will rule the world, and then we will see
> The world becoming golden and full of ancient works.[23]

Petrarch's sonnet is topically, polemically engaged in ecclesiastical politics. Gower's new Arion passage (like the 'Toledo Letter') is not. But the Church is central to Gower's view of apocalyptic decline and 'division' in

---

[20] McGinn, *Visions*, esp. pp. 33–4, 43–50, 70–76, 85–6, 168–79; Reeves, 'Development of apocalyptic thought', pp. 45–6; Lerner, 'Black Death', p. 544.

[21] Lerner, *Powers of Prophecy*, esp. p. 118 n. 6.

[22] Roger of Howden, *Chronica*, ed. William Stubbs, 4 vols (London, 1868–71), ii, p. 291, trans. in McGinn, *Visions*, p. 153; see also Lerner, *Powers of Prophecy*, pp. 190–91.

[23] Petrarch, Lyric 137, in *Petrarch's Lyric Poems: The Rime Sparse and Other Lyrics*, ed. and trans. Robert M. Durling (Cambridge, MA, 1976), lines 12–14; McGinn, *Visions*, p. 244. The earliest extant English translation of a Petrarchan sonnet, in Chaucer's *Troilus and Criseyde*, was produced in the 1380s: Ernest H. Wilkins, 'Cantus Troili', *ELH*, 16 (1949), 167–73; Patricia Thomson, 'The "*Canticus Troili*": Chaucer and Petrarch', *Comparative Literature*, 11 (1959), 313–28.

the Prologue: Avignon remains a byword for 'Pompe' and a Church interested in 'erthly thinge' is characteristic of the present age of iron and clay (*Confessio*, Prol., lines 304–7, 328–33, 851–80). Petrarch's historical scheme, in which a corrupted Church is cleared out for a new peace with a lay ambience, is more strenuous than but similar to Gower's. As a distinctively lay version of the apostolic renewal or 'ad pristinum statum' theme popular in medieval apocalyptic, the new Arion passage is implicitly anticlerical.[24]

Regardless of the affinities between the 'Toledo' dispensation and Arionic renewal, between Petrarch's and Gower's golden ages future, however, it remains that the *Confessio* Prologue is not finally chiliastic: it speaks in hope and not conviction about the future (and rather furtive hope at that). Arion's successor is sought-after, not predicted and divinely sent. Also, the social renewal he would inspire would delay rather than further the completion of history. (These are the third and fourth of the four salient aspects by which I earlier characterized the Prologue's apocalyptic.) The supreme earthly renewal in a truly chiliastic text enters into the sequence of the End times, so that its reversing the moral stamp of the world is already fully part of the final divine plan. In his 'holding role', the new Arion is less like a Last World Emperor and more like the *Katechōn*, the last line of defence against the final evil and the divine retribution that will end the world. But the *Katechōn* is already present and forestalling, not sudden and radically reformative in the fashion of a new Arion. In the writings of Cola di Rienzo (c.1314–1354), revolutionary and excommunicate, and later papal senator and victim of a Roman mob, Saints Dominic and Francis figure as forestallers of chastisement, but an unknown pastor will introduce the chiliastic age of the Holy Spirit.[25]

The *Katechōn*, then, has less profound power than a new Arion, while full-blown chiliastic prophecy has none of Gower's circumspection about the prospect of social renewal. The best way to calibrate Gower's exegetically engaged, careful and idiosyncratic Prologue in relation to apocalyptic discourse may be to say that its main line of apocalyptic is capped by an attenuated form of chiliasm.

---

[24] For Gower's disenfranchisement of the clergy in the *Confessio* more generally, see Larry Scanlon, *Narrative, Authority, and Power: The Medieval Exemplum and the Chaucerian Tradition* (Cambridge, 1994), pp. 248–67.

[25] Cola di Rienzo, 'Letter 49' (to Charles IV, 1350), in *Vom Mittelalter zur Reformation*, ed. Konrad Burdach, 6 vols (Berlin, 1912–39), ii, pp. 192–6, trans. McGinn, *Visions*, pp. 241–3. See also Cola di Rienzo, *The Life of Cola di Rienzo*, ed. and trans. John Wright (Toronto, 1975); Reeves, *Influence of Prophecy*, pp. 318–19. Fraternal and other religious orders were often identified as major players in the End times, for good or evil. See, e.g., McGinn, *Visions*, pp. 158–67, 200–221, 234–8; Kerby-Fulton, *Reformist Apocalypticism*, pp. 19–22, 133–64, 192–3.

Social and Political Renewal

The very incompleteness of Gower's chiliasm opens a space in which poetry can work personally and politically. Because the rehabilitation of history is not inevitable, it is all to play for in the poem's project of personal reform for the sake of the divided world.[26] The Prologue's peculiar isotope of chiliasm, a connection between personal and social transformation, and the transformative potential that Gower implicitly claims for his own poetry are all brought to bear in the call for Arionic renewal.

I have so far focused on the *Confessio*'s Prologue, where the poem's apocalyptic model of history is set out and then inflected by hope for a new Arion. I have only gestured to a reading of the poem as a whole.[27] The political ambition of the Prologue, and the new Arion passage in particular, only fully makes sense in the light of the penitential narrative of the main part of the poem. The intersection of chiliasm and penance (incorporating confession) gives the poem's apocalyptic idea of history its special politically enabling quality.

The penitential gravity of the *Confessio*'s frame narrative comes home at the end of the poem in the micro-apocalyptic that overtakes the lover as he discovers the complete persona of 'John Gower':

> And forth withal [Venus] tok me tho
> A wonder Mirour forto holde,
> ...
> And thanne into my remembrance
> I drowh myn olde daies passed,
> And as reson it hath compassed,
> I made a liknesse of miselve
> Unto the sondri Monthes twelve,
> ...
> The Wynter wol no Somer knowe,
> The grene lef is overthrowe,
> The clothed earthe is thanne bare,
> Despuiled is the Somerfare. (*Confessio*, VIII, lines 2820–56)

Venus's mirror supplies *personal* 'apocalyptic' in an apocalypse – a supernaturally mediated vision of the lover's end. As he views his age-ravaged face we have not only an elegant re-imagination of a 'learn to die' trope such as we find in book VII of the *Vox* (for example, lines 920–47, 1121–4,

---

[26] Cf. Kerby-Fulton, *Reformist Apocalypticism*, noting that an element of contingency in a prophecy of Bridget of Sweden is 'typical of the tension one often finds in reformist apocalypticism between the promise of certain chastisement and the hope that repentance will forestall it' (p. 106).

[27] On the relationship between the poem's political historical Prologue and its amatory confession narrative, see also James Simpson, *Sciences and the Self in Medieval Poetry: Alan of Lille's Anticlaudianus and John Gower's Confessio Amantis* (Cambridge, 1995), esp. pp. 139–48, 211–17; and *Reform and Cultural Revolution*, The Oxford English Literary History, 2, 1350–1547 (Oxford, 2002), pp. 121–48, 219–23; A. J. Minnis, 'John Gower, *sapiens* in ethics and politics', *MÆ*, 49 (1980), 207–29; and *Medieval Theory of Authorship*, pp. 177–82; Elizabeth Porter, 'Gower's ethical microcosm and political macrocosm', in *Gower's Confessio Amantis: Responses and Reassessments*, ed. A. J. Minnis (Cambridge, 1983), pp. 135–62.

1465–6); we have also a properly apocalyptic field of imagery, the individual imagined in terms of the world, its 'clothed earthe', and its cycle of seasons made terminal: 'The Wynter wol no Somer knowe.' There are echoes of the disordered-world imagery of the Prologue's apocalyptic – especially the 'bare' trees, 'leves grene', 'somer floures' and the resonant term 'overthrowe', which links the old lover and Nebuchadnezzar's statue 'nyh overthrowe' (*Confessio*, Prol., lines 884, 969). Thus, at each end of the poem, an apocalyptic sense of imminence is produced or imitated when a review of time collapses the wonder of the past onto a senescent present that seems barely able to take the strain.

History, for the *Confessio*, is poised between apocalyptic and penance because penance can change the world. Penance trails prophecy in an apocalyptic logic; and penance, like apocalyptic, is a confrontation with the Last Things – death, Judgment, heaven and hell.[28] The lover's quasi-apocalyptic shock finally allows penitential lessons to take effect by overthrowing his will, and these lessons will support him on his new path set out by Venus's judgment.[29] This kind of personal re-ordering cumulatively, on a population-wide scale, would mark a new 'age of Arion'. The fundamental importance of the new Arion passage from this penitential-transformative perspective is that it links moral reform to political history as cause to effect rather than vice versa. The penitential freight of orthodox apocalyptic emphasizes rewards for individual souls in the next world and urges a turning away from this world. The gospel of Matthew depicts an 'every person for themselves' historical crisis in which the good will abandon doomed society for the spiritual lifeboats of contemplative faith and personal suffering or martyrdom: 'Then they that are in Judea [in the End times], let them flee to the mountains. And he that is on the housetop, let him not come down to take any thing out of his house' (Matthew 24. 16–17). The basic point of the salvation theology of Augustine of Hippo (354–430) was to disentangle Church and empire, so his eschatology separates salvific history from temporal institutions and degrades political relations as blind, malignant, impossible.[30] *Vox clamantis* advocates a consonant shedding of the world: 'Because the flesh is frail [...] The spirit should shun this world and hope for future things [*hunc mundum spernat speretque futura*]' (*Vox*, VII, lines 1111–13).[31] Even if the

---

[28] Peck records Lee Patterson's comment that penance is apocalyptic on a personal level: 'Gower and the Book of Daniel', p. 162. Cf. Peck's non-apocalyptic coordination of penance and history in the *Confessio* in the same article, pp. 159–60, 172–80.

[29] See Elliot Kendall, *Lordship and Literature: John Gower and the Politics of the Great Household* (Oxford, 2008), pp. 101–18. For the politics of penitential subject-formation, see also Michel Foucault, *The History of Sexuality*, trans. Robert Hurley, 3 vols (London, 1979–88), i, esp. pp. 58–9; John M. Ganim, 'Chaucer, Boccaccio, confession and subjectivity', in *The Decameron and the Canterbury Tales: New Essays on an Old Question*, ed. Leonard Michael Koff and Brenda Deen Schildgen (London, 2000), pp. 130–33.

[30] See Robert A. Markus, *Saeculum: History and Society in the Theology of St Augustine*, rev. edn (Cambridge, 1989), esp. pp. 41–4, 53–6, 133–5.

[31] Cf. the *Confessio*'s warning that high secular office will offer no shelter from divine punishment (*Confessio*, V, lines 1921–4). This passage is part of a specifically clerical critique. It draws on material from Gregory I, *Homilia XVII, XL*, in *Homiliarum in Evangelia libri duo*, in

behaviour to be rewarded involves socially productive virtues like charity (the prime criterion for separating sheep and goats in Matthew 25. 32–46), then historical pessimism enfeebles it socially. Gregory the Great's encouragement in his homily on Ezekiel 2. 6 to 'imitate those deeds of good men that we are able to' seems socially frail in its immediate context of apocalyptic horrors and worldwide desolation: 'Let us therefore despise with all our being [*Despiciamus ergo ex toto animo*] this present – or rather extinct [*exstinctum*] – world'.[32] Penance is only a function of this kind of apocalyptic history, not also a corrective to it.

Gower's *Confessio* Prologue, conversely, looks to a fully socialized and institutional response to the End times. Arionic renewal would yield harmony between lords and commons, and even the Prologue's preliminary advice about preparation for Judgment focuses on social, conciliatory forms of justice and couples 'worldes welthe' and salvation:

> In hevene is pes and al acord,
> Bot helle is full of such descord
> That ther may be no loveday:
> Forthi good is, whil a man may,
> Echon to sette pes with other
> And loven as his oghne brother;
> So may he winne worldes welthe
> And afterward his soule helthe. (*Confessio,* Prol., lines 1045–52)

The first and last goal of moral reform, 'pes' is the antidote to the social 'division' elaborated by the Prologue. In a communal sense, as the (king's) peace, it remains the main objective in Venus's instructions to the reformed 'John Gower' for his future life (*Confessio*, VIII, line 2913). The Prologue passage is clear that peace between individuals would be good policy for salvation, but in the first place it would anticipate Arionic renewal.

Gower's attenuated chiliasm expresses a radical but not revolutionary politics. Chiliasm can imagine change in a language of restoration, a forward-looking nostalgia for apostolic, ancient or pristine values, whatever its political content.[33] The new Arion passage is conservative in content as well as rhetoric. Its ideal community of lords and commons in 'good acord' distils a brand of elite politics. In this conservatism, the *Confessio* belongs to an apocalyptic mainstream in the Middle Ages. If, in some modern discussions, especially following the work of Norman Cohn, there has been a tendency to associate apocalyptic, and chiliasm above all, with popular political insurgency, then the *Confessio* adds to the counter-examples. As the broadly conservative work of a non-clerical but nonetheless elite writer, it

---

PL, 76, col. 1148 that Gower had previously used in the *Mirour de l'Omme* (lines 20065–88) and, with irony, in the *Vox* (III, lines 903–8).

[32] Gregory I, *Homilia VI*, 24, in *Homiliarum in Ezechielem prophetam libri duo*, in PL, 76, col. 1011, trans. McGinn, *Visions*, p. 63 (modified).

[33] Cf. Petrarch's and Gower's golden ageism (above, pp. 52–3). On the distinction between 'radical' and 'revolutionary' notions of reform, see Reeves, 'Originality and influence', p. 294.

supports the view of researchers such as Lerner who argue that 'chiliasm was not just [or indeed primarily] the ideology of lunatic-fringe "fanatics" and uprooted classes' and that it was culturally more embedded than any 'occasional product of materially dislocating disasters'.[34] Apocalyptic writers like Gower, and their primary audiences, may have felt that their values were gravely threatened, and their social groups may have been living through notable economic and political change (as the late medieval English aristocracy certainly were), but this did not mean that their texts spoke for genuinely disadvantaged groups in society.[35]

The new age of Arion fits what I take to be the *Confessio*'s core politics. These are uncentralized and principally unofficial or semi-official, based on lordship.[36] The new Arion would not restore or bring in a golden statue: the golden tyrant Nebuchadnezzar is for the poem an alloyed ideal and, while the figure of Arion's successor *may* represent a poetically inspired or enlightened monarch, there is little sign of strong centralized rule. Gower has imagined King David and kingship more generally in terms of social musicianship in the *Mirour de l'Omme*.[37] Even if such symbolism is to the fore in a reader's mind, however, Arion's political role is seemingly informal, inspirational and even remote, not arbitrary and commanding or legislative, still less vigorous and military like a Last World Emperor's. Richard Firth Green sees Arion as a supreme mediator while discussing processes of unofficial or semi-official dispute resolution.[38] If Arion is a monarch then he fits a medieval ideal of the polity in which the aristocracy hold dominion under a monarch who guarantees that dominion and who can resolve conflict within the aristocracy as a final resort.[39]

The society perfected by a new Arion, monarch or not, would be light on kingship and official governance. The passage's focus is on lords and commonalty bound together in 'love', which implicitly puts away the more formal *law* as well as melancholy.[40] The prospect is less structured than the golden age of the past described at the Prologue's beginning (*Confessio*, Prol.,

---

[34] Robert E. Lerner, 'Medieval prophecy and religious dissent', *Past and Present*, 72 (1976), 3–24 (p. 19). See also McGinn, *Visions*, pp. xix, 28–35. Cf. Norman Cohn, *The Pursuit of the Millenium: Revolutionary Millenarians and Mystical Anarchists of the Middle Ages* (London, 1957; rpt 1970), esp. pp. 209–17, which basically understands medieval apocalypticism as the millenarianism of western Europe's dispossessed poor. More recently it has been claimed that 'chiliasm has […] always had a distinctly subversive political character, and ruling groups invariably oppose it': Richard Landes, 'The fear of an apocalyptic year 1000: Augustinian historiography, medieval and modern', *Speculum*, 75 (2000), 97–145 (p. 104).

[35] For the economic situation of the aristocracy in late-fourteenth-century England, see Christopher Dyer, *Making a Living in the Middle Ages: The People of Britain 850–1520* (London, 2003), pp. 265–97, 330–62. For my argument that this is a significant context for the production of the *Confessio*, see Kendall, *Lordship and Literature*, pp. 36–41, 57–64.

[36] I have discussed the lordship politics of the *Confessio* at length in *Lordship and Literature*.

[37] *Mirour*, lines 22875, 22897–920.

[38] Richard Firth Green, *A Crisis of Truth: Literature and Law in Ricardian England* (Philadelphia, PA, 1999), pp. 175–8; Cf. Kendall, *Lordship and Literature*, pp. 185–7.

[39] Christine Carpenter, *Locality and Polity: A Study of Warwickshire Landed Society, 1401–1499* (Cambridge, 1992), pp. 351–2, 616–29; Kendall, *Lordship and Literature*, pp. 242–6.

[40] *Confessio*, Prol., lines 1068–9. For medieval ideas of 'love' and 'law' in the context of dispute resolution, see Michael Clanchy, 'Law and love in the Middle Ages', in *Disputes and Settle-*

lines 93–117). There, the 'privilege of regalie', 'Justice of lawe' and 'reule of governance' all feature (*Confessio*, Prol., lines 102–3, 108). But social stability rests equally on less formal elements, including the 'worschipe' or social capital of lords, and love or 'charite' (*Confessio*, Prol., lines 105–6, 110). In the context of a polity in which aristocrats looked to variously formal means of power, including their own personal relations, the king and the common law, these two views of golden age society are not exactly at odds with each other. Even for a pre-monetary age of innocence (*Confessio*, V, lines 1–21), Gower does not explicitly set aside monarchy or draw conclusions for landed power in an economy in which 'al was set to the comune' (line 5). In Arionic polity, however, there is an unquestioned emphasis on less formal kinds of authority and a seigneurial milieu.

Here, characteristic linguistic equilibrium, and especially the chiasmus of 'the comun with the lord, | And lord with the comun also' (*Confessio*, Prol., lines 1066–7), embody society's tranquillity and good order, and the chiasmus implies an ethos of mutual responsibility and reciprocity.[41] This ethos is highly idealized and euphemistic of power relations, and Gower's poem never proposes that 'good acord' grows from commons' and lords' sharing of the *same* responsibilities or proper conduct. *Comun* and *lord* remain very different political categories. It is the identity of these pre-End-time players and the direction of the euphemizing that are revealing of the poem's politics. With neither Church nor empire in evidence, and in tune with the *Confessio*'s politics as a whole, harmony depends on an ideal of clearly hierarchical but mutually interested and unlegislated, unobjectifiable lay aristocratic power apocalyptically authorized as the apotheosis of history.

Much rides, then, on rediscovering Arionic music. And rather than a princely political mediator, Arion's successor, with his enigmatic, musical *modus operandi*, might bear a passing resemblance to John Gower. The poem's confessional mimesis of one individual's poetically orchestrated reform spurs the comparison. The Prologue's apocalyptic-Arionic theory gives such reform unusual political impetus, which springs strikingly to view when the body of the poem is read as itself an imitation of Arion's song.

---

ments: *Law and Human Relations in the West*, ed. John Bossy (Cambridge, 1983), pp. 47–67. See also Green, *Crisis of Truth*, e.g. pp. 176–86.

[41] On Gower's 'rhetorical mimesis' of balance, see Helen Cooper, '"Peised evene in the balance": a thematic and rhetorical topos in the *Confessio Amantis*', *Mediaevalia*, 16 (1993), 113–39 (quotation at p. 115).

Chapter 5

Gower's Poetics of the Literal

ROBERT R. EDWARDS

Critics have long worked within a settled, if not wholly satisfying, consensus about John Gower's narrative art in the *Confessio Amantis*: whatever else he may be as a moralist, social thinker or political theorist, Gower is a poet of narrative economy. Early in the last century, G. C. Macaulay noted Gower's 'gift of clear and interesting narrative' and his 'natural taste for simplicity'.[1] Near mid-century, Derek Pearsall observed that Gower gives 'local, imaginative truth to general, abstract truth', while Arno Esch found a 'directness of description' in Gower's tales.[2] In recent decades Gower's narrative economy has furnished a rationale for other important approaches. A wide range of comparative studies has catalogued Gower's abbreviation of stories from romances, chronicles and, most especially, Ovid.[3] Narrative economy underwrites our understanding of 'moral Gower'. Charles Runacres, for instance, stresses the importance to Gower's ethical analysis of 'the particulars of human behaviour and experience as they are recorded in his *narraciones*'.[4] The same case could be made for the utility of Gower's narratives as social

---

[1] G. C. Macaulay, 'John Gower 6. The English *Confessio Amantis*', in *The Cambridge History of English and American Literature*, eds A. W. Ward, A. R. Waller, W. P. Trent, J. Erskine, S. P. Sherman and C. Van Doren, 18 vols (Cambridge, 1907–1921), vol. 2; rpt in Peter Nicholson, ed., *Gower's Confessio Amantis: A Critical Anthology* (Cambridge, 1991), pp. 12–13. I cite other landmark articles and essays in Gower criticism in the form reprinted in Nicholson's anthology.

[2] Derek Pearsall, 'Gower's narrative art', *PMLA*, 81 (1966), 475–84 (p. 478); rpt in Nicholson, *Gower's Confessio Amantis*, p. 68; and Arno Esch, 'John Gower's Erzahlkunst', *Chaucer und seine Zeit: Symposion für Walter F. Schirmer*, ed. Arno Esch (Tübingen, 1968), pp. 207–39; and trans. Linda Barney Burke, 'John Gower's narrative art', in *Gower's Confessio Amantis: A Critical Anthology*, ed. Peter Nicholson (Cambridge, 1991), p. 86.

[3] See Götz Schmitz, 'The priesthood of genius: a study of the medieval tradition', in *Gower's Confessio Amantis: A Critical Anthology*, ed. Peter Nicholson (Cambridge, 1991), p. 137 on the Troy story; see Esch, 'John Gower's Erzahlkunst', p. 137 n. 33 on romance and p. 97 on Trevet; see Pearsall, 'Gower's narrative art', p. 75 on Ovid's Jason and Medea; and Julia Creswell, 'The tales of Acteon and Narcissus in the Confessio Amantis', *Reading Medieval Studies*, 7 (1981), 32–40; and Siân Echard, 'Introduction', in *Companion*, p. 17.

[4] Charles Runacres, 'Art and ethics in the "exempla" of *Confessio Amantis*', in *Gower's 'Confessio Amantis': Responses and Reassessments*, ed. A. J. Minnis (Cambridge, 1983), pp. 106–34 (p. 115).

commentary and what Anne Middleton termed the 'public poetry' of the late fourteenth century.[5]

Beneath this consensus runs a paradox that C. S. Lewis identified in describing something like the ground zero of Gower's narrative: 'In this kind of narrative, so spare, so direct, and so concentrated on the event, it is not easy to distinguish the merit of the telling from the intrinsic merit of the story.'[6] Lewis has a more practical aim here than the theoretical concerns with plot and story elaborated by the Russian Formalists or with Bakhtin's reflections on genre, chronotope and the world. He delineates precisely the qualities that have offered critics and readers very little interpretative leverage. How are we to give an analysis of Gower's narrative that goes beyond a mere description or restatement of its action? What artistic or conceptual features can we find in the narrow interval between telling and story? Hence the attraction of Gower's exemplarity, for exemplarity offers a figurative approach to interpretation that remains historically grounded in medieval literary practice. Yet the fit between example and precept in the *Confessio Amantis* is inexact and often problematic. Books by Larry Scanlon, J. A. Mitchell, Peter Nicholson and Elizabeth Allen have marked a serious and nuanced re-examination of what exemplarity might entail in the late Middle Ages. In various ways these scholars map a shift in emphasis from the formal properties of literary discourse to the hermeneutic role of readers.[7]

If Gower's narrative economy is paradoxical in the way Lewis described, it nonetheless remains a literary effect with important artistic and cultural stakes. In particular, it represents an effort to construct a poetics of the literal within the richly figurative frames afforded by the dream vision, penitential dialogue and moralizations of the *Confessio Amantis*. By poetics I mean not just the compositional techniques derived from rhetoric in the Middle Ages but the underlying suppositions and entailments of such practice – the necessary conditions we can infer about writing as well as the consequences that follow for shaping imaginative discourse. By literal I mean both linguistic denotation and history – the relation of words and things within a system of signs and *res gestae*, things done and said by human agents and known on credible witness, preferably eye witness or contemporary testimony. The literal, as Henri de Lubac notes in his account of the exegetical tradition, is the *prima significatio* of a text, the *prima expositio* of a commentator and the *primus intellectus* of a reader.[8] It is conveniently expressed in the exegetical

---

[5] Anne Middleton, 'The idea of public poetry in the reign of Richard II', *Speculum*, 53 (1978), 94–114.

[6] C. S. Lewis, 'Gower', in *Gower's Confessio Amantis: A Critical Anthology*, ed. Peter Nicholson (Cambridge, 1991), p. 26.

[7] Larry Scanlon, *Narrative, Authority, and Power: The Medieval Exemplum and the Chaucer Tradition* (Cambridge, 1994); J. Allan Mitchell, *Ethics and Exemplary Narrative in Chaucer and Gower* (Cambridge, 2004); Peter Nicholson, *Love and Ethics in Gower's 'Confessio Amantis'* (Ann Arbor, MI, 2005); and Elizabeth Allen, *False Fables and Exemplary Truth in Later Middle English Literature* (New York, 2005).

[8] Henri de Lubac, *Exégèse médiévale: Les quatre sens de l'écriture*, 4 vols (Paris, 1959–64), pp. 425–6; Gilbert Dahan, 'L'éxégèse chrétienne de la Bible en Occident médiévale: XIIe–XIVe siècle', rev. E. Ann Matter, *Speculum*, 77 (2002), 1272–4, observes that Lubac's schematization of

commonplace 'littera gesta docet'. But, as Lubac goes on to explain, the substance of literal meaning proves inseparable from the mode of literal meaning: if the literal means history, history implies some kind of narrative ('Historia est rerum gestarum narratio').

Moreover, in medieval theories of reading the literal includes other kinds of discourse besides historical narrative, such as proverbs, parables and the law. It operates through figurative as well as denotative language, through images as well as statements and descriptions. The literal claims its ground outside the order of language. As Aquinas explains, literal meaning arises from the intent of the author; and God, as the author of scripture, has the power to signify his meaning through both language and things. Consequently, the things signified by words also have signification.[9] Aquinas's account of the literal, drawing on Augustine, not only identifies it with the historical sense but also includes the causes of events (*aetiologia*) and the harmony (*analogia*) between passages in the Bible (*Summa theologiae* 1a.1.10 ad 2). A poetics of the literal thus complicates rather than simplifies the *verba-res* connection that lies at the base of both sign theory and the practice of exegesis.[10] Equally important for a narrative poet, it is only from the literal sense, not figurative senses, that arguments and proofs can be adduced: 'cum omnes sensus fundentur super unum, scilicet litteralem; ex quo solo potest trahi argumentum, non autem ex his quae secundum allegoriam dicuntur' ('for all senses are based on one – that is, the literal – from which alone can argument be drawn and not from those that are said to be according to allegory' (*Summa theologiae* 1a.1.10 ad 1)).[11] The terms of demonstration and persuasion, hence the expository and argumentative power of narrative, are based in what language signifies and in what history records.

Gower's literalism has usually been framed as an issue of poetic style. Genius connects plain speech and truth-telling in his discussion of rhetoric in book VII of the *Confessio Amantis*, where rhetoric is stabilized by grammar and logic and these two arts 'serven bothe unto the speche' (*Confessio*, VII, line 1529). The connection is confirmed in Gower's authorial leave-taking at the end of the poem: 'y have do my trewe peyne | With rude wordis and with pleyne' (*Confessio*, VIII, lines 3121–2). As Götz Schmitz, J. D. Burnley, Helen Cooper and others have insisted, the technical resources of style serve

---

the four senses of Scripture 'has proved too rigid to encompass all categories of medieval understanding of the Bible' (1272).

[9] St Thomas Aquinas, *Summa theologiae*, ed. John Fearon, OP (Cambridge, 2006) 1a.1.10: 'ipsae res significatae per voces, etiam significant aliquid'. The power of things to signify other things, Aquinas remarks, distinguishes God from man who can, like God, signify through linguistic signs.

[10] David W. Hiscoe, 'Heavenly sign and comic design in Gower's *Confessio Amantis*', in *Sign, Sentence, Discourse: Language in Medieval Thought and Literature*, eds Julian N. Wasserman and Lois Roney (Syracuse, NY, 1989), pp. 228–44 (pp. 230–31), on Augustine's insistence that words recall 'spiritual realities that exist prior to and independent of the verbal instruments we use to call them up'.

[11] Alastair Minnis, 'Fifteenth-century versions of Thomistic literalism: Girolamo Savonarola and Alfonso de Madrigal', in *Neue Richtungen in der hoch- und spätmittelalterlichen Bibelexegese*, eds Robert E. Lerner and Elisabeth Müller-Luckner (Munich, 1996), pp. 163–80, usefully reviews Thomistic doctrine and traces its influence in the fifteenth century.

a thematic purpose in Gower's critique of ornament and in his use of devices that symbolize forms of order.[12] Diane Watt has argued that the concept of right speech is gendered male.[13] John Burrow reminds us that Gower writes in a variety of styles across his French, Latin and English works and that, consequently, his decision to employ a plain style is a considered artistic choice.[14] Nor is it the case that Gower writes without using rhetorical figures or that his narrative action and details lack symbolic resonance. Masayoshi Ito shows, for example, that Gower frequently turns to figures of wordplay across his major works.[15] Robert F. Yeager has emphasized how the simple objects and furniture of Gower's tales acquire a meaning beyond their immediate functions in a narrative plot.[16] The majority view remains, however, the one Burrow voices in his appraisal of Gower's poetic styles: 'The poem's prevailing mode of meaning is literal', by which he means 'literal exemplification'.[17]

Gower's literalism encompasses other important dimensions besides poetic style that we must examine in order to appreciate his narrative art fully. On the level of narrative technique, the *Confessio Amantis* exploits the broad resources that exegetes had claimed for the literal as a primary means of linguistic signification. Within his stories, Gower turns to devices such as enigmas and material objects in order to structure narrative action. On a thematic level, he uses narrative as a means to disclose the ideological formations that both constitute and threaten the social order within a realm of mutability and division. In this aim, as we shall see, the *Confessio Amantis* demonstrates an important continuity with Gower's earlier works and with the 'prophetic literalism' that underwrites their literary programs.

Word and Conceit

In the Prologue to the *Confessio Amantis* Gower imagines a 'tyme passed' (*Confessio*, Prol., line 94) of plenitude, justice and social harmony. This Golden Age is also a period of virtuous linguistic practice and signification:

---

[12] Schmitz, 'The priesthood of genius', pp. 120–29; J. D. Burnley, 'Chaucer, Usk, and Geoffrey of Vinsauf', *Neophilologus*, 69 (1985), 284–93; Helen Cooper, "Peised Evene in the Balance': a thematic and rhetorical topos in the *Confessio Amantis*', *Mediaevalia*, 16 (1993), 113–39; and Edwin T. Craun, *Lies, Slander, and Obscenity in Medieval English Literature: Pastoral Rhetoric and the Deviant Speaker* (Cambridge, 1997).

[13] Diane Watt, 'Literary genealogy, virile rhetoric, and John Gower's *Confessio Amantis*', *PQ*, 79 (1999), 389–415.

[14] J. A. Burrow, 'Gower's poetic styles', in *Companion*, pp. 239–50 (p. 239). Earlier, Lewis, 'Gower', p. 21, and Esch, 'John Gower's Erzahlkunst', pp. 119, 140, emphasized that Gower had multiple styles available to him across his literary corpus.

[15] Masayoshi Ito, *John Gower, The Medieval Poet* (Tokyo, 1976), pp. 199–290.

[16] R. F. Yeager, 'John Gower's images: "The Tale of Constance" and "The Man of Law's Tale"', in *Speaking Images: Essays in Honour of V. A. Kolve*, eds R. F. Yeager and Charlotte Morse (Asheville, NC, 2001), pp. 525–57. Lewis, 'Gower', pp. 22–3, begins the process of reclaiming Gower as a poet who appeals to the visual, particularly to movement, by which Lewis means 'actions and events'.

[17] Burrow, 'Gower's poetic styles', pp. 239–50 (pp. 247, 248).

'The word was lich to the conceite | Withoute semblant of deceit' (*Confessio*, Prol., lines 113–14). Authorial intention is directed to the alignment of verbal signs and perception, and perception corresponds in turn to objects of experience within reality. As Gower quickly makes apparent, the Golden Age is a heuristic fantasy that serves to define by contrast the fallenness of later periods and particularly that of the present moment. For language, fallenness manifests itself in inevitable slippage and misuse and in intentional abuse and deception, so that the full power of signification is lost and irrecoverable, hence impossible. Against this background, Gower's literalism operates as a project to recover signification so that words align with ideas and ideas align with things in order to advance a project of reform.

The enigmas that Gower treats within his narratives map various possibilities of reform. The stories of Florent and Apollonius anchor opposite ends of the *Confessio Amantis* yet embody a similar mechanism. In both tales, the enigma serves as an initial narrative given for which the appropriate circumstances – the truth conditions – must be inferred so that a narrative reversal can occur. Florent presents a solution (female sovereignty) to the riddle 'What alle wommen most desire' (*Confessio*, I, line 1481) to win the judicial wager on his life and to scandalize his scheming antagonist by revealing 'the privite, | Which alle wommen most desire' (*Confessio*, I, lines 1660–61). He then enacts his solution by surrendering sovereignty to his wife who poses the choice of being beautiful by day or night and who is herself released from her stepmother's curse. Antiochus's riddle is presented as more enigmatic, having no stable formulation to be 'unlocke' (*Confessio*, VIII, line 424) by an incisive verbal solution that fulfils all its conditions.[18] Instead, Apollonius solves the enigma by giving a name to the thing that it refers to: 'It toucheth al the privete | Between thin oghne child and thee' (*Confessio*, VIII, lines 425–6). His answer is directed to the literal truth that proceeds from Antiochus's intention and lies beyond verbal formulation, a 'privete' connecting father and child. In subsequent phases of the story, the same literal truth will confront Artestrathes as he accedes to his daughter's choice of Apollonius over three princely suitors. It recurs for Apollonius as he later encounters Thais in a dangerous and partially eroticized scene of reunion.[19] If the repetitions do not trace a complete reform of attachments within patriarchy, they nonetheless exhibit successful strategies for redirecting the intimacy of fathers and daughters within the social and political orders.

The Trump of Death uses literal signification to tell a story of recognition leading to individual reform. The recognition again occurs in several phases. The king of Hungary's brother is offended by the king's generous

---

[18] For a reading of Antiochus's riddle, see Steele Nowlin, 'Narratives of incest and incestuous narratives: memory, process, and the *Confessio Amantis*'s "Middel Weie"', *JMEMS*, 35 (2005), 217–44 (esp. p. 227): 'the riddle refers not only to Antiochus's secret, but to Gower's narrative technique'.

[19] Larry Scanlon, 'The riddle of incest: John Gower and the problem of medieval sexuality', in *Re-visioning Gower*, ed. R. F. Yeager (Charlotte, NC, 1998), pp. 93–127, emphasizes the enduring complications of patriarchal authority and exchange.

and deferential reception of two elderly, impoverished pilgrims before the court at a moment of high ceremony. The king recognizes in 'here ymage' (*Confessio*, I, line 2230) the lesson of his own mortality and the power of death to level social distinctions and privilege. When he orders the trumpet blown before his brother's gate, his brother recognizes it as a sign of death but cannot grasp the significance: 'he the sothe noght forthi | Ne wiste, and ther was sorwe tho' (*Confessio*, I, lines 2150–51). The truth behind the sign is not merely the brother's overbearing pride but the events that have led to his chastisement – his exaggerated sense of dignity, his direct reproach to the king, his presumption in saying that the king owes an apology to his nobles. After he leads his family in smocks and shirts to seek pardon, the king admonishes his brother, 'only for a trompes soun | Hast gon despuiled thurgh the toun' (*Confessio*, I, lines 2217–18). The display of abasement has in fact reproduced the initial public sight of the two old pilgrims and led to an understanding of the strong analogy between the scenes. As so often in Gower, the exemplary meaning is a lesson in reading.

Elsewhere in the *Confessio Amantis*, enigmas establish the literal truth that drives narrative movements. In the tale of Lucrece, the downfall of Tarquin and Arruns prophesied by Phoebus is effectively set in motion when Brutus understands the 'entente' (*Confessio*, VII, line 4742) of the prophecy, though the conclusion is deferred until the final look shared by Lucrece and Brutus to ratify his promise of vengeance (*Confessio*, VII, line 5088). Similarly, Ulysses's dream discloses the 'tokne of oure aqueintance' (*Confessio*, VI, line 1542), a 'signe [...] | Of an Empire' (*Confessio*, VI, lines 1561–2), that Ulysses understands only belatedly when he recognizes that Telegonus rather than Telemachus is the son prophesied to slay him (*Confessio* VI, line 1744). The tale of Lycurgus marks one extreme of the power of the literal to determine action. In his governance of Athens Lycurgus achieves a political ideal of 'justice and equité | In forthringe of comun profit' (*Confessio*, VII, lines 2956–7) following a law originating in 'goddes sonde' (*Confessio* VII, line 2962). The problem he faces is to induce his subjects to follow the law over time – that is, to preserve its literal meaning. The 'wonder thing' (*Confessio*, VII, line 2942) that he devises to further this end is a pretext: he claims that Mercury has commanded him to leave Athens to receive information for the city's welfare, and he secures the promise of its citizens to maintain his laws during his absence. Accepting exile and abandonment of his princely office, he makes the law an enduring literal truth of politics and civic life.

Another form of Gower's literalism can be seen in the material objects of his narrative, which show the same capacity as fit words to shape narrative and reveal the contingencies of its social vision. In telling the story of Rosiphelee, Genius's explicit aim is to warn Amans (gratuitously, it seems) of the dangers of idleness in love. Despite her reluctance to love, the 'lusti Maide' (*Confessio*, IV, line 1248) Rosiphelee finds herself in the eroticized landscape of the *locus amoenus*, playing the role of courtly observer. That role famously serves Machaut and Chaucer as an enabling fiction for poetry, but for Rosiphelee it functions to show how meaning becomes direct and concrete. The procession of mounted women she sees pass through the landscape represents the noble life through the richness and beauty of their ornament. The woman Rosiphelee detains and questions is the anomalous figure who trails behind the group, carrying their halters and bearing herself 'A riche bridel for the nones | Of gold and precious Stones' (*Confessio*, IV, lines 1353–4). The bridle signifies her late conversion to love; it is a recognition of her good will (*Confessio*, IV, line 1427) but a punishment for her delay in acting.

Rosiphelee grasps the *analogia* of the woman's story – 'I am riht in the same cas' (*Confessio*, IV, line 1440) – but Gower reveals at the same time the larger social drama that frames exemplarity. The woman suffers not because she has transgressed the law of love but because transgression entails a loss of social identity. She is 'bot as here horse knave' (*Confessio*, IV, line 1399), the stable boy trailing behind the women and carrying their tack. Fixed in her subordinate position, she has suffered social as well as physical death. Genius reveals the cultural investments that shape the governing moral and erotic precepts of this scene: 'Among the gentil nacion | Love is an occupacion' (*Confessio*, IV, lines 1451–2). Peter Nicholson glosses 'occupacion' as 'service, duty, effort, discipline, "travail"', but another meaning that Gower uses, in a pejorative sense, is 'preoccupation'.[20] That the literalism of the story disrupts convention is clear from the text. The Latin marginal gloss to this passage quickly cancels out the disclosure – 'Non quia sic se habet veritas, set opinio Amantum' ('it is not truth but the opinion of lovers') – and Genius soon displaces love 'paramours' into the honest love of marriage and child-bearing. In the meantime, love stands revealed to Rosiphelee not as a unifying power in creation or unacknowledged domain in her makeup but as a practice of social privilege and exclusion.

The signifying power of material objects shows itself fully in the tale of Albinus and Rosemund. Genius tells the story as a warning against Avantance (boasting, vainglory), the fourth species of pride. Albinus makes the skull of Gurmond, Rosemund's father, into an object of literal significance 'To kepe and drawe into memoire | Of his bataille the victoire' (*Confessio*, I, lines 2475–76) over Gurmond. He transforms it, though, into an aesthetic object, a simulacrum of a griffin's eye adorned with stones and engraving and polished with workmanship to efface its origin and semiotic value: 'no signe of the Skulle is sene' (*Confessio*, I, line 2544). The trajectory of Gower's narrative follows the shift between metonymic object and metaphorical artefact. The stability of the tale – 'that love time in reste' (*Confessio*, I, line 2487) when Albinus and Rosemund 'love ech other wonder wel' (*Confessio*, I, line 2489) – coincides with the period in which Gormund's skull is not recognized for what it actually is. The sign returns to its literal meaning at the height of Albinus's accomplishment, 'As he that hath his world achieved' (*Confessio*, I, line 2498) when he aligns the military, political and domestic spheres in the displays of chivalric ceremony. He gives the skull to Rosemund at the

---

[20] Nicholson, *Love and Ethics*, p. 223, cf. pp. 235–6 on echoes of Rosiphelee later in book IV. MED, s.v. *occupacioun* , 4b, citing *Confessio* V, lines 195–8: 'And if worschipe / I axe and of the world lordschipe, / That is an occupacion / Of proud ymaginacion.'

feast, with the order 'Drink with thi fader, Dame' (*Confessio*, I, line 2551). For Gower's readers, the command hovers between a grisly directive to consume along with her father and an order to drink through the agency of her father. For Albinus's entourage, the explanation is simple and direct: 'thanne al oute | The kyng in audience about | Hath told it was hire fader Skulle' (*Confessio*, I, lines 2555–7). As Yeager notes, the shock of narrative and moral recognition is 'an exercise in how we ought to read'.[21]

Albinus's disclosure of the literal sets in motion a plot of betrayal and vengeance that undermines a successful dynastic marriage, the loyalty of his liegeman Helmege and the prosperity of his kingdom, as Rosemund and Helmege flee with his treasure after killing him. The tale's ironies are part of its narrative artistry. As the Latin gloss at line 2405 maintains, a prideful man wishing to extol his fame overturns it with his own mouth. The wine that Rosemund drinks from Gormund's skull becomes the literal poison that the duke of Ravenna arranges for Rosemund and Helmege to drink as their final punishment for violence against the social order. Beyond its monitory function, Gower's story is a foundational narrative. Albinus is the first Lombard king, and his pride stems from a synthesis of power in a chivalric world that speaks obsessively of arms and love, effectively transposing the two. Victory over Gormund leads immediately to marriage with Rosemund and then to the display of royal power as he compels those 'obeisant to his heste' (*Confessio*, I, line 2502) to make themselves known as subjects to his wife. Albinus shows in his acts and speech – in the literalism of *res gestae* – that the figure of the 'Lombard tyrant' so vivid for Gower's age and his political imaginary is present from the very beginning; it resides not just in pride but in the very structure of chivalric kingship.

Prophetic Literalism

At the beginning of book I of the *Confessio Amantis* Gower claims to abandon the poetics that informs his earlier writing. He resolves to

> [...] treten upon othre thinges.
> Forthi the Stile of my writinges
> From this day forth I thenke change
> And speke of thing is noght so strange [...]. (*Confessio*, I, lines 7–10)

'Stile' in this passage refers to the content or poetic matter of his writing, and it is coordinated semantically with 'othre thinges', other topics of poetic invention.[22] The shift in subject matter is reinforced here by a related, concrete use of 'stile', which is the pen or stylus used by the poet to write his material. Gower's turn to his new topic – the love that drives and regulates the animate world – is usually taken to imply a specific move away from the *Vox*

---

[21] R. F. Yeager, *John Gower's Poetic: The Search for a New Arion* (Cambridge, 1990), p. 117.
[22] *MED*, s.v. *stile*, n2b, quoting this passage; see also Burrow, 'Gower's poetic styles', 245. Peck glosses the term as 'style', as does Schmitz, 'The priesthood of genius', p. 117.

Clamantis and its mode of visionary politics.[23] Love, by contrast, is ostensibly a 'thing [...] noght so strange' because it is not unusual or extraordinary as a poetic topic nor is it recondite and oblique in its manner of expression.[24]

Gower positions himself as a poet moving consciously to a new topic in a different mode of expression, but his narrative depends to a significant degree on the techniques used in earlier works.[25] Alastair J. Minnis has argued that in the *Vox* Gower uses the spiritual and intellectual visions applied to prophecy as well as the figure of the preacher-poet.[26] Gower, in fact, does not abandon his earlier poetics in the *Confessio Amantis* so much as carry it forward and recontextualize it in a new project. The subject of the *Mirour de l'Omme* is not 'chose controvée' ('imaginary matter') but a true account of the workings of sin, which is defined literally and paradoxically as nothing ('nient').[27] In the Prologue to book I of the *Vox*, Gower insists that his dream vision, a sustained fugue of transformations among the lower social orders occasioned by their loss of reason and discipline, directly signifies the conditions of his time: 'Hinc puto que vidi quod sompnia tempore noctis | Signa rei certe commemoranda ferunt' (*Vox*, Prol. I, lines 15–16) ('Hence, I think that the dreams I witnessed at nighttime furnish memorable tokens of a certain occurrence').[28] However grotesque, the countless monstrous forms ('Innumerabilia monstra') of the vision are 'Signa rei', literal signs with real referents. Gower's poetic and political conceit is that the common mob devolves to animals before his eyes in a reverse incarnation perhaps more Ovidian and classical than Christian: 'Ecce dei subito malediccio fulsit in illos, | Et mutans formas fecerat esse feras' (*Vox*, I, lines 175–6) ('behold, the curse of God suddenly flashed upon them, and changing their shapes, it had made them into wild beasts'). In the Prologue to book III of the *Vox*, the poetic role that Gower assumes abjures divine mysteries; its warrant lies, he insists, in 'humana [...] vox communis' and its concrete subject matter

---

23 Nicholson, *Love and Ethics*, p. 3.
24 *MED*, s.v. *straunge*, adj. 2b and d; Peck glosses it as 'foreign' (2c).
25 The turn from one literary form to another has its most successful exponent in Ovid, the poet whose work Gower echoes repeatedly. At the beginning of the *Amores*, Ovid's project turns from the higher genre of epic to the lesser (and less stable) genre of love poetry: 'Arma gravi numero violentaque bella parabam | edere, materia conveniente modis' (*Amores* 1.1.1–2). One lesson of the *Amores* is that abandoned topics are never actually banished. The language of epic is recuperated within love elegy: 'Militat omnis amans, et habet sua castra Cupido' (*Amores* 1.9.1). Ovid's turn is also a conscious move away from Vergil and the *cursus honorum* of classical authorship represented by epic, georgic and bucolic works in Vergil's oeuvre and formalized in the apocryphal *ille ego* opening to his works reported by Donatus. In the poem 'Eneidos Bucolis', likely to have been composed by Ralph Strode, the 'Philosophus' mentioned in the poem's rubric, Gower's three major works, each in a different language, are equated structurally with Vergil's three genres.
26 Alastair J. Minnis, *Medieval Theory of Authorship: Scholastic Literary Attitudes in the Later Middle Ages*, 2nd edn (Aldershot, 1988), pp. 168–77. Minnis's discussion of the literalism of the *forma prophetialis* includes Gower's adaptation of the academic prologue in the *Vox* and Gower's authorial position as an instrumental or secondary efficient cause of the work after God, the primary *auctor*.
27 *Miroir*, p. 3, ll. 13 and 54; *The Mirror*, p. 3.
28 *Vox*, Macaulay, iv, p. 20; John Gower, *The Major Latin Works of John Gower*, trans. Eric Stockton (Seattle, 1962), p. 50.

is 'moderna mala' (*Vox*, Prol. III, lines 55–6).[29] Here, too, Gower objectifies his role in the image of his stylus. He asks, 'Vt nichil abrupte sibi presumat stilus iste' (*Vox*, Prol. III, line 51) ('that this piece of writing may incorporate nothing inconsiderately'), just as earlier he claims to write in a 'stilus stillatus' (*Vox*, Prol. II, line 19), a 'tenuous style of writing' (Stockton's translation), which carries the additional sense of a mode of writing that instills its meaning drop by drop.

The paradoxical literalism of the *Vox Clamantis*, its concretion of images within an allegorical structure, provides a staging for the vernacular artistry of Gower's narrative in the *Confessio Amantis*. The voice of Sophia that speaks to the distraught poet-narrator of the *Vox* while quoting Ovid (*Fasti*, I, line 483) reveals literally and definitively that his alienation and terror stem not from punishment but from divine anger (*Vox*, I, 16, line 1550). Her speech accords directly with the explanatory function that Aquinas calls *aetiologia*. The ship in which the dreamer seeks refuge with the fearful nobility displaced by the rebels is a transparent figure for the Tower of London: 'figurat enim dictam turrim similem esse naui prope voraginem Cille periclitanti' (rubric to *Vox*, I, l, line 17) ('Indeed, he pictures the said tower to be like a ship near the whirlpool of the perilous Scylla'). In Gower's satiric portrait of monastic corruption later in the *Vox*, personification allegories take over the cloister, giving literal form to abstract virtues and vices and putting them into action and social performance: 'Mortuus est dompnus Paciens, viuitque professus | Murmur' (*Vox*, IV, 7, lines 327–8) ('Abbot Patience is dead, and the monk Grumbler lives on'). Likewise, his admonition that a king must avoid lust and find lawful pleasure only in his consort draws on the historical record of the Old Testament, notably the examples of David, Balaam and Saul (*Vox*, VI, 12, lines 853–916).

A repeated theme that emerges in the *Vox* is the efficacy of literal meaning. Gower sees in the Old Testament a resource especially adapted to the aims of pastoral care: 'Legis enim veteris scripture sunt memorande, | Quo bonus exemplum pastor habere queat' (*Vox*, III, 13, lines 1115–16) ('The Scriptures of the Old Testament should be borne in mind. In this way the good shepherd can have a guide'). He then elaborates on the passage from Genesis 30. 37 in which Jacob peels part of the green bark off poplar, almond and plane-tree rods in order to expose the underlying whiteness. In Genesis, the incident is connected to fertility and prosperity. In the tradition of biblical commentary this 'historical narrative', as Gregory the Great calls it, signifies the lives and teachings of the ancient fathers.[30] Gower emphasizes the utility of the immediate and external meaning: 'Cortex saluatur, cum litera sola tenetur, |

---

[29] Gower stages a historical moment for the authoritative popular voice in the *Cronica Tripertita*, where the clamour of the people for justice is accepted as law by Henry IV (*Cronica* III, line 373).

[30] Gregory the Great, *Moralia in Job* 21. 1 *Sancti Gregorii Moralia in Job*, ed. Marcus Adriaen, 2 vols. (Turnholt: Brepols, 1979); cf. Rupert of Deutz, *De sancta trinitate et operibus eius*, ed. Hrabanus Haacke, 4 vols. (Turnholt: Brepols, 1971–2) *Liber VII, in Genesim VII*, p. 472. Gower, *The Major Latin Works*, trans. Stockton, p. 400, notes that Gower's immediate source is Peter of Riga's *Aurora*.

Et pastor sensu simplice pascit oues' (*Vox*, III, 13, lines 1123–4) ('The bark is saved when the letter alone is held to, and the pastor feeds his flock on the outward meaning'). In the matter of pastoral care, the literal also provides a defining contrast. The speech of ecclesiastical greed and abuse imputed to Clement VII turns on the conscious misalignment of signs and meaning, and Gower adds the grammatical play that Clement lacks the required prefix that would accurately name him – *inclemens* ('unmerciful' (*Vox*, III, 10, lines 955–6)).[31] In his remarks on mendicant preachers, Gower warns against the *duplex verbum* that separates the mind from God: 'Est simplex verbum fidei bonus vnde meretur' (*Vox*, IV, 22, line 1073) ('The simple word is good, and accordingly merits trust'). By extension, poetic composition itself requires caution, for adornment overlies the simple meaning of words.[32]

In the *Confessio Amantis*, then, Gower draws on a strain of prophecy that reaches back to the *Vox* and the *Mirour*. All three works combine dimensions of prophecy that St Paul originally distinguished and that subsequently came to inform Christian theology. In I Corinthians 14. 6, St Paul asks, 'quid vobis prodero nisi si vobis loquar aut in revelatione aut scientia aut prophetia aut in doctrina'? ('what shall I profit you, unless I speak to you either in revelation or in knowledge or in prophecy or in doctrine'?). Prophecy is about the unfolding of narrative and about instruction (the two are conflated in early commentary on Paul).[33] The implicit narrative of the *Mirour* – from the nothing of sin to reform to the intercession of the Virgin – is subordinated to its instructional aims. The original plan of the *Vox* is made prophetic by the subsequent addition of Gower's dream vision as a new opening book and the transition at the end of the poem to the *Cronica Tripertita* as a monitory fulfilment of precepts directed to the social estates. In the *Confessio Amantis* the overall narrative trajectory is prophetic in its forward movement toward a conclusion that Genius knows at the outset but Amans and the reader

---

[31] In the *Mirour* (lines 18,505–792), a similar ventriloquized speech is imputed to the Roman Curia; see Macaulay, iv, p. 384, and Gower, *The Major Latin Works*, trans. Stockton, pp. 397–8.

[32] For the phrase, 'Aurea dicuntur lingua' (*Vox*, IV, 22, line 1072), Macaulay, p. 393 notes the common variant 'verba'.

[33] John Cassian, *Iohannis Cassiani Conlationes xxiiii*, ed. Michael Petschenig (Vienna: Gerold, 1886), conlatio 14, cap. 8, p. 405, connects *revelatio* with allegory, *scientia* with tropology, *prophetia* with anagogy and *doctrina* with 'simplicem historicae expositionis ordinem'. Sedulius Scottus, *Sedutii Scotti Collectaneum in apostolum*, ed. Hermann Josef Frede and Herbert Stanjek, 2 vols. (Freiburg: Herder, 1996–7) (vol. 2, in epist. ad corinthos I, cap. 14, p. 434), follows Cassian's scheme; he glosses *doctrina* as 'in historia secundum litteram'. For Peter Lombard, *Collectanea in omnes Pauli apostoli Epistulas* (I ad Corinthos, cap 14) in *PL* 191, 1665, *scientia* illuminates faith, *prophetia* expounds scripture regarding the future, *doctrina* deals with habit and *revelatio* shows things made through the spirit. Aquinas (*Summa theologiae*, 2a2ae, 174.1) distinguishes the prophecy of divine predestination, foreknowledge and denunciation. Richard K. Emmerson, 'The prophetic, the apocalyptic, and the study of medieval literature', in *Poetic Prophecy in Western Literature*, eds Jan Wojick and Raymond-Jean Frontain (Madison, NJ, 1984), pp. 40–54, remarks that medieval Christian exegetes conflated the prophetic, which operates in times of chaos, with the apocalyptic, which operates in times of oppression: the prophetic is concerned with the present and is not predictive, while the apocalyptic is predictive and future-oriented, cf. p. 46.

come to understand only at the end of the poem.[34] Within individual stories, such as those of Nebuchadnezzar and Daniel or Alexander and Nectanabus, narrative action frequently turns on the realization of signs and mysteries within time. In the same measure, the poem speaks to power and instructs the nation and its people in spiritual, social and moral reform, following the authority and model of the Old Testament prophets.[35] From the standpoint of poetics, perhaps the most interesting work of prophecy in the *Confessio Amantis* can be seen in the pressure of history as it bears on structures of cultural belief which are seemingly positioned outside time and contingency, beyond deliberation and debate. Prophecy in this sense operates poetically through a literalism that makes visible the systems of power that organize life and experience in a social world of division, reversal and mutability. Put another way, Gower uses concrete particulars and the 'tale plein' (*Confessio*, VIII, line 497) to deconstruct the mystification and fantasies of ideology.[36]

The Tale of the Three Questions demonstrates a case where a contest of wit uncovers the artificial constructions that determine social life. Petro's daughter, Peronelle, offers not just abstract solutions to the questions that King Alphonse poses in a rivalry that began as a contest over intellectual authority with her father; her answers coalesce in the evocative phrase 'some good word' (*Confessio*, I, line 3204).[37] She then goes on to solve the tale's second problem, the king's thwarted desire for her. His desire appears after Peronelle has answered the three questions, leaving Alfonse 'inly glad and so wel paid' (*Confessio*, I, line 3324). He responds, in other words, to the intellectual elegance of her 'good word' and only afterward gazes on her face and invests 'al his pris' (*Confessio*, I, line 3329) in her. Critics have seen vestiges of the Annunciation and of the practice of queenly intercession in Peronelle's answers.[38] Her solutions present what Winthrop Wetherbee has called 'the concrete embodiment of Gower's message' in the iconic figure of the daughter's humility overcoming pride.[39] Both parts of the tale, however, are structured by the larger, abiding question of *gentilesse*: does nobility stem

---

[34] J. A. W. Bennett, 'Gower's "Honeste Love", in *Patterns of Love and Courtesy: Essays in Memory of C. S. Lewis*, ed. John Lawlor (London, 1966), pp. 107–21.

[35] Echard points out in *Companion*, p. 8, that across Gower's works, the prophetic voice ranges from moral lament or outrage in the *Mirour de l'Omme* to that of the distant observer in the *Confessio Amantis*.

[36] My formulation of prophecy here draws on the insights of Angus Fletcher, *The Prophetic Moment: An Essay on Spenser* (Chicago, MI, 1971), p. 5: 'The method of prophecy is to hold the eternal and the ephemeral in simultaneous co-presence, balancing stable principle against unstable reality'. Jane Aptekar's review of Fletcher's book (*Renaissance Quarterly*, 24 (1971), 560–63 (p. 560)) insists that prophecy 'is not prediction; it is visionary criticism of society and history, in the mode of Jeremiah, Virgil, Milton, and Blake'.

[37] The phrase recurs, again with a sense of concrete embodiment, in Amans's acknowledgment that he seeks 'A lusti touche, a good word eke' (*Confessio*, V, line 7147) from his lady.

[38] Patrick J. Gallacher, *Love, the Word, and Mercury: A Reading of John Gower's 'Confessio Amantis'* (Albuquerque, NM, 1975), pp. 37–40; Misty Schieberle, '"Thing which a man mai noght areche": women and counsel in Gower's *Confessio Amantis*', *CR*, 42 (2007), 91–109. For a larger view of female counsel, see Carolyn P. Collette, *Performing Polity: Women and Agency in the Anglo-French Tradition, 1395–1620* (Turnhout, 2006).

[39] W. Wetherbee, 'Genius and interpretation in the *Confessio Amantis*,' in *Magister Regis: Studies in Honor of Robert Earl Kaske*, ed. Arthur Groos (New York, 1986), pp. 241–60 (p. 259).

from lineage or virtue? Peronelle's three answers to Alphonse, especially the first, reveal the insubstantial base of social differences, while she resolves the king's erotic dilemma by asking for her father's advancement to a peerage, which makes her eligible to be a royal wife. This last move Russell Peck has identified as the middle term of Alphonse's syllogism.[40] But, as Yeager points out, the solution leaves unchanged the original objection to the marriage.[41] It serves, we might infer, to uncover the real question, which is the logic of social difference. Can a subordinate truly be a rival? Can a humble daughter speak for a father and overcome a prideful king? Do reason and wit generate desires that trump hierarchy?[42] At the end, Genius confidently situates the tale in the authority of Spanish chronicle history, whose established social world the literal narrative has meanwhile demystified as a set of contingent arrangements of power and pleasure.[43]

Gower's historical parable echoes the critique of social difference and the claims of power that runs through other classical and medieval exempla in the *Confessio Amantis*. In the tale of Alexander and the pirate, the 'Rovere of the See' (*Confessio*, III, line 2369), a 'Pilour' (*Confessio* III, line 2372) and a 'famous man' for his violence and theft (*Confessio*, III, line 2373), argues to Alexander, after his capture, that only the conventional 'name' (*Confessio*, III, line 2392) and the fact of poverty distinguish him from the Emperor: 'Oure dedes ben of o colour | And in effect of o decerte' (*Confessio*, III, lines 2394–5). When Alexander takes him into his service, he changes the name to knight and gives him land to remedy his poverty, but the essential actions, styled now as 'gret prouesce of armes' (*Confessio*, III, line 2416), remain unchanged. Piracy co-opted by imperial service passes under the rubric of chivalry; as the marginal gloss explains, 'sic bellicosus bellatori complacuit' ('thus one warrior was pleased by another'). A similar demystification underlies the tale of Adrian and Bardus, which centres on justice to the poor and the enforcement of covenants made with them. The comic reduction of the Roman senator Adrian, a 'gret lord' (*Confessio*, V, line 4939) in Gower's narrative, is conveyed directly in the rubric, which explains that the tale shows how beasts naturally excel ungrateful humans. The thematic focus on what Andrew Galloway has identified as the naturalizing of social differences contrasts the spontaneous generosity of the ape and the serpent with the arrogance and bad faith of Adrian after Bardus rescues all three

---

[40] Russell. A. Peck, *Kingship and Common Profit in Gower's Confessio Amantis* (Carbondale, IL, 1978), p. 57.

[41] R. F. Yeager, 'John Gower and the *exemplum* form: tale models in the *Confessio Amantis*', *Mediaevalia*, 8 (1982), 307–35 (p. 329).

[42] The attraction of Peronelle's wit delineates this exemplum from the biblical story of Apemen and Cirus (I Esdras. 3–4), which emphasizes the immediate erotic power of 'hire goodly lok' (*Confessio* VII, line 1890); see also Gardner Stillwell, 'John Gower and the last years of Edward III', *SP*, 45 (1948), 454–71, for application to Edward III and Alice Perrers.

[43] The reading I offer here diverges from the assertion in John Hurt Fisher, *John Gower: Moral Philosopher and Friend of Chaucer* (New York, 1964), p. 195, that the Tale of the Three Questions is 'a general illustration of the virtue of humility with neither romantic nor political implications'. The issue is not Gower's ethical bent, which Fisher established as one foundation of modern Gower criticism, but the collateral effects produced by exemplarity.

from a pit.[44] But the difference is not merely between natural beneficence and ingratitude. The key moment, repeated three times, resides in Bardus's anticipation: he expects to rescue a man but instead saves three creatures in the same predicament. That the ape and serpent follow natural law while Adrian must be constrained by positive law and imperial edict only qualifies the fundamental identity of the patrician Adrian as a similitude of a man and a companion of serpents.

The arbitrary nature of social difference shows up clearly in the betrayal of the False Bachelor. Gower sets the tale, like that of Alexander and the pirate, in the liminal borderland of the marches and in a historical frame of natural law rather than grace and Christian faith. The Emperor's son, desiring the fame of chivalry, proves his worth in service to the Sultan of Persia: 'above alle his pris deserveth | This knightly Romein' (*Confessio*, II, lines 2624–5). He is given the ring that conveys the Sultan's daughter and empire to him, in a seemingly natural continuation of empire building at the margins, but his companion steals the token and claims both for himself. The announced aim of the tale is to illustrate the vice of supplantation, but the effect is to demonstrate the vulnerability of the Persian nobles, who are bound by the Sultan's compact, and the limits of Roman power, which cannot act against a crowned monarch in place without compromising its own political legitimacy. The confessed traitor must be returned to Rome for justice, but on the margins of Roman authority his claims to monarchy cannot be countered by the rightful claims of the Emperor's son. Gower's gloss on the tale ends with a literal description of the power of substitution within a political system and not the final disposition of justice: 'Et sic seruus pro domino desponsata sibi Soldani filia coronatus Persie regnauit' ('And so the servant having married the Sultan's daughter in place of his lord and been crowned king ruled over Persia').

The narratives that Gower assembles from the 'Croniques' reveal the mobility of social relations and the pressures of history on political authority. Gower's prophetic literalism goes further, however, to address the social risk from within established regimes of power. The master narrative here is arguably the tale of Lucrece, in which the prerogatives of noble families and freeborn men are compromised by tyranny exercised on their women. In a sequence of vignettes in book VI Gower uses the principal species of gluttony to frame monitory tales of social turmoil. Gluttony is a sin against reason and self-regulation, but Gower locates it specifically in the operation of power: 'Delicie cum diuiciis sunt iura potentum' (*Confessio*, VI, ii) ('Sensualities, along with riches, are the laws of the powerful').[45] Thus, the wedding of Pirithous and Ipotacia ends in the bride's abduction as drink and lust inflame friends and neighbours invited to the ceremony. The Spanish rulers Galba and Vitellus share a 'sori felaschipe' (*Confessio*, VI, line 544) of gluttony and drunkenness that leads them to prey on wives and maidens but

---

[44] Andrew Galloway, 'The making of a social ethic in late-medieval England: from "Gratitudo" to "Kyndenesse"', *Journal of the History of Ideas*, 55 (1994), 365–83 (p. 378).

[45] The translation is by Andrew Galloway, from Peck.

leaves them 'healdede slain' (*Confessio*, VI, line 594) when justice befalls them. Nero is an icon of sensuality, 'which ayein kinde manyfold / His lustes tok' (*Confessio*, VI, line 1156–7), acting against citizens and women out of both curiosity and appetite.

The tale of Athemus and Demophon marks one logical endpoint of Gower's reflections on history and power. The aftermath of the Trojan war emerges here, as in the late classical and medieval Troy narratives, as a period of political instability. Athemus and Demophon, like other returning monarchs, find themselves disavowed by subjects who have made other arrangements in the interim, and so the kings form alliances 'To vengen hem of thilke oultrage | And winne ayein here heritage' (*Confessio*, III, lines 1775–6). The first aim outruns the second, however, as 'Folhaste' (*Confessio*, III, lines 1787), a species of anger, aligns their grievance with the intemperance of the young warriors who join them. In a passage that Gower largely adds to his source, Nestor averts their plans to put their people to the sword by demonstrating the literal impossibility of their intentions: 'To what final conclusioun | Thei wolde regne Kinges there, | If that no people in londe were' (*Confessio*, III, lines 1817–19).[46] He offers a prophetic definition – at once instructive and visionary – of kingship cancelling itself in the act of asserting its right to violence against the subjects who constitute its conditions of existence.

The poetics of the literal adds an important dimension to our understanding of Gower's poetry. It complements his professed exemplarity and his choice of the 'middel weie' (*Confessio*, Prol., line 17) by demonstrating what is at stake in the precepts and values that his poem expounds. It reminds us thereby that moral, political and poetic Gower are the same poet, though in complex ways. Moreover, it recontextualizes Gower among late-fourteenth-century English poets. Gower's self-reflexive comments about lust and lore, earnest and game, unlike Chaucer's ambiguity or Langland's ambivalence over the power of imagination, have generally had the effect of containing his poem rather than signalling its nuances and subtleties. In his turn to the literal, Gower reveals himself as a poet with the same capacity for radical critique and discovery that we have long valued in his metropolitan contemporaries.

---

[46] Gower's source is the *Roman de Troie*; Macaulay notes that Nestor's speech in the *Confessio Amantis* is 'for the most part original', Macaulay, ii, p. 499.

Chapter 6

Romance, Popular Style and the *Confessio Amantis*: Conflict or Evasion?

GEORGE SHUFFELTON

Given the scope of Gower's *Confessio Amantis,* sometimes the most surprising choices are the omissions, the stories Gower chooses *not* to tell. In book IV's discussion of Sloth and the various sins of idleness in love, Genius turns to the need for young men to remain active lest they lose the love of their ladies. It is, on the face of things, an ideal subject for romance, as Genius recognizes:

> For if thou wolt the bokes rede
> Of Lancelot and othre mo,
> Ther miht thou sen hou it was tho
> Of armes, for thei wolde atteigne
> To love, which withoute peine
> Mai noght be gete of ydelnesse.
> And that I take to witnesse
> An old cronique in special,
> The which into memorial
> Is write, for his loves sake,
> Hou that a kniht schal undertake. (*Confessio*, IV, lines 2034–44)[1]

This is, I think, an interesting move for Genius – and by extension Gower – to make. Genius acknowledges that a fourteenth-century English audience looking for feats of chivalry in the service of love would most naturally read 'books of Lancelot' or other romances. More specifically, the Vulgate *Lancelot* offers plenty of examples of Lancelot momentarily falling into knightly 'sloth' before once again serving his lady heroically – the *Chevalier de la Charrette* episode would seem particularly apt for the point Genius is making here, and he seems to acknowledge as much in these lines.[2] Yet

---

[1] *Confessio* references in this article are from Peck.
[2] E. D. Kennedy suggests that Lancelot's crossing of the sword bridge may be behind these lines: 'Gower, Chaucer, and French prose Arthurian romance', *Mediaevalia*, 16 (1993), 55–90. Kennedy argues that Gower appreciated French romance for the same reasons he appreciated Ovid, as 'sexually risqué stories that were nonetheless edifying and conducive to virtue' (p. 79). Yet Gower admits his debt to Ovid in ways that he does not do for French romance.

without quite saying that he won't tell such stories, Genius turns away from such romances towards his preferred sources in 'old cronique'.

This substitution of 'old cronique' for books of Lancelot becomes a little stranger when Genius begins his next tale immediately after these lines. It is an Ovidian story, the tale of the battle between Hercules and Achelous (or Achelons, for Gower) for the hand of Deianira. But the tale has been considerably altered from its source in the *Metamorphoses*, and has come to look much more like a short romance. In Ovid, the tale is told by Achelous and from his perspective, and it presents Hercules as a thuggish brute, 'accensae non fortiter imperat irae' ('unable to master his burning anger any longer'), who nonetheless prevails.[3] It begins rather abruptly, with the rival claims of both suitors to Deianira's father, Oeneus. Achelous, thinking that 'turpe deum mortali cedere' ('it is a shame for a god to yield to a mortal'), points out that he is a river god of Oeneus' own country, unlike Hercules, a foreigner and the product of an adulterous union between Jove and Alcmena (*Metamorphoses*, IX, line 16). Gower has Genius narrate the tale in the third person, and turns Achelous' taunt into a praise of the 'hih lignage' of Hercules, establishing him as a 'noble kniht,' the proper hero of a romance (*Confessio*, IV, lines 2064, 2053). And Gower borrows from two archetypal varieties of romance villains in turning the river god Achelous into a giant and a sorcerer. What had been a wrestling match in Ovid turns into knightly combat in Gower, and it concludes not with Achelous bemoaning his fate but with Hercules obtaining the love of his lady, 'sche for whom he hadde served' (*Confessio*, IV, line 2129).

Gower always tailors his sources to the local needs of his text, and his changes to the tale of Hercules and Achelous are not really more radical than other kinds of alterations he makes to other Ovidian material.[4] But here the changes seem particularly odd: immediately after *not* delivering a romance where one would seem obviously called for, Gower has instead reshaped a story of 'old cronique' into a romance, without either fully conforming to the expectations of the genre or fully acknowledging what he has done. The changes do not merely involve 'medievalizing' his source through anachronism, but a realignment of the perspective, function and narrative movement of the original so that it shares crucial resemblances with romance. Though perhaps unusually devious in being prefaced by Genius's disclaimer, this move is perfectly typical of the *Confessio Amantis* as a whole in its preference for subtle compromise between genres rather than explicit, acknowledged conflict. Gower's own description of his work as *compilatio*, his claim that

---

[3] Ovid, *Metamorphoses*, ed. G. P. Goold, 2 vols (Cambridge, MA, 1984) ii, IX. line 28. Subsequent references are to line numbers in this edition; translations are my own.

[4] The questions surrounding Gower's treatment of Ovid have, of course, been widely considered. Selected contributions to the discussion include Götz Schmitz, 'Gower, Chaucer and the classics: back to the textual evidence', in *John Gower: Recent Readings*, ed. Robert Yeager (Kalamazoo, MI, 1989), pp. 209–23; Thomas Hatton, 'John Gower's use of Ovid in Book III of the *Confessio Amantis*', *Mediaevalia*, 13 (1989), 257–74; and the essays collected by Peter G. Beidler, ed., *John Gower's Literary Transformations in the Confessio Amantis* (Washington DC, 1982).

'tanquam fauum ex variis floribus recollectum, presentem libellum ex variis cronicis, historiis, poetarum philosophorumque dictis [...] studiosissime compilauit', deliberately effaces the possible generic differences between 'cronique', poetry and philosophy.[5]

Gower's treatment of the tale of Hercules and Achelous offers an opportunity to re-explore his treatment of romance and other popular genres, and in turn an opportunity to qualify several recent readings of the *Confessio Amantis*. Several recent readings have paid close attention to Gower's handling of romance (though not, to my knowledge, to this moment in book VI). These readings share some common perspectives and even, perhaps, a shared conclusion: the conflict between romance and other genres in the *Confessio* (especially *exempla*) presents an ethical/moral challenge for Amans and the reader.[6] William Robins, for example, argues that in the *Confessio* 'romance and exemplarity come to stand less as genres than as two distinct modes', and 'the convergence of modes in any one story is thus also a potential conflict'.[7] By the *Confessio*'s end, 'Amans casts off an exclusively romance conception of his relation to the world, but has not therefore committed himself to an exemplary model. [...] Amans/Gower is finally positioned as a subject who has to adjudicate between the competing narrative modes that constitute his ability to think about himself.'[8] Simon Meecham-Jones shares this sense of the text's tension between romance and other genres, but argues that the conflict entails a more decisive rejection.[9] Where Robins defines the romance mode by its emphasis on contingency and chance, Meecham-Jones instead sees in romances 'patterns of divine intervention in the course of human events', in opposition to Gower's 'rigorous secularity' and 'schematic and designedly practical dissection of moral possibility'.[10] This model of romance fails 'to articulate an *achievable* strategy which every reader could rehearse in their own conduct' and thus 'it must be rejected as being insufficient for Gower's purpose.'[11] Jeremy Dimmick, by comparison, finds a similar conflict *within* the various kinds of romances in the *Confessio* (and

---

[5] 'He has assiduously gathered this book from various chronicles, histories, and sayings of poets and philosophers, like a honeycomb drawn from various flowers.' These lines, part of the Latin marginalia which appears in different forms in different manuscripts, are taken from Peck's transcription of Oxford, Bodleian Library MS Bodley 294, though they also appear in other manuscripts and seem to be part of the author's second recension; Peck, p. 287. For further consideration of Gower's work as *compilatio*, see Kurt Olsson, *John Gower and the Structures of Conversion: A Reading of the 'Confessio Amantis'* (Cambridge, 1992), pp. 5–11.

[6] All of these readings thus owe much to the influential work of James Simpson, who sets forth the idea of Amans as reader making ethical choices in *Sciences and the Self in Medieval Poetry: Alan of Lille's Anticlaudianus and John Gower's Confessio Amantis* (Cambridge, 1995), pp. 252–71.

[7] William Robins, 'Romance, *exemplum*, and the subject of the *Confessio Amantis*', *SAC*, 19 (1997), 157–81 (p. 169).

[8] Ibid., 175.

[9] Simon Meecham-Jones, 'Questioning romance: Amadas and Ydoine in Gower's *Confessio Amantis*', *Parergon*, 17, 2 (2000), 35–49.

[10] Ibid., 46.

[11] Ibid.

not just between the exemplary mode and romance in general). Dimmick sees certain romances as more conducive to Gower's moral purposes than others, and suggests that those romances which emphasize social reintegration (e.g. the Tale of Constance) rather than individual wish-fulfilment play a key role in the *Confessio*'s moral argument.[12] In other words, Amans must learn to prefer ethically valuable romances over bad ones.

Each of these persuasive arguments considers romance primarily in structural, rather than formal, terms, just as each critic ultimately reads the *Confessio* in moral terms – surely very reasonable responses to Gower's stated aims. But Middle English romance, whether defined as a mode or a genre, can also be considered as a flexible set of styles, tropes and figures. It is a popular form, perhaps even what we might loosely call popular culture, a category definable mostly by what it is not: not classical, not biblical, not otherwise authoritative. In short, the popular is that which is not 'old cronique', the category that Genius so consistently steers Amans towards. Thinking about Gower's treatment of popular literary genres in formal terms, I would argue, offers insight into his remarkably inclusive – even idealistic – cultural politics.

Making this kind of argument depends on distinctions between popular and elite forms of culture in Gower's England, distinctions that are hard to make and even harder to agree on. Perhaps no one would be prepared to create for fourteenth-century England the sort of elegant schematic diagrams that Pierre Bourdieu has applied (with a theorist's confidence) to the nineteenth-century French art market.[13] Stratifying vernacular writing in England by class has rarely been a convincing exercise. Yet the fact that late medieval culture was not perhaps as rigidly segmented or stratified as that of some later periods seems to be does not mean that there were not perceivable hierarchies between kinds of cultural products – between a romance and a tale from Ovid, or between a homespun proverb and a quotation from Justinian's *Digest*. And surely Gower too perceived them acutely, given the attention all his works pay to hierarchies of class and language. Winthrop Wetherbee has recently suggested that 'Gower's primary theme in the *Confessio Amantis* is culture', and Gower's relationship to high and low culture has long served a crucial role in his critical reception, even as critics have disagreed about just where he belongs on this continuum.[14] But Gower, I would like to suggest, mostly recognizes cultural distinctions by refusing to exploit them, avoiding their oppositions whenever possible. Rather than parody, critique or directly reject cultural modes, either high or low, Gower works to integrate them without fully acknowledging that he does so.

---

[12] Jeremy Dimmick, '"Redinge of Romance" in Gower's *Confessio Amantis*', in *Tradition and Transformation in Medieval Romance*, ed. Rosalind Field (Cambridge, 1999), pp. 125–37.

[13] For example, Pierre Bourdieu, *The Field of Cultural Production*, ed. and trans. Randal Johnson (New York, 1993), p. 49.

[14] W. Wetherbee, 'Rome, Troy and culture in the *Confessio Amantis*', in *On John Gower: Essays at the Millennium*, ed. R. F. Yeager (Kalamazoo, MI, 2007), pp. 20–42 (p. 20).

Obviously, Gower does not always handle the genre of romance as indirectly or delicately as he does in the Tale of Hercules. Book VII's Tale of Apollonius of Tyre is unquestionably a romance. It certainly derives from romance, preserves its romance plot, and runs about as long as many other Middle English romances. 'Greek' romance plots featuring dispersed families rather than warfaring knights appear with some frequency in French and Middle English romance, though usually these popular romances manage to include some knightly combat, as in (for example) *Sir Isumbras*, where the wandering hero fights several battles on the way to recovering his lost family and lost identity. Gower's Tale of Apollonius is just such a romance, but he does not popularize his sources by including such chivalric touches, and instead deliberately attenuates this tale's connections to romance. The Latin marginalia calls this a 'mirabile exemplum' rather than a romance, and at its outset Genius carefully establishes its authoritative pedigree from a 'cronique in daies gon', naming the *Pantheon* as its source (*Confessio*, VIII, lines 271–2). Once again, when Gower flirts with romance he makes clear his preference for Latinate, written sources – old cronique – over French or Middle English popular romances from oral traditions.

Something similar happens in Gower's Tale of Florent in book I, which more closely resembles a romance than analogues such as the *Wife of Bath's Tale*. Florent fights battles, and his loathly lady, far from delivering sermons about 'gentilesse', turns out to be a princess of Sicily. Gower's Tale thus ends on a triumphant note, with its romance hero having overcome obstacles, won his beautiful bride and secured a wealthy inheritance. But rather than acknowledge the true genre of the tale, Genius introduces it as another 'gret ensample' that can be found 'In a cronique' (*Confessio*, I, lines 1404–5). Dimmick argues that this only 'seems at first glance to be' a romance of wish-fulfilment 'disguised as an *exemplum*'; the tale ultimately rewards Florent for curbing his knightly will for *aventure* rather than exercising it.[15] Dimmick's argument presumes a rather narrow definition of romance, since many romances, from Chrétien's *Yvain* to *Sir Gowther*, involve some similar restraint of chivalric impulsiveness and the desire for *aventure*. Exemplary romances that operate in both modes simultaneously are not uncommon. But what seems notable here is Genius's calling it an *exemplum* rather than a romance, surely a partial description at best. This seems entirely consistent with the *Confessio*'s deliberate vagueness on the genres of its material.

If the prevailing formal scheme of the *Confessio* involves effacing or refusing to acknowledge the presence of popular forms like romance, Gower nevertheless allows the style and language of popular romance to sneak in. In book IV, Genius tells the Tale of Rosiphelee as an example of a young woman reluctant to serve the demands of love. Like a good romance heroine, Rosiphelee goes riding by herself in a landscape highly reminiscent of the genre, and here Gower's diction betrays the debt to romance rather obviously. In a 'schawe' ('grove') Rosiphelee watches a parade of handsomely

---

[15] Dimmick, '"Redinge of Romance"', p. 128.

dressed women ride by, and from 'under a linde' she sees a bedraggled woman ride at the back of the procession, before learning that this wretched straggler is a dead woman who had refused to love when alive (*Confessio*, IV, lines 1295, 1341). Romances frequently place events 'under a linde' and 'under a schawe'; though not words limited to romance, the majority of the *MED*'s attested quotations for 'schawe' and 'linde' come from texts such as *William of Palerne*, *Guy of Warwick*, *Octavian*, *Athelston*, *Gamelyn* and various tales of Robin Hood. With its spooky vision of the dead and its lush natural setting, this entire scene recalls nothing so closely as the moment in *Sir Orfeo* when the hero encounters Heurodys riding among the King of Fairy's otherworldly retinue.[16] In his self-imposed exile in the wilderness, Orfeo watches 'The king o fairy with his rout', a group of 'Sexti levedis on hors ride, | Gentil and jolif as brid on ris' (*Orfeo* 283; 304–5). Rosiphelee likewise sees 'clad in o suite a route | Of ladis, wher thei comen ryde | Along under the wodes syde' (*Confessio*, IV, lines 1306–8). Or perhaps a closer analogue is the otherworldly *pastourelle* at the outset of *Sir Degarré*, when a princess (who has refused marriage, though in this case at the command of her father) and her retinue lie down underneath a chestnut tree. The princess then encounters a fairy knight, who rapes her and thus begets Sir Degarré.[17] Rosiphelee's encounter carries the same charge of violent sexual coercion, although in the Tale of Rosiphelee this encounter has the immediate effects of an *exemplum* – reform – rather than serving as the generative dilemma of a romance. Yet Gower has clearly drawn from the idiom of Middle English romance in order to make the episode so powerful. In particular, he has used romance conventions of otherworldly encounters in the wilderness in the same way that these romances use the trope, making the boundary between the natural and supernatural serve as the stage for a psychic drama of unrecognized desires. Immediately before Rosiphelee sees the 'route' of ladies, she observes the springtime mating of 'bestes in her kinde', and this moment 'began there a querele | Betwen love and hir oghne herte, | Fro which sche couthe noght asterte' (*Confessio*, IV, lines 1299, 1302–3). Gower employs romance conventions adeptly and thoughtfully, but once again without acknowledging that he is doing so in any explicit way.

Gower also seems willing to employ popular styles at particular moments, especially when he wishes to describe fast-moving events. At these moments, his four-stress lines become increasingly paratactic and more closely resemble the four-stress couplets of many fourteenth-century Middle English romances. For example, book I's quickly told Tale of the Trojan horse follows a romance-driven style especially visible in the action of lines 1162–71, when Gower wishes to dispatch a series of events in short order. The rhyme couplet 'yare'/'fare' in lines 1165–6 is relatively unusual for Gower (and even more unusual for Chaucer) but it appears commonly in works like *Havelok* and *Guy of Warwick*. Gower relies on the popular diction

---

[16] See *Sir Orfeo*, *The Middle English Breton Lays*, eds Anne Laskaya and Eve Salisbury (Kalamazoo, MI, 1995), lines 281–330. Subsequent references are to line numbers in this edition.

[17] See *Sir Degarré* in *The Middle English Breton Lays*, eds Laskaya and Salisbury, lines 37–140.

of romance for other moments of narrative economy or temporal transition, as when he uses a word such as 'enderdai' that, again, appears virtually nowhere in Chaucer, Lydgate or Hoccleve but everywhere in popular Middle English lyrics and romances.[18] Somewhat more frequently, he uses formulaic temporal phrases like 'ilke stounde' or 'a litel stounde', and even 'the montance of a mile', formulas so indispensable for tail-rhyme romances that works such as *Lybeaus Desconeus* seem to feature them in every stanza.

Along with oral formulas we ought to consider Genius's fondness for proverbs, though this fondness does not necessarily mark his discourse as especially popular, given the nearly universal use of proverbs across the entire range of medieval genres. Still, the proverbs Genius chooses seem to come from the domain of homespun wisdom at least as often as they come from the schoolroom, the law, the Bible or other sententious sources. When Genius remarks in book V's discussion of Avarice that 'He was wys that ferst made mede', he relies on a proverb also endorsed by *Havelok* and *Sir Tristrem* (*Confessio*, V, line 4720).[19] *Havelok* and a number of Middle English lyrics also feature his proverb 'Old senne, newe schame', and Genius's outburst of proverbs in book III, lines 1615–58, what one editor has called a *'tour de force* of proverbs', shares its wisdom with texts such as *The Proverbs of Hendyng, The South English Legendary, The Towneley Plays, Generydes* and various lyrics and carols.[20]

One final example of this pattern recalls the curious indirection of the Hercules and Achelous example with which I started, and has served several other readers as evidence for arguments about Gower's engagement with romance. In book VI the Lover confesses to a kind of gluttony that involves gorging on the delicacies of seeing and hearing about his lady. The passage features heavily the traditional language of Middle English love lyric and romance, as Amans imagines his lady's fair white hands, body round and middle small, and so forth and so on. And Amans takes special solace in 'redinge of romance | Of Ydoine and of Amadas, | That whilom weren in mi cas, | And eke of othre many a score' (*Confessio*, VI, lines 878–81). Yet in recalling these moments of escapist fantasy, Amans recognizes that they provide only temporary respite that 'endureth bot a throwe | Riht as it were a cherie feste' (VI, lines 890–91). The reminder that the joys of romance reading, like all worldly pleasures, last only as long as a cherry harvest recalls not only the warning issued by the Prologue of the *Confessio* – 'For al is bot a chirie faire' – but also a long line of proverbial cherry fairs in Middle English penitential lyrics, carols and courtesy books such as *How the Wise*

---

[18] For 'enderdai' in the *Confessio*, see book I, line 98 and book V, line 7400. No complete concordances exist for Lydgate's and Hoccleve's works, so there may be instances of the word *enderdai* (or its variants) that have escaped my notice. But variants of the word do not appear in any of the electronically searchable texts of these authors.

[19] *Havelok the Dane, Four Romances of England*, eds Ronald B. Herzman, Graham Drake and Eve Salisbury (Kalamazoo, MI, 1999), line 1635; *Sir Tristrem, Lancelot of the Laik and Sir Tristrem*, ed. Alan Lupack (Kalamazoo, MI, 1994), lines 626–7.

[20] For 'old sinne makes newe shame', see *Havelok the Dane*, eds Herzman *et al.*, line 2461. Peck refers to the *'tour de force* of proverbs' in the note for III, lines 1615–58 (Peck, p. 367).

Man Taught His Son (Prol. 454).[21] In other words, the popular escapist fantasies of romance run into the popular sententiousness of folk wisdom. And Amans, without the help of Genius or his 'old cronique', seems perfectly capable of recognizing this on his own.

Genius does not censure Amans's reading habits, and instead excuses Amans's escapist fantasies as petty rather than truly dangerous self-indulgence. But if Genius forgives these tastes he does not cater to them either, and his following tale of Dives and Lazarus could be seen as a gentle rebuke to all forms of luxury, romance reading included. Indeed, Meecham-Jones uses this particular episode to argue that Gower rejects the moral vision of romance, with its comforting reassurance of divine providence, in favor of a more rigorous morality based on individual responsibility.[22] Wetherbee draws the slightly different conclusion that, for Gower, 'the calculated naiveté ... of romance sets off the dangers of chivalric individualism.'[23] There are surely other ways of explaining this alleged rejection as well, and Gower's treatment of romance might usefully be connected to his critiques of crusading, the Anglo-French war and aristocratic militarism more generally.

Again, readings of the *Confessio* that depict a conflict between romance, *exemplum* and other genres, and that view this conflict as part of Gower's moral vision, seem to me very persuasive. But such readings do not reflect the remarkable *lack* of conflict at the 'surface' of the text, where different genres and styles interact without a hint of tension or even explicit acknowledgment that such differences exist. Genius goes out of his way to avoid direct rejections of romance or any other genre, instead co-opting them into the very flexible category of 'olde cronique', a category which also seems capable of a range of popular styles. This question of whether or not the *Confessio* rejects or subordinates romance has a direct bearing on Gower's relationship to popular English verse more broadly, since critics have most often figured this, too, as a series of rejections. John Burrow's admirably focused account of Gower's English style concludes that 'Gower avoids certain expressions of [the] "popular" kind at least as carefully as does Chaucer' and that 'a suitably qualified reader – an *elegans lector* from the London intelligentsia, perhaps – would have been impressed by the relative absence of ... commonplace English poeticisms.'[24] This kind of judgment has a long history behind it, beginning with the many fifteenth-century paeans to Gower as one of those who, like Chaucer and Lydgate, raised crude English into something more noble and aureate. This is the Gower who, in George Ashby's words, helped create a 'fresshe douce englisshe ... not used before.'[25] Thomas Warton's praise for Gower's 'cultivation of his native

---

[21] *How the Wise Man Taught His Son*, in *Codex Ashmole 61: A Compilation of Popular Middle English Verse*, ed. George Shuffleton (Kalamazoo, MI, 2008), line 68.
[22] Meecham-Jones, 'Questioning romance,' p. 46.
[23] W. Wetherbee, 'Classical and Boethian tradition in the *Confessio Amantis*', in *Companion*, pp. 181–96 (p. 196).
[24] John Burrow, 'Gower's poetic styles', in *Companion*, pp. 239–50 (p. 243).
[25] *Active Policy of a Prince*, in George Ashby, *George Ashby's Poems*, ed. Mary Bateson, EETS e.s. 76 (London, 1899), lines 5–6.

language', C. S. Lewis's similar praise of his plain style's 'politeness' that is 'noble rather than urbane', and R. F. Yeager's more recent assessments of him as Augustan in refinement and decorum, all follow in this same critical tradition.[26] In Yeager's words, 'Gower decided to write in English, even as he rejected as crude and moribund its native poetic traditions'.[27]

This assessment also would seem to accord with the general sense of Gower as an elitist in other political dimensions. Corroborating evidence for this picture might include his laureate desire to speak directly to kings and princes, his scathing contempt for rebellious peasants, the relative distance of his Southwark retreat from Westminster's sordid politics and London's filthy lucre, and his insistence on framing his vernacular in scholarly Latin.[28] The fact that both Gower's ardent supporters and harshest critics have contributed something to this picture suggests just how and why it can be convincing.

But while this may be the prevailing or most common portrait of Gower's cultural politics, it is not the only one. Siân Echard cites an anonymous review essay from 1858 that celebrates Gower as one who celebrated the language of the common people, without any 'sickly notions about the courtly or superrefined phraseology'.[29] More recently, Russell Peck has praised Gower's 'folkloric instinct', calling the *Confessio* a 'cultural treasury'.[30] And there are ample reasons to think of Gower as a popularizer, even if this seems initially hard to reconcile with his more familiar roles as conservative social critic, adviser to princes and moralizing prophet. Gower made more Latin literature available to Middle English readers than any other contemporary; more specifically, the *Confessio* can be seen as the first sustained attempt to translate Ovid into English. The *Confessio* also makes biblical history, astronomy, scientific lore and Aristotelian ideas available to new audiences. Encyclopedias are quintessentially popularizing works, and book VII ought to rank Gower with John Trevisa as one of the very first encyclopedists in English. And many fifteenth-century readers clearly did view the *Confessio* as a 'cultural treasury', whether they raided it for favourite tales, like the London grocer Richard Hill in his miscellany of carols, courtesy texts and practical wisdom, or whether they excerpted more 'scientific' material, like the compiler of Longleat 174, who included book VII's account of the fifteen

---

[26] Thomas Warton, *The History of English Poetry from the Close of the Eleventh to the Commencement of the Eighteenth Century*, 4 vols (London, 1778), ii, p. 2; C. S. Lewis, *The Allegory of Love* (Oxford, 1939), p. 201; R. F. Yeager, *John Gower's Poetic: The Search for a New Arion* (Cambridge, 1990), pp. 11–16.

[27] Yeager, *John Gower's Poetic*, p. 13.

[28] For Gower's pose of laureate authority and its possible influence on poets like Lydgate, see Robert Meyer-Lee, *Poets and Power From Chaucer to Wyatt* (Cambridge, 2007), pp. 36–7. For his treatment of the 1381 revolt, see Steven Justice, *Writing and Rebellion: England in 1381* (Berkeley, CA, 1994), pp. 207–13. On the cultural politics of Gower's dwelling in Southwark, see Robert Epstein, 'London, Southward, Westminster: Gower's urban contexts', in *Companion*, pp. 43–60.

[29] 'John Gower and his works', *The British Quarterly Review*, 53 (1858), 8; quoted in Siân Echard, 'Introduction', in *Companion*, p. 13.

[30] Peck, pp. 9–10.

stars in a collection of mostly medical texts.[31] In this sense the *Confessio* belongs alongside scruffy hodgepodge collections like *Ypotis* and the *Seven Sages of Rome* – popular texts in every sense of the term.

Exaggerating these portraits of Gower leaves us with might seem to be an unbridgeable divide between the elitist, scholastic, reluctant late-comer to English who forged a new poetic medium by turning his back on older ones, and the more popular and populist Gower, lover of folk wisdom and poet of the common tongue. But this seems to be exactly the kind of divide that the *Confessio* works so hard to bridge, in its consistent willingness to marry high and low, to tell stories from Ovid in the language and style of *Havelok* and *King Horn*. Certainly one can read Gower's 'middel weie' as a series of rejections: a refusal to commit to any one genre or literary style. But describing it this way seems to me against the spirit of the *Confessio*, which shows far more evidence for a desire to evade the tensions between distinct cultural forms than an interest in exploiting them.

Here the customary comparison to Chaucer seems inevitable and revealing. Chaucer, after all, exploited the tensions between genres and styles in explicit – and explicitly political – ways, tying literary form to ideology in ways that Gower never did. *The Canterbury Tales* dramatizes the conflict of literary genres in the form of competing and largely irreconcilable class perspectives. When popular idiom meets refined, courtly style in *The Canterbury Tales*, the meeting is staged as the Miller's combative quitting of the Knight; when Chaucer adopts the form and style of popular romance, it is as self-conscious parody (almost akin to blackface minstrelsy) in *Sir Thopas*. Where Gower discreetly plays with genre and popular style without directly acknowledging it, Chaucer stages pyrotechnic displays like the *The Nun's Priest's Tale*.[32] A similar comparison might be made between Gower and Langland, insofar as Langland, like Chaucer, is a contemporary whose engagements with popular genres and styles may be configured as a series of conflicts, competitions and rejections. Again, Gower seems remarkable for his desire to evade such conflicts rather than exploit them.

This desire surely stems from Gower's acutely self-conscious sense of his idealized audience. As has often been recognized, Gower continually represents himself as speaking both for and to the collected public. And of course the *Confessio* begins on a populist note, with its famous declaration that since 'fewe men endite | In oure Englissh, I thenke make | A bok for Engelondes sake' (*Confessio* Prol., lines 22–4). This habit of speaking to a broad audience, imagined as the entire nation undifferentiated and unparticularized, runs across Gower's work, from the prophetic voice of *Vox Clamantis* to the

---

[31] For a recent account of Hill's book, see David Parker, *The Commonplace Book in Tudor London* (Lanham, MD, 1998), pp. 37–88. On the Longleat manuscript, see Kate Harris, 'The Longleat House extracted manuscript of Gower's *Confessio Amantis*', in *Middle English Poetry: Texts and Traditions, Essays in Honour of Derek Pearsall*, ed. A. J. Minnis (York, 2001), pp. 77–90. On the fifteen stars passage, see O'Callaghan's essay in this volume.

[32] Derek Pearsall describes *The Nun's Priest's Tale* as 'like a fireworks display that has got into the hands of a pyromaniac'; Pearsall, *The Canterbury Tales* (London, 1985; rpt 1993), p. 231.

direction of his *Treatise for Married Lovers* 'a tout le monde en general'.[33] Part of the desire to play the role of Arion, to restore unity to a fractured polity, involves this imagination of a universal audience, undivided by taste or cultural distinctions. This may seem naive or merely idealistic. But, as I hope I have suggested, at the level of his more intricate manoeuvres Gower's cultural politics are sly, sophisticated and evasive even as they aim at this optimistic ideal of inclusion.

---

[33] See the preface to Gower's *Traitié Pour Essampler Les Amantz Marietz* in Macaulay, i, p. 379.

Chapter 7

John Gower: Prophet or Turncoat?

NIGEL SAUL

For an historian, particularly a political historian, one of the key questions about Gower relates to his consistency. Was he actually, as Chaucer called him, 'moral Gower'? Did he stick to a consistent set of positions throughout his career? Or did he trim his views to suit the changing political wind? To be precise, was he a man of integrity? Or did he sink in his later years into the role of sad apologist for the Lancastrian monarchy?

The question which is raised here is hardly a new one. It is a quite old – not to say, a slightly old-fashioned – one. It was first raised in the early eighteenth century, when Thomas Hearne, the editor and antiquary, accused Gower very specifically of being a turncoat by switching the dedication of the *Confessio Amantis* from Richard II to Henry, earl of Derby, later King Henry IV.[1] To Hearne, the rededication smacked of opportunism and ingratitude. In Hearne's view Gower went on to compound the evil after 1399 by turning out what amounted to crude Lancastrian propaganda (for example, the *Cronica Tripertita*). The notion of Gower as a political turncoat has generally been rejected by modern critics of his work: their emphasis is firmly on 'moral Gower'. Yet the idea that in later life he compromised his integrity refuses to fade away. In recent years it has been given a new lease of life in the work of Terry Jones and Paul Strohm on the Lancastrian 'propaganda machine', which has demonstrated the sheer scale of the Lancastrian disinformation campaign after 1399. Terry Jones, for example, has argued that Gower, 'the aging poet, wrote what he thought the usurper wanted him to say'; Gower, he argues, 'went back into his past writings and tried, as best he could, to alter the record, so it would appear that his admiration for Henry and misgivings about Richard pre-dated the usurpation'.[2] It is not the intention of this essay to focus exclusively on the narrow and sometimes technical issue of Gower's rewriting of history after 1399, although that matter will certainly be considered; the main aim will be, rather, to use the issue of Gower's rewritings to initiate a broader exploration of the poet's ideas and their significance in late-fourteenth- and early-fifteenth-century

---

[1] For Hearne and the charge of political opportunism, see J. H. Fisher, *John Gower: Moral Philosopher and Friend of Chaucer* (London, 1965), p. 26.
[2] T. Jones, 'Was Richard II a tyrant? Richard's use of the books of rules for princes', in *Fourteenth Century England, V*, ed N. E. Saul (Woodbridge, 2008), pp. 130–60 (p. 156).

political debate. It has long been recognized that Gower's works provide a convenient measure of the mainstream political thinking of his age. The suggestion has been made, indeed, that the main objection to Gower is not so much that he was a timeserving opportunist as that his output amounts to little more than a collection of everyday commonplaces – in the words of Janet Coleman, 'an encyclopaedia of current prejudice and ideals.'[3] The issue of whether Gower's writings should be treated with scepticism needs to be considered not so much because, in his later years, they were Pavlovian reactions to changes of political leadership but because they were never very interesting in the first place. In other words, if 'moral' Gower was not actually a turncoat, was he still fairly unpersuasive in the role of social prophet?

Gower certainly lived through eventful times, and the crises of his adulthood are amply reflected in his poetry. It is partly for this reason that historians are drawn so strongly to his works; they can be cherry-picked for examples of contemporary comment. In 1377, on the death of Edward III, the boy king Richard II came to the throne and a conciliar government was put in place to lead the country until he came of age. In 1381, in the wake of the levying of the third poll tax, the commons of south-east England rose in rebellion, taking over the capital for three days in mid-June. In 1387–8 growing criticism of the king's policies culminated in the Appellant takeover of government and the cleansing of the Augean stables of the court in the aptly named Merciless Parliament. In 1390, after the ebbing of the Appellant tide, Richard reasserted his authority, dismissing the Appellant-appointed ministers and embarking on the creation of a more authoritarian style of kingship which stressed the subject's obligation of obedience to the ruler. Finally, in 1397 and 1398 came the sequence of events which was to culminate in the king's downfall: in July 1397 his arrest and destruction of the former Appellant lords, his creation of a new courtier nobility endowed with the former Appellants' lands and his exiling of the two junior Appellants, Mowbray and Bolingbroke; and in June 1399 his departure for Ireland, followed, in the autumn, by his deposition and the accession of his cousin, Henry IV.

Scholars have attempted to trace Gower's responses to these crises – and, in particular, to the twists and turns of court politics – in the successive revisions that he made to his poems. Gower constantly reworked his poetic corpus to take account of his changing views on the great issues of the day. In the first version of the *Vox Clamantis*, written sometime before 1388, when he had grieved over the state of the realm, he had held the young Richard himself free of blame; in the headnotes to the Epistle to the king in book VI he had addressed the king in affectionate terms, implicitly blaming misgovernment on the lords and council. By the time he revised the *Vox*, however, his attitude had become less sympathetic. The king was now criticized for following the advice of foolish young counsellors and for failing to impose self-discipline on himself, self-discipline being the founda-

---

[3] Janet Coleman, *English Literature in History, 1350–1400* (London, 1981), p. 129.

tion of sound government; Richard should be more attentive to fair justice, he said; he should banish the false flatterers, protect the poor and hold back from pride and gluttony. There is further evidence of Gower's disenchantment with Richard in his amendments to the last of his great works, the *Confessio Amantis*. In the versions of the poem circulating earliest Gower had included tributes to Richard in both the Prologue and Epilogue. In a first stage of revision he replaced the prayer for Richard in the Epilogue with a prayer for the better governance of England. Then, at a later stage, he revised the Prologue, excising the original dedication to Richard in favour of one to Henry of Lancaster. Gower's enthusiasm for Henry, later Henry IV, was also to find expression in the poems of his last years, notably the *Cronica Tripertita*, which was probably conceived as a sequel to the *Vox Clamantis*, and 'Rex celi deus'.

In the traditional dating of Gower's works, the changes of outlook found in the *Vox* and the *Confessio* are held to have occurred in the 1380s and the 1390s, so constituting a commentary on Richard's policies as king. It is suggested that the first datable stage of revision in the surviving copies is represented by the revised Epilogue to the *Confessio Amantis*, in which the prayer for England takes the place of the original prayer to the Creator for Richard himself, the marginal commentary to the revised Epilogue being dated 14 Richard II (22 June 1390 to 21 June 1391). It is further suggested that the second datable stage of revision is represented by the new Prologue to the same poem, in which the dedication to Richard is replaced with one to Henry, a change dated at line 25 to 16 Richard II (22 June 1392 to 21 June 1393). In Gower's other great work, the *Vox Clamantis*, it is argued that the first stage of revision is represented by the replacement of the lines sympathetic to the young Richard in book VI with the lines condemning him for his reliance on foolish counsellors. A further stage of revision is then represented by lines 545–54 in book VI, chapter 7, which contain the theme of a pestilence of vices afflicting the country, a theme more fully worked out in the *Carmen super multiplici viciorum pestilencia*, datable to Richard's twentieth year (22 June 1396 to 21 June 1397). A final stage of revision, it is suggested, was carried out after 1399, and consisted of rewritings at the end of book VII, chapter 25. At lines 1479–81 Gower includes a reference to the *Cronica Tripertita*, which he is known to have completed only after Richard's death in Pontefract Castle in February 1400. In Malcolm Parkes's view this pattern of textual revision is entirely characteristic of the pattern of reworking generally associated with the transmission of texts by medieval authors.[4] We need only call to mind the careful revision to which William Langland subjected his great poem *Piers Plowman*.

If it is possible to accept, in very broad terms, the stages of revision suggested in this reconstruction, it is nonetheless difficult to be confident

---

[4] M. B. Parkes, 'Patterns of scribal activity and revisions of the text in early copies of works by John Gower', in *New Science out of Old Books. Studies in Manuscripts and Early Printed Books in Honour of A. I. Doyle*, eds R. Beadle and A. J. Piper (Aldershot and Brookfield, 1995), pp. 80–121, 84.

about the exact dates to be assigned to those stages. In the traditional view, associated with Macaulay, the greater part of the rewriting was done in Richard's reign, the marginal commentaries in some cases actually noting the dates of the changes. It is precisely this view, however, which has been subjected to criticism recently by Terry Jones.[5] The apparently firm dating of the rededication to Henry 'of Lancaster' of the *Confessio* to Richard's sixteenth year (June 1392–June 1393) presents particular problems. In the first half of the 1390s Henry was generally referred to by his title 'earl of Derby', his father, John of Gaunt, holder of the ducal title, being referred to as 'of Lancaster'. Gower's use of the form 'of Lancaster' points to the possibility that he made the revision only after Henry had succeeded his father (i.e. after February 1399), dating the change retrospectively to lend it authenticity. If this were the case, the change could be seen as forming part of the extensive Lancastrian-sponsored rewriting of history which occurred after the Lancastrian takeover in 1399. Terry Jones has argued that most, if not all, of the revisions which Gower made to his works should be dated to the years after 1399. It is on the strength of this view that he sees Gower as a turncoat, a timeserver who turned out works to suit the needs of his Lancastrian masters or patrons. If, as Janet Coleman says, Gower's ideas are no more than an encyclopaedia of commonplaces, even worse, in Jones's view, they are not even his own ideas; they are those of his Lancastrian paymasters.

Unfortunately, the matter of the dating of Gower's revisions to his poems is probably one which will never be resolved to general satisfaction. It might be supposed that a solution of sorts could be provided by close analysis of the textual history of the early manuscripts of the works. It is highly unlikely, however, that this is actually the case. As Parkes and Fisher have separately shown, the process of piecemeal excision and revision can certainly be traced in the earliest extant manuscripts. The problem, however, is that none of these manuscripts is a holograph copy. Without exception, they date from the last years of Gower's life, in some cases from after his death, and are the products of first-generation transmission. What we are observing is a process of scribal revision the precise relationship of which to the mental process of Gower's own revisions is unfortunately beyond recovery.

The point can be illustrated by reference to the scribal history of the earliest extant manuscripts as reconstructed by Malcolm Parkes. Parkes has identified some twenty or more scribes who worked on the six manuscripts in which the text has been revised. The scribe whose work appears most prominently and repeatedly in the group is the writer he identifies as scribe 4. In one early manuscript, Glasgow, Hunterian Library MS T. 2.17 (Macaulay's G), this writer appears to have worked in three stints. In the first he entered Gower's 'first-stage' revision at *Vox*, VI, vii, lines 555–80 ('Rex puer indoctus' for 'Stat puer immunis'); in the second a number of further small revisions to the *Vox* coupled with the addition of the *Cronica*

---

[5] Jones, 'Was Richard II a tyrant?'; *idem*, 'Richard II: royal villain or victim of spin', *The Times* (4 October 2008).

Tripertita and copies of the minor poems and other texts; and in the third and last inserting the poems 'Rex celi deus' and 'O deus immense'. Parkes suggests that the second stint belongs to the years 1401–2, when Gower was losing his eyesight, and the third to shortly after his death in 1408. In another manuscript of the *Vox*, BL MS Harley 6291 (Macaulay's H), scribe 4 completed two stints, the first comprising Gower's first- and second-stage revisions, and the second comprising further revisions and the addition of the *Cronica Tripertita*. The presence of this last work indicates that the second stint of work was undertaken sometime after c.1403. In a third text of the *Vox*, All Souls College, Oxford, MS 98 (Macaulay's S), scribe 4 completed four stints, the first two comprising the same revisions as in G but with the addition of the *Cronica*, the third consisting of the addition of the minor poems, and the fourth of the addition of 'O deus immense' with the heading 'Carmen quod Johannes Gower adhuc vivens super principum regimine ultimo composuit'. The third and fourth stints must be dated to shortly before 1408.

The pattern of scribal activity revealed by these revisions is hardly such as to imply that they were made under the direction of a single guiding hand, least of all Gower's own. A century ago Macaulay ventured the suggestion that a number of the earliest surviving manuscripts of Gower's works were copied in the poet's own 'scriptorium', in some cases (notably that of the Fairfax manuscript of the *Confessio*) under the poet's direct personal supervision.[6] In the light of the number and diversity of the hands involved in making the revisions, Macaulay's suggestion, while tempting, must now be considered highly unlikely. Parkes is surely right to argue that some, if not all, of the early surviving copies were made for the circle of Gower's immediate friends and associates who formed the first audience for his works. Among such people might be numbered Sir Arnald Savage, the Kent MP and sometime Speaker of the House of Commons, and William Denne, clerk of the king's chapel, both of whom Gower named as his executors. Parkes suggests that the revisions were entered at different times into copies which already belonged to Gower's readers, and that they were transcribed from different exemplars.[7] The work of revision, he suggests, affords clear insights into the complex first stages in the transmission of Gower's texts. For precisely that reason, however, it is of little or no assistance in shedding light on just when Gower thought up the revisions in the first place.

Given the complex processes involved in the composition and early transmission of Gower's major works, there is probably a strong case for discarding any notion of textual stability in them at all. The works were produced in an age when poetry was recited as well as read, and it is plausible to suppose that they were in a state of revision almost from the moment of their creation. The suggestion has recently been made that the composition of one work in particular, the *Confessio Amantis*, should be seen in such

---

[6] Macaulay, ii, pp. cxxx–cxxxi; and iv, pp. lx–lxi.
[7] Parkes, 'Patterns of scribal activity', pp. 96–8.

terms. Wim Lindeboom's argument, based on a close study of the texts, is that the *Confessio* was composed around 1388–9 and then presented orally and in instalments in the 1390s before being added to and amended under Henry IV.[8] The re-dedication of the poem to Henry, earl of Derby, which a marginal gloss dates to Richard's sixteenth year, could in this view be interpreted as a response to Henry's growing public prominence as his father sought to position him as a possible successor to the childless Richard II.[9] In Lindeboom's view the process of textual revision to the *Confessio* went on well into Henry IV's later years and was not just a response to the immediate circumstances of the usurpation. Lindeboom accounts for the survival of so many texts of the poem that include the story of Richard meeting Gower on the Thames – a shade unexpected given the evidence of early Lancastrian censorship – by supposing that they were produced in Henry's final years, when memories of the usurpation were fading. In the case of Gower's most important political poem, the *Vox*, there is at least some evidence to support the suggestion that the poet undertook the earliest textual revisions in response to changes in his own attitude to Richard's policies as king. The constant emphasis which Gower places on Richard's youth, surprising at a time when the king was growing to manhood, may well have owed something to the Appellants' use of a critique of youth to justify the imposition of political controls on him.[10] It seems likely that a *terminus ante quem* for the revisions which Gower made to the texts in person is found in the onset of his blindness in Henry IV's first year (30 September 1399–29 September 1400), a date which Gower himself gives us. Once his eyesight had gone he could have exercised only limited personal control over revisions to the texts. This is a point generally overlooked by those who see him driven to extensive re-writes in the wake of the Lancastrian usurpation in 1399.

It is thus something of an oversimplification to suppose that Gower's revisions were made for the most part shortly after 1399 as an immediate reaction to the Lancastrian revolution. They were made over a longer period and in response to a variety of factors. Considerations of reader expectation and textual transmission were involved, as well as those of political manipulation and hamfisted censorship.

Even if these suggested modifications to Terry Jones's views are not altogether accepted, there is another way in which the matter of Gower's shifting allegiances can be approached. Let us suppose, for the moment, that Gower undertook all the revisions required of him in the opening months of

---

[8] W. Lindeboom, 'Rethinking the recensions of the *Confessio Amantis*', *Viator*, 40 (2009), 319–48.
[9] Lynn Staley, 'Gower, Richard II, Henry of Derby, and the business of making culture', *Speculum*, 75 (2000), 68–96. A possible rejoinder to Terry Jones's point that Henry was usually styled 'earl of Derby', not 'Henry of Lancaster', in these years might be that in the accounts of his expedition to Prussia Henry is referred to as 'Henry of Lancaster, earl of Derby' ('... Henrici Lancastrie Comitis Derbie ...'): L. Toulmin-Smith, ed., *Expeditions to Prussia and the Holy Land made by Henry, Earl of Derby* (London, 1894) p. 291.
[10] Christopher Fletcher, *Richard II. Manhood, Youth and Politics, 1377–99* (Oxford, 2008), see esp. chap. 8.

Henry IV's reign while his eyesight remained; and let us suppose, too, that he undertook the work at the very time when the Lancastrian censors were imposing their clampdown. Does this necessarily prove that Gower undertook the work of revision unwillingly? Does it necessarily imply that he was forced into rewriting the history of Richard's reign and hailing the new Lancastrian dawn when he did not actually want to? It is highly unlikely that such was the case. There is no evidence at all that Gower wrote a single word against his will. It may have been, as Terry Jones suggests, that some of the chroniclers whose work was called in after 1399 were forced with gritted teeth to amend anti-Lancastrian passages which they had written years earlier. Such circumstances, however, could hardly be said to have applied to Gower. At no point had Gower ever written anything unfavourable to the Lancastrian cause. Everything that we know about his attitude to the house of Lancaster, both before and after 1399, suggests that he was both genuine and committed in his allegiance to the family's interests. On his death in 1408 he was shown on his tomb effigy in St Mary Overey, Southwark, with the Lancastrian Ss collar round his neck. Gower simply cannot be said to fall into the category of some unprincipled poetaster willingly turning out 'hack' propaganda to justify a new political order. He was a thoughtful writer who embraced the Lancastrian cause with warmth. He wrote in support of Henry IV because he genuinely admired and approved of him. He saw Henry's kingship as promising the fulfilment of his own deeply held aspirations for society. It was not Gower who had changed his position by the late 1390s, it was Richard. The hopes which Richard had aroused in his early years by 1399 had gone; in Gower's view, it was the Lancastrian challenger who now offered the best prospects for the future.

Whether or not Gower amended his works only after 1399 is actually, then, a question which has surprisingly little bearing on the coherence of his views on political issues of his day. At whatever date the amendments were made, they still articulate a view of Richard's kingship and of contemporary social ills which accorded with Gower's view of society as a whole. Gower's body of ideas, while continually evolving, was both more consistent and more coherent than some recent critics have allowed. As J. H. Fisher wrote nearly half a century ago, Gower's works are informed by a general philosophy, an outlook on the world, which makes them more than the sum of their parts. Broadly speaking, there is a consistent body of ideas running through all his works, from *Mirour de l'Omme* in the 1370s to the *Confessio Amantis* in the 1390s and the lesser poems later, a body of ideas which transcends day-to-day, year-to-year issues. The case can also be argued that politics is one of the major themes of Gower's work, even in the *Confessio Amantis* – a poem which, although ostensibly about love, shows that selfless divine love leads to political harmony, justice and peace. There is no avoiding, therefore, the matter of Gower's political views; they are central to a serious understanding of his work. So what did Gower have to say? If an attempt is made to summarize his views, or to summarize their essence, two key ideas stand out. One is the idea of ethical self-government; and the other a concern for the common profit. Neither idea was new, both having been articulated many times before. But their very age and antiquity lent them authority. The important question is how Gower treated them.

Gower found the idea of ethical self-government in two main sources – the Pseudo-Aristotelian *Secretum Secretorum* and that widely read 'mirror for princes' treatise, Giles of Rome's *De Regimine Principum*.[11] Both authorities argued for a relationship between the ethical health of the individual and the political health of the realm. The good king, they believed, was the good man. Good governance, in other words, was dependent on ethical self-rule by the king himself. We see these ideas incorporated in the Epistle to King Richard in book VI of the *Vox Clamantis*. In chapter 8 we read:

> You who subdue others, strive to conquer yourself. If you wish to be a king, rule yourself and you will be one. By what right could a man who does not even rule over the workings of his own mind say that he was a king? The sovereign cannot confer well-being upon others so long as he is not ruler of himself as he should be.[12]

Much earlier in the *Mirour de l'Omme*, drawing in the main on examples from Biblical history, Gower had shown how man's good or sinful nature affected his relationship with the physical universe. Now, in the *Vox Clamantis*, some five or six years later, he developed the relationship not with the physical universe but with the political macrocosm. Following Giles of Rome, he maintained that ethical self-governance issued forth to embrace the governance of the household and ultimately the governance of the realm. The king's ability to rule himself became in this way the foundation of the good governance of the state.

We will return to that point in a moment. But in the meantime let us look briefly at the other key principle which informed Gower's thought, a concern for the common profit.[13] The notion of the common profit, or common good, was one of the commonplaces of ancient and medieval political thought. Kings and princes, set over men by God, were expected to work for the general good of their subjects. If they failed to do so, and put their own interests first, then they were considered tyrants. According to Roman law, when public taxation was granted to the king it was given in the name of the common profit. For Gower, the notion of the common profit referred to men's moral responsibilities, their duty both individually and collectively in their estates to work for the wellbeing of the community. All groups in society, Gower believed, were dependent on one another. If one group were to neglect its duties, it followed that others would suffer – more than that, indeed, the defective group itself would be among the sufferers; for to diminish others was to diminish oneself. Equally, however, a joy in the good fortune of others is a source of strength to the common profit. For Gower, the common profit was upheld by the good governance of the king

---

[11] E. Porter, 'Gower's ethical microcosm and political macrocosm', in *Gower's 'Confessio Amantis': Responses and Reassessments*, ed. A. J. Minnis (Cambridge, 1983), pp. 135–62.
[12] John Gower, *The Major Latin Works of John Gower*, trans. Eric Stockton (Seattle, 1962), p. 234.
[13] Russell A. Peck, *Kingship and Common Profit in Gower's 'Confessio Amantis'* (Carbondale, IL, 1978).

ruling according to both kinds of law, natural and positive. The king must rule justly. He must curb the sinfulness of his officers. He should resemble King David, the good harpist, tuning the discordant strings – his subjects – into perfect harmony.

Gower's king, it should be noted, is no 'roi fainéant'. He is a powerful figure, one in full enjoyment of the majesty of his office. Gower takes a lofty view of the divinity of kingship. In the heading to chapter 18 of his Address to the king in book VI of *Vox* he says that the king should elevate himself through the prerogative, and rule magnificently in the eyes of his subjects, while presenting himself as humble in the sight of God.[14] Gower viewed the king's estate as free towards all other than God. The king had to be free to sustain the burden of government. If it were otherwise, the kingdom could not stand firm because the king would be unstable.

The lofty nature of Gower's conception of kingship is worth emphasizing because in its essentials it differed little from the views articulated by Richard II himself and his advisers. This is a point which has perhaps hitherto been insufficiently appreciated. Scholars have become so absorbed with the idea of Gower as a critic of Richard that they have tended to overlook what the two had in common. If Gower believed that the king should be free towards all other than God, then so did Richard himself: he and his ministers said as much on a number of occasions. If Gower believed that the king should exercise the power of the prerogative, then so again did Richard; he insisted as much in parliament in 1392. Above all, if Gower believed that the king should rule magnificently, then Richard revealed himself as magnificence personified: we need only consider the evidence of the treasure he accumulated, detailed in the inventory compiled on his deposition.[15] What Gower articulated, and what Richard practised, was a highly exalted form of kingship. Kingship had to be exalted to curb the malpractices of the evildoers and to uphold the divinely established order.

Gower's emphasis on a strong kingship is not an aspect of his thought which has received much emphasis in recent criticism. Nonetheless, it is there all the same. Nor should we be surprised at what we find. These were ideas espoused not just by Richard, not just by Gower, but by virtually all of the ruling class at the time. Ever since the catastrophe of the Black Death the members of the first and second estates had been concerned at the crumbling of the social hierarchy and the assertiveness of the lower orders. This concern had grown to panic proportions in the wake of the Peasants' Revolt. The general view of the political elite was that a strong and commanding kingship was needed to restore and uphold order. Hence the mantra, so often reiterated, of the need for obedience. In his keynote speech to the parliament of 1383, in the aftermath of the Revolt, Richard's chancellor, Sir Michael de la Pole, had said that proper obedience to the king was 'the sole foundation of all peace and quiet in the realm'. In the next decade,

---

[14] Gower, *The Major Latin Works*, trans. Stockton, p. 247.
[15] The National Archives, Public Record Office, E101/411/9. An edition of this inventory is currently being prepared by Dr J. Stratford.

in the Revenge Parliament of 1397, a subsequent chancellor, Edmund Stafford, bishop of Exeter, declared that in a well-governed realm 'every subject should be duly obedient to the king and his laws'. And lest it be thought that the mantra came only from the mouths of well-heeled Ricardians, it is worth remembering that the rhetoric of obedience was also articulated by none other than Archbishop Arundel, Henry IV's future counsellor, in his earlier incarnation as Richard's chancellor. In 1395 Arundel said in parliament that the king's subjects had an obligation 'to honour, cherish and obey the king, and to employ all their power in his service'.[16]

That Gower should have articulated a case of a broadly comparable sort for an exalted kingship may, at first sight, appear surprising given the evidence of his growing disenchantment with Richard in the 1390s. Yet, in fact, such an outlook is only to be expected, for Gower was nothing if not a thoroughgoing social conservative. He was committed to the idea of a divinely ordained social order. Having lived through the Peasants' Revolt he was determined to see the lower orders kept in their proper place. If we see him today as a dyed-in-the-wool reactionary, he was only articulating what was then a broadly held consensus. And another point needs to be remembered: the political manual from which Gower derived so many of his political ideas, Giles of Rome's *De regimine principum*, was one from which others in the political establishment picked up ideas; the courtiers, higher nobility and many of the senior administrators knew their Giles of Rome too. Simon Burley, Richard's childhood magister and political mentor, for example, owned a copy and there can be little doubt, as Richard Jones once said, that he set Richard to work reading it.[17] Giles, too, believed in an ascendant monarchy, and said that the first duty of a ruler's subjects was to obey him. The authoritarian kingship of Richard II was in many ways a textbook example of Egidian ideas in practice. What we have here is a body of thought espoused by most or all of the ruling class because it offered a solution to the most pressing social problem of the day: the dissolution of the social hierarchy and the need to reinforce obedience.

So why, in that case, did Gower not remain steadfast in his support for Richard's exalted kingship? Why did he so completely turn away from him? The answer is again to be found in the writings of Giles. Giles, while stressing the need for obedience to the king, as noted above, had also said, as we have already seen, that the beginning of good governance was the king's own self-governance. The king must rule himself before he can rule others: he must practise ethical self-discipline. This body of ideas is encapsulated in the first book of *De regimine*. Gower picks up the drift in book VI of *Vox Clamantis*, the Address to Richard. Thus in chapter 8: 'The sovereign cannot confer wellbeing on others so long as he is not ruler of himself.'[18] Or, later,

---

[16] For full references to these passages, see N. E. Saul, *Richard II* (New Haven, CT, and London, 1997), p. 386.

[17] R. Jones, *The Royal Policy of Richard II: Absolutism in the Late Middle Ages* (Oxford, 1968), p. 161.

[18] Gower, *The Major Latin Works*, trans. Stockton, p. 234.

in chapter 18: 'If a king is vain, greedy and haughty, so that he torments his kingdom, the land subject to him suffers.'[19]

Gower's view was that Richard was altogether too selective in his reading of Giles's tract. Just as historians today cherry-pick Gower, so Gower thought Richard was cherry-picking Giles. While Richard willingly lapped up all the later passages about the subjects' duty of obedience, he largely overlooked the earlier section about the ruler's need for self-rule. Gower saw the young Richard as wilful, undisciplined, lacking in self-control, giving free rein to favourites, incapable of ruling either himself or his household. It is not difficult to find episodes in Richard's record which could have lent substance to these views. We can take the affair of the Mortimer inheritance, for example, which the chronicler Walsingham tells us about in his account of the year 1382.[20] In December 1381 Edmund Mortimer, earl of March, had died in Ireland, and his vast inheritance fell to the crown as a royal wardship for the duration of the minority of the earl's son and heir. Immediately, a host of minor but ambitious suitors beat a path to the king's door, begging grants of lands and lordships pertaining to the inheritance. Richard, in a spirit of generosity, acceded to their requests and sent letters to the chancellor, Richard, Lord Scrope, authorizing the preparation in their favour of letters under the great seal. Scrope, however, desiring the king's profit, refused to comply, saying that the king was impoverishing himself by such profligacy. Hearing of this, Walsingham says, Richard flew into a rage, insisted that the chancellor carry out his will, and, when the chancellor still refused, dismissed him. That was in July 1382, quite early on in the reign, but when Richard's true colours were already emerging. Alternatively, we might think of an episode recorded by the Monk of Westminster a few years later, in 1385: Richard's quarrel with the archbishop of Canterbury. The archbishop, William Courtenay, had criticized Richard for harbouring courtiers who had plotted against the life of the duke of Lancaster: a disgraceful episode which Gower would have thought unworthy of a king. When the king and the archbishop passed one another one day in boats on the Thames near Lambeth, the row flared up again; the king drew his sword and would have run the archbishop through had he not been restrained by his companions.[21]

Richard's wilfulness was a matter of such concern to Gower because in his writings he consistently chose to emphasize the character and wisdom necessary to a just king. For him the king, the head of the body politic, the seat of wisdom and reason, was the person who guided and directed the limbs, his subjects. Gower believed that in an ordered state reason should rule, not bestial passion. And reason characteristically found expression in sound laws – laws which it was the king's duty to enforce. The wilful behaviour of the king, therefore, sat ill with the principle of the rule of law. Richard's lack of self-rule disqualified him as a dispenser of justice. This is

---

[19] Gower, *The Major Latin Works*, trans. Stockton, p. 248.
[20] Thomas Walsingham, *The Chronica Maiora of Thomas Walsingham (1376–1422)*, eds and trans D. Preest with J. G. Clark (Woodbridge, 2005), pp. 186–7.
[21] *The Westminster Chronicle, 1381–94*, eds L. C. Hector and B. F. Harvey (Oxford, 1982), p. 116.

a view for which it is possible to find support not only in the *Vox* but in the *Confessio Amantis*. In a recent article Kathryn McKinley has shown how in two of the tales in book V (Jason and Medea, and Tereus) Gower uses the relationship of husband and wife as a metaphor for the political relationship between the king and the realm, in this way providing himself with a framework within which to offer reflections on proper governance and self-rule.[22]

Gower's misgivings about Richard, evident already by the mid 1380s, could therefore only have strengthened with time, as the true character of the king's rule became clearer. As Richard's reign developed there were increasing indications that he chose to elevate will over reason, considering will to have the force of law. A telling episode was found in the king's confiscation of the liberties of the City of London in 1392. Early in 1392 the Londoners had unwisely refused the king a loan, and in June he revoked their liberties (their right of self-government), ruling the city through a warden, until in August the city fathers submitted, agreeing to give him a corporate loan of £10,000. Here was a most striking demonstration of the royal will overriding man-made law, played out right on Gower's doorstep and within his sight. Richard was a king unusually interested in the relationship between the king and the law. Back in 1387, when he had faced opposition from his baronial and parliamentary critics, he had demonstrated this interest by submitting questions about the legal standing of royal authority to the judges, receiving answers wholly favourable to the prerogative. Three years later, in 1390, he was presented with a book of statutes, now at St John's College, Cambridge, which reveals his interest in legal precedent, in particular in the statutes shackling Edward II, which he sought to overthrow.[23] He seems to have been attracted by the political possibilities of Roman law. The saying attributed to him in the deposition articles about the laws of England being in his mouth or in his breast was of course an adage of Roman law. Richard's conception of law sat ill with Gower's. In particular, it sat ill with his advice to him in the Epistle that, while as king he was above the law, as a just man he should nonetheless live under the law; he should govern his actions moderately.

To sum up these observations: although Gower was to turn against Richard by stages by the late 1390s, the differences between the two men were actually narrower than often supposed. In the years after the Great Revolt of 1381 the members of England's ruling elite were remarkably united in their views on the maintenance of the social order and on the need for obedience to royal authority. They had all read the same advice books, chief among them Giles of Rome's *De regimine principum*, a sourcebook for Richard's views as well as Gower's. Gower's falling out with Richard was rooted in one thing above all – his belief that the king lacked self-discipline and was ruled by will rather than reason, a defect which disqualified him

---

[22] Kathryn McKinley, 'Lessons for a king from John Gower's *Confessio Amantis*', in *Metamorphoses: The Changing Face of Ovid in Medieval and Early Modern Europe*, eds Alison Keith and Stephen Rupp (Toronto, 2007), pp. 107–28.
[23] Cambridge, St John's College, MS A. 7.

as a dispenser of justice. This was the perception not only of Gower but of others: Archbishop Arundel, for example. It is worth remembering that Arundel, the future pillar of the Lancastrian establishment, was a one-time committed Ricardian. It was Arundel, no less, who had articulated the rhetoric of obedience as Richard's chancellor in the 1390s. Arundel's trajectory from the one camp to the other directly paralleled Gower's. Both men saw Richard's discordant reliance on will as untuning the social order. If they both became ardent Lancastrians, it was because they saw Henry IV as the more effective guarantor of a stable social order. In that respect, arguably they were right.

Chapter 8

The Parliamentary Source of Gower's *Cronica Tripertita* and Incommensurable Styles[1]

DAVID R. CARLSON

Gower's last long piece of writing, the *Cronica Tripertita* of early 1400, is written in the most verbally ornate style the poet used: 1062 lines of Leonine hexameters (though with a single pentameter line *in fine*), the rhymes consistently disyllabic, with also some couplet formations; not having quite the complexity of the work of some near-contemporary Anglo-Latin poets, perhaps; yet Gower sustained what was for others fundamentally a lyric style over the course of a lengthy historical ennarration. Though unparalleled, even original in style, the poem is also altogether derivative in its substance and shape: the *Cronica* makes verse of 'Les record et proces del renunciacion du roy Richard le second apres le conquest, et de lacceptacion de mesme la renunciacion, ensemblement oue la deposicion de mesme le roy Richard' – hereafter 'Record' – insinuated into the public records of parliament late in 1399 and put about otherwise, in various forms, by those then essaying to master England. The verse-form Gower used for the *Cronica* is highly mannered, by comparison with his earlier Latin poems; the Latin prose source on which he based his work is also in a highly mannered style,

---

[1] The title of this paper acknowledges the influence of the work of Matthew Giancarlo, especially *Parliament and Literature in Late Medieval England* (Cambridge, 2007), where the notion of 'parliamentary literature' is developed to mean both the literature of parliament itself, in the form of bills of complaint and other procedural records, and parliament in the contemporary literature, in the form of representations of parliament and repetitions of the forms of parliamentary documents in non-parliamentary writing; also, 'Murder, lies, and storytelling: the manipulation of justice(s) in the parliaments of 1397 and 1399', *Speculum*, 77 (2002), 76–112; and Emily Steiner, *Documentary Culture and the Making of Medieval English Literature* (Cambridge, 2003). Quotations from Gower's Latin are from Macaulay; quotations from the Record are from the edition in *The Record and Process of the Renunciation and Deposition of Richard II (1399) and Related Writings* (Toronto, 2007), pp. 23–65, cited by line number parenthetically (1–989), abbreviated *Deposition*; for ease of cross-reference also supplied are the page and column (416a–424b) of the edition in vol. III of the *Rotuli parliamentorum: ut et petitiones, et placita in parliamento*, eds Richard Blyke, John Strachey et al., 8 vols (London, 1780–1832), abbreviated *Rotuli*, by means of which the passages can also be located in the (vastly preferable) *Parliament Rolls of Medieval England*, gen. ed. Chris Given-Wilson, CD-ROM version (Leicester, 2005), abbreviated *Parliament Rolls*, which has the *Rotuli* locations embedded in it. Other references to the parliamentary rolls are to the editions in *Parliament Rolls*, though by means of the *Rotuli* locations. English translations are the present writer's doing, with the exception of the verse translations of Gower, courtesy of A. G. Rigg.

though differently mannered: grotesquely verbose, largely by consequence of constant synonym-mongering and clausal repetition, yielding periods so distraught that even the persons responsible for them lost grammatical way sometimes, having also an idiosyncratic word-set taken over from Law French, with admixture of unliterary but precise Anglicisms.[2]

The incommensurability of the stylistic extremes of the two pieces of writing made Gower's undertaking the more difficult, and his difficulties would have been compounded by another peculiarity of the source, in turn the product of its peculiar limitations, which were institutionally determined. Strictly, the Record recounts a single day's events, and only such business as was transacted in parliament (or the parliament-like assembly), at Westminster, 30 September 1399. Because, strictly, it records only the particular parliamentary process, the Record cannot itself give a temporally ordered recounting of the sequence of events culminating in Richard II's deposition that might stand on its own as narrative or provide a basis for narrative directly. First, the Record records, the assembly was informed that Richard had resigned the throne, though this had happened the day before and as a result of Richard's prior agreement to resign, in August 1399, to which reference must also be made. Next, the assembly decided to accept Richard's resignation, though its acceptance required consideration first of ways in which Richard had earlier violated his responsibilities as king – thirty-three particular violations making up the 'Articles of Deposition' that comprise the bulk of the document – the violations in turn requiring consideration of Richard's formal undertakings still earlier, when he became king, particularly the 'Coronation Oath' that he had had to swear first in 1377 and again in 1388. Having considered Richard's particular malfeasances the assembly accepted Richard's resignation and passed a 'Sentence of Deposition' on him. The throne thus vacated was claimed formally by Richard's cousin Henry Bolingbroke, who offered his own explanation of prior events, before the assembly, and Henry's claim was vindicated (or accepted or made good by some kind of elective acclamation): the assembled 'estates, with the people as a whole, did consent as one, without any difficulty whatsoever or hesitance, that the duke aforementioned ought reign over them' (Record 797–9 = 423a). Henry's enthronement was physically enacted. A sermon was pronounced *ad status*. Parliament was called anew, by authority of the new king, and a date for the coronation ceremony was announced. Dispersal was to ensue. The Record then ends with an appended report of a delegation's delivery to Richard the next day of the assembly's 'Sentence of Deposition', encompassing its formal, legal withdrawal of fealty from him.

By its nature, as documentation only of a particular parliamentary process, the Record is always subject to this kind of involution of narrative. It must refer to prior events; but it can do so only by attesting what happened in parliament at Westminster on the particular day. In other words, tangled

---

[2] There is some comment on the style of the *Cronica* in my own 'A rhyme distribution chronology of John Gower's Latin poetry', *SP*, 104 (2007), 15–55; and on the Record, in *Deposition*, pp. 7–8.

up with the document's linear recounting of the assembly's doings on the one day is an embedded involute narrative of a (selected) prior sequence of events leading up to the culminating moment that the document attests immediately.

Matters of Fact

Disinvolution of the chronology of selected prior events embedded in the Record makes immediately clear Gower's fundamental dependence on it for what makes the organization of the *Cronica tripertita* tripartite. Excepting the 1377 coronation, remarked upon only in passing, the earliest matter made reference to in Gower's parliamentary source is the Appellants' Coup of 1387–8, though the anachronistic terminology is inimical to the purposes of both poet and prose source – 'A work of humankind ['opus humanum'] it is, to seek out peace and follow after it', in Gower's introductory description; 'for this is what the three noblemen did, of whom mention is made below, when faith was among them' (*Cronica*, Prol. Pr.) – including tendentious accounting of the coup's origin in Richard's resistance against the November 1386 'Commission of Governance' imposed on him by the magnates to supervise his finances, and concluding with the doings of the Appellants' 'Merciless Parliament', by which Richard's resistance was punished. The Record omits mention of the intervening decade, 1388–97, of Richard's personal rule, as does the *Cronica*. The next matter embedded chronologically in the Record is that of Richard's vengeance against the 1387–8 Appellants, including the doings of his 'Revenge Parliament' of 1397: 'the work of hell ['opus inferni']', as Gower describes it, serves as matter for the second book of the *Cronica*: 'to disrupt peace and to put to death the just persons of the realm' (*Cronica*, Prol. pr.). The third part of the *Cronica* centres on 'the work in Christ ['opus in Cristo']' – namely, 'to put proud persons down from on high and to lift the lowly up' – which, in the parliamentary record, consists of Richard's deposition and Henry's installation. Broadly speaking, the structures of the Record and the *Cronica* are the same. However, Gower displaces the relatively narrow legal issues of his source text, most notably the emphasis on Richard's perjury on which the Record relies for justification, in favour of explanations for these events as justified 'by right divine ['iure superni']' (*Cronica*, Prol., line 4). Divine movement is certainly implicit in the Record, but Gower's *Cronica* foregrounds it: 'for this is what God did', Gower asserts: 'the hated Richard he cast down from his throne, and he caused the pious Henry, beloved of all affection, to be raised above in glory' (*Cronica*, Prol., pr.).

Other constructions and selections of events in this period are conceivable, differing from the particular choices shared by the *Cronica* and the Record. In fact, other contemporary accounts of the same events make different choices. It was not inevitable, as if necessitated by something inherent in the nature of the events themselves, that Gower and the Lancastrian parliamentary account should have settled on the same selection and construction.

Rather, the basic coincidence or coherence of these two accounts bespeaks their interdependence. That said, Gower must have used other sources too from time to time, both written and oral, as well his own inventions. The *Cronica* and the Record frequently converge in their particular selections, organisation and explanation of these events, but beyond sharing the same basic tripartite scheme the *Cronica* shows a consistent pattern of Gower's overwhelming dependence on the one documentary source.

A clear instance of Gower's particular reliance on the Record for building the details of a subsection of his own poem comes in the *Cronica*'s second book, treating the events of Richard's Revenge Parliament, which initially met at Westminster from 17–29 September 1397. The records of that parliament (with corroboration from other witnesses) demonstrate that appeals of treason were brought against the Duke of Gloucester, and the earls of Arundel and Warwick on the parliament's opening day, 17 September 1397. Furthermore, the earl of Arundel's younger brother Thomas Arundel, archbishop of Canterbury, was impeached of treason on 20 September; the earl of Arundel was tried and condemned on 21 September, Gloucester on 24 September, Thomas Arundel on 25 September and Warwick on 28 September, before the parliament's prorogation on 29 September. Separate matters were also transacted in the parliament's continuation in its 'Shrewsbury sessions', held on 28–9 January 1398.[3]

Gower and the 1399 Record use the same order for describing these events, an order deriving from political–oratorical considerations rather than historical–chronological ones: first the disposition of Gloucester and finally that of the archbishop Thomas Arundel; between them those of the earl of Arundel and Warwick, Warwick coupled with John Cobham. Gloucester had a kind of primacy that the Record writers and Gower might have recognised independently; the Record characterises him in detail in a way it does for no one else ('uncle to the king himself, likewise son of Edward of revered memory, late king of England' (238–40 = 418a)); Gower's remarks also stress this matter of royal descent ('O regale genus' (*Cronica*, II, line 39)), by virtue of which Gloucester belongs first, Richard's destruction of him being the most unnatural of his crimes on the occasion, and hence most terrifying from the perspective of a ruling class whose prerogatives derived from patrilineal heredity:

> Heu! Quis iam viuit, vnquam qui talia sciuit,
> Sic regis natum per regem mortificatum?
> Heu! Quia regalis stirps Anglica, tam specialis,
> Regis precepto periit sine crimine cepto.
>
> (*Cronica*, II, lines 109–12)

> (Alas, who living now has known of such a thing,
> That thus a king's son should be slaughtered by a king?

---

[3] *Parliament Rolls* III, 349–56, 357–9, 372, and 376–82.

> Alas, that royal stock, an English duke sublime,
> Should die by king's command, convicted of no crime!)

Removal of the archbishop to the rhetorically emphatic final position may have had to do with similar considerations, his primacy in the spiritual sphere matching Gloucester's in the secular. Rather, or also, it may have to do with personal influence: various considerations indicate that Thomas Arundel had a hand in or direct influence over the composition of the Record, and he was connected with Gower.[4]

By contrast with the Appellants' 'Merciless Parliament' of 1388, the victims on this later occasion were few; in fact, the only person whom the 'Revenge Parliament' executed was the earl of Arundel. Both the Record and Gower, however, inflate the list of Richard's victims by singling out for attention the minor figure John Cobham, 3rd Baron Cobham (d. 1408), associating him with Warwick among Richard's victims.[5] Like Warwick, Cobham was sentenced only to exile in the Channel Islands, and he too survived to be rehabilitated early in the reign of Henry IV; otherwise, his case was not like those of the great Appellants, nor was his trial adjacent to theirs. Cobham had been appointed to the 1386 Commission of Governance, though the appointment seems inadequate to explain either Richard's malign attention years later or the Lancastrian notice marked in the *Cronica* and the Record still later. And, in any case, Cobham's indictment and trial came only 28 January 1398, in the very brief Shrewsbury sessions of 28–9 January 1398, continuing the Revenge Parliament that had been prorogued at the end of September 1397, when Cobham was one of only two further persons against whom Richard proceeded by parliamentary means. The other person arraigned at the Shrewsbury sessions goes unmentioned by Gower and the Record.[6]

---

[4] Strictly speaking, the evidence is only a manuscript presentation and some lines of verse Gower addressed to Arundel, indicating that Gower sought his patronage: see esp. John Hurt Fisher, *John Gower: Moral Philosopher and Friend of Chaucer* (London, 1965), pp. 99–100, pp. 105–6; and M. B. Parkes, 'Patterns of scribal activity and revisions of the text in early copies of works by John Gower', in *New Science Out of Old Books: Studies in Manuscripts and Early Printed Books in Honour of A. I. Doyle*, eds Richard Beadle and A. J. Piper (Aldershot and Brookfield, 1995), pp. 92–3. For the Archbishop's hand on the Record, see Chris Given-Wilson, *Chronicles of the Revolution 1397–1400: The Reign of Richard II* (Manchester, 1993), p. 183 n. 15.

[5] The granddaughter of this 3rd Baron Cobham married Sir John Oldcastle (d. 1417), being Oldcastle's fourth wife, who had from her the title 'Lord Cobham', which has occasioned some confusion about the figure whom Gower mentions.

[6] For Cobham's indictment and trial, see *Parliament Rolls* III, 381–2. Gower's information about this figure may indicate personal knowledge: 'Transtulit ad sedem se Cartusiensis ad edem' (2.220) (literally, 'he transferred himself to the seat, to the house of the Carthusians'), i.e. the London Charterhouse, though the phrasing is sufficiently awkward to make the text seem suspect; also, for the notion that Cobham was a victim of Exchequer malice: 'voluit quem tollere fiscus' (2.221) (where the technical term *fiscus* is confirmed by rhyme); and 'fiscus sine iure reduxit' (2.222). The other person tried at the same time, whom Gower does not mention, was Thomas Mortimer, who killed Edward de Vere's lieutenant Thomas Molineaux in battle: see *Parliament Rolls* III, 380–81. For more on this episode see James L. Gillespie, 'Thomas Mortimer and Thomas Molineux: Radcot Bridge and the appeal of 1397', *Albion*, 7 (1975), 161–73.

The basic article in the Record dealing with the Westminster sessions of the 1397 Revenge Parliament (232–57 = 418a) has, first, the arrests of Gloucester, Arundel and Warwick (Richard 'capi et arestari fecit'); Gloucester's export, imprisonment and murder (the king again 'occulte suffocari, strangulari, et murdrari inhumaniter et crudeliter fecit'); the judicial murder of Arundel ('dampnabiliter decapitari fecit'); and the disposition of Warwick and Cobham (ostensibly, Richard 'perpetuis carceribus mancipauit'). Gower's verse narrative imposes the same artificial construction: the arrests (*Cronica*, II, lines 29–76); Gloucester's complex disposition (II, lines 83–118); the earl of Arundel's disposition (II, lines 119–58); and what was done with Warwick and Cobham (II, lines 159–232).

Incidentals too, mentioned only in passing in the same article of the Record, in subordination, are likewise developed in Gower, again in the same order that the parliamentary record uses: the king's prior pardon of the three great Appellants ('in pleno parliamento de assensu eiusdem pardonasset') concluding the Merciless Parliament in 1388, at *Cronica*, II, line 1516: 'Set magis vt tuti maneant de lege statuti, | Hii regis querunt cartas, quas optinuerunt' ('In order to protect themselves, by law secured, | They asked the king, and royal charters they procured'); Richard's deception of the same men in the meanwhile: 'vultum hillarem et benignum' ('he had made them show of his gracious and benign disposition') –

> Ecce scelus magnum: latitans quasi vulpis in agnum,
> Sic dolus expectat quos ira tirannica spectat.
> O fraus, Oque dolus, quos rex sub ymagine solus,
> Dum scelus exhausit, tam longo tempore clausit!
> Sed magis ad plenum tunc fuderat ille venenum.
>   (*Cronica*, II, lines 21–5)

> (O what a crime was this: like a fox in wait for lambs,
> Guile lies in wait for those that tyrant's anger damns.
> What fraud and guile the king concealed for such long time
> Alone, with feigning face, till he fulfilled his crime!
> At last he fully poured his poison out.)

Richard's use of armed force for intimidating parliament ('his own parliament, set about with great men at arms and bowmen for the people's intimidation'), probably with reference to the infamous Cheshire praetorians): 'Rex iubet arma geri' (*Cronica*, II, line 34) ('The king sends out a call to arms');[7] the matter of the earl of Arundel's special pardon and the earl's invocation of it at his parliamentary trial ('adducing both a charter of the said general pardon and a charter of the pardon in special granted him afterwards'), 'Pretendens regisque sigilla sub ordine legis | Cartam monstrauit,

---

[7] See esp. Record 258–273 = 418b. For comment, John M. Bowers, '*Pearl* in its royal setting: Ricardian poetry revisited', *SAC*, 17 (1995), 115–19; also R. R. Davies, 'Richard II and the Principality of Chester 1397–9', in *The Reign of Richard II: Essays in Honour of May McKisack*, eds F. R. H. Du Boulay and Caroline M. Barron (London, 1971), pp. 267–70; and James L. Gillespie, 'Richard II's archers of the crown', *Journal of British Studies*, 18 (1979), 14–29.

qua tucior esse putauit' (*Cronica*, II, lines 126–8) but 'Non fuit' ('He shows the royal seals, just as the law prescribes. | He showed the charter, thinking he'd the safer be | But no!'); finally, the confiscations that followed the trials ('wickedly confiscating their lands and tenements') and Richard's redistribution of the spoils ('giving them to their accusers'), including: 'capit ex toto terras herede remoto' (*Cronica*, II, line 202) ('He seized all the estates and set aside the heir') and 'Regis fautores super hoc tamen anteriores | Fraudibus obtentum concludunt parliamentum' (*Cronica*, II, lines 272–3) ('What's more, the royal sycophants, then first in time, | Prorogued the parliament, now seized by treachery').

Points of Motive

Matters of fact are rearranged in the same way by both Gower and the Record, contrary to the actual sequence of events. Gower's *Cronica* and the Record converge, too, on peculiar imputations of motive in an absence of evidence in fact or action, and share an idiosyncratic explanation for the inception of the troubles between leading magnates and the king that resulted in the Appellants' Coup in November–December 1387, for example.

About a year earlier, in November 1386, a 'Commission of Governance', to remain in place for a year, had been imposed on the young monarch, ostensibly to supervise the household expenditure.[8] Chronologically the earliest matter embedded in the Record – in fact about a third of the way into the document, in the first of its 'Articles of Deposition' (190–202 = 417b–418a) – essays to explain what happened (first) by Richard's rejection of sage council for dissipation with immature favourites instead and (second) by an intention on Richard's part to harm those whom he felt had imposed the 'Commission of Governance' on him: 'for the realm's governance, certain prelates and other temporal lords had been chosen and deputed, to labour in good faith, with all at their disposal, towards the end of the realm's governance within its own proper ways and means.' Gower, too, has it explicitly that the royal favour shown 'personis indignis' was shown to young persons, unworthy by virtue of their youth, whose council the king yet preferred to that of those older and wiser persons legally deputed to rule. 'Tunc aderant tales iuuenes', Gower has it, 'qui sunt speciales, | Laudantes regem' (*Cronica*, I, lines 35–6): ('Such young men stood beside that he called "special friends", | Who praised him'):

---

[8] For the parliamentary Commission itself, see *Parliament Rolls* III, 221–2 (also in S. B. Chrimes and A. L. Brown, *Select Documents of English Constitutional History 1307–1485* (London, 1961), pp. 136–7); a somewhat fuller form of the commission was later promulgated as statute: see *The Statutes of the Realm*, eds J. Caley et al., 11 vols in 12 (London, 1810–28), II, pp. 39–43 (also, *Parliament Rolls* III, 349–50, excerpted in Chrimes and Brown, *Select Documents*, pp. 169–70, and *Statutes of the Realm*, II, 95–8). In general, see J. J. N. Palmer, 'The parliament of 1385 and the constitutional crisis of 1386', *Speculum*, 46 (1971), 477–90; and on the cognate statutes, D. Clementi, 'Richard II's ninth question to the judges', *EHR*, 86 (1971), 96–113, pp. 100–103.

> Stultorum vile sibi consilium iuuenile
> Legerat, et sectam senium dedit esse reiectam.
> Consilio iuuenum spirauerat ille venenum,
> Quo bona predaret procerum, quos mortificaret.
> Sic malus ipse malis adhesit, eisque sodalis
> Efficitur, tota regis pietate remota.
> Tunc accusare quosdam presumpsit auare,
> Vnde catallorum gazas spoliaret eorum.
> Tres sunt antiqui proceres quos regis iniqui
> Ira magis nouit, et eos occidere vouit. (*Cronica*, 1, lines 15–24)
>
> (Unsound advice from foolish youth he took as guide;
> The wiser thoughts of older men he cast aside.
> By young men's counsel he breathed out a deadly breath
> To seize the nobles' goods and bring them to their death.
> Thus he became their friend, as bad with bad combined;
> All royal sense of mercy was put out of mind.
> He then presumed, from avarice, false charges to contrive,
> Some men of all their wealth in order to deprive.
> The wrath of wicked king marked out three older men,
> All nobles: these he vowed to kill right there and then.)

The intention to harm, even to murder, that Gower imputes here to Richard is imputed likewise in the Record, in advance of any evidence to the effect in Richard's actions. Out of interest in the 'bona procerum', 'greedily', the Record alleges, 'a compact was struck between him and his co-conspirators, the king yet intending to bring in charges of high treason against the aforementioned lords, both spiritual and temporal, who were labouring but for the realm's benefit'; and 'the like king intended afterwards to initiate process of law for the destruction of the duke of Gloucester and the earls of Arundel and Warwick and the rest of the lords, with whose doings and actions the aforesaid king was exceedingly incensed, especially inasmuch as they were desirous of the same king remaining under but good goverance' (213–17 = 418a).

Here, as in Gower too, the king moves forward his plan to harm the magnates by means of a suborning of his judges. In August 1387 Richard posed the justices of the realm a series of ten questions concerning the 1386 'Commission of Governance', seeking to establish its legality and, if it were found illegal, the culpability of those responsible for its establishment. Richard received written responses to his enquiry: without naming names, the judges found that such persons as might have been responsible for such a thing as the 1386 Commission might be liable to be treated 'tanquam proditores' or 'ut proditores', as if they were guilty of treason, the penalty for which was death and forfeiture.[9] Both the Record and Gower exculpate these same justices by asserting that they had acted under coercion: they

---

[9] The questions themselves survive, with their answers, in several contexts, with some variation of content; modern English translation of them is incorporated in S. B. Chrimes, 'Richard II's questions to the judges, 1387', *Law Quarterly Review*, 72 (1956), 376–81.

were 'Munere corrupti suadente timoreque rupti' (*Cronica*, I, line 29) ('By suasive gifts seduced and broken down by fright'), in Gower's relatively efficient phrase; in the 'Articles of Deposition' it is alleged that the king 'induced the justices of the realm to corroborate his criminal proposition by fear of death and bodily torture, with violence', expressly again 'intending to destroy the said lords' (202–4 = 418a), and that King Richard, 'by various threats and menaces, even by fear of death, did induce, cause, and compel them, in their own persons, to answer him, [...] above and beyond their own will, and otherwise than they would have answered him had they enjoyed their proper rights and not been subject to such coercion' (207–12 = 418a). The justices themselves used the same claim in their own defence at their parliamentary trial in the 'Merciless Parliament' in February 1388.[10]

That Richard 'intended to bring in charges of high treason' against anyone in particular at the time, as is charged in the 'Articles of Deposition', never became clear. The questions to the justices were to remain secret, but of course they did not; the Appellants struck first, their coup ensuing, before Richard could act. Nonetheless, Gower matches the Record here too with his suggestion that Richard's aim was the death of those who became the great Appellants of 1387–8: 'et eos occidere vouit' (*Cronica*, I, line 24) ('these he vowed to kill'). The common notion basic to both Gower and his source in the parliamentary record was a speculation: the king intended them harm, so the Appellants' doings were strictly self-defensive.

It could be that the convergence of the *Cronica* and the Record in this interpretation was due to parallel conceit, but deriving independently. A decade or more after the fact, in the political circumstance created by the usurpation, any apologist would impute the most malign of intentions to the deposed king and the noblest to the Appellant Lords in an absence of concrete evidence in action or event to indicate one way or another, or in despite of evidence. Gower need not have had a source for such a conceit, it might be felt, being perfectly capable of speculating in this same way all on his own. Cumulatively, however, the pattern of Gower's dependence on the Record is so pervasive, for points big and little, in matters of fact and interpretation, that positing other sources (including Gower's own capacity for invention) is uneconomical: whenever possible, as much as possible, Gower used the 1399 parliamentary record. As a poet, he had other worries.

Invention and the Verbal Issue

The pattern of Gower's dependence on the Record, not only for broad structure but also for various particulars of selection, arrangement, emphasis and interpretation, continues well into his final book. However, in *Cronica* III the matter of Gower's own inventions, as well as problems of his use of sources other than the Record, becomes critical (strictly, no longer a matter

---

[10] See *Parliament Rolls* III, 238–40.

of a 'parliamentary source' for the *Cronica*). Gower must eventually leave the one official record, because it gives out. Since, by its nature, the Record must end with the events of the one day it accounts directly, 30 September 1399, for subsequent events that he would tell – the Henrician coronation and parliament of 1399 October (*Cronica*, III, lines 308–99, only announced in the Record), the 'Epiphany Rising' or 'Revolt of the Earls' of 4–15 January 1400 (*Cronica*, III, lines 400–431), and the death and interment of the former king Richard II in February 1400 (*Cronica*, III, lines 432–61) – Gower necessarily had recourse to other sources, including talk, autoscopy and his own capacity for invention.

In fact, at other points in the *Cronica* too, Gower had recourse to such non-parliamentary sources at points where the Record was reticent or silent. About the dispositions of various aristocratic corpses and body-parts, apparently of considerable interest to Gower, likewise the post-revolutionary fates of some minor though still noble persons, the parliamentary source tells nothing.[11] When such extra-parliamentary doings as interested Gower took place in or near London, his reports appear to be well informed and are informative; when such events transpired remote from the metropolis, Gower was more often thrown back on his own invention. The chief instance of Gower's invention encompasses the events of the Henrician invasion of England, inescapably illegal in numerous ways and so understandably not much detailed in the Record. Gower obtained good information from elsewhere, it would appear, about the Bristol killings of Scrope, Bussy and Green on 29 July 1399 (*Cronica*, III, lines 168–85).[12] Otherwise, even on such basic points as Henry's place of return to England – though the landing in force precisely at Ravenspur was widely reported, Gower has only the epic-sounding and approximately correct 'Aquilonica littora cepit' (*Cronica*, III, line 143) ('The duke made landfall in the North') – not to mention more consequential matters, such as the number and sequence of Henry's meetings with Richard in August, Gower was bound to have recourse to his own invention.[13]

---

[11] On the disposition of Gloucester's remains, see *Cronica* 2.99–104 and 2.117–118, where Adam Usk may have comparable information: *The Chronicle of Adam Usk 1377–1421*, ed. and trans. Chris Given-Wilson (Oxford, 1997), pp. 84–5; and on the disposition of the earl of Arundel's, see *Cronica* 2.153–158, where the nearest analogue is in Thomas Walsingham, *Annales*, ed. Henry Thomas Riley, in *Johannis de Trokelowe, et Henrici de Blaneforde, monachorum S. Albani, necnon quorundam anonymorum Chronica et Annales*, Rolls Series 28, vol. 3 (London, 1866), pp. 218–19, though see also *The Chronicle of Adam Usk*, pp. 82–3. At *Cronica* 3.256 and 273 Gower makes reference to Humphrey Bohun (c.1381–1399), the son and heir of the late Thomas of Woodstock, duke of Gloucester, who is not mentioned in the parliamentary record, though he is noticed elsewhere: see David R. Carlson, 'English poetry, July–October 1399, and Lancastrian crime', *SAC*, 29 (2007), 379 and n. 9; at *Cronica* 3.137 and 258, Gower makes reference to Thomas Fitzalan (1381–1415), son and heir of Archbishop Arundel's brother, Richard Fitzalan, earl of Arundel, whose restoration to dignity in the 1399 October parliament, by petition of commons, was noted in official records: *Parliament Rolls* III, 435–6.

[12] On the sources to do with this episode, including Gower, there is comment in Carlson, 'English Poetry, July–October 1399', 375–418.

[13] On the sources for the invasion and the August meetings, see especially the comments of James W. Sherborne, 'Perjury and the Lancastrian Revolution of 1399', *Welsh History Review*, 14 (1988), 217–41.

Already in *Cronica* I Gower resorts to literary-topical invention, where his parliamentary source was largely out and he did not have other sources of intelligence concerning events remote from London: in his account of the Battle at Radcot Bridge, near Oxford, of 20 December 1387, Gower may nonetheless have once used the 'ipsissima verba' of the Record. In the course of the Appellants' Coup, at meetings near and in London on 15 and 17 November 1387, the Appellants made formal appeal of treason against five Ricardian officers and favourites to the king and his representatives, and a parliament for trying these appeals was then set for February 1388. In the Appellants' view, any military action on Richard's behalf in the meanwhile was treacherous: a violation of the agreement already in place to go to parliamentary trials, and so their official account in the Record makes of events another instance of Richard's perjury; for, despite the agreement, it was later alleged, the king had sent Robert de Vere 'into Chester', 'clandestinely' yet 'with the king's writ and banner' ('cum suis literis et vexillo'), whereabouts de Vere 'did rouse to arms and did induce to insurrection no few persons against the aforesaid lords and magnates, the guardian-keepers of the realm and commonweal, raising up the king's banner ('vexillum eius') against the very peace he had sworn publicly to maintain, whence had arisen throughout the whole of the realm homicides, kidnaps, rapines, and other wrongs to no end' (220–31 = 418a). In Gower, for the same military action: 'Ducit Aper [sc. Vere] gentes, quas concitat arma gerentes' ('The Boar assembles people, stirring them to fight') (*Cronica*, I, line 75), from the Record: 'ibique nonnullas gentes ad arma commouit'; the same motive is alleged: 'vt hiis pergat proceresque per omnia spergat' ('so he may freely march and nobles put to flight') (*Cronica*, I, line 76), from the Record: 'et contra dictos dominos et magnates regni et reipublice seruitores insurgere fecit'; as is also the same improbably dire consequence: 'Quo regnum periat' ('To bring the realm to ruin') in Gower (*Cronica*, I, line 72), from the Record: 'unde homicidia, captiuitates, dissensiones, et alia mala infinita per totum regnum secuta fuerant'.

The Record has no details of battle, however: remote from events, and other sources absent, Gower must invent, and his inventions may have been prompted by a particular recurrent term in the official source: 'vexillum' – an allusion to the ubiquitous 'Venantius Fortunatus' hymn of Christ's triumph, known by its opening phrase 'Vexilla regis' – twice in this one article of deposition but nowhere else in the Record: 'rex clanculo ducem Hibernie, cum suis literis et vexillo, ad partes Cestrie destinauit' and 'vexillum eius contra pacem per eum iuratam publice erigendo', and once in Gower: 'Regis vexillum fatue signauerat illum' ('The royal banner, foolishly, had signed his rights') (*Cronica*, I, line 66). The poet does more by way of developing the conceit of antitypical parallels between Christ in triumph and Vere in defeat than does the parliamentary record: the battle at Radcot Bridge occurred, like the crucifixion, on a Friday, Gower emphasises: 'Cum Venus incepit lucem' (*Cronica*, I, line 79) ('The day of Venus dawned'); Vere made his escape from the battlefield by passing through water 'fugiens set Aper vada transit' (*Cronica*, I, line 85) ('The Boar fled through the stream'), and Gower treats his immersion, derisively, mockingly, as a baptism for him, a type of the crucifixion: Vere emerges as if 'de fonte renatus' (*Cronica*, I, line 86) ('there he was baptized again'). Gower must have had sources other than the Record (or other portions of the parliamentary record) for his information on Vere's military humiliation, although the poet resorts also to speculative elaborations here. However, the liturgical drift and tenor of Gower's literary-topical elaborations may have been prompted by the terms of the Record nonetheless – there is the verbal parallel. The parallel occurs in a passage where, generally again, Gower and the Record have the same tendentious selection and sequence of events; but the allusion to Fortunatus (if allusion there be) may well have occurred to both writers independently and, in any case, the verbal parallels are neither close nor extensive. An unsettling phenomenon, nonetheless: there are no better verbal parallels between the *Cronica* and its source in the Record than this single use of *vexillum*, such as it is.

Examples could be multiplied but only to more of the same effect: Gower did not draw from the verbal fabric of the Record for making the *Cronica*. Verbal parallels do not reveal his dependence, or even much suggest it, though the reasons are not far to seek: 'causa metri', though not quite as strictly as the term intends. For some kinds of post-classical Latin poets quoting is easy, perhaps the easiest thing to do; even turning prose into verse can present few problems if rhyme is not involved.[14] No such procedures were available to Latin poets working with Leonines, however: nor prose nor ancient (i.e. unrhymed) verse can be made to fit so readily. Gower knew the passage in the *Aeneid* describing *Fama*'s malign pervasion, for example:

> it Fama per vrbes,
> Fama, malum qua non aliud velocius vllum:
> mobilitate viget virisque adquirit eundo. (*Aeneid*, IV, lines 173–5)
>
> ('All about the cities goes Rumour, Rumour herself, than whom no other evil travels more quickly: she grows from going, gaining strength by movement.')

For he quotes the passage in the unrhymed *Vox clamantis*: 'Sperserat ambiguas huius vaga Fama per vrbes | Rumoris sonitum' ('Fame wanders through the doubtful towns and spreads | This rumour's sound') (*Vox*, I, lines 1231–2) and again: 'volat inclita Fama per orbem' (*Vox*, VII, line 9) ('renowned Fame flies throughout the world'). On the other hand, 'Fama volans creuitque climata cuncta repleuit' (*Cronica*, III, line 338) ('To all points of the realm the rumour spread and grew') and 'Quod sic decreuit rex fama perambula creuit; | Per mundum totum scelus hoc erit amodo notum' ('The king's decrees were spread by rumour far and wide; | His crime henceforth will be well known on every side') (*Cronica*, III, lines 120–21) – both from

---

[14] An extended instance is analysed in Bernard André, 'De sancta Katharina carmen "Cum Maxentius imperator" and De Sancto Andrea Apostolo "Si meritis dignas" (*c*.1509–1517)', *Sacris Erudiri*, 46 (2007), 440–50.

the *Cronica*, and so both rhymed – may recall the Virgilian passage, perhaps by alluding to the exceptionally well-known phrases.[15] They do not quote, however. They cannot. In this way generally for Leonine verse, prosodic constraints determined or delimited the possible extent of verbal debt.

In the case of the *Cronica*, the rhyming poet's technical problems were compounded by the nature of the prose with which he had to work. Gower might have quoted himself or other near-contemporary rhyming Latin poets; translating the mannered prose of official sources into the equally but differently mannered verse style Gower chose was not possible. The Record and cognate official documents are not in some quotidian 'sermo humilis', but in an idiosyncratic, highly elaborated style peculiar to the peculiar documentary class. 'Idem tamen rex, machinans viis et modis quibus poterat eundem archiepiscopum Cantuariensem opprimere, et in nichilum redigere statum eius' ('Again: yet the king, contriving by all the ways and means he could dispose to tread down the same archbishop of Canterbury, and to reduce him in status to nullity') (635–7 = 421b): how to turn such a remark into disyllabically rhymed hexameters? Here is Gower's essay, it appears, substantively close though verbally not at all alike: 'Tramite subtili latitans plus vulpe senili | Rex studet in fine Thomam prostrare ruine' ('By stealth, on crafty path, than aged fox more sly, | The king contrives to bring the bishop down from high') (*Cronica*, II, lines 249–50).

The *Cronica* is a difficult poem from a technical perspective, composed in the most ornate Latin verse style Gower ever elaborated for himself. Moreover, Gower's narrative is complexly re-assembled from a disorderly source and supplemented from other disparate materials. For the substance of events that the poem treats, Gower can be shown to have drawn from time to time on various sources of several kinds: on other parts of the public records, of the parliaments of October 1399 and 1388; on talk going around, though only the kind of anti-Ricardian talk, official or quasi-, that can be paralleled in the work of pro-Lancastrian writers like Walsingham and Adam Usk; on his own personal connections among the grand; and, finally, on his own (considerable professional) capacity to invent, especially when bound to tell of events he could know little about and which occurred remote from his base in London. Above all, however, there was for Gower the Record. The pattern of his persistent substantive dependence on it, again and again, whenever possible, even in the absence of extensive verbal parallels, indicates that the poet had use of this official source. Inasmuch as he did, Gower's work in the *Cronica* is in effect an official verse panegyric of the Lancastrian advent. The initiating agency is not on record in the evidence; nonetheless, Gower obtained or someone provided him with a copy of the Record itself, and Gower rendered his service, in verse, completing his

---

[15] Quasi-proverbial, in fact: see Hans Walther, *Proverbia Sententiaeque Latinitatis Medii Aevi: Lateinische Sprichwörter und Sentenzen des Mittelalters in alphabetischer Anordnung*, 6 vols (Göttingen, 1963–9), nos 5091, 6852, 8288, 8827, 8840; and used also in Chaucer, *House of Fame*, lines 1368–76.

poetical apology soon after February 1400. Also, at about the date of the completion of the Record, Gower began to be remunerated by the Lancastrian regime.[16]

---

[16] On this point, see esp. Fisher, *John Gower*, pp. 68–9 and p. 342 nn. 7–8; see also my 'Gower *pia vota bibit* and Henry IV in 1399 November', *ES*, 89 (2008), 377–84.

Chapter 9

John Gower's Legal Advocacy and 'In Praise of Peace'

CANDACE BARRINGTON

In his second and final English poem, known to us as 'In Praise of Peace', John Gower declares to King Henry IV, 'Mi liege lord, tak hiede of that Y seie' ('Praise', line 82); he thereby presents himself as the king's adviser, a role in all of Gower's poems identified as the 'most significant' by George Coffman.[1] Subsequent essays by Paul Strohm, Frank Grady and Michael Livingston have shown how 'In Praise of Peace' confirms this advisory role by presenting Gower as an insider able to repeat the official Lancastrian argument justifying Henry's claim to the English throne but also able to demonstrate an uncomfortable awareness of internal contradictions in the Lancastrian claims, especially the problem inherent in claiming that military conquest justified removing a legitimate king from power.[2] Gower's English verses sidestep this problematic justification, instead crediting Henry's ascent to his noble blood, God's choice and the desire of the English people, echoing an argument devised by Henry's propagandists.[3] Once the first stanzas establish his *bona fides* as a loyal Lancastrian, Gower then makes 'his voice all the more essential', as Michael Livingston argues, by helping Henry 'better understand and implement God's will': that 'the best rule is that which leads to peace', a direction contrary to the new king's policy.[4] That is, Gower attempts to combine in the poem both the Lancastrian propaganda and a criticism of the regime. As these readings show, the poem demonstrates the delicacy of finding 'a place from which, and the voice in which, to speak'.[5] What role, the poem asks, allows the poet to be heard by those he would scold? Because the voice of royal adviser so pervades 'In Praise of Peace', Gower's readers have generally not looked beyond that

---

[1] G. R. Coffman, 'John Gower in his most significant role', *University of Colorado Studies* Series B, no. 2, 4 (1945), 52–61.
[2] Paul Strohm, 'Saving the appearances: Chaucer's *Purse* and the fabrication of the Lancastrian claim', in *Chaucer's England: Literature in Historical Context*, ed. Barbara A. Hanawalt (Minneapolis, MN, 1992), pp. 21–40; Frank Grady, 'The Lancastrian Gower and the limits of exemplarity', *Speculum*, 70 (1995), 552–75; *John Gower: The Minor Latin Works*, p. 1.
[3] Grady, 'The Lancastrian Gower'; Strohm, 'Saving the appearances', 21–2, 33.
[4] *John Gower: The Minor Latin Works*, p. 6.
[5] Siân Echard, 'Introduction', in *Companion*, p. 9.

role. In doing so, readers have encountered textual self-contradictions seemingly explained only by authorial waffling, a characteristic not generally associated with the poet's voice.

To appreciate fully Gower's strategies for advising peace to a king who militarily overthrew his predecessor, I suggest that, in addition to his advisory role, Gower performs in the poem the role of legal advocate to the king. Recognizing this second role helps to untangle the structural logic behind the way the poem keeps working against itself, presenting an argument and then undermining it a few stanzas, even a few lines, later. Such an apparent contradiction opens the poem: the Latin proem incorporates all four possible Lancastrians claims – divine selection, legal right, popular support and conquest – while the first three English stanzas downplay conquest as a justification for crowning Henry king of England. Subsequent contradictions in the poem have led Frank Grady to claim that the multiple discussions on peace were diversionary tactics rather than advice Gower expected the king to consider seriously. Gower, Grady explains, repeatedly tries 'to distract his audience from [the poem's] manifest contradictions by plunging ahead on the theme of peace'.[6] Limning the structural logic behind those apparent contradictions will restore the rather audacious nature of Gower's enterprise, one which extends to presenting his verse as a vehicle for transforming Henry from a usurper reliant on martial force to a monarch who, motivated by juridical pity, consolidates his power by ensuring his people have recourse to stable laws and efficient courts. When legal advocacy is seen as an essential role in the poem, 'In Praise of Peace' is less 'a valediction to the mirror-for-princes genre' and more a man-of-law's novel strategy for earning the king's trust and attention.[7]

To understand Gower's performance as legal advocate, I suggest we recognize the poem's set of legal gestures, gestures that would have come to him easily – even 'naturally' – because he was probably associated with the legal profession. To make this argument, I will not review the data pointing to Gower's legal career. Rather, I accept the most recent assessment of his life records, which finds 'highly plausible that part of the younger Gower's education would have taken place in the Inns of Court of London … [and] that Gower pursued a legal career'.[8] With that in mind, we can assume that, through serious reading, studious observation and reiterative performance, he learned the arcane and privileged knowledge of the common law, mastered the technicalities of procedure and the art of pleading, and absorbed the 'detailed doctrine and general modes of thought and discourse' of legal principles.[9] After a lifetime immersed in the legal profession's intricacies

---

[6] Grady, 'The Lancastrian Gower', p. 565.
[7] Ibid., p. 570.
[8] John Hines, Nathalie Cohen and Simon Roffey, '*Iohannes Gower, Armiger, Poeta*: records and memorials of his life and death', in *Companion*, pp. 23–41 (p. 25).
[9] J. H. Baker, *An Introduction to English Legal History*, 4th edn (London, 2002), p. 65.

and unforgiving demands, Gower's modes of thought and behaviour would have been shaped into the *habitus* of a man of law.[10] Anyone whose career had been spent at court would have found it difficult to avoid performing within these authoritative, and now naturalized, parameters.

As I explore the ramification of these legal gestures, I am interested in the ways 'processes of legal thought and practice' shaped Gower's self-presentation and his poem.[11] Because I am extending the scholarship of Richard Firth Green, who has forcefully and productively advocated that we read law and literature 'as parallel forms of discourse', I will not examine the poem in ways scholars frequently think about their intersection.[12] I am not looking for mimetic depictions of fictive documents or legal processes; instead, I will locate unselfconscious gestures learned and practised at law courts. When bundled together, these gestures impart to the poem the performative force of a legal argument without requiring it to reach the status of a legal argument.

In order to delineate these gestures drawn from contemporaneous legal life, I will divide them into three categories: semantic, procedural and illocutionary. The semantic gestures incorporate into the English text a legal terminology – primarily an Anglo-Norman lexical pool, England's legal language between the thirteenth and seventeenth centuries. The procedural gestures reflect two standard processes for developing a legal case, presenting a writ and pleading. The illocutionary gestures instantiate the roles of participants in the legal process, here the man-of-law in his dual roles as both advocate and adviser, plus the royal judge instantiated as the kingdom's final guarantor of justice. Recognizing that these three sets of gestures create a legal poetics leads us to see how the poem seeks to do more than either advocate for or advise the king; the poem begins to help to transform Henry IV into the king he promised to be yet failed to become.

Semantic Gestures: the Legal Lexis

Gower's first of two semantic gestures is to fill the English poem with a lexis drawn from legal documents and court records. Though this lexis includes some surviving Anglo-Saxon and Latin legal terms, it primarily derives from Anglo-Norman. This lexical dominance reflects the late medieval practice of conducting and recording legal proceedings in the French dialect associated with England's earlier Norman and Angevin ruling class, a dialect that for convenience's sake I refer to as 'law French' (though that term does not

---

[10] Pierre Bourdieu, *Outline of a Theory of Practice*, trans. Richard Nice (Cambridge, 1977); Michel de Certeau, *The Practice of Everyday Life*, trans. Steven Rendall (Berkeley, CA, 1984); Marvin Carlson, *Performance: A Critical Introduction* (New York, 1996). For an exemplary application of these theories to medieval literature, see Susan Crane, *The Performance of Self: Ritual, Clothing, and Identity During the Hundred Years War* (Philadelphia, PA, 2002).
[11] Anthony G. Amsterdam and Jerome Bruner, *Minding the Law* (Cambridge, MA, 2000), p. 2.
[12] Richard Firth Green, *A Crisis of Truth: Literature and Law in Ricardian England* (Philadelphia, PA, 1999), p. xvi.

appear in the written records until much later). The use of law French in English courtrooms continued long after Anglo-Norman ceased to be used elsewhere in England.[13] Besides ensuring that professionals trained in the specialized argot could monopolize control of the courts, this linguistic conservatism provided England with a specialized body of terms whose native equivalents did not carry the same legal associations.[14] Even when cases were conducted wholly or partially in English, technical legal vocabulary borrowed from law French was regularly slipped into the written record.[15] Anglo-Saxon, Latin and, most significantly, law French together provided a corpus of legal terms assimilated by fourteenth-century English as it gradually became the vehicle for judicial thought and practice.[16]

'In Praise of Peace' abounds with these assimilated legal terms. Identifying them, however, is not a simple matter of finding those 'termes queinte of lawe' rejected by Chaucer's Shipman.[17] Locating this legal lexis requires us to compare Gower's semantic corpus with that of coeval legal documents, a process expedited by John Alford's *Glossary of Legal Diction* and John Baker's *Manual of Law French*.[18] For the modern reader, examples of late medieval code-switching from non-legal English to legal English are not always readily apparent. The passage of time has diminished their earlier legal associations, so that many of these terms have become fully absorbed into common Modern English discourse and have a light hold on any judicial connotations. Many, especially those with English roots, are visible only in 'context alone, particularly the way in which they are joined with other words'.[19] In all, Gower's poem includes at least 125 words associated with legal discourse.[20] Collectively, these legal terms remind us of Gower's natural recourse to a judicial vocabulary and signal that 'In Praise of Peace' deserves a polysemous interpretation wherein legal definitions are read alongside the non-legal ones.[21]

---

[13] J. H. Baker, *Manual of Law French*, 2nd edn (Aldershot, 1990), pp. 1–4.

[14] W. M. Ormrod, 'The uses of English: language, law, and political culture in fourteenth-century England', *Speculum*, 78, 3 (2003), 773–8.

[15] Paul Brand, 'The languages of the law in later medieval England', in *Multilingualism in Later Medieval Britain*, ed. D. A. Trotter (Cambridge, 2000), pp. 66–7; Jane Roberts, 'A Lancashire lease', in *People and Texts: Relationships in Medieval Literature*, eds Thea Summerfield and Keith Busby (Amsterdam, 2007), p. 173; William Rothwell, 'Aspects of lexical and morpho-syntactical mixing in the languages of medieval England', in *Multilingualism in Later Medieval Britain*, ed. D. A. Trotter (Woodbridge, 2000), p. 219.

[16] William Rothwell, 'English and French in England after 1362', *ES*, 6 (2001), 539–99; Peter Goodrich, 'Literacy and the languages of the early common law', *Journal of Law and Society*, 14, 4 (1987), 433–6.

[17] II, line 1189.

[18] John A. Alford, ed., *Piers Plowman: A Glossary of Legal Diction* (Cambridge, 1988); Baker, *Manual of Law French*. See also Janet Bately, '"Here comes the judge": a small contribution to the study of French input into the vocabulary of the law in Middle English', in *Placing Middle English in Context*, eds Irma Taavitsainen *et al.* (Berlin, 2000), pp. 255–75.

[19] Alford, *Piers Plowman: A Glossary*, p. xi.

[20] See http://www.english.ccsu.edu/faculty/Barrington/default.htm (accessed 22 March 2010), for a copy of 'In Praise of Peace' highlighting each word drawn from the legal lexicon and a chart listing each of the poem's legal terms along with its definition.

[21] Alford, *Piers Plowman: A Glossary*, pp. xi–xiv.

Gower's second semantic gesture is to link a law French term with an English synonym. This paratactic redundancy appears in Englished law books and legal records in order to emphasize a point that might not be clearly established by the English term alone. These fixed phrases of paired synonyms survive in popular conceptions of modern legal discourse, including 'null and void', 'to have and to hold', and 'law and order'.[22] Although it might seem more apt to classify these phrases as syntactical structures, their history reveals that they evolved from the semantic problem of integrating the vernacular English and the professional discourse of law French. Besides granting a large element of redundancy that seeks to prevent misunderstanding, misdirection or ambiguity, these collocates preserve the verbal convention by which English was transformed into a language fit for conveying legal weight: Middle English legal documents frequently linked a word of English origin with a word of Anglo-Norman or Old French origin to signal the legal weight the English term needed to bear.[23] Gower uses similar word pairs repeatedly, at least twenty-five times, throughout the poem; we find, for example, in the first sixty lines 'serve and wirche' (20), 'pees and reste' (35), 'ordeigne and take' (58) and 'cleime and axe' (59), each of which combines an English word with its law French synonym.[24] Many times, these synonymic pairs could be explained as line fillers that allow Gower to maintain his metrical regularity. But they occur so frequently in the 385-line poem that they constitute a mindset accustomed to emphasizing a given point by pairing synonyms, often one a native term traceable to Anglo-Saxon, the other a similarly defined Anglo-Norman loan word.[25]

Together, these two semantic gestures anglicizing late medieval England's legal register allow us to rethink and expand the semantic status of the poem's lexical choices.[26] Our awareness of this possible register, created by the legal connotations of terms and phrases embedded in fifty-one of fifty-five stanzas, provides us with a new way of understanding the lines with a legal slant. Consequently, at the same time that the poem calls for peace a parallel legal reading considers the principles of common-law justice.[27] This parallel reading is so pervasive that it provides a second level of coherence. For example, the Christological passage explaining Christ's intervention in divine justice can also be read as establishing the essentially Christian nature of the common-law courtroom by contrasting it to the regressive 'bataile', trial by battle, that the Crusades amount to:

> To give ous pes was *cause* whi Crist dide;
> Withoute pes may no thing stonde *availed*.
> Bot now a man mai sen on everi side

---

[22] David Mellinkoff, *The Language of the Law* (Boston, 1963), pp. 120–22.
[23] Roberts, 'A Lancashire lease', pp. 168–9.
[24] Other instances occur at lines 58, 62, 80, 102, 154, 155, 175, 179, 194, 195, 207, 227, 274, 276, 288, 300, 322, and 359.
[25] Mellinkoff, *Language of the Law*, p. 25.
[26] Lech Morawski, 'Law, fact and legal language', *Law and Philosophy*, 18 (1999), 471.
[27] Only stanzas 1, 7, 31 and 51 exhibit neither semantic gesture.

> How Cristes feith is every dai *assailed*,
> With the paiens destruid, and so *batailed*
> That for *defalte* of help and of *defence*
> Unethe hath Crist His dewe reverence.
>
> ('Praise', lines 190–96, emphasis mine)

The Anglo-Norman legal terms 'cause', 'availed', 'assailed', 'batailed', 'defalte' and 'defence', as well as the two synonym pairs – 'destruid and [...] batailed' and 'of help and of defence' – ask us to consider the pagan assaults on Christianity as not only military clashes on the battlefield but also trials by battle ('bataile'). Reread through the lens of legal discourse, the pagans become the party undermining the legal action, or 'cause', settled by Christ's crucifixion. Through their assaults on the Christian faith they have removed justice from the realm of the courtroom and returned it to the battlefield, where the undefended Christian is forced to retreat to the less just trial by battle. In essence, identifying the legal subtext allows us to see Gower integrating concerns about two threats to England's peace: pagan incursions and common-law courts weakened by internal military strife.

The breadth of the legal lexicon also permits Gower to take rather bold stands. In a stanza decrying any 'prevé counseillour' ('Praise', line 128) who might advise against peace, the poem urges the king to '[l]ete God ben of this counseil in this cas' (line 129). Influenced by the words 'prevé counseillour' in the previous line, the reader is initially inclined to imagine God as a member of the king's inner circle. The addition of 'in this cas', however, invokes the legal context, and the reader is positioned to imagine God not as an adviser to the king in 'matters of state', but as an adviser in 'matters of law' who reviews a 'set of facts' with his client and reminds him that one man should not kill another 'withoute cause of dedly forfeture' (133) – that is, without a legal suit demanding 'loss of life [...] as punishment for a crime'.[28] God's concerns, in this reading, rest with the legality of the king's actions. Moreover, God as the king's legal 'counseil' joins John Gower, who, as we will see, presents himself to the king as both legal advocate and legal adviser in the form of Henry's IV's man-of-law.

Procedural Gestures: Common-Law Courts

In conjunction with the semantic gestures, two procedural gestures create a deeper layer of meaning by arranging these words in a way that echoes medieval courts' organizational protocol: writs (which initiated legal proceedings) and pleadings (which determined the issues before the court). Together, these gestures reflect a man-of-law's assumptions about the way competing points of views could be integrated and even reconciled. And

---

[28] Alford, *Piers Plowman: A Glossary*, q.v. 'counseil' and 'forfeture'; Baker, *Manual of Law French*, q.v. 'cas' and 'cause'.

more to Gower's purposes, the procedural gestures become a subtle means by which Gower can insert his counsel alongside his advocacy.

The first procedural gesture reflects the writ, the necessary trigger for legal action in medieval England's common-law courts. Written in Latin, the writ established the terms on which the demandant made a legal claim.[29] The Latin proem heading 'In Praise of Peace' functions in similar ways by articulating the four justifications for his ascension that Henry of Lancaster provided parliament: hereditary descent, divine grace, conquest and the election of the people. Echoing pertinent writs with such words as 'petisti', 'restituisti', 'renovata' and 'succedent', it reminds us of writs invoking the *assize of novel disseisin*, a case asserting the plaintiff's right to recover control of an estate.[30] Reference to a writ would have been a natural gesture for Gower to begin his case for peace. Because peace in England requires universal recognition of Henry's legitimate proprietorship of England, the writ-like proem lays out the foundational terms for the Lancastrian claim to the throne.

Gower's second procedural gesture uses the formulas of legal pleadings to structure the poem. Although I am not labelling the poem an exercise in legal pleading, I am saying that this poem reflects a mindset shaped by late medieval courtroom pleadings. These common-law pleadings and procedures were not codified or even spelled out in theoretical discussions of jurisprudence until the middle of the fifteenth century, when Sir John Fortescue wrote *De natura legis naturae*.[31] Until then, our knowledge of the technicalities of late medieval common-law pleadings comes from cases recorded in the Year Books kept by students attending court and taking notes.[32] From these Year Books we can resurrect the shape of common-law pleadings, 'the system of rules and principles that governed the forms into which parties cast their claims or defenses in order to set an issue before the court'.[33] Thus, the first move in civil pleadings was the plaintiff's 'count' or 'tale', in which the plaintiff staked his case, keeping strictly to the terms of the original writ.[34] In response, the defendant offered either a demurrer or a plea. With a demurrer, the defendant raised an issue of law by admitting the facts but arguing that those facts did not give the plaintiff any cause of action. A plea, on the other hand, could take many forms. For our purposes, the most pertinent plea was the confession and avoidance. Briefly, the confession and avoidance stated that 'additional facts rendered the claim unenforceable,

---

[29] Anthony Musson and W. M. Ormrod, *The Evolution of English Justice: Law, Politics and Society in the Fourteenth Century* (Houndmills, 1999), pp. 18–19, 23.

[30] On this legal background see F. W. Maitland's discussion at http://www.fordham.edu/halsall/basis/maitland-formsofaction.html#Select%20Writ (accessed 29 December 2009).

[31] J. W. Tubbs, *The Common Law Mind: Medieval and Early Modern Conceptions* (Baltimore, MD, 2000), p. 53.

[32] Tubbs, *The Common Law Mind*, p. 42.

[33] 'Common-law pleadings', *West's Encyclopedia of American Law*, 2nd edn (Detroit, 2008). Alan Harding, *A Social History of English Law* (Gloucester, MA, 1966; rpt 1973), p. 124.

[34] W. S. Holdsworth, *A History of English Law* (London, 1903–9), pp. 472–84.

even if the plaintiff's facts were true.'[35] No matter the defendant's plea, the plaintiff could respond by arguing against the newly introduced facts using the same kind of responses available to the defendant, a step called the plaintiff's replication. The case continued, back and forth, alternating from plaintiff to defendant and back to plaintiff, until they reached a contestable point – an issue of law or an issue of fact – for which one side or the other had the advantage, meaning that one of the attorneys could not argue convincingly against the newly introduced facts.

Before examining how pleading structures 'In Praise of Peace', I want to highlight three significant aspects of common-law pleading. First, pleading followed a back-and-forth movement between two positions. Second, each position had to respond to the newly introduced facts of the previously articulated position. Third, the case could be won on a point that seemed to have little to do with the original case. Together, these three aspects resulted in a structure something like this:

> A is true.
> Yes, A is true but that doesn't matter because of B.
> Okay, B is somewhat true, but what about C?
> Granted C is true, but D proves my case (even though D has little to do with A!)

Without understanding the legal framework undergirding it, we may find such an argument aimless and contradictory. However, for someone trained and practised in the common-law system of pleading, such argumentative forms as the confession and avoidance would have become a set of naturalized gestures easily incorporated into any writing that argues a point, including a poem.

To see how the principles of common-law pleading structure 'In Praise of Peace', we need to refer to the poem's structural divisions noted by Michael Livingston in his recent TEAMS edition. Based on the Trentham manuscript, the only manuscript copy of the poem, Livingston's edition correctly notes the rubricated capitals beginning ten of the poem's fifty-five stanzas.[36] Considering these divisions and the poem's concern with unity, Livingston proposes we understand the poem as a 'mathematical proof in the guise of poetry' that demonstrates 'the best rule is that which leads to peace'.[37] Yes, but. (Here's my own confession and avoidance.) *Yes*, the manuscript directs the reader to notice the division and to expect a developing argument within each segment, *but* the poem evokes more than a straightforward mathematical theorem. That is, if we see the poem through the lens of legal pleading – with its back-and-forth movement in which the alternating segments accept some elements of the previous segment's arguments and refute other elements – then we can understand both the logical sequence

---

[35] John Jay McKelvey, *Principles of Common-Law Pleading*, 2nd edn, revd (New York, 1894; rpt 1917), pp. 69–163.
[36] Some but not all of the rubricated capitals were marked in Macaulay.
[37] *John Gower: The Minor Latin Works*, p. 6.

of the argument and the reason the poem repeats an argument only to rebut it a stanza or two later.

When understood in the art of pleading's terms, 'In Praise of Peace' comprises two voices responding to the Lancastrian claim established in the one-stanza Latin proem, thereby allowing Gower to present two voices and two arguments: the first voice advocates the king's position by justifying Henry's war when he brought armed forces back into England; the second voice advises the king to pursue peace for the nation. Allowing the poet to present both sides, legal pleading's flexible formulas provide a framework for thinking through and presenting two arguments: one the king wants to hear, the second less attractive to his immediate goals. The first voice appears in the first fifteen English stanzas ('Praise', lines 1–105), forming the first section and articulating a plea similar to a confession and avoidance. Yes, these English stanzas agree, Henry's 'ancestrie' (line 12) plus the will of God and of the 'londes folk' (line 13) have positioned him to rule England. However, this first voice argues, the fourth element was not conquest but the 'lawe of riht' (line 55), which is better than conquest; that is, unlike conquest, which is the means by which a tyrant grieves the world (lines 47–49), peace, the 'chief of all the worldes welthe' (line 78), is the ultimate goal of a king who makes 'werre upon his right' (line 66). So this first section accepts three Lancastrian justifications while revising the fourth to demonstrate that this particular war was not naked aggression but a commendable military exercise because its ultimate goal was to restore the 'lawe of riht' (line 56), which in turn will bring peace to the kingdom. This section provides, in effect, a legal advocacy for Henry's claim to the throne. Here, the first voice suggests, is a way he could use the law and its protection of landholders' rights to defend his usurpation of the crown.

In section two ('Praise', lines 106–47), a second voice introduces a dissenting position that immediately proclaims, 'The werre is modir of the wronges alle' (line 106), including passing over the laws of a kingdom (line 110). Less concerned with legalities, this voice advises the king by invoking the greater principle of peace. While accepting that peace is the highest good, it denies that peace can ever be achieved by war. The first voice returns in the third section (lines 148–68) with the interjection 'Ha'. Yes, this voice agrees, it is good to avoid war, but sometimes war is necessary in the 'cause of rihtwisnesse' (line 149). The dissenting second voice returns in the fourth section (lines 169–96) to question how the cause of righteousness could ever be served by war when the Old Law of Moses forbids manslaughter and Christ died to create peace. Moreover, this voice adds, peace is primarily impeded by internal wars, which make Christian lands vulnerable to pagan invasions. The original English voice rebuts in the fifth section (lines 197–252) by first accepting that the infidels are a problem, then adding that invading infidels are why Christian knights must be militarily ready to protect the divided Church. In the sixth section (lines 253–94), the dissenting voice grants that Christendom's peace is unrealized because of the Church's internal dissension, pagan incursions and greedy kings; however, kings must try to serve peace because the long-term fortunes of war are unknown. In the seventh section (lines 295–329), the original voice agrees that no one knows the long-term consequences of our actions and that peace is wonderful; however, peace requires either that both parties agree to it or that one party is strong enough to pity the other and withhold aggression. In the eighth section (lines 330–57), the second voice finally agrees with the original: Yes, exactly, peace depends upon pity. The ninth section (lines 358–78) restates the point upon which both agree: pity is the answer. And the tenth section (lines 379–85) concludes with a request that all Christian kings establish peace before more evil occurs by dealing with the war, installing in Rome the 'rightful pope', keeping love and pity close at hand and maintaining the law.

By resting on 'pite' as the point where both advocate and adviser agree, the poem settles on a legal instrument whose nature Andrew Galloway has identified as 'menacing and unreliable'.[38] For monarchal pity can be expressed in two ways. It could be displayed as a compassionate respect for justice, thereby '[generating] good policy, including the lifting of onerous obligations, relief of taxes, and the preservation of great men's inheritances for their heirs' – certainly the manifestation of pity grounded in the law that Gower advocates and advises for Henry. Pity could also been seen as the 'arbitrary gestures of grace proffered through and as sheer power', which when wielded by Richard II was seen as an instrument of terror springing from the king's desire, as easily withdrawn as granted.[39] Because pleading has taken both advocate and adviser to the same resolution, the principle of pity is presented as less a political tool to be exercised arbitrarily and more a point of view grounded on principles of common-law justice.

When combined with the semantic gestures, the two procedural gestures point to the specific legal domain of the king's common-law courts, whose hallmark duties were to distribute and protect the property rights of the proprietary classes.[40] These courts ensured the relative peace of the nation because they provided the baronial class an alternative to the battlefield for settling property disputes. Simply put, for a man-of-law, this cluster of performative gestures would have been a natural way to think abstractly about the conditions, causes and obstacles to peace. But, as noted by Frank Grady, proposing peace to a king who gained the throne through armed aggression could be a fruitless, if not risky, business. The alternating, two-voice structure of pleading allows Gower to present two arguments. The first advocates Henry's position; the second advises Henry to consolidate his power through non-military means, particularly by exerting royal pity and maintaining the law.

---

[38] Andrew Galloway, 'The literature of 1388 and the politics of pity in Gower's *Confessio Amantis*', in *The Letter of the Law: Legal Practise and Literary Production in Medieval England*, eds Emily Steiner and Candace Barrington (Ithaca, NY, 2002), pp. 67–104, p. 68.
[39] Galloway, 'The literature of 1388', pp. 89 and 93.
[40] For a succinct definition of these distinctions, see Musson and Ormrod, *The Evolution of English Justice*, pp. 8–10.

Illocutionary Gestures: Transformative Texts

'In Praise of Peace' goes beyond simply advocating the Lancastrian cause and advising Henry to reinvigorate the courts. Two illocutionary gestures make Gower into Henry's man-of-law and Henry into the ensurer of justice in England. By making real the proper roles for each man – a man-of-law preserves his lord's legal rights, while the king ensures those legal rights – the poem begins the process of imaginatively revitalizing the royal courts.

The first illocutionary gesture has Gower establishing himself in the role of Henry's legal counsel by identifying himself as Henry's 'liege man' ('Praise', line 374) and calling Henry his 'liege lord' (lines 82, 92 and 358), terms generally connoting a feudal relationship in which a man served his lord in either the martial or legal realm.[41] Although this gesture, in and of itself, does not automatically equate with legal discourse, it does remind us that during the late fourteenth century the average attorney was not a freelancer taking any client who knocked on his door. Instead, most attorneys were associated with a baronial household and joined armed knights as defenders of a lord's landholdings.[42] Rather than operating on the battlefield, they conducted their defence in the courts. In addition to receiving fees for their services, these retained attorneys would often have been given robes, such as the one with striped sleeves that Gower mentions owning in *Mirour de l'Omme* – 'Ainz ai vestu la raye mance' (*Mirour* XXI, line 772 ('Before, I have worn striped sleeves') – to signify a close identity with a nobleman.[43] Despite their similarity to robes associated with legal seigneurial guilds during the next century, robes such as Gower's had a different significance in the fourteenth-century household, deriving from the customary distribution of identifying wardrobes to the household's retained knights. When presented to a man-of-law rather than a man-of-arms, the robes continued to signify a similar form of maintenance, reminding us that a seigneurial attorney was a retainer-at-law, a knight who 'seeks no armour but is willing to conquer with his tongue'.[44] By identifying himself in this capacity, Gower can play the role of one whose professional interests align perfectly with King Henry's.

In saying that Gower positions himself in the poem as the king's man-of-law, I am not claiming that Gower served in that capacity within the Lancastrian household. Granted, we can date a liege relationship to 1393, marked by the presentation of an annual pipe of Gascony wine and the

---

[41] For the Parliamentary commons' practice of addressing the king as 'liege lord', see Judith Ferster, *Fictions of Advice: The Literature and Politics of Counsel in Late Medieval England* (Philadelphia, PA, 1996), pp. 125 and 135.

[42] K. B. McFarlane, *The Nobility of Later Medieval England* (Oxford, 1973), p. 12.

[43] My own translations with aid from John Gower, *Mirour de l'Omme*, trans. William Burton Wilson, rev. Nancy Wilson Van Baak (East Lansing, 1991). See also *Mirour* XXIV, line 273, part of an extended passage on the legal profession, which identifies these robes with lawyers.

[44] J. H. Baker and S. F. C. Milsom, *Sources of English Legal History: Private Law to 1750* (Guildford, 1986), p. 101; Musson and Ormrod, *The Evolution of English Justice*, pp. 37–9.

Lancastrian livery collar. The collar was such an integral part of Gower's self-presentation that on the poet's much-remarked tomb, around the neck of the stone image, a collar of Ss, fastened with the device of a chained swan, boasts of his affinity with the Lancastrians, the greatest seigneurial retinue of fourteenth-century England.[45] The formal recognition of Gower's Lancastrian affinity, coupled with the man-of-law's propensity to see himself serving his lord's proprietary interests, would make it easy to transfer those gestures so that he speaks from the *habitus* of Henry's man-of-law. Therefore, without assuming that Gower served as a man-of-law for the Lancastrians, we can expect him to act like a man-of-law in regards to Henry. By addressing King Henry as his 'liege' and incorporating the panoply of legal gestures into his poem, Gower adopts the role of the attorney and establishes a basis for understanding the speaker's commitment to preserving his lord's legal rights. As already noted in the pleading's two voices, the defence of Henry's rights comes in two forms: legal advocacy justifying Henry's claim to the throne and legal advice calling for peace through the reinvigoration of the royal courts.

Gower's second illocutionary gesture comes about when he speaks directly to the king, thereby making Henry the ultimate arbitrator and judge. Gower reaffirms the identity of his intended audience through the generous use of Henry's name and title ('Praise', lines 1, 120, 155, 274, 358 and 265), of second-person pronouns (especially in the first four and the final four stanzas) and of imperative verbs. Thus, the English poem opens with a direct address, 'O worthi noble kyng, Henry the Ferthe'. Each subsequent second-person pronoun reconfirms this address by asking us to imagine the king reading this written document presenting the case for peace. And because the official lexicon and structures of legal documents and processes mark this poem with the authenticating tags of the court, reading the poem requires the same skills of discernment as those of a judge. When the poem commands the king to '[b]eholde and see the world uppon this point' ('Praise', line 276) it imaginatively prepares the king for his primary adjudicative role reviewing the case before him in order to protect rights and prevent trespasses.

We can begin to understand this illocutionary gesture's import when we remember that the immediate context for the poem is Henry's promise to reform the royal judiciary after his deposition of Richard II. From the beginning of his reign domestic peace was impeded by two judicial challenges: asserting the primacy of the law after gaining the crown through extra-legal means, and maintaining peace at home without resorting to factionalism

---

[45] Simon Walker, *The Lancastrian Affinity, 1361–1399* (Oxford, 1990), pp. 1–7. Despite its vaunt, the collar reveals that within the Lancastrian retinue, Gower's position was humble. According to the Duchy of Lancaster records, the collar was comparatively inexpensive, only 26s 8d. Even the silver collar given to Derby's butler was worth 56s 8d, and Henry's own gold collar cost £26 8s 11d. Macaulay, vol. iv, p. xvii. See also Ronald W. Lightbown, *Mediaeval European Jewellery, with a Catalogue of the Collection in the Victoria and Albert Museum* (Hong Kong, 1992), pp. 245–70.

and internal war. He first publicly addressed these challenges soon after his coronation:

> Sires, I thanke god and yow Spirituell and Temporell and all the States off the lande. And I do yow to vndirstonde that hit is nat my wille that no man thynk that by wey off conqest I wolde disherite eny man off his heritage, ffraunchieses, or other Rihtes that him ougt to have, ne to putte him oute off that he hath and hath hadde by goode lawes and custumes off the Rewme: excepte thes persones that haue ben ageyns the goode purpos and the comvne profyte off the Rewme.[46]

In these post-coronation remarks, Henry turned away from the events leading up to his possession of the throne – which he baldly labelled as 'conquest' – and declared what he would not do as their king. He would not deprive anyone of their traditional rights, and he would not ignore those who trespass against the common good. Henry's speech, then, acknowledged his authority and his duty to grant or restore rights as well as to prosecute or redress trespasses against the king's peace. Yet, by formulating them in negative terms, he betrayed his own awareness of the difficulties of instigating judicial reform. Much to the weaker landholders' chagrin, his proposal to review the royal courts remained unfulfilled during his reign. His dubious title to the throne precipitated a series of baronial revolts. Factionalism, which had begun to threaten the effectiveness of the king's courts during Richard II's reign, completely disabled them during Henry's rule. The king had no standing army or policing force; instead, he had to depend on the barons and their armed retinues to enforce the courts' decisions. Not surprisingly, this strategy contributed to rather than reduced the judicial chaos. After the rebellion of the earls in 1400 failed and its ringleaders were lynched by mobs, the king's council met to consider measures to restore order. This brief attempt to restore judicial order was followed by Henry's near-abandonment of the common-law courts. In the end, his regime resorted to detecting and prosecuting conspiracy rather than maintaining public order. By the time Gower composed 'In Praise of Peace', Henry was stuck in a cycle of violent aggression with few means for escape.[47]

Within this context, the poem's legal conceits introduce Henry to the adjudicative process when it asks him to read the poem. Alongside affirming Henry's right and duty to assume his role within the rightful order, this gesture means the king begins to fulfil his judicial role by reading the poem. With this illocutionary gesture, the poem moves beyond advocacy and advising to shaping Henry into the sort of king that Gower imagines to be the best. Through strong monarchal control of the courts, peace can be

---

[46] *The Chronicles of London*, ed. C. line Kingsford (Oxford, 1905), p. 46.
[47] Christine Carpenter, 'Law, justice, and landowners in late medieval England', *Law and History Review*, 1, 2 (1983), 205–37; Chris Given-Wilson, *The Royal Household and the King's Affinity, 1360–1413* (New Haven, CT, 1986); Musson and Ormrod, *The Evolution of English Justice*, p. 138; Theodore F. T. Plucknett, *Early English Legal Literature* (Cambridge, 1958), pp. 35–40; K. B. McFarlane, *Lancastrian Kings and Lollard Knights* (Oxford, 1972), pp. 61–101.

assured because the 'lawe of riht' prevails and no one need resort to factionalism or internal war.

Beyond the incorporation of this cluster of six performative gestures associated with legal discourse lies a final, nearly invisible gesture: a sense of how efficient Gower expected his poem to be. Like any late medieval man-of-law he would not have expected immediate results, for he knew that litigation was a drawn-out, long-term project, requiring persistence and patience.[48] When he dared to transport his audience of one to the legal realm, an area Henry had previously rejected when he invaded England and one he subsequently failed to control fully, Gower must have suspected his poem would not quickly yield favourable outcomes. In truth, the poem exhibits little faith that the much desired judicial reform or its concomitant peace will soon arrive. Beyond the illocutionary gestures he can imagine no immediate realization of his advice. Instead, he frames its fulfilment in terms of the king's 'pacience' and consigns its record to the memory of saints who will praise him for 'perdurable gloire' ('Praise', line 371). Thus, perhaps the most significant consequence of Gower's legal gestures and advocacy role is his acceptance that the case will be deferred indefinitely.

[48] Harding, *A Social History of English Law*, p. 121.

Chapter 10

Se-duction and Sovereign Power in Gower's *Confessio Amantis* Book V*

ANDREEA BOBOC

In book V of the *Confessio Amantis* Gower surprisingly compares perjury, a serious crime in the king's court, to amatory seduction, a lesser moral offence which ecclesiastical courts ranked in importance well behind rape and adultery.[1] These dissimilar wrongdoings share a motive – 'coveitise', which, according to *MED*, means both 'immoderate desire for acquiring worldly goods or estate' and 'strong sexual desire' for women.[2] The comparison between lands and women as objects of desire is warranted by men's proprietary interest in their sisters', wives' or daughters' chastity:

> ... Sicut agros cupidus dum querit amans mulieres,
> Vult testes falsos falsus habere suos.
> Non sine vindicta periurus abibit in eius
> Visu, qui cordis intima cuncta videt.
> Fallere periuro non est laudanda puellam
> Gloria, set false condicionis opus.
>
> (In the same way, a cupidinous lover seeks women as if he were seeking lands: he desires his own false witnesses. But not without punishment will the perjurer live in the sight of whoever sees all the secrets of his heart. To deceive a girl by perjury is not a praiseworthy glory but an action of false contract.)[3]

The Latin ('sicut ... agros ... mulieres') supports the fusion of sexual and property desire and also the subsequent transformation of 'cupidus amans' into 'periurus', whose epithet is echoed to emphasize his wrongdoing ('periuro'). These lines, which introduce the tales of *Confessio* book V, preface

---

* I am grateful to Elisabeth Dutton, Kathleen Kennedy and Theresa Tinkle, whose probing questions made this a better essay.
[1] For perjured jurors, see Frederick Pollock and Frederic W. Maitland, *The History of English Law*, 2nd edn (Cambridge, 1968), vol. 2, pp. 541–2. For amatory seduction, see James A. Brundage, 'Rape and seduction in the medieval canon law', in *Sexual Practices and the Medieval Church*, eds Vern Bullough and James Brundage (Amherst, NY, 1994), pp. 141–8 (pp. 146–8).
[2] *MED*, s.v. *coveitise* (n.) 1 and 2.
[3] Unless otherwise specified, in this essay all *Confessio* quotations are from Peck. This ref. p. 98.

Gower's intriguing contention that seduction and perjury might be legally equivalent. Yet even if one equates the objects of their desire, perjury and seduction are hardly alike: unlike the property thief, the covetous lover ('cupidus amans') might escape punishment and even take pride ('laudanda gloria') in his sexual conquests. Widespread misogynist views of women as tempting daughters of Eve ensured modest penalties for medieval seducers. Ecclesiastic courts levied small fines, occasionally flogging those perpetrators who were either unwilling to marry their victims or too poor to pay compensation.[4] If seduction was such a minor offence in the eyes of the law, why does Gower liken it to the weightier perjury ('periurium') and false contract ('false conditionis opus')?

Importantly, all three *Confessio* tales involving perjury – the *Tale of Achilles and Deidamia*, the *Tale of Jason and Medea* and the *Tale of Prixus and Helle* – also entail the seductions of kings. Royal or political seductions differ from amatory ones phenomenologically – that is, through the collective, outward manifestations that characterize them as acts or processes. While amatory seductions typically rely on blandishments and false promises to induce a woman to surrender her chastity, political seductions are perpetrated by means of perjury and false witnessing. Notably, smooth talk, commonly associated with amatory seduction, plays no part in these tales. This differentiates seduction from 'flaterie'[5] and the related 'glosinge'.[6] Verbal seduction is mentioned only in passing in the prefatory discussion between Genius and Amans (*Confessio*, V, lines 2895–902), and never again discussed; nor is sexual intercourse in these tales ever seduction's ultimate goal.

Until seduction appears nominally in the English vernacular of the sixteenth century, its lexical gap is filled phenomenologically by the description of its manifestations.[7] James Brundage notes the absence of a technical term for amatory seduction (that is, illicit coitus achieved by arts and blandishment) in Roman and medieval canon law, although its modus operandi is understood and differentiated from other sexual offences ('stuprum') from the thirteenth century.[8] In the absence of an English word, Gower would have conceptualized seduction in Latin, in which 'seducere' means 'to lead astray; to lead away from the right path'.[9] The noun 'seductor' appears in the legal context of treason, as 'seditio regis' (sometimes spelled 'seductio regis'), as early as 1305. As J. G. Bellamy writes, William Wallace is tried and publicly outlawed in the king's court 'ut seductor, praedo et felo' (i.e. as a seditionist, robber and criminal).[10]

---

[4] Brundage, 'Rape and seduction', pp. 141–8 (p. 147).
[5] *MED* s.v. 'flaterie' (n.) 'dishonest praise, flattering behavior, coaxing speech'.
[6] *MED* s.v. 'glosinge' (ger.) '(c) smooth or deceitful talk; adulation, blandishment, cajolery, flattery; also, an instance of this'.
[7] According to the *OED*, the noun 'seduction' is first documented in 1526, though the verb 'seduct' appears as early as 1490.
[8] Brundage, 'Rape and seduction', pp. 141–8 (p. 147).
[9] See, for instance, Augustine, *Confessions*, ed. J. J. O'Donnell (Oxford, 1992), 2.3.8.
[10] *Chronicles of Edward I and Edward II*, I, 141, cited in J. G. Bellamy, *The Law of Treason in England in the Later Middle Ages* (Cambridge, 1970), p. 36.

In describing seduction phenomenologically for the political domain Gower draws on the discursive traditions of Latin as the language of law but also of the church, where seduction is often presented as a 'conspiracy of signs' against the Elect.[11] In the Vulgate, Christ foretells the rise of false Christs and prophets who will attempt to seduce even the Elect by showing signs and wonders: 'Exsurgent enimi pseudochristi et pseudoprophetae et dabunt signa et portenta ad seducendos si potest fieri etiam electos' (Mark 13.22).[12]

When Gower equates seduction with perjury and false contract, he proposes a public context for what was previously understood as a private, sexual offence. Throughout *Confessio* book V amatory seductions are subordinated in significance to royal seductions. In effect Gower criminalizes seduction in the political arena by presenting it as a 'conspiracy of signs' against sovereign power: perjurers, false witnesses and even fabricated sensorial experiences all conspire to lead the king astray in conduct or belief and trigger his imprudent or arrogant response, which ultimately leads to his or his realm's ruin. Political seduction (hereafter spelled se-duction to differentiate it from amatory seduction) operates via a complex legal and moral apparatus of deception, which includes not only perjury (in the legal sense of false oath) but also breach of promise, producing false witnesses, lying by omission, breach of contract and treason. All these moral and criminal failings involve reneging on truth – and are presented by Gower at a time when, as Richard Firth Green has argued, the concept of truth was itself caught up in a cultural shift from a social system based on personal, oath-based relationships to a centralized bureaucracy reliant upon documentary records.[13] At his deposition in 1399, perjury was among the crimes imputed to Richard II in a political context that, according to Richard's detractors, intentionally undermined the institutions of truth production.[14] In warning against se-duction's disastrous effects on kingship, Gower's tales extend the late medieval tradition of *Fürstenspiegel* (advice for princes) in a new and compelling direction.

Fürstenspiegel generally teach the king how to choose good over bad counsel.[15] Se-duction, however, either suspends the sovereign's choice or leads it astray by creating an alternative reality in which signs are reordered according to the seducer's agenda. In this context, Gower shows, the king appears weak and easily misled – perhaps another oblique reference to Richard II's deteriorating leadership. In the person of the se-duced king,

---

[11] For the definition of seduction as a 'conspiracy of signs', see Jean Baudrillard, *Seduction*, trans. Brian Singer (New York, 1990), p. 2.

[12] *Biblia Sacra Iuxta Vulgatam Versionem*, ed. Robert Weber, 4th edn (Stuttgart, 1994).

[13] Richard F. Green, *A Crisis of Truth: Literature and Law in Ricardian England* (Philadelphia, PA, 1999).

[14] *Chronicon Adae de Usk, 1377–1421*, ed. Sir E. M. Thompson, 2nd edn (Oxford, 1904), p. 181, cited in *English Historical Documents: 1327–1485*, ed. A. R. Myers (New York, 1969), pp. 179–80.

[15] Judith Ferster, *Fictions of Advice: The Literature and Politics of Counsel in Late Medieval England* (Philadelphia, PA, 1996).

human fallibility and power are united to destructive ends. To appreciate fully what these tales reveal about the dangers of se-duction to sovereignty, however, one must first expose the challenges posed by the sovereign power to the moral and legal order.

Giorgio Agamben argues that the sovereign power challenges the moral and legal order because sovereignty belongs to the law, but, at the same time, paradoxically constitutes itself outside it.[16] Although since the *Magna Carta* the English monarchy had not been absolute in the sense that Agamben puts forward, his biopolitical theory of sovereignty applies to at least one moment in Richard II's kingship: in October 1386, the Appellants sought to bring the King constitutionally 'sub iure', that is, under the control of the parliament;[17] in August of the following year, however, Richard succeeded in obtaining judicial opinions that he was 'supra iure'.[18] If a sovereign may be both subject to the law and an exception to it, those subject to his power may be exposed to violence and even made liable to be killed as soon as the sovereign suspends the law and invokes a 'state of exception'.[19] In exercising power over 'bare life', which is the part of the political subject's existence excluded from the juridical order instituted by the sovereign power, the sovereign becomes 'the threshold on which violence passes over into law and law passes over into violence'.[20] It is tempting, therefore, to read the se-ductions from book V of the *Confessio* as an oblique critique of the ongoing struggle between Richard and his nobility at the expense of his subjects.[21]

Se-duction endangers the sovereign by encouraging him to take exception to the legal and moral order. Once law and morality are suspended, his subjects become exposed to the violence that the state of exception unleashes upon them. In all three tales, se-duction victimizes not only the king but also his family and subjects, who are figures of 'bare life'. Sometimes the king's se-duction exposes his subjects to violence unwittingly. In the *Tale of Achilles and Deidamia*, for instance, the king's misfortune has devastating

---

[16] Giorgio Agamben, *Homo Sacer: Sovereign Power and Bare Life*, trans. Daniel Heller-Roazen (Stanford, CA, 1995), p. 15.

[17] Lee Patterson, *Chaucer and the Subject of History* (Madison, WI, 1991), p. 157.

[18] J. J. N. Palmer, 'The parliament of 1385 and the constitutional crisis of 1386', *Speculum*, 46 (1971), 477–90.

[19] As Agamben points out, 'the state of exception is not a special kind of law (like the law of war); rather, insofar as it is a suspension of the juridical order itself, it defines law's threshold or limit concept.' See Giorgio Agamben, *State of Exception*, trans. Kevin Attell (Chicago, MI, and London, 2005), p. 4.

[20] Agamben, *Homo Sacer*, p. 32. On p. 8 Agamben defines the 'bare life' as 'the life of the *homo sacer* (sacred man), who *may be killed, yet not sacrificed*' (italics in the original).

[21] For other examples of poetry read as political commentary see Ferster, *Fictions of Advice*; David Wallace, *Chaucerian Polity: Absolutist Lineages and Associational Forms in England and Italy* (Stanford, CA, 1997); Lynn Staley, *Languages of Power in the Age of Richard II* (University Park, PA, 2005); Diane Watt, *Amoral Gower: Language, Sex, and Politics* (Minneapolis, MN, 2003); Yoshiko Kobayashi, '*Principis Umbra*: kingship, justice and pity in John Gower's poetry', in *On John Gower: Essays at the Millenium*, ed. R. F. Yeager (Kalamazoo, MI, 2007), pp. 71–103; and Kathryn McKinley, 'Lessons for a king from Gower's *Confessio Amantis*', in *Metamorphosis: The Changing Face of Ovid in Medieval and Early Modern Europe*, eds Alison Keith and Stephen Rupp (Toronto, 2007), pp. 107–28.

consequences for his kingdom, which is left without the protection of a male ruler.

King Lichomede is led astray (se-duced) to his inevitable downfall by perjury and false witnessing, which encourage a display of his own naiveté, imprudence and arrogance. Afraid that her son will die at Troy as prophesied, Thetis resolves to dress young Achilles in feminine attire and pass him off as an innocent maiden. To ensure that her trick works, Thetis charges her women servants on their oath to act as false witnesses: 'Whereof she hath hire wommen bede I And charged be here othes alle I [...] I That thei discovere noght this thing, I Bot feigne and make a knowleching' (*Confessio*, V, lines 2988–93). Ironically, oaths are here aligned with falsity, not truth. Gower depicts the truth crisis of his age as so acute that witnesses swear to deceive. But false witnessing also works here via an astute performance of gender which is taken as a signifier for gender itself: the phoney oaths of Thetis' female servants add credibility to Achilles' performance.

Achilles is a veritable Trojan horse: he is the vehicle of his mother's betrayal, but he himself is not made culpable in the poem; he is presented as an inexperienced youth who takes the whole business of dressing up in jest (*Confessio*, V, lines 3010–13) and obeys his mother without understanding the reason behind her orders: 'Achilles herde his moder telle I And wiste noght the cause why' (*Confessio*, V, lines 3028–9). Afterwards, at King Lichomede's invitation, he keeps company with Deidamia and ends up sleeping with her but does so without the guile of amatory seduction. Genius reports simply that nature takes its course: Gower changes his source so that the young lovers have consensual sex.[22] The private seduction of Deidamia, for which Amans makes Thetis fully culpable, is subordinated in significance to Thetis' se-duction of the king in the public arena.[23] Gower relies on natural law not only to normalize the behaviour of the young lovers but also to show Thetis as a ruthless se-ducer, who knowingly sacrifices Lichomede's dynastic interests.

The king's se-duction brings about consequences more pernicious than anyone would have imagined. It fails to prevent the evils it was supposed to avert and instead breeds new ones: Achilles still goes to war and ultimately dies; Deidamia gives birth to an illegitimate son, Pirrus; Lichomede is driven to distraction by shock at the divine betrayal (*Confessio*, V, lines 3190–91). But, if this is a cautionary tale, what benefit might a king derive from it, given that the perjurer is also a goddess? How can a king guard against se-duction when the gods themselves engineer his downfall? The

---

[22] In Statius, by contrast, Achilles rapes Deidamia in a cave. Statius, *Achilleid*, ed. and trans. D. R. Shackleton Bailey (Cambridge, MA, 2004), I, 640–50.

[23] The subordination of amatory to political seduction becomes even more apparent when Amans calls Thetis, and not Achilles, the actual seducer. Thetis appears unnatural and depraved because she destroys what Genius regards as the 'natural' bond between women. How can any woman – asks Genius – be safe from men's 'untrouthe' if women themselves betray their sex: 'If o womman another guile, I Wher is ther eny sikernesse?' (*Confessio*, V, lines 3204–5).

paradox is meant to caution as well as flatter the king by pointing out the magnitude of his task.

All signs thus conspire against King Lichomede. He is led into making the wrong decision by Thetis's status and credibility, which in turn is bolstered by her women's complicity and Achilles' cross-dressing. The king's own senses betray him when Achilles appears to him disguised as a girl: 'He was a womman to beholde' (*Confessio*, V, line 3021). Nevertheless, Lichomede is not without blame. Though se-duction relies on a 'malicious use of signs', it also requires the participation of victims who offer their trust in return for the pleasure of being se-duced.[24] Lichomede prefers the lesser pleasure of being a beneficent host to the greater satisfaction of protecting his kingdom.

Lichomede's hospitality is as excessive as his delight ('gret gladnesse'). In bidding strangers a welcome that disrupts personal and social boundaries he demonstrates pride, a cardinal sin against which the manuals for princes warn.[25] Boundaries are precisely what define households, communities or kingdoms.[26] When Lichomede reorganizes those boundaries around the needs of strangers and places his guests' demands above his safety requirements as a host, parent and king, he abdicates his royal responsibility to protect his subjects. Certainly, Lichomede is right to offer Thetis and her 'daughter' Achilles hospitality according to their rank and in a manner that projects his largesse and power,[27] but he fails to evaluate the potential dangers that hospitality entails.[28] Several Chaucerian tales – the *Miller's*, *Shipman's* and *Reeve's* – and Gower's own *Tale of the Rape of Lucrece* – chronicle the dangers associated with incautiously admitting strangers.[29] While hospitality suggests order and munificent government in a household or realm, it also brings the threat of disorder and death.[30] A good host

---

[24] Baudrillard, *Seduction*, p. 2.

[25] See, for instance, *The Governance of Kings and Princes: John Trevisa's Middle English Translation of the* De Regimine Principum *of Aegidius Romanus*, eds David C. Fowler, Charles F. Briggs and Paul G. Remley (New York and London, 1997), bk I, pt II, chap. XXVI. Herein the king is advised to balance magnanimity with humility. Also see *Secretum Secretorum*, ed. Robert Steele (Oxford, 1920), p. 185.

[26] Felicity Heal emphasizes the necessity of boundaries in hospitality: 'to allow total openness would have been to deny the significance of [the] transition [from stranger to guest], and hence of the integrity of the household and its head.' *Hospitality in Early Modern England* (Oxford, 1990), p. 8.

[27] Christine D. Pohl describes medieval hospitality as 'strategic' because it reinforces social boundaries and existing patterns of wealth and power. See *Making Room: Recovering Hospitality as a Christian Tradition* (Cambridge, 1999), p. 50. Felicity Heal also notes the 'mandatory quality' of medieval hospitality as being informed by both Christian and chivalric codes of behaviour; see *Hospitality in Early Modern England*, p. 5.

[28] Lichomede trusts blindly and eagerly; he does not test, though testing would have been possible, as Ulysses' later ploy to uncover the identity of the disguised Achilles demonstrates.

[29] According to *Secretum Secretorum* a king should be 'foreseeing the issues of events' (p. 185). For prudence as a legitimizing principle for a king, see Marco Toste, 'Virtue and the city: the virtues of the ruler and the citizen in the medieval reception of Aristotle's *Politics*', in *Princely Virtues in the Middle Ages: 1200–1500*, eds I. P. Bejczy and C. J. Nederman (Turnhout, 2007), pp. 73–98.

[30] Marcus Waithe, *William Morris's Utopia of Strangers: Victorian Medievalism and the Ideal of Hospitality* (Cambridge, 2006), esp. pp. 1–33.

graciously opens his house to strangers while prudently putting his most treasured possessions away.

Lichomede falls prey to se-duction in the absence of counsel, understood here as a much-needed, clear-headed perspective on a situation for which the king lacks objectivity: 'As he that wot noght hou it ferde | Upon the conseil of the nede' (*Confessio*, V, lines 3040–41). If caution seems gratuitous, perhaps even offensive, in the face of Thetis' status and implicit credibility, this is because the king is only too delighted to believe her after being se-duced not only by Thetis' false oaths but also by her request of hospitality: 'Of such record, of such witnesse, | He hadde riht a gret gladnesse | Of that he both syh and herde' (*Confessio*, V, lines 3037–9). Throwing all caution to the wind, he allows the disguised Achilles to sleep in the same bed as his comeliest daughter, Deidamia. By acting on his own accord and without counsel, Lichomede inadvertently institutes a state of exception with dire consequences for his family and kingdom. Deidamia's dalliance precipitates the king's downfall. The later unmasking of Achilles as a man by Ulysses and his companions, who have come to take him to battle, proves that crafty and timely counsel would have saved both Lichomede and his kingdom.

If the celestial guest in the *Tale of Achilles and Deidamia* arouses the reader's sympathy on account of her motherly love, no such mitigation is available for Jason, who behaves abominably as both a guest and a king. Jason is an opportunist who wants the best for himself on every occasion and does not shrink from breaking the law and reducing his subjects to 'bare life' to obtain it; he best embodies the blending of perjury and the insatiable desire for fame, lands and women. His many crimes, which include oath-breaking, lying by omission, theft and breach of contract (including a marriage contract), are all rooted in the same sin: 'cupiditas'. Ironically, since Medea keeps all her oaths, she becomes the virtuous counterpoint to Jason's vices, despite her own heinous crimes.[31] Russell A. Peck's estimation that 'for Gower, sin is a psychopathic condition',[32] seems nowhere more apparent than in Jason.

To magnify Jason's sins, Gower has him believe that he deserves his good fortune, a conceit that will ultimately cause his downfall. Readers know, however, that Medea is in charge of Jason's ventures. Medea's instructions to Jason to obtain the Golden Fleece occupy over 120 lines (*Confessio*, V, lines 3505–633) and detail the perils and challenges that Jason will encounter: this reinforces the magnitude of his task as well as his sheer unpreparedness. The magical gifts that Medea gives Jason are indispensable to his success – to emphasize this, Gower gives us a second account of the dangers (*Confessio*, V, lines 3690–735). Jason finds every challenge exactly as Medea describes, and is able to overcome each only by following her advice – for example, Medea's miraculous gifts ensure that Jason survives battling the dragon (*Confessio*, V, lines 3711–16).

---

[31] Natalie Grinnell has discussed Gower's emphasis on Medea's humanity as a wronged wife. See 'Medea's humanity and John Gower's romance', *Medieval Perspectives*, 14 (1999), 70–83.
[32] Peck, p. 3.

Though the merit is all Medea's, Jason takes full credit for the success of his enterprise, even though people gossip behind his back, wondering how he could have possibly succeeded (*Confessio*, V, lines 3822–7). One could argue that Medea's merit is also Jason's, since husband and wife are one according to the legal doctrine of 'couverture' and the Church. If husband and wife are one in flesh, however, they could not be more disparate in ethics. Medea, bound by decorum and natural modesty, does not right matters, while Jason, blinded by victory, lies by omitting her crucial involvement. This moral failure is merely the first step in a series of crimes that include: violating the laws of hospitality by absconding with his host's daughter and treasure; taking Creusa publicly as a wife despite being married in secret to Medea; and willfully bastardizing any future offspring he might have with Creusa as a consequence of the unlawfully contracted second marriage.[33] When Jason does not break contracts, he avoids making them: instead of publicly acknowledging his marriage to Medea and coming to an understanding with her father regarding her dowry, he disappears with both the king's daughter and the king's treasure, by night, like a common thief.

Gower emphasizes Jason's moral decay and downward spiral into crime as a clear consequence of his cupidity for riches, fame and women. The accomplished, despicable Jason stands in sharp contrast to the aspiring, likable Jason from the beginning of the tale, a self-reliant knight capable of real affection; when he arrives at the court of Medea's father, King Lamedon, he and Medea are smitten with one another at the same time: 'Here hertes bothe of on accord | Ben set to love, bot as tho | Ther mihten be no wordes mo' (*Confessio*, V, lines 3390–92). The relationship is based on mutual affection, not self-interest or gratitude. Once 'cupiditas' for the Golden Fleece comes into play, however, self-interest changes Jason so that he twice forswears. Though Jason makes his marriage vows to Medea conditional on his success in obtaining the Golden Fleece, he is legally bound to them as soon as he consummates their marriage.[34] When Jason publicly marries Creusa, he does so as a fully culpable bigamist, even though his first vows were clandestine. By giving Medea the romantic lead and by dedicating only two lines to Jason's sexual conquest of Creusa, 'For he another hath received | Which dowhter was to King Creon' (*Confessio*, V, lines 4194–5), Gower downplays the importance of sexual seduction and focuses instead on Jason's pride, which se-duces him into believing that he deserves what he has amassed through 'cupiditas'.

---

[33] Gower's readers would have interpreted the legal consequences for Jason's offspring from their own perspective. According to the English ecclesiastic statute 1 Salisbury 79 (1217 × 1219), a person cannot contract a marriage while being already married to another person. The first marriage creates for the second an impediment, which if wilfully ignored turns any children who might result from the second marriage into bastards. See Conor McCarthy, *Marriage in Medieval England* (Cambridge, 2004), pp. 153, 64. Even subsequently legitimated and very successful bastards, such as Katherine Swynford and John of Gaunt's children, the Beauforts, were barred from ever acquiring the royal dignity. See Chris Given-Wilson and Alice Curteis, *The Royal Bastards of Medieval England* (London, 1984), p. 150.

[34] Henry Ansgar Kelly, *Love and Marriage in the Age of Chaucer* (Ithaca, NY, and London, 1975), p. 206.

The *Tale of Jason and Medea* shows that pride leads kings to believe that there are no moral limitations to desire. Pride and 'cupiditas' appear closely related, since Jason abandons Medea for a king's daughter opportunely, just as he himself becomes king (*Confessio*, V, lines 4187–95). His actions speak volumes about his royal qualifications and foreshadow disaster for his family and kingdom. Jason loses his wife, his children, his new bride; and only Medea's timely escape to Athena's heavenly court prevents his turning murderer, too. Following Medea's infanticide, Jason is left 'in gret destresse' (*Confessio*, V, line 4222), with no heirs to bear his name and continue his lineage.

Still more astonishing than Jason's pride is his imprudence. In repudiating Medea, he not only dismisses his wisest and most devoted supporter but also misguidedly reduces her to 'bare life' – that is, the disenfranchised legal subject over which sovereignty can exercise its power of life and death. Jason fails to recognize that Medea represents a version of 'bare life' in name only, since her abilities are not limited by any juridical order but only by her own desire: 'Lo, what mihte eny man devise, | A womman schewe in eny wise | Mor hertly love in every stede, | Than Medea to Jason dede?' (*Confessio*, V, lines 4175–8). Gower emphasizes Jason's moral debts to Medea by enumerating the sacrifices she made on his behalf. Once Medea realizes that her love has been abused, however, she settles the score with unparalleled cruelty. As an empowered form of 'bare life', Medea stands symbolically for a king's most valuable supporters, whom the king cannot exclude from the juridical order without causing deep rifts in the body politic. Always in the se-ductive company of undeserved successes, Jason takes exception to legal and moral order by violating the law of marriage and the moral laws of hospitality, gratitude and prudence.

In turning both legality and morality into the political casualties of se-duction, Gower aligns them in a manner that would strain the sensibilities of modern law-makers but that certainly satisfied the medieval understanding of crimes as also being sins. As Stanley Fish has pointed out, 'morality is something to which [modern] law wishes to be related, but not too closely' because 'a legal system whose judgments perfectly meshed with our moral institutions would be thereby rendered superfluous.'[35] Nevertheless, morality complements legality in ways useful for the punishment of offenders. Even when criminals escape justice in a court of law, morality ensures their condemnation in the court of public opinion, which sometimes works as a compensatory arena to legal justice. This holds especially true for a medieval context, in which one could be repudiated legally and socially for 'mala fama'.[36] Ironically, Jason's credibility and chivalry are thrown into doubt by the people's gossip precisely at the moment when he publicly takes credit for them.

---

[35] Stanley Fish, *There Is No Such Thing as Free Speech, and It's a Good Thing, Too* (Oxford and New York, 1993), p. 141.

[36] See Thelma Fenster and Daniel Lord Smail, eds, *Fama: The Politics of Talk and Reputation in Medieval Europe* (Cornell, 2003).

Gower's strategic discussion of morality alongside law in book V of the *Confessio Amantis* unmasks se-duction as a multifaceted threat to sovereign power. If Jason's self-seduction prompts him to rid himself of his faithful wife, the faithless wife of King Athemas in the *Tale of Prixus and Helle* se-duces him into destroying his own lineage. Yno, the maidenly wife of the older, gullible King Athemas, finds herself in violation of both legal and moral order when she sets about eliminating her husband's heirs from a previous marriage. Like the goddess Thetis, she subjects her victim to a 'conspiracy of signs', in which her servants become her accomplices in perjury, destruction of the realm and attempted murder. No reason is given for Yno's behaviour: perhaps she wants the king's realm for her future heirs, or perhaps the motive is irrelevant because Gower focuses on kings who allow themselves to be led astray. After Yno destroys the country's harvest by having boiled corn sown in the fields, she has false priests swear that her husband's children are the reason for the famine because they upset the goddess Ceres (*Confessio*, V, lines 4292–306). Yno suggests that the king's heirs be destroyed to restore order and prosperity in the kingdom, a proposal to which the king grimly agrees: 'The king [...] | [...] seith that levere him is to chese | Hise children bothe for to lese, | Than him and al the remenant | Of hem whiche are aportenant | Unto the lond which he schal kepe (*Confessio*, V, lines 4313–18). The king's misplaced trust in his wife, combined with his desire to save his realm and himself, makes him fall victim to her malefic use of signs and invoke a state of exception on his offspring. Though the king appears here as an unsuspecting victim, his lack of control over his own household renders him blameworthy.[37]

Yno's many perjuries anticipate some of the later changes made to the 1352 Statute of Treason, especially with respect to 'treason by words' introduced in 1402 by Henry IV's judges.[38] Yno's words and actions qualify as treason because she incites the people against the king's eldest son and heir, Prixus, who barely escapes death through Juno's last-minute intervention. While Prixus is safely carried to the isle of Colchos by the golden ram, his sister is not so lucky: frightened by the watery ride on the ram's back, she falls in and drowns. Once again, the king's subjects are reduced to 'bare life' by the sovereign's state of exception. Yno's treason seems unlikely because of her gender and her position within the royal family. The wording of the 1352 Statute clearly designates a male perpetrator from outside the royal family as the main suspect in cases of treason: 'en cas quant homme face compasser ou ymaginer la mort nostre seignur le roi, ou ma dame sa compaigne, ou de lour fitz primer et heir; ou si homme violast la compaigne le roi; et la

---

[37] *The Governance of Kings and Princes* dedicates a whole book of advice to the king's correct governing of marriage and household.
[38] J. G. Bellamy (*The Law of Treason*) writes that 'in 1402 there occurred at least five such cases of treason four of which were connected with the affair of the false Richard ... In the king's bench the judges were of the opinion that the words were intended to excite the people against their king to the destruction of the realm' (p. 116).

eisne fille le roi nient marie; et la compaigne a l'eisne fitz et heir du roi …'.[39] In choosing a tale in which the king's wife is the offender, Gower warns against treason that might come from inside the royal family. He anticipates the revisions in the extended law of treason of 1397, which generalizes the language describing the perpetrator from 'any man' ('homme)' to 'everyone' ('chescune').[40]

In all three tales from book V, Gower downplays the significance of private, sexual conquests in relation to the more substantial crime of political se-duction, warning that se-duction never concerns just the king, but has wide-ranging and often disastrous consequences for the law and the 'bare life'. He contributes to the late-fourteenth-century legal imagination by presenting us with three tales in which political se-duction emerges in relationship to well-established crimes (perjury, false witnessing and false contract). Although it has become commonplace to identify the king's wife metaphorically with the king's realm,[41] Gower complicates this paradigm by presenting Medea and Yno as exceptional embodiments of 'bare life' that resist the king's state of exception. Both women escape punishment after perpetrating heinous crimes upon the king's realm. Gower's scenario of high treason, whereby the king's own wife is the traitor, is a sinister expansion of petty treason into the political realm. Verbalized for the first time in 1352, the provisions for petty treason included wives slaying their husbands.[42] When queens kill (or attempt to kill) the royal heirs instead, they cut deeply into the king's body politic.

Paradoxically, just as se-duction endangers sovereign power, it can also limit the king's liability for oppressing his subjects. By exposing the workings of se-duction as a perjurers' plot in the cases of Kings Lichomede and Athemas, Gower suggests that a sovereign might turn his subjects into 'bare life' unintentionally, or else pursue exceptionalism only as a last resort. One may think Lichomede too unwary of strangers or Athemas too trusting of his wife, but both are caught in such evil conspiracies that their fates arouse more pity than reproof, and the damage they inflict on their subjects appears accidental. Only Jason injures the 'bare life' deliberately. Ironically, he too is the victim of a 'conspiracy', though one of his own making: Jason is successful in every feat so that, in his pride, he becomes convinced of his invincibility and merit.

Once the se-duced king invokes exceptionalism, however, sovereignty itself is called into question: 'What is a king in his ligance', asks Gower in

---

[39] *The Parliament Rolls of Medieval England*, eds C. Given-Wilson, P. Brand, A. Curry, R. E. Horrox, G. Martin, W. M. Ormrod and J. R. S. Phillips (Leicester and Woodbridge, 2005) (hereafter cited as *PROME*), II, p. 239a: 'in the event that any man plots or plans the death of our lord the king, my lady his consort or their first son and heir; if any man rapes the king's spouse, the king's eldest daughter when unmarried or the spouse of the king's eldest son and heir …'. The crime of rape unmistakably genders the perpetrator as male.
[40] *PROME*, III, p. 351b.
[41] See, for instance, Wallace, *Chaucerian Polity*, and Staley, *Languages of Power*.
[42] *The Statutes of the Realm*, eds J. Caley et al., I, p. 319, quoted in *English Historical Documents: 1327–1485*, p. 403.

book VII, 'Wher there is no lawe in londe'? (*Confessio*, VII, lines 2698–9). Whenever the king's authority ('ligance') dissolves into anarchy, it becomes irrelevant whether his subjects have been intentionally injured or not. As Gower writes in *Mirour de l'Omme*, 'the king's sickness hurts those who are not responsible for the sin; for often the people suffer because the king's obviously outrageous sins are offensive to God.'[43] Se-duction magnifies the king's shortcomings because it incites him to commit other sins against which *Fürstenspiegel* warn, such as arrogance, imprudence and ingratitude. In the political arena, se-duction resembles a snowball which sets in motion an avalanche of wrongdoings on both sides: the side of the false witnesses and perjurers who aid the seducer and the side of the king who takes exception to the juridical order. If sin is part disorder, as Aquinas writes in *Summa Theologiae*, then by encouraging an array of crimes and sins and stripping political subjects down to 'bare life', se-duction promotes social and political disorder.[44] Since se-ductions cause the suspension of law in all three tales, Gower obliquely advocates the need for making the sovereign obedient to the law and denying him the privilege of imposing the 'state of exception'.

Perhaps Gower saw the subordination of the sovereign to the law as a solution for offsetting the disorder in England, where Richard II and his subjects were often at odds with one another. Lee Patterson has described the 1380s as 'a time of disheartening turbulence for England [...] a nation threatened by enemies from without and dissension from within'.[45] After 1381 Richard engaged in a long and bitter struggle with his established aristocracy, whom he sought to replace with a 'new courtier nobility' of his own creation.[46] Nigel Saul writes that Richard and his senior magnates lacked both a common vision and a political understanding with regard to the distribution of patronage.[47] Richard's partiality toward men of humble origins such as Simon Burley and Michael de la Pole, who were richly rewarded for their services, and his association with men like Robert Vere, the Earl of Oxford, incensed the more established nobility (the Appellants), who manufactured a story of Richard's political se-duction by his evil councillors to justify their opposition.[48]

Gower offers competing perspectives on the se-duction of kings: Lichomede and Athemas are unsuspecting victims, while Jason is clearly guilty. Though all seducers operate via false oaths and witnesses, they are depicted in turn as illustrious outsiders (Thetis), scheming insiders (Yno), or even the king's own failings (Jason's pride and imprudence). One may speculate that the victimized kings represent earlier, sympathetic depictions of Richard, while Jason stands for later condemnatory portrayals of Richard,

---

[43] John Gower, *Mirour de l'Omme*, trans. William Burton Wilson, rev. Nancy Wilson Van Baak (East Lansing, 1992), p. 298.
[44] St Thomas Aquinas, *Summa Theologiae* – vol. 25, sin: 1a2æ. 71–80, ed. John Fearon, O. P. (Cambridge, 2006), 1a, 2æ. 72, 8.
[45] Patterson, *Chaucer and the Subject of History*, p. 156.
[46] Anthony Tuck, *Richard II and the English Nobility* (New York, 1974), p. 86.
[47] Nigel Saul, *Richard II* (New Haven, CT, and London, 1997), p. 129.
[48] Christopher Fletcher, *Richard II: Manhood, Youth, and Politics, 1377–99* (Oxford, 2008), p. 171.

in which writers such as Gower imputed disregard for the law to him.[49] Of course, the fictive se-ductions in *Confessio* V cannot be aligned with any specific historical events, but, as he revised his work, Gower appears to have commented on aspects of Richard's kingship with which he had become disillusioned.[50] One of these aspects was Richard's resistance to counsel that did not originate with his inner circle of favourites. Not surprisingly, all se-ductions take place in the absence of counsel: Jason wilfully acts of his own accord, while Athemas and Lichomede simply lack the opportunity to discover the truth.

Throughout *Confessio* V political se-duction is clearly differentiated from flattery. Flatterers operate within the king's own reality, so that the king believes 'that all is well, whatevere he doth', as Gower himself states later (*Confessio*, V, line 2195). Se-ducers, however, create or perform an alternative reality for the king by subjecting him to a conspiracy of signs made up of lies, false oaths and phoney identities. As Deborah Lyn Houk has pointed out, 'the performance of seduction entails substituting appearances for prior reality, thereby creating a new space of reality that encompasses seducer, seduced, and all those who believe it to be real.'[51] In this new reality, Gower's kings appear isolated and easy to manipulate into imposing the state of exception on their subjects.

Perhaps it was the 'bare life' that Gower worried about the most. Textual evidence supports this view: in 1391 Gower replaced the *Confessio*'s tribute to Richard with a prayer for the state of the realm.[52] For a poet who understood himself as crying out with the voice of the people, the king's se-duction was not a private offence but a public crime that threatened the social and political order.

---

[49] Saul, *Richard II*, p. 436.
[50] *Ibid.*, p. 437.
[51] Deborah Lyn Houk, 'The Politics of Seduction: Comparing Balzac and Sand' (unpublished PhD dissertation, Univ. of Pennsylvania, Philadelphia, 1997), p. 204.
[52] See Macaulay, ii, p. 2; iii, pp. 468–75. G. B. Stow has written on the deletion of the dedication to Richard; see 'Richard II in John Gower's *Confessio Amantis*: some historical perspectives', *Medievalia*, 16 (1993), 3–31. See also the essay by Saul in this volume.

Chapter 11

The Fifteen Stars, Stones and Herbs: Book VII of the *Confessio Amantis* and its Afterlife

TAMARA F. O'CALLAGHAN

As M. A. Manzalaoui has noted, to choose book VII of John Gower's *Confessio Amantis* as a topic is to load oneself with the handicap of a subject most critics have found particularly dull.[1] Furthermore, the passage from book VII describing the fifteen stars, stones and herbs is a subject most critics have entirely dismissed. With the exception of Patricia Eberle,[2] those few scholars who have deigned to comment on the passage find it to be simply pedantic.[3] While each of the previous six books of the *Confessio* focuses on one of the deadly sins, book VII is immediately a significant digression, for it does not discuss lechery, as expected, but describes 'al that to a king belongeth' (*Confessio*, VI, line 2413).[4] The book is, in fact, a 'mirror for princes', a handbook of instruction for a young king;[5] thus it elaborates the theme of kingship set out initially in the Prologue. Why, then, does Gower include a seemingly obscure and uninspiring passage on the fifteen stars, fifteen stones and fifteen herbs? How does such a passage fit into the poem's primary theme of kingship and secondary theme of love? By exploring the passage in light of the scientific treatises of the period, examining other references to stars,

---

[1] M. A. Manzalaoui, '"Noght in the Registre of Venus": Gower's English mirror for princes', in *Medieval Studies for J. A. W. Bennett*, ed. P. L. Heyworth (Oxford, 1981), p. 159.
[2] Patricia Eberle, 'Miniatures as evidence of reading in a manuscript of the *Confessio Amantis* (Pierpont Morgan Ms. M. 126)', in *John Gower: Recent Readings*, ed. R. F. Yeager (Kalamazoo, MI, 1989), esp. pp. 321–5. I must express my thanks to Patricia Eberle for encouraging me to pursue this topic and, in particular, the illumination sequence in Pierpont Morgan MS M.126.
[3] George L. Hamilton, 'Some sources of the seventh book of Gower's *Confessio Amantis*', *MP*, 9 (1912), 343, and 'Studies in the sources of Gower', *JEGP*, 26 (1927), 511–13; P. J. Heather, 'Precious stones in the Middle-English verse of the fourteenth century', *Folklore*, 42 (1931), 224–6 and 244–5; and George C. Fox, *The Mediaeval Sciences in the Works of John Gower* (New York, 1966), pp. 80–81. Only Kate Harris notes a limited interest in the passage by subsequent readers of Gower's text, suggesting that a few may have read the poem for 'lore' rather than for love stories, but she is somewhat dismissive of the significance; 'The Longleat House extracted manuscript of Gower's *Confessio Amantis*', in *Middle English Poetry: Texts and Traditions, Essays in Honour of Derek Pearsall*, ed. A. J. Minnis (York, 2001), pp. 77–8 and 88–90.
[4] Translations of the Latin poetry are supplied by John Gower, *The Latin Verses in the 'Confessio Amantis': An Annotated Translation*, eds Siân Echard and Claire Fanger, with A. G. Rigg (East Lansing, MI, 1991).
[5] Manzalaoui, '"Noght in the Registre of Venus"', pp. 159–83.

stones and herbs as they are found throughout the poem and determining the reception of the passage in the centuries immediately following Gower's death we begin to understand the importance such a presentation held for its author and his audience.

The theme of kingship and good governance is established in the Prologue and pervades the entire work. Book VII provides the greatest elaboration on this theme, resulting in the seeming divergence from the poem's principal narrative. It is presented as Aristotle's teaching to Alexander the Great and focuses on the two types of knowledge needed to be an effective ruler: theoretical knowledge, including theology, physics and mathematics, with a brief digression on the four elements, humours and parts of the world; and practical knowledge, including the five moral principles or points of policy – truth, liberality, justice, pity and charity. In this scheme, astronomy and astrology are the last of the four branches of mathematics, after arithmetic, geometry and music. Book VII is based on two major works: Brunetto Latini's *Li Livres dou Tresors*, in which mention is made of Alexander's education by Calistre and Aristotle, and the *Secretum secretorum*, a letter supposedly written by Aristotle to Alexander, instructing him on the proper behaviour for a king.[6] However, neither source text refers to the fifteen stars, stones and herbs which the *Confessio* lists at the end of a long discussion on astronomy. The catalogue is straightforward and didactic in nature, yet no one has adequately explained why Gower chose to include it or how the passage relates to the poem as a whole. G. C. Macaulay cites as the source the treatise *Liber Hermetis de xv stellis et de xv lapidus et xv herbis, xv figures, etc.*, and this has been generally accepted: George Hamilton notes that Gower may have translated either Jofroi de Watreford's French version of the *Secretum secretorum* or some other Latin source, but does not elaborate.[7] In fact, one of the difficulties in analyzing Gower's discussion of the fifteen stars, fifteen stones and fifteen herbs is determining precisely what source or sources he could have used.

Macaulay's citation of an Hermetical tract on the stars, stones and herbs refers to one of a number of extant astrological treatises attributed to Hermes the Egyptian, or Hermes Trismegistus. Works ascribed to him can be traced back to the first century AD, and many philosophers who followed him claimed that he wrote thousands of volumes of mystic works. Only seventeen or eighteen fragments now survive under the general rubric of the Hermetic corpus, of which several tracts describe the relation of herbs to the planets, signs of the zodiac, or thirty-six decans – that is, a division of ten parts, or ten degrees, of the zodiacal sign.[8] These treatises attribute magical virtues to plants, include prayers to be repeated when plucking the herb

---

[6] Macaulay, p. 522; Hamilton, 'Some sources', 334.

[7] Hamilton, 'Studies', 511–12.

[8] The association of specific plants with the heavenly bodies is a particularly old tradition, dating to sometime between the second century BC and the first century AD. Although the individual association of plants with the sun, moon, planets, signs of the zodiac and the decans was common, their association with the fixed stars was much rarer. See Jim Tester, *A History of Western Astrology* (Suffolk, 1987), especially pp. 24 and 62–3.

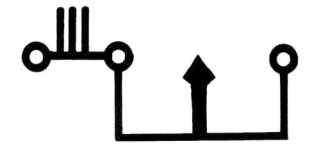

Figure 1. *Carectus* of the Pleiades. Book of Enoch: Oxford, Bodleian MS. e Museo 52 (xv, English). Drawn by John Hines.

and explain the healing powers of the astronomical figures of the decans when they are engraved on stones.[9] The particular treatise on the fifteen stars, stones and herbs, and the fifteen images to be engraved on the stones, is usually attributed to Hermes, but occasionally ascribed to another mystic writer, Enoch the patriarch.[10]

One such manuscript attributed to Enoch is the fifteenth-century Oxford, Bodleian Library MS. e Museo 52, ff. 44–47. The treatise presents five parallel columns: four with the headings 'stellae', 'lapides', 'herbae' and 'carectus', and a final column describing the 'virtus' of the four: for example, the second row refers to the constellation, the Pleiades, with the corresponding gemstone of crystal, herb of fennel, and the 'character', sometimes referred to as the star's sigil or 'occult sign' (Figure 1). All possess the power to gather demons and the spirits of the dead, call the winds and make what is hidden and secret known to the bearer. Additional details under the names of many of the stars refer to the individual star's cardinal position and the sign of the zodiac in which it appears. Other manuscripts, such as the early-fourteenth-century MS BL Harley 1612, fols 15–18[v], describe each star's 'occult sign', which must be carved on the gemstone when the constellation affecting its operation was favourably situated in the sky. In this way, the influence of the desired star could be maintained even when the star was not present.[11] One of the Hermetical manuscripts cited by Macaulay as a source for Gower's description of the fifteen stars, stones and herbs, Oxford, Bodleian Library MS Ashmole 341, is very similar to the Oxford 'Book of Enoch' manuscript: dated after the mid-thirteenth century, it too provides diagrams of each star's corresponding 'carectus.' The other manuscript to which Macaulay refers, Oxford, Bodleian Library MS Ashmole 1471, is dated late fourteenth century and provides no diagrams or drawings of any kind.

How influential was this work attributed to Hermes or Enoch in the Middle Ages? At least eight manuscripts from the thirteenth and fourteenth centuries survive, suggesting that the concept of the fifteen stars, stones, herbs and images was well received.[12] Although he often disagrees with

---

[9] Lynn Thorndike, *A History of Magic and Experimental Science During the First Thirteen Centuries of Our Era*, 4 vols, 2nd edn (New York, 1923; rpt 1929), vol. 1, pp. 287–92.

[10] Thorndike, *A History of Magic*, vol. 1, p. 340. MSS ascribed to Hermes: BL MS Harley 80; BL MS Sloane 3847; BL MS Royal 12 C XVIII; Berlin MS 963, fol. 105; Vienna MS 5216, 15th c., fols 63[r]–6[v]. MSS ascribed to Enoch: BL MS Harley 1612, fol. 15[4]; Wolfenbuttel MS 2725, 14th c., fols 83–94[v]; Bibliothèque Nationale (BN) MS 13014, 14th c., fols 42–5.

[11] Joan Evans, *Magical Jewels of the Middle Ages and the Renaissance Particularly in England* (Oxford, 1922), pp. 97 and 108–9.

[12] Lynn Thorndike and Pearl Kibre, *A Catalogue of Incipits of Medieval Scientific Writings in Latin* (Cambridge, MA, 1937).

Hermes on matters of detail, Albertus Magnus, the thirteenth-century philosopher, acknowledges that Hermes, of all the ancients, gives the most probable reason for the power of stones. In his *Mineralium*, Albertus concurs that heavenly power operates through the stars and constellations to impress powers into every specific form of stone.[13] These powers may also be attributed to various herbs, for 'si verum est, mirabile est valde, et absque dubio coelesti virtuti deputandum; quas Hermes mirabiles esse dicit in lapidus et etiam in plantis'.[14] Such powers must be well understood for stones and herbs to accomplish the marvellous by means of natural magic.

The works of two other philosophers, Heinrich Cornelius Agrippa (1486–1535) and Marsilio Ficino (1433–1499), demonstrate the extent to which the theory of the fifteen stars, stones and herbs enjoyed popularity in the Middle Ages. In *The Medieval Sciences in the Works of John Gower*, George Fox makes a cursory reference to the list of fifteen stars, stones and herbs that parallels Gower's own catalogue almost exactly.[15] The passage can be found in Agrippa's fifteenth-century work *De occulta philosophia*. However, it is much more complete than Fox leads one to believe, for it includes the earthly animals and herbs governed by the zodiacal signs as well as the stars, stones and herbs. The differences between the two lists are not great, the most significant being the inversion of the stars *Algol* and *Aldeboran* and the position of *Venenas* as the eleventh star on Gower's list and the eighth on Agrippa's. Nevertheless, Agrippa cites the Arab mathematician, Thābit ibn Qurrah al-Harrānī (836–901), as his source, as well as Hermes.[16] In his late-fifteenth-century treatise *De vita triplici* Ficino also refers to Thābit ibn Qurrah al-Harrānī as the source for his list of stars with their corresponding stones and herbs.[17] In addition, he includes the zodiacal position of the stars within his catalogue. Ficino lists only fourteen stars because he combines the star 'Alderboran' with 'Alhaiot' and is missing stones for Andromeda/Algol, Wing of the Crow and 'Alcameth'. Otherwise, his choice of names and ordering of the stars, stones and herbs is closer to Agrippa's than to Gower's.

Gower refers to Thābit ibn Qurrah in connection with sorcery rather than astronomy. In his catalogue of magicians and works on magic in book VI Gower includes 'thymage | of Thebith' (*Confessio*, VI, lines 1420–21), the full title of which is *De imaginibus*, a treatise describing the fabrication and use of statuettes for conjuration.[18] Gower initially claims, however, that the

---

[13] Albertus Magnus, *Mineralium*, in *Opera Omnium*, ed. August Borgnet (Paris, 1890), book 2, tr. 1, c. 2–3.
[14] Albertus Magnus, *Mineralium*, book 2, tr. 2, c. 10. 'If it is true, it is very wonderful, and without doubt to be attributed to a heavenly power, those things which Hermes declares to be marvellous in stones and also in plants.'
[15] Fox, *Mediaeval Sciences*, p. 81.
[16] Henry Cornelius Agrippa, *De occulta philosophia*, ed. Karl A. Nowotny (Graz, Austria, 1967), book 1, chap. 32.
[17] Marsilio Ficino, *De vita triplici, libri tres*, ed. Martin Plessner (Hildesheim, Germany, 1978), book 3, chap. 8.
[18] Thābit ibn Qurrah al-Harrānī, *De imaginibus*, in *The Astronomical Works of Thabit b. Qurra*, ed. Francis J. Carmody (Berkeley, CA, 1960).

source of his discussion on the fifteen stars, stones and herbs is a magician, Nectanabus:

> Among the whiche forth withal
> Nectanabus in special,
> Which was an Astronomien
> And ek a gret Magicien,
> And undertake hath thilke emprise
> To Alisandre in his apprise
> As of Magique naturel
> To knowe, enformeth him somdel
> Of certain sterres what thei mene;
> Of whiche, he seith, ther ben fifteen,
> And sondrily to everich on
> A gras belongeth and a Ston,
> Wherof men worchen many a wonder
> To sette thing bothe up and under.
> (*Confessio*, VII, lines 1295–1308)

Accordingly, each of the fifteen stars has an associated herb and gemstone which allow man to work wonders through natural magic. Gower cites Hermes as source only at the end of this passage:

> Thus have I seid hou thei be founded,
> Of every sterre in special,
> Which hath his herbe and Ston withal,
> As Hermes in his bokes olde
> Witnesse berth of that I tolde. (*Confessio*, VII, lines 1434–8)

He later refers to Hermes as the astronomer with the greatest experience in the science (*Confessio* VII, lines 1476–80).[19] Although there is no extant evidence that Nectanabus wrote a tract on the fifteen stars, stones and herbs, Gower's reference to him as his source is not surprising given the presentation of Nectanabus in the *Confessio Amantis*.[20] In book VI, Genius tells Amans the tale of Nectanabus, a renowned magician who, upon seeing queen Olimpias, greatly desired her (*Confessio*, VI, lines 1789–2366). He prophesied to her that she would beget a child by a god, Amos, and then, in the shape of Amos, impregnated her with Alexander the Great. Aristotle taught the boy philosophy, and Nectanabus astronomy. One night, while observing the stars, Nectanabus prophesied his own death at the hands of his son. To prove the magician wrong, Alexander threw him from the tower to his death, thereby fulfilling the prophecy. By casting Nectanabus in the role of Alexander's teacher of astronomy, Gower not only portrays him as extremely knowledgeable about the heavens and the stars, but also establishes him as

---

[19] It is important to note that Gower does not retract Nectanabus as the source for the passage, but merely adds Hermes. Consequently, I disagree with Manzalaoui's claim that, at this point, Gower 'steps out of the story and gives his true source' (Manzalaoui, '"Noght in the Registre of Venus"', p. 166).

[20] On Nectanabus, see also Knapp's essay in this volume.

a reliable authority on the fifteen stars, stones and herbs presented in book VII as part of Alexander the Great's education.

But why fifteen stars? Gower is not the only vernacular writer to make mention of them – they appear in *Paradiso*, where Dante emphasizes their brightness:

> Let him who would conceive what now I saw
> (And let him hold the image in his mind,
> While I am speaking, firmly as a rock)
> Imagine, first of all, the fifteen stars
> That are so bright they pierce the densest air.[21]

The number fifteen is used not for any associated 'magical' quality but because of astronomical tradition. In their analyses of the stars and their properties, both Agrippa and Ficino emphasize the superiority of the fifteen stars: Agrippa describes them as 'stellae insigniores', more eminent than the rest,[22] and Ficino notes that the stars selected are the 'maiores', or greater ones, which astrologers say 'have learned from Mercury and these have great authority'.[23] Fifteen of the fixed stars somehow exceed all the others in terms of virtue. This idea seems to have originated with Ptolemy, who considered these fifteen stars to be of the first magnitude because they are the brightest and, therefore, the most visible.[24] A chart in his *Almagest* indicates the comparative declinations of the 'easily recognizable' stars as recorded by the school of Timocharis, by Hipparchus and by Ptolemy himself.[25] Not surprisingly, these are the same stars described by Gower, Agrippa and Ficino. It seems very probable that Ptolemic tradition has determined the number, especially given Agrippa's and Ficino's references to the elevated status of the fifteen stars. Ptolemy believed these particular stars to be superior to all others, and succeeding philosophers may have extrapolated from his comments and attributed magical powers to them, thereby making them spiritually as well as physically superior.

Thus Gower's use of the fifteen stars, stones and herbs is less surprising than it initially appears: when viewed within the context of astronomical tradition, his entire discussion begins to take on a logical form. After describing the seven planets and their natures (*Confessio*, VII, lines 721–946), Gower goes on to discuss the twelve signs of the zodiac and their appropriate stars, only omitting the constellation for Aries (*Confessio*, VII, lines 955–1270). He then lists the fifteen stars with their corresponding stones and herbs (*Confessio*, VII, lines 1281–438). The structure is very similar to Agrippa's section on astronomy in book I of *De occulta philosophia*,[26] which

---

[21] Alighieri Dante, *Paradise*, in *The Divine Comedy*, trans. Kenneth MacKenzie (London, 1979), Canto 13, lines 1–5.
[22] Agrippa, *De occulta philosophia*, book 1, chap. 32.
[23] Ficino, *De vita triplici*, book 3, chap. 8.
[24] Thorndike, *A History of Magic*, p. 340, n. 1.
[25] Ptolemy, *Almagest*, trans. G. J. Toomer (London, 1984), pp. 330–32.
[26] Significantly, Agrippa is viewed as a figure who does not necessarily pursue 'occult' knowledge for the right reasons, but rather for the 'demonic' purposes about which Gower

devotes a chapter to each of the planets and describes the zodiacal signs and their powers, as well as the fifteen stars, stones and herbs, within a single chapter. Although considerably longer, the order of Agrippa's discussion on astronomy is the same as Gower's.

However, stars, stones and herbs are not major motifs in the *Confessio Amantis*: Gower only occasionally mentions their influence. In the tale of Jason and Medea both stars and herbs have magical effects.[27] As a sorceress, Medea calls upon the stars to help her cast her spells (*Confessio*, V, line 3978–9). She also uses herbs as part of her 'art magique' (*Confessio*, V, line 3947) as well as medicinally to soothe Jason after a long journey (*Confessio*, V, line 3947) and to heal the wounds of his father, Eson (*Confessio*, V, lines 4161–6). In the tale of Ulysses and Telegonus Genius describes Ulysses as the perfect ruler, complete in his knowledge of all things, including the 'strengthe of herbes' (*Confessio*, VI, line 1408). Genius also acknowledges the power of stones in a lengthy description of the Philosopher's Stone, a mineral which

> Transformeth al the ferste kynde
> And makth hem able to conceive
> Through his vertu, and to receive
> Both in substance and in figure
> Of gold and selver the nature. (*Confessio*, IV, lines 2560–64)

He does not doubt the stone's power, but considers the craft lost because present-day seekers of the Philosopher's Stone desire riches rather than the wisdom the mineral promises (*Confessio*, IV, lines 2590ff.). The connection between magic and stones is further complicated by the example of the prudent serpent, the Aspidis, who bears the 'Ston noblest of alle', the Carbuncle, 'in his hed' (*Confessio*, I, lines 463–7).

This episode inverts the usual 'magical' abilities of the stone: in this case, it is not the gemstone which bestows the power to enchant, but rather another type of 'carectus' employed by man for the purpose of obtaining the jewel. The asp prevents the spell, 'carecte', of men who attempt to steal his jewel from having any effect by placing one ear flat against the ground and plugging the other ear with his tail (*Confessio*, I, lines 468–77). Thus, long before book VII, the reader is introduced to the unusual term 'caractus' and its association with magical power. Gower is clearly familiar with this unusual technical scientific term not commonly found in Middle English.[28]

Gower's references to the magical abilities of the stars, stones and herbs are significant in that they represent part of a larger theme, the role of magic in love. Book VI, which supposedly focuses on the sin of gluttony in love, is also devoted to the influence of magic over lovers. Genius warns Amans of the plight of the desperate lover who will use any means to gain his beloved, regardless of the folly or sin involved:

---

cautions in his poem; see D. P. Walter, *Spiritual and Demonic Magic from Ficino to Campanella* (London, 1958), p. 75.

[27] On Jason and Medea, see also Boboc's essay in this volume.

[28] In fact, Gower appears to be the only author in Middle English to use it.

> Riht as he secheth Sorcerie
> Of hem that ben Magiciens,
> Riht so of the Naturiens
> Upon the Sterres from above
> His weie he secheth unto love,
> Als fer as he hem understondeth.
> In many a sundry wise he fondeth;
> He makth ymage, he makth sculpture,
> He makth writinge, he makth figure,
> He makth his calculations,
> He makth his demonstraciouns;
> His houres of Astronomie
> He kepeth as for that partie
> Which longeth to thinspeccion
> Of love and his affeccion;
> He wolde into the helle seche
> The devel himselve to beseche,
> If that he wiste forto spede,
> To gete of love his lusti mede. (*Confessio*, VI, lines 1336–54)

Such a lover views the magical arts merely as a method for obtaining his own ends, not as a skill through which greater knowledge may be sought. There are no limits to which he will not go, for he would seek the devil in hell if the demon could help him. Genius offers four cautionary tales: the tale of Ulysses and Telegonus, in which Ulysses uses magic to flee the sorceress, Circe, only to be later killed by their son (*Confessio*, VI, lines 1391–788); the tale of Nectanabus, in which the magician uses the art of shape-shifting in order to impregnate Queen Olimpias with his child, who he later prophesies will bring about his own death (*Confessio*, VI, lines 1789–2366); the tale of Zoroaster, in which Zoroaster learns the art of magic only to be slain by a Syriac king (*Confessio*, VI, lines 2367–83); and the tale of Saul and the Witch, in which Saul forbids sorcery, but secretly practises it himself, thereby bringing about his rapid death (*Confessio*, VI, lines 2384–90).

Gower's attitude toward magic is one of belief and caution. He clearly does not doubt that the magical arts exist, for he makes mention of many of them; however, he repeatedly warns against using them for selfish purposes. A Latin verse preceding the four tales of magic describes two types of sorcery – natural magic and 'black' magic:

> When Love is goaded, he will dare to do
> What rising pleasure orders, fearing nought.
> The lover tries in turn the power of the plants,
> And all that stars and strength of hell may do.
> The evil task that God won't aid him with
> The fool performs with devil's conjurings.
> He sets his nets, he's heedless for himself,
> Provided he can catch the naked bird.[29]

---

[29] Gower, *The Latin Verses in the 'Confessio Amantis'*, eds Echard and Fanger, p. 71.

Natural magic refers to the powers inherent in objects such as stars, stones and herbs. Although, as Echard and Fanger note, Gower makes clear in this verse and in the main narrative that powers of nature and the elements can be misused, he does not take a firm line in the poem against all magic.[30] He warns of the perils of its misuse – for example, linking Nectanabus's death directly to his abuse of magic: 'Nectanabus his craft miswente, | So it misfell him er he wente' (*Confessio*, VI, lines 2360–61). Magic, especially in the form of necromancy, can easily allow a man 'to do folie' (*Confessio*, VI, lines 2364–6). Nevertheless, Gower devotes much of book VII to the natural magic that an ideal king needs to rule effectively. Alexander learned astronomy to help him govern his empire (*Confessio*, VII, lines 1277–80), and so, by using the magic transmitted by the stars to such earthly objects as stones and herbs, a man may better judge his course of actions. Such magical arts are only permitted if they are employed 'to good entente' and 'be weie of kinde' (*Confessio*, VI, lines 1305 and 1304) – that is, by way of nature or 'natural' magic.

The illuminations of Pierpont Morgan MS M. 126, a late-fifteenth-century English manuscript of the *Confessio Amantis*, support the supposition that Gower's medieval audience was familiar not only with magic but also with the concept of the fifteen stars, stones and herbs.[31] With 108 illuminations,[32] it is the most richly decorated manuscript of the poem. Although more than half of the fifty extant manuscripts of the *Confessio Amantis* have some illumination, most have only two miniatures: an illustration of Nebuchadnezzar's Dream of Precious Metals (cf. *Confessio*, Prol., lines 604–24) and a picture of Amans kneeling before Genius (cf. beginning of book I).[33] Only Oxford New College MS 266 and Pierpont Morgan MS M. 126 have a full sequence of miniatures: those of the New College manuscript are limited to scenes from Gower's narrative exempla and total only thirty-two; thirteen are missing, having been cut out of the manuscript at some point in its history, and the remaining ones are in poor condition.[34] In contrast, the Pierpont Morgan manuscript has an extraordinarily full pictorial sequence illustrating scenes from the poem's frame, the narrative exempla and, most curiously, the education of Alexander the Great by Aristotle as described in book VII of the poem.

Pierpont Morgan MS M.126 is remarkable for the unusual distribution of its miniatures as well as their number: these features have been docu-

---

[30] *Ibid.*, pp. 70–71, n. 102.
[31] Certainly, his original royal patron, Richard II, appears to have had an interest in the occult sciences, although to exactly what degree is the matter of some debate; see Hilary M. Carey, *Courting Disaster: Astrology at the English Court and University in the Later Middle Ages* (New York, 1992), pp. 92–116.
[32] There should be 110 illuminations, but the miniatures on f. 48v ('The Tale of Constantine', II, lines 3187–496) and fol. 171v ('Cruelty of Leontius', *Confessio*, VII, lines 3267–94) are missing.
[33] Jeremy Griffiths, '*Confessio Amantis*: the poem and its pictures', in *Gower's 'Confessio Amantis': Responses and Reassessments*, ed. A. J. Minnis (Oxford, 1983), pp. 163–78.
[34] Peter C. Braeger, 'The illustrations in New College Ms. 266 for Gower's conversion tales', in *John Gower: Recent Readings*, ed. R. F. Yeager (Kalamazoo, MI, 1989), pp. 275–310.

naturalis operacione specialius contenut·

Pon sundry cwacion
Stant sondry operacion
Som worcheth this som worcheth that
The fyir is hoot in his astate
And brenneth what he may atteyne
The water may the fyre restreyne
Which is moyst and cold also
Of other thing it fareth right so
Upon this erthe amoung us here
And for to speke in this matiere
Upon the heuene a man may fynde
The sterres ben of sondry kynde
And worchen many sondry thynges

Figure 2. Pierpont Morgan Ms. M.126, f. 158r. Nectanabus instructing Alexander the Great.

mented by Eberle. Of the 106 surviving illuminations, book VII contains fifty-four, just over half.[35] This is an important exception both to the general rule that illustrations tend to be concentrated in the earlier part of secular manuscripts and to the tradition of distribution in illuminated *Confessio* manuscripts. Book VII also concentrates the largest number in the penultimate book. The large number is not even proportional to the length of book VII; book V, the longest of the eight books, has only thirteen miniatures, while book VI, the shortest, has three. Even more surprisingly, subsection iv of book VII, the section devoted exclusively to astronomy, contains thirty of the fifty-four miniatures allotted to book VII.[36] Given the location and cost of producing so many illuminations, one must assume that the content of book VII was of great importance to the patron who requested the manuscript.

The reader is immediately aware of the ease with which one can locate book VII in this particular manuscript. From the Prologue to the end of book VI illuminations filling the width of one column and the length of twelve lines appear every four pages or so. By book VII, illuminations are much more frequent, culminating with the four to six smaller illuminations per page within the section on astronomy. It appears that the patron of this manuscript did not intend simply to read the poem through in order, but wished to locate this section quickly, and without question the attraction lay in the astronomical portions of the text. The first twelve miniatures of the section are fairly standard depictions of the twelve signs of the zodiac, each set outdoors with the appropriate constellation shown in the sky. The next miniature (Figure 2) marks the division in the text between the zodiacal signs and the fifteen stars, stones and herbs. It shows Nectanabus teaching Alexander not in a library surrounded by books but in a field. Alexander is dressed as a king, with an elaborate crown, robe and sceptre, reinforcing the fact that this book is a mirror for princes.[37] Nectanabus is directing Alexander's gaze to an open field covered with thirty-two multi-coloured jewels and twenty-two varieties of plant. Above are twenty-two stars, the sun and the moon. Thus far in the text no mention has been made of the stars with their corresponding stones and herbs, but, with this miniature, the illuminator has prepared the reader for the passage to come.

The next three folios contain individual illuminations of each of the fifteen stars, stones and herbs (Figure 3). Again, each miniature is set outdoors. The stars are fairly large, elaborately stylized in gold leaf, and occupy the upper left corner of each picture. The stones are all uniform in shape but varied in colour, and are centrally located. The herbs appear in the bottom right corner of each miniature, each drawn as accurately as space permitted (Figure 4). These illuminations are eye-catching and neatly mark off the transitions in

---

[35] I thank Martha Driver and William M. Voelkle (curator of medieval and renaissance manuscripts at the Pierpont Morgan Library) for help in determining a definitive number of extant illuminations.

[36] Eberle, 'Miniatures as evidence of reading', pp. 320–22.

[37] The significance of Alexander's regalia in relation to other illuminations depicting crowned figures in the manuscript and to the theme of kingship in the poem is part of another study in progress.

Figure 3. Pierpont Morgan Ms. M.126, f. 158v. The first five of the fifteen stars, stones, and herbs.

Figure 4. (Pierpont Morgan MS. M. 126, f. 158v (left column, bottom). The Pleiades (Clota), Crystal, Fennel. (Not to scale.)

the text from one set of stars/stones/herbs to the next. The patron's request that such a passage be so heavily illuminated is most likely to originate from a desire to learn of the magical powers held by stones and herbs by virtue of their particular star. If, as Martha Driver has argued,[38] the patron of Pierpont Morgan MS M.126 was Elizabeth Woodville, the wife of Edward IV, it seems she had a serious interest in the occult sciences.[39]

How, then, does this series of astronomical illuminations fit into the overall pictorial plan of the Pierpont Morgan manuscript? Surprisingly, the iconography appears in other illuminations throughout the manuscript. Stylized stars drawn in liquid gold appear in miniatures illustrating outdoor scenes from episodes throughout the *Confessio Amantis*. Excluding the fifty-four miniatures in book VII, eighteen of the remaining fifty-four in the manuscript have gold stars set against azure-blue skies.[40] The second illumination in the manuscript and the first to illustrate stars is that of Arion bringing concord to the world. In the Prologue, Gower mourns for the days when Arion's harp brought harmony to the prelapsarian world of man (*Confessio*, Prol., lines 1053–65). The accompanying illumination shows Arion playing

---

[38] Martha Driver, 'Printing the *Confessio Amantis*: Caxton's edition in context', in *Re-Visioning Gower*, ed. R. F. Yeager (Asheville, NC, 1998), pp. 282ff.

[39] Carey briefly discusses Elizabeth's association with royal astrologers in *Courting Disaster*, pp. 156 and 161–2.

[40] A full analysis of all eighteen illuminations as well as of the other illuminations depicting stars in book VII is not possible here, so discussion will be limited to a representational sampling.

Figure 5. (a) Pierpont Morgan Ms. M.126, f. 8v. Venus, the God of Love, and Amans. (b) Pierpont Morgan Ms. M.126, f. 77v. Ulysses feigning madness. (Not to scale.)

his harp under fourteen stars as two men shake hands and a dog nuzzles a rabbit, a wolf nuzzles a sheep and a lion nuzzles a deer: even though stars are not mentioned in the textual description of the scene, the harmony found on earth is depicted as extending to the heavens. The only miniature to illustrate the poem's frame depicts Venus, the God of Love, and Amans outdoors. As the God of Love's fiery dart pierces Amans's exposed heart, ten stars shine down as if portents of his fate (Figure 5a). Many illustrations include stars even when the episode of the poem illustrated takes place during the day. In the miniature from the Tale of Nauplus and Ulysses, Ulysses is ploughing a field with two foxes and sowing it with salt in an unsuccessful attempt to feign madness and avoid fighting in the Trojan war (Figure 5b). The poem states explicitly that Ulysses performs this peculiar act 'erli the morwe day' (*Confessio*, IV, line 1829) – early the next day – however, sixteen stars depicted in the sky overhead suggest that Ulysses is fated to fight the Trojans. Stars gleam in the sky as Dido commits suicide on a stony shore and Aeneas sails away from Carthage (Figure 6a). Although Gower does not mention it in his version of the tale of Dido and Aeneas, the classical story tells how Aeneas lingered in Carthage too long and departed for Italy only at the insistence of Jupiter's messenger, Mercury. The stars shown here suggest the influence of the heavens on the scene below – that Aeneas's departure and Dido's death are divinely ordained.

Constance is an example of unquestioning obedience to the will of God. The miniature in Pierpont Morgan MS M. 126 shows her being cast out to sea in a rudderless boat by her mother-in-law as her husband (the king) and his courtiers look on (Figure 6b). Under the starry sky, Constance sits with hands pressed together as though in prayer, a pose that clearly illustrates her submission to God's will. These miniatures illustrate, literally, the significance of the passage on the fifteen stars, stones and herbs – that heavenly bodies influence the actions of those on earth.

The control that the stars exert over the earth and its inhabitants is clearly expressed by the Latin verse which precedes the section on astronomy in book VII:

> By starry law the lower things are ruled,
> But now and then that rule may prove deceptive.
> With God's help wise men dominate the stars;
> And Fate quite rightly brings on new surprises.

Astronomy reveals just how the heavens rule over this earth:

> Benethe upon this Erthe hiere
> Of alle thinges the matiere,
> As tellen ous thei that ben lerned,
> Of thing above it stant governed,
> That is to sein of the Planetes.
> The cheles both and ek the hetes,
> The chances of the world also,
> That we fortune clepen so,

Figure 6. (a) Pierpont Morgan Ms. M.126, f. 68v. Dido and Aeneas. (b) Pierpont Morgan Ms. M.126, f. 32v. Constance. (Not to scale.)

> Among the mennes nacion
> Al is thurgh constellacion,
> Wherof that som man hath the wele,
> And som man hath deseses fele
> In love als wel as othre thinges;
> The stat of realmes and of kinges
> In time of pes, in time of werre
> It is conceived of the Sterre. (*Confessio*, VII, lines 633–48)

It would seem that a king must understand this 'descending' view of authority in order to govern well. The science of astronomy will provide him with powers greater than those he already possesses, allowing him to know in advance his destiny and that of his people. However, the science serves also to remind the king that he, too, is subject to a higher power – the authority of God. The illumination sequences of the zodiac signs and the fifteen stars, stones and herbs sensitize the viewer to the images of stars throughout Pierpont Morgan MS M. 126. Each time we see stars in an illumination, we are subtly reminded that the heavens rule the actions of those on earth.

Starry skies in daytime settings can be found in other fifteenth-century manuscripts, both French and English. Books of hours frequently depict skies filled with stars, in keeping with the calendric nature of the genre. Star-filled skies are also found in manuscripts of vernacular poetry: they illustrate narrative episodes from Lydgate's *Troy Book*, Christine de Pizan's *L'Epître d'Othéa* and Boccaccio's *De claris mulieribus*. However, the illumination sequence of the fifteen stars, stones and herbs in Pierpont Morgan MS M. 126 is unusual in the number and detail of its miniatures. That someone should select the passage for such comprehensive illustration is evidence that the *Confessio* was being read much like an encyclopaedia. While no clear exemplar has been determined for Pierpont Morgan MS M. 126, several miniatures, most notably that of Nectanabus instructing Aristotle the Great (Figure 2), resemble those found in illustrated manuscripts of Bartholomeus Anglicus's *De proprietatibus rerum*,[41] which reinforces the impression that the poem was read by some as a reference work. The patron who commissioned the manuscript viewed the *Confessio Amantis* as a book of wisdom and magical lore rather than a poem on love and vice. Such an interpretation of the manuscript is further supported by the appearance, in the final twelve folios, of an incomplete and unsystematic index, written by the scribe that copied the poetic text. Indices in manuscripts of grammar texts and encyclopaediae are not uncommon in the fifteenth century; however, they are very unusual in manuscripts of vernacular poetry. Such an index, if it had been effectively completed, would have allowed the user of the Pierpont Morgan

---

[41] Two fifteenth-century French manuscripts of Batholomeus's work have similar illuminations: one manuscript was sold by Sotheby's in June 1990 and is in private hands, possibly in Switzerland; the other is BN MS francais 9141, fol. 217^v, which represents Geography with two figures looking out over a landscape in a manner similar to that of Nectanabus and Alexander.

manuscript to read the text in an order other than that originally designed by the author: it emphasizes the encyclopaedic nature of the manuscript.

Pierpont Morgan MS M.126 is not the only manuscript to highlight Gower's passage on the fifteen stars, stones and herbs, although it does so with considerable visual appeal. At least two other manuscripts include this passage in some form. Longleat House MS 174, a medical collection in Latin and English, includes it in full: Kate Harris has demonstrated that this indicates another reader for whom Gower's work was 'lore' more than 'love'.[42] BL MS Sloane 3847, a miscellany of astronomical texts and 'diverse' magic spells collected between the fifteenth and seventeenth centuries, also includes Gower's passage as a simple list. Although Harris notes the similarities between this manuscript and the Longleat House MS, she is fairly dismissive of its significance.[43] The Sloane manuscript, in fact, places Gower's passage alongside the source first identified by Macaulay, for, on fols 84 to 100, the treatise on the fifteen stars, stones and herbs attributed to Hermes Trismegistus appears prefaced on fol. 83 with the list of fifteen stars, stones and herbs according to Gower.[44] Without question, Gower's inclusion of the stars, stones and herbs in the *Confessio Amantis* strongly indicates that he and his audience must have held an understanding, however superficial, of astronomical lore. This is not to suggest that Gower was an expert in the field himself, but he did have an active interest in the subject, and so did his audience, as the manuscript tradition attests.[45] For at least three of Gower's readers, book VII, with its 'educational' focus and the astronomical wisdom it presents, was the most important part of the *Confessio*. Gower's inclusion of the material in book VII, and its reception, calls into question traditional views of the poem which regard the love-vision as central and book VII as a digression, or which see the poem as appealing to some presumed interest of Richard II, and perhaps of Henry IV, in 'courtly love'. Under the influence of the passage of the fifteen stars, fifteen stones and fifteen herbs, 'moral' Gower is transformed into 'scientific' Gower.

---

[42] Harris, 'The Longleat House extracted manuscript', p. 88.
[43] *Ibid.*, p. 90.
[44] As Harris notes (*ibid.*, pp. 89–90), the list is clearly drawn from Thomas Berthelette's 1554 edition of the *Confessio*, for the folio is headed with a title indicating that Gower dedicated his poem to Henry IV.
[45] The same is true about Gower's discussion of alchemy, which appears in a Bodleian Ashmole manuscript and in the *Theatrum chemicum Britannicum* of 1652.

Chapter 12

'Of the parfite medicine':
Merita Perpetuata in Gower's Vernacular Alchemy

STEPHANIE L. BATKIE

When one speaks of models of virtuous, productive labour in the medieval period, the alchemist is not a figure that springs immediately to mind. In the sixteenth century Reginald Scot lambastes those who made use of alchemical language and practices as 'ranke couseners, and consuming cankers to the common wealth, and therefore to be rejected and excommunicated from the fellowship of all honest men', a forceful opinion which is far from unfamiliar in earlier centuries.[1] In fact, outside of those who claim to practise alchemy and produce texts of their own, it seems that little good can be said about it. Alchemy is satirized, condemned and generally mistrusted. It is probably heretical. Its literature fails to describe it clearly because the practice is a shadowy, immoral sham. False coining, charlatanry and out and out theft – all were dangers when entering into an alchemist's laboratory, to say nothing of violent explosions and other experimental disasters. In short, there is a reason that Dante condemns alchemists to one of the lowest circles of Hell.

Yet it is in this very environment of mistrust and suspicion that Gower writes book IV of the *Confessio Amantis*, with its surprising validation of alchemy as the highest possible form of human labour. The 'problem' with Gower's treatment of alchemy, I will argue, has less to do with its presence in the poem and more to do with the plainness of its presentation. After all, there are many things that Gower might well find attractive about the practice of alchemy – its focus on unification and purity, its demands for studious discipline, the faith it puts in divine intervention – but all of these qualities are dwarfed by the science's insistence on transformational labour and the virtue of its adepts. This last element, that of labour (both textual and material) is critical to Gower's characterization of alchemy as a remedy for the sin of Sloth but also to the larger confessional framework of the poem. Through alchemy Gower shows his audience how to become virtuous readers who are able to materially change themselves through the abstract and immaterial world of the text. He does not, however, write like an alchemist; he

---

[1] Reginald Scot, *Reginald Scot's the Discoverie of Witchcraft*, ed. Montague Summers (London, 1930), p. 216.

rejects alchemy's form even as he celebrates its meaning. The translation of alchemy from a technical Latinate discourse to the vernacular *exemplum* we find in the poem, inapproachable and inactionable, reveals the deep gulf between Gower's vision of the art as an idealized system of miraculous purification and as a defunct practice made inoperable by the degeneration of the human condition. This paper will argue for a reading of Gower's vernacular alchemy as a model of transformational textual labour in order to show how the form of the poem works to create virtuous reading subjects.

*

In order to understand Genius's one-sided lecture on alchemy in book IV, we need to see it first as an abstract system of transformation and unification, the end of which is the miraculous creation of a material so pure that its very perfection is contagious. Multiplication, most commonly multiplication of gold or silver, is the physical result of a successful alchemical transformation, but, for the alchemists, the creation of precious metals is the sign through which a far more monumental accomplishment is read; the creation of the Philosopher's Stone is the material, visible proof of divine perfection brought to earth through human labour and skill. Gower says of the stone:

> It makth multiplicacioun
> Of gold, and the fixacioun
> It causeth, and of his habit
> He doth the werk to be parfit (*Confessio*, IV, lines 2574–7)

Furthermore, this perfection is accomplished through chemical contact that allows 'vertu' to pass from the Stone to the material to be transmuted:

> This mineral, so as I finde,
> Transformeth al the ferste kynde
> And makth hem able to conceive
> Thrugh his vertu, and to receive
> Bothe in substance and in figure
> Of gold and selver the nature. (*Confessio*, IV, lines 2559–64)

The metaphor of conception is a common one in alchemical literature, though slightly at odds with alchemical theory in that it suggests that the Stone injects an element (its perfection and virtue) into the base matter whereas, in fact, the alchemists understood the Stone to draw out contaminants from the lead or copper, leaving the purer gold or silver behind. Arnold of Villanova describes the Holy Grail of the alchemists as such: 'That there abides in nature a certain pure matter, which, being discovered and brought by art to perfection, converts to itself proportionally all imperfect bodies that it touches.'[2] Gower chooses to emphasize the former, allowing the 'vertu' of the Stone to materialize into a transferable, transactional component, the

---

[2] J. Read and F. H. Sawyer, *Prelude to Chemistry: An Outline of Alchemy, Its Literature and Relationships* (New York, 1937), p. 119

quintessence of its perfect purity, in order to draw readers' eyes along the path of transformation. Virtue becomes a reified quality that flows from the Stone to the base matter in the alchemical exchange, and, more importantly for Gower, it increases in quantity with every use.

This miraculous virtue, however, can only come from the unflagging and faithful labour of the true alchemist, one who carries the mark of divine election and a purified soul. Alchemy consists of two sides of the same coin, so to speak: what is known as esoteric, or philosophical alchemy, and exoteric, or practical alchemy.[3] The first involves the purification and perfection of the adept himself, achieved primarily through his own labour over the art and through divine election, while the second (and more commonly depicted) form is the alchemy that is associated with strange-looking vessels, foul odours and smoking furnaces. Gower, in book IV, follows the traditional exoteric formula to the letter.

While explaining the alchemical theory of the maturation of metals to the dutiful Amans, Genius lectures that the alchemist's labour is ultimately more powerful than nature's, and that the perfection of metals comes through the removal of lesser elements in a hierarchical scale that moves from lead to gold or silver. The Philosopher's Stone works on other, baser metals because of its ability to act as a reified symbol of perfection. It becomes for Gower, as for the alchemists, emblematic of productive and valuable labour in its ability to both embody virtue and, more importantly, to multiply it through diligent and effective labour. The just adept, chosen by God for his wisdom and purity, will complete the work and be rewarded with material proof that can be multiplied again and again. His inner virtue becomes embodied in the Stone, which, in turn, reproduces that same virtue in everything it touches.

Although there is no narrative *exemplum* accompanying the alchemical lecture in book IV we can see this same logic of contagious goodness played out in the 'Tale of Adrian and Bardus' in book V of the *Confessio*. In the tale, Bardus, a poor woodsman, rescues Adrian, a wealthy nobleman, from a pit in return for half of Adrian's worldly goods, but not before he inadvertently does the same for an ape and a serpent. Predictably, once saved, Adrian refuses to deliver payment, but the animals, unbidden, reward Bardus for his aid. The ape provides a stack of wood for Bardus to sell in the marketplace, while the serpent offers a 'ston mor bright than a cristall' (*Confessio*, V, line 5066). Bardus sells the stone to a jeweller for gold coins, yet once he returns home he finds the gold and the stone together in his purse. Over the following days, the same scenario plays out again and again: he sells the stone, only to find it returned to him as before. Eventually, the tale of the miraculous stone reaches the ears of the Emperor, Justinian, who calls Bardus to court, hears the story and reconciles the debt between Adrian and Bardus by ordering half of Adrian's worldly goods to go to the formerly

---

[3] For what I have found to be the very best summary of alchemical theories and practices, both succinct and thoughtful, see chapter 1 of Stanton J. Linden, *Darke Hieroglyphicks: Alchemy in English Literature from Chaucer to the Restoration* (Lexington, KY, 1996).

poverty-stricken woodsman. The larger import of the tale is a story about both the dangers of Adrian's unkindness (in its standing as a sub-species of Avarice) and also the inevitable and natural separation of the classes – a rift that only the exercise of just law through royal administration can bridge.[4] The appearance of a miraculous stone that continually produces gold as a reward for virtuous action, however, must certainly resonate with the extended description of the alchemical Stone in the previous book. Bardus's magical stone mimics the physical capabilities of the Philosopher's Stone inasmuch as it provides the owner with material wealth, but it also becomes a marker of virtue and an instrument for social change.

The stone is a signifier of the perceived value of Bardus' labour, and its circulation not only profits the character but effects narrative progress as well. Bardus' labour is, as many have commented upon, not entirely without self-interest – he is motivated first and foremost by the promise of riches and the lure of a leg up on the social ladder – but in the tale's system of labour and reward it is only his action, not his mindset, that is accounted for. Justinian resolves the broken verbal contract and reinstitutes social order only because rumours of the stone's powers reach his royal ears, not because Bardus' good deed circulates on its own. Even if, as Russell Peck suggests, the end of the tale serves to 'remind man of the virtue of his rationality which, when rightly assessed and justly administered, is more potent than even the 'vertu' of the serpent's stone', the right rule of law, in all its rationality, is visible only because of the material and verbal circulation of the symbol of Bardus' worthy work.[5] Without the stone, the *exemplum* would be a negative one that demonstrates the hollowness of verbal contracts and, by association, human speech and reason; with the stone, however, Gower can bring the tale to a successful and satisfying conclusion. Virtuous labour (if not virtue itself) is reified in the tale in order to become a socially and individually effective instrument, multiplied again and again in Bardus's purse and magnified into an antidote to legislative and civic disorder.

Like the power of the serpent's stone, the multiplying and purifying properties of the Philosopher's Stone circulate in the poem (and in the world) as a marker for the value of the labour of the alchemists, hard at work in their laboratories and at their furnaces. In this economy of surplus, however, the familiar relationship between labour and product dissolves as the representation of labour, the Stone, overtakes the work required to produce it and transforms into a producer in its own right. Once set in motion, the produc-

---

[4] For more on this tale and its place as a social and moral *exemplum*, see Patrick J. Gallacher, *Love, the Word, and Mercury: A Reading of John Gower's 'Confessio Amantis'* (Albuquerque, NM, 1975), pp. 154–5; Andrew Galloway, 'The making of a social ethic in late-medieval England: from "Gratitudo" to "Kyndenesse"', *Journal of the History of Ideas*, 55 (1994), 378; Peter Nicholson, *Love and Ethics in Gower's 'Confessio Amantis'* (Ann Arbor, MI, 2005), pp. 88–9; Russell A. Peck, *Kingship and Common Profit in Gower's Confessio Amantis* (Carbondale, IL, 1978), pp. 116–19; Peck pp. 10–14. For a description of the serpent's stone as a magical object, see P. J. Heather, 'Precious stones in the Middle-English verse of the fourteenth century', *Folklore*, 42 (1931), 217–64 (p. 371).

[5] Peck, *Kingship and Common Profit*, p. 119

tive power of the Stone enacts the alchemist's initial virtuous labour again and again; it is both a reward for labour and a continual reproduction of labour itself. Unlike gold, which, as Peggy Knapp rightly reminds us, is an 'unstable metaphor, symbolizing both perfection and avarice in medieval Christian discourse', the Stone is always a repository for (and a product of) virtue and a source of perfection.[6]

Gower seizes upon the Stone's promise of perpetually productive labour as the ideal form of 'busyness' to combat the sin of Sloth, but also as a larger model for virtuous work of all kinds. More specifically, he allows the alchemical pattern of production to shape a picture of readerly labour, both in Genius's lecture in book IV and in his presentation of reading elsewhere in the poem. Through his careful framing of Genius's alchemical lecture, Gower transmutes the physical labour of the alchemists into textual labour that will change readers as fundamentally as distillation, calcination or fixation changes metal. Because the decay of alchemy as a functioning science prevents the Philosopher's Stone from functioning as a physical object, its effect in Gower's poem must work not on material elements, but on the internal life of the readers who encounter it. In alchemical theory the physical Philosopher's Stone must be both signifier and signified at once in order to initiate transmutation of base matter.[7] The ability to be and to represent simultaneously is the source of the Stone's transformative power and is the miracle of the alchemist's art. The Stone is not only perfect, it is perfection, not only pure, but purity. Gower reminds us, however, that this miraculous collapse of the sign is no longer possible given the loss of alchemical knowledge and the disintegration of the world's order and, as such, the Stone can now exist only as a textual trace.[8] The poem therefore re-locates the transformative powers of the physical stone to its textual representation in book IV and, in doing so, allows alchemy to become a textualized practice that works on the reader in the same way that the Stone works on copper and lead.

---

[6] Peggy A. Knapp, 'The work of alchemy', *JMEMS*, 30 (2000), 575–99 (p. 576).

[7] For Brian Vickers this collapse of the sign is a tendency for all 'occult' practices and literatures. He writes, 'One constant feature of the occult is its tendency to turn concepts into essences, abstract into concrete, to reify and hypostatize metaphors and ideas. In Saussurian terms, the line separating signified and signifier is removed, and the two concepts fuse as one.' Brian Vickers, 'On the function of analogy in the occult', in *Hermeticism and the Renaissance*, eds Ingrid Mekel and Allen G. Debus (Washington DC and London, 1988), pp. 265–92 (p. 283).

[8] In a sense, this is both the most surprising and the most important statement Gower makes about alchemy. He allows that the practice does not work, but he is careful in his qualification – alchemy *no longer* works, meaning that at one point it was not just feasible, but practically possible. Previously, alchemy worked in the exact manner as the alchemists claimed, 'Bot *now* it stant al otherwise' (IV, line 2580) because the understanding that must lie behind the language has been lost, even as the world has fallen into fragmentation and ruin. And yet Gower is careful to return to the past glories of the art at the end of Genius' lecture: 'Bot noght forthi, who that it knewe, | The science of himself is trewe' (V, lines 2597–8). The result is that what once was the idealized symbol of practiced labour can now be read as an unreachable and abstract *exemplum* only.

This is not done without precedent. Gower's reformation of alchemy from the material to the poetic appropriates the long-standing traditions of esoteric, or philosophical, alchemy and its creation of what Stanton J. Linden calls 'a way of life for its most devout disciples: a vast religious and philosophical system aimed at the purification and regeneration of their lives'.[9] In esoteric alchemy, the 'practical' work of the laboratory fades in favour of the 'theoretical' work of understanding the alchemical principles at work in transformation; purification of the soul becomes associated with contemplative textual study and esoteric (inward) searching for divine truths hidden in the natural world. The exoteric focus on the perfection of metals through physical labour becomes in esoteric alchemy the perfection of the self through textual labour. Following this tradition, Gower's treatment of alchemy in the *Confessio* suggests that the most valuable and applicable aspect of the art is its continual requirement of inward, transformational reading.

Gower does not, however, appropriate this quality of alchemical reading, its ability to act on its readers, without a fundamental intervention into how language is deployed by the alchemists in their manuscripts. The literature of medieval alchemy is renowned for being unwelcoming and intentionally impenetrable. Petrus Bonus, an influential fourteenth-century alchemist and physician, describes alchemical texts in his *Margarita preciosa novella* as 'a pathless thicket of contradictions and obscure metaphors'.[10] While speaking from a privileged position as a clearly established alchemical authority, Bonus nevertheless voices one of the most prevalent criticisms levelled against the alchemists: the opacity of their texts and deliberate obfuscation of their secrets. And yet nearly every medieval alchemist, Bonus included, continues to write with 'studied obscurity of expression' even as they deplore its effects, namely, that readers are doomed to 'flounder along through these great works, with only here and there a glimmering of light, which vanishes as soon as one approaches it more closely'.[11] The alchemical text offers one of the most unusual forms of medieval textuality available to us, in that it structures its language around the hope of not being understood by anyone – even, presumably, by those who already know the secrets of the art. In doing so, it uses language to create a barrier between readers and meaning for the express purpose of initiating laborious and frustrating study. The difficult language becomes a barrier to understanding that must be struggled with, and it is the effort of this struggle that will, in the end, transform the alchemist.[12] In the same way that fire purifies metals, alchemical language will purify its readers – not easily, but permanently.

---

[9] Linden, *Darke Hierogliphicks*, p. 8

[10] Pietro Antonio Boni, *The New Pearl of Great Price; a Treatise Concerning the Treasure and Most Precious Stone of the Philosophers. Or the Method and Procedure of This Divine Art; with Observations Drawn from the Works of Arnoldus, Raymondus, Rhasis, Albertus, and Michael Scotus*, trans. Arthur Edward Waite (London, 1963), p. 111.

[11] Boni, *New Pearl*, p. 114.

[12] Of course, the other primary result of difficult language is to hide the truths of the art from the unworthy or the mercenary. The effect of alchemical discourse is twofold: it winnows out the unelect even as it elevates and perfects the chosen few. Bonus assures the faithful

This technique is clearly not something Gower incorporates into his alchemical presentation. The dominant voice of Gower's discussion of the science is the same as the rest of the *Confessio*, which renders even the most ostensibly erudite of alchemical terms as a litany of rhyming vocabulary. The passage revels in the lilting -cion suffixes endemic to the discourse and allows the prominence of the Latinate terminology to emphasize the steady and unified rhythm of the poetry:

> Bot what man that this werk beginne,
> He mot awaite at every tyde,
> So that nothing be left aside,
> Ferst of the distillacion,
> Forth with the congelacion,
> Solucioun, descencion,
> And kepe in his entencion
> The point of sublimacion,
> And forth with calcinacion,
> Of veray approbacion
> Do there be fixacion
> With tempered hetes of the fyr
> Til he the parfit elixir
> Of thilke philosophers ston
> Mai gete … (*Confessio*, IV, lines 2510–24)

The clustering of technical jargon embodies the strict control of the alchemists over the materials of their art, and the way their labours all work towards the ideals of order and unification. And yet, for all the poetical and aural weight given to the Latin terms, this is still not alchemical language as we would expect to find it in texts of the period. It remains a vernacular transmutation of the discourse that capitalizes on vocabulary to demonstrate the sonorous but empty effect of alchemical terminology. But Gower's language, the 'middle way' of his vernacular, does incorporate aspects of alchemical reading even as it resists the impenetrable discourse that, for the alchemists, is so much a part of their art. He appropriates the purifying and active process of studious reading alchemy requires and integrates it into his vernacular poetic style. Reading and study become a form of labour that produces results in the same way that the Philosopher's Stone, as a product and receptacle for virtuous labour, produces gold.

We can see this process rehearsed in one of the few *exempla* in the entire poem that uses ethical reading as a distinguishing marker of character. In

---

that, 'These are very good and human reasons, then, why this Art should not be revealed to everybody. Moreover, it is delivered to us in obscure terms, in order that the student may be compelled to work hard in its pursuit. We do not prize that which costs us nothing; it is our highest delight to reap some great benefit as the reward of our labour. Therefore, it would not be good for you if this knowledge were to come to you after reading one book, or after spending a few days in its investigation. But if you are worthy, if you possess energy and the spirit of perseverance, if you are ready to study diligently by day and by night, if you place yourself under the guidance of God, you will find the coveted knowledge in God's own good time.' Boni, *New Pearl*, pp. 131–2.

the 'Tale of Diogenes and Aristippus', both characters are Athens-educated and have recently returned to Carthage to pursue the ends of their learning. But whereas Diogenes immerses himself in continued study and humble, private work, Aristippus uses his ability to manipulate knowledge and language in the service of a prince. He installs himself at court and becomes a flatterer in order to gain worldly rewards of gold and riches from the beguiled nobleman. Reading and careful study are turned into monitors of natural virtue to the extent that Aristippus's greedy fawning becomes a lens through which readers can see his discordant and unreasonable mind. He has gained enough mastery over language to use it to his own ends, but Diogenes models himself after Reason and the truth of nature, using his reading as an ethical check against the temptations of political and economic advancement:

> Bot Diogenes duelte stille
> At home and loked on his bok.
> He soughte noght the worldes crok,
> For vein honour ne for richesse,
> Bot all his hertes besinesse
> He sette to be vertuous (*Confessio*, VII, lines 2266–71)

Flattery is an example of deceitful speech that both goes against nature and obscures the line between representation and truth (as traced by language); Diogenes, marked by his dedication to study, and therefore to reason, refuses to follow the path of flattery even through it brings with it the promise of gold and other worldly treasures. Study becomes a way of both instilling and practising virtue, which, in turn, results in ethical action. Right reading, therefore, is reading that follows nature and elevates the internal state of the reader first, who then in turn becomes a representation of kindly order through his actions in the world. In this sense, Aristippus reads like a bad alchemist: he uses his knowledge as a strategy for self-aggrandizement and profit (the ability to speak well, for him, equals the ability to flatter and produce gold) and in doing so debases himself and the learning he misapplies. The understanding of Diogenes' performance of study, on the other hand, of finding virtue through reading, which, in turn, makes virtue visible in the surrounding world, is esoteric alchemical reading defined.[13] 'Besinesse' is transformed into 'virtuous' in a near-rhyme that trumps the 'richesse' Diogenes so rightly rejects.[14]

---

[13] Nicolette Zeeman has a similar reading of the medieval notion of study and labour. Her approach complements my own here in her insistence that we see the work of reading as part of a larger social history of labour and devotion. Nicolette Zeeman, '"Studying" in the Middle Ages – and in *Piers Plowman*', *NML*, 3 (1999), 185–212.

[14] Chaucer, of course, famously juxtaposes the failed 'busyness'/business of the alchemists in *The Canon's Yeoman's Tale* with the successful 'busyness' of devotion and piety in the legend of St Cecilia found in *The Second Nun's Tale*. When we place Chaucer's depiction against Gower's portrayal of alchemy, we see yet another example of how unique the alchemical presentation in the *Confessio* is – Gower manages to offer alchemy as both a failed and a successful example of labour without resorting to open satire or condemnation. If anything, his language suggests regret at the loss/capitalistic corruption of alchemical knowledge

Aristippus' false flattery stands, then, in direct opposition to Diogenes' virtue-producing reading in the tale, first in how each character approaches learning after returning to Carthage, but more importantly in how their resulting speech becomes a reflection of how study, both false and true, produces action in the world. The result of virtuous reading is the multiplication of truth: when he attempts to re-educate Aristippus though his own powers of language, Diogenes is attempting to reproduce his understanding of reason and nature in another. Like the power of the Philosopher's Stone, truthful reading begets truthful speech. Conversely, the danger of flattery, as Gower says explicitly, lies in its power to obscure truth. The flatterer undermines the connection between language and meaning by filling his target's ears with 'feigned wordes' that 'make him wene | That blak is whyt and blew is grene' (*Confessio*, VII, lines 2187–8). Reading and study are not solitary and self-involved acts; rather, the tale deploys them as the impetus for direct action and result in the social and political arena, reproducing themselves to either positive or negative ends. Not only does the labour of learning transform Diogenes and Aristippus, it has the potential power to change those they interact with, prince or peer.

Apart from the warning against flattery as a temptation for both the powerful and the power-hungry, the active effects of reading and study that emerge as central concerns in this particular tale resonate throughout the rest of the poem, including book IV's alchemical lecture. Alchemy in Gower is 'the parfit medicine' (*Confessio*, IV, line 2624) in a material and in the spiritual sense. Materially, the bodies and spirits of metals are 'cured' of their imperfections through the contagious purity embodied in the Philosopher's Stone; commensurately, human perfection, indicated by health, improved sensory perception and even immortality, is accomplished through the same basic principle of exposing a corrupted material, the human body, to a hyper-perfect material, a potable form of the Stone known as the Elixir of Life. When ingested, the Elixir supposedly purges the gross, corporeal body and draws out the impurities that run rampant throughout, effectively returning the body to as close a prelapsarian state as is possible this side of the divine.[15] Spiritual redemption, on the other hand, is solely the product of laborious study and divine election. Unfortunately, the labour of transformation that the alchemical passage has been leading to, both as a material process and an elevating reading practice, disappears into Amans's silence in the face of Genius's exposition, giving us one of the most profound examples of misreading in the entire poem. He has missed his opportunity for self-redemption and failed to read alchemy as a model for the way in which he must address the faults of his soul in order to craft himself into

---

and an urge to locate similar mechanisms of productive virtue in other, more accessible, discourses.

[15] Instead of dividing alchemical production between the Philosopher's Stone and the Elixir of Life, Gower tells of three different stones: the 'lapis vegetabilis', the 'lapis animalis' and 'minerall'. This modification from traditional alchemical theory is unique to Gower. See George Gillespie Fox, *The Mediaeval Sciences in the Works of John Gower* (New York, 1966), pp. 114–35.

a proper lover. In some sense, this should not be surprising. Amans, after all, is a figure of the will and, as James Simpson observes, is only interested in listening to what will directly affect his ability to woo his lady: 'Amans, then, as desire, desires only the fulfilment of his very self; the logic of his listening to Genius for so long a time can only be that he sees, or rather hears in Genius what he wants to.'[16] In this way, Amans (like Aristippus) reads like a false alchemist. Only interested in one thing, Amans rejects the more difficult textual labour described by Genius in the same way that a mercenary or foolish alchemist will gravitate towards the quick, chemical operations while disregarding the esoteric, inward aspects of the art. In the words of Petrus Bonus,

> Yet one who can perform the practical operations of Alchemy is not yet an Alchemist, just as not every one who speaks grammatically is a grammarian. Such persons still lack that knowledge of the causes of things which exalts the mind of man, and raises it to God.[17]

The imagination that serves Amans so well in identifying with the lovers in Genius's *exempla* deserts him now when it is most needed; because he focuses on personal identification with characters, the abstractions and value of the alchemical lecture pass ineffectually by, unheard and unheeded.

If Amans's silent misreading is bound up with his all-encompassing desire, and Genius's call for productive labour cannot draw his attention beyond the scope of his longing for love, then the narrative voice of the authorial Gower must urge his external readers to fill the void. This theme, as Simpson points out, is a recurring one throughout the poem: 'Gower's is a reader-oriented aesthetic, where the reader must participate in the construction of meaning through the activation of higher powers of the world than those represented from within the poem.'[18] Amans's silence corresponds to Gower's vernacularization of alchemy by opening a space for readers to begin to make their own meaning, independent of the poem's narrative force. They are not, as Amans is, driven by a desire to simply become better lovers (or, at least, Gower seems to hope they are not), and as a result they have the potential to activate the transformative power of textual interpretation for themselves. The 'bok for Engelonde's sake' engages readers through absence: absence of textual difficulty, absence of examples of right reading and absence of workable transformations. Even the one narrative transformation we do see, that of Amans into John Gower in book VIII, serves as an erasure of an authoritative voice rather than a poetic elevation. Amans's process of tempering the force of his wilful spirit with the guidance of reason is not one that a reader may approximate and, unlike alchemical transformation, does not pass beyond the confines of the poem. The virtue Amans gains is not contagious on its own terms and the writing that we read (Amans/

---

[16] James Simpson, *Sciences and the Self in Medieval Poetry: Alan of Lille's Anticlaudianus and John Gower's Confessio Amantis* (Cambridge, 1995), p. 151.
[17] Boni, *New Pearl*, p. 138.
[18] Simpson, *Sciences and the Self*, p. 254.

Gower's production), with its 'rude wordis and with pleyne' (*Confessio*, VIII, line 3122) cannot, as alchemical language does, instigate productive labour. What it can do, however, is open a new kind of vernacular reading that relies on Simpson's 'reader-oriented aesthetic' by leading readers to assume responsibility for their own understanding.

*

If we follow Larry Scanlon's definition of the medieval *exemplum* as 'a narrative enactment of cultural authority', then Gower's use of alchemy doesn't seem to be an *exemplum* at all.[19] Even though it appears as part of a larger story (Genius's education and confession of Amans), it in and of itself is not a narrative, and it would be difficult to call Gower's unusual literary acceptance of alchemy sympathetic with the wider cultural opinion of the day. Furthermore, as a distant and even defunct science, it doesn't seem able to be an 'enactment' of anything whatsoever (or, at least, of anything valuable.) And yet we have seen that alchemy is in fact more than a strange and dismissible interjection into the otherwise orderly pattern of the poem thus far, and rather that it offers a unique opportunity to examine Gower's selective appropriation of an inaccessible example of transformation. If we ought, as I suggest, to read the poem's alchemical diversion as an *exemplum* for virtuous textual labour, we must accept a form of reading that moves through readers who, in turn, deploy the effects of that reading. Diane Watt characterizes Gower's vernacular poetics as language that encourages readers to experiment with meaning-making as they read, even as the stylistics of the poem are designed 'to communicate rather than to withhold learning'.[20] This experimentation, without the benefit of esoteric, obscure language as an impetus to labour, is the engine that drives transformation in Gower's audience. Contemplative study generates virtue and understanding, which then determine how readers interact socially and politically in the world.

Transformative reading moves beyond the confines of the narrative and textual *auctoritas* to create a system of redemption on a broad, macrocosmic scale. To refashion one reader is not enough to generate the fundamental societal change Gower hopes for in the Prologue, and he is unwilling to rely on the fit but few audience members who will respond to difficult discourses such as those of alchemy. Rather, the ambition of the *Confessio* is to offer a vernacular poetics that relies on its simplicity to engage a different form of textual contemplation, one wherein readers must work to distance themselves from the text in order to construct meaningful interpretations.[21] *Auctoritas* has shifted from author to readers in a remarkable and unprecedented way. Readers must resist Genius's packaged moralizing to form meaning that speaks to them; they must look past Amans's silences, his

---

[19] Larry Scanlon, *Narrative, Authority, and Power: The Medieval Exemplum and the Chaucerian Tradition* (Cambridge, 1994).
[20] Diane Watt, *Amoral Gower: Language, Sex, and Politics* (Minneapolis, MN, 2003), p. 21.
[21] For what is still the most elegant and convincing description of Gower's poetics, see R. F. Yeager, *John Gower's Poetic: The Search for a New Arion* (Cambridge, 1990).

pouts and his myopic complaints; and, most importantly, they must overtake Gower's deliberate self-effacement in the face of his daunting task. Interpretation is activated in order that the transformation of one reader becomes the transformation of many, rendering that which is above (the larger social construct) to be like that which is below (the newly reformed individual). The *Confessio* traces the experimental outline of a new form of the vernacular that evades definition, becoming mutable and insubstantial even as it attempts to affect readers in fundamental ways. In the end, for the text to generate *merita perpetuata* in the individual and social sphere, the plain must work, and work hard, to evolve into the productive.

Chapter 13

Inside Out in Gower's Republic of Letters

KARLA TAYLOR

In *I Henry IV* Shakespeare found the perfect metaphor to stage the political tumult of Gower's England. Facing off against his erstwhile supporters in the climactic battle of Shrewsbury, Henry, the traitor turned king, spreads confusion by disguising several lieutenants in his own coat of arms, so that the rebels cannot recognize the true king. The Earl of Douglas's military frustration adumbrates Henry IV's political problem as well:

> DOUGLAS Another king? They grow like Hydra's heads.
> I am the Douglas, fatal to all those
> That wear those colors on them. What art thou
> That counterfeit'st the person of a king?
> (*I Henry IV*, V. 4. 26–9)

To Henry's reply, 'I will assay thee', Douglas responds, 'I fear thou art another counterfeit, | And yet in faith thou bearest thee like a king' (*I Henry IV*, V. 4. 35, 36–7).[1] The interchange offers counterfeiting – the illicitly multiplied image of the king's face struck in metal – as a metaphor for the crisis of legitimacy after Henry's deposition of Richard has allowed many claimants to spring up in place of one.

Under the metaphor lies the language of alchemy: Douglas expects 'colors' to reveal the true king, while Henry 'assays' Douglas's true mettle/metal. Since alchemical colours are unreliable signs of identity, Douglas resolves to kill all who bear the king's coat of arms. Shakespeare's alchemical metaphor recasts the political problem as epistemological: not just a matter of illicit multiplication, more fundamentally it suggests the loss of a whole world of sacramental continuity in which the face of things had made visible their invisible inward identities.

In linking alchemical language to the tumultuous changes of the late fourteenth century, Shakespeare was anticipated by Gower. Gower's commitment in the *Confessio Amantis* to the reformation of individual and public governance, and to a poetic language that refers plainly and truly, will not surprise readers of this volume. What is surprising, however, is that his

---

[1] William Shakespeare, *I Henry IV*, *The Riverside Shakespeare*, ed. G. Blakemore Evans (Boston, 1997), p. 921.

model for plain, truthful transformation is alchemy. Gower's endorsement of alchemy in *Confessio* book IV is at odds not only with the usual exposés of transmutation, but also with his own intolerance of fraud in language and deed.[2] Alchemy frequently exemplified the human failings against which Gower ordinarily directed sorrow or scorn. What, then, does he gain from his departure from sceptical fourteenth-century treatments of it as quackery, fraud or an expense of time and spirit? Gower characterizes alchemy in terms that suggest it as an imaginative model reconciling sacramentalism with change, both within and to the vernacular, without succumbing to the increasingly divisive theological polemics that threatened to align the vernacular with heresy. As book VII's Lucretia story shows, Gower's alchemical model reconciles political change with the poetics and referential ethics of the *Confessio*.

It was scarcely a promising model. Accusations of fraud dogged the alchemy in the fourteenth century. From early on, the transmutation of metal was linked to false imitation; thus Dante puts Griffolino d'Arezzo and Capocchio da Siena in hell as counterfeiters of metals and apes of nature.[3] The threat of counterfeiting prompted Pope John XXII's 1317 decretal 'Spondent quas non exhibent', which forbade the pretended use of alchemy to deceive others and to pass off counterfeited money as legal tender.[4] According to the usual account (derived from the hostile inquisitor Nicolaus Eymericus), the pope suppressed alchemy because the transmutation of base metals into gold did not accord with nature.[5] John's decretal became part of the literature warning against the science itself. But John banned only false alchemists who promised what they did not produce; known to have supported scientific alchemy for medical purposes, he was also reputed to have practised it himself. His vast fortune was rumoured to have come from alchemical sources.[6] In the logic of 'Spondent quas non exhibent', false transmutation by dishonest pseudo-alchemists resembles and enables the counterfeiting of money. In both cases, a visible image is duplicated in order to deceive: the alchemist's false image of gold, and the counterfeiter's doubly false image of the king's face. Pope John was outraged not by alchemy as such, but rather by the illicit multiplication of coins, for counterfeiting was widely held to subvert the state.[7]

---

[2] Peck, ii, IV. lines 2451–632.
[3] *Inferno* 29, lines 109–39. For Capocchio's representation of the story of Christ's passion on his fingernails see Benvenuto da Imola, *Comentum super Dantis Aldigherij Comoediam*, cited from *Divine Comedy*, ed. and trans. C. S. Singleton (Princeton, NJ, 1970–75), vol. I, Part II, pp. 541–3.
[4] John W. Spargo, 'The Canon's Yeoman's Prologue and Tale', in *Sources and Analogues of Chaucer's Canterbury Tales*, eds W. F. Bryan and Germaine Dempster (Chicago, MI, 1941), pp. 691–2; trans. in J. R. Partington, 'Albertus Magnus on alchemy', *Ambix*, 1 (1937), 15–16.
[5] See Will H. L. Ogrinc, 'Western society and alchemy from 1200 to 1500', *JMH*, 6 (1980), 114; and Lynn Thorndike, *A History of Magical and Experimental Science During the First Thirteen Centuries of Our Era*, 4 vols (New York, 1923–58), vol. 3, p. 515.
[6] Thorndike, *A History of Magic*, vol. 3, p. 34; and Ogrinc, 'Western society', 114–15.
[7] According to Nicolaus Eymericus, *Directorium inquisitorum* (Rome, 1585), 'more true and more judicious is the opinion of those who consider her [alchemy] destructive to the state'

Counterfeiting also preoccupied English rulers, although they sometimes fostered rather than forbade practical alchemy. In 1329 Edward III summoned Johannes de Rous and William Dalby to show him how to make gold and silver to replenish state coffers.[8] Less reliable stories relate Edward's efforts to enlist alchemy to support his wars.[9] He was no more favourably disposed than John XXII toward counterfeiters, however; in 1374 the chaplain William de Brumley was prosecuted for making counterfeit gold pieces according to the alchemical teachings of William Shuchirch.[10] Richard II shared his grandfather's attraction to alchemy.[11] But in 1403, the same year Shakespeare portrays him as multiplying kings on the Shrewsbury battlefield, Henry IV forbade the multiplication of gold and silver as a capital felony.[12] In this sphere, as in others, he was concerned to protect his legitimacy, and thus to control the value of the king's face in trustworthy coinage. After 1436, the economic pressure of war led English kings to license alchemists to practise their art, thus replenishing state coffers through entirely unmysterious fees.[13]

The official suppression of practical alchemy resulted chiefly from its assimilation to counterfeiting. Its potential for fraud derived from two other aspects: uncertainty as to whether it perfects or subverts nature, and its characteristic profusion of terms. Proliferating signs dominate alchemical texts, where gold might masquerade as the sun, or mercury as a dragon, and where any substance or process hides behind layers of cover-names to frustrate the uninitiated.

The multitudinous cover-names paradoxically grow out of the core philosophical assumption of alchemy: the fundamental unity of all matter. This monism makes it possible for any red or yellow base metal to stand in for

---

(p. 477); see Ogrinc, 'Western society', 125, who cites the prohibitions against alchemy by French and English kings as well as by Venice and Nürnberg in order to protect coinage from counterfeiting. The 1352 English Statute of Treasons includes counterfeiting: 'si homme contreface les grant ou prive sealx le roi, ou sa monoie'; see 25 Edward III, st. 5, c. 2, quoted from S. B. Chrimes and A. L. Brown, eds, *Select Documents of English Constitutional History 1307–1485* (London, 1961), p. 77.

[8] Ogrinc, 'Western society', 118–19, citing Thomas Rymer, *Foedera, conventiones, literae, et cujuscunque generis acta publica, inter reges Angliae*, 3rd edn (The Hague, 1739–45), p. 24.

[9] E. M. Holmyard, *Alchemy* (New York, 1957), pp. 102–7; Ogrinc, 'Western society', 119.

[10] E. H. Duncan, 'The literature of alchemy and Chaucer's Canon's Yeoman's Tale: framework, theme, and characters', *Speculum*, 43 (1968), 633–4; H. G. Richardson, 'Year books and plea Rolls as sources of historical information', *TRHS*, ser. 4, 5 (1922), 38–40. For French kings and alchemy, see Ogrinc, 'Western society', 119.

[11] Wilhelm Ganzenmüller, *Die Alchemie im Mittelalter* (Hildesheim, 1967), p. 107; Duncan, 'The literature of alchemy,' 634; Dorothy Waley Singer, with Annie Anderson, *Catalogue of Latin and Alchemical Manuscripts in Great Britain and Ireland Dating From Before the XVI Century*, vol. 3 (Brussels, 1931), pp. 781–2, includes a document from the Close Rolls of Richard II (1393) concerning Johannes Pygas, a monk of Bristol who made 60 groats of alchemical silver bearing the likeness of the king's coinage.

[12] 4 Henry IV, in *The Statues of the Realm*, ed. T. E. Tomlins (London, 1816), vol. 2, p. 144. For Hoccleve's concern for coinage see Robert Meyer-Lee, 'Thomas Hoccleve and the apprehension of money', *Exemplaria*, 13 (2001), 173–214.

[13] F. Sherwood Taylor, *The Alchemists: Founders of Modern Science* (London, 1962), p. 103, reports that 20 licenses were issued for alchemy during the fifteenth century; a 1445 case refers to transmuation as *transubstantiare*, as does Henry VI's appeal to the clergy after 1436; see Ogrinc, 'Western society', 119.

gold, for instance; in the alchemist's analysis, the shared colour expresses the essential identity of pyrite (fool's gold) with the noble metal it resembles. The cover-names draw in a universe of resemblances – sun and moon, male and female, gold and silver, sulphur and quicksilver – expressing the unity underlying disparate phenomenal appearances. But the resulting terminological maze is impenetrable without a master to provide the secret key. In the face of growing scepticism, alchemical language grew ever more obscure in order to protect the secrets of transmutation from hostile eyes.[14] Problems of reference dominated the texts Gower is likely to have known.

Hence Gower's fellow poets also regarded alchemy with suspicion, as much for misleading language as for material fraud. Langland castigates its 'gynful speche', or deliberately deceptive speech.[15] So does Chaucer, whose *Canon's Yeoman's Tale*, although heavy with the stench of the laboratory, finally concerns fraudulent language. Its dense thickets of alchemical terminology – English, but virtually incomprehensible without Latin and Arabic – expose a language used not to foster understanding, but to block it. The Yeoman's daunting alchemical jargon thus proves a hermetic anti-vernacular, and his 'slidynge science' a despairing analogy to Chaucer's own reformative poetry.[16] Poetry resembles either the smooth-talking alchemist's confidence game or the explosive failures of the Canon and his Yeoman, who are thwarted by a heavy material world set against change. Here only names can change. The tale ends with a verbal shell-game that frustrates the quest for the 'secree of the secretes' (*Canon's*, VIII, line 1447) with a laboratory recipe that never gets past its first enigmatic direction: 'Take the stoon that Titanos men name' (*Canon's*, VIII, line 1454). Titanos is glossed as Magnasia, which is water made from the four elements – but what this is remains forever unspoken, since alchemists are sworn to secrecy.[17] The abortive quest implies both that multiplication of terms has no consequence outside language and that material transmutation cannot be expressed in words. The analogy between alchemy and poetry suggests

---

[14] As Dorothee Metlitzki points out in *The Matter of Araby in Medieval England* (New Haven, CT, 1977), p. 82, hermetic *Decknamen* were the means by which alchemical secrets were both transmitted to initiates and kept hidden from everyone else. The association of secrecy and allegory is exemplified by Petrus Bonus's *Pretiosa margarita novella* (c.1335), one of the most important fourteenth-century alchemical works. Petrus asserts that the essential secrets of alchemy are so simple that they can be learned in an hour from a master, without whose instruction they are impenetrable; see Ogrinc, 'Western society', 110; and Holmyard, *Alchemy*, p. 138.

[15] William Langland, *Piers Plowman: The B Text*, eds George Kane and E. Talbot Donaldson (London, 1975), B 10, lines 213–19.

[16] *Canterbury Tales*, VIII, 733. For alchemy as an analogue to poetry, see David Raybin, '"And pave it al of silver and of gold": the humane artistry of *The Canon's Yeoman's Tale*, in *Rebels and Rivals: The Contestive Spirit in The Canterbury Tales*, eds Susanna Greer Fein, David Raybin and Peter C. Braeger (Kalamazoo, MI, 1991), pp. 189–212.

[17] *The Canon's Yeoman's Tale*'s brilliant satire labels the endlessly deferred reference of alchemical texts 'ignotum per ignocius', glossing the unfamiliar by the more unfamiliar (VIII, line 1457); see Lee Patterson, 'Perpetual motion: alchemy and the technology of the self', *SAC*, 15 (1993), 25–57.

that ethical change and verbal art are incommensurate; in both cases, transformative efforts can continue only in bad faith.

Gower's alchemy is also a model for his poetic practice.[18] Its placement (*Confessio*, IV, lines 2457–632) among the mechanical arts suggests a belief in its material principles. Appearing in a list of human inventors and discoveries that suit the natural world to human use, it follows Saturn's invention of 'chapmanhode' (*Confessio*, IV, line 2447) and coinage from metal; metal prompts a glance at metallurgy as the prelude to alchemy. The discovery of Latin language, grammar and rhetoric ensues (*Confessio*, IV, lines 2633–71). Alchemy's placement, between the representation of value in metal coins and verbal sciences, constructs it as a form of natural rhetoric, at once material and representational.

Despite this resolutely material basis, Gower's understanding of alchemy seems entirely textual. Perhaps owing to his conception of it as a natural rhetoric, he protects its textual aspects from any taint of deceit. Alchemy in the *Confessio* is literally guileless. Here the potential for fraud and self-delusion troubles only its practice, which even Gower does not defend. Modern alchemists are no more successful than Chaucer's hapless Canon and his Yeoman – not because human beings are irremediably greedy or the material world stubbornly resistant, but because they no longer know as much as the ancients or their Arab successors. Contemporary ignorance notwithstanding, 'The science of himself is trewe | Upon the forme as it was founded' (*Confessio*, IV, lines 2598–9).

Thus Gower criticizes alchemy for falling away from a true essence he nevertheless endorses. His knowledge of the 'trewe' science seems restricted to general encyclopaedic accounts such as Vincent of Beauvais's thirteenth-century *Speculum maius*.[19] He cites as an authority Avicenna, who was perhaps its best-known sceptic (*Confessio*, IV, lines 2610–12).[20] Moreover, he chooses precisely the wrong descriptor in asserting that the great alchemical inventors – Hermes, Geber, Ortolan, Morien, and Avicenna – wrote 'pleinli / Upon this craft' (*Confessio*, IV, lines 2613–14). Alchemical texts are anything but 'plein', in both senses: clear and complete. They stress their own incompleteness, since they do not disclose their secret of secrets; and even the

---

[18] R. F. Yeager, *John Gower's Poetic: The Search for a New Arion* (Cambridge, 1990), pp. 165–9, explains Gower's treatment of alchemy as an analogue to his own poetic labour, and stresses the unity among heterogeneous elements that makes alchemy 'quite close to the center of Gower's poetic' (p. 165).

[19] Vincent (*c*.1190–*c*.1264), the first Western encyclopaedist to treat alchemy as an important branch of learning, also classified it under the mechanical arts, after mining metals. He believed transmutation was feasible: 'From the words of the above-mentioned authors it appears that alchemy is, in a sense, false. But the ancient philosophers as well as the artists of our own time have proved that it is true'; *Speculum maius*, II.11. 106, quoted from Ogrinc, 'Western society', p. 105.

[20] Both Avicenna and Albertus Magnus were credited with having written alchemical treatises, their scepticism notwithstanding. Albertus considered transmutation theoretically possible, but focused on fraudulent alchemy; see *De mineralibus*, III, treatise 1, chaps 1–9; see Ogrinc, 'Western society', p. 105.

simplest texts are opaque, owing both to the difficulty of materials and procedures and to their forbidding allegorical language.

Two aspects of alchemy in particular are imbricated in the ethical, poetic and political concerns of the *Confessio*: it is the science at once of face value and of transformation. Gower's spare account stresses the capacity of alchemical transformations to render the natural world legible, from observable accident to inner substance.[21] Metals are classified according to the degree to which they 'ben accordant' (*Confessio*, IV, line 2491) to gold or silver; by removing impurities obscuring natural resemblances to these 'tuo principal extremites' (*Confessio*, IV, line 2489), alchemy allows true essences to emerge visibly:

> And so thurgh kinde resemblant,
> That what man couthe aweie take
> The rust, of which thei waxen blake,
> And the savour and the hardnesse,
> Thei scholden take the liknesse
> Of gold or selver parfitly. (*Confessio*, IV, lines 2492–7)

This passage evinces a remarkable faith in appearances. Alchemy restores the visible image of gold or silver, whose essence has been present all along, but whose properties have been hidden by rust. Throughout, Gower stresses its ability to make likenesses true. It is the science of reliable reference.

The faith alchemists placed in the reliability of observable surfaces led to their extraordinary attention to colour. Again Chaucer provides vivid illustration. The Canon's Yeoman's mesmerizing catalogue of reagents and processes captures the play of surface colour: 'Waters rubifiyng', 'albificacioun' and 'citrinacioun' (*Canon's*, VIII, lines 797, 805, 816). The incantatory words enact the power of alchemy to blear the eye and enthrall the mind through the sheer weight and stuffness of its materials.

Still, serious alchemists too sought to change the colour of metals by treating surfaces. Colour was regarded as an activity, and hence a spirit ('pneuma'); alchemists invented elaborate, multinecked vessels and techniques to distill liquids that attacked metals, successively blackening, whitening, yellowing and reddening them.[22] While most such efforts led to nothing (or to explosions), sometimes the colour of the reagent and the product coincided. Thus when white arsenic was added to copper, the resulting copper arsenide resembled silver in colour and lustre.[23] Sometimes the result went beyond resemblance: base gold alloys turned red when heated with iron sulphate, alum and salt, since the sulphuric and hydrochloric acids formed during this process removed the base metals from the surface and left a thin layer of purified gold. No touchstone could distinguish the resulting

---

[21] Albertus and Thomas Aquinas used Aristotelian terms to contrast transmuted and real gold. The former acquired the properties ('accidentia') of natural gold but not its inner substance ('essentia'); see Ogrinc, 'Western society', p. 128.
[22] Taylor, *The Alchemists*, p. 44.
[23] *Ibid.*, p. 32.

metal from solid gold, for the surface was indeed pure.[24] Alchemists lacked the modern touchstone of qualitative analysis to tell them that the change was only superficial. Their best techniques told them that they had transmuted the metal, and that the transformed surface – always signalled by colour – revealed inward, essential change as well. The golden surface was the visible emanation of true gold beneath. For an alchemist, all that glitters must indeed be gold.

It is this devotion to the continuity of surface and depth that Gower means in describing alchemy as 'plein'. Alchemical continuity embodies a kind of sacramentalism, the visible sign of an invisible truth, to paraphrase Augustine, that makes it an apt model for Gower's ideal integrity of reference in all spheres – politics and ethics as well as language. This 'plein' continuity, legible rather than strictly literal, first appears in the Prologue's evocation of a lost golden age when:

> Of mannes herte the corage
> Was schewed thanne in the visage;
> The word was lich to the conceite
> Withoute semblant of deceite. (*Confessio*, Prol., lines 111–14)

Here ethical integrity is a form of referential integrity. In an idea and rhyme that recur throughout the poem, Gower correlates outside to inside, so that the heart's 'corage' – an inner orientation or intention – is manifest in the 'visage'. In contrast, the negative phrasing of the last line associates outer 'semblant' with 'deceite', the condition of the Prologue's diminished, divided present. The metaphor suggests legibility rather than identity. The continuity it evokes might have been expressed with the lexical alternative 'chere', but Gower instead splits it into two words.[25] Instead, the 'corage'/'visage' rhyme makes interpretative reading a necessary bridge between meanings whose identity had once been simply presupposed. The specifically poetic means of rhyme and artfully balanced couplets make inner intention contiguous with outward manifestation in face and deed, linguistic reference and ethical action.

Alchemy, like modern chemistry, was also the science of transformation. Its 'plein' surface-to-depth continuity depended on human fabrication to bring it to light. Gower's account correlates the science of transmutation with his own transformative poetry. He aligns its seven arduous processes, through which impure materials are purified into 'the parfit Elixir | Of thilke philosophres ston' (*Confessio*, IV, lines 2522–3), with the moral, ethical and political transformations he seeks through Amans's confession of the seven deadly sins. The mineral stone tempers, refines and purifies other metals so

---

[24] *Ibid.*, p. 25.

[25] In the early 1390s a new meaning of 'chere', as deceptive expression of feigned emotion, first appeared in Gower and Chaucer; sv. 'chere', definition 3, quoting *Confessio*, II, line 2061 ('Ne feigned I semblant ne chiere') and *The Canterbury Tales*, IV, lines 535–6 ('Out of the child he hente | Despitously and gan a cheere make, | As thogh he wolde han slayn it'). *MED*, http://quod.lib.umich.edu/m/med (accessed November 2009).

>   That al the vice goth aweie
>   Of rust, of stink, and of hardnesse.
>   And whan thei ben of such clennesse,
>   This mineral, so as I finde,
>   Transformeth al the ferste kynde
>   And makth hem able to conceive
>   Thurgh his vertu, and to receive
>   Bothe in substance and in figure
>   Of gold and selver the nature. (*Confessio*, IV, lines 2556–64)

Gower begins with metallurgy, modulates through terms of moral transformation, and ends with the sacramental terms of an ideal integrity of reference: the transmutation of metals takes place in both substance and appearance. Alchemy, in short, promises that the face of nature can be *made* plainly legible.

Since alchemy offers a natural, unmiraculous model for transformation, figured reliably and legibly, it compactly organizes the central concerns of the *Confessio*. The problem with alchemy was that it slipped too easily into fraud and threatened to subvert the state by counterfeiting both nature's metal and the king's face on coins. Having shielded alchemy from the suspicion of offences against political authority and referential truth, Gower can use it to forge his ideal of kingship in book VII. The analogy between alchemy and the ethics of kingship rests on the referential integrity assumed by both: tangible properties are tokens of inner meaning, and the truth embraced with the king's 'hole herte' also guarantees that 'his word be trewe and plein' as a 'tokne of that withinne' (*Confessio*, VII, lines 1730–31, 1737). Ethical reformation and right political rule come together in Aristotle's education of Alexander: learn to govern the self so that one may also govern others well. The truth embraced in the kingly heart evinces itself primarily as fidelity in language; notably, however, Genius's ideal king does not wear it in his face, but rather rules with a calculated dissimulation (*Confessio*, VII, lines 3545–52, discussed below). In the key tale of Lucretia, such politic dissimulation plays a key role in transforming her death into political reformation. As the brief appearance of alchemical language in this story suggests, alchemy's reconciliation of reliable reference with transformation provides a model for understanding the story not only as an ethical and political exemplum, but also as a drama in which the wrenching failure of Gower's ideal 'pleinness' is transmuted into a new, vernacular form.

The rape of Lucretia has always been a political myth.[26] In Livy's account, Lucretia proves her peerless virtue when her husband Collatinus and the son of the Roman tyrant, Sextus Tarquinius, observe her unawares. Inflamed by her virtue, the Tarquin takes advantage of Collatinus's hospitality and rapes her. She sends for her male relatives, tells them what has happened, and despite their faith in her innocence, kills herself. Her cousin Lucius

---

[26] Livy, *History of Rome*, trans. B. O. Foster (Cambridge, 1952), I, 52–60; *The Early History of Rome*, trans. Aubrey de Selincourt (Harmondsworth, 1960), pp. 76–85. Gower's main source is Ovid, *Fasti*, II, lines 685–852; see *Fasti*, ed. James George Frazer (Cambridge, 1967).

Junius (nicknamed Brutus) takes her bloody body to the forum and instigates a revolt in which the Tarquinian tyrants are driven from power. From Lucretia's rape, the Roman republic is born.

In the *Confessio*, Lucrece's virtue is transparently legible, for she is committed to the same face value integrity found in Gower's alchemy. Gower repeatedly stresses her utter commitment to the bond between inner virtue and outward expression. When the tyrant's son Arrons starts the competition over wifely virtue, Collatin proposes that they settle it in a 'trewe assay' (*Confessio* VII, lines 4785, 4778–9). They find Lucrece diligently at work, her words and thoughts fixed on her husband. She laments Collatin's absence in word and the expressive language of the body, as suggested in an odd demonstration of reading from outside to inside:

> With that the water in hire yhe
> Aros, that sche ne myhte it stoppe,
> And as men sen the dew bedroppe
> The leves and the floures eke,
> Riht so upon hire whyte cheke
> The wofull salte teres felle. (*Confessio*, VII, lines 4830–35)

Because Lucrece's physical expression is a natural reflex of inward intention, the passage starts with a scientifically observed process from which it infers tears. The dew simile confirms her tears as natural feeling rather than calculated performance. In both words and salt tears, Lucrece expresses 'The menynge of hire trewe herte' (*Confessio*, VII, line 4837). Alone among the Romans, for whom tyranny has severed 'herte' from 'semblant', Lucrece's 'chiere' conjoins 'visage' and 'corage' (*Confessio*, VII, lines 4733–4, 4832 et passim). It is this natural oneness that Arrons fractures when he rapes her.

Arrons embodies tyranny in the consistent split between his friendly 'countienance' and his rapacious 'corage' (*Confessio*, VII, lines 4859, 4875). Devastatingly, the rape transplants his doubleness into Lucrece: 'And thus he broghte hire herte in doute' (*Confessio*, VII, line 4982). 'Doute' means not only fear, but also doubt or uncertainty; etymologically it points to doubleness or division ('dubitum'). At the moment of crisis, Lucrece is invaded by the opposite of everything she has so far embodied. She literally disintegrates within.

The rape has no witnesses: not its victim, not its poet. Lucrece herself faints, and the narrative retreats into euphemism – that is, a division between verbal surface and intended meaning:

> And he, which al him hadde adresced
> To lust, tok thanne what him liste,
> And goth his wey, that non it wiste
> (*Confessio*, VII, lines 4988–90)

This narrative swoon both mirrors Lucrece's loss of consciousness and captures the elusive division that will wrack her. With no experience of the rape itself, but only of her 'doute' in the instant before fainting, she has no inner 'corage' to which her words and tears can later refer. It is a fatal absence. In an inversion of Lucrece's doubled heart, Gower's words (as euphemisms do) refer only improperly; he does not call rape by its name. Nevertheless, no reader can doubt his reference. The improper face of Gower's euphemism is more legible than Lucrece's once-transparent purity of heart.

Lucrece's terrible 'doute' becomes the dilemma that eventually kills her. Having lost her transparent 'pleinness', she weeps 'as sche to water scholde' (*Confessio*, VII, line 5018) and 'desguises' her hair and clothes in mourning. But she can express no inside that does not correspond to her violated outside. Alchemical language conveys Lucrece's newly troubled expression:

> And sche, which hath hire sorwes grene,
> Hire wo to telle thanne **assaieth**,
> Bot tendre schame hire word delaieth,
> That sondri times as sche **minte**
> To speke, upon the point sche stinte.
> And thei hire bidden evere in on
> To telle forth, and therupon,
> Whan that sche sih sche moste nede,
> Hire tale betwen schame and drede
> Sche tolde, noght withoute peine. (*Confessio*, VII, lines 5040–49)

The alchemical language points to the trap: Lucrece's trust in surfaces. She is true as touch, but because she cannot withstand a division between accidence and essence, her 'assay' is bound to fail. The alchemical language may even extend to 'minte', which means primarily 'intended', but may also suggest coinage, the effort to stamp a face on metal.[27] Even when she is finally able to tell her story, Gower retreats into indirect discourse, and we cannot read her words.

Lucrece's suicide is a last attempt to obliterate 'doute' and communicate the content of her heart as something other than 'schame and drede':

> A naked swerd, the which sche bar
> Withinne hire mantel priveli,
> Betwen hire hondes sodeinly
> Sche tok, and thurgh hire herte it throng.
> (*Confessio*, VII, lines 5066–9)

It is as if Lucrece has turned herself inside out. With her inward innocence no longer legible from her violated body, she makes her heart's blood physically and directly visible. By stripping her heart bare, she annihilates her intolerable illegibility to herself.

And still her death would be insufficient without someone to speak for her. Lucrece is half an alchemist; her 'pleinness' embodies reliable face value

---

[27] *MED*, sv. 'minte'; 'minte' n. (2), meaning 'intention', is attested in the late fourteenth century, but 'minte' n. (3), meaning the making of coins, is also current from 1225. The verb 'minten', in the sense of 'to mint coins', is not attested until after the period covered by the *MED*, but I suggest that this usage draws on both meanings. http://quod.lib.umich.edu/m/med (accessed November 2009).

but is for that reason especially vulnerable to 'doute', taking *in* what Arrons so violently imposed *on* her from without. She lacks the *science* of transformation. For that she needs Brutus. Brutus is alchemy's other half, a transformational reagent not bound by Lucrece's rigid fidelity to the literal. His effectiveness results from a skill at fabrication resembling the dissimulation of Genius's ideal king:

> A king schal make good visage,
> That no man knowe of his corage
> Bot al honour and worthinesse.
> For if a king schal upon gesse
> Withoute verrai cause drede,
> He mai be lich to that I rede;
> And thogh that it be lich a fable,
> Th'ensample is good and resonable.
>
> (*Confessio*, VII, lines 3545–52)

The calculated self-governance here undoes the difference between tyrants and just rulers.[28] It is hardly the ideal of Lucretian 'pleinness', without fraud or disguise. The wording instead suggests a fabricated image: the king should deliberately inscribe virtue on his 'visage' to communicate only the virtuous intentions of his 'corage'. The negative phrasing of the first part suggests that he may have motives that he does not allow others to read in his face; the second part seems to suggest that a king should terrorize his subjects only if he has good reason to do so. The lack of 'pleinness' in the king's 'visage' is embodied in the inverted, interrupted syntax of the passage, which, in doubling the calculated fabrication of the king's governance, obscures his unnerving resemblance to the tyrants Genius has just warned against in a series of graphic narratives.

Genius cannot finally distinguish good kings from tyrants, since both wilfully stamp their faces with whatever motives they wish others to read in them. But the Lucretia story offers, in Brutus, a less troubling, and more fictional, version of the ethics of political reference. He is a skilled rhetorician and even a poet. His disguise, stressed in Livy and Ovid as the enforced division between inner intent and outward expression under tyranny, survives here only in his name, which Latin readers would recognize as 'stupid, dull, insensate, without reason', and thus at odds with his penetrating intelligence. His skill at metaphor enables him to solve the enigmatic oracle warning the Tarquinians that they will be avenged by the first man to kiss his mother (*Confessio*, VII, lines 4730–32). Brutus alone drops and kisses the earth (as Gower helpfully explains, 'th'erthe of every mannes kinde | Is moder' (*Confessio*, VII, lines 4743–4)). He summons his rhetorical and poetic skill to transform the silenced, dead Lucrece into a symbol with which he incites regime change. The man who had previously 'Toward himself his herte kepte' now pulls the bloody sword from Lucrece's heart, with 'manlich

---

[28] Elizabeth Allen, *False Fables and Exemplary Truth in Later Middle English Literature* (New York, 2005), p. 81.

herte' has her body carried to the 'marketplace', and rouses the assembled citizens so that 'every mannes herte is trembled' by his tale (*Confessio*, VII, 5083–104). The heart transplant from Lucrece to Brutus to the people is poetic sleight of hand, a discursive cohesiveness substituting for a political change that is never quite specified. Through it, I believe, Gower means to recuperate Lucrece's lost 'pleinness': Brutus fabricates a way by which *he* can bring *her* heart to full outward expression and implant it in others too. His poetic capacity makes Lucrece into a potent symbol in the marketplace, through which he brings about 'betre governance' (*Confessio*, VII, line 5123).

It is a specifically vernacular resolution, the founding fable for a tentatively imagined English republic of letters. Its vernacular specificity is subtly expressed in Brutus's name, which echoes that other Brutus, the 'ferste joye' of England's 'newe Troye' in the Ricardian recension of the Prologue.[29] Second, it is suggested by the setting in the marketplace, the place of collective action and conversation. Finally, the description of the populace as the 'comun clamour' (*Confessio*, VII, line 5115), known by the sound and collectivity of their speech, recalls Gower's own earlier representation of the sounds of the English populace. The word recalls the 1381 rebels depicted in the *Vox Clamantis* as having 'brutorum species irracionis', the appearance of irrational beasts, and characterized insistently by the sounds of their clamorous, inarticulate speech.[30] Gower scarcely advocates another popular uprising. But this English 'clamour' suggests a change, if not to a political republic then perhaps to a vernacular republic. To the extent that the tellingly unspecified 'betre governance' includes political renovation, it does so as an outgrowth of the ethical and linguistic integrity restored by a collective, eloquent, vernacular 'comun clamour' roused by Brutus's well-directed poetic skill.

So what *does* Gower gain from alchemy? In part, it offers a way to sever the vernacular from political sedition and especially from religious dissent. Next to theology, alchemy was the most important medieval science of change, an organized body of natural knowledge that sought to account for changes in the properties of things. Most broadly, it offers Gower a sphere through which to work out his resistant endorsement of change. When Gower asserts both his belief in alchemical theory and his critique of contemporary prac-

---

[29] See the setting for Richard II's commissioning of the *Confessio* in the first recension:
   As it bifel upon a tyde,
   As thing which scholde tho bityde,
   Under the toun of newe Troye,
   Which took of Brut his ferste joye,
   In Temse whan it was flowende (Prologue, *35–9).

'Brut' echoes the Latin verses that open the *Confessio*, where Gower promises an English poem: 'Qua tamen Engisti lingua canit Insula Bruti | Anglica Carmente metra iuuante loquar' ('Nevertheless in the tongue of Hengist in which the island of Brutus sang, with Carmentis' aid I will utter English verses').

[30] *Vox Clamantis*, Macaulay, iv; John Gower, *The Major Latin Works of John Gower*, trans. Eric Stockton (Seattle, WA, 1962), p. 54. The verb forms *clamat*, *clamavit* predominate; see Steven Justice, *Writing and Rebellion: England in 1381* (Berkeley, CA, 1994), pp. 207–18. Yeager, *John Gower's Poetic*, pp. 153–4, discusses bestialization as loss of reason; see *Vox*, I, lines 177–8.

tice, he reconciles his commitment to reformative change with the conservative's unhappiness with actual changes in his social world. Gower was a reformer who never met a reform he liked; for such a person, what better model for transformation than alchemy? As a theory of change, alchemy is deeply attractive because it appeals to an underlying lack of change; it aims to strip away the 'rust' of deceiving appearances and return things to their true natures, once hidden and now made truly visible. Committed to an integrity of reference that gives a visible face to the inner, invisible workings of nature and the human heart, Gower finds in alchemy a rebuttal to Lollard iconoclasm (its tendency to devalue images, external forms and sacraments) in favour of an unmediated relation between believer and deity, or a truth unaffected by the materiality of human language. Not least, the natural rhetoric of alchemy offers him a way to imagine a role for vernacular poetry in the ethical and political reforms of the *Confessio*. Sadly, however, Brutus's 'betre governance' remains as nameless and elusive as the 'ignotum per ignocius' that haunts *The Canon's Yeoman's Tale*.

Chapter 14

Gower's Business: Artistic Production of Cultural Capital and The Tale of Florent

BRIAN GASTLE

The prologue to the first recension of the *Confessio Amantis* describes the now-famous patronage scene, wherein King Richard commands that the narrator 'som newe thing I sholde boke' (*Confessio*, Prol., line 51).[1] This scene takes place upon the Thames, 'under the toun of newe Troye', after the narrator has left his own boat and come aboard the royal barge at the king's request. It is one of the few literal manifestations of London we have in Gower's poetry and remarkable also in its representation of literary patronage. As Robert Epstein states, 'It becomes difficult to find in Gower's writing any association with the City of London or its suburbs.'[2] Rather, Epstein continues, comparing Gower's separation from London with the famous portrait of Gower removed from the globe, Gower 'is of the world but not in it'.[3] So too is the Thames passage a representation of this, since the narrator is looking upon London, but is separate and apart from it in the river. I am not so much interested here in the historical veracity of this event, something which has been much debated in the past, and which will probably never be verified.[4] Instead, I am interested in addressing why Gower chose to narrate this section of the poem in the way that he did, both in the body of the poem and in the attendant marginal notations. Gower, on the barge, traverses a river that, like contemporary cartographic representations of the globe, splits his world in three: suburban Southwark and its mélange of professions, the courts of Westminster, and the economic, artistic and political hub of the city of London itself. In this opening scene Gower,

---

[1] All quotations from Gower's works are taken from Macaulay. First and second recension references will be marked by an asterisk. For discussions of differences, both scribal and thematic, between the recensions, see especially Peter Nicholson, 'Gower's revisions in the *Confessio Amantis*', *CR*, 19 (1984), 123–43, as well as Dhira B. Mahoney, 'Gower's two Prologues to *Confessio Amantis*', in *Re-visioning Gower*, ed. R. F. Yeager (Asheville, NC, 1998), pp. 17–37, and Derek Pearsall, 'Manuscripts and illustrations', in *Companion*, pp. 61–97 (pp. 93–4).

[2] Robert Epstein, 'London, Southwark, Westminster: Gower's urban contexts', in *Companion*, pp. 43–60 (p. 57).

[3] Epstein, 'London, Southwark, Westminster', p. 43.

[4] See, for example and summary of this debate, Frank Grady, 'Gower's boat, Richard's barge, and the true story of the *Confessio Amantis*: text and gloss', *Texas Studies in Literature and Language*, 44 (2002), 1–15.

rather than inhabiting the margins, becomes the poetic centre for this urban environment, and that centre (the Thames) is unabashedly commercial.

Whether or not the meeting ever happened, or actually happened in the way narrated, in this opening scene Gower capitalizes upon the cultural and economic role of the Thames to position himself, as poet, apart from the confines of London and yet able to comment upon the various political and social machinations of his mercantile urban environment. I would suggest that, while most of the *Confessio* focuses upon artistic, philosophical, theological and political issues, this opening scene evokes a mercantile undercurrent, if you will, influencing and defining Gower's artistry. These mercantile concerns, and Gower's own changing position on the role of business, are played out in the various recensions of the Prologue. Furthermore, I suggest that Gower returns to these concerns in subtle ways in The Tale of Florent, and Chaucer recognizes and amplifies those concerns in his own, more clearly mercantile, version in *The Wife of Bath's Tale*. Gower's business – artistic production of cultural capital – may not be overtly urban (or even overtly mercantile) but it certainly begins in the economic and political centre of England's most urban and trade-conscious locale. For when Gower looked upon the city of London, he meant business.

Gower's (or the narrator's) presence on the Thames is not surprising, since the Thames was used regularly for local transportation between London, Southwark and Westminster, and it was apparently common for the clerks of Chancery to travel between the Temple and Westminster by boat.[5] So even if Gower had retired from his supposed legal career by the 1370s, as Fisher suggests,[6] such transport would not have been out of place. Although his residence at the Priory of St Mary Overey was extremely close to London Bridge, it would make sense for him, given his self-proclaimed 'illness', to travel by water-taxi rather than make the trek to London by the bridge.

While we hear nothing of a companion on that boat, there is a silent other in the background of this event. It seems unlikely that the somewhat infirm Gower would be rowing himself, 'As I be bote cam rowende' (*Confessio*, Prol., line 40*) but we hear nothing of the waterman who takes him to his destination, nor do we hear about Gower paying for his journey, a point to which I shall return. I am interested in that omission of detail because it would appear to speak to Gower's casual inattentiveness to workaday matters within his poem. Yet the language he will go on to use to describe his project belies this seeming ignorance. Once on the barge, the narrator states that the King:

> Hath this charge upon me leid,
> And bad me doo my besynesse
> That to his hihe worthinesse
> Som newe thing I sholde boke (*Confessio*, Prol., lines 48–51*)

---

[5] James Field Willard, 'Inland transportation in England during the fourteenth century', *Speculum*, 1, 4 (1926), 361–74 (p. 362).
[6] John Fisher, *John Gower: Moral Philosopher and Friend of Chaucer* (New York, 1964), pp. 59–60.

Gower's use of the term 'business' here is interesting and, I would suggest, calculated. It is not a particularly unusual term for Gower – he uses it over forty times in the *Confessio* – but his application of it does appear strategic. He most commonly uses it (about half the number of usages in the poem) in book IV when addressing the sin of Sloth. For example, Idleness is characterized as that 'which alle labour set behinde | And hateth alle besinesse' (*Confessio*, IV, lines 1084–85) and 'with thi grete besinesse | Thou miht atteigne the richesse | Of love' (*Confessio*, IV, lines 513–15). Nicola Masciandaro, in *The Voice of the Hammer*, points out that in Gower's approach to the history of work in book IV, 'Material labour is thus valued as temporal, earthly, and merely useful, whereas mental labour is valued intrinsically as enacting and producing transcendental value.'[7] Similarly, Genius returns to the term 'business' in book VII when discussing sloth during the teaching of Alexander. But unique to the use of the term 'business' in the Prologue is the fact that it refers to the poet's own business, a fact attested to by the syntax of the rest of that line. The narrator is told some new thing he 'sholde boke'. The verb 'boke', to compose or write, reflects the command of the king, who also links that endeavour with the narrator's business. As Gregory Sadlek points out, 'Gower's favoured labour ideology is one that presents work as a necessary but positive human activity, one whose value derives not merely because it is an antidote to idleness but primarily because of its material contribution to the common profit.'[8] In this instance, the narrator's business, according to his king, is explicitly the craft of composition, and like any craft it requires work and hopefully leads to some form of remuneration. It is both his 'busy-ness' and his 'business' and will lead to artistic (if not monetary) profit.

Concurrently, in the margins of many first and second recension manuscripts, just prior to the king's request for the narrator to do his business, is a summary marginal note in Latin:

> Hic declarat in primis qualiter ob reuerenciam serenissimi principis domini sui Regis Anglie Ricardi secundi totus suus humilis Iohannes Gower, licet graui infirmitate a diu multipliciter fatigatus, huius opusculi laboures suscipere non recusauit, sed tanquam fauum ex variis floribus recollectum, presentem libellum ex variis cronicis, historiis, poetarum philosophorumque dictis, quatenus sibi infirmitas permisit, studiosissime compilauit.
>
> (Here he declares particularly how, because of reverence of the most serene prince, his lord king of England Richard II, his own and humble John Gower, although long wearied in many ways by grave illness, did not refuse to take up the labours of this little work, but instead has most zealously compiled the present little book from various chronicles, histories, and sayings of poets and philosophers, like a honeycomb gathered from various flowers, to the extent that his infirmity allowed him.)[9]

---

[7] Nicola Masciandaro, *The Voice of the Hammer* (Notre Dame, IN, 2007), pp. 84–94 (p. 85).
[8] Gregory M. Sadlek, *Idleness Working: The Discourse of Love's Labour from Ovid through Chaucer and Gower* (Washington DC, 2004), p. 171. For a discussion of Gower's use of the term 'business' elsewhere in the *Confessio* see pp. 190–200.
[9] Translations of Latin passages in the *Confessio* are Andrew Galloway's, from Peck.

This note appears in the margin at or between lines 34–5 of a number of first and second recension manuscripts. As Olsson points out, in *John Gower and the Structures of Conversion*, the 'variis floribus' trope may indeed underscore Gower's views of the *Confessio* as a form of 'compilatio', and the 'honeycomb' image certainly foreshadows appropriately the interconnectedness of the *Confessio* narratives.[10] But that particular metaphor also partakes of the common link between bees and laudable workaday behaviour. Petrarch, in *De otio religioso*, will compare the work of monks to that of bees, and in *Le Familiari* 1.8 he will even compare bees' work to that of poets.[11] And Chaucer, apart from his infamous swarm of bees fleeing Satan in *The Summoner's Tale* prologue, has his Host invoke the bee metaphor in the epilogue to *The Merchant's Tale* to characterize how busy wives deceive their husbands. But it is bees' direct association with work or labour, as well as their affiliation with social order and monarchical control, attested to in both scriptural and contemporary medieval accounts, that I am interested in applying to this instance.

The narrator agrees to 'take up the labour' ('laboures') of his 'little work' ('opusculi'), and while referring to the *Confessio* as a little work is certainly a literary trope (and a rare moment of humour given that few scholars, and probably no students, have ever referred to the *Confessio* as 'little'), it also neatly transitions into the iconic 'little workers' that close this marginal note. Alexander Neckam, in his *De Laudibus Divinae Sapientiae*, identifies bees as laudatory parallels for human behaviour because of their work ethic,[12] whereas in his *De Naturis Rerum* he culls material from the *Georgics* to use them as examples of good rule.[13] For Neckham, 'ingeniosus' is linked to the physical labour of bees, and both the ingenuity and work of the bee exceeds that of people. So too does the bee exceed humanity when it comes to works of art, given the bee's production of honey. By invoking the bee, Gower's 'opusculi laboures' similarly posits the process of literary production via 'compilatio' as an exemplary form of artistic production. His work then becomes cultural capital that will partake of both artistic and mercantile markets as it is reproduced, transmitted and disseminated. While *The Merchant's Tale* epilogue in *The Canterbury Tales* likens deceptive women to being as 'bisy as bees' (line 2422), Gower's evocation of their honey production focuses upon the laudable aspects of their work.

Both Pliny the Elder, in *Naturalis Historia*, and Isidore of Seville, in *Etymologies*, relate that bees select a king to rule them and order their societies

---

[10] Kurt Olsson, *John Gower and the Structures of Conversion: A Reading of the 'Confessio Amantis'* (Cambridge, 1992), pp. 5–10.

[11] For a discussion of Petrarch's use of the trope, see Susanna Barsella, 'Boccaccio, Petrarch, and Peter Damian: two models of the Humanist intellectual', *MLN*, 121, 1 (2006), 16–48 (p. 33), and Amy W. Goodwin. 'The Griselda Game', *CR*, 39, 1 (2004), 41–69 (p. 45).

[12] Alexander Neckam, *Alexandri Neckam De naturis rerum libri duo: with the poem of the same author, 'De laudibus divinæ sapientiæ'*, ed. Thomas Wright (Oxford, 1863), p. 491 (IX, lines 223–30).

[13] In Chapter 163, Neckam evokes an image of the 'king' bee without a sting to argue for mercy among monarchs.

much like humans, in that they wage war, post sentries and adopt a class system which includes drones, workers and warriors. The later medieval bestiary tradition continues this focus on bees' social order.[14] Chaucer will echo this tradition in *The Parson's Tale*, when the Parson points out that bees choose a king without a sting to reflect the pity that should be inherent in a person of gentility:

> Now been ther generale signes of gentillesse, as … to be benigne to his goode subgetis, wherfore seith Senek, "Ther is no thing moore covenable to a man of heigh estaat than debonairetee and pitee, / and therfore thise flyes that men clepen bees, whan they maken hir kyng, they chesen oon that hath no prikke wherwith he may stynge." (*Parson's*, X, lines 464–8)

In *Li Livres dou Tresor*, a work with which Gower was familiar, Brunetto Latini will, after first describing their physical development, begin his description of bees by praising their industry and the products of their labour: honey and wax. He will then go on to describe their almost communistic social order wherein each bee's work is the same as another's, as is their food. The social order of bees, according to Latini's *significatio*, culminates in unswerving devotion to their king:

> In short you should know that they love their king very much, and they have such faith and courage that they throw themselves into the peril of death to protect their king and to rescue him. As long as the king is hale and hearty, they are unswerving in their faith and judgment, but when he dies or is lost, they lose their faith and judgment in such a way that they lose and destroy their honey and destroy their hives. (*Li Livres*, I, lines 154–6)[15]

So a lost king not only results in chaos in the hive but also leads to destruction of produced goods and proletarian output. The mode of production, the hive, is destroyed along with the goods produced, the honey, and for Gower that honey represents his own work. The association of bees with monarchy and power is especially intriguing given Gower's positioning of the reference in the first recension against his meeting with Richard on the Thames. Gower's revision of the prologue in the later recensions redirects the acknowledgement away from King Richard to Henry, and that revision also removes the marginal gloss likening Gower's *compilatio* project to the work of bees. In so doing the final version erases much of Gower's focus on artistic and cultural production as the work or business of poets.

In that first recension, as Russell Peck notes, 'Gower turns his expression of allegiance into an epitome of a true subject's right relationship with his liege lord, thus adding an important touch to the theme of kingship and

---

[14] See, for example, Bartholomaeus Anglicus's *De Proprietatibus Rerum*, which serves as a source of bee lore for *Mum and the Sothsegger*. In *Mum*, the bee 'of alle bestz beste is ygouverned | Yn lowlynes and labour and in lawe eeke' (997–8) and represents both exemplary work and exemplary rule, although as a political poem *Mum* is more interested in the latter (*Mum and the Sothsegger Edited from the Manuscripts Camb. Univ. Ll. iv. 14 and Brit. Mus. Add. 41666*, eds Mabel Day and Robert Steele, EETS o.s. 199. (Oxford, 1936), lines 987–1086).

[15] Brunetto Latini, *Li Livres dou Tresor*, eds and trans Paul Barrette and Spurgeon Baldwin (New York, 1993), p. 118.

common profit which he is preparing to develop.'[16] Peck believes the third recension is not merely a revision, but that it amounts to an 'obliteration [...] a total disenchantment with Richard'.[17] In addition, since the final version of the *Confessio* removes Richard's commission, it also deletes the call by Richard for the poet to 'do his business'. But that revision does not altogether remove language that associated Gower's poetic work with mercantile endeavours. The revision of the passage that originally evoked Richard includes a diatribe against tyrants:

> The worthi princes that tho were,
> The bokes schewen hiere and there,
> Wherof the world ensampled is;
> And tho that deden thanne amis
> Thurgh tirannie and cruelte
> Right as thei stonden in degre,
> So was the wryting of here werk. (*Confessio*, Prol., lines 45–51)

So, says the narrator, the world is full of examples of worthy princes, and as for those who 'did amiss' because of cruelty and tyranny, just as much as they were cruel and tyrannical, as Gower puts it, 'so was the writing of their works'. That is a rather interesting line, since the 'writing' may refer to the representations of deeds but it may also refer to the writing itself: the more cruel the tyrant, the more explicit the work depicting that tyrant's actions, but perhaps also the more significant and important is the work of the author who represents those deeds.

Gower turns from the works of the tyrant (interesting in itself, given the turn away from Richard to Henry) and the works of the chronicler of the tyrant's deeds to his own work as he continues: 'Thus I, which am a burel clerk | Purpose for to wryte a bok' (*Confessio*, Prol., lines 52–53). The 'ignorant clerk' motif is, of course, a commonplace for medieval authors, but it is worth noting that Gower, who elsewhere seems so removed from the workaday life of his contemporary London environment, here at the beginning of the *Confessio* will acknowledge his own work as a form of cultural and political production, for

> Thogh I seknesse have upon honde
> And longe have had, yit woll I fonde
> To wryte and do my bisinesse
> That in som part, so I gesse
> The wyse man mai ben avised. (*Confessio*, Prol., lines 61–5)

In this later version of the Prologue, Gower refers to his business as writing. But rather than receiving a command from his monarch, the narrator motivates himself to apply his craft for the benefit of his nation, 'For this prologe is so assised / That it to wisdom al belongeth' (*Confessio*, Prol., line 67–8).

---

[16] Russell A. Peck, *Kingship and Common Profit in Gower's 'Confessio Amantis'* (Carbondale, 1978), p. 7.
[17] *Ibid.*, p. 8.

So, in all versions of the Prologue, Gower figures his artistic production as his work, his business in multiple senses of the term. But some key elements of mercantile activity have changed from the earlier versions. Gone is the physical locale of London and the Thames, and therefore gone too is the urban economic backdrop for the poem. As Peck points out, the earlier version is a 'nostalgic autobiography',[18] whereas the later version focuses upon the increasing social and political decay of England. The earlier version is written 'for King Richardes' sake, whereas the later version is 'for Engelondes sake'. But the earlier version localizes the rule of Richard, positioning him on the economic and military highway of the Thames. So too does it localize the work of the poet, since Gower himself surveys the tripartite London just as he will survey the tripartite social classes later in the Prologue, and just as he will survey the tripartite world in that classic image of him shooting his arrows. While there is nothing particularly surprising about a poet referring to his or her 'works' or to the 'business' of poetry, I would suggest that Gower's use of the term is calculated, given its other uses in the *Confessio*.

Apart from the use of the term in his admonitions against Sloth later in the *Confessio*, Gower will use it one final time at the end of the poem in book VIII in the earlier recension:

> And for this cause in myn entente
> This povere bok heer I presente
> Unto his hihe worthinesse,
> Write of my simple besinesse,
> So as seeknesse suffre wolde. (*Confessio*, VIII, lines 3049–53*)

This passage mirrors the opening patronage scene in which Richard commands the narrator to write the book, to do his business. But this return to artistic production as business appears only in the earlier recension – the Ricardian version – of the poem. Later versions offer a prayer for England and kingship rather than for Richard in particular. And the final section on kingship in the later versions begins by foregrounding a king's power over clerk, knight, lawyer, merchant and labourer. The earliest of the versions, therefore, is most rife with recognition of poetic production as business, and so too does it most situate that work, at least for Gower, in the environs of London. While Gower rarely touches upon work and labour throughout the rest of the *Confessio*, we can see moments where that preoccupation with artistic production as cultural work emerges. In fact, I believe that his work was perceived in those economic terms, to some extent, by at least one of his contemporaries, for while Richard implored (if not employed) Gower to work, Chaucer recognized in the *Confessio* Gower's interest in artistic production as work.

Gower has not benefited from Chaucer's reputation as accessible or relevant to mundane issues such as labour and mercantile activity. In some

---

[18] Ibid, p. 8.

ways this is a result of Chaucer's own characterization of Gower as 'Moral Gower'. How might his reputation have changed had Chaucer named him 'Happy Gower' or, alliteratively, 'Giddy Gower'? Stuck as he is with the nomenclature of 'Moral Gower', Gower suffers, as Derek Pearsall puts it, 'the odour of unsuccess'[19] that extends from the early modern period to the present. I would extend Pearsall's comment by saying that, in the meantime, Chaucer has benefited from the reek, or stench, of success (both good Old English words as opposed to Gower's French 'odour'). But, as the concern with labour evidenced by the first recension suggests, Gower is not perhaps as far removed from the workaday aspects of humanity as he may first appear, and I believe Chaucer himself recognized that in him. True, Chaucer's success may derive from the humour found in *The Miller's Tale* or the Summoner's Prologue, a kind of ribaldry that is all but absent in Gower, but Chaucer and Gower found common ground, and common utility, in tales like The Tale of Florent and the Wife of Bath's version of that tale.

Much, of course, has been written of the two versions of this story. Gower is more interested in the political while Chaucer is in some ways more personal in his engendering of the tale. As Peter Beidler puts it, 'Gower's tale demonstrates how a cautious and near-perfect knight *does* behave in a dangerous and hostile situation, whereas Chaucer's tale shows how an impulsive and most imperfect knight *learns how to* behave in a far less threatening situation.'[20] So, Beidler suggests, Gower's is reflective – it portrays or shows an ideal – whereas Chaucer's is didactic – it instructs through character development. However, Florent does indeed learn something through the course of the tale, a lesson echoed and amplified by Chaucer's version. While not as overtly and blatantly mercantile as Chaucer's version, Gower's tale portrays a knight within a traditional courtly romance who comes to experience and learn from the economic realities of marriage, realities that were constantly changing in the economic and social landscape of the late fourteenth century. This education in marital commodification is then an extension of the interest in artistic work as labour delineated in the Prologue.

Given her propensity for merchandising both her cloth and her sexuality, and her appeal towards feminine authority in both prologue and tale, the Wife of Bath exemplifies a highly stylized literary representation of late medieval mercantility. She is, as R. A. Shoaf states, 'a figure of the commercial idiom and the commercial imagination',[21] and, as Mark Amsler demonstrates, her power, mercantile or otherwise, extends far beyond that figure, 'a power – sexual, economic, textual, and political – which is peculiar to England and the fourteenth century'.[22] She participates in those fourteenth-century discourses which characterize the relations – often problematic – between

---

[19] Derek Pearsall, 'The Gower tradition', in *Confessio Amantis: Responses and Reassessments*, ed. A. J. Minnis (Cambridge, 1983), p. 194.
[20] Peter G. Beidler, 'Transformations in Gower's *Tale of Florent* and Chaucer's *Wife of Bath's Tale*', in *Chaucer and Gower: Difference, Mutuality, Exchange*, ed. R. F. Yeager (Victoria, B.C., 1991), pp. 100–114 (p. 101).
[21] R. A. Shoaf, *Dante, Chaucer, and the Currency of the World* (Norman, OK, 1983), p. 175.
[22] Mark Amsler, 'The Wife of Bath and women's power', *Assays*, 4 (1986), 67–83 (p. 68).

aristocratic ideals, merchants and merchant marriages. Chaucer's own position within the merchant communities of London would have offered opportunities to experience the active role that women played within those communities and the effect women had upon merchant companies. And this experience, 'though noon auctoritee', is explicit in, among others, the characterization of the Wife of Bath and the commodification of her body.[23] *The Wife of Bath's Tale* – like the romances told by other mercantile and quasi-mercantile pilgrims – despite its apparently lofty concerns, plays out its narrator's anxiety regarding trade, women's role in economic activity and, perhaps most importantly, conjugal debt. While the tale revolves around a traditional chivalric quest narrative, the quest of this tale is readdressed as a negotiation of debt and surety. Arthur, the supreme legal authority, abdicates his legal authority to Guenevere. She, in turn, refigures the punishment by positing it in economic terms, which reflects the transgression against property inherent in the knight's rape of the maiden. The loss of the maiden's virginity would, to Chaucer's and Gower's contemporaries, have been seen as a trespass against the value of the maiden in marriage negotiations. So Guenevere points out to the knight: '"Thou standest yet", quod she, "in swich array / That of thy lyf hastow no surety"' (*Wife*, III, lines 902–3). The 'surety' to which she refers is certainly 'assurance' that he will live, but so too does that term evoke the language of mercantile and political contracts which demand collateral. Asking him to find out what women most desire, Guenevere continues:

> And if thou kanst nat tellen it anon,
> Yet wol I yeve thee leve for to gon
> A twelf-month and a day, to seche and leere
> An answere suffisant in this mateere;
> And suretee wol I han, er that thou pace,
> Thy body for to yelden in this place. (*Wife*, III, lines 907–12)

In the Prologue, the Wife of Bath's body is commodified through her five marriages, the body depreciating in value as her economic wealth appreciates. In Chaucer's version of the tale itself, the knight is forced into negotiating for his *corpus*. Guenevere negotiates for his life, and holds his body as surety for that life, and the old woman subsequently enters into a similar contract with him. It is tempting to wonder (considering to what use the old hag plans to put the knight's body) whether, when Guenevere requires him 'thy body for to yelden', it is necessarily his life that she will require of him, or whether she, like the hag, may find more use for it alive than dead. The hag's bargaining for the knight's body is in any case a reversal of the

---

[23] For discussions of the commodification of the Wife of Bath's body see especially both Laurie Finke, '"All is for to selle": breeding capital: sexual economies in the Wife of Bath's Prologue and Tale', in *Geoffrey Chaucer: The Wife of Bath: Complete, Authoritative Text with Biographical and Historical Contexts, Critical History, and Essays from Five Contemporary Critical Perspectives*, ed. Peter G. Beidler (New York, 1995), pp. 171–87, and Carolyn Dinshaw, *Chaucer's Sexual Poetics* (Madison, WI, 1989).

standard negotiation with (or on) a woman's body, such as we later see in the Franklin's and Shipman's tales.

Such contractual negotiations rely upon the legal and social aspects of marriage as well as upon the authority of women within contemporary mercantile communities.[24] While Guenevere's language is courtly, echoing, among other sources, the language of the formal duel, in which one proves 'on one's body' that one is in the right, in the context of the hag's bargain and the question Guenevere wants answered Guenevere acts as a *femme sole*, contracting for the body of the knight. The legal power over the knight which her husband commands is officially withdrawn in favour of the power of the wife – she is conducting business on her own account, and the repercussions of that contract are, according to English law, divested from the goods and activities of her husband.[25] The Wife's interests are such that even Arthurian romance is a vehicle for the discussion of essentially mercantile issues, particularly when those issues are complicated by the advent of businesswomen. For Chaucer's and Gower's audiences, marriage was essentially a contract to be negotiated and figured in terms of property.

Gower's scene is not wholly devoid of such contractual obligation, but the initial contract in his scene evokes feudal obligation and social standing more than business dealings. Branchus's grandmother proposes the task, but in Gower's version it is the Knight who invokes and writes the contract, saying he wishes the proposal 'under seales write' (Florent, 1.1474), and, when he agrees to the task, 'under his seal he wrot his oth' (Florent, 1.1487). Both Chaucer's version and Gower's version depend upon the knight's return, but Gower's is more documentary. Twice he recounts the document in which Florent signs his oath and affixes his seal. Affixing of the seal authorizes the contract by associating the agreement with Florent's personal and familial history. Unlike the contractual negotiation of Chaucer's version, Gower's initial agreement echoes vassalage and feudal obligation. This is not wholly unexpected given the generic constraints within which Gower was writing, but it may also point to recognition in Chaucer's version of the untrustworthiness of the rapist knight's promise (given the nature of the transgression). He must yield his body as collateral or surety because his word, his reputation, his seal, is no longer sufficient.

---

[24] A comparable moment in contemporary literature is Margery Kempe's negotiations with her husband in *The Book of Margery Kempe*. Margery's desire for a 'chaste marriage' is initially thwarted by her obligations to her husband. Ultimately, she can secure her desire for chastity by agreeing to pay her husband's debts, another instance of a wife's body figured in economic terms and defined by a specific exchange value. For discussions of these issues in the *Book of Margery Kempe* see Nona Fienberg, 'Thematics of value in *The Book of Margery Kempe*', MP, 87, 2 (1989), 132–41, and Lynn Staley, *Margery Kempe's Dissenting Fictions* (University Park, PA, 1994), p. 40.

[25] For a discussion of single women, widows and wives operating as *femme sole* see Amy M. Froide, 'Marital status as a category in early modern England', in *Singlewomen in the European Past 1250–1800*, eds Judith M. Bennett and Amy M. Froide (Philadelphia, PA, 1999), pp. 246–8 and Brian Gastle, '"as if she were single": working wives and the late medieval English *femme sole*', in *The Middle Ages at Work: Practicing Labour in Late Medieval England*, eds Kellie Robertson and Michael Uebel (New York, 2004), pp. 41–64.

Shortly after this scene in both versions the old woman arrives to proffer a 'sufficient' answer. In Chaucer's version, when the old woman fulfils her end of the bargain with the knight, giving him the answer which allows him to (technically) fulfil the quest narrative, she requires his body as compensation, 'that thou me take unto thy wyf', not unlike the way in which Guenevere required it as collateral. His first reaction is to offer alternative payment: 'Taak al my good and lat my body go' (*Wife*, line 1061). He attempts a restitution or substitution of goods ('good') for what was originally contracted ('body'), a response reminiscent of the Pardoner's interruption to Alison's prologue. Like the Pardoner, the knight associates the marriage contract with a transfer of the body as real property, inverting the traditional image of the woman's body as part and parcel of the goods associated with the marriage dowry. The Wife's tale, then, is a further response to the Pardoner's interruption, picking up on the Pardoner's initial critique of the marriage contract as a devaluation of the husband's body as well as the wife's. The hag of Alison's tale answers the knight's despair using both aristocratic and mercantile language. She not only insists upon the letter of the law, requiring her pound of flesh, but launches into a diatribe concerning her gentility (or social worth) despite her poor background, saying: 'Heere may ye se wel how that genterye | Is nat annexed to possessioun' (*Wife*, lines 1146–7) – that possession which increasingly dictated social standing in London society over class designation. In general, wives or widows assumed the same social standing as their spouses. As Sylvia Thrupp states:

> Wives of veteran merchant wardens were not slow to assume the equivalent prefix of mistress or, better still, of my Lady, which set them apart from the wives of other merchants. Wives of Wardens in the lesser companies seem to have been content to be called 'goodwife'.[26]

The Wife of Bath herself exhibits this interest in social positioning when she walks ahead of all other women in church. Those who made the most money (i.e., those who could afford membership in the livery) were afforded the respect of rank appropriate to the prestigious (pseudo-aristocratic) merchant classes.

The corresponding passage in Gower's version portrays a similar recognition by Gower of the workaday aspects of marriage, especially the economic subtleties associated with secular union. In Gower's version, Florent is given the terms of the contract prior to agreeing to it. That in itself dissociates the story from the folklore motif of the 'rash promise' present in and capitalized upon in Chaucer's version. *A priori* terms characterize the arrangement more as a traditional contractual obligation wherein the parties are privy to the terms and agree before executing the contract, and such contracts were, since Bracton,[27] associated with oaths and pacts and required *quid pro*

---

[26] Sylvia Thrupp, *The Merchant Class in Medieval London, 1300–1500* (Ann Arbor, MI, 1948; rpt 1989), p. 24.

[27] Henry de Bracton (c.1250) in his *De Legibus et Consuetudinibus Angliae* provided the basis for much of later medieval civil law and policy, including mercantile contracts and marriage

quo to be binding. Mercantile contracts require consideration, or value for transmittal; offering something for nothing isn't a contract, it is a gift. In The Tale of Florent the Old Woman will reinforce the contractual nature of the agreement by stating:

> 'I bidde nevere a betre taxe',
> Quod sche, 'bot ferst, er thou be sped,
> Thou schalt me leve such a wedd,
> That I wol have thi trowthe in honde
> That thou schalt be myn housebonde'. (Florent, I, lines 157–61)

She asks for no other payment – 'I bidde nevere a betre taxe' – than for him to agree to marry him. The marriage becomes appropriate compensation or consideration for the answer she provides. Interestingly, the *Middle English Dictionary* defines this particular instance of 'taxe' as a fine, penalty or fee. But the primary definition (both in ME and in MnE) of 'tax' is a price levied by a sovereign or government.[28] The few other instances of the word in the *Confessio* imply a requirement or payment (and always, interestingly, rhyme 'taxe' with 'axe' as a form of 'ask').[29] This fairly peculiar use of the word by Gower, associating 'tax' with both a payment and a request, links the marriage contract with the social obligation of the individual. Payment in this case becomes the knight's name in marriage. Furthermore, in Gower's tale, when trying to negotiate for some other payment, Florent spells out all of the goods that he offers instead of his troth:

> Florent behihte hire good ynowh
> Of lond, of rente, of park, of plowh,
> Bot al that compteth sche at noght. (Florent, I, lines 565–7)

Gower does not need a subsequent diatribe as Chaucer does – the rant against the aristocratic presumption that wealth is tantamount to gentility – because Florent exhibits that disposition here. The specific goods he offers are all real property: land, rental income, game land and farmland. These are the 'goods' of the landed gentry and aristocracy, but the tale leads him to recognize he is not exempt from contemporary contractual responsibili-

---

contracts. For a discussion of his influence on later English contract law see especially William M. McGovern, 'Contract in medieval England: the necessity for quid pro quo and a sum certain', *The American Journal of Legal History*, 13, 3 (1969), 173–201 (pp. 181–3).

[28] *MED*: tax(e) (n.) Pl. *taxes, taxus*. (a) An obligatory contribution levied on persons, possessions, property, etc. by a sovereign or government, impost; also, the rate at which a tax is levied [quot. 1455]; within the ~, on the tax rolls; (b) a fine, penalty; also [1st quot.], a fee; – ?with punning ref. to task(e) n. (b) (a1393) Gower CA (Frf 3) 1.1556: What schal I have to my mede? ... I bidde nevere a betre taxe ... bot ferst ... Thou schalt me leve such a wedd ... That thou schalt be myn housebonde.

[29] Six other instances appear in *Confessio*: 'Wherof the holi cherche is taxed, / That in the point as it is axed' (Prol., lines 267–8); 'The king thes thre demandes axeth, / And to the knyht this lawe he taxeth' (I, lines 3107–8); 'The double of that his felaw axeth;/ And thus to hem his grace he taxeth' (II, lines .333–4); 'Whan Salomon his bone hath taxed, I The god of that which he hath axed' (VII, lines 3905–6); 'Foryive and grante al that is axed I Of that his fader hadde taxed' (VII, lines 4701–2); 'And in this wise his lawe he taxeth, /That what man that his doghter axeth' (VII, lines 361–62)

ties. If his agreement to the terms were merely a manifestation of his courtly ideals, Florent would not thereafter pursue the line of thought he does.

The subsequent rationalization by Florent – that the Old Woman will die soon and he can keep her on an island alone until then – is really one of the more pragmatic and unknightly things we see him do. It is also one of the more humorous moments in the tale (and one upon which Chaucer cannot capitalize in his version). But it certainly does not accord with the belief that Genius is presenting an uncomplicated exemplum for Amans. That pragmatic and humourous moment derives immediately from Florent's experience negotiating for his life, negotiating for his nuptials and negotiating for his worldly goods. So, whereas Chaucer's version shows a rapist knight learning to behave in a way the Wife of Bath desires, The Tale of Florent offers a traditional romance knight learning to behave more pragmatically given the economic and social context of marriage negotiations, even though that commercialization appears in a more traditional medieval romance narrative.

Medieval romances tend to be among the most stylized and tropaically rigorous of all literary genres: a genre generally devoted to highly stylized diction, aristocratic and chivalric civility and idealized relationships, or, as Derek Pearsall puts it, 'a narrative of the life of an idealized warrior aristocracy, in which prowess in feats of arms and dedication to the service of women are the principal subjects.'[30] Traditionally, these narratives often mask the necessity for the everyday or the mundane; their non-aristocratic characters are largely character parts, so to speak. Interest in the commonplace, the workaday and (not coincidentally) the financial had, by the end of the fourteenth century throughout Europe, become increasingly associated with mercantile activity, whose business it was to supply comfort, wealth and luxury rather than more moral or spiritual commodities. Despite their increasing financial power, a merchant's place in the traditional romance, if any, could only be a subordinate one. But Gower's Tale of Florent, for all its adherence to the traditional romance, offers a glimpse into the intrusion of fiscal reality upon courtly ideals, a glimpse Chaucer amplifies and repositions for his own narrator. Concomitantly, the Prologue to the *Confessio* is interested in this issue to varying degrees.

Something essential seems to have changed between the first and final versions of the Prologue with respect to Gower's attitudes towards the role business played in England's development, to Gower's attitudes towards labour, and to his understanding of poetic production as cultural work. As Masciandaro states:

> Gower's attitude towards work is bound up with status concerns in ways that betray its class origins. Gower's representation of the virtuousness of *besinesse*, however significant as part of the moral discourse of the *Confessio*, bears social meaning [...] it constitutes an attempt not merely to defend the honor of work, but to define it in terms that are adaptable to aristo-

---

[30] Derek Pearsall, *The Canterbury Tales* (London, 1985), p. 114.

cratic values. In turn, material production occupies an ambiguous position in Gower's scheme.[31]

As I hope I have shown, in the revision history of the Prologue Gower approached his artistic work as a form of material production, and one which was imbricated with the political and economic development of England. Chaucer's version of Gower's Tale of Florent becomes a literal transmission of the cultural capital that tale represents. In the Ricardian recensions (in both the verse and in the Latin marginal notations), Gower was more interested in explicitly positing his work as the labour of the realm. Chaucer appears to have recognized the mercantile elements of Gower's courtly tales. But that does beg the question of the revision, the removal of the patronage scene, the erasure of the Thames and the absent boatman. Why place Richard on the iconic Thames in the earlier versions and not place Henry there later? Why erase London entirely from that part of the final version? If anything, it would seem more appropriate to associate the well-liked Henry with the urban merchants of London who were later to support him. And finally, whatever happened to Gower's boat and the absent boatman? Perhaps, like many of us who have taken taxis, that mercantile exchange of money for services rendered was so commonplace for Gower that it did not bear mentioning, even though the call for Gower to compose, to do his business, was worthy of remark. And while the scene is crucial, yet frustratingly incomplete, even in that incompleteness the boat is juxtaposed against the royal barge of the king's, a boat Gower could hardly have wanted us to assume he was rowing in his infirmity but whose boatman was never described or even mentioned, an absent 'primum mobile'. Perhaps, like many, Gower was unaware of and unconcerned with this invisible member of the service industry. Perhaps that juxtaposition of the London trade with the aristocratic barge sufficed to establish his poetics of work. Perhaps (whether the event occurred or not), as Gower went about his own work he felt the job of the boatman was none of his business.

---

[31] Masciandaro, *Voice of the Hammer*, p. 94.

Chapter 15

Genius and Sensual Reading in the *Vox Clamantis*

MATTHEW IRVIN

When Gower made Genius a central figure in the *Confessio Amantis* he had already employed Venus's priest once before, in *Vox Clamantis* book IV, chapters 13–14. Chapters 13 and 14 seem to be a rather typical indictment of weak-willed femininity, as suggested by the heading of Chapter 13: 'Hic loquitur vlterius de mulieribus, que in habitu moniali sub sacre religionis velo professionem suscipientes ordinis sui continenciam non obseruant' (Here, he [Gower] speaks further concerning the women who, in the habits of nuns making profession of vows under the sacred veil of religion, do not observe due continence).[1] However, Gower redirects and modifies this misogynist cliché through the inclusion of the male Genius, a sensual double for the supposedly intellectual masculine ecclesiastical institution, and the real target for his critique. Genius appears as a part of the ecclesiastical institution in both the *Confessio Amantis* and the *Vox Clamantis*, but while the ecclesiastical nature of his role in the *Confessio* is contestable,[2] in the *Vox* he clearly functions as not only a confessor but also a bishop and scholar of theology. A close examination of his appearance in the *Vox Clamantis* shows how the sensual (feminine) pleasures of reading can subvert the supposedly prudential forms of masculine, institutional interpretation.

In the *Confessio Amantis*, and in its model, Jean de Meun's section of the *Roman de la Rose*, confession to Genius is a substitution, made visible by Genius's re-vestment by Venus.[3] I wish to concentrate upon the institutional substitution that occurs, as the institutional forms that produce conscience and moral prudence (here, auricular confession) remain essentially the same, but their content is significantly altered. Gower, describing the failure of the institutional Church in *Confessio Amantis* book V, remarks upon the strange change of content: 'The forme is kept, bot the matiere | Transformed

---

[1] *Vox*, chap. XIII. All Gower quotations are from Macaulay. Unless otherwise noted, translations are mine.
[2] Almost the entire history of modern criticism on the *Confessio Amantis* deals with the 'dual nature' of Genius as ecclesiastical priest and priest of Venus, starting with G. C. Macaulay's remarks in his 'John Gower 6. The English *Confessio Amantis*', in *The Cambridge History of English and American Literature*, vol. 2, *The End of the Middle Ages*, eds A. W. Ward and A. R. Waller (Cambridge, 1908), pp. 153–78 (p. 172).
[3] Cf. Guillaume de Lorris and Jean de Meun, *Le Roman de la Rose*, ed. Daniel Poiron (Paris, 1974), 19447ff.

is in other wise' (*Confessio*, V, lines 1872–3).[4] This sentence is not immediately logical: how can the form remain if the matter is trans*formed*? Upon consulting the *Middle English Dictionary*, one finds that Gower is extremely inventive with the word 'forme', especially in uses concerning literary form and literary production. Gower accounts for some of the earliest uses of 'forme' to mean 'the way in which something is done or made; manner, mode, fashion'; 'style of writing'; 'the exact wording of a text, formulation'; 'the correct or appropriate way of doing something: established process or procedure; customary or traditional usage; prescribed ritual; formal etiquette'; 'pattern of a manufactured object; fashion in clothing, style, cut'; and 'the essence of a thing, the formative principle, that which causes a thing to be what it is'.[5] Even the last definition, which is more metaphysical than the rest and comes with the very technical discussion by Genius of the creation of the universe in book VII, line 214, late in the *Confessio* and contained within the 'formally' different section dealing with advice to princes, still involves (artistic) production, only with God as the artist.

> Riht so the hihe pourveance
> Tho hadde under his ordinance
> A gret substance, a gret matiere,
> Of which he wolde in his manere
> These othre thinges make and forme.
> For yit withouten eny forme
> Was that matiere universal,
> Which hihte ylem in special. (*Confessio*, VIII, lines 209–16)

Like Gower's production of 'new som matiere' (*Confessio*, Prol., line 6), God's 'gret matiere' is produced through categories of knowledge, Gower through 'olde wyse' (*Confessio*, Prol., line 7), and God through his 'hihe pourveance'. However, in the divine creation, 'ordinance' (government), will (what God 'wolde') and 'manere' of production are in perfect harmony. This is the goal of the ruler in Gower's Aristotelian political theory: 'Practique [...] techeth hou and in what wise | Thurgh hih pourveied ordinance | A king schal sette in governance | His realme, and that is Policie' (*Confessio*, VII, lines 1679–83). Gower is using the vocabulary of divine creation ('hih pourve[ance]' and 'ordinance') but also takes into account the different 'wise/wyse' in which, in the practical world, such setting can proceed. The relationship between divine production, artistic production and political action relies upon a Christian–Aristotelian distinction between 'actio' (acting) and 'factio' (making). In the contingent world the king acts politically, and his corresponding category of knowledge is *prudentia*; the writer makes, and his corresponding category of knowledge is *ars*.[6] God's action

---

[4] Cf. *Vox*, IV, line 50, for a discussion of the *forma* of monks as a purely exterior appearance.
[5] 'forme', *n.*, *MED*. Cf. definitions 5(a), 6(a, d), 8(a), 11(b), 14b(a). It is interesting to note that Chaucer is solely responsible for all the first uses of 'forme' which deal with Platonic 'forms', in his *Boece* (14a).
[6] Aristotle, *Ethica Nicomachea*, VI iv, in Grosseteste's translation from St Thomas Aquinas, *In decem libros ethicorum Aristotelis ad Nicomachum expositio* (Rome, 1949).

and production are not contingent (because of his providential knowledge), and furthermore are identical; human knowledge of divine action is *scientia*. The relations between these kinds of action and kinds of knowing rely upon analogies: contingent action is analogous to divine action and, in the contingent world, action and production are analogous; contingency itself allows for the knowledge of analogous rather than identical relationships. Aristotle makes these analogies at the very beginning of the *Ethica*[7] specifically to examine their limitations. The potential to misunderstand the limitations of these analogies is what requires the *prudens*, the masculine authority in political, œconomical and ethical situations capable of judging the mean in contingent cases.[8] Genius as confessor should be prudent in precisely this way, and institutional forms are designed in order to promote prudence in general.

James Simpson, one of the few critics of the *Confessio Amantis* to deal at all with Genius's appearance in the *Vox Clamantis*, draws upon this same passage from *Confessio* book VII to discuss the informing action of Genius in terms of the divine forming of matter. There, God is compared to an artist whose forming of matter '[brings] elements to their fullness, or perfection'.[9] Genius's act of forming, Simpson claims, is similarly artistic; 'The role of the shaper, or informer, is shared by Genius, since he informs stories to bring them to an ideal, proper form.' It is also pedagogical, and 'brings the soul, through self-knowledge, to that proper, ideal form'.[10] However, that 'ideal form', which is important to Simpson's overall argument that the *Confessio Amantis* is a 'humanist psychological allegory',[11] is more consistent with Chaucer's Platonizing use of 'forme' in the *Boece* than Gower's Aristotelian use of 'forme' in his English (and Latin) poetry. Simpson collapses *ars* and *doctrina*, and sees literary form 'tending towards a state of perfection',[12] while I argue that Gower is particularly concerned about the results of taking analogy as identity.[13]

Looking to Gower's own artistic production, one becomes aware that the 'forme' in which matter is expressed is always contingent, as in the king's practical lawmaking. The *Confessio*, which uses variations on the word 'forme' as a motif, first uses it in reference not to Gower's own writing, but

---

[7] Aristotle, *Ethica*, I i. His text begins by putting together 'Omnis ars, et omnis doctrina' (Every art, and every teaching), only to rigorously separate them in *Ethica*, VI.
[8] The *prudens* has the experience in practical affairs to make proper decisions; cf. *Ethica*, VI viii.
[9] James Simpson, *Sciences and the Self in Medieval Poetry: Alan of Lille's Anticlaudianus and John Gower's Confessio amantis* (New York, 1995), p. 3. For his reference to Genius's appearance in *Vox*, cf. p. 154.
[10] Simpson, *Sciences and the Self*, p. 5.
[11] *Ibid.*, p. 135.
[12] *Ibid.*, p. 6.
[13] I oppose to Simpson's humanist and Platonist reading (a reading which better allies the *Confessio* with Alan of Lille's work) an Aristotelian reading of Gower, which better aligns the *Confessio* with more contemporary work. For a similar and relatively contemporary English discussion of prudence, cf. *The Governance of Kings and Princes: John Trevisa's Middle English Translation of the* De Regimine Principium *of Aegidiius Romanus*, eds David Fowler, Charles F. Briggs and Paul G. Remley (New York, 1997), I, ii, lines 6–9, pp. 47–54.

to Genius's speech, and in Genius's own words: 'Of my presthode after the forme | I wol thi schrifte so enforme' (*Confessio*, I, lines 275–6). In the *Vox Clamantis*, Genius functions not to identify but to divide the essence of the thing from its outward appearance. In the *Confessio Amantis*, the entire relationship between the personae of Genius and Amans depends upon the substitution inherent in his priesthood, where the outward form remains while the essence is changed; in the *Vox Clamantis*, Gower develops this substitution through Genius, but on the verbal level: a word that retains its outward form when its matter is transformed is a *paranomasia*, a pun. Words that should produce a harmony (though still not an identity) between divine ordinance, will and style are subjected to a paranomastic transformation into sensual meanings.

Genius appears in the section of *Vox Clamantis* book IV that deals with the continence of nuns. Arguing that erring nuns are less culpable than monks due to the frailty of their sex, Gower suggests a corresponding textual problem:

> Et que scripta sciunt, magis omnibus hee laicali
> Ex indiscreto crimine sepe cadunt.
> Simpliciter textum dum sepe legunt, neque glosam
> Concernunt, vt agant scripta licere putant:
> Leccio scripture docet illas cuncta probare,
> Sic, quia cuncta legunt, cuncta probare volunt.
> Crescere nature sunt iura que multiplicare,
> Que deus in primo scripsit ab ore suo;
> Hecque dei scripta seruare volunt, quoque iura
> Nature solita reddere mente pia. (*Vox*, IV, lines 563–74)

> (And those who know the scriptures, more than all others, often fall on account of an indiscreet crime of the laity. They often read the text simply, and are not concerned with the gloss, so that they think that the scripture permits them to act as they do; the reading of scripture teaches to [ap]prove all things, thus, because they read all things, they wish to [ap]prove all things. The laws of nature are to increase and multiply, which God in the beginning wrote from his own mouth; and these scriptures of God they wish to obey, and also the accustomed laws of Nature they wish to administer with a pious mind.)[14]

As E. W. Stockton points out, the women's reading error is exactly the same as that pointed out by Conscience to Lady Meed in *Piers Plowman* B III lines 333–9; it is a reading that lacks the context and clarity of instruction that a gloss would provide.[15] The sexual incontinence of the nuns derives from separating the form of the words (as text) from the form of the words (as essence), thus allowing a change in content that better satisfies their sensual

---

[14] Canons apparently have the opposite problem, glossing too much: cf. *Vox*, IV, lines 355–6.
[15] John Gower, *The Major Latin Works of John Gower*, trans E. W. Stockton (Seattle, WA, 1962), p. 421. The propriety of Conscience pointing out this error on the authority of the ruler of the Christian commonwealth suggests the commonality of this problem for Gower's milieu.

wills. They read Romans 15. 4 ('Quæcumque enim scripta sunt, ad nostram doctrinam scripta sunt'; For what things soever were written were written for our learning) and I Thessalonians 5. 21 ('Omnia autem probate'; prove all things)[16] without reasoning out the proper, decorous relationship to the institutional and moral forms (here, the gloss) that would order their verbal content. It allows paranomasia, such as the pun on *probare* as both 'to test' and 'to approve', a pun that Gower will use later in the *Confessio*.[17] Though God writes down the Law of Nature *ab ore suo* into the book of Genesis, the authority of Nature's words depends upon their inclusion in Divine Law, a formal code that is transmitted through the institution of the Church.[18] This is the nuns' 'laicali [...] crimine'; they refuse the formal constraints of the *clericali* and interpret according to their individual wills, specifically in their femininity (traditionally sensual). Gower ironically reproduces their self-deception, as they sin with *mente pia*, and his repetition of the verb *volo* emphasizes the will's domination. He introduces Venus and Genius to specify the failure of institutional forms of conscience and prudence, established to protect the nuns against incontinence, but instead stimulating and helping to excuse it:

> Scribitur, hec grana que non capiet bona terra,
> Nil sibi fructificant, set peritura iacent:
> Que tamen et qualis sit terra patet monialis,
> Est ibi nam decies multiplicata Ceres:
> Et quia sic teneres subeunt pondus mulieres,
> Ocia quandoque de racione petunt.
> Accidit in Veneris quod sumunt ergo diebus
> Carnes pro stomachi debilitate sui:
> Nam Venus ingenuis Genio comittit alumpnis
> Fercula quod nimphis preparet ipse sui.
> Set gula sepe grauat nimiumque replete tumescit,
> Dum dolet oppressa de grauitate cibi.
> Est nimis offa grauis, ventrem que tincta veneno
> Toxicat, et dubium mortis inesse dabit;
> Esca set occulto que sumitur, est vbi nulla
> Lux, nocet et morbos sepe dat esse graues.
>
> (*Vox*, IV, lines 579–94)

(It is written that the seeds which good earth will not receive do not bear any fruit at all, but lie dying. And yet a nun should be the kind of earth which lies in readiness, for there the seeds are multiplied tenfold. And since frail women sustain such a

---

[16] All Latin Biblical citations are to *Biblia Sacra iuxta Vulgatam versionem*, ed. Robert Weber, 4th edn (Stuttgart, 1969), while all English versions follow the Douai–Rheims translation.

[17] Cf. *Confessio*, IV, vi, lines 1–2.

[18] While several critics, most prominently Larry Scanlon, have suggested a strong strain of anti-clericism in Gower's writing, I do not see in any of Gower's work a move towards the elimination of the power of the ecclesiastical institution in spiritual matters. His critique of the failures of the institutional Church suggests its reform, not its destruction. Cf. Larry Scanlon, *Narrative, Authority, and Power: The Medieval Exemplum and the Chaucerian Tradition* (New York, 1994), pp. 248–67.

heavy burden, sometimes they rightly seek rest and quiet. Therefore it happens on Venus's days they eat meat because of their weak stomach. For to Genius, Venus entrusts her worthy foster daughters the pork dishes which he should prepare for his own nymphs. But when sated, their maw often grows too heavy and swells up because it is in pain, troubled by the weight of the food. The swelling is too burdensome, and being tainted with poison, it is toxic to the stomach, and will bring on a fear of death. On the other hand, the food which is eaten secretly in the dark is injurious, and often causes heavy illnesses.) (trans. Stockton, p. 179)

I give Stockton's translation to illustrate how easy it is to miss the complicated Latin punning that drives this passage. Gower uses paranomasia to produce a sensual and sexual reading of the parable of the sower and the seed (Luke 8. 5–15). Instead of the seed being the gospel, and the good earth being the righteous, Gower suggests that the nuns are the good earth, and the seed semen, which will cause them to multiply. When women are pregnant (that is, holding a burden), then rightly they should seek rest; and it is allowable for them to make Fridays into 'days of Venus' by eating meat (as pregnant women were allowed during times of abstinence).[19] Gower creates a parallel between Genius's nymphs (lay women, Genius's nymphs on account of their active participation in procreation) and Venus's adopted daughters (the nuns, engaging in illicit sexual love, and therefore adopted daughters of Venus); the meat properly for the nymphs is given to the adopted daughters, the meat also functioning as a metaphor for sexual intercourse. For, after their eating of the meat, that which ate it (the 'gula', the gullet, with associations of gluttony, and as a metaphor for the vagina/womb) is heavy; that is, the nuns become pregnant.[20] This being too heavy (that is, becoming too obvious), the nun attempts to poison the stomach (here it seems likely that Gower is referring to a technique of abortion). Such secret 'eating' causes heavy illnesses. In the marginalia is written, 'Nota quos Genius secundum poetas Sacerdos Dee Veneris nuncupatus est' ('Note that according to the poets, Genius is called the priest of Venus').[21] This is a

---

[19] John Mirk notes that 'woymen with child' are given a dispensation: *Mirk's Festial: A Collection of Homilies by Johannes Mirkus*, ed. Theodore Erbe, EETS e.s. 96 (London, 1905), p. 82. Cf. C. M. Woolgar, 'Group diets in late medieval England', in *Food in Medieval England*, eds C. M. Woolgar, D. Serjeantson and T. Waldron (New York, 2006), p. 192. For fasting as a 'crucial component of the reputation of religious women' in the late Middle Ages, cf. Caroline Walker Bynum, *Holy Feast and Holy Fast: The Religious Significance of Food to Medieval Women* (Berkeley, CA, 1987), p. 76, referring to André Vauchez, *La Sainteté en Occident aux derniers siècles du moyen âge d'après les procès de canonisation et les documents hagiographiques* (Rome, 1981), pp. 224–6, 347–8, 405–6, 450–51. Bynum makes the wider point that fasting is not only a particular concern of religious women during the late Middle Ages but was also bound up with male consideration of female weakness.

[20] The word 'gula' has already been the focus of an ingenious Latin pun in book IV: 'Fit modo curtata monarchorum regula prima, | Est nam re dempta, sic manet ipsa gula' (*Vox*, IV, lines 127–8) ('In such a way has the first rule of the monks been severed, for the 're' (thing, important part) is thrown out, so that all that remains is the 'gula' (stomach)').

[21] It has been noted that this marginalia is not in the same hand as that of the main text, although it is contemporary. It is enough to remark that an educated reader would not only

reference to the *Roman de la Rose*, and prepares the reader for Genius's institutional role in the sensual, feminine interpretation of texts.

Genius and Venus are not merely goads to incontinence, features of their individual flesh or representations of universal temptation; through Genius, they take over the institutional forms that would work against the flesh. In the next few lines of the *Vox*, Genius becomes a confessor:

> Quas Venus et Genius cellas modo rite gubernant,
> Carnis non claustri iura tenere docent:
> Conuentus custos Genius confessor et extat,
> Et quandoque locum presulis ipse tenet:
> Sub specie iuris in claustro visitat ipsas,
> Quas veniens thalamis, iure negante, regit.
> Sit licet in capa furrata, dum docet ipse,
> Nuda tamen valde iura ministrat eis:
> Iudicio Genii pro culpis sunt lapidate,
> Set neque mortalis aggrauat ictus eas. (*Vox*, IV, lines 595–604)

> (Venus and Genius steer the cells of the cloister in the fashion of their rite, and teach [the nuns] to hold the laws of the flesh, not enclosure. Genius the confessor exists as protector of the convent, and sometimes he holds the place of bishop. Under the appearance of law he visits those in the cloister, coming to their bedchambers, he rules them, law having been cast aside. Though he might be in a furred cap while he teaches them, nevertheless nude he strenuously administers the laws to them. By the judgment of Genius they are stoned [weighed down, made pregnant] for their sins, but he does not grieve them with a stroke of death.)

The women's reading practice quoted above commits a very specific error: it ignores the gloss produced by the institution to guide reading – in a sense, the conscience of the text. This is, however, only a small part of the issue. The section by and large excuses women because of their weak will; its real target is the action of Genius.[22] Genius patently usurps institutional roles, exchanging the 'lex menti' for the 'lex in membris' to produce the women's errant readings.[23] Gower's language communicates the form of this exchange, as the authority of Venus and Genius (implied by the use of 'gubernant') transforms the cells by the rite into brothels ('cella' meaning both the room of a cloister and the room of a brothel). In the word 'cella' Gower literally reproduces (by paranomasia) the sensual reading by means of the presence of Venus and Genius. Genius takes on several roles in the

---

realize but would consider it important enough to the meaning of the poem to note that this Genius is Jean de Meun's (if not also Alain de Lille's).

[22] While Gower no doubt shared his culture's belief in the relative weakness of male and female will, he seems to be using this belief less for its misogyny than to expose male clerical sin, and especially the allowance of continued incontinence. The passage also requires little manipulation to render it an allegory of the feminine will and male intellect in general, in the spirit of Augustine's interpretation of Adam and Eve in Augustine's *Confessions*, ed. J. J. O'Donnell (Oxford, 1992), XIII xxxii (p. 47).

[23] Cf. Romans 7. 23.

next few lines, as confessor, bishop and teacher. While Gower is certainly making an obvious allusion to male clerics in the convent being a risk to sexual continence, Genius's roles as confessor, bishop and teacher are also instrumental in the failure of prudence. It is to the authority of Genius that the women refer, as did the nobles of the *Roman de la Rose*. As such, the urgings of Genius to procreate sexually arrive 'sub specie iuri' (under the form of the law) but are not such in content. They, like the *cellae*, are transformed: under their law, the virgin who fornicates is stoned, but here in the sense of becoming pregnant.[24] Once again, Gower forces the reader to interpret in two ways, emphasizing the production by Genius of misreading.

Genius, taken as the spirit of procreation, is not inherently sinful, but depends upon a decorous relation between the form of procreation and the matter procreated. Returning to the first section of *Vox Clamantis* book IV quoted above, the presence of Genius produces feminine sin by encouraging misreading not only through paranomasia but also through grammatical confusion. In *Vox*, IV, line 569, Gower paraphrases the law of 'nature', 'crescite et multiplicamini' (Genesis 1. 28); but the subjects of this law are cloistered nuns, not laywomen; they are the matter. Their form of procreation must be appropriate to them as subjects. As Aquinas argues in his question on virginity, while natural and divine law demands that mankind procreate, it does not demand that each individual do so (as natural law demands that each individual eat). Specifically, mankind requires an increase and multiplication of spiritual things as well, and therefore it is right and necessary that some abstain from sexual procreation in order to benefit mankind as a true Christian commonwealth.[25] Gower returns again and again to the problem of spiritual increase as generically appropriate to humankind, and humankind's sin resulting from a failure of interpretation.[26] This is the very sensual failure of reading that occurs in the misinterpretation of Luke 8. The subject of the parable in Luke 8 is spiritual increase. Gower's intentional misinterpretation interprets it physically, and fails to draw distinctions among different kinds of people, specifically clergy and lay people. This produces the unnatural relationship to Venus and Genius, one expressed through grammatical confusion. The nuns are 'alumpnis' 'foster-daughters' of Venus, and Venus does not represent simply a concept, but a whole set of real practices, the 'res' to which the word 'Venus' refers.[27] They are involved, but should not be involved, in those practices; therefore they are *foster* daughters. Gower goes further, producing a powerful association through a typical technique for him, double adjective agreement. Gower makes use of a possible confusion

---

[24] The reference in line 603 is to Deuteronomy 22. 23–4.
[25] St Thomas Aquinas, *Summa Theologiae*, trans. Fathers of the English Dominican Province (Allen, TX, 1981) II–II, Q. 152, 2, reply to objection 1: the objection quotes Genesis 1. 28 to argue that virginity is unlawful.
[26] Most notably, Gower articulates the importance of spiritual rather than literal increase in his *Traitié pour essampler les amantz marietz*, II, lines 1–3, which is found appended to nine copies of the *Confessio*.
[27] Cf. Teresa Tinkle, *Medieval Venuses and Cupids: Sexuality, Hermeneutics, and English Poetry* (Stanford, CA, 1996), esp. pp. 42–77.

in agreement between 'ingenuis', 'alumpnis' and 'nimphis'. According to word order, it would make more sense for 'ingenuis' to modify 'alumpnis', and one could (as Stockon does) render it into English as 'worthy foster daughters'. However, 'ingenuis' is not such a simple term; there are a number of possible meanings, ranging from 'innate, natural' to 'well-born' to 'befitting a free person' (in terms of morals).[28] In its meaning as 'natural' 'ingenuis' is strictly the opposite of 'alumpnis' ('adopted'), and would seem better suited semantically to modify 'nimphis', which are already referred 'Genio' (to Genius), the word adjacent to 'ingenuis' and thus connected to it by polyptoton. The reader is left with two possibilities: one can refer 'ingenuis' to 'alumpnis' with considerable irony (for certainly the foster daughters of Venus are indeed unworthy, and certainly not noble, as the entire passage suggests), or read 'ingenuis' and 'alumpnis' as opposites and refer 'ingenuis' to 'nimphis' in the next line, translating it the 'natural nymphs of Genius' (those married women who by their nature belong to Genius; that is, to procreation). Neither reading is grammatically erroneous, and either choice causes some confusion concerning nature and value. Genius's place in the line, and his polyptoton with 'ingenuis' locates him at the centre of the confusion of feminine identity and value. The confusion of 'ingenuis' and 'alumpnis' is a problem (literally and allegorically) of the nature of things: in order to make sense of the lines, a reader must not only be able to parse the grammar, but understand ethically the sorts of relationships the grammar allows.

This is precisely what the presence of Genius makes impossible for the nuns, instead encouraging a sensual and finally incontinent reading practice. Such a practice exists not only in spite of but through the very institutional forms and authorities designed to mitigate it: confession, orders of enclosure and education; confessors, bishops and scholars. Gower's extraordinarily dense and allusive poetry in this section does not simply indicate or satirize this reading practice, but exposes the means by which institutional forms are used to facilitate it. Those means are substitutions, false equivalents which seem like prudence, especially paronomasia and personification. These are parts of the poetic art. In Aristotelian terms, what Gower is articulating is the transformation of *doctrina* into *ars,* and the confusion that results from the lack of a prudential guide. Genius, the very spirit of *factio*, production, impersonates the *prudens*, the confessor, the bishop and the scholar upon whom especially the weak of will rely for spiritual direction. Reading Gower's *Vox Clamantis*, which is rife with verbal art, educates the reader less by precept than by experience. After all, the clerics he harangues do not lack for *regulae*; they have just substituted them with *gulae*, allowing themselves and their charges to read sensually while keeping the form of religion. I also wish to suggest that in the *Confessio Amantis* Genius continues to represent a sensual reading practice, but one massively extended by Gower and demanding from its readers an equally extended critical engagement.

---

[28] 'Ingenuus, adj.', *Dictionary of Medieval Latin from British Sources*, Fascicule I: A–B (London, 1975).

Reading Genius's persona in the *Confessio* with his brief appearance in the *Vox* can begin to illustrate Gower's larger poetic and political goals. Both texts encourage not the exclusion of love and sex, but the inclusion of them within a larger political and institutional discourse, and the necessity for a *prudens* to experience their possibilities in order to properly act morally and politically. The *Vox* and the *Confessio* are two related poetic projects in the interpretation of which the effect and affect of poetic form are central, and part of a poetic tradition that includes, most notably, Jean de Meun and Alain de Lille.

Chapter 16

Irony v. Paradox in the *Confessio Amantis*

PETER NICHOLSON

Some of the best of the recent published criticism of the *Confessio Amantis* has given us some challenging new ways of understanding both the structure of the poem and the nature of Gower's moral project. To cite only three examples: we have James Simpson's recasting of the entire dialogue between Amans and Genius as a kind of *psychomachia* between Will and Imagination; Diane Watt's argument, in *Amoral Gower*, that instead of advocating a single stable morality the poem actually offers a sustained critique of the possibility of any consistent moral principles; and J. Allen Mitchell's argument that what morality is provided in the poem is all contingent and conditional, depending as it does upon the circumstances and upon the active participation of the reader.[1] These are three very different claims and in many ways they would be difficult to reconcile, but they do have some common threads. First, they are fundamentally ironic in nature: things are not what they seem in the *Confessio*; more specifically, they offer alternatives to reading the poem as a series of straightforward moral lessons addressed by a priest to his penitent. And, like earlier ironic readings, which saw Genius simply as a flawed priest offering a false morality,[2] they are based upon the same perceived problems in the poem, notably what are viewed as its inconsistencies, either in its overall structure (comparing, for instance, the beginning to the end), or between lessons, or even within single passages, which are interpreted as reflecting either the inadequacies of Genius as moral instructor or as either the inability or the refusal of Gower himself to advance a coherent morality.

The charge of inconsistency is itself worth examining. The apparent contradictions may not be so great if one reads with a clear eye for distinctions and with a sensitivity to the argument that Genius presents, both about

---

[1] James Simpson, *Sciences and the Self in Medieval Poetry: Alan of Lille's Anticlaudianus and John Gower's* Confessio Amantis (Cambridge, 1995); Diane Watt, *Amoral Gower: Language, Sex and Politics* (Minneapolis, MN, 2003); and J. Allan Mitchell, *Ethics and Exemplary Narrative in Chaucer and Gower* (Cambridge, 2004).

[2] See, among several others, Thomas J. Hatton, 'The role of Venus and Genius in John Gower's *Confessio Amantis*: a reconsideration', *Greyfriar*, 16 (1975), 29–40; and David W. Hiscoe, 'The Ovidian comic strategy of Gower's *Confessio Amantis*', *Mediaevalia*, 13 (1987), 257–74. See also Russell A. Peck, 'The problematics of irony in Gower's Confessio Amantis', Mediaevalia, 15 (1993), 207–29, who offers a valuable discussion of the meaning of 'irony' as it applies to this poem.

the nature of sin and about the bases of moral conduct, and while they may render that argument somewhat more complex, they do not for that reason necessarily undermine it. But it is also necessary to give some consideration to the justification for inferring a conceptual structure so different from the one that Genius himself presents. The distinction between the poet and the speaker that allows displacing Genius in this way is a habit of reading encouraged by the example of Chaucer, but the *Confessio* is very different, particularly from Chaucer's later works, and our willingness to detect irony at every turn may not be as appropriate for Gower as it is for his better-known contemporary.

Chaucer's poetry, especially in his most mature work, is marked throughout by an awareness that the same words and the same actions can be understood in more than one way, and our experience of reading is a constant process of discovery of that which is unexpressed.[3] *The Pardoner's Tale* offers a particularly straightforward example and, though perhaps the most 'moral' of *The Canterbury Tales*, it illustrates one type of effect that lay well beyond the range of Gower. When the 'riotoures' learn of the ravages of Death they determine not just to seek him but also to put him to death: 'He shal be slayn, he that so manye sleeth, | By Goddes dignitee, er it be nyght' (*Pardoner's Tale*, VI, lines 700–701). Their vow turns the simple story of how the three companions kill one another out of greed into something much more powerful, a tale of how greed blinds them both to the nature of their own actions and to the spiritual reality that lies behind the material, a blindness embodied in their lack of understanding of their own quest. It is this lack of understanding, rather than their drunkenness, swearing, greed, theft or murder, that receives its proper reward at the end, and we as readers are put in the position of knowing better, of being able to perceive in the revellers' own words the significance of which they are unaware, the meaning that is confirmed in the tale's outcome. That contrast between the reader's understanding and the speaker's understanding is one of Chaucer's most characteristic devices. Comic examples include Nicholas's boasting of his own cleverness in *The Miller's Tale* (I, lines 3298–300); January's declaration of his expectations of marriage in *The Merchant's Tale* (IV, lines 1263–6; 1637–54); and the entire conversation between the Summoner and the devil in *The Friar's Tale*, in which the Summoner's wish for the devil's companionship, his interest in his abode, his eagerness to learn and his encouragement of the seizure all reveal a spiritual blindness not very different from that of the revellers in *The Pardoner's Tale*. The irony is the greater, in examples such as these, the more that the characters' words or actions draw our attention to the truth of which they are unaware, and the more that that truth is validated in the events that follow.

Chaucer's most extended use of irony in narrative occurs in *Troilus and Criseyde*, in which the characters' words and actions are repeatedly either

---

[3] The bibliography on Chaucer's use of irony is immense, but one may still consult with profit, if only for its catalogue of examples, Germaine Dempster, *Dramatic Irony in Chaucer* (Stanford, CA, 1932).

unknowingly apt or unknowingly inapt, in both cases pointing our way to the understanding that they do not possess. In the first part of the poem the effect is comic: when Troilus mocks other lovers (*Troilus*, I, lines 183–205), we know that he is simply betraying his ignorance of the vulnerability that he shares with other mortals; when Criseyde debates with herself on whether she should submit to love (*Troilus*, II, lines 694–812) we see a display of feeling that is possible only for someone who is already in love, and we are put in the position of understanding her feelings better than she does; and when Pandarus arranges for Troilus to ride by Criseyde's window (*Troilus*, II, lines 1010–22), we know, but he does not, that his machinations only mirror reality, for Criseyde has already seen Troilus ride by (*Troilus*, II, lines 610–58). Chaucer uses irony here as a way of giving substance to the force that is shaping the characters' lives that lies beyond their control and in many respects beyond their comprehension. In book III the ground starts to shift: the moment of the characters' greatest happiness is tinged with allusions to what is going to follow, in the long discussion of Criseyde's fidelity (*Troilus*, III, lines 771–840; 988–1054), and in the sorrows they experience at parting (*Troilus*, III, lines 1415–1526; 1695–1701), including their blame of Apollo for his intrusion upon their lives (*Troilus*, III, lines 1464–70; 1702–08). If we are willing to ignore the hints in order to share their joy, it becomes impossible to do so as the poet turns to tragedy with the Prohemye to book IV. In the long scene in which the two lovers debate what to do (*Troilus*, IV, lines 1254–701) we are allowed to see that each of the reasons that Criseyde offers for giving in to the exchange is false and that each of the reasons that Troilus offers for fleeing Troy is true; and, as we observe their choice, the irony of the Trojans' decision to trade Criseyde for the traitor Antenor (*Troilus*, IV, lines 197–210) is small compared to that of Troilus and Criseyde's willing submission to what we know will destroy them.

In *Troilus and Criseyde* Chaucer deploys irony in order to explore the characters' lack of knowledge of their fates. In the General Prologue and elsewhere in the *Canterbury Tales*, he deploys it to examine the characters' lack of knowledge of themselves and to pierce beneath the masks by which they present themselves to others. In the most memorable portraits in the General Prologue (the Knight, the Squire, the Monk, the Prioress, the Wife), the narrator – with a straight face and entirely uncritically – emphasizes what the pilgrims find most important about themselves, and he presents them as they themselves wish to be seen, but usually in such a way as to draw our attention to a judgment or assessment that he does not express and of which the pilgrim is unaware. The narrator's uncritical mimicry of the pilgrim's voice is matched by – and may be modelled on – his report of the pilgrims' tales. In that each tale is also a self-presentation, it too is 'ironic' to the extent that we learn from it something more about the teller of which he or she is unaware. In the case of the Merchant, who betrays his own self-loathing in his portrait of January, or the Wife of Bath, whose most secret wishes are transferred to the old hag, the revelation is deeply personal. And once we are put in the position of assessing the pilgrims' performances in this way, we are offered a constant invitation to perceive a significance that they themselves do not express, if only to recognize the limitations in each teller's view of experience in contrast to that of the other pilgrims as expressed in their very different tales.

In the *Confessio Amantis* the possibility of irony of the latter sort is foreclosed by Gower's choice of a very different frame. All the tales are told by Genius: the distancing from each teller that results simply from multiplying the number of speakers, none of whom has greater authority than any other, does not occur, and there is therefore not the same invitation to see each tale as a mere performance. But Gower's choice of a different framing device is only one token of the broader and more substantial differences between these two poems. For irony is not just a device for Chaucer, it is a habit of mind. It is an awareness of the limitations of our knowledge, both of our destinies and of ourselves, and of the subjectivity of all expression; and it is that awareness, rather than any moral assessment, that provides an underlying theme of Chaucer's major poetry. Gower's interests are manifestly very different, and they are reflected not just in his frame but also in his very different handling of both his characters and his tales.

It is difficult to find examples of any of the types of irony that are most characteristic of Chaucerian narrative anywhere in the *Confessio*. In the largest number of Gower's tales the possibility of irony simply doesn't arise since they offer straightforward moral lessons with very little plot. These include the emblematic examples of particular sins or virtues, the tales in which one character receives instruction from another and the very small number of allegorical tales and natural analogies.[4] There is also little room for irony in tales in which virtue receives its just reward. But even in the tales in which a sinner receives a punishment (about 40% of the tales in the poem), in which the potential for irony is seemingly the greatest, Gower appears deliberately to have made the choice not to exploit it. In the tale of Midas, for example (*Confessio*, V, lines 141–332), which is rich with the possibility of self-delusion, Gower gives Midas two long speeches neither of which serves either to display his foolishness or to put us in a morally superior position. In the first (*Confessio*, V, lines 189–216) he lays out the proper and orthodox view of what he sees as his three alternatives, and in the second (*Confessio*, V, lines 234–45), in which he chooses gold, he gives an assessment of its power that is difficult to contradict and that is in no way belied by anything that follows. Midas obviously gives too little thought to the consequences of his choice of gift, but Genius holds him guilty neither of the desire for gold nor of a lack of foresight but merely of a lack of 'mesure' (*Confessio*, V, lines 247–8). In other similar cases the characters are given no opportunity to reflect at all. The tale of Narcissus (*Confessio*, I, lines 2275–366) illustrates the same lesson on the power of love that is learned by Troilus, but, unlike Troilus, Narcissus does not proclaim his immunity to love, nor does he even decide not to love; much less does

---

[4] On the classification of the tales according to the way in which they create their moral lesson, see the discussion in my *Love and Ethics in Gower's 'Confessio Amantis'* (Ann Arbor, MI, 2005), pp. 82–94 and nn.

he mock those who have fallen victim to love. 'No strengthe of love bowe mihte | His herte' (*Confessio* I, lines 2286–7) is all that Genius says. Neither Narcissus's choice nor his lack of self-awareness is even in question; he is simply unmoved, until Love decides to overthrow him. In the same book the tales of Capaneus (*Confessio*, I, lines 1977–2009) and Nebuchadnezzar (*Confessio*, I, lines 2785–3042) illustrate much more serious forms of pride and the potential for irony is again inherent, but in each Gower suppresses from his source the direct speech that precedes the character's punishment.[5] Genius describes them as boasting (*Confessio*, I, lines 1986–8; 2958–61), but we do not hear their boast, and we are neither put in a position of knowing better than they nor allowed to anticipate the consequences of which they are unaware.

In all these cases Gower is much less concerned with the difference between the characters' understanding and ours than he is with the precise definition of their shortcomings, and in this these tales they are typical of the *Confessio* as a whole. Gower's characters are guilty of real and specific faults which are announced in advance and they are shown acting out these faults, but they do not, as a rule, get a chance to display their lack of awareness either of their situation or of themselves. None proclaims himself wiser than he really is, nor does any mock a character who is about to outwit him; much less does any of Gower's characters draw our attention in any way to that which we recognize but of which he or she is unaware. There is no instance in the *Confessio* in which we are in a position to understand a character's feelings better than the character does, none of a character saying something either unknowingly apt or unknowingly inapt,[6] and nothing that comes close to the persistency of error of the Pardoner's revellers or the Friar's summoner.

Nor is there any character who unwittingly brings justice upon himself directly through his own action. There are several tales, of course, in which the punishment is particularly appropriate to the sin, but except in the cases of hastiness or neglect ('Pygmaleon', 'The Foolish Virgins', 'Grosseteste'),[7] the punishment is imposed by someone else (either human or divine) acting as an agent of correction. Often the agent has been provoked, as Paulina is by Albinus's boasting (*Confessio*, I, lines 761–1059), but, as in this tale, there is usually little direct link between the fault itself and the punishment. Even Crassus, who is guilty of covetousness, is actually punished only for the stupidity of allowing the mirror to be destroyed, and only after falling victim to the philosophers' elaborate plot to deceive him (*Confessio*, V, lines 2031–224). There is no mere poetic justice in Gower, much less are there any characters like Troilus and Criseyde who innocently make the choices that result in their destruction. The only 'tragedies' in the poem concern those who are victimized by others, and in these (for instance, 'Mundus and

---

[5] See Macaulay's note to *Confessio*, I, line 1980 ff., and Daniel 4. 30.
[6] The only possible exception: the young girl who weeps for the death of her dog 'Perse', which her father takes as foretelling the death of Perseus (*Confessio*, II, lines 1780–804).
[7] *Confessio*, IV, lines 371–436; 250–60; 234–43.

Paulina', 'The False Bachelor')[8] Gower works hard to elicit our sympathy for the victim – one of his most effective tools for the condemnation of the sinner. But even in tales such as 'The Trojan Horse' (*Confessio*, I, lines 1077–189; in which the Trojans are cast as the victims of deceit) or Paris and Helen (*Confessio*, V, lines 7195–585; in which Cassandra's role is so severely diminished), the emphasis remains fixed on the moral lesson, not on the ways in which the characters act in ignorance of the destiny that we foresee.

In the two cases that might be cited as exceptions, the ignorance is itself part of the moral lesson. The tales of Ulysses and Nectanabus that occur together in the second half of book VI (*Confessio*, VI, lines 1391–778; 1789–2366) seem to offer the only real examples of dramatic irony in the *Confessio*, but they do so for a specific thematic purpose. Both tales are full of ominous references to the two characters' lack of knowledge and to the inevitability of fate. Ulysses is given a mysterious dream that suggests that either he or his son will receive death at the hands of the other (*Confessio*, VI, lines 1541–48). Unaware of the son that he has had with Circe, he imprisons Telemachus and we then watch as Telegonus, bearing the pennon of the dream, eagerly seeks out his father, and, when they fail to recognize one another, slays him. Nectanabus, too, is given a portent of his death at the hands of his son which he fails either to comprehend or to believe (*Confessio*, VI, lines 2295–6; 2302–5), and Alexander, provoked to disprove even so equivocal a prophecy, unwittingly fulfils it. Both tales concern men who are not as wise as they need to be; more importantly, their lack of knowledge of their fate is offered as a token of a broader lack of understanding of God's purpose (*Confessio*, VI, lines 1571–4; 1789–94). These tales mark an important transition between the godlessness of characters such as Nero (cf. *Confessio*, VI, lines 1256–60), which is manifested in an ignorance of moral law, and Genius's exposition of the foundation of moral law, as taught by Alexander's other teacher, Aristotle, which occupies book VII. It does happen that we are put in a position of seeing more than the characters do in these two tales, but Gower's interest lies not in the gap between their knowledge and ours but in their lack of understanding compared to God's.

There are also some important scenes in which family members fail to recognize one another in both 'Constance' (*Confessio*, II, lines 587–1603) and 'Apollonius of Tyre' (*Confessio*, VIII, lines 271–2008), but the effect that Gower aims for is not irony but pathos, as the momentary deferral of the reunion heightens the reader's participation in the characters' joy. Elsewhere, we are simply not given that advantage of knowing more than the characters do, except for the instruction that Genius provides on what is right and what is wrong. Whether out of a difference of habit of mind or simply because it did not suit his moral purpose, Gower betrays virtually no awareness that words can have a meaning unknown to those who utter them. There is no invitation to read any of the characters' speeches in more than a single way to discover a significance that the characters or the narrator does not

---

[8] *Confessio*, I, lines 761–1059; II, lines 2501–781.

express. In Gower's narratives, at least, irony is simply not a characteristic mode.

In assessing whether there is a consistent underlying pattern of irony in Genius's discourse, as opposed to what happens in the tales, one must acknowledge at once that the priest's lessons are marked by a vast amount of purely conventional morality (including his earnest advocacy of 'trouthe') and by his enormous sympathy for the innocent victims of sin. There is also no evidence that Genius's judgments of his characters are not to be shared, especially of those (and there are very many) of whom he disapproves. If problems arise, it is with the few that he does not condemn as strongly as he might be expected to (including, on occasion, Amans) and with the apparent inconsistency between his declarations of the irresistibility and irrationality of love and his insistence upon rationally guided moral conduct. But this is precisely where it is necessary to insist upon some distinctions, for there are at least three very different ways in which love is said to be irrational in the poem, and they have very different moral consequences. The first is the innate susceptibility to *naturatus amor* (I vv. 1–4) that humans share with other creatures and which only the most saintly can escape (*Confessio*, VIII, lines 2330–36), which in that sense is beyond rational control: 'For wit ne strengthe may noght helpe, | And he which elles wolde him yelpe | Is rathest throwen under fote' (*Confessio*, I, lines 25–7).[9] The second is the arbitrariness and unpredictability of the distribution of love's rewards, which is also apparently irrational and beyond human control:

> For love is blind and may noght se,
> Forthi may no certeinete
> Be set upon his jugement,
> Bot as the whiel aboute went
> He yifth his graces undeserved. (*Confessio*, I, lines 47–51)[10]

And the third applies to the conduct of those who are in love, which can be either rational or irrational but which is, or at least ought to be, subject to human control, and that is the difference.

At a key moment in the middle of book III, Genius tells Amans, in effect, 'I know that you can't help being in love, but that's not an excuse for behaving badly' (*Confessio* III, lines 1194–9; see also III, lines 1870–79). That very distinction is enacted in the opening scene, in which Amans's subjection to love is confirmed by Cupid's arrow but in which he is immediately compelled to submit his behaviour to examination in the confession. The principal consequence, in fact, of emphasizing the naturalness and irresistibility of love is to shift attention away from the choice of whether or not to love and onto the ethical issues that arise regarding conduct in love, and

---

[9] See also *Confessio*, I, lines 91–2; II, lines 2580–85; III, lines 344–50; III, lines 389–91; III, lines 1194–5; III, lines 1873–5, etc.

[10] See the entire passage from which the quotation is taken, *Confessio*, I, lines 39–60, plus 1 vv. 5–6, I, lines 2490–93; III, lines 1462–72; V, lines 4546–60, the tale of 'Jupiter's Two Tuns', VI, lines 325–90 (esp. lines 663–4); and VIII, lines 2231–5.

thus to make the need for moral regulation of the lover's conduct all the more compelling. This is what the confession is about. Amans is examined on his behaviour as a lover; but he is not corrected simply for being in love, for there is nothing that he can do about it. The only time that Genius recommends that Amans abandon his love occurs just before the conclusion (*Confessio*, VIII, lines 2060–148), but he withdraws his advice almost as quickly as it is offered, and it serves to demonstrate only the futility of the suggestion. When Cupid withdraws his dart several hundred lines later and Amans is finally freed of his compulsion to love, it is not by his choice or in any way as a result of the confession but because of another natural force over which he has no control. While both the onset and the withdrawal of love are beyond rational governance, however, the lover's conduct is not, as Genius demonstrates as he proceeds point by point through the confession. Love cannot be controlled, but it must be regulated. Within the terms that Genius sets out, that is not a contradiction, though it does pose a paradox. Love is both beyond and also necessarily subject to reason: that simple proposition helps account for a great many of the more puzzling features of the *Confessio*, and it also provides a model – better than 'irony' – for the conceptual structure of the poem.

One aspect of that paradox is represented in Genius's dual allegiance, both to Venus and to God. He is a paradoxical figure, to be sure, but not a contradictory one, for more than any of his predecessors he embodies the reconciliation between love and moral regulation that it is the purpose of the poem to advocate, and while consistently conceding the overwhelming force of love he also urges, even more consistently, the need for the proper moral guidance of the lover's conduct. Venus too embodies some of the central paradoxes in the poem, though in a different way. Gower presents us with several Venuses, and the one who appears in the frame – who descends from the heavens (*Confessio*, VIII, lines 2941–4) and assumes the morally regulatory role implied by her summoning of Genius to hear Amans's confession – has little in common with the Venuses who appear in several of the tales, who are also quite different from one another;[11] and she is not even necessarily the same as the goddess that Amans prays to, who confers her 'grace' upon despairing lovers (*Confessio*, I, lines 132–7).[12] The diversity of Venus's appearances in the poem illustrates what we might consider Gower's tolerance for inconsistency,[13] but it is a particularly functional example as each of her different manifestations embodies one of the many different – paradoxical – aspects of the human experience of love.

---

[11] Compare, for instance, 'Pygmaleon' (esp. *Confessio*, IV, lines 419–23), 'Vulcan and Venus' (V, lines 635–725), 'Leucothoe' (V, lines 6715–19).

[12] She is also very different from the euhemeristic deity that Genius exposes as a fraud in his denunciation of pagan religions (*Confessio*, V, lines 1382–443). On the variety of portrayals of Venus in medieval literature see Teresa Tinkle, *Medieval Venuses and Cupids: Sexuality, Hermeneutics, and English Poetry* (Stanford, CA, 1996).

[13] Other deities, several of the more important exemplary human figures and even Amans himself also take on different roles according to the needs of the immediate lesson.

Some of the paradoxes inherent in the experience of love were already deeply inscribed in the love poetry with which Gower was most familiar. 'Est amor egra salus, vexata quies, pius error', he writes in the opening epigram to book I (I vv. 7); and a few lines later he refers in English to 'thilke unsely jolif wo' (*Confessio*, I, line 88; see also IV, lines 1212–15). He gives another version of the traditional oxymora in his Balade XLVIII and again in the Latin verses that he appends to the *Traitié*.[14] In extending his exploration of these paradoxes from the emotional to the moral realm, Gower not only places love in a different relation to reason; he also ascribes a paradoxical role both to love and to Nature. The passages in which Nature is said to inspire the behaviour of which Nature disapproves are well known,[15] and they will perhaps appear less troubling in view of the pervasiveness of paradox elsewhere in the poem. Compared to his predecessors Jean de Meun and Alain de Lille, Gower seems here and elsewhere to have heightened both the moral peril that Nature poses and also her potential for good, but he leaves the paradox unresolved and, in most cases that the poem considers, the moral issues that she raises are not sufficiently answered by Nature herself. Love, too, is obviously an occasion for moral peril and inspires much of the most irrational conduct of the characters in the tales, as Genius points out in passages that are also frequently cited in the criticism,[16] but there is also a morally normative love that Genius cites at least as often that is much more powerful than the morally normative Nature. Love is injured and offended by misconduct;[17] and to be 'obedient' to love means more than just succumbing to love: it means adhering to the laws of proper and worthy conduct.[18] One of the recurring themes of Genius's lessons – and more evidence of his success at serving two masters – is that the good conduct that he urges is required not just by universal moral law but also by love itself – or at least by the type of love that Genius advocates for Amans. In books I–V in particular he insists that, for lovers like Amans, the needed escape from the moral dangers associated with love and for most of its specific sins can be found – paradoxically – in love itself. 'Love makes me angry and sullen', Amans proclaims throughout book III. 'Love asketh pes', Genius tells him in reply (*Confessio*, III, line 1647), and this conversation, in one or another form, is one of the leitmotifs of the confession.

Love forbids Pride, Envy, Wrath, Sloth and the many forms of Avarice in love and Avarice for love. Love demands Humility, Charity, Patience, Gener-

---

[14] *Confessio*, I, lines 375–6; 392.
[15] *Confessio*, III, lines 169–88 (cf. VIII, lines 214; 222); IV, lines 484–95.
[16] E.g. *Confessio*, I, lines 772–5; I, lines 1051–2; III, lines 152–88; III, lines 1473–5; IV, lines 3523–6; IV, lines 3545–6. The latter two passages refer to Iphis, whose love is specifically marked as 'unwys' (IV, line 3529). In other similar cases, it is not love generally that is held to blame but a specific sort of unregulated love. Cf. IV, lines 1472–7; V, line 2632; VIII, lines 165–8, VIII, lines 187–8; VIII, lines 2009–11.
[17] E.g. I, lines 745–60; I, line 1056; I, lines 1200–1204, I, lines 1217–21; V, lines 5224–5.
[18] E.g. III, lines 1645–7, IV, lines 2296–304; IV, lines 2317–19; IV, lines 2326–9; V, lines 4362–5; V, lines 6053–8; V, lines 6130–34.

osity, Selflessness and, above all, the constant effort to be good.[19] These are not small lessons, but they pose another paradox, at least from the point of view of Amans, who is still hoping, after all, that all of this instruction will bring him closer to success. From that perspective, some of Genius's instruction seems not just unhelpful but almost contradictory. In book II, for instance, Amans is taught that love requires him to be charitable, even, or even especially, to his rivals (e.g. *Confessio*, II, lines 201–10; 2435–45). In book III, in which his anger is directed against love itself because of his persistent ill luck, he is taught that love requires that he accept his destiny with equanimity (e.g. *Confessio*, III, lines 1613–58). In book IV the principal lesson for Amans is that he must continue his faithful, virtuous service to his lady even without the prospect of any reward.[20] Book V is a bit different, because there Amans's dogged fidelity is held up as an example of commendable behaviour (the sinners are the characters such as Tereus and Jason, with whom he has virtually nothing in common), but he does get scolded when he betrays his expectation of some reward (*Confessio*, V, lines 4435–566; 5176–225). And, going back to book I, the central lesson on Obedience, with all of the promise implicit in *The Tale of Florent* (*Confessio*, I, lines 1407–1861), is immediately followed by the lesson on Presumption (*Confessio*, I, lines 1883ff.). Gower draws many of these lessons from a tradition of French love poetry that valued commitment to love – without regard to whether or not that love was reciprocated – as constituting its own reward: one becomes a better person for serving love without expectation, and only after one has proved oneself worthy in that way does love occasionally bestow its rewards.[21] Amans naturally has some difficulty with the concept, but what seems most unhelpful – and most paradoxical – from the point of view of one who is focused upon *sped* is from a broader perspective the highest form of celebration of the moral worthiness of love.

'Paradox' is thus written into every level of Genius's instruction. Most of the seeming inconsistencies in the poem are actually the elements in Genius's analysis of the complexity of the human experience of love, and they form part of an argument in favour of the highest degree of moral expectation. But there is a further paradox that extends beyond Genius's instruction on love, and it is manifested in one respect in the inconclusiveness of the ending. Many have been troubled by the lack of a permanent resolution at the end, in the form, for instance, of a final reconciliation between Nature and Reason.[22] It is not just that the advice to abandon love proves

---

[19] A more detailed exposition of the lessons summarized in this paragraph may be found in my *Love and Ethics* (see n. 5 above).

[20] Such is the tenor of many of the exchanges between Amans and Genius, but particularly in *Confessio*, IV, lines 2228–330, perhaps the central passage in book IV, in which Genius turns the question from how one may best earn the rewards of love to how service to love provides its own reward in the form of the virtuous conduct that it inspires.

[21] Nicholson, *Love and Ethics*, pp. 9–30.

[22] E.g. Michael D. Cherniss, *Boethian Apocalypse: Studies in Middle English Vision Poetry* (Norman, OK, 1987), pp. 116–18; and the influential studies of Hugh White: 'Division and failure in Gower's Confessio Amantis', *Neophilologus*, 72 (1988), 605–7, 613–15; 'Nature and the good in Gower's Confessio Amantis', in *John Gower: Recent Readings*, ed. R. F. Yeager (Kalamazoo,

impossible to implement but that all of the ethical instruction that Genius provides to Amans fails to turn him into a perfect human being. But, at least in the ordinary Christian view, such is the condition of the fallen world. The imposition of reason upon conduct is always tentative, and temporary, and incomplete. That may be one of the most compelling pieces of wisdom that the poem offers, and it does so through its very form and not just in the ending. The apparent ceaselessness of the struggle is represented in the very fact of the confession, with its infinitely expandable catalogue of sins and with its structure, in which Amans, no matter how much he has been taught, is always starting over with a new lesson and with the necessity of another moral choice. The impossibility of perfection is manifested throughout the poem in the contrast between Amans and the characters in the tales, which, while illustrating ideals that Amans is expected to strive for, also depict a world in which choices are rather simpler than they are for Amans and in which rewards are generally more immediate and more direct. The same impossibility is also embodied in his lack of success in love, or perhaps it would be better to say in his parallel quests to please both his lady and his confessor. The world doesn't guarantee success in love any more than it makes it easy to be good, so Amans must continue to struggle, but without any assurance of reaching either of his goals. With respect to his moral quest, the poem is about both the need for moral governance in a fallen world *and* the elusiveness of perfection. And that is perhaps the biggest paradox that it offers: that we are constantly obliged to strive for an ideal that we cannot ever fully achieve. That is the inevitable result of our fallen condition, but again, it merely makes a continued effort all the more necessary.

To sum up the central paradoxes of the poem: love cannot be controlled, but it must be regulated; love can be the occasion for sin, but it can also be conducive to the highest forms of virtue; love requires a constant effort, but it does not promise any reward – in fact, one becomes most worthy of love's rewards by loving without expectation; and we must constantly aspire to a moral ideal that we know that we are incapable of achieving. Irony is not a characteristic mode for Gower, but paradox is, and it is unnecessary to ascribe the conflicting lessons in the poem either to a deficient instructor or to a poet who was not fully committed to them. Things are what they seem in the *Confessio Amantis*, but they are far from simple, and taking the poem at its word does not simplify it; it restores its complexity. And as Gower, like Chaucer, embraces in his own way fallen human nature – including both the inevitability of sin and the necessity of virtue – he offers in the *Confessio* not just instruction on how to behave but a mirror of human moral experience in all of its bewildering complexity.

MI, 1989), pp. 12–14; and *Nature, Sex, and Goodness in a Medieval Literary Tradition* (Oxford, 2000), 203–19. See also Tinkle, *Medieval Venuses*, p. 192; Watt, *Amoral Gower*, p. 160.

Chapter 17

Sinning Against Love in *Confessio Amantis*

J. A. BURROW

Confessio Amantis was, I believe, the first medieval poem to apply the priestly scheme of the Seven Deadly Sins systematically to the cause of love. Since that scheme of the Sins purported to cover the whole of human experience, one might suppose that Gower would have found a great deal to his purpose in treatments of love to be found in the clerical tradition, as if the job were already half done for him there. But this was evidently far from the case. The nearest way to see this is to read Gower's own earlier general treatment of the Sins in his *Mirour de l'Omme*. The exposition of them there is very long and elaborate, with each of the Seven Sins having five sub-species, or 'daughters' as they are called. Many of these daughters bear the same name as species of sin in the *Confessio*; yet a reader of the *Mirour* will find very little in it that anticipates the world of the English poem. There is nothing at all under four of the Sins (Anger, Sloth, Covetousness and Gluttony). Under Pride, a single stanza concerns the lover who boasts of a secret love (*Mirour*, lines 1909–20); and the section on Envy devotes a single stanza, again, to Malebouche, who makes young ladies blush by gossiping about their affairs (*Mirour*, lines 2701–12). Rather more substantially, the treatment of Foldelit, under Lechery, has 150 lines on the foolish pleasures of young women in love with love and on the young men who languish for them without food or sleep (*Mirour*, lines 9277–432). But these few passages amount to very little out of a total of 9000 lines. On this evidence – and, I think, on any evidence – Gower had to do most of the work himself when he came in the *Confessio* to map the scheme of the Seven Sins onto the life of Amans.

Gower's latest project, then, was a challenging one; and I want to touch here on some of the difficulties as well as the opportunities that it presented, sketching out what might be called a cost/benefit analysis. But first let me say something about the position that Genius occupies in the poem. Gower's contemporary readers would have been acquainted with the delicate double part played by household priests. These were men who owed allegiance both to God and also to the lord or lady by whom they were retained, men like Richard II's Dominican confessors or William Dunbar at the court of James IV of Scotland. The position of such priests placed them, as it were, both above and below their human patrons, at once a 'father' and a follower. When preaching or hearing confessions they would speak as priests; but on other occasions they could be treated simply as dependants and called upon to perform household tasks like drafting documents or carrying messages.[1] These contemporary realities are mirrored in the world of the *Confessio*, where Genius is represented as a Christian priest retained in the household of a great lady. He is subject to her commands, but he is also a holy father who performs the high offices of the priesthood.

However, the position of Genius differs from that of an ordinary household priest in one significant particular. The great lady whom he serves is herself divine. So his service of her can properly extend even into his priestly work as a confessor, as it should not do in ordinary circumstances: he may speak not only in the cause of God but also in the cause of his lady, Venus. He explains this unusual double obligation to Amans early on in their encounter:

> So thenke I to don bothe tuo,
> Ferst that myn ordre longeth to,
> The vices forto telle arewe,
> Bot next above alle othre schewe
> Of love I wol the propretes,
> How that thei stonde be degrees
> After the disposicioun
> Of Venus, whos condicioun
> I moste folwe, as I am holde.
> For I with love am al withholde. (*Confessio*, I, lines 253–62)

In these lines Genius does not seem altogether clear about his priorities. He owes a duty 'ferst', he says, to his order as a Christian priest, but also 'above alle othre' to Venus, 'For I with love am al withholde', that is, retained. So one might perhaps expect that, in his conduct of the ensuing confessions, these two loyalties will on occasion come into conflict. But I find little trace of such conflict. I agree broadly, in fact, with Peter Nicholson, who throughout his recent study stresses what he describes as 'the fundamental harmony rather than opposition between God's ethical demands and love's'.[2] When Genius turns, as he regularly does, from describing a sin in general to his application of it to the specific case of love, the moral issue most often remains very recognizably the same. Hypocrisy in a lover does not differ from hypocrisy as the Church understands it. Indeed, I find only one place where this 'harmony' positively breaks down. Treating Idleness in book IV, Genius speaks of those who refuse love altogether, a species of idleness which he exemplifies by the story of Rosiphelee. From this he concludes that

---

[1] The contrast of roles is marked in the *Roman de la Rose* by a change of clothing: Jean de Meun's Genius, the priest of Nature, hears his lady's confession dressed in his ecclesiastical vestments; but, when he prepares to carry Nature's message to the God of Love, he strips them off and puts on 'sa robe seculiere': Guillaume de Lorris and Jean de Meun, *Le Roman de la Rose*, ed. Félix Lecoy (Paris, 1965–70), lines 19401–8.

[2] Peter Nicholson, *Love and Ethics in Gower's 'Confessio Amantis'* (Ann Arbor, MI, 2005), p. vi.

> Love is an occupacion,
> Which forto kepe hise lustes save
> Scholde every gentil herte have. (*Confessio*, IV, lines 1452–4)

In asserting that 'every gentle heart' is actually *obliged* to be a lover, Genius does for once overstep the mark – girls like Rosiphelee, after all, could always properly dedicate themselves to a life of virginity in a nunnery. So here, for the only time in the poem, the margin steps in with a downright caveat: 'Non quia sic se habet veritas, set opinio Amantum' – that is, 'Not because the truth has it so, but such is the opinion of lovers'.

The general harmony of which Nicholson speaks does not mean, however, that Gower elides or blurs his transitions between sins in general and sins against love. On the contrary, he has Genius mark them very clearly. Telling his exemplary stories, the confessor leaves Amans in no doubt about which of them concern love and which do not; and when he expounds a sin, he marks the love-sin out from the wider type to which it belongs. On both occasions, he will often mark the distinction – twenty-one times, in fact – by the use of the phrase 'in love's cause'.[3] And this is backed up in the Latin sidenotes by no less than thirty-four occurrences of the corresponding Latin expression, 'in amoris causa'.[4] These sidenotes (which I confidently ascribe to the poet himself) may also mark the same distinction in more technical terms, when they speak of a sin as treated either *simpliciter*, simply as a whole, or *specialius*, that is, more specifically in the cause of love. Thus, when Genius discusses Disobedience 'he first declares the nature of this vice *simpliciter* and then deals particularly with that Disobedience which in the court of Cupid frequently hinders the cause of love by its folly. On this matter the confessor questions Amans *specialius*.'[5]

Throughout the *Confessio* Genius illustrates his teachings with exemplary narratives, some of sin *simpliciter*, others of sin *specialius*. Although there was, of course, a long tradition of general moral exempla, no one before Gower, so far as I know, had attempted to assemble stories devoted *specialius* to the seven sins against love, each of them with their several branches. Gower was widely read in legends and histories, Latin and French, and some of his choices of exempla must have been very easy to make. The story of Tereus, for example:

---

[3] Genius uses the phrase, with small variations, twenty-one times: *Confessio*, I, line 1911, I, line 3437, II, line 232, II, line 2436, III, line 339, III, line 1328, III, line 1464, III, line 1682, IV, line 140, IV, line 245, IV, line 2194, IV, line 2693, V, line 4225, V, line 5548, V, line 6483, V, line 6709, V, line 7033, VI, line 478, VI, line 1239, VII, line 17, VIII, line 273. Amans uses it too: I, line 1342, I, line 2261, I, line 2371, IV, line 1605, V, line 3228, V, line 4371, V, line 6488, VIII, line 2550, VIII, line 2746, VIII, line 2812.

[4] In the sidenotes to *Confessio* I, line 98, I, line 2405, I, line 2682, II, line 101, II, line 454, II, line 589, II, line 1926, II, line 2382, II, line 2503, III, line 421, III, line 785, III, line 1333, III, line 1688, IV, line 80, IV, line 374, IV, line 542, IV, line 733, IV, line 890, IV, line 1619, IV, line 2199, IV, line 3319, V, line 1975, V, line 2863, V, line 3251, V, line 4784, V, line 5554, V, line 6079. V, line 6147, V, line 6716, V, line 7197, VI, line 1393, VIII, line 3, VIII, line 2068, VIII, line 3108.

[5] Sidenote to *Confessio*, I, line 1240. Elsewhere, *simpliciter* at I, line 576, I, line 1887, I, line 3069; *specialius* at I, line 9, V, line 8, VIII, line 3108.

> Now list, mi Sone, and thou schalt hiere,
> So as it hath befalle er this,
> In loves cause how that it is
> A man to take be Ravine
> The preie which is femeline. (*Confessio*, V, lines 5546–50)

The rape of Philomena by Tereus is one of those stories where men treat women as their 'prey', winning them either by force or trickery. Such stories suited Gower's project very well, and the *Confessio* has many of them, notably the tales of Mundus and Paulina, the False Bachelor, and Nectanabus. Classical and medieval sources were equally rich in examples of that other kind of love-sin where men break their promises and leave women in the lurch. So book IV (Sloth) draws on Ovid's *Heroides* for the sufferings of Dido, Penelope and Phyllis; and book V has the long story of Jason's breach of promise with Medea.

However, appropriate stories such as these did not always come so readily to hand, and Gower can be seen sometimes having to settle for second best. In his first three books he stretches a point to include offences committed not by lovers themselves but against them by others – 'Sins against Love' in a different sense of that phrase. So book III illustrates its treatment of melancholy Wrath with the tale of Canace and Machaire, and here the sin in question is the violent response of their father to the two siblings, not – emphatically not – their own incestuous passion. Again, Gower may resort to stories which touch on his moral point only obliquely or in passing, as in the long tale of Albinus and Rosemund. This story turns on the moment when Albinus tricks his wife Rosemund into drinking out of a goblet made from the skull of her defeated father: '"Drink with thi fader, Dame", he seide'. It is left for a Latin sidenote here to explain that Albinus is boasting about his love as well as about his victory; but this is hardly enough to establish the point of what proves to be quite a long story. Another long tale that leaves its declared point behind is that of Apollonius of Tyre, where the incestuous relations between Antiochus and his daughter play no further part in events once Apollonius has set out on his travels.

Gower's main project, however, was to apply the scheme of the Seven Sins to the single case of Amans, and here he faced difficulties of a quite different kind. The exemplary stories told by Genius *in amoris causa* most often involve actions which, in one way or another, can readily be seen as sinful – very evidently so in cases such as that of Tereus. By the standards of legendary or historical story-telling, however, Amans can hardly be said to have *done* anything at all. His confessions describe his life as a lover in the form of what Gérard Genette calls 'iterative narrative', where, as Genette puts it, 'a single narrative utterance takes upon itself several occurrences together of the same event'.[6] So Amans bundles many occurrences

---

[6] Gérard Genette, *Narrative Discourse: An Essay in Method*, trans. Jane E. Lewin from Genette's *Figures III* (Ithaca, NY, 1980), p. 116.

together and recalls them in the present tense that English uses for repeated or customary doings, as in 'I go to London every week.' No particular occasion or event is singled out as critical. Here is one typical example of this narrative manner, from the section on Sacrilege. Amans and his lady are in church.

> Bot I wold stele, if that I mihte,
> A glad word or a goodly syhte;
> And evere mi service I profre,
> And namly whan sche wol gon offre,
> For thanne I lede hire, if I may,
> For somwhat wolde I stele away.
> Whan I beclippe hire on the wast,
> Yit ate leste I stele a tast,
> And otherwhile 'grant mercy'
> Sche seith, and so winne I therby
> A lusti touch, a good word eke,
> But al the remenant to seke
> Is fro mi pourpos wonder ferr. (*Confessio*, V, lines 7137–49)

Characteristically, this is the worst that Amans can find to confess in the matter of Sacrilege: he sometimes does steal a touch and a word from his lady on occasions when he leads her up for the offering in church. The insignificance of these little so-called thefts is pointed up when Genius goes straight on to tell of the abduction of Helen by Paris from a temple of Venus, a very much more momentous example of sacrilegious theft by a lover.

So here we have a single lover who does almost nothing and gets almost nowhere in his devotion to his lady. His story – if indeed you call it that – is quite without dramatic incident. Yet it is to this pusillanimous subject that Genius confines himself as confessor, turning from sin *simpliciter* to the sins of love before questioning Amans only about the latter, as he promised at the start:

> I wol thi schrifte so enforme,
> That ate leste thou schalt hiere
> The vices, and to thi matiere
> Of love I schal hem so remene
> That thou schalt knowe what thei mene.
> (*Confessio*, I, lines 276–80)

In his responses Amans also confines himself to his matter of love, for he is, of course, all and only a lover. His confessions, though, are much more varied and interesting than one might expect. Questioned about a particular Sin against Love, he may respond with a more or less absolute denial; or he may admit that he has indeed done wrong; or he may confess to the sin, not in what he has done, but in his feelings, wishes or thoughts. These three options of response, alone or in combination, allow Gower considerable freedom of invention in composing the lover's confessional speeches.

*

In the *Confessio* Gower presents the Seven Sins in the same Gregorian order that he adopted in his *Mirour de l'Omme*.[7] In the *Mirour* each of the Sins has its five 'daughters', and the English poem follows suit, but only in its first three books (Pride, Envy and Wrath). In these books, furthermore, the five daughters or sub-types are exactly the same as in the French. In both poems, for instance, Pride divides into Hypocrisy, Disobedience, Arrogance, Boasting and Vainglory. It seems to be the case that after book III Gower found greater difficulties in accommodating the schemes and terminology of the *Mirour* to his new purpose, and he certainly takes increasing liberties with them thereafter, as we will see. By comparison, Pride, Envy and Wrath lent themselves quite readily to being re-imagined as Sins against Love; and especially in book II, on Envy, the costs of Gower's project were quite outweighed by its benefits.

In this book the confessions of Amans all evoke a setting in what he calls the Court of Cupid (*Confessio*, II, line 39); that is, gatherings where love is in the air. On social occasions such as these, gentlemen enter into competition with each other for the favour of ladies – and especially, Amans imagines, for the favour of the lady he loves. So throughout this book the objects of his envious feelings are his rivals, real or supposed. Of the five *Mirour* sub-types of Envy, the first two are sins that may be committed only in feeling and in thought: Sorrow for another's Joy, and Joy for another's Sorrow (the latter not nowadays understood as a form of Envy). So, under the first of these heads, Amans confesses that, when he sees young men approach his lady, converse with her and even whisper in her ear, their joy causes his sorrow. This is not exactly jealousy, for Amans protests that he trusts the lady completely: 'For no mistrust I have of hire | Me grieveth noght' (*Confessio*, II, lines 53–4). It is purely Sorrow for another's Joy. Nor does this bitter feeling cause him to do or even say anything at all. In this he is comically unlike the giant Polyphemus, who, in the confessor's exemplum, inspired by his frustrated passion for Galatea, crushes her lover Acis to death under a landslip. As Amans remarks after being told this story:

> Mi fader, this ensample is good;
> Bot how so evere that it stod
> With Poliphemes love as tho,
> It schal noght stonde with me so,
> To worchen eny felonie
> In love for no such Envie. (*Confessio*, II, lines 211–16)

Amans will never 'worchen eny felonie', but he has his own sort of envious doings, as he confesses under the third *Mirour* head, Detraction. For he takes pains to spread evil reports about his rivals and to malign them in conversation with his lady. Here Amans gives a very convincingly muddled account of his envious responses to what he calls the 'yonge lusty route' of the lady's admirers. He declares that his lady can perfectly well look after herself; she

---

[7] On the order of the Sins, see Morton W. Bloomfield, *The Seven Deadly Sins* (East Lansing, MI, 1952), pp. 105–6 etc.

will not be taken in by false declarations of love; she 'holds her thumb in her fist'. Yet he is still afraid that plausible men may succeed in 'enchanting her innocence', so he takes every opportunity of alerting her to their evil intentions. His own motives, however, are by no means pure, for he goes on in a very crisp couplet to admit that he would be just as ready to malign a rival who was truly and honourably in love: 'For be thei goode, or be thei badde, | I wolde non my ladi hadde' (*Confessio*, II, lines 513–14). Confessional self-analysis here yields a convincing psychological portrait. It is the case of Malebouche – recalled from the *Roman de la Rose* at II, line 389 – but seen from a new point of view. The lover is here not the victim of detraction but the perpetrator of it. Amans is Malebouche.

The fourth sub-type of Envy is Falssemblant. Here, for the first time in book II, the immediate response of Amans is to deny all culpability. Certainly he does not, like the lover in the *Roman de la Rose*, enlist Faus Semblant directly in his campaign against the resistance of the lady. But he does go on to admit to more devious deceits. When he suspects men of fancying his lady, he 'feigns company' with them and, if his suspicions are confirmed, he maligns them in conversation with her. This is another variation upon the *Roman de la Rose*: in the French, Faus Semblant sets out to frustrate Malebouche, but here he provides him with materials for his backbiting.

In the fifth and final sub-type, Supplantation, Amans responds to his confessor's questioning by distinguishing between thought and deed. He would dearly *like* to supplant all his rivals in the lady's affections, but he *can't*. Genius responds to this admission with an even-handed judgment:

> Mi goode Sone, as of Supplant
> Thee thar noght drede tant ne quant,
> As for nothing that I have herd,
> But only that thou hast misferd
> Thenkende, and that me liketh noght,
> For godd beholt a mannes thoght. (*Confessio*, II, lines 2429–34)

In this Book of Envy, as most often in the poem elsewhere, Amans has little to confess in the way of sinful doings – only, in this book, speeches of detraction and false-seeming. His life as a lover is lived largely in his thoughts and feelings – some of them sinful, as Genius observes – and he cannot bring himself to do anything much at all. In this respect he resembles not the lover in the *Roman de la Rose* but those polite, timorous lovers who are to be found in the fourteenth-century *dits amoreux* of Jean Froissart and Guillaume de Machaut.[8]

After his first three books, as I observed earlier, Gower progressively abandons the fivefold divisions of the *Mirour* and has to allow himself increasing freedoms in his handling of the remaining Sins against Love. In particular, he begins to draw upon new figurative ways of applying the terminology of the Sins to the love-life of Amans. There is an early instance of this already

---

[8] See most recently Nicholson, *Love and Ethics*, pp. 9–30 etc.

in book III, in the treatment of Contek or Strife, a sub-type of Wrath. Challenged by Genius here, Amans denies this 'as of the dede' but confesses to what he calls 'hertes contek', or mental strife (*Confessio*, III, line 1132), described allegorically as a battle in his heart between Reason and Passion. But it is in books V and VI (Avarice and Gluttony) that such extended figurative applications become frequent, as Nicholson observes.[9] It is not difficult to see why this should be so. Pride, Envy and Wrath lie directly in the emotional path of a lover, but Avarice and Gluttony do not. So one may say that Gower was forced by the demands of his project into resorting to non-literal applications. But here the benefits clearly outweigh the costs.

The long and elaborate Book of Avarice has many examples of both literal and metaphorical interpretations. The distinction between them appears very distinctly in the section on Covetousness, where Genius first takes the sin figuratively as 'covoitise of love', that is, a promiscuous desire for many women, and then literally, as desire for a woman for her gold and her land. Amans, of course, denies both. More interesting is the treatment of Avarice. This is distinguished from Covetousness in the customary way: 'That on hold and that other draweth' (*Confessio*, V, line 1981), that is, Avarice holds on to what it has got where Covetousness reaches out for more. In his presentation of Avarice, so understood, Genius first plays on the verb *have* when describing a miser as one who cannot be said truly to own possessions that he never puts to use: 'Thus hath he, that he noght ne hath'; his possessing is such that he possesses nothing. Rather, it is his possessions that own him: 'For good hath him and halt him teid' (*Confessio*, V, lines 47–56). Replying *in causa amoris*, Amans confesses that, if he were lucky enough to possess his lady, he would indeed keep her to himself; but in actual fact he is not the possessor but the possessed: 'For I am hadd and noght ne have' (*Confessio*, V, line 113). It is a remarkable passage, not least for the sequence of six couplets of punning rhyme (*rime équivoque* in French) with which Amans expresses his dream of single possession:

> And in this wise, taketh kepe,
> If I hire hadde, I wolde hire kepe,
> And yet no friday wolde I faste,
> Thogh I hire kepte and hielde faste.
> Fy on the bagges in the kiste!
> I hadde ynogh, if I hire kiste.
> For certes, if sche were myn,
> I hadde hir levere than a Myn
> Of Gold; for al this worldesriche
> Ne mihte make me so riche
> As sche, that is so inly good.
> I sette noght of other good. (*Confessio*, V, lines 79–90)

Sexual possessiveness here figures as a kind of avarice, especially in the coupling of 'kiste' (kissed) with 'kiste' (strongbox) and 'myn' (my beloved)

---

[9] See *ibid.*, pp. 71–5.

with 'Myn' (goldmine).[10] A little later Genius draws an analogy between Avarice and sexual jealousy, summing it up in a formal *comparatio*:

> That oon wolde have his bagges stille,
> And noght departen with his wille,
> And dar noght for the thieves slepe,
> So fain he wolde his tresor kepe;
> That other mai noght wel be glad,
> For he is evere more adrad
> Of these lovers that gon aboute,
> In aunter if thei putte him oute.
> So have thei bothe litel joy
> As wel of love as of monoie. (*Confessio*, V, lines 601–10)

This comparison between Avarice and jealousy, as Nicholson observes,[11] was by no means a commonplace. It may have come to Gower, in fact, as a happy inspiration thrown up in the working out of his project. The jealous lover or husband, like the miser, is so afraid of losing his 'treasure' that its possession gives him no joy.

Equally suggestive is the treatment in this book of Usury as a Sin against Love. In its literal sense, Usury stands here for any inordinate profiting from a transaction, getting a lot for a little. So, by analogy, a usurious lover will be one who wins more love from his lady than he himself devotes to her. Predictably, Amans pleads not guilty of this offence. Indeed, he boldly suggests that the fault lies rather with his lady, for has she not purchased the whole of his heart with nothing more substantial than a single 'looking of her eye'? To this argument Genius objects:

> Sche mai be such that hire o lok
> Is worth thin herte manyfold;
> So hast thou wel thin herte sold,
> Whan thou hast that is more worth. (*Confessio*, V, lines 4542–5)

A lady's glances – like the lady's kisses in *Sir Gawain and the Green Knight* – cannot be valued in the way that commodities are valued; nor can the balance of profit and loss in affairs of love between two people be easily determined. It is a courtly and somewhat precious thought, but not without a wider bearing on human relationships.

Book VI, on Gluttony, confines itself to just two of the subheads in the *Mirour*, Drunkenness and Delicacy, setting aside the other three 'daughters' (immoderation in appetite, consumption, and expense). Both these vices have only figurative applications *specialiter* to the cause of love. In his account of Drunkenness, Genius first condemns the everyday vice and then likens

---

[10] 'Rime équivoque' is highly recommended (as against its inartistic opposite, flat repetition of the same word) in the French poetic manuals known as Second Rhetorics: *Receuil d'arts de seconde rhétorique*, ed. E. Langlois (Paris, 1902). Discussion in Alastair Minnis and Ian Johnson, eds, *The Cambridge History of Literary Criticism*, vol. 2: *The Middle Ages* (Cambridge, 2005), pp. 455–61.

[11] Nicholson, *Love and Ethics*, p. 267.

it to the condition of those who suffer from the 'maladie of lovedrunke' (*Confessio*, VI, lines 110–11). In his long response, in which he confesses to being lovedrunk, Amans plays some ingenious variations on the theme of love as a drink. Thinking about the lady, he says, is meat and drink to him, but the drink is bitter-sweet, leaving him with dry lips and an unquenched thirst. Again, it is the lack of his love-drink that makes him drunk; but if only the lady would look favourably upon him, he would sober up and be happy:

> As I am drunke of that I drinke,
> So am I ek for falte of drinke;
> Of which I finde no reles:
> Bot if I myhte natheles
> Of such a drinke as I coveite,
> So as me liste, have o receite,
> I scholde assobre and fare wel. (*Confessio*, VI, lines 285–91)

Paradoxes such as these express the bipolar confusion of his love-experience more powerfully than conventional oxymorons like the confessor's talk of 'jolif wo' (*Confessio*, VI, line 84).

The second of these sins of the mouth, Delicacy, is distinguished from Drunkenness – more sharply than in the *Mirour* – as concerning only food. Genius explains that 'delicate' eaters are never content with common foods and seek out 'metes strange' (*Confessio*, VI, line 659). Eaters like these correspond, by analogy, to lovers who cannot be satisfied by their lady's favours and to husbands who find other women more desirable than their wives. Amans responds by denying any such fault. His lady, he says, grants him no favours at all, but if she were to allow him even as little as a friendly look, he would be only too happy with that. He does, however, go on to confess to a different kind of delicacy, indulged in when he sees his lady and thinks about her afterwards. These sights and thoughts are the titbits upon which he is forced to feed. A long and characteristic passage here (*Confessio*, VI, lines 727–950) cleverly adapts to the idiom of Gluttony the three comforts that Cupid offers the lover in the *Roman de la Rose*: Sweet Looking, Sweet Speech and Sweet Thought.[12] Amans expresses, for instance, the gluttonous relish with which he gazes at those portions of the lady's flesh that are visible at her face, neck and hands. But these, as Amans complains, are no more than small and insubstantial foods:

> Bot yit is noght mi feste al plein,
> Bot al of woldes and of wisshes,
> Therof have I my fulle disshes,
> Bot as of fielinge and of tast,
> Yit mihte I nevere have o repast. (*Confessio*, VI, lines 922–6)

I come now to the section on Lechery, which concludes the lover's confession in no less than 2000 lines of book VIII. I must admit that I have consid-

---

[12] Guillaume de Lorris and Jean de Meun, *Roman de la Rose*, lines 2629–748.

erable difficulty in understanding what Gower does in this part of the poem. Why did he choose to confine the exchanges between Genius and Amans here, at such great length, to a single topic? And why Incest?

Let me suppose that, as on previous occasions, Gower's mind went back to his *Mirour*. There, as usual, Lechery had five daughters: Fornication, 'Stupre' (sexual violation), Adultery, Incest and 'Foldelit'. Citing that same list, G. C. Macaulay observed that 'nearly all of these subjects [...] have already been treated of more or less fully'.[13] They have indeed figured in many of the stories that Genius tells, so Gower would have seen little opportunity here to introduce a fresh and interesting batch of exempla. More disheartening, however, would be the prospect of applying any or all of the *Mirour* list to the particular case of Amans. There could be no question of a lover such as this actually committing any of the five, unless perhaps he were to admit to Foldelit. Nor did any of them allow of an extended, figurative application, for they are all already Sins against Love. Perhaps Amans might have confessed to committing some of them in his heart, if not in deed? Fornication, perhaps? Yet could Amans ever do anything as gross as fantasizing about sexual intercourse? I think not. It seems, in fact, that Amans could only have gone on responding to Genius with a monotonous series of unqualified negatives – never a 'Yes, guilty', not even a 'Yes, if only'.

So one may imagine that Gower is cutting his losses here when he selects just one sin from the *Mirour* list. But why did he choose Incest? Perhaps because it was a fresh topic (not addressed as such in the tale of Canace and Machaire)? Or was he keen to use the story of Apollonius of Tyre? I do not know. In the event, anyway, he devotes serious attention to the topic, focusing on it quite sharply through no less than 2000 lines. The opening history of marriage is specifically concerned with the historical development of the prohibited degrees as they were extended in scope from the time of Adam and Eve to the present day, and it concludes by condemning those who offend against modern canonical rules as no better than creatures without reason, cocks or stallions (*Confessio*, VIII, lines 159–63).[14] Challenged by the confessor, Amans very briefly denies culpability – he has never been tempted by any incestuous desire. Yet Genius persists, telling stories of men in love with their sisters or daughters, including Apollonius of Tyre, before warning Amans once more that he should not 'take lust as doth a beste' (*Confessio*, VIII, line 2025). The lover then, rather wearily, again acquits himself of guilt 'in this point', and his confession is concluded.

*

The end of the confession is marked, at book VIII, line 2068, by a Latin sidenote announcing that the whole *confessio super Amoris causa* is now, from this point on, a thing of the past. It is *finita*. Yet more than a thousand lines of the poem still remain, and we may expect there to learn what we are to make of Amans and the kind of love that he represents. What judgment is

---

[13] Macaulay, i, II, p. 536.
[14] See generally Elizabeth Archibald, *Incest and the Medieval Imagination* (Oxford, 2001).

the poem to pass upon him? This is a large and controversial question, upon which much might be said; but I must confine myself here to the opinions expressed by Genius. How does his confessor judge Amans?

At the end of his last confession, Amans called upon Genius for his 'hole conseil', that is, his full, definitive assessment of the case. In response, the confessor promised to turn from 'truffles' (fanciful trifles?) to 'trouthe':

> Mi sone, unto the trouthe wende
> Now wol I for the love of thee,
> And let alle othre truffles be. (*Confessio*, VIII, lines 2060–62)

So Genius goes on to offer what he calls his 'conclusion final' – in keeping, he says, with his priestly order:

> Forthi to speken overmore
> Of love, which thee may availe,
> Tak love where it mai noght faile:
> For as of this which thou art inne,
> Be that thou seist it is a Sinne,
> And Sinne may no pris deserve,
> Withoute pris and who shal serve,
> I not what profit myhte availe. (*Confessio*, VIII, lines 2084–91)

These are uncompromising truths. 'Tak love where it may noght faile'. The love to which Amans has confessed is directed towards an object that cannot promise any lasting satisfaction; and it is to be condemned wholesale as 'a Sinne'. Despite the absence of specifically theological language, we may be reminded here of the epilogue to Chaucer's *Troilus*: since all sublunary loves are bound to disappoint, one must look elsewhere for an attachment that will not fail.

Gower himself enunciates a rather similar view when he comes to his own farewell to love at the very end of the *Confessio*. Yet Genius's 'conclusion' proves to be anything but his 'final' word on Amans; for, in what follows, things change. In particular, the identification of Amans as 'John Gower' allows him to make his 'beau retret' from love on the grounds of old age and incapacity. So it is to an Amans who is no longer a lover that Genius pronounces what is indeed his final judgment, his last word. Amans has recalled his confession and asked the priest for absolution, to which Genius replies:

> [...] Sone, as of thi schrifte
> Thou hast ful pardoun and foryifte;
> Foryet it thou, and so wol I. (*Confessio*, VIII, lines 2895–7)

In the course of their scenes together Amans has several times looked forward to receiving from Genius his absolution and the appropriate penances;[15] yet

---

[15] Absolution: III, line 596; Penances: I, line 1972, II, line 2316, II, line 3514; III, line 2746, IV, line 1226, IV, line 3500, V, line 6699.

now, when the solemn moment has evidently arrived, the priest makes no more than an unceremonious allusion to a 'full pardon' that has already been granted (when?) and exempts him from any further obligations in the matter. 'Foryet it thou, and so wol I'!

I find these parting words from Genius to be more in keeping with his general conduct as a confessor than his more otherworldly judgment earlier. In his scenes with Amans he rarely found any reason to blame him at all severely. On more than half of the forty occasions when he challenged Amans about a sin, the lover had no fault to confess, or only a fault so trifling that Genius could dismiss it as 'a game'. Nor, on the other occasions, did the sin amount to much – not, certainly, by comparison with the behaviour of other lovers in the exemplary stories. There is, consequently, a general lack of heavy moralizing in the confession scenes, and Amans is left free to expatiate on what his own life as a lover has felt like.

And expatiate he does, to a total of more than 3000 lines. It is extraordinary that so many lines should be devoted to the confessions of a man who is, as his name declares, all and only a lover – and one who at no point makes any real progress in the pursuit of his lady. The whole account, in fact, confines itself to just one (admittedly protracted) phase in the affair, with nothing about the origins of his passion and nothing, of course, about any happy developments to come. However, the scheme of the Seven Sins serves to impose a principle of order upon the long account that Amans gives. It is not a narrative or chronological principle, as in the usual love-stories, but an analytical one, taking the Sins successively in their Gregorian sequence. So Amans's experience of love is represented – synchronically, as it were – by all his affirmative or negative responses to the questions that Genius puts; and these responses, these yeses and nos, rather like the pixels in digital photography, build up to a very full and detailed, though always conventional, picture of the life of a disappointed lover. The result is a very distinctive contribution to the courtly Matter of Love, unmatched both in the love lyrics and in love narratives of the time. This, I think, is the greatest benefit that Gower derived from his project: his mapping of the Seven Sins onto the life of Amans.

Chapter 18

The Woman's Response in John Gower's *Cinkante Balades*

HOLLY BARBACCIA

In John Gower's Anglo-French lyric cycle, the *Cinkante Balades*, the five-poem woman's series marks a critical moment. Gower positions the woman's response within the last fifth of the cycle, grouping her apparently contradictory poems together as a self-contained series, Balades 41–44 and 46. Mathematically one-tenth of the whole, the woman's response to the male speaker nevertheless occupies much emotional space in the cycle.[1] Gower's male speaker begs for, describes and reacts to the woman's poems repeatedly in his own Balades. Comparing her and her replies to diamond, marble, rock and crystal, the male speaker learns to praise his beloved's stony resistance. He tries to use his poems to wear her down, but, ultimately, her Balades polish and refine his: in fact, the woman's response reflects and corrects his poetic vocabulary. Only in the wake of the woman's series can the male speaker find poetic honour and comment on love's virtue. Thus Gower suggests that the woman and her reply illuminate and clarify whole text.

Yet, while the woman's response has attracted some critical attention, it has not received a thorough treatment. Lynn Wells Hagman claims that the woman's poems 'tell a little story of her own', but she concludes that the 'mistress' section does not end on a particularly strong note'.[2] Instead she argues that, as the male speaker has 'progressively less and less to do with the actual love situations' involving the woman, 'Gower himself' emerges

---

[1] London, BL, MS Additional 59495, the 'Trentham' MS (c.1399), contains two Balades numbered 'IIII', so the cycle technically includes fifty-one numbered Balades, forty-six belonging to the male speaker. However, all poems after the second Balade IIII are numbered as if the cycle only contains fifty total Balades; I number and 'count' the Balades accordingly throughout this paper.

[2] Lynn Wells Hagman, 'A study of Gower's *Cinkante Balades*' (unpublished doctoral dissertation, University of Detroit, 1968), pp. 95, 99. Note that Hagman concludes that the woman's series ends with a whimper because she accepts G. C. Macaulay's premise that the woman rejects the male speaker and accepts a new lover in Balade 44. For this view, see Macaulay, pp. lxxviii, xxvii. More recently, scholars appear to adopt the simpler approach of assuming that the woman addresses a single male speaker whom she first rejects and then accepts. See, for instance, R. F. Yeager, *John Gower's Poetic: the Search for a New Arion* (Cambridge, 1990), p. 107, and William Calin, *The French Tradition and the Literature of Medieval England* (Toronto, 1994), pp. 380–85.

and leads the cycle to 'progress in moral tone toward the climax' in the unnumbered Marian coda Balade following the numbered cycle in the manuscript.[3] In Hagman's reading the Virgin replaces the earthly woman of the male speaker's poems as the object of Gower's own desire. Likewise, Russell Ralph Cressman argues that the male speaker's initial fascination with the woman and 'fin amour' gives way to Gower's increasing emphasis on 'vrai amour', what he calls 'brotherly love'. 'Fin' and 'vrai amour' both finally find themselves 'subsumed within *bon amour*', which Cressman alleges corresponds to 'divine love', the love ultimately endorsed and embodied by the Virgin.[4]

R. F. Yeager has given the woman's response more sustained attention, observing that 'Gower, in the persona of the Lady, weaves into her poems lines from lyrics by Guillaume de Machaut, Eustache Deschamps, Jean Froissart, and Oton de Grandson while also creating the sense through her Balades that 'she has read the poems of the [male speaker], and kept them close enough to quote back to him his own lines in paraphrase.' Yet, not unlike Hagman and Cressman, he also claims that:

> Gower maneuvers his reader from the first five balades dedicated to conjugal love through the history and 'conversation' of his lovers [...] to the conclusion of the cycle, first in the didactic, theoretical balades concerned with the 'rationality' of true lovers to (finally) the supra-rational love due the Virgin, whose model as a seldom-requited, loyal lover exceeds all human examples touted by the tradition of the courtly lyric. No Jason, no Aeneas, no Lancelot (and certainly no Guinevere) ever loved like the Mother of God. And that was, apparently, Gower's point ...[5]

Yeager concludes that the text thus presents us with a vision of the 'lovers progressing steadily' as they become 'beings capable of moral choices', leaving the conventional rhetoric of love poetry behind even as the cycle proceeds towards 'Gower's moral conclusion'.[6] In Yeager's reading, the lovers' conversation becomes a route by which the male speaker approaches the Virgin and Gower broaches his moral lesson.

Critics who see the *Cinkante Balades* culminating in the Marian Balade often also urge us to proceed *through* the woman's response series. However, I would argue that Gower encourages us to move towards and linger over that group of poems as a key to the whole text. In fact, the first forty Balades, as well as Balades 45 and 47, revolve around the woman and her reply. Only in the light of her response can the male speaker produce his moral insights about love and honour in Balades 48–50. In fact, from the cycle's first Balade the male speaker insists upon the importance of his and his beloved's poetic exchange. In the *envoi* to Balade 1, the speaker equates exchanging Balades and oaths with exchanging hearts and bodies, offering himself through his

---

[3] Hagman, 'A study', p. 99
[4] Russell Ralph Cressman, 'Gower's *Cinkante Balade's* and French court lyrics' (unpublished doctoral dissertation, University of North Carolina at Chapel Hill, 1983), p. i.
[5] R. F. Yeager, 'John Gower's French', in *Companion*, pp. 137–51 (p. 147).
[6] *Ibid.*, p. 148.

writing: 'Par cest escrit, ma dame, a vous me rens' (line 25).[7] The speaker's refrain reiterates that his heart ('coer', with a pun on 'corps', body) remains in his lady's 'grace', the symbolic place from which she grants erotic mercy and pleasure. In Balade 2, the speaker makes it clear that he hopes for her replies in reward for his 'long' (line 11) service:

> Le jour qe j'ai de vous novelle oï,
> Il m'est avis qe rien me grievera:
> Porceo, ma chiere dame, jeo vous pri,
> Par vo message, quant il vous plerra ... (*Balades*, 2, lines 17–20)

> (On the day I hear some news of you, it seems to me nothing can cause me grief: therefore, my dear lady, I pray for your message, whenever it pleases you.)

Thus, as it implies an amorous servitude and a lyric conversation already underway, the cycle also begins to anticipate the woman's response and to represent her reply itself as a reward for service. Throughout the Balades that follow, the speaker alludes directly and indirectly to the woman's reply, creating a presence from her and her responses' absence.

As his steadfast heart and thought fly towards the absent woman faster than the 'falcon de sa Mue' on poetic wings of hope and desire, the speaker's frustrated desire dismembers him (*Balades*, 8, lines 3, 4). But the lover finds himself paradoxically unified: serving his beloved renders him all hers entirely (*Balades*, 8, line 16). Because she lives at a different court, the speaker must send the woman his 'coer et corps' 'Milfoitz le jour' through the Balades (*Balades*, 5, line 26; 6, line 18). Still, he fantasizes about direct mental communion:

> Si mon penser saveroit a sa venue
> A vous, ma doulce dame, reconter
> Ma volenté, et a sa revenue
> Vostre plaisir a moi auci conter,
> En tout le mond n'eust si bon Messager (*Balades*, 8, lines 8–12)

> (If my thoughts could know the way to come to you, my sweet lady, to recount my will, and on their return, to also recount your pleasure to me, in all the world there would not be such a good messenger.)

He contents himself with sending his heart, mind and body through the lyric missives 'Centmillfoitz' times a day 'en lieu' of himself (*Balades*, 8, line 13, line 7). His 'coer', 'corps' and 'joie' together compose and send the poem, and Balade 8 concludes with the speaker 'En bon espoir, tanque jeo vous revoie' (*Balades*, 8, lines 23, 25).

Repeatedly, the male speaker asks for the woman's reward for services rendered in the form of a poetic response. He begs for erotic mercy, pity, grace and 'ameisté complie' from his lady and tries to serve her in 'faitz

---

[7] All citations of the *Cinkante Balades* refer to Macaulay.

et ditz' (*Balades*, 10, line 21; 11, line 4). But she will not show even 'un poi plus amerouse' (Balade 11, refrain). The speaker also asks for a 'favour' of 'reguard', perhaps a message agreeing to show him her eyes and the 'grace' of her 'figure' (*Balades*, 12, line 7, line 21). Here, the speaker may make a play for literary as well as literal eye contact, since 'figure' can refer to her poems as well as her body, and since the 'cure' he requests can represent textual as well as sexual healing (*Balades*, 12, line 27). He urges her to answer him, since he deserves a gift and should have a reward for his service, reminding her of her 'franchise' and 'largesce' – her nobility, generosity and freedom (*Balades* 28, line 8). He asks her:

> Dame, u est ore celle naturesce,
> Qe soloit estre en vous tiel temps jeo vi,
> Q'il ne vous plest de vostre gentilesce
> Un soul salutz mander a vostre ami? (*Balades* 28, lines 1–4)

> (Lady, where is now that nature which many times I have seen in you, that it now does not please your gentleness and courtesy to send a single salute to your friend?)

He offers 'ceo dit' in remembrance of him and asks her to send back her own 'beals ditz' (*Balades*, 28, lines 23, 24).

But the lady's silence increasingly becomes the speaker's theme. Her 'desdeigne' renders him borderline aphasic in Balade 14 (line 8). With no sustenance but his own thoughts to keep his hope alive, the speaker likens himself to a 'Chamaeleon', not because he changes his colours but because he, too, lives on 'l'air sanz plus' (*Balades*, 16, lines 1, 2).[8] The speaker goes on to complain that although his lady has a masterful command of language, she says nothing to him: 'Ma dame, qui sciet langage a plentée, | Rien me respont' (*Balades*, 17, lines 17–18). Like a silent 'Sibille', she has not returned 'un mot' to the speaker's 'requeste', and the more he prays to her, the less she understands or responds to him (*Balades*, 19, line 14; *Balades*, 18, line 20, refrain). When she does reply to his prayers, he hears only a 'basse vois' whispering one 'mot': 'nay' (*Balades*, 17, lines 21, 23). That small, hateful word adorns its 'sentence' with 'grant dolour' (*Balades*, 17, line 24). In Balade 30, the *'danger'* – resistance, but now also physical danger – represented by her 'parole' disturbs the waters he sails (line 4). Refusing him any 'mot de confort', the lady's personified Danger says 'nai' and, when he speaks, he transforms the 'chiere porte' into 'mort' for the speaker (*Balades*, 30, lines 16, 19, 20).

At the same time the speaker alludes to and fantasizes about the woman's ability to transform him with her words: her use of language profoundly impacts his. The speaker carries within himself the 'essample' of her 'bon noun' (*Balades*, 21, line 25). In Balade 24, with her 'mein' she inscribes her

---

[8] Compare this with Genius' description in *Confessio*, I, lines 2699–711, of chameleon-like lovers who cycle through lyric poetic modes as quickly as they change clothing. That the chameleon here does *not* symbolize change may underscore the male speaker's fidelity, perhaps to the strict limitations of his Balade form as well as to the lady.

'propre noun' upon the text of his heart (lines 1, 2). He registers his lady's writing inside him when he cannot say any name but hers during the chaplain's litany and lesson (*Balades*, 24, line 5). Even so, he implies that she adopts and transforms the signs he sends her through his poems. She accepts the rose for her 'desport' and rejects him (*Balades*, 37, line 4). Adopting 'la ruge Rose', the symbol which represents her, the 'plus belle' 'flour des flours', she appears to allow his poesy into her 'parclose', but she shuts him out (*Balades*, 37, line 3; *Balades*, 9, line 41; *Balades*, 37, line 8). Refusing his love, she treats his poems instead as the 'plus joiouse chose' (*Balades*, 37, line 1). She remains 'franche', free to enjoy the rose without feeling the prick of love, but the chains of the speaker's amorous desires bind him, and he finds himself stuck with a different symbol for his beloved – 'L'urtie' ('stinging nettle': *Balades*, 37, refrain, line 24).

Even as he emphasizes the woman's powerful ability to use and transform his poetic signs, the male speaker produces a range of metaphors to decry his lady's 'durtée', her inflexibility and hardness (*Balades*, 17, line 1). Offering nothing but 'rien', she becomes 'fiere | Com Diamant, qe n'est de riens fendu' (*Balades*, 18, lines 22–3). As 'piere Daiamand' attracts iron, so she draws his heart to her (*Balades*, 38, line 1). Her seemingly 'tendre oraille' proves harder than 'la rochiere' (*Balades*, 18, lines 5, 12). Taking up an Ovidian image, the male speaker compares his poems to 'Les goutes d'eaue'; unlike those drops, though, his lyrics cannot erode his lady's 'dure piere' (*Balades*, 18, lines 1, 2). One can even pierce 'marbre', but his beloved always closes her ear to the speaker's poetic 'matiere' (*Balades*, 18, lines 19, 18). The male speaker wishes his own writing could change her the way hers changes him, imagining that, like 'Pigmalion', he could use his 'oreisoun' – his poem as well as his prayer – to transform his lady's poetic 'image' from 'piere en char' (*Balades*, 24, lines 10, 11, 12). But as her adamantine ear withstands lyric corrosion, so the woman's 'visage', faced with the male speaker's 'paroles', refuses to transform (*Balades*, 19, lines 3, 2). Her face remains a reflective but unimpressionable 'Mirour d'onour' and provides a 'tresbeal mirour' which ravishes the speaker's gaze (*Balades*, 21, line 25; *Balades*, 22, line 19). She may have left her mark on his heart, and she may take in some of his poetic signs, but *his* image only moves across her heart and body's surface. Finally, even the woman's 'beals ditz' emerge as stony objects. He tells her to keep her ring and brooch, asking for no 'autre Juel' from the lady but her 'ameiste certeine' offered as an 'enseigne' 'd'amour', probably a love Balade answering his (*Balades*, 33, lines 8, 9, 19).

In its condensed, prismatic Balades, the long-deferred, long-anticipated woman's response reflects these complaints. Her brief series covers steep emotional terrain, from the depths of rejection to the heights of erotic reciprocation. The series' seemingly erratic arrangement in fact demonstrates an internal logic, as she first reflects the male speaker's laments and then transforms both their suffering into mutual, joyous pleasure. Immediately, the woman's response takes up and reverses the theme of her free use of 'enseignes', turning it back on him. In Balade 41, she criticizes all lovers (including the male speaker) who use seduction language to serve their own desire: 'Les lievres de la bouche q'ensi ment | Cil tricheour tant beal les sciet movoir' (*Balades*, 41, lines 17–18). Conflating literary with sexual foreplay, the woman suggests that the male speaker, like any treacherous lover, wants to love a hundred women and so promises each one that he will love her alone (*Balades*, 41, lines 9–11). Throughout the Balade the woman addresses any lovers who meet her description, but in her *envoi* she zeroes in on a specific 'tu', a man who appears 'au matin un et autre au soir' (*Balades*, 41, line 25). She, it seems, would know.

She refers to the kind of duplicitous lover who fills his 'loialté' with 'falsetés' to betray many women (*Balades*, 42, line 3). She describes the male speaker's 'fals', 'feinte' 'parole' and his shattered promises (*Balades*, 42, lines 13, 14). Again, she represents his verbal transgressions as sexual ones: symbolically, her lover has made someone else pregnant. By filling his oaths with falsehoods he has engendered 'fraude et malengin' upon 'conscience' (*Balades*, 42, lines 22, 21). As if this weren't bad enough, in Balade 43 she calls the male speaker more treacherous even than Jason to Medea, Aeneas to Dido, Theseus to Ariadne or Demophon to Phyllis. More common than the 'halte voie', he takes all lovers who come his way (*Balades*, 43, line 14). Even as they rebuke him, the woman's complaints about the male speaker proclaim his amorous and poetic potency, giving the lie to his own previous accounts of verbal impotence. Her words reinvigorate his.

Her Balades echo his language directly as she adopts and improves upon his poetic lexicon. He compared himself to Menelaus abandoned by Helen (*Balades*, 40, lines 5–6); she ups the ante and calls him the Hector of the boudoir, for while Hector armed himself hastily in Troy the male speaker strips just as quickly to hop into bed (*Balades*, 43, lines 9–10). He promises to serve as her 'chivaler': she contrasts him with Lancelot, Tristan and Florent, who guarded their loyalty (*Balades*, 7, refrain; *Balades*, 43, lines 17–20). Where he has sent his heart, body and mind through his Balades, she returns punishment, rejection and 'nonchaloir' (*Balades*, 41, lines 26, 27). He called her free and himself tightly bound; she accuses him of going free while she suffers 'en destroit' (*Balades*, 43, line 23). He called her a mirror of honour; she calls him the 'mirour des mutabilitées' on which she finds 'l'image' of false lovers depicted (*Balades*, 42, lines 17, 18). The woman transforms the male speaker's complaints into her own, taking his lyric expressions of amorous suffering and using them to speak her own 'voir dit' (*Balades*, 41, line 5).

As she turns to accept him, she continues echoing his poems. Adopting the male speaker's image of her own hyperbolically impenetrable marble ear, she transforms it into an 'oreille trespercée' (*Balades*, 44, line 10). Addressing his claims about her face's unchanging hardness, she reminds him of her flesh, describing her 'rugge' flush of shame (*Balades*, 46, line 17). Insisting upon the 'colour' he makes her turn, she also reveals how deeply his poems have changed and affected the colours of her own rhetoric (*Balades*, 46, line 20). Acknowledging that the male speaker has already given her his 'corps et coer', she validates his bawdy word-play by adopting it and reciprocating it in her own Balades (44, line 3). Indeed, she refers to the rights and rites of sexual love: she loves him according to nature's 'droite' and proclaims that 'Droitz est q'amour vous rende sa droiture' (*Balades*, 46, line 24). She highlights the erotic reciprocation enacted by the poetic exchange: 'Ceste ma lettre, quoique nulls en die, | Ove tout le coer envoie a vo noblesce; | Q'au tiel ami jeo vuill bien estre amie' (*Balades*, 44, lines 23–5). She says she will hold on to the 'point d'acord' – the erotic and poetic bond they have forged – for the rest of her life (*Balades*, 44, line 20). She compensates the male speaker for his service through her letter's praise, which also conveys her 'coer' and 'corps'.

In fact, not only does the female speaker reflect the male speaker's poems; she also mixes her echoes of his poems with references to contemporary French baladeers. She asserts her own poetic competency, claiming that, even though she had loved the male speaker before, from now on she will sing, 'C'est ma dolour, qe fuist ainçois ma joie': her refrain paraphrases Guillaume de Machaut's 'C'est ma dolour et la fin de ma joie' (*Balades*, 43). Likewise, her catalogues of treacherous legendary lovers and loyal chivalric ones evoke Oton de Grandson's Balade beginning 'Ho! doulce Yseult, qui fus a la fontaine | Avec Tristan, Jason et Medea' and perhaps also allude to Jean Froissart. In Balade 44, where the lady accepts the lover just as passionately as she rejected him in the first three lyrics of her series, she paraphrases Eustache Deschamps's Balade beginning 'Belle, blanche, blonde, bonne, agreable'. Her Balade begins by addressing her lover as 'Valiant, courtois, gentil et renomée', a line patterned loosely on Deschamps's opening blazon of his beloved's features (*Balades*, 44, line 1). Her lines 'Si jeo de Rome fuisse l'emperesse, | Vostre ameisté refuserai jeo mie' also evoke Deschamps's Balade's refrain, 'Telle dame estre empereis de Romme' (*Balades*, 44, lines 5–6).

By paraphrasing Machaut, Grandson, Froissart, Dechamps and the male speaker in practically the same breath, the woman speaker puts them on equal footing; she thus elevates her beloved's Balades and his poetic reputation. She describes accounts of the male speaker's 'halte fame', 'prouesce' and 'valour' flying through the land like an 'aigle', and the reports of his 'noble port' and 'fiere estature' circulate within her court and through her Balades (*Balades*, 44, line 8; *Balades*, 46, lines 9, 11, 1, 16). Rhyming 'promesse' with 'prouesse', she attaches his reputation to his vows, declaring now the truth of his 'loial, verrai' words as forcefully as she decried their falseness earlier (*Balades*, 44, lines 2, 9). Finally, she uses her 'poair' to 'procure' his 'honour' (*Balades*, 46, line 12). Having given her reply, the woman falls silent again, but with a difference: 'Si parler n'ose, ades jeo penserai' (*Balades*, 46, refrain).

As her initial rejection of the speaker resolves into praise and acceptance, Gower structures the woman's series to bring the lovers' voices into harmony. Her two celebratory Balades, 44 and 46, enfold the male speaker's most significant poem, Balade 45, praising her. There, he corrects his own use of poetic signs from earlier in the sequence. He had complained about her attractive but impervious hardness and had prayed his poems might turn her from stone to flesh. Now he turns to praise her resistance of him, since it has led him to clarify his own poetry. Reflecting the new light her series of poems has shed on his poetry, he compares her to the 'cristall, qe les autres eslumine' (*Balades*, 45, line 2). The crystal, when touched, cures and renders more 'preciouse' and 'fine' the thing that touches it through its own medicinal 'vertu' ('virtue' or 'property') (*Balades*, 45, lines 5, 4). He claims 'El Cristall dame om porra bien noter | Deux propertés semblable a vo covine: | Le Cristall est de soi et blanc et clier' (*Balades*, 45, lines 15–17). His revised metaphor for the lady's hardness emphasizes her brightness, transparency, virtue and clarity as well as her attractiveness and resistance. Indeed, 'ma dame [de] la durtée' becomes 'El Cristall dame' in a near-epithet reminiscent of Dante's *donnapetra*, another stony lady resembling the kind of transparent gemstone that clarifies others. Similarly, it seems that by drawing the male speaker's poetic signs into her own Balades and clarifying them, mixing them with lines and phrases from the French baladeers, and using them to speak of her own pain and desire, the Cristall dame has refined the male speaker and his poems.

Indeed, by comparing the woman with the crystal, the speaker finally does appear to refine and correct his own poetic signs as he turns towards the concluding Balades. Apparently he can only accomplish this clarification after the woman has provided him with her example. The male speaker's Balade 47, the last one explicitly addressing the woman, reflects back upon 'l'istoire' of 'fin amour', the 'bien et mal' (*Balades*, 47, lines 15, 16). The Balade ends with an *envoi* divided in equal parts between joy and sighs as the lover still paradoxically languishes in the 'santé d'amour' (*Balades*, 47, line 24). The male speaker may still complain that love makes him ill, but now he sees that the pain contains its own cure.

After this Balade, the cycle proceeds in the philosophical direction the male speaker's Balade 45 predicted. In a final series of three Balades the speaker describes love abstractly. Balade 48 explores 'merveilouse' amorous oxymora: love is bitter and sweet, easy and grievous, pleasant and perilous, low and high, near and far, humble and disdainful (line 1). Love's infernal paradise turns the 'aignelle' 'fiere' and the 'leon humein', yet 'En toutz errours amour se justefie' (*Balades*, 48, line 19, refrain).[9] Balade 49 delineates an explicitly Christian hierarchy of rational love, suggesting that 'Amour' (already established in the cycle as sexual love) instructs lovers as well in divine, neighbourly and matrimonial love. This poem's refrain introduces the final two Balades' theme, that 'amour', like a 'droite miere', gives birth to 'honour'. Therefore, claims the speaker, anyone who seeks 'boun amour' simultaneously seeks his own fame, glory and goodness (*Balades*, 49, line 22). Balade 50's refrain and conclusion suggest that whoever looks for 'l'original' of honour discovers that 'Amour s'acorde a nature et resoun' (*Balades*, 50, lines 27, 28). The penultimate stanza returns to Balade 30's image of the waters the lady's 'danger' perturbed, suggesting now that only 'malvois',

---

[9] Perhaps in this imagery one might detect an oblique reference to Gower's marriage with Agnes Groundolf (1398). Gower's heraldic arms sported leopards' or lions' heads; the imagery of lion and lamb transforming into one another might conceivably evoke the union.

wicked lovers will lose the rudder of honour in such tempests (*Balades*, 50, line 19). Thus the final Balades claim that lovers who seek good love and its offspring, honour, will find smooth sailing on the sea of fortune. In Balade 50, in fact, the very phrase 'bones mours', the good morals governed by Love, almost merges with 'bon amour', good love, itself (*Balades*, 50, line 3).

Finally, the unnumbered coda Balade may appear to leave sexual love behind as it praises the 'Virgine et miere', but even this poem re-evokes the woman speaker and her poems (line 8). At first glance the male speaker – or perhaps Gower – seems to renounce earthly desires and attachments, saying he should abandon his service to all ladies except for 'ma dame pleine de franchise' (line 11). But, even here, the speaker suggests that 'Amour de soi est bon en toute guise, | Si resoun le governe et justifie' (lines 1–2). The Balade seems to confirm that 'bon amour' wears many forms even as it evokes the cycle's original female object of praise, already identified as a lady full of 'franchise'. An indivisible trinity of beloveds – Mary, Amour (the other 'droite miere' mentioned in the cycle) and the woman addressed throughout the numbered Balades – emerges. In fact, the 'amie' praised in the coda Balade explicitly hearkens to the Cristall dame: after all, she offers her lovers as a reward 'perdurable amour' – enduring, or eternally hard, love (line 14). Like Petrarch's *canzone* 366, Gower's coda Balade apparently praising Mary functions as a palimpsest, revealing *dame* through *dame*.

Thus the cycle's final words on Love seem predicated on the moral clarity the female speaker's reply produces. Not until she draws in and corrects his language can the male speaker use his Balades to properly describe love. Only after the woman has replied can the male speaker see the truth of her and Amour's nature: her stony resistance has refined his poetry, and her free use of his signs has unbound and reattached them to new and better meanings. Amour and Mary both reflect the speaker's stony dame, and she reflects them as well as the male speaker. In turn, the woman's Balades function as the male speaker's touchstone, generating praise out of his own complaints and producing and reproducing his poetic 'honour'. Within the woman's series, the male speaker's best lyric efforts crystallize. So, it seems, do Gower's.

Chapter 19

Rich Words: Gower's *Rime Riche* in Dramatic Action*

KIM ZARINS

Close readings of Gower's poetry are not as common as broader or more thematic assessments, but such attention highlights the linguistic skill which makes Gower fit to stand with Chaucer among England's early makers of poetry. This essay will compare the two poets by exploring a particular formal aspect, namely *rime riche*, in which rhyme partners appear identical but diverge in meaning. Rich rhyme has received attention from scholars in diverse periods and provinces, most notably in Tony Hunt's recent book on Gautier de Coincy, *Miraculous Rhymes*.[1] A medieval aesthetic that used such rhymes was once described almost apologetically by scholars, as though it were a phase of mannerism now outgrown, but medievalists today are not alone in appreciating rich rhyme, as Marjorie Perloff's recent discussion of W. B. Yeats attests.[2] There is growing awareness of how rich rhymes, in medieval poetry as much as modern, can be not just ornamental to a poem's surface but at the heart of a poem, pointed and integral to its purpose.

Rime riche in medieval poetry is very frequent, featuring in 650 couplets of the French and English poetry of Gower alone.[3] It reflects sophisticated literary culture, and Hunt has deepened our sense of the sententious, virtuoso and satirical nature of the device in the hands of a poet like Gautier, who positions many of his rich rhymes at the end of miracle tales as a moralizing coda. Rhyme reflects the poet's brilliant, authoritative voice. But what is the dramatic power of *rime riche*? What brilliance and authority are conferred upon a character who speaks with such rhymes, and on what level do fellow characters hear them? As in Gautier and Chaucer, the majority of *rime riche* couplets in Gower's *Confessio Amantis* are delivered by a narrator, Genius,

---

* I give deepest thanks to these generous readers of this essay in forms early and late: Andrew Galloway and Winthrop Wetherbee, both of Cornell University, Maura Nolan of the University of California at Berkeley, and Russell Peck of the University of Rochester.
[1] *Miraculous Rhymes: The Writing of Gautier de Coinci* (Cambridge, 2007).
[2] Marjorie Perloff, 'The sound of poetry/the poetry of sound: the 2006 MLA Presidential Forum', *PMLA*, 123, 3 (May 2008), 751.
[3] See Masayoshi Ito, *John Gower, The Medieval Poet* (Tokyo, 1976), pp. 214–31; R. F. Yeager, *John Gower's Poetic: The Search for a New Arion* (Cambridge, 1990), pp. 33–44; Alexandra Hennessey Olsen, *'Betwene Ernest and Game': The Literary Artistry of the 'Confessio Amantis'* (New York, 1990); Charles A. Owen, Jr, 'Notes on Gower's Prosody', *CR*, 28, 4 (1994), p. 408.

yet Genius's sententious style is not meant for our ears alone. Amans reacts to Genius's *rime riche* couplets in a sophisticated 'couplet war', in which the frame narrative's fictional characters indeed hear rhyme. That rhyme impresses a fictional audience is borne out in Chaucer's use of the device, delivered by the noble Black Knight, wily Pandarus and others; however, there is less 'quyting' of rhyme in Chaucer than one might expect given the centrality of verbal payback to the competition of his Canterbury pilgrims, particularly his Miller and Knight.

For the characters inside the pilgrims' tales, couplet wars and 'quyting' rhymes are rarer than in the *Confessio*, in which *rime riche* couplets serve to undermine morally dubious authority, mainly of kings who oppress their subjects. The empowered voices of these kings' subjects in turn possess an alternative authority, as commoners use *rime riche* to question kings and as women like Peronelle and Thaïse use it to confront men and have the final word. By bestowing this sententious device on peasants and women Gower not only enriches his critique of kingship but confers poetic power on the peasants and women making that critique.

Eat Your Words: Rich Rhyme, the Rich, and Gower's Pot Pie

Rich rhyme operates on seeming repetition, and that repetition in sound if not sense can put an edge on exchanges between characters. In the *Confessio*, Amans and Genius sometimes share a couplet, with one character speaking and the other responding within the same rhymed space (e.g., *Confessio*, IV, lines 1117–18; V, lines 1373–4; V, lines 1381–2). Late in book III Genius speaks in a fatherly, authoritative way to Amans, who replies politely yet renders his submissive words ambiguous by completing Genius's couplets with jingling rich rhymes:

> 'Mi sone, er we departe atwinne,
> *I schal behinde nothing leve'.*
> 'Mi goode fader, be your leve
> Thanne axeth forth what so you list ...'
>
> 'Mi sone, art thou coupable of Slowthe
> *In eny point which to him longeth?'*
> *'My fader, of tho pointz me longeth*
> To wite pleinly what thei meene ...'
> (*Confessio*, III, lines 2750–61; italics mine)[4]

This passage demonstrates how pointed colloquial turns of phrase can be. Amans's seemingly deferential 'be your leve' artfully weaves Genius's speech into his own response. Charles Muscatine, in a different context, called this repetition in dialogue the 'hollow echo of agreement' and a kind of verbal

---

[4] All quotations from the *Confessio* in this article are from Peck.

fencing.[5] Here, and throughout the *Confessio*, Amans seems to compete with Genius over rhyme and the authority it confers. Genius employs 179 *rime riche* couplets in the tales and another 139 couplets in dialogue with Amans, who thus is on the receiving end of this sententious device but 'quytes' this discourse with his own conspicuous stock of rich rhyme (Amans/Gower uses 96 rich rhymes). Amans may only be Genius's pupil and 'son', but he is a chip off the old sententious block. Even as he pretends to confess his ignorance meekly (he does not know what Sloth in its variations might 'meene'), he demonstrates his ear for Genius's words and the feisty wit to spin them into words of his own.[6]

Stephen Knight points out that verbal repetition, not double entendre, is Chaucer's primary mode of punning.[7] This play with repetition includes 'quyting' rhyme with rhyme. Most famously, the Miller vows to 'quite with the Knightes tale', and quites not only the tale's content but also its rhyme (3119). The Knight uses two seemingly identical words to describe the flames seen by Emelye, a girl caught between two seemingly identical men, as she prays to Diana:

> But sodeynly she saugh a sighte queynte,
> For right anon oon of the fyres queynte,
> And quyked agayn, and after that anon
> That oother fyr was queynt and al agon;
> And as it queynte, it made a whistelynge
> As doon thise wete brondes in hir brennynge
> 			(*Knight's Tale*, I, lines 1475–80)

Emelye's sexual anxieties linger unspoken in the couplet; 'queynte' is repeated three times, but the sexual reference of the noun on which the verb puns is denied, and metaphors of sexual passion are displaced by more literal fires. As if in reaction to this passage, the Miller brilliantly if ungraciously exposes this resisted definition of 'queynte', grabbing at the lewder definition even as Nicholas grabs Alison while her husband is away: 'As clerkes ben ful subtile and ful queynte; | And prively he caughte hire by the queynte' (*Miller's Tale*, I, lines 167–8). In this 'queynte' quyting, the Miller not only appropriates the Knight's subject matter for his fabliau but rhymes tit for tat against the Knight's careful couplet. This case of hearing a rhyme and responding in kind reveals Chaucer's development of rich rhyme throughout his poetic career, not just in the earliest poems such as *Book of the Duchess*.

Chaucer's use of *rime riche* has been downplayed in Gower scholarship. In his foundational study Masayoshi Ito tabulated *rime riche* in Chaucer and

---

[5] Charles Muscatine, *Chaucer and the French Tradition* (Berkeley, CA, 1957), pp. 156–7.
[6] At VI, lines 1358–64, Amans performs the same act of linguistic skill coupled with pretended ignorance:
   'Mi sone, if thou of such a lore | Hast ben er this, I red thee leve.' | 'Min holi fader, be youre leve ... | I wot noght o word what ye mene.'
[7] Stephen Thomas Knight, *Rhyming Craftily: Meaning in Chaucer's Poetry* (Sydney, 1973), p. 50.

Gower, noting that Gower employs 383 *rime riche* couplets in his *Confessio* and 241 in his *Mirour de l'Omme*, while Chaucer employs only 111 in his entire corpus.[8] However, these numbers refer to *rime riche* couplets, and Chaucer uses the device artfully if less conspicuously in his stanzas on 81 occasions.[9] It seems important to stress the continuity between these two authors before exploring their differences in qualitative, not just quantitative, terms. Both authors use *rime riche* as a site for verbal play and poetic authority that glosses narrated action; the Miller, moreover, gains a poetic edge over his social superior by appropriating the authoritative heft of *rime riche* six times in his Prologue and Tale. There may be a similar aspect of social ambition in the Merchant's eight instances of rich rhyme (in *The Canterbury Tales*, only *The Knight's Tale*, with twelve instances, makes more use of it).

In the fictive world of Chaucer's tales, however, it is for noblemen, the rich, to speak with rich rhyme. Chaucer's *rime riche*-speakers abound with knights, including young Arcite and old January, the knight from *The Squire's Tale*, one-dimensional Thopas and the complex Black Knight. Chaucer uses this French rhyme to mark a higher social valence to their speech, a poet's means to confer refined 'Frankish fare' as a separate species of speech on the lips of courtly men.[10] Rich rhymes reflect their knightly pursuits of honour and love; Arcite, January and Troilus all pursue a maiden ('may') either in May or as well as they may, a little pun to show courtliness. The Black Knight has eight of the poem's fifteen *rime riche* couplets and they reveal his cultured grief, aestheticized in courtly terms that Geoffrey so famously misunderstands. It is a matter of station for men like the Black Knight to speak so. Even Hector, noted as a plain speaker and even 'inarticulate', uses rich rhyme and thereby puns on what is here and what one *hears* (*Troilus*, I, lines 121–3).[11] Hector's language reflects his rank.

These themes of social ambition, wealth and power are prominent in book V of the *Confessio*, in which avarice is explored from complex angles – not just greed for lucre, but power over people. Amans fails to discern the camouflaged presence of the vice, for he uses the poem's most conspicuous *rime riche* cluster to claim that he lives without avarice, but his rhymes reveal an avarice which is erotic, not financial:

> And in this wise, taketh kepe,
> If I hire hadde, I wolde hire kepe,
> And yit no friday wolde I faste,
> Thogh I hire kepte and hielde faste.
> Fy on the bagges in the kiste!
> I hadde ynogh, if I hire kiste.
> For certes, if sche were myn,
> I hadde hir lever than a Myn

---

[8] Ito, *John Gower*, p. 215.
[9] Ito, *John Gower*, p. 230.
[10] *Sir Gawain and the Green Knight*, line 1116, in *The Poems of the Pearl Manuscript*, eds Malcolm Andrew and Ronald Waldron, 5th edn (Exeter, 2007).
[11] Knight, *Rhyming Craftily*, pp. 65, 76.

>   Of Gold; for al this worldesriche
>   Ne mihte make me so riche
>   As sche, that is so inly goode.
>   I sette noght of other goode. (*Confessio*, V, lines 79–90)

Each *rime riche* couplet tries to differentiate Amans's desire from avaricious behaviour but, because Amans uses the same words for both, the differences collapse. In the first two couplets it is for other people to 'kepe', or take heed, and 'faste'. However, Amans pairs these lines with identically spelled words that convey an opposing, acquisitive and rapacious meaning. He will 'kepe' and 'hielde faste' his lady, a vow that blurs together the languages of love and money, so that even as he distinguishes his beloved from financial goods, his lady proves to be just a different kind of 'goode' for his 'kiste' or moneybox. The couplet is a *kiste*, encasing the lady in a sphere of rich rhyme: artful couplets, grasping and spilling over with breathless enjambment, are aural confections with which Amans imagines hoarding the object of his desire.

Two kings later in the book use similar *rime riche*-styled chests to trick and entrap their subjects. In The Tale of the Two Coffers a king tests his grumbling men, who apparently have not been compensated in quite some time, with a guessing game of pick-the-right-chest, like that in *The Merchant of Venice* except that the two chests have identical exteriors: 'Anon he let tuo cofres make / Of o semblance and of o make (*Confessio*, V, lines 2295–6).[12] Gower's rhyme parallels the action of the king, who in essence manufactures a *rime riche* object, identical without though different within. The emphasis on oneness – 'o semblance', 'o make' and one rhyme – frames the two possible outcomes: the knights and officers will win either a fortune or nothing. They pick the wrong chest, and this supposedly teaches them not to grumble against their king. So authoritative is the non-verbal, false riddle (false because it demands an arbitrary choice and cannot be intellectually decoded), and so sententious the *rime riche*, that Genius never questions the king's treatment of his men. Deflecting attention from himself to the chests, the king crafts a moral that hinges on the grumbling men's failure to differentiate between identical exteriors rather than on his own actions. The scene reveals how duplicity – seeming sameness belying difference, a *rime riche* technique – is a source for abused power, as the king misleadingly diverts attention from his own behaviour to that of his subjects.

The following Tale of the Beggars and the Two Pastries presents a similar guessing game, but complicated by alternative authority, empowered with *rime riche*, which challenges the emperor and moralizes on his actions. A beggar cries out to the Emperor Frederick: 'Ha, lord, wel mai the man be riche / Whom that a king list for to riche' (*Tale* V, lines 2397–8). This is

---

[12] Just as rhyme is the key to this coffer, so in Shakespeare's play, rhyme solves the riddle: 'Tell me where is Fancy bred, | Or in the heart or in the head? | How begot, how nourished?' (*Merchant* III ii, lines 65–7) Portia's rhyme points to the answer: lead. Debra Fried, 'Rhyme puns', in *On Puns*, ed. Jonathan Culler (New York, 1988), pp. 83–99 (p. 84).

literally a rich rhyme, and the cry, 'Ha,' is not jocular but rather a cry for attention, shared by other characters in need including Ariadne, Procne and Rosiphelee (who also follow up their call with *rime riche*). The plea and embellished rhyme elevate the beggar's speech, though a fellow beggar retorts that God will help whom he will. As though the Emperor would one-up the beggar's *rime riche*, he invites both beggars to dinner and offers a gustatory version of *rime riche*, two pastries identical in appearance but nothing alike inside – one is ordinary, while the other contains florins. Frederick has the unsuspecting poet-beggar choose which culinary homonym he will have. He chooses the pot pie, which leaves his fellow with the pastry filled with florins, rich rhyme indeed.

The stated Boethian moral is that the beggar who uses *rime riche* looks for human help while the other man counts on God, and all got their just deserts. However, this is also a tale about a king reacting against his subject's words and reinforcing his sovereignty over sententious discourse. It is for the king to instruct, not be instructed. The king does not reward intelligence but vaunts his own wit and arbitrary power, playing God even as he facilitates the message that he is not God. Quite deliberately, he sets the *rime riche* scene: two seemingly identical pastries are given to two seemingly identical beggars, but both pairs are revealed as internally different, one valuable, one base. While the beggar's wordplay is crafted to pair pauper and king, the king's act pairs the beggars, who, like *rime riche*, are the same outside but different within. The Emperor delivers both his pies and his point and so seems to make the beggar eat his words, yet the beggar uses *rime riche* a second time to criticize the king with a moralizing coda:

> Nou have I certeinly conceived
> That he mai lihtly be deceived,
> That tristeth unto mannes helpe;
> Bot wel is him whom God wol helpe ...
> (*Confessio*, V, lines 2423–6)

The beggar tones down his rhyme word and his ambitions from getting *riche* to getting mere 'helpe', but, even as he moralizes over his error, he blames Frederick, who deceived him 'lihtly', making a game out of a pauper's request. The beggar's couplet pairs the king with God: though similar in their power over men, they differ at heart. One should trust God, not just because God is good, but because the king betrays trust.

This king is as avaricious as Adrian, the Roman nobleman who falls into a pit and calls 'Ha' for help from the pauper Bardus, inverting the action of Two Pastries by making the nobleman beg (*Confessio*, V, line 4970). If rescued, Adrian vows to give half his fortune to the peasant Bardus, who, after heaving out a monkey and snake, suspects that he is the butt of a practical joke and needs verbal reassurance before trying again:

> 'What wiht art thou in Goddes name?'
> 'I am,' quod Adrian, 'the same,
> Whos good thou schalt have evene half.'

Quod Bardus, 'Thanne a Goddes half
The thridde time assaie I schal.' (*Confessio*, V, lines 5013–17)

The echo rhyme resounds with Bardus's enthusiasm at being offered half. Again, pauper and prince are paired, and though their diction conveys their opposite social classes, they come together under the rhyme. Bardus's interjections, 'Goddes name' and 'Goddes half', reflect his simplicity, yet the second stock phrase 'quytes' the rhyme word, so Adrian and Bardus share equal space within a couplet hardened by colloquial *rime riche* into a compact under God. Adrian, of course, fails to live up to his half of the bargain until Justinian holds him accountable. Though Genius criticizes only Adrian, the duplicitous kings of the Tales of Two Coffers and Two Pastries similarly degrade their own word by playing games of rich rhyme halves.

Traditionally, rich rhyme is largely the province of the rich. Apart from Chaucer's frame narrative, only once in *The Canterbury Tales*, in *The Clerk's Tale*, does a commoner – or at least someone who speaks with the *vox populi* – use *rime riche*, to ask his lord to marry and provide an heir. He broaches the topic by asking Walter to respect the passage of time: 'thenketh, lord, among youre thoghtes wyse | How that oure dayes passe in sondry wyse' (*Clerk's Tale*, IV, lines 116–17). The phrasing conveys the simple wisdom in the man's reasonable request. Although Walter seems to comply, he reacts like Frederick and 'quytes' his subject's speech with an uneven marriage that mirrors Walter's uneven relationship with his subjects. Chaucer's narrator suggests his sympathy for Walter's subjects in rich rhymes that describe Griselda's patient suffering (*Clerk's Tale*, IV, lines 380–82; 1087–90; 1129–32), but in Gower it is not the narrator who voices this imbalance in power, but the peasants. Bardus completes a *rime riche* couplet in such a way to remind Adrian to live up to his words. They halve a couplet just as they are to halve a fortune, and Bardus is entitled to both. Similarly, in Two Pastries Gower allows the beggar to 'quyte' his superior directly. Exposing the emperor's duplicity, not to mention folly, in arbitrarily putting coins into a pastry, the tale's true gold lies in the pauper's words.

Mi Weie: The Riches of Women's Words

Rime riche is sententious rhetoric often used to moralize with skill and authority. Wise men such as Solomon and the physician Cerymon speak with *rime riche* in the *Confessio*, but clever villains like Boniface and Perseus exploit this tool of persuasion, underscoring duplicity in the repeated couplet rhyme. Chaucer's characters also use *rime riche* to persuade: Theseus uses *rime riche* twice in his 'First Mover' speech, and Pandarus dominates over Troilus and Criseyde with rhymes – eleven rich rhyme couplets and another thirteen rich rhymes in stanzas. Just as Pandarus's words abound in proverbs, so his *rime riche* lends a pat finality to his logic.

In Chaucer, rich rhyme's rhetorical power is markedly gendered. Theseus and Pandarus move the hearts of passive women – respectively sister-in-law and niece – through their speech: Emelye is largely voiceless and Pandarus verbally outmanoeuvres Criseyde. Muscatine has praised Criseyde's rhetorical fencing with Pandarus and her ability to recycle his language with a punch; her rich rhymes show this talent, but ultimately her linguistic skill underscores her lack of agency.[13] For example, just before the bedroom scene, Criseyde uses *rime riche* not to declare her autonomous authority but rather to relinquish it:

> 'Than, em,' quod she, 'doth herof as yow list.
> But er he come, I wil up first arise;
> And for the love of god, syn al my trist
> Is on yow two, and ye ben bothe wise,
> So werketh now in so discret a wise,
> That I honour may have, and he plesaunce:
> For I am here al in your governaunce.' (*Troilus*, III, lines 939–45)

Criseyde repeats Pandarus's rich rhyme on 'wise', which he used a hundred lines before in the same conversation, not to 'quyte' him but to put herself under his governance, paradoxically showing her lexical power in her abdication of will (*Troilus*, III, lines 851–2). Perhaps her sharpest fighting words occur the next morning, when Pandarus enters the bedroom and asks 'how kan ye fare?' She 'quytes' his trite greeting with a rich rhyme that turns the word 'fare' on its head: 'God help me so, ye caused al this fare [...] for al youre wordes white' (*Troilus*, III, lines 1563–7). Pandarus had previously upbraided Criseyde for not taking action quickly: 'For al among that fare / The harm is don, and fare-wel feldefare!' (*Troilus*, III, lines 860–61). Criseyde's rhyme brilliantly exposes the colour of Pandarus's seemingly transparent 'wordes white'. At the same time, however, she succumbs to his verbal fare in word and deed.

Of twenty-nine speakers of rich rhymes in Chaucer's corpus, only eight are women (Criseyde, Antigone, the Wife of Bath's hag, Cecilia, Pertolete, Anelida, Alcyone and Dame Abstinence); counting the Canterbury pilgrims (nine men and two women) would make the ratio even more imbalanced. Even when Chaucer finally gives a woman like Criseyde the sententious power of *rime riche* her words usually serve the interests of men, rather than critiquing and remaking authority. In Gower's *Confessio*, by contrast, twenty-one characters in the tales use *rime riche*: eleven men and ten women. Gower's even-handedness lends authority to women's speech and brings into question the argument that in Gower's text proper speech is the sole province of men.[14] It is almost axiomatic in criticism that Gower prizes plain speech over rhetorical sophistication, yet to combat challenges and abuse women reveal their linguistic power in a public domain.

María Bullón-Fernández distinguishes between public and private spheres when she contrasts the private reaction to rape by Antiochus's

---

[13] Muscatine, *Chaucer and the French Tradition*, pp. 56–7.
[14] Diane Watt, 'Literary genealogy, virile rhetoric, and Gower's *Confessio Amantis*', PQ, 79 (1999), 389–415 (pp. 393–4).

passive daughter to the proactive, public use of language by Thaïse, who is sent to Leonin's brothel but uses the displacing power of language to free herself.[15] Unlike Antiochus's daughter, Thaïse can manipulate words through riddles, an ability that complements her use of *rime riche*. To escape from the brothel, she tells Leonin's man,

> If so be that thi maister wolde
> That I his gold encresce scholde,
> It mai noght falle be this weie;
> Bot soffre me to go mi weie
> Out of this hous wher I am inne,
> And I schal make him for to winne
> In som place elles of the toun. (*Confessio*, VIII, lines 1449–55)

Thaïse's speech is a more sophisticated version of the Miller's demand to tell his tale 'or elles go my weie'; there, the Host 'quytes' him with rich rhyme and retorts, 'a devel wey!' (*Miller's Prologue*, A, lines 3133–4), but Thaïse's speech – from its opening conditional clause to its hypothetical scenarios – allows her to rationalize her insistence on virginity in ways Leonin can appreciate. Female agency is made palatable by the riches she can make for him in a public space, at a women's school, rather than a private one, and the financial 'encresce' candy-coats the 'encresce' in rhyme that converts 'this weie' to 'mi weie'. *Rime riche* makes the path from 'hous' to 'toun' the way to 'winne'.

Thaïse's gift with language is usually attributed to her father, but her mother, the unnamed princess of Pentapolis, similarly expresses in *rime riche* her need to control her sexuality. Writing to her father to declare love for her tutor Apollonius rather than the three princes seeking her hand, she, like Thaïse, insists on having her 'weie':

> I wol non other man abide.
> And certes if I of him faile,
> I wot riht wel withoute faile
> Ye schull for me be dowhterles. (*Confessio*, VIII, lines 900–903)

In his notes to this passage Russell A. Peck observes that Gower's source letter expresses no lovesickness that could lead to death.[16] However, her agonized desire for a potentially mismatched union (Apollonius's royalty is yet unknown) replays Antiochus's consuming desire for his daughter. Nowhere is that verbal echo clearer than in Antiochus's riddle:

> Hierof I am inquisitive;
> And who that can mi tale save,
> Al quyt he schal my doghter have;

---

[15] Maria Bullón-Fernandez, *Fathers and Daughters in Gower's 'Confessio Amantis'* (Cambridge, 2000), p. 55.
[16] Peck, VIII, line 335 n.

> Of his ansuere and if he faile,
> He schal be ded withoute faile. (*Confessio*, VIII, lines 410–14)

In many ways Gower overlaps the fathers and daughters of Antioch and Pentapolis to contrast the relationships between father and daughter, but the princess's couplet sets her up against Antiochus rather than his voiceless daughter. In writing to her father the princess takes charge of her life in terms that challenge Antiochus's tyranny. If Apollonius solves Antiochus's riddle, he will be 'Al quyte' with marriage; the princess's rhyme, in turn, 'quytes' Antiochus's falsehood with truth, subverting labyrinthine speech with plain knowledge. She 'quytes' Antiochus unknowingly, but that does not detract from her agency in moving from confinement and confusion to naming her beloved and proposing marriage. A story that begins with a daughter whose will is suffocated by her father offers her counterpart in a daughter who makes her will known, actively forming her 'weie' much as her own daughter will later do, too.

The shared rhyme on 'faile', however, ominously points to the trap of language that repeats because words fail, and so mirrors the deaths Antiochus and she propose. At her supposed death at sea, 'lich' is rhymed with 'lich' to underscore Apollonius's sorrow – there is nothing *like* it – before her corpse, her 'lich' (*Confessio*, VIII, lines 1075–6). The simile of sorrow dissolves as words turn in on themselves in deadly sameness, but these rhymes can also heal. Whereas Amans used rich rhyme to put his lady into an imaginary 'kiste', when the physician Cerymon discovers the princess's 'kiste' (1230), he uses rich rhyme to restore her:

> [He] seith, 'Ma dame, yee ben hiere
> Wher yee be sauf, as yee schal hiere
> Hierafterward; forthi as nou
> Mi conseil is, conforteth you
> For trusteth wel withoute faile,
> Ther is nothing which schal you faile …'
> (*Confessio*, VIII, lines 1211–16)

Cerymon's words mark not an end but a beginning, predicated on language originally spoken by Antiochus to curse. Repetition works as part of the healing process, restoring the princess to life almost by incantation. If readers consider the tale a lesson for Apollonius in escaping Antiochus's taint, the princess passes the test first. She has endured desire and death and experiences language reversed and remade. As her body recovers, so does her authority: 'time com that sche was hol; | And tho thei take her conseil hol' (*Confessio*, VIII, lines 1257–8). She has lost everything, or thinks she has, but begins her rebirth as an abbess of Diana.

Cerymon's triple soundplay on 'hiere' is interesting because five out of the seven instances of this rich rhyme are spoken by women: Rosiphelee, Procne, Ariadne, Lucrece and Peronelle, as well as Chaucer's Alcyone and Cecilia. Men use this rhyme as well, but Gower's Cerymon and Nectanabus and Chaucer's Hector use it to comfort and inform their female audience.

Gower's women, however, use it to demand that an audience simply listen.[17] For unfortunate lovers like Ariadne and Procne, their couplets protest their misfortune. Ariadne addresses Theseus with *rime riche* after Theseus has already abandoned her. Nevertheless, as she says, 'al the world schal after hiere' what he has done to 'this woful womman hiere' (*Confessio*, V, lines 5445–6). She cannot directly reach Theseus's ears, but she can tell the world of his faithlessness. These women may not change their fate, but, like the beggar in the Tale of Two Pastries, they offer a for-the-record critique of those who abused their power and relationships.

In the Tale of Three Questions Peronelle uses this rhyme pair strategically to change a man's behaviour. Her verbal tactic and larger strategy use her femininity to control her king and determine her own way. Peronelle and King Alphonse are set publicly and lexically against one another, not just during the riddle contest, but also with the *rime riche* couplets that describe them as wise. In the opening lines, the emphasis on wisdom is a subversive indication of the king's pride:

> A king whilom was yong and *wys*,
> The which sette of his wit gret pris.
> Of depe ymaginaciouns
> And strange interpretaciouns,
> Problems and demandes eke,
> His *wisdom* was to find and seke;
> Wherof he wold in sondri *wise*
> Opposen hem that weren *wise*.
> (*Confessio*, I, lines 3067–74; italics mine)

The repetition of 'wise' underscores that King Alphonse lacks the true wisdom to rule justly. As the *rime riche* suggests, he is not wise but acts 'in sondri wise' to tease wise men with verbal tricks. Because the knight Petro answers his riddles easily, the jealous king devises three more which Petro must answer correctly or die. The king intends to establish his wisdom and Petro's folly, but becomes a tyrant in the process.

Peronelle, too, is called wise, but the couplets feminize her wisdom:

> Arraied in hire beste wise
> This maiden with hire wordes wise
> Hire fader ladde be the hond [...] (*Confessio*, I, lines 3223–4)

> And sche the king with wordes wise
> Knelende thonketh in this wise. (*Confessio*, I, lines 3344–5)

From these couplets one would never guess that she is a riddle master, for they focus on her intercessory role as Petro's daughter. The attention to

---

[17] Chaucer's Cecilia seems fit company for Gower's women. She follows up a colloquial phrase with a direct accusation: 'sooth to heere [...] thou hast maad a ful gret lesyng heere' (*Second Nun's Tale*, VIII, lines 477–9). Her burn-the-bridges critique is not designed to persuade her judge but to embrace her martyrdom; it is also rhetorical flare from a character noted for her plain speech.

Peronelle's dress points to her feminine strategy in managing the king, not unlike the biblical Esther who dresses herself exquisitely before approaching her lord – there, too, on a mission to save her people from a king's arbitrary orders. Wisely arrayed with feminine dress and kneeling posture, Peronelle uses humility as a mask to save her father and be an agent in her own exchange between men.[18]

Without threatening the king's pride, Peronelle holds the position of power by retelling and answering the three riddles while the king looks on in silence. The scene reverses expected male–female roles of who should speak or be silent, as dramatized in *The Wife of Bath's Tale*, in which the Wife as narrator gives the rapist knight little direct discourse yet praises his stellar year-awaited performance before a hushed court of ladies:

> To every wight comanded was silence,
> And that the knyght sholde telle in audience
> What thyng that worldly wommen loven best.
> This knyght ne stood nat stille as doth a best,
> But to his questioun anon answerde
> With manly voys, that al the court it herde.
> (*Wife of Bath's Tale*, III, lines 1037–42)

Like Criseyde, whose lexical power serves men, the Wife pairs the knight's 'manly voys' with the authority of *rime riche*. He is a front man delivering a canned answer, yet that seems good enough for the Wife, Guinivere's court, and the hag who marries him. The play on 'best' hints at the beastliness of rape – the assurance that he is not a beast opens the possibility that he is one – but Chaucer's women seem to admire show over substance and in doing so sacrifice their power for his pleasure.

Peronelle, by contrast, steals the show. She is not only described with *rime riche* but speaks it, a version of walking the walk and talking the talk which Alphonse lacks. She effortlessly cuts through the king's labyrinthine three riddles with three clarifying *rime riche* couplets, the most rich rhymes given to any character in the *Confessio*'s tales, used here to 'quyte' the king's three-part attack. The riddles misleadingly revolve around the language of valuation, but Peronelle's rich rhyme draws out the concealed truth, as with her answer to the second riddle:

> [That] Which most is worth and most is good
> And costeth lest a man to kepe,
> Mi lord, if ye woll take kepe,
> I seie it is humilité. (*Confessio*, I, lines 3272–5)

Buttressed with *rime riche*, her answer conveys a pat, proverbial sentiment and draws on homespun yet non-negotiable wisdom, just the right verbal tactic to address a king sensitive to his intellectual supremacy. Counselling him to 'take kepe' and teaching him the answer as if he did not know it,

---

[18] Bullón-Fernandez, *Fathers and Daughters*, p. 72.

Peronelle turns the tables on her king and hints that he has issued a riddle about humility without keeping any humility for himself.

With each rich rhyme, Peronelle's instruction of her king becomes more explicit. On the third occasion she advises him,

> That ye such grace and such justice
> Ordeigne for mi fader hiere,
> That after this, whan men it hiere,
> The world therof mai speke good. (*Confessio*, I, lines 3318–21)

Peronelle never accuses the king of ungracious and unjust behaviour, but states that the way the king acts toward her father here will be universally known not if but when 'men it hiere'. The language is proactive – dwelling not on what has happened, but on what will happen, with real and public consequences for the king. Given such words, the king has no reasonable choice but to compensate Petro for attempting to murder him and steal his goods. Immediately securing her father's promotion, she secures her own and rises from commoner to queen. The king earlier comments that he would have married her if she were his equal (her father is only a 'bachilier' (*Confessio*, I, line 3338); she reminds the king of his public statement, points out that she is now his peer, and proposes a marriage he cannot refuse: 'A kinges word it mot ben holde' (*Confessio*, I, line 3369). An English version of the Latin maxim 'Stet verbum regis', her phrase indicates that 'when a king has made a judgment, that "verbum" is final and cannot be changed, even if the king should wish to do so.'[19] While her couplets are water-tight, his words are easy targets for her judgments, and she operates like Bardus and Justinian combined, forcing the king to share power with her.

Rime riche is only one means for a character to enrich speech, but, uniquely, it uses sameness to speak with difference. Though most *rime riche* speakers within Chaucer's tales are rich men, Gower seems interested in diversifying these sententious voices to include peasants and women and empowers them in the way he best understood – by giving them poetic power to make their couplets sing. Though Chaucer's pilgrims delight us with their mixed estates and unlikely camaraderie, Gower presents mixed voices that are not just playful, but match and even outdo authority. Bardus's simplicity is ultimately honoured; Peronelle moves the king with her 'wordes wise', and Thaïse sings 'lich an angel', winning over all who hear her voice (*Confessio*, VIII, line 1671). Gower graces peasant and female speech with *rime riche* like overtones of Arion's restorative music, to make the world a richer one by helping kings listen rather than speak.

---

[19] Thomas D. Hill, '*Stet Verbum Regis*: why Henryson's husbandman is not a king', *ES*, 86, 2 (April 2005), 129.

Appendix[1]

1. 21 speakers of *rime riche* in Gower's *Confessio Amantis* (excluding Genius, Amans/Gower, and Venus)

Antiochus VIII, lines 413–4 faile
Ariadne V, lines 5445–6 hiere
Bardus (completes Adrian's line with RR) V, lines 5015–6 half
Beggar (Two Pastries) V, 2397–8 riche; V, lines 2425–6 help
Boniface II, lines 2883–4 laste
Cephalus IV, lines 3219–20 armes
Cerymon VIII, lines 1211–2 hiere; VIII, lines 1215–1216 faile
Constantine II, lines 3247–8 wise
Diana V, lines 6277–8 touche
Lady addressing Rosiphelee IV, lines 1381–2 leve; IV, lines 1419–20 laste
Lucrece VII, lines 4817–8 hiere
Lycurgus VII, lines 2981–2 fare
Nectanabus VI, lines 1877–8 hiere; VI, lines 1939–40 behote / be hote
Penelope IV, lines 167–8 wente
Peronelle I, lines 3253–4 maii; I, lines 3273–4 kepe; I, lines 3319–20 hiere
Perseus II, lines 1659–60 kepe
Princess of Pentapolis VIII, lines 901–2 faile
Procne V, lines 5857–8 hiere
Rosiphelee IV, lines 1369–70 hiere
Solomon VII, lines 3901–2 regne
Thaïse VIII, lines 1451–2 weie

2. 29 speakers of *rime riche* in Chaucer's corpus (excluding Canterbury pilgrims and Chaucer as a narrator)

Abstinence *RR*, lines 535–6 thought
Alcyone *BD*, lines 93–4 here
Anelida *AA*, lines 333–6 drye
Antigone *TC*, II, lines 848–50; II, lines 870–73 laste
Arcite *CT* I, lines 1511–2 may
Baronage to Love *RR*, lines 5939–40 wise
Black Knight *BD*, lines 615–16 werre; lines 621–2 halt; lines 629–30 floures/flour ys; lines 931–2 harmed / harm hid; lines 659–60 chek her/chekker; lines 883–4 herte; lines 1089–90 say; lines 1271–2 weyes
Calkas *TC*, IV, lines 81–2 leve/leeve
Cecilia *CT* VIII, lines 477–9 heere

---

[1] For this appendix I consulted J. D. Pickles and J. L. Dawson, *A Concordance to John Gower's 'Confessio Amantis'* (Wolfeboro, NH, 1987); Max Kaluza, *Chaucer und der Rosenroman: Eine Litterargeschichtliche Studie* (Berlin, 1893).

Commoner *CT* IV, lines 116–17 (ClT) wyse
Criseyde *TC*, II, lines 100–103 rede; III, lines 942–3 wise; III, lines 1563–6 fare (completes rhyme); IV, lines 1231–2 dede; V, lines 690–91 longe; V, lines 975–8 was; V, lines 1084–5 leve
Diomede *TC*, aweye/weye at *TC*, V, lines 93–6; V, lines 104–5 meene/mene; V, lines 884–6 se
Eagle *HF*, lines 747–8 see
False-Semblant *RR*, lines 7093–4 prophetis/prophet is; lines 7301–2 forwardis (completes rhyme)
Friar *CT* III, lines 1747–8 (*SumT*) chese
Hag *CT* III, lines 1155–6 (*WBT*) dedis/deed is
Hector *TC*, I, lines 121–3 here
January *CT* IV, lines 1913–4 may
Judge *CT* VI, 173–4 heere
Knight *CT* V, lines 145–6 (*SqT*) heere
Love places/place is *RR*, lines 6119–20; he(e)re/heere *RR*, lines 6223–4 and 6797–8
Pandarus *TC*, I, lines 617–9 longe; I, lines 667–70 sore; I, lines 687–9 vices/vice is; I, lines 697–8 wise; I, lines 932–4 love; I, lines 961–4 (and 959) wyse; I, lines 991–2 wise; II, lines 191–3 ben; II, lines 443–5 see; II, lines 513–6 to and fro; II, lines 545–6 longe; II, lines 1031–3 harpe; II, lines 1628–9 here; II, lines 1644–5 here; III, lines 151–2 yerne; III, lines 254–6 meene; III, lines 291–2 dede; III, lines 774–5 calle; III, lines 785–7 wente; III, lines 851–2 wise; IV, lines 531–2 fare; IV, lines 582–4 me; V, lines 380–83 fowles/foul is
Priest *RR*, lines 7687–8 wise
Summoner *CT* III, lines 1767–8 (*SumT*) placis/place is
Theseus *CT* I, lines 1837–8 lief/leef; A lines 3031–2 se
Third tercel eagle *PF*, lines 464–7 here
Thopas *CT* VII, lines 817–18 thee
Troilus *TC* I, lines 536–7 laste; I, lines 1047–8 laste; IV, lines 543–4 here; V, lines 422–5 may; V, lines 1409–12 may; V, lines 1717–20 may; V, lines 1353–6 moore

Chapter 20

Florent's *Mariage sous la potence*

RICHARD F. GREEN

In his contribution to a recent collection of essays on the English 'Loathly Lady' tales, Russell A. Peck makes a persuasive case for John Gower's Tale of Florent being 'the first sustained Loathly Lady narrative in English literature', and thus the direct source of Chaucer's *Wife of Bath's Tale*.[1] This narrative tells of a knight accused of murder (though he has in fact killed his man in a fair fight) who is offered a reprieve on condition that he can discover what it is that all women most desire. At his wit's end to answer this conundrum, he encounters a Loathly Lady who offers to supply the answer on condition that he marry her. He ponders this offer for a while:

> Now goth he forth, now comth ayein
> He wot noght wat is best to sein,
> And thoghte, as he rode to and fro,
> That chese he mot on of the tuo,
> Or forto take hire to his wif
> Or elles forto lese his lif. (*Confessio*, I, lines 1569–74)

After carefully weighing his options, he decides to accept the offer – his life is saved, and the tale ends happily when the hag is magically transformed into a beautiful young damsel. We learn that her hideous shape had been due to a stepmother's curse and that only by winning both the 'love and sovereinete' of a knight that 'alle othre passeth of good name' (*Confessio*, I, lines 1847–9) had the lady been able to break the spell – Florent satisfying the second condition by having the good sense to defer to her judgment in the solution of a riddle. Chaucer's *Wife of Bath's Tale* follows a similar pattern, except that the initial offence is the more shameful one of rape, the Loathly Lady offers her solution in exchange for an unspecified favour (only later does the knight learn that it is to be marriage), and the motif of the stepmother's curse is dropped. Two later stories – 'The Wedding of Sir Gawain and Dame Ragnell' and 'The Marriage of Sir Gawain' – displace Gower's narrative motifs even further.

---

[1] Russell A. Peck, 'Folklore and powerful women in Gower's "Tale of Florent"', in *The English 'Loathly Lady' Tales: Boundaries, Traditions, Motifs*, eds S. Elizabeth Passmore and Susan Carter (Kalamazoo, MI, 2007) pp. 100–145.

Peck places particular emphasis on the folklore conventions that Gower employs: 'the tone of "The Tale of Florent",' he writes, 'is that of a folktale, particularly in the way it stages itself. Characters [...] are perceived by their function, working within a matrix of performing typologies [...] They live within the lexias of folk motifs and types that scholars like Stith Thompson and Antti A. Arne have concerned themselves with.'[2] In support of his claim that Gower himself 'put together the basic narrative as we know it',[3] Peck imagines the poet deliberately reconfiguring these traditional folk motifs and adapting them to new uses. Attractive as this hypothesis is, it still does not wholly meet the objections raised by J. K. Bollard to Sigmund Eisner's more conventional source study,[4] for even if he wishes to argue that earlier manifestations of the Loathly Lady furnished Gower with folkloric building blocks rather than a ready-made plot, Peck must still show that such blocks contained within themselves the narrative kernel of 'The Tale of Florent'. The closest of these manifestations in time and space to Gower and Chaucer is the Loathly Lady who initiates the second movement of Chrétien de Troyes' *Perceval*, turning up at Arthur's court to curse the young knight just after he has returned, as he believes, in triumph. She figures in a number of continuations and imitations of *Perceval*, and even features in an interlude staged at Edward I's marriage feast in 1299: 'the third course was followed by the entrance of the Loathly Damsel on a bony nag, charmingly made up with a nose a foot long, a goitre on her neck, and teeth projecting a finger's length from her wry mouth.'[5] However, as Bollard points out, 'transformation is not a significant development in these tales; the Loathly Lady does not demand favours of the hero, nor does she [...] deliver him from a sentence of death.'[6] Irish tales of the transformation of Erin are superficially closer in theme but far more remote from late-fourteenth-century London. Even here, however, as Bollard has again demonstrated, 'the similarity [...] lies primarily in the simple presence of the transformation incident alone. In each group the occasion for that transformation is different, both structurally and thematically'.[7] Most significantly, the central episode in these tales is a test of the hero's fitness to rule Ireland, so that the sovereignty in question is finally a male not a female one.

In none of these Irish analogues (nor in the French ones for that matter) is the hero whose actions initiate the transformation under sentence of death for a previous crime, nor does the transformed hag have it in her power to save his life, but there is a folklore custom, apparently widespread in Gower's day, that offers a clear analogy for both these conditions. More-

---

[2] *Ibid.*, p. 106.
[3] *Ibid.*, p. 100.
[4] J. K. Bollard, 'Sovereignty and the Loathly Lady in English, Welsh and Irish', *LSE*, n.s. 17 (1986), 41–59; and Sigmund Eisner, *A Tale of Wonder: A Source Study of The Wife of Bath's Tale* (New York, 1957).
[5] Roger S. Loomis, *Arthurian Literature in the Middle Ages: A Collaborative History* (Oxford, 1959) pp. 558–9.
[6] Bollard, 'Sovereignty', 45.
[7] *Ibid.*, p. 56.

over, this custom, recorded in the folklaw of several European countries in the Middle Ages and early modern period, fully accords with another aspect of The Tale of Florent noted by Peck – the marked air of legality that Gower conveys: 'An interesting aspect of Gower's version', he writes, 'is the emphasis placed upon the legality of all proceedings [...] Control of the law (*lex positiva*) may usually be thought of as a feature of patriarchy, but in this instance it is the women who are determined to use it to their advantage.'[8] The custom I have in mind strikes me as quite as likely as any of the folktales so far adduced to have provided Gower, directly or indirectly, with the mainspring of what Peck calls the 'narrative syntax' of The Tale of Florent – it is the custom of *mariage sous la potence*.

In the summer of 1468, while Charles the Bold was awaiting the arrival of his new bride, Margaret of York, in the town of Bruges, a young man called Hernoul, the bastard son of Hernoul de la Hameyde, lord of Condet, was brought before him accused of murder. The duke, evidently determined to show his impartiality, decided to make an example of this young aristocrat, and turned a deaf ear to all the pleas of his family and friends for clemency. Hernoul's plight generated enormous public sympathy, and the spectacle of his execution drew large crowds. Georges Chastellain describes the procession to the gallows in some detail: the handsome young man ('bel de visage plus que autre') with his long golden locks ('beaux crins blonds'), 'as elegantly dressed as if he were going to a wedding' ('aussi honnestement vestu que pour aller à noces'), was driven in a cart followed by a great crowd, which included:

> a multitude of poor, foolish women, who followed after him and who cried and wept piteously for him and asked to have him in marriage (*et le demandoient avoir en mariage*), which was always refused them, for no one would have dared, for fear of the prince, even though they would have liked to have had the power to do it, for there wasn't even a lawyer who didn't weep for the pathos of the case.[9]

Chastellain is here describing the operation (ineffective in this instance) of the curious but little known medieval custom generally referred to as '*le mariage sous la potence*' (or marriage at the foot of the gallows).

The earliest firmly attested instance that I know of comes from the second half of the thirteenth century in Aurillac in the Midi. A man called Raymond Aoust, convicted of seriously injuring a fellow citizen, was led to the gallows but pardoned at the last moment because a woman sought his hand in marriage: 'et cum Ramundus Augusti duceretur ad furchas et esset prope, quedam mulier petit eum habere in maritum et habuit' ('and when Raymond was led to the gallows and was approaching them, a certain woman sought to have him in marriage, and had him').[10] The custom is also recorded in

---

[8] Peck, 'Folklore', p. 110.
[9] *Oeuvres de Georges Chastellain, 5: Chronique*, ed. Kervyn de Lettenhove (Brussels, 1864), pp. 403–4.
[10] Roger Grand, 'Justice criminelle: procédure et peines dans les villes aux XIIIe et XIVe siècles', *Bibliothèques de l'école des chartes*, 102 (1941), 103.

the fourteenth century: in Peronne in Picardy in 1382, Hennequin Doutart was taken in a cart to the gibbet and a halter placed around his neck: 'then came there Jehenette Mourchon, called Rebaude, a young woman, born in the town of Hemaincourt, as suppliant, requiring of the Provost or his Lieutenant, that she might have the said Doutard in marriage if it might please him, and he was led away and returned to prison', where he was later pardoned.[11] In 1430 the Bourgeois de Paris describes the beheading of ten criminals:

> the eleventh was a handsome young man about twenty-four years old; he was stripped and waiting for the blindfold, when a young woman, born in the Halles, came and asked boldly for him, and made such a good bargain ['tant fit par son bon purchas'] that he was led back to the Chastelet, and they were later married.[12]

In the sixteenth century the practice fell under the sceptical gaze of learned jurisconsults like André Tiraqueau and Jean Papon. Tiraqueau's opinion in *De legibus connubialibus* (1513) that, whatever may have happened in the past, it was certainly no longer to be seen in France ('qu'il ne sçait, si par deuant celà a esté prattiqué en France, mais qu'il sait bien, que de son temps il n'est point prattiqué') is cited in Papon's *Recueil d'arrests notables des cours souveraines de France* (1565), and Papon himself insists that, whatever it is, it's not the law ('Quoy qu'il en soit, celà ne se peut faire de droit').[13] Nonetheless, as is often the way, even in France it hung on in folklore and popular belief until at least the end of the seventeenth century. Esprit Fléchier, in his *Mémoires sur les grands-jours d'Auverne*, tells the story of a man condemned to the galleys who persuades a girl of dubious virtue ('une fille qui fût tombée en quelque faute') to marry him, 'croyant de bonne foi que c'était un ordre inviolable dans la justice [...] qu'un homme qui pouvait être aimé ne devait point être puni'.[14] Fléchier gives a drôle account of their prison courtship, whose ends, alas, are frustrated when it comes to the attention of the authorities.

Whatever was the case in France, the custom was still very much alive in the Low Countries, Belgium, Germany and Austria well into the sixteenth century and beyond; it would be possible to cite a number of actual instances from each of these countries, but one example may stand for all. In Hildesheim, Saxony, in 1554,

> Zacharias Koch and Bernard Steinberg had been brought to the public scaffold when two servant girls thrust themselves forward, bedecked with green garlands and dressed in bridal gowns, and requested the prisoners for their husbands. In answer to their prayers, as is the custom ['ut moris

---

[11] Jean Gessler, 'Le mariage sous la potence', *Le Folklore Brabançon*, 7, 37/38 (1927–8), 115–35 (118). See also the supplementary notes by F. Van Es and Charles Didier in *Le Folklore Brabançon*, 7, 42 (1928), 340–43, and by Archer Taylor, *Journal of American Folklore*, 40 (1947), 185.

[12] Gessler, 'Le mariage', 118.

[13] Jean Papon, *Recueil d'arrests notables des cours souveraines de France* (Paris, 1601), fol. 545^v (bk 24, tit. 10); I am grateful to Ian Maclean for verifying this quotation for me.

[14] Esprit Fléchier, *Mémoires de Fléchier sur les Grands-Jours d'Auvergne*, ed. Yves-Marie Bercé (Paris, 1984), p. 242.

est'], the prisoners were released, as soon as the executioner's fee had been paid, and the marriage of both couples was celebrated next day in St. Paul's Church: Zacharias Koch married Angela Papen and Bernard Steinberg married Adelaide Bejern.[15]

Hardly surprisingly, the learned jurisconsults of early modern Europe were generally at a loss to explain this strange custom (though Jean Papon does remark facetiously, 'some say in jest, that releasing the condemned man to the girl is no remission of his sentence, because marriage will prove a greater punishment for him than death'), but one rationalization, usually credited to Spanish jurists, depended upon the woman concerned being a prostitute. It is not simply, as de Grati puts it, that it is 'a greater punishment to marry a whore than to die by the sword',[16] but, in the words of the great seventeenth-century jurist Carpzovius: 'whoever leads a straying prostitute from the path of error, does a great work of charity, and that may be of benefit to him in the pardoning of sinners',[17] or, as the English common lawyer, John Manningham, wrote in 1602: 'It is the Custome (not the lawe) in Fraunce and Italy that yf anie notorious professed strumpet will begg for hir husband a man which is going to execution, he shal be repreived, and shee may obteine a pardon and marry him, that both their ill lives may be bettered by soe holie an action.'[18] Gessler doubts that all the women who begged a husband at the gallows steps were prostitutes, but one case we have already noted, that of the Picard Hennequin Doutart whose neck was saved by 'Jehenette Mourchon, called *Rebaude*' in 1382, proves that some certainly were.

The relevance of all this to The Tale of Florent should by now be obvious. Florent is under sentence of death and his life depends upon marriage to a woman who has it in her power to choose or reject him. Because the question of marriage is raised only after the riddle has been solved this aspect of the story is barely hinted at in Chaucer's *Wife of Bath's Tale*, but in Gower it is absolutely fundamental. References to Florent's imminent death and the Loathly Lady's power to prevent it pepper the text. When she first meets him she predicts: 'Thi deth is schapen and devised, | That al the world ne mai the save, | Bot if that thou my conseil have' (*Confessio*, I, lines 1544–6). She asks him what reward she must have, 'if I for the so schape, | That thou thurgh me thi deth ascape?' (lines 1551–2), and when he recoils from the prospect of marrying her she reminds him that 'And if thou go withoute red, | Thou schalt be sekerliche ded' (lines 1565–6). Faced with the inevitable choice, 'That chese he mot on of the tuo, | Or forto take hire to his wif | Or elles forto lese his lif' (lines 1572–4), he comes to the sensible decision, 'If that non other chance | Mai make my deliverance, | […] I schal thee wedde' (lines 1583–7), and before supplying him with the solu-

---

[15] Gessler, 'Le mariage', 124.
[16] *Ibid.*, 121.
[17] *Ibid.*, 125.
[18] John Manningham, *The Diary of John Manningham of the Middle Temple, 1602—1603*, ed. Robert Parker Sorlien (Hanover, NH, 1976), p. 153.

tion to the riddle she generously agrees to release him from his bargain, 'if eny other thing | Bot that thou hast of my techyng | Fro deth thi body mai respite' (lines 1591–3). In other words, in the sixty or so lines leading up to the answer to the riddle, Gower makes six separate allusions to the Loathly Lady's power to commute Florent's death sentence. Chaucer, by contrast, has only the brusque statement, 'I dar me wel avante | Thy lyf is sauf, for I wol stonde therby' (*Wife of Bath's Tale*, III, lines 1014–15).

Even more striking is the way that the motif of *mariage sous la potence* acts as a kingpin for the underlying folklore syntax of The Tale of Florent. For a condemned man whose slim hope of life depends upon a woman's favour, the question of 'what alle wommen most desire' (*Confessio*, I, line 1481) is far from being a merely academic one; perhaps the handsome young Hernoul de la Hameyde hoped that he had found an answer when he dressed for his execution, 'as elegantly as if he were going to a wedding' – and indeed had it not been for the duke's implacability he might well have been successful. Similarly, the second riddle – foul by day and fair by night? Or, rather more crudely, as Chaucer has it, foul and faithful or fair and untrustworthy? – has a particular resonance for a man who has been given no real choice in picking his marriage partner and who finds himself allied to a woman about whom he knows almost nothing. If, as in one interpretation of the custom of *mariage sous la potence*, he suspects he may have married a prostitute, the riddle takes on an even greater urgency, and from this perspective the point that Peck makes about the epithet 'coise' is particularly interesting. The reprieved Florent returns home,

> And prively withoute noise
> He bringth this foule grete Coise
> To his Castell in such a wise
> That noman myhte hire schappe avise.
> (*Confessio*, I, lines 1733–6)

'Coise', apparently from the French *cuisse*, 'thigh', is unique as an epithet here, so it would be unwise to place too much weight on it, but taken together with the hag's eagerness 'to pleie and rage' (*Confessio*, I, line 1769) on her wedding night, it may indeed, as Peck suggests, hint 'at male fears of woman's sexuality'.[19]

Though I have been arguing that *mariage sous la potence* could well have furnished Gower with a cultural, if not a narrative, source for The Tale of Florent, the comparative scarcity of evidence for the custom in medieval England must be conceded. The earliest English reference seems to be in the play *Arden of Faversham*, published in 1592: one of the manservants, who is plotting to murder Arden, says to an accomplice:

> Why, say I should be took, I'll ne'er confess
> That you know anything; and Susan, being a maid,
> May beg me from the gallows of the shrive.

---

[19] Peck, 'Folklore', pp. 114–15.

His partner replies, 'Trust not to that, Michael'; but he remains confident: 'You cannot tell me; I have seen it.'[20] Ten years later we find the lawyer, John Manningham, writing in his diary; 'In England it hath bin used that yf a woman will beg a condemned person for hir husband, shee must come in hir smocke onely, with a white rod in hir hand, as Sterrill said he had seen.'[21] And in the seventeenth century the antiquarian John Aubrey, after quoting the jurist John Jacob Wissenbach on the existence of the custom in Germany, adds, 'the same custome is at London, of wch I remember one instance.'[22] One other seventeenth-century English example, however, appears to count against this, since the setting of *A most sweet song of an English Merchant, borne at Chichester* (*ESTC*, S120228) is Germany, which might seem to imply that the author regarded the custom as foreign. The Englishman, condemned to death for murder, makes his last goodnight on the scaffold:

> This was no sooner sp[o]ke[n]
> But that to stint his griefe,
> Ten goodly Maids did proffer him,
> For loue to beg his life:
> This is our law, quoth they,
> We may your death remoue,
> If you in lieu of our good will,
> Will grant to vs your loue.
> ...
> Braue Englishman, quoth one,
> 'Tis I will beg thy life:
> Nay, quoth the second, it is I,
> If I must be thy wife:
> 'Tis I, the third did say;
> Nay, quoth the fourth, 'tis I:
> So each one after other said,
> still waiting his reply. (*A most sweet song* stanzas 7 and 8)

His situation is somewhat reminiscent of Macheath's at the end of the *Beggar's Opera*, and luckily it has a similarly happy outcome. One final detail might, however, be held to show a survival of the custom even in the folk memory of the early eighteenth century: Daniel Defoe describes condemned felons riding to Tyburn 'as neat and trim as if they were going to a wedding'.[23] This observation is usually taken to illustrate their remarkable *sang-froid*, but (as in the case of the Burgundian nobleman Hernoul de la Hameyde) it may also attest to some faint hope of a marital reprieve.

I cannot leave these stories without quoting what is in many ways the most remarkable of all. It comes from the autobiography of a freed slave

---

[20] *The Tragedy of Master Arden of Faversham*, ed. M. L. Wine (London, 1973), pp. 14–15. (I, i, lines 165–9).
[21] Manningham, *Diary*, p. 153.
[22] John Aubrey, *Remains of Gentilisme and Judaisme*, ed. James Britten (London, 1881), p. 126.
[23] Daniel Defoe, *Street-robberies, consider'd* (London, 1728), p. 52. Defoe's authorship has been questioned.

called Olaudah Equiano, published under the title of *The Interesting Narrative* in 1789. In 1784 Equiano had sailed to New York:

> While we lay here, a circumstance happened which I thought extremely singular: – One day a malefactor was to be executed on a gallows; but with condition that if any woman, having nothing on her but her shift, married the man under the gallows, his life was to be saved. This extraordinary privilege was claimed; a woman presented herself; and the marriage ceremony was performed.[24]

It would be helpful to be able to claim this New York example as a dramatic late survival of an old, though rarely recorded, English folk custom; unfortunately, there's always the possibility that it may have been a Dutch rather than an English survival.

Whether or not Gower might have encountered the custom of *mariage sous la potence* in late-fourteenth-century London is, however, not crucial to my argument. He need only have been aware of the existence of such a custom, or even of the popular attitude to capital punishment that informs it, in order to have constructed The Tale of Florent out of its folkloric implications. This is what I mean by calling *mariage sous la potence* a cultural rather than a narrative source. Of course, there remains the possibility that the custom might have given rise to an earlier narrative resembling The Tale of Florent, which was known to Gower; if so, it would not have been the only time that *mariage sous la potence* had inspired a folktale.

I have left to the end a particularly tantalizing 'soft-analogue' (to use Beidler's terminology),[25] a story that actually connects the custom of *mariage sous la potence* with the figure of a Loathly Lady. The earliest appearance of this story seems to be in the *Scomata* attributed to John Geiler of Kayserberg (1445–1510) and printed by Johan Adelphus Müling in the *Margarita Facetiarum*:

> A certain man was being led, blindfolded, to be hanged, when he was told that there was a certain woman there who wished to marry him and redeem him from the gallows. He asked that his eyes should be unbound. As soon as he could see her, he saw her thin lips and sharp nose, and said 'Never! I'd rather hang than marry such a one'.[26]

Some such story was evidently known to Michel de Montaigne, who writes:

> Everyone has heard the story of the Picard who was presented with a young woman as he stood on the ladder, who, as our laws sometimes allow ['comme nostre justice permet quelque fois'], could have saved his life had he wished to marry her. He, after staring at her for a while, saw that she was

---

[24] Olaudah Equiano, *The Interesting Narrative and Other Writings*, ed. Vincent Caretta (New York, 2003), pp. 223–4. I thank my colleague David Brewer for this reference.

[25] Even Peter Beidler's clear-headed and capacious taxonomy of source-types doesn't cover the sense I have in mind, though 'soft-source' is the closest. 'New terminology for sources and analogues: or, let's forget the lost French source for *The Miller's Tale*', SAC, 28 (2006), 225–30.

[26] [Geiler, John, of Kayserberg] (attrib.), *Scomata*, in *Margarita Facetiarum* (Strasburg, 1508). No foliation.

lame; 'The noose! the noose!' says he, 'She limps'. And they say much the same in Denmark of a man who was condemned to be beheaded: he was standing on the scaffold when he was offered the same choice; he refused because the girl they presented to him had hanging jowels and a very sharp nose.[27]

Montaigne's second story is a version of one that seems to have been known all over Europe and which usually concluded with a characteristic couplet. This example comes from Normandy: 'Lèvres serrées, nez pointu? | J'aime mieux être pendu!' ('Shrivelled lips and beaky nose? | I'd rather hang than marry those!'). In Dutch it is: 'Scherp geneusd en dun gelipt: | hangen, hangen!'[28] Here is a Walloon example: 'Tennès lepps è bètchow narenne! | Hanguenne! Hanguenne!'[29] And, finally, one from southern Germany: 'A spitzig Nasen, spitzig Kinn, | da sitzt doch der Teufel drin; | mach lieber Gingerl, Gangerl' ('Pointy nose and pointy chin, shows the devil dwells within; I rather go dingle, dangle').[30] In other words, when Montaigne says that everyone has heard the story of the man who finds marriage, literally, a fate worse than death, he seems likely to have been speaking the truth.

While there is no evidence that Gower could have known such a story (even though Florent's debating with himself about whether to accept the Loathly Lady's offer inevitably brings it to mind), it does prove how readily a custom like *mariage sous la potence* could pass into folktale. If, as Peck suggests, we owe The Tale of Florent to Gower's own ingenuity then the possibility that he was inspired by this custom seems to me extremely strong. I have already argued that the two riddles that Florent is faced with grow naturally out of the scenario of the gallows wedding, and in the context of the first book of *Confessio* Gower could hardly have found a better way to represent the humbling of male pride and the concomitant wisdom of obedience to a woman's will.

---

[27] *Essais* I: 14, Michel de Montaigne, *Oeuvres complètes*, eds Albert Thibaudet and Maurice Rat (Paris, 1962), p. 51.
[28] Both from Gessler, 'Le mariage', 128.
[29] F. Van Es and Charles Didies, 'Encore le mariage sous la potence', *Folklore Brabançon*, 7, 42 (1928), 343: 'bètchow narenne' (pointed nose).
[30] Johannes Bolte, 'Begnadigung zum Stricktagen oder zur Heirat', *Zeitschrift des Vereins für Volkskunde*, 27 (1917), 236.

Chapter 21

Why did Gower Write the *Traitié*?*

CATHY HUME

R. F. Yeager's 2005 article asks: 'Why *did* Gower write two sequences of ballades in French?'[1] In this essay I want to reopen the question of why one of the two sequences, the *Traitié pour essampler les amantz marietz*, was written, and propose a new reason for its composition, a new intended audience and perhaps a new date. It must be said that the *Traitié*'s framing material discourages this kind of investigation: Gower makes clear statements about the reason for its composition and its intended audience. The modern title of the poem, given to it by Macaulay, comes from the prose passage that appears after the *Confessio Amantis* and before the *Traitié* in most *Traitié* manuscripts. Gower says that he has written 'a tout le monde en general un traitié selonc les auctours pour essampler les amantz marietz, au fin q'ils la foi de lour seintes espousailes pourront par fine loialté guarder, et al honour de dieu salvement tenir' ('a treatise for all the world generally, following the authorities, as an example for married lovers, in order that they might be able to protect the promise of their sacred spousal through perfect loyalty, and truly hold fast to the honour of God').[2] There is also an apparently clear indication of the date of composition. The poem ends with some Latin verse, of which the final lines are: 'Hinc vetus annorum Gower sub spe meritorum | Ordine sponsorum tutus adhibo thorum' ('Thus I, Gower, old in years, in hope of favour, / Safely approach the marriage bed in the order of husbands').[3] Since we know that Gower married Agnes Groundolf in 1398, Macaulay makes the reasonable assumption that it must have been written around that date, in 1397–8.[4] In some ways it seems a pity to unsettle all this. However, the poem's glaring unsuitability either as an occasional piece written for the author's own marriage or as a poem of advice on how to maintain a good Christian marriage must prompt a reassessment.

---

* I am grateful to John Burrow for reading an early version of this paper, and to Jane Gilbert and Mark Ormrod for stimulating conversations about it.
[1] R. F. Yeager, 'John Gower's audience: the Ballades', *CR*, 40 (2005), 81–105 (p. 81).
[2] Macaulay, i: p. 379. Translations from the Ballades in this article are from R. F. Yeager, ed. and trans., *John Gower: The French Balades* (Kalamazoo, MI, forthcoming 2010).
[3] Translation that of R. F. Yeager in John Gower, *John Gower: The Minor Latin Works*, ed. and trans. R. F. Yeager (Kalamazoo, MI, 2005), pp. 32, 33.
[4] Macaulay, p. lxxxiii.

The *Traitié* is a sequence of eighteen ballades, which take the standard form of three seven-line rime royal stanzas, where the final line of each stanza is a refrain.[5] (The exception is the final ballade, where an extra stanza acts as an envoy.) The opening ballades give the impression that the poem will offer a general consideration of marriage, beginning with its conventional Christian justifications. The first ballade deals with the body's governance by the soul's reason; the second with the conflicting desires of body and soul; the third with procreation and man and woman as one flesh; and the fourth with the qualities of a good marriage, which should combine love and fidelity and should not be contracted out of avarice. But from this point on the poem is almost monotonously focused on adultery and its ill effects, the tone is for the most part hectoring, and the refrains are either reproving or speak of punishment and vengeance: 'c'est grant peril de freindre l'espousaile' ('Great peril it is to break a marriage') (*Traitié*, VII) and 'Horribles sont les mals d'avolterie' ('Horrible are the evils of adultery') (*Traitié*, IX), for example.

Both content and tone make the *Traitié* deeply unsuitable as a celebration of marriage. As Yeager has commented, it seems unlikely that Agnes, who was probably Flemish or English, 'would have approved of a matched set of eighteen Anglo-French ballades with a Latin apparatus, mostly condemning adultery [...] as a suitable celebration of her marriage'.[6] The focus on adultery makes it equally unsuitable as Gower's own private meditation on his reasons for marrying. As Yeager goes on to conclude, it must be a real 'unlikelihood that Gower's wedding had anything whatsoever to do with why he composed *Traitié*'.[7] Perhaps Gower's mention of his marriage in the Latin coda to the poem was more a way of marking its date of completion than an explanation for its undertaking.

What of his claim that it is written 'a tout le monde en general [...] pour essampler les amantz marietz' ('... for all the world generally ... as an example for married lovers')? Again, the subject matter sits oddly with this idea. Generic advice on marriage was a fairly well-established subject for writing in both verse and prose at this period. The *Menagier de Paris* is a roughly contemporary manual on marriage written *c*.1392–4 by an ageing Parisian husband for his wife, expanding beyond its original brief to cover how she might take care of another husband beyond his death.[8] It includes three books, one of which has a chapter on chastity, but that sits alongside other chapters on how to be a loving companion to one's husband, how to care for him, how to restrain him from error, obedience, and discretion. The second book covers managing servants and food. These same broad areas are covered in Christine de Pizan's *Livre des trois vertus* (1405) and the fourteenth-century English poem *The Good Wife Taught her Daughter*, which

---

5   On ballade form, see James I. Wimsatt, *Chaucer and His French Contemporaries: Natural Music in the Fourteenth Century* (Toronto, 1991), esp. pp. 30 and 60.
6   Yeager, 'Gower's audience', pp. 87–8.
7   *Ibid.*, p. 88.
8   *Le Menagier de Paris*, eds Georgine E. Brereton and Janet M. Ferrier (Oxford, 1981).

is closer in length to the *Traitié*.⁹ Similar material is also found in medieval sermons on marriage, which, as Rüdiger Schnell has shown, tend to talk about fidelity alongside the importance of loving and caring for one another, mutual help, bringing up children, negotiating everyday conflicts and the need for husbands to give their wives reasonable freedom and not beat them.¹⁰

One might argue that the idiosyncratic material in the *Traitié* reflected Gower's eccentric view of marriage, and that he believed the only important thing to say on the subject was that adultery should be avoided.¹¹ However, in lines 17137–748 of the *Mirour de l'Omme* (probably written before 1377) he writes about marriage as the third daughter of chastity.¹² There he makes some of the same general points as in the opening section of the *Traitié*: marriage is a sacrament; it allows procreation and avoids lechery; one should not marry for avarice. But he also discusses marriage as companionship, and explains the role of male government and female obedience and tolerance, the importance of paying the marriage debt, how to cherish one's wife, how to have a harmonious marriage, and the need to avoid jealousy. He describes the good examples of biblical wives, some wives' bad advice and gossiping; and he covers good household management. In summary, Gower knew how to say all the things that medieval writers of advice on marriage normally said, and yet he chose not to do so in the *Traitié*. Coupled with the general unsuitability of its content, this must shake our belief in Gower's claim that he wrote it as advice for married couples.

An alternative approach to the *Traitié* has found some critical favour. I mentioned above that it frequently appears after *Confessio Amantis* in the manuscripts. The apparently authorial prose that connects them, which I quoted above, begins: 'Puisqu'il ad dit cit devant en Englois par voie d'essample la sotie de cellui qui par amours aime par especial, dirra ore apres en François a tout le monde [...] ('Because the preceding poem in English was by way of example of the foolishness of those in particular who love in a courtly manner, now the subsequent treatise will be in French, for all the world ...)'. Accordingly, Yeager has suggested that 'Gower composed *Traitié* specifically as an addition to *Confessio Amantis*' and that it was 'plainly intended to replicate the form of the *Confessio*', while John Fisher thought instead in terms of the 'eventual association' of the two poems, because the *Traitié* 'summed up [the] major themes' of the *Confessio*.¹³ The connec-

---

9   Christine de Pizan, *Le Livre des trois vertus*, eds Charity Cannon Willard and Eric Hicks (Paris, 1989). *The Good Wife Taught Her Daughter*, eds Tauno F. Mustanoja, Annales Academiæ Scientiarum Fennicæ, BLXI, 2 (Helsinki, 1948).
10 Rüdiger Schnell, 'The discourse on marriage in the Middle Ages', *Speculum*, 73 (1998), 771–86.
11 For a reading of the *Traitié* as a presentation of the marriage ideology of Gower's class see Emma Lipton, *The Politics of Sacramental Marriage in Late Medieval English Literature* (Notre Dame, IN, 2007), esp. pp. 82 ff.
12 In addition to Macaulay's edition, I have made use of John Gower, *Mirour de l'Omme*, trans. William Burton Wilson, rev. Nancy Wilson Van Baak (East Lansing, MI, 1992).
13 Yeager, 'Gower's audience', p. 92; John H. Fisher, *John Gower: Moral Philosopher and Friend of Chaucer* (London, 1964), p. 84.

tions that Yeager and Fisher see between the two poems cannot be disputed: both are largely composed of exemplary stories of love, and many of those stories are found in both; as far as style is concerned, both have unusual Latin marginal glosses. If we go on to consider why Gower might have wanted to connect these texts, a few possibilities present themselves. The *Traitié* might function as a kind of brief advertisement for, or clever virtuoso French reworking of, the *Confessio*. This seems to be how Yeager conceives of the connection.[14] Alternatively, the *Traitié* might be intended to work as a corrective or correlative to the moral message of the *Confessio*: if love outside marriage must be rejected, or if the *Confessio* has seemed unduly playful, here is the orthodox line on marriage.

To take these possibilities in turn, I find the idea that the *Traitié* was intended to advertise the content of the *Confessio* unpersuasive. It has none of the variety, inventiveness or interest of the *Confessio* – even allowing for the fact that it is so much shorter – because everything in the *Traitié* always comes back to the evil of adultery. The differences are clear when we compare the exemplary stories that appear in both poems, and how they are moralised in each case. In seven cases (Nectanabus and Alexander; Ulysses and Telegonus; Hercules and Deianira; Jason and Medea; Agamemnon and Clytemnestra; Helen, Paris and Menelaus; Procne, Tereus and Philomela) the *Traitié* moral is that adultery will be punished. These compare with *Confessio* moralizations about the evils of sorcery, false-seeming, swearing false oaths, murder, sacrilege and rape: a blind eye is frequently turned to adultery. In the remaining cases (Tarquin and Lucrece; Mundus and Paulina; Valentinian; and Lancelot and Tristan), *Traitié* moralisations about sexual sin, the foolishness of love and the virtue of chastity contrast with more diverse morals in the *Confessio*. Although the *Confessio* mentions sexual virtue and sin in relation to Tarquin and Valentinian, it also moralises on righteousness, trickery and lies, prowess and drunkenness. As well as flattening out the diverse morals of the *Confessio*, the *Traitié* fails to suggest the colour or interest of the *Confessio* stories. To take just one example: the story of Nectanabus is a wonderful story in book VI of the *Confessio*, with Nectanabus tricking queen Olimpias with elaborate magic and stories about the god Amos. In the *Traitié*, all we are told is that Nectanabus 'l'espouse au roi Philipp ad violé' ('The wife of King Philip, he ravished') (*Traitié*, VI, line 4). Then, instead of the delightfully cruel twist in the tale in which Nectanabus is teaching Alexander and Alexander throws him off a roof to disprove what he is telling him, the *Traitié* states that Alexander killed for no reason other than the general principle that adultery is avenged. If the *Traitié* was written as a companion piece for the *Confessio*, one would expect it to reflect its rich variety: if anything, the contrasts between them tend to suggest that the *Traitié* preceded the *Confessio*.

As for the idea that the *Traitié* works as a moral corrective, this, too, seems unsatisfactory, partly since several of its stories do not crop up in

---

[14] Yeager, 'Gower's audience', pp. 92 and 96.

the *Confessio*. Pharaoh, Sarai and Abraham, Lancelot, Tristan and Gawain are mentioned either not at all or in passing in the *Confessio*. They would be odd choices, then, to include in a summary of or a response to that work. All this argues that the *Traitié* is working to an agenda of its own, and that its association with the *Confessio* is an afterthought rather than the real reason for its composition. The fact that in three manuscripts it appears independently of the *Confessio* tends to support that view.[15]

With all these ideas about the *Traitié*'s original purpose discarded, we can return to the poem to see what other evidence it offers. What is most striking, in my view, is that it shows signs of being addressed to a reader (or readers) who is (or are) already engaged in adultery. This is first suggested simply by the poem's focus on adultery rather than other marital crimes such as cruelty or neglect. It is also perhaps implied by the emphasis on adverse consequences rather than simple moral principle. Although Gower states early in the poem, in Ballade V, that marriage is a sacrament that must be honoured, the content of the rest of the poem suggests that he considered an argument based on Christian morality alone insufficient.[16] This tends to suggest that this first and most obvious line of argument had already failed, or that the case was so grave that a range of arguments must be marshalled. Accordingly, grisly murder and vengeance are presented as the natural consequences of adultery. Nectanabus and Ulysses are killed by their sons in Ballade VI, Hercules by his wife in Ballade VII; Medea and Procne kill their children to be avenged on their fathers in Ballades VIII and XII, and so on. The 'peril' of adultery (*Traitié*, VII, refrain), rather than its sinful nature, is the main emphasis. At the same time there is some appeal to worldly honour: the refrain of Ballade V is 'Sa foi mentir n'est pas a l'omme honeste' ('He who falsifies a promise is no honest man'), while Ballade XVI argues that, although many have prowess in battle, 'Qui sa char veint, sur toutz doit porter pris' ('Who overcomes his flesh, over all ought he to bear the glory').

Moreover, there are several indications that the point at issue is not embarking on adultery but carrying on with it, failing to repent of it, or failing to stop when warned. That he is addressing a current adulterer may explain as strategic Gower's admission that this category of sin has some superficial appeal and pleasure. In Ballade X, Paris 'se faisoit gai' ('was joyful') during his affair with Helen, 'Mais puis tornoit toute sa joie en wai' ('But thereafter all his joy turned to woe') (Ballade X, lines 4–5); similarly, Pharaoh's enjoyment of his affair with Sarai is short-lived, 'Pour son delit covient au fin doloir' ('For its delight sorrow must be its end') (Ballade XIII, line 20). Adultery seems fun now, Gower concedes, meeting his reader

---

[15] The beginning of the poem is missing in the Trentham and All Souls MSS, but in the Glasgow MS there is an alternative French prose introduction which does not mention the *Confessio*, but otherwise is similar to the connecting passage in the other MSS. See apparatus in Macaulay.

[16] The tendency to offer a secular rather than a Christian approach is also observed by Lipton, *Politics of Sacramental Marriage*, p. 75.

halfway, before going on to point out that it will end badly. Elsewhere, he explicitly cautions against *carrying on* with adultery:

> Cil avoltiers qui fait continuance
> En ses pecchés et toutdis se delite
> Poi crient de dieu et l'ire et la vengeance. (Ballade IX, lines 1–3)
>
> ('Those adulterers who persevere / In their sins, and always delight themselves, / Little fear the anger of the vengeance of God').

And Ballade XV says that 'Cil q'est guarni et nulle garde prent' ('He who is warned and takes no care') should carry the weight of his folly. Gower appears to be shaping his message for a sinner who is in danger of failing to reform, rather than someone who needs to be cautioned against a sin that he might commit – which would be odd in a poem genuinely addressed to a general audience. Perhaps the clearest indication of this, and one of the few places where the poem takes a rest from its angry, hectoring tone, is the ballade about King David, Ballade XIV. Here, Gower acknowledges sympathetically that 'Trop est humaine char frele et vileine' ('Human flesh is exceedingly frail and base') (Ballade XIV, line 1) and that we need God's help to defend ourselves against sin. David does sin through adultery and murder, but he also repents – he 'se prist si fort a repentir' ('himself very forthrightly acted to repent') (Ballade XIV, line 16) – so that in the end God has mercy on him. The point of this exemplum is that repentance after great sin is worthwhile: it has meaning principally for a sinner who might wonder despairingly whether there was any point in repentance.[17] Finally, this implied sinning addressee seems to be male. As Emma Lipton has argued, in the *Traitié* 'Gower de-emphasizes the role of women entirely, focussing instead on the role of their husbands.'[18] Gower takes no interest in the adulterous behaviour of Sarai, Guinevere or Helen, but is exclusively concerned with the immorality, punishment and possible repentance of their male lovers.

Almost as marked as the poem's preoccupation with adultery is its preoccupation with kings. Above I noted the contrast between the *Traitié* and the material on marriage in the *Mirour de l'Omme*. But there are striking similarities between the *Traitié* and the *Mirour*'s material on the estate of kings (lines 22225–3208). One is that the *Mirour* includes a long discussion of King David, who, as we saw above, is the subject of Ballade XIV of the *Traitié*. First, the *Mirour* discusses David as a negative exemplar:

> Du Roy David je truis escrit
> Que pour son charnel appetit
> Du Bersabée, qu'il ot conu,

---

[17] This is also implied by Lipton's observation that the *Traitié*'s purpose is 'to persuade wicked people to reform themselves' and that it emphasises man's control over his own fate: *Politics of Sacramental Marriage*, p. 78.
[18] *Ibid.*, p. 67.

> Vilainement fuist desconfit;
> Car Rois ne serra ja parfit
> Q'est de sa frele char vencu. (*Mirour*, lines 22819–24)

> ('Of King David I find written that he was basely discomfited because of his carnal appetite for Bathsheba. No king will be perfect who is vanquished by his frail flesh.')[19]

It then goes on to present David as a positive exemplar for 'chascun Roy' (line 22875) in six points. One is his penitence, which should inspire the king to his own penitence (lines 22945–56). So, in both poems David is upbraided for his adultery but praised for repenting. In Ballade XIV Gower does not make the point that adultery is specifically inappropriate for a king, as he does in line 22823 of the *Mirour* – but this idea comes up elsewhere, as we shall see. Here, what interests me is that David, who is an exemplar for kings in the *Mirour*, is given an exemplary function that works very similarly in the *Traitié*.

Another aspect of the *Mirour* story of David is God's vengeance. Gower explains:

> Dedeinz la bible qui lira
> Des Rois, sovent y trovera
> Qe pour les mals que Rois faisoit
> Non soulement dieus se venga
> Sur le Roy mesme, ainz pour cela
> Trestout le pueple chastioit. (*Mirour*, lines 22825–30)

> ('He who reads of the kings in the Bible will often find there that, for an evil committed by the king, God not only took vengeance on the king himself but also punished all the people.')

Accordingly, God avenged himself on David's people for his base behaviour. Gower explains why God acts in this way towards the end of this section of the *Mirour*:

> Car si la povre gent mesfait,
> Dont sont du siecle chastiée;
> Mais si ly Rois fait malvoisté,
> N'est qui pourra sa Royalté
> Punir, ainz quit de son forsfait
> Irra tout a sa volenté,
> Tanque la haulte deité
> Luy fait ruer de son aguait. (*Mirour*, lines 23128–36)[20]

> ('For if the lesser people do wrong, the misdeed is turned back on them, and they are punished for it by the world. But if the king does wrong, there is no one who can punish his royalty, and thus

---

[19] Translations from the *Mirour* are by William Burton Wilson: Gower, *Mirour de l'Omme*.
[20] Gower makes the same point in *Vox Clamantis*, VI, line 7498. See Russell A. Peck, 'The politics and psychology of governance in Gower: ideas of kingship and real kings', in *Companion*, pp. 215–38 (p. 226).

he goes about at his own will, free from his transgression, until the Deity on high makes him fall into his own snare.')

Since no earthly power can punish the king, God is forced to take the matter into his own hands. The same principle is at work in Ballade XIII of the *Traitié*, which explains that when Pharaoh had had his will of Sarai, 'Soubdeinement, ainz qe l'en scieust pour quoi, | Par toute Egipte espandist la morine' ('Suddenly, before he knew why, / Throughout all Egypt spread the murrain') (Ballade XIII, lines 15–16). But, more generally, this understanding could be seen to pervade the *Traitié*, with its constant references to God's vengeance, such as 'Freinte espousaile dieux le vengera' ('A broken marriage God will avenge') (Ballade VIII, refrain).[21] I suggested above that the poem's relative lack of emphasis on purely moral arguments might imply an addressee who had already shown indifference to them. But it is striking that there is no suggestion of legal sanction either. Immediate divine justice, which the *Mirour* presents as primarily appropriate for kings, is the main punishment for adultery in the *Traitié*.[22]

A third point of similarity between the two texts is their treatment of the fall of princes. The *Mirour* says:

> [...] si ly Rois ad plus poer,
> Tant plus vers dieu est acomptable.
>   Qui plus en halte estage monte,
> S'il en cherra, mal se desmonte,
> Dont trop se blesce; et tout ensi
> Par cas semblable tant amonte
> Ly Rois, qui tous estatz surmonte;
> S'il soit des vices assailly
> Et soit vencu, tant plus failly
> Serra coupable et malbailly,
> Qant a son dieu rendra l'acompte. (*Mirour*, lines 23111–21)

('if the king has more power, he is all the more accountable towards God. Whoever mounts to a high level comes down hard if he falls from it, and thereby he hurts himself greatly. And likewise, the king is in the same high position, for he surmounts all the other estates. If he is assailed by vices and overcome by them, he shall be found all the more wanting and guilty and brought to ruin when he render account to his God.')

These ideas are reiterated in two of the *Traitié* refrains: 'Si haut pecché covient en bass descendre' ('Thus high sin must needs be brought low'), in Ballade X, and 'En halt estat falt temprer le pooir' ('Power in high estate must be controlled') in Ballade XIII.[23] People of high estate should not abuse

---

[21] R. F. Yeager notes the pervasive references to vengeance in *John Gower's Poetic: The Search for a New Arion* (Cambridge, 1990), p. 89.
[22] Lipton makes a similar observation: *Politics of Sacramental Marriage*, p. 79.
[23] I am taking 'haut' in Ballade X to refer to the noble class of the sinner, which seems to me to be the most probable meaning. See *AND*, s.v. *halt*.

their power, and if they do they will fall all the harder. For these comments to have any direct relevance to the reader, Gower needs to be addressing someone of high – probably at least princely – estate.

Indeed, throughout the *Traitié*, the stories seem to be angled to suggest that adultery harms kings in particular. The reference to Lancelot and Tristram is oblique: all that is really said about them is that their 'sotie' ('folly') remains 'en memoire' ('in memory') (*Traitié*, XV, line 3).[24] But the Latin gloss spells out the significance more clearly: Lancelot had an affair with 'Gunnoram regis Arthuri uxorem' ('Guinevere, wife of King Arthur'), and Tristam with 'Isoldam regis Marci aunculi sui uxorem' ('Isolde the wife of his uncle King Mark'), and the consequence of this adultery concerning kings was great misfortune and pain.[25] Agamemnon is another king who is a victim of adultery. Although Gower tells his story very concisely, in two stanzas only, he finds room to introduce him by saying that he 'ot soubtz sa governance | De les Gregois toute la flour eslite' ('had under his governance / All the select flower of the Greeks') (*Traitié*, IX, lines 8–9). Practically everyone in the poem is a king or a king's relative – Helen is 'l'espouse a roi de Grece Menelai' ('The wife of the king of Greece, Menelaus') (*Traitié*, X, line 2); Nectanabus had been 'rois' ('king') in Egypt (*Traitié*, VI, line 2); Procne and Philomene are the daughters of 'le noble roi d'Athenes Pandeon' ('the noble king of Athens, Pandeon') (*Traitié*, XII, line 1) – and the space it takes to explain this constantly seems out of proportion in the brief narratives. But the point seems to be that adultery is the particular enemy of royalty, bringing about their deaths and downfalls. Conversely, the gloss to Ballade XVI refers to the praiseworthiness of a generic 'Princeps' guarding himself against lechery, implying that the moral that should be drawn from the story of Valentinian has relevance for princes rather than a general audience.[26]

Gardiner Stillwell described the *Mirour* section on kingship as 'loaded with significance for the politics of his [Gower's] contemporaries' in its critique of Edward III's actions.[27] As Stillwell says, phrases such as 'ils font ore' ('they nowadays') (*Mirour*, line 22241) make it clear that a criticism of current practice is intended, rather than a general discussion of possible failings of the royal estate. One of the main targets of Gower's criticism is the evil influence of women over the king. Stillwell goes on to show that Gower reworks a biblical story to give particular prominence to a courtier's argument that women are stronger than the king:[28]

---

[24] Also noted by Yeager, *John Gower's Poetic*, p. 90.
[25] Translations of French and Latin by Yeager, *French Balades*.
[26] However, against this Jane Gilbert argues that 'the exemplars' princely rank gives the text a limited universalism by acting as a figure for the *ipse* or sovereign masculine self': 'Men behaving badly: linguistic purity and sexual perversity in Derrida's *Le Monolinguisme de l'autre* and Gower's *Traitié pour essampler les amantz marietz*', *Romance Studies*, 24 (2006), 77–89 (p. 81). For a similar view, see Lipton, *Politics of Sacramental Marriage*, pp. 83–4.
[27] Gardiner Stillwell, 'John Gower and the last years of Edward III', *SP*, 45 (1948), 454–71 (p. 454).
[28] Stillwell's references for this story are confusing, but it appears in the book that is called Esdras I in the Apocrypha of the King James Bible.

> Mais ly secondes respondy,
> Qe femmes sont plus fort de luy;
> Car femmes scievont Roy danter:
> L'essample veons chascun dy. (*Mirour*, lines 22777–80)

> ('The second responded that women are stronger than the king because women can tame the king; we see an example of this every day.')

The story concludes with the assertion that:

> Voir dist qui dist femme est puissant,
> Et ce voit om du meintenant:
> Dieus pense de les mals guarir,
> Q'as toutes loys est descordant,
> Qe femme en terre soit regnant
> Et Rois soubgit pour luy servir. (*Mirour*, lines 22807–12)

> ('He speaks the truth who says that woman is powerful, and that is visible nowadays. May God save us from these evils, for it is in discord with all laws that a woman should rule in the land and should subject the king to serve her.')

Although the woman who has this inappropriate power is not named, the reference is generally taken to be to Alice Perrers, with whom Edward III had a notoriously public affair, and whose influence was notably deplored by Thomas Walsingham in the St Albans Chronicle.[29] Could the similarities between this section of the *Mirour* and the *Traitié* be taken further: could Edward III's affair with Alice Perrers have prompted Gower to write the *Traitié* in order to encourage the king to break it off?

We know that Gower liked to address poems to kings: to Richard II in *Vox Clamantis* and the first version of the *Confessio*; *Cinkante Ballades*, 'In Praise of Peace' and the second version of the *Confessio* to Henry IV. We have also seen that the Alice Perrers affair concerned Walsingham, who claimed that 'the whole populace desired Alice's condemnation' and 'longed for her downfall'.[30] If we take the references to kings that pervade the *Traitié* to imply that a king was the intended addressee, Edward III, the only king in Gower's lifetime who had a notorious affair, is the most likely candidate. Alice Perrers seems to have become Edward's mistress around 1364; Queen Philippa did not die until 1369, so the affair was initially adulterous on Edward's side. 'It was not until after the queen's death ... that her relationship with Edward III became public', but during the 1370s it was flaunted.[31] Any adultery at this point could only have been on Alice's side. Mark Ormrod has shown that she was married to one Janyn Perrers, but that he was probably dead by the time Alice conceived Edward's acknowledged

---

[29] *The St Albans Chronicle: The 'Chronica maiora' of Thomas Walsingham, vol 1, 1376–94*, eds and trans John Taylor, Wendy R. Childs and Leslie Watkiss (Oxford, 2003), pp. 42–7.
[30] *St Albans Chronicle*, p. 57.
[31] C. Given-Wilson, 'Perrers [married name Windsor], Alice (d. 1400/01)', *ODNB*.

son John Southeray.[32] Subsequently, she married William Windsor, possibly in 1373–4 when he was temporarily in England.[33] Walsingham reports that this marriage was revealed at the Good Parliament in May 1376, and that on hearing this revelation Edward 'became very frightened, swearing [...] that he did not know she was married, and that if he had known she had a husband, he would in no way have entertained this sinful liaison'.[34] At this point Alice was cast off, but by October she had been pardoned, returned to Edward, and remained with him until his death – to Walsingham's disgust. The accuracy of Walsingham's account has been disputed, but it seems clear that Alice was married to Windsor by November 1376, when she was accused of having tried to exert influence on his behalf.[35]

If the affair was the occasion and Edward the addressee of the *Traitié*, the period between October 1376 and Edward's death in June 1377 seems the most likely point for its composition. Edward had been conducting the affair with Alice Perrers for many years, but only now did it publicly emerge that it was adulterous; although he had initially shown remorse at this new degree of sinfulness, that was apparently insufficient to stop him from resuming the affair. With Edward's health in danger from October 1376 onward Gower might have felt that the time was ripe for a diplomatically subtle but persuasively targeted poem on the subject of the dangers of adultery for kings in particular, which held out the promise that it was never too late to earn God's forgiveness through repentance – even when one had continued to sin in the face of proper warnings. Can this date of composition be countenanced, given that the *Traitié* has normally been dated around twenty years later? On the face of it there is no real obstacle to seeing this as the date of original composition of the French verse. (Of course, the prefatory prose and Latin verse could not have been written until after the composition of the *Confessio* and shortly before Gower's marriage respectively.) Macaulay's dating, as we have seen, was based on the Latin verse alone, while Fisher suggested that the *Traitié* had to be dated to after 1386, or the period of the composition of the *Confessio*, because of their shared theme and treatment; but I have already argued that this is an unhelpful way of thinking about the composition of the *Traitié*.[36] As Yeager has said, there is 'no way to establish an unequivocal chronology for the French poems', and he has entertained the possibility of their being written and rewritten over the years.[37] In fact, according to what he has shown about the fashion for ballades with envoys after 1390, it would actually be more comfortable to assume that the *Traitié* was written before that date, and Gower's choice of the French language

---

[32] W. M. Ormrod, 'Who was Alice Perrers?', *CR*, 40, 3 (2006), 219–29 (p. 224).
[33] Given-Wilson, 'Alice Perrers'.
[34] *St Albans Chronicle*, p. 47.
[35] Given-Wilson, 'Alice Perrers'.
[36] Fisher, *John Gower*, p. 85.
[37] Yeager, 'John Gower's French', in *Companion*, pp. 137–51 (p. 137). For the idea of writing and rewriting, see Yeager, 'Gower's audience', 82.

for this poem would be readily explained by French being the dominant language of Edward's court.[38]

Another possibility is that the intended addressee is John of Gaunt, the other notorious royal adulterer of the period.[39] Gaunt's affair with Katherine Swynford began around 1371–2, roughly at the same time as his second marriage, to Constanza. Their affair seems to have been well known in the 1370s, but to have caused some scandal around 1381–2 which caused Katherine to withdraw from court until 1389, when she again lived openly with Gaunt. Constanza died in 1394, and Gaunt and Katherine married and had their four children legitimated by papal dispensation.[40] A couple of points seem to make Gaunt a more plausible addressee than Edward: Gaunt was married himself, and thus might seem a more appropriate recipient of a poem on the sin of adultery (albeit that the poem is often concerned with unmarried men's affairs with married women); and the date of the poem could be pushed later, perhaps between 1389 and 1394. There is the problem that the poem's obsession with kings seems less relevant to a king's uncle – but Gaunt styled himself king of Castile and León following his marriage to Constanza, and might have been thought to be susceptible to flattery on this basis, which would subtly remind him of the importance of that marriage.[41] It has been suggested that Gower snubbed Gaunt by omitting to mention him in the *Cronica Tripertita*, but this does not necessarily rule out an earlier attempt to write him a monitory poem.[42]

But of course what I have just proposed flies in the face of everything Gower tells us about the *Traitié* at its opening and close: that it should be read as a companion piece to the *Confessio*, that it is associated with his own marriage, and that it is for a general audience. The final French stanza-envoy reads as follows:

> Al université de tout le monde
> Johan Gower ceste Ballade envoie;
> Et si jeo n'ai de François la faconde,
> Pardonetz moi qe jeo de ceo forsvoie:
> Jeo sui Englois, si quier par tiele voie
> Estre excusé; mais quoique nulls en die,
> L'amour parfit en dieu se justifie. (*Traitié*, XVIII, lines 22–8)

('To the community of the entire world / John Gower this Balade sends: / And if I do not have eloquence in French, / Pardon me when I go astray with it: / I am English – thus I seek in such a

---

[38] On the fashion for envoys, see Yeager, 'Gower's audience', 92. On the French culture of Edward's court, see 'John Gower's French', p. 144.
[39] I am grateful to Mark Ormrod for suggesting this possibility to me in conversation.
[40] Chris Given-Wilson and Alice Curteis, *The Royal Bastards of Medieval England* (London 1984), pp. 147–50.
[41] Simon Walker, 'John, duke of Aquitaine and duke of Lancaster, styled king of Castile and León (1340–1399)', *ODNB*.
[42] See Anthony Goodman, *John of Gaunt: The Exercise of Princely Power in Fourteenth-Century Europe* (Harlow, 1992), p. 15.

way / To be excused; but whatever anyone may say about it / Perfect love justifies itself in God.')

It reiterates the point of a general address, in line 22, and apologises, rather conventionally, for defects in Gower's French. But does Gower protest too much? Are the envoy, the prefatory French prose and the concluding Latin all a way of deflecting our attention from the daring agenda and addressee of the original poem? Yeager has drawn attention to how unusual Gower's opening prose is, with its apparently unnecessary comment that the *Traitié* is in French and unfulfilled promise that the *Traitié* will give advice 'selonc les auctours' ('according to the authorities').[43] Could it be that all of this material is designed to act as a smokescreen, to suggest generality, conventionality, and assert that the *Traitié* is, as others have assumed it to be, a mirror of the *Confessio* that differs only in its language? If so, the reason for this smokescreen would be Gower's desire to give his elegant (if rather hectoring) ballade sequence a longer life once its original purpose had been superseded: events moved on, whether or not Gower ever delivered the poem to either Edward or Gaunt, and the poem could no longer stand on its own. Perhaps there may even be an alternative way of reading Gower's closing apology. He asks us to excuse him if he goes astray – 'qe jeo […] forsvoie' ('if I go astray') – or says anything 'incongrua', as the gloss has it, by considering that he is English. Could he be partly apologising for indecorously bold words motivated by patriotism? Whether these closing speculations are well-founded or not, I hope to have demonstrated that Gower's *Traitié* is so far out of line with conventional advice on marriage, so specifically focused on the question of adultery and the importance of breaking it off once it has begun and so suggestively connected with the *Mirour*'s material on kingship that we must reject Gower's claim that it was originally composed with 'tout le monde' ('all the world') in mind.

---

[43] Yeager, *John Gower's Poetic*, pp. 86 and 91. He goes on to argue that these signal Gower's intention to engage with the courtly love tradition of French poetry and challenge it on its own ground.

Chapter 22

Rival Poets: Gower's *Confessio* and Chaucer's *Legend of Good Women*

JOHN M. BOWERS

The *Man of Law's Tale* was based on the account of Constance's travels written first by John Gower, and *The Wife of Bath's Tale* derives from the Tale of Florent in *Confessio Amantis*.[1] The fact that both of Chaucer's source-texts occur early in Gower's collection even suggests some preliminary access to the *Confessio* as a work-in-progress in the late 1380s. In addition to sharing manuscripts back and forth, literary rivalry can be detected in Chaucer's attempts at re-writing these tales, some playful competition rather than the quarrel speculated by Thomas Tyrwhitt in the 1770s.[2] In *The Man of Law's Prologue*, Chaucer encrypts a sly portrait of Gower as the legal professional, who held power of attorney while Chaucer travelled to Italy in 1378,[3] but also a severe critic of his poetry; in *The Man of Law's Tale*, Gower's alter ego narrates a new and improved version of his own tale of Constance.

This paper explores further the collegial exchanges between the two poets in terms of the *Confessio* and the *Legend of Good Women* by proposing that influence, as such, continued to flow in the direction proposed by John Leland around 1540 – 'de Govero plura in Chaucero dicemus' – from Gower to Chaucer. My argument requires two radical claims. First, the received chronology of Chaucer's canon needs adjusting in order to position the *Legend* in the F Prologue as well as the G version later than Gower's collection datable to the early 1390s. And second, Gower (b. 1330?) assumes the position of an older brother asserting influence and generating anxiety for his slightly younger contemporary Chaucer (b. 1340?), something like the competitive relationship better documented between Petrarch and Boccaccio. No weakling in this challenge for making literary history, Chaucer qualifies as one of Harold Bloom's 'strong poets' who 'make that history by misreading one

---

[1] Peter Nicholson, 'Chaucer borrows from Gower: the sources of the *Man of Law's Tale*', in *Chaucer and Gower: Difference, Mutuality, Exchange*, ed. R. F. Yeager (Victoria, B.C., 1991), pp. 85–99; and Peter G. Beidler, 'Transformations in Gower's *Tale of Florent* and Chaucer's *Wife of Bath's Tale*', in *Chaucer and Gower*, ed. R. F. Yeager, pp. 100–14.

[2] John Hurt Fisher, *John Gower: Moral Philosopher and Friend of Chaucer* (London, 1965), pp. 26–36, puts to rest the legend of some serious quarrel.

[3] Fisher, *John Gower*, pp. 57–8, on Gower's 'professional involvement in the law'.

another so as to clear imaginative space for themselves'.[4] Chaucer plays with his adaptations of tragic love-stories in the *Legend*, while both *Legend* Prologues take Gower's lucky encounter with Richard II on the royal barge and recast the scene as Chaucer's nightmarish interrogation before the tyrannical God of Love.

Placing the *Legend* anywhere in the chronology of Chaucer's career has always been problematic, not least because the Prologue survives in two distinct versions. George Kane's article 'Outstanding problems of Middle English scholarship' made the point that our confidence about dating medieval texts seldom relies upon much hard evidence: 'Many discussions came nowhere near agreement but simply lapsed; and it could happen that the rhetorical skill of a proponent rather than the excellence of his evidence would establish his opinion'.[5] In terms of dating Chaucer's works, Kane noticed a 'disturbing complacency about his chronology', and yet his stern reminder that 'the suggestion of authoritative, agreed conclusions reached by the best kind of argument which editorial blandness and the veneer of print convey is gravely misleading'[6] has made absolutely no impact upon the orderings established more than a century ago by the scholarly guesswork of Bernhard ten Brink, Walter W. Skeat and John S. P. Tatlock.[7] Editors are obliged to make decisions about ordering an author's works, of course, but those speculations achieve quite different status when later Chaucer scholars treat as 'facts' the guesses of their predecessors. E. Talbot Donaldson, Albert C. Baugh and Baugh's student John H. Fisher adhered to the oeuvre's chronology established by Skeat's Oxford edition.[8] F. N. Robinson's 1933 'Canon and chronology of Chaucer's writings' was retained verbatim in his second edition of 1957 and largely adopted by Larry Benson in the 1987 third edition of *The Riverside Chaucer*.[9] 'As far as I know', Kane observed, 'there has been no attempt of real scope on the subject since Tatlock's youthful work in 1907'.

Thirty years after Kane's challenge, Kathryn Lynch's article 'Dating Chaucer' starts with Derek Pearsall's description of Chaucerian chronologies as 'a spider's web of hypothesis' and proceeds to characterize any attempt at devising a narrative of the poet's development based on the *Riverside*

---

[4] Harold Bloom, *The Anxiety of Influence* (Oxford, 1973), p. 5.
[5] George Kane, 'Outstanding problems of Middle English scholarship' (1977), in *Chaucer and Langland: Historical and Textual Approaches* (Berkeley, CA, 1989, pp. 228–41 (p. 235).
[6] Kane, 'Outstanding problems', p. 235.
[7] Bernhard ten Brink, *Chaucer: Studien zur Geschichte seiner Entwicklung und zur Chronologie seiner Schriften* (Münster, 1870); W. W. Skeat, *The Chaucer Canon* (Oxford, 1900); and John S. P. Tatlock, *The Development and Chronology of Chaucer's Works* (London, 1907).
[8] Geoffrey Chaucer, *The Complete Works of Geoffrey Chaucer*, ed. W. W. Skeat, 6 vols (Oxford, 1894); *Chaucer's Poetry: An Anthology for the Modern Reader*, ed. E. T. Donaldson (New York, 1958), pp. 868–9; *Chaucer's Major Poetry*, ed. Albert C. Baugh (New York, 1963), pp. xix–xxi; and *The Complete Poetry and Prose of Geoffrey Chaucer*, ed. John H. Fisher (New York, 1977), p. xiii.
[9] Geoffrey Chaucer, *The Poetical Works of Chaucer*, ed. F. N. Robinson (Boston, 1933), pp. xxiv–xxv; *The Works of Geoffrey Chaucer*, ed. F. N. Robinson, 2nd edn (Boston, 1957), pp. xxviii–xxx; and *The Riverside Chaucer*, gen. ed. Larry D. Benson, 3rd edn (Boston, 1987), pp. xxvi–xxix.

Chaucer's agreed-upon chronology as 'speculation and wishful thinking'.[10] As evidence of intransigence, few have rushed to endorse Helen Cooper's advocacy of re-dating *The House of Fame* to the late 1380s – that is, after the completion of *Troilus*, when the English poet had reason to consider his own candidacy as a famed author. Cooper argues convincingly (to my mind) that Chaucer projects himself as the 'Englyssh Gaufride' helping to support the history of the Trojan War (*House*, 1464–70) as indeed *Troilus* had done so brilliantly,[11] while the ending, with its hurly-burly of pilgrims, pardoners and shipmen exchanging 'tydynges', looks forward to the *Canterbury Tales* as the poet's next work.

What was the original evidence for dating *House of Fame* a decade earlier? This question pertains to the dating of the *Legend* as well. First, the octosyllabic couplets required close proximity to *Book of the Duchess*, usually dated between Blanche of Lancaster's death in 1368 and John of Gaunt's remarriage in 1372.[12] This argument presumes that Chaucer became a hostage to whatever verse-form he used at any given period and was incapable of reverting to prior practices. For some, 'metrical determinacy' continues to require back-dating the rhyme royal narratives in the *Canterbury Tales* to the 1380s, along with *Troilus*. With his *Confessio* begun in the late 1380s, Gower's octosyllabic couplets would have encouraged Chaucer's return to this verse-form in *House of Fame*. But the general development of Chaucer's prosody actually works in favour of dating of the *Legend* to the mid-1390s and bestowing upon the *Tales* the distinction of introducing iambic pentameter couplets to English poetry, an innovation in verse-form otherwise begrudgingly bestowed upon the *Legend* Prologue.

Second, and more relevant to the *Legend*, the genre of dream-vision forced *House of Fame* early into Ten Brink's French period in the poet's career, even though the poem responds deeply to Chaucer's forward-looking encounters with Italian literary culture.[13] Here the poet grapples with Petrarch's notion of literary fame in a three-part vision parodying the *Divine Comedy* so obviously that John Lydgate called the work 'Dante in Inglissh'.[14] The presumption that dream-visions belonged to Chaucer's early career forced the *Legend* to as early a date as possible, immediately after *Troilus*, to which the Prologue makes steady reference, but still at an uncomfortably late date.

Why all the fuss about re-dating? The return to literary history in the form of New Historicism makes dating Chaucer's works urgent in ways previ-

---

[10] Kathryn L. Lynch, 'Dating Chaucer', *CR*, 42 (2007), 1–22 (pp. 2–4), citing Derek Pearsall, *The Life of Geoffrey Chaucer* (Oxford, 1992), p. 3.

[11] Helen Cooper, 'Welcome to the *House of Fame*: 600 years dead: Chaucer's deserved reputation as "the father of English poetry"', *TLS* 5091 (27 October 2000), 3–4, and 'Chaucerian representation', in *New Readings of Chaucer's Poetry*, eds Robert G. Benson and Susan J. Ridyard, intro. Derek Brewer (Cambridge, 2003), pp. 7–29.

[12] Lynch, 'Dating Chaucer', 4–5, reviews speculation dating *Book of the Duchess* anywhere from 1368 to 1399.

[13] Ten Brink, *Chaucer: Studien* (1870), proposed the resilient three-part division of the poet's career into French, Italian and English periods.

[14] John Lydgate, *Fall of Princes*, ed. Henry Bergen, EETS e.s. 121–124 (Oxford, 1924–7) (Part I, pp. 8–10, book I, lines 281–357).

ously lacking for New Criticism with its neglect of historical context and Exegetics with its assumption of an unchanging medieval culture. But if the *Legend* is meaningfully embedded in its historical moment, we need those dates. The challenge becomes doubly complicated when aligning Chaucer's career with contemporary textual productions like Gower's *Confessio*, begun, we guess, in about 1387. Internal testimony indicates that Gower completed the first version about 1390; the second recension followed by 1392 with references to Richard II and Geoffrey Chaucer removed; and the third version was finished in about 1393.[15]

Always lurking in discussions of the Chaucer–Gower connection is the fact that we dislike conceding that a genius such as Chaucer was subject to influences from any English contemporaries. One means of cordoning him off from unwanted interference from fellow writers has been to banish them from his immediate environment. Once upon a time William Langland was safely rusticated in the Malvern area, although Derek Pearsall and Caroline Barron have forcefully reasserted Skeat's view of *Piers Plowman* as a London poem.[16] As another metropolitan writer, Langland's influence becomes legible in Chaucer's Plowman as well as the estates satire of the General Prologue.[17] And the *Gawain* Poet was long exiled to some manorial court in Cheshire until Michael Bennett began making the case for relocating this courtly poet instead among the numerous Cheshiremen recruited into King Richard's household from the late 1380s.[18] The Squire's allusion to Sir Gawain when his own weird, helmetless knight on horseback bursts into a royal banquet (*Tales*, V, 89–97) sounds like Chaucer's recollection of *Sir Gawain and the Green Knight*.[19] This recent scholarship suggesting Langland and the *Gawain*-Poet as London contemporaries underscores the well-attested fact that Gower never left London, or at least went no further than Southwark.

John Fisher rightly compares the collaborative interplay between Chaucer and Gower to the creative conjunction of Wordsworth and Coleridge. 'The

---

[15] Macaulay, i, pp. xxi–xxiii; see also Peter Nicholson, 'The dedications of Gower's *Confessio Amantis*', *Mediaevalia*, 10 (1984), 160–80.

[16] Caroline M. Barron, 'William Langland: a London poet', in *Chaucer's England: Literature in Historical Context*, ed. Barbara Hanawalt (Minneapolis, MN, 1992), pp. 91–109, and Derek Pearsall, 'Langland's London', in *Written Work: Langland, Labor, and Authorship*, eds Steven Justice and Kathryn Kerby-Fulton (Philadelphia, PA, 1997), pp. 185–207. Linne R. Mooney, 'Chaucer's scribe', *Speculum*, 81 (2006), 97–138, confirms the Londoner Adam Pinkhurst as the copyist of the Trinity B.15.17 *Piers Plowman* as well as the Hengwrt and Ellesmere manuscripts of the *Canterbury Tales*.

[17] My book *Chaucer and Langland: The Antagonistic Tradition* (Notre Dame, IN, 2007) suggests that much of Chaucer's output took shape in response to *Piers Plowman*.

[18] An expert on medieval Cheshire, Michael J. Bennett launched this revisionist project in '*Sir Gawain and the Green Knight* and the literary achievement of the northwest midlands: the historical background', *JMH*, 5 (1979), 63–88, and it has gained a certain orthodoxy in his 'The historical background', in *A Companion to the 'Gawain'-Poet*, eds Derek Brewer and Jonathan Gibson (Cambridge, 1997), pp. 71–90. See also John M. Bowers, *The Politics of 'Pearl': Court Poetry in the Age of Richard II* (Cambridge, 2001).

[19] J. R. R. Tolkien, '*Sir Gawain and the Green Knight*' (1953), in *The Monsters and the Critics and Other Essays*, ed. Christopher Tolkien (London, 2006), pp. 72–108 (pp. 73, 100, 108. n. 30), took the *Squire's Tale* as evidence that Chaucer knew *Gawain* and probably its author also.

relationships between the works of the two poets ... can be explained only by assuming that Chaucer and Gower were in constant communication, passing their manuscripts back and forth frequently at least up to 1386 and again after 1390.'[20] More than the short-lived relationship between Erasmus and Sir Thomas More that produced *Praise of Folly* and *Utopia*, one imagines the long-term masculine chumminess, along with the friendly rivalry and mutual prodding, that developed between C. S. Lewis and J. R. R. Tolkien – along with the murkiness about who influenced whom.[21] Gower's dropping of the 'Chaucer greeting' from his second version of *Confessio* has been variously interpreted as some personal falling-out or parting of the ways politically. Gower's hostility to Lollard divisiveness – 'Of scisme causeth forto bringe | This newe secte of Lollardie' (*Confessio*, Prol. 349 ff.) – combined with Wycliffite controversies during the 1390s may have intensified differences with a writer who maintained ties with the Lollard knights Clanvowe and Clifford and incorporated Lollard attitudes in his *Canterbury Tales*.[22] Carolyn Dinshaw investigates the legend of a quarrel, one male writer pitted aggressively against another, as a fantasy that constructs our literary history: 'This Gower was to play the lumbering fall guy to the nimble and free-spirited Chaucer'.[23]

In terms of the *Legend*, Fisher imagined a collegial process of parallel composition, with each poet responding to a royal command from Richard II, and he identified five points of similarity between the *Confessio* and the Prologue to the *Legend*: '(1) the appearance of the king and queen of love; (2) general details of setting and dress such as the "swote pleine", the fiery darts, the pearl crowns, the company of lovers; (3) the displeasure of the king of love with the poets; (4) the intercession of the queen of love; and (5) her assignment of a confession or penance which provides motivation for a collection of stories'.[24] Paul Strohm laid the groundwork for post-dating the *Legend* Prologue in his study 'Queens as intercessors', which links Queen Alceste with Queen Anne in her petitionary role during the royal entry into London in 1392.[25] The account of the entry by Richard Maidstone (d. 1396) culminates with the scene in Westminster Hall where Queen Anne begs for mercy on London's behalf.[26] I believe Chaucer had this highly theat-

---

[20] Fisher, *John Gower*, pp. 32–3.
[21] Humphrey Carpenter, *J. R. R. Tolkien: A Biography* (Boston, 2000), pp. 204–5.
[22] Alcuin G. Blamires, 'The Wife of Bath and Lollardy', *MÆ*, 58 (1989), 224–42; Paul Strohm, 'Chaucer's Lollard joke: history and the textual unconscious', *SAC*, 17 (1995), 23–42; and Katherine Little, 'Chaucer's Parson and the specter of Wycliffism', *SAC*, 23 (2001), 225–53, build upon the longstanding view that Chaucer aligned himself with the reform-minded Lollard knights; see K. B. McFarlane, *Lancastrian Kings and Lollard Knights* (Oxford, 1972), pp. 148–76, and Steven Justice, 'Lollardy at court', in *Cambridge History of Medieval English Literature*, ed David Wallace (Cambridge, 1999), pp. 670–73.
[23] Carolyn Dinshaw, 'Rivalry, rape and manhood: Gower and Chaucer', in *Violence Against Women in Medieval Texts*, ed. Anna Roberts (Gainesville, FL, 1998), pp. 137–60 (p. 139).
[24] Fisher, *John Gower*, pp. 235–50 (p. 240).
[25] Paul Strohm, 'Queens as intercessors', in *Hochon's Arrow: The Social Imagination of Fourteenth-Century Texts* (Princeton, NJ, 1992), pp. 95–119.
[26] Richard Maidstone, *Concordia (The Reconciliation of Richard II with London)*, ed. David Carlson, trans. A. G. Rigg (Kalamazoo, MI, 2003).

rical public display specifically in mind when writing the F Prologue of the *Legend*. The untimely death of Richard's beloved consort in 1394 prompted the revision of the G Prologue with removal of the reference to the queen 'at Eltham or at Sheene' (*Prol. F*, lines 496–7).[27] The beginnings of the *Legend* project can then be dated between Richard II's 1392 royal entry and Queen Anne's 1394 death.

Chaucer would have considered the dream-vision a courtly genre at whatever point in his decades-long career he put quill to parchment. Negotiations for the marriage of Richard II and Anne of Bohemia during 1380–81 had provided the occasion for *Parliament of Fowls*, even though its indebtedness to Boccaccio signalled Chaucer's discovery of Italian poetry. This aviary debate-poem in turn inspired Sir John Clanvowe's *The Boke of Cupide, God of Loue*, datable to 1389 because of its commendation to Queen Anne at Woodstock in that year.[28] Indeed, the Anglo-French truce of 1389 marked a turn in courtly tastes, as French culture was no longer the enemy's culture. Eleanor Prescott Hammond was unbothered that Chaucer, in the Prologue to the *Legend*, 'returned to French models after those of Italy had become familiar to him'.[29] My own work on *Pearl* suggests several cultural factors behind Chaucer's revisiting of the courtly dream-vision in the 1390s, particularly King Richard's embrace of French artistic styles when arranging his marriage to the French king's daughter during 1395–96. The shrewd opportunist Jean Froissart saw an opening in 1395 and returned to England with a book of his poetry luxuriously prepared as a gift for Richard II, who showed himself a proficient speaker of the French language as well as a connoisseur of French love-poetry.[30] The elegiac *Songe Vert* provides the surprising example of a French dream-vision written in England during the mid-1390s.[31]

Re-dating the *Legend* affords a way of approaching anew the interplay between the two poets who made efforts at naming each other: Chaucer commends 'moral Gower' near the end of *Troilus* (V, line 1856), and Gower has Venus claim Chaucer as 'mi disciple and mi poete' near the end of the *Confessio* (VIII, 2941*–57*). The current *Riverside Chaucer* retains Robinson's agnosticism regarding the *Legend* that 'the date of composition ... cannot be established' and 'the dating of the collection remains uncertain' (p. 1059). Yet the logic of the absence of evidence equalling evidence of absence has prevailed to support the scholarly orthodoxy that 'the F Prologue was composed sometime in the period 1386 at the earliest to 1388 at the very latest, since the General Prologue to the *Tales* would surely have been

---

[27] John Hurt Fisher, 'The revision of the Prologue to the *Legend of Good Women*: an occasional explanation', *South Atlantic Bulletin*, 43 (1978), 75–84, makes a forceful case for dating the revised G Prologue to 1395–7.

[28] John Clanvowe, *The Works of Sir John Clanvowe*, ed. V. J. Scattergood (Cambridge, 1975), p. 52 (lines 281–5).

[29] Eleanor Prescott Hammond, *Chaucer: A Bibliographical Manual* (New York, 1908; rpt 1933), p. 71.

[30] George B. Stow, 'Richard II in Jean Froissart's *Chroniques*', *JMH*, 11 (1985), 333–45, and Bowers, *The Politics of 'Pearl'*, pp. 156–9 and 179–80.

[31] Ethel Seaton, '*Le Songe Vert*: its occasion of writing and its author', *MÆ*, 19 (1950), 1–16.

mentioned, in Alceste's catalogue of the poet's writings, after that date' (p. 1060).[32] Elsewhere I have suggested that the *Legend* Prologues, including the G Prologue after 1394, fail to mention the General Prologue because Chaucer was writing his *Tales* as a 'closet' project not meant for courtly readers, particularly Richard II, but intended instead for future generations of readers – us – while the *Legend* became his offering for courtly readers like Edward, Duke of York, who quoted the poem in his *Master of Game*.[33]

Shifting the *Legend* backward six years (or so) is not drastic in the great scheme of things, but it has some noteworthy implications in the context of Chaucer's creative output as well as that of his literary relations with his contemporaries. For example, Sir John Clanvowe's *Boke of Cupide* is datable to the late 1380s because its author died outside Constantinople in 1391[34] and therefore this work contributed to Chaucer's depiction of the touchy, temperamental God of Love in the *Legend* Prologue, not the other way around as generally presumed.[35] Much as we dislike the idea that Chaucer might have been influenced by great contemporaries like Langland, we recoil at the notion he might have been indebted to lesser talents like Clanvowe, normally designated as an early Chaucerian imitator after quoting the 1380s version of the *Knight's Tale* known as 'The Love of Palamon and Arcite'.[36] By appropriating the God of Love from the *Boke of Cupide*, Chaucer actually operated as a Clanvowian imitator.

In his *Tales*, Chaucer engages in a number of inside jokes with his friend Gower. He models the 'Man of Law' partly after Gower, who served as one of Chaucer's own attorneys as early as 1378.[37] He places into the mouth of the Man of Law spiteful comments about his own incompetence as a poet – 'That Chaucer though he kan but lewedly | On metres and on rymyng craftily (*Tales*, II, 47–8) – and then adds dismissive remarks about the 'unkynde abhomynacions' of incest tales concerning Canacee and Apollonius who happen to figure in the *Confessio*, thereby using Gower's fictional alter ego to mock the senior poet's own sex-subjects. Apparently unable to recognize Chaucer as a fellow pilgrim – another joke in view of the well-documented personal relationship between the two men – the Man of Law proceeds to a lengthy, seemingly well-informed list of the tragic lovers from

---

[32] This reasoning follows Robert W. Frank, Jr, *Chaucer and 'The Legend of Good Women'* (Cambridge, MA, 1972), pp. 1–10.

[33] John M. Bowers, 'Chaucer after Retters: the wartime origins of English literature', in *Inscribing the Hundred Years' War in French and English Cultures*, ed. Denise N. Baker (Albany, NY, 2000), pp. 91–125 (pp. 108–13).

[34] Siegrid Düll, Anthony Luttrell and Maurice Keen, 'Faithful unto death: the tomb slab of Sir William Neville and Sir John Clanvowe, Constantinople 1391', *Antiquaries Journal*, 71 (1991), 174–90.

[35] Lisa Kiser, *Telling Classical Tales: Chaucer and the 'Legend of Good Women'* (Ithaca, NY, 1983), pp. 62–70.

[36] On Clanvowe as a member of the original audience of 'The Love of Palamon and Arcite', see my article 'Three readings of *The Knight's Tale*: Sir John Clanvowe, Geoffrey Chaucer, and James I of Scotland', *JMEMS*, 34 (2004), 279–307.

[37] Fisher, *John Gower*, p. 61.

Chaucer's 'Seintes Legend of Cupide'. These allusions have been taken as evidence that the *Legend* must pre-date Fragment II of the *Tales*.

But there has always been a problem, because the Man of Law's list does not correctly match the lover-martyrs in our received texts – and, specifically, seven of his tragic lovers are absent from the *Legend*: Deianira, Hermione, Hero, Helen of Troy, Briseyde, Laodamia and Penelope.[38] Did Chaucer later delete these instalments? Or was he 'deliberately and comically falsifying the contents of his Legendary as part of characterizing the narrator or tweaking his colleague John Gower'?[39] Gower gets back his own because his *Confessio* includes the seven missing ladies plus seven others actually included in Chaucer's *Legend*: Thisbe, Dido, Medea, Lucrece, Ariadne, Phyllis and Queen Alceste herself. Does this overlap represent jesting acknowledgement that Gower had already portrayed these tragic heroines? And does the Man of Law's reference to a substantial volume – 'Whoso that wole his large volume seke' (*Tales* II, 60) – return to self-mockery on Chaucer's part for producing a collection far smaller than described here?

Philomena and Cleopatra, missing from the Man of Law's roster, may be evidence that Chaucer continued compiling the *Legend* after writing the *Man of Law's Prologue*. Or perhaps professional jealousy prompted omitting Philomela from the catalogue because Gower's version was longer and arguably better.[40] The absence of Cleopatra from the Man of Law's name-list remains mysterious since both F and G Prologues have Alceste ordering the poet to start with the Egyptian queen: 'At Cleopatre I wol that thow begynne' (F, line 566, G, line 542).[41] As a striking innovation, Chaucer's version describes the queen leaping naked into a snake-pit: 'Among the serpents in the pit she sterte | And there she ches to have hire burying' (*Legend* F, lines 6997–8).[42] Gower says she died in a cave: 'Cleopatras which in a Cave | With Serpentz hath hirself begrave' (*Confessio*, VIII, lines 2573–4). Macaulay traces this account to Vincent of Beauvais, with the now-familiar report of her dying in her tomb ('in mausoleum').[43] To my mind, the more likely trajectory leads from mausoleum to cave to snake-pit, not from mausoleum to snake-pit to cave – with Chaucer extrapolating grotesquely from Gower's bare description.

I imagine the *Legend* as a work-in-progress during the 1390s when Chaucer composed Fragment II of the *Tales* and some of the tragic heroines mentioned by the Man of Law were planned, but never finally executed. Lynch agrees: 'Chaucer may not be accounting for what he *has* written but

---

[38] See *The Riverside Chaucer*, p. 855n.
[39] Lynch, 'Dating Chaucer', 6.
[40] On the inferiority of Chaucer's version, see Derek Pearsall, 'Gower's narrative art', *PMLA*, 81 (1966), 475–84 (pp. 478–9).
[41] *Riverside 3* hedges on sequence: 'Gower's brief account of Cleopatra (*Confessio*, VIII, lines 2571–7) is probably based on Chaucer's legend' (p. 1066).
[42] V. A. Kolve, 'From Cleopatra to Alceste: an iconographic study of *The Legend of Good Women*' (1981), in *Telling Images: Chaucer and the Imagery of Narrative II* (Stanford, CA, 2009), pp. 28–65.
[43] Macaulay, iii, II, lines 456 and 547.

offering a prospectus of what he *plans* to write'.[44] The scope of this unrealized project is certainly no more ambitious than the 120 stories announced for *The Canterbury Tales*. Even *Riverside 3* admits uncertainty about dating *The Legend of Thisbe*: 'Chaucer's and Gower's versions seem related, but it is hard to say which came first' (p. 1067). As evidence of the ongoing unstable status for the *Legend* – proceeding 'yer by yere' (F, 479–85) – there remains the mystery of Chaucer's title in his *Retraction*: *The Book of the XXV Ladies*. We have at most ten ladies, if we count Hypsipyle and Medea separately, far short of twenty-five. Yet Duke Edward of York's *Master of Game* also refers to Chaucer's work as 'The Twenty-Five Good Women'. Not simply repeating the wording of the *Retraction*, York quotes from memory the Prologue's arresting phrase about the key of remembrance: 'ffor as Chaucer saiþ in this prologe of the xxv. good wymmen. Be wryteng haue men of ymages passed, for writyng is þe keye of alle good remembraunce.'[45] As a member of Richard II's inner circle, did York know a larger expanded version of the *Legend* – the Man of Law's 'large volume' – which did not survive Lancastrian efforts at eradicating Ricardian court culture after 1399?[46] Simon Horobin's identification of Bokenham's extensive translation of the *Legenda Aurea* as a greatly expanded version of his *Legends of Holy Women* suggests the existence of variant collections, some shorter and some longer.[47]

Much as Chaucer fostered an image of himself without English-language antecedents and certainly without contemporary rivals, his London was a lively arena of literary competition and one-upmanship in which he was not clearly destined to become the winner in terms of posterity. He could have had good reason to feel insecure around 1392. Langland's *Piers Plowman* had gained a national readership and was already attracting imitations such as *Pierce the Plowman's Creed* (c.1393). Michael Bennett's evidence suggests that the *Gawain* Poet would have benefited from the patronage which Richard II lavished upon other Cheshiremen in his household. And Gower had completed the substantial works *Mirour de l'Omme* in French and *Vox Clamantis* in Latin as well as the ambitious English story-collection *Confessio Amantis*.[48] Chaucer's later triumph as the Father of English Poetry obscures the fact he had cause to view himself as a lesser poet writing only in English during the early years of the 1390s.

All biographical evidence suggests that Chaucer was quite capable of composing texts in French – though not, I think, the 'Ch' poems of the Pennsylvania manuscript[49] – and his decision to write exclusively in English,

---

[44] Lynch, 'Dating Chaucer', 6.
[45] Edward, Second Duke of York, *The Master of Game*, eds William A. Baillie-Grohman and F. N. Baillie-Grohman, intro. Theodore Roosevelt (London, 1904), pp. 3–4.
[46] Bowers, *The Politics of 'Pearl'*, pp. 186–95.
[47] Simon Horobin, 'A manuscript found in the library of Abbotsford House and the lost legendary of Osbern Bokenham', *English Manuscript Studies, 1100–1700*, 14 (2007), 132–64.
[48] R. F. Yeager, 'Learning to speak in tongues: writing poetry for a trilingual culture', in *Chaucer and Gower: Difference, Mutuality, Exchange*, ed. R. F. Yeager (Victoria, B.C., 1991), pp. 115–29.
[49] James I. Wimsatt, *Chaucer and the Poems of 'Ch' in University of Pennsylvania MS French 15* (Cambridge, 1982).

which looks so natural in historical hindsight, gave grounds for a literary 'inferiority complex' in terms of Gower's achievements in French *and* Latin.[50] Chaucer's weak Latin, as evidenced by his reliance upon a French translation of the *Consolation of Philosophy* when producing his English *Boece*, might well have intensified his embarrassment when compared with his friend's proficiency. Even the English-language *Confessio* came equipped with an armature of glosses as well as Latin verses extensive enough for a free-standing modern translation.[51]

In the 1390 *Confessio* Gower describes himself being recognized by Richard II on the Thames, receiving a gracious welcome aboard the royal barge, but then feeling anxious over the royal commission to write 'som new thing' in a book:[52]

> And natheles this world is wilde
> Of such jangling, and what befalle,
> My kings heste schal nought falle,
> That I, in hope to deserve
> His thonk, ne schal his will observe.
>   (*Confessio*, Prol., lines 68*–72*)

Then something happened by the completion of the 1392 version which caused Gower to drop the barge scene and allude darkly to dangerous times:

> The cause whi it changeth so
> It needeth nought to specifie,
> The thing so open is at ye
> That every man it mai beholde. (*Confessio*, Prol., lines 32–5)

What had happened? Every Londoner understood that 1392 marked the year when Richard II, enraged over the city's refusal to grant a £5000 loan, moved three major offices of government to York and threatened more violent retributions.[53] Only the magnificent royal entry (plus the money) placated the monarch, while leaving Londoners sufficiently embittered that they later welcomed the usurper Henry IV. As Strohm has suggested, the entry's drama of regal wrathfulness and queenly intercession bears compar-

---

[50] Tim William Machan, 'Medieval multilingualism and Gower's literary practice', *SP*, 103 (2006), 1–25, and more specifically R. F. Yeager, 'Gower's French audience: the *Mirour de l'Omme*', *CR*, 41, 2 (2006), 111–37.

[51] John Gower, *The Latin Verses in the 'Confessio Amantis': An Annotated Translation*, eds Siân Echard and Claire Fanger, with A. G. Rigg (East Lansing, MI, 1991). On Chaucer and Latin, see John M. Bowers, 'Latinity, colonialism, and resistance', in *Chaucer: Contemporary Approaches*, eds Susanna Fein and David Raybin (University Park, PA, 2009), pp. 114–29.

[52] Frank Grady, 'Gower's Boat, Richard's Barge, and the True Story of the *Confessio Amantis*: Text and Gloss', *Texas Studies in Language and Literature*, 44 (2002): 1–15, and Joyce Coleman, '"A Bok for King Richardes Sake": Royal Patronage, the *Confessio*, and the *Legend of Good Women*', in *On John Gower: Essays at the Millennium*, ed. R. F. Yeager (Kalamazoo MI, 2007), pp. 104–21.

[53] Caroline M. Barron, 'The quarrel of Richard II with London, 1392-7', in *The Reign of Richard II: Essays in Honour of May McKisack*, eds F. R. H. Du Boulay and Caroline M. Barron (London, 1971), pp. 173–201; see also Nigel Saul, *Richard II* (New Haven, CT, 1997), pp. 436–7.

ison to Chaucer's nightmare in the *Legend* Prologue. The poet-dreamer had earned the anger of the God of Love (aka Richard II) for writing *Troilus*, with its unflattering description of female inconstancy but, more particularly, I believe, with its unflattering portrait of the youthful prince's romantic histrionics and sexual fumbling, even his homosocial intimacy with Pandarus as a fictional stand-in for Robert de Vere, Earl of Oxford. The monastic historian Walsingham alleged that Richard and Robert engaged in 'obscene familiarity',[54] and a line-count indicates that Troilus actually spends more time in bed with Pandarus than with Criseyde. As confessor to John of Gaunt in the Lancastrian affinity, Maidstone in his *Concordia* praised King Richard with the backhanded compliment 'beautiful as Troilus', which hit an already sore spot.[55] The God of Love's displeasure in the *Legend* has to do less with Chaucer's unflattering portrayal of ladies and more with his unflattering portrait of Richard's Trojan alter ego.[56] The Kafkaesque paranoia of the *Legend* Prologues reflects Chaucer's insecurity at the court of an increasingly volatile monarch inclined to favour the Cheshire author of *Pearl*.[57] While Chaucer retreated into the largely covert enterprise of the *Canterbury Tales*, Gower marshalled his revisions of the *Confessio* to bolster his secondary bid for goodwill within the Lancastrian affinity.

Nor was Chaucer's primacy in the nascent English literary tradition secure during the decade after his death in 1400. After Gower's self-promotion through the dedication of his revised *Confessio* to Gaunt's son Henry, he received the Lancastrian 'Ss' collar, later represented on his tomb statue, and he attained the distinction as the first English poet to have work translated abroad, first into Portuguese and then Castilian Spanish, very possibly during his lifetime.[58] He lived long enough into the Lancastrian era – dying in 1408 – to write the anti-Ricardian *Tripartite Chronicle* and dedicate his French *Cinkante Balades* to Henry IV after Christine de Pizan turned down Henry's invitation to the English court.[59] Though Adam Pinkhurst distinguished himself by copying Hengwrt and Ellesmere, his colleague Scribe D

---

[54] Thomas Walsingham, *Historia Anglicana*, ed. Henry Thomas Riley, 2 vols (London, 1863–4), ii, p. 148: 'tantum afficiebatur eidem, tantum coluit et amavit eundem, non sine nota prout fertur, familiaritatis obscoenae'. See Tison Pugh, *Queering Medieval Genres* (New York, 2004), 'Queer Pandarus?', pp. 82–95.

[55] See my '"Beautiful as Troilus": Richard II, Chaucer's Troilus, and figures of (un)masculinity', in *Men and Masculinity in Chaucer's 'Troilus and Criseyde'*, eds Tison Pugh and Marcia Smith Marzec (Cambridge, 2008), pp. 9–27.

[56] Derek Brewer, 'Chaucer's anti-Ricardian poetry', in *The Living Middle Ages: Studies in Mediaeval English Literature and Its Traditions*, eds Uwe Böker, Manfred Markus and Rainer Schöwerling (Stuttgart, 1989), pp. 115–28.

[57] Michael J. Bennett, 'The court of Richard II and the promotion of literature', in *Chaucer's England: Literature in Historical Context*, ed. Barbara Hanawalt (Minneapolis, MN, 1992), pp. 3–20.

[58] R. F. Yeager, 'Gower's Lancastrian affinity: the Iberian connection', *Viator*, 35 (2004), 483–515, and Joyce Coleman, 'Philippa of Lancaster, queen of Portugal – and patron of the Gower translation?', in *England and Iberia in the Middle Ages*, ed. María Bullón-Fernández (New York, 2007), pp. 135–65.

[59] David R. Carlson, 'Gower on Henry IV's rule: the endings of the *Cronica Tripertita* and its texts', *Traditio*, 62 (2007), 207–36, and J. C. Laidlaw, 'Christine de Pizan, the Earl of Salisbury and Henry IV', *French Studies*, 36 (1982), 129–43.

copied two other early manuscripts of *The Canterbury Tales* – Corpus 198 and Harley 7334 – but also included in his résumé an astonishing eight manuscripts of the *Confessio*.[60] Scribe D's Christ Church MS 148 has original arms indicating completion for one of Henry IV's sons, probably Thomas, Duke of Clarence, while his Bodley MS 294 bears the erased motto of Humphrey, Duke of Gloucester, as evidence of magnate readership entirely lacking even in the richly produced Ellesmere Chaucer.[61]

Treating the *Confessio* as the cornerstone of a new vernacular canon, these high-quality manuscripts attest that Gower worked diligently enough as a promoter of the Lancastrians to become temporarily their most-favoured poet.[62] More than a decade earlier the direction of influence that I have been suggesting from the classical tales of the *Confessio* to the *Legend* – and the two quite different encounters with their Ricardian authority-figure, and Chaucer's playful caricature of his friend as the Man of Law – all confirm Gower's preeminence as *the* London author of English, Latin and French poetry during the 1390s as impetus for Chaucer's competitive, creative responses in his *Canterbury Tales* but also in his *Legend of Good Women*.

---

[60] A. I. Doyle and M. B. Parkes, 'The production of copies of the *Canterbury Tales* and the *Confessio Amantis* in the early fifteenth century', in *Medieval Scribes, Manuscripts and Libraries: Essays Presented to N. R. Ker*, eds M. B. Parkes and A. G. Watson (London, 1978), pp. 163–210; Kathryn Kerby-Fulton and Steven Justice, 'Scribe D and the marketing of Ricardian literature', in *The Medieval Professional Reader at Work*, eds Kathryn Kerby-Fulton and Maidie Hilmo (Victoria, B.C., 2001), pp. 217–32; John M. Bowers, 'Two professional readers of Chaucer and Langland: Scribe D and the HM 114 Scribe', *SAC*, 26 (2004), 113–46; and Mooney, 'Chaucer's scribe'.

[61] Doyle and Parkes, 'The production of copies', Appendix C: evidence of original owners, pp. 208–9.

[62] M. B. Parkes, 'Patterns of scribal activity and revisions of the text in early copies of works by John Gower', in *New Science out of Old Books: Studies in Manuscripts and Early Printed Books in Honour of A. I. Doyle*, eds Richard Beadle and A. J. Piper (Aldershot, 1995), pp. 81–104.

Chapter 23

Reassessing Gower's Dream-Visions

ANDREW GALLOWAY

Even by his apologists Gower is not considered a master of the dream-vision, though he has gained a minor – I think too minor – reputation as one of its demolishers. Most surveys of medieval dream-vision poetry fail to include his uses of dream-visions at all. A. C. Spearing's foundational discussion *Medieval Dream-Poetry* omits Gower, no doubt because the *Confessio Amantis* has as a whole only a questionable claim to being in the dream-vision tradition.[1] Kathryn Lynch's *High Medieval Dream-Vision* includes the *Confessio* but, in some ways more strangely, does not focus mainly on Gower's explicit dream-visions, in that poem or others. Instead, Lynch treats the *Confessio* as a whole as an example of how features of the genre have survived outside their original habitat: features such as the figure of Genius and a philosophy of 'the way that the world is organized to reflect God's plan', for which she has in mind precedents like Alan of Lille and the *Roman de la Rose*.[2]

These evasions are kinder than some of the direct attention. To consider Gower's explicit handling of the genre most commentators turn to the *Vox Clamantis* book I, with its depiction of the 'Peasants' Rebellion' of 1381 in which domesticated or other normally placid animals are monstrously transformed. But this work is often treated as an embarrassing sport in the dream-vision genre. Maria Wickert, still the work's most attentive commentator, notes its structural awkwardness in which, for instance, the author 'obviously had difficulty padding out' the description of an entire spring day before falling asleep, because, she ingeniously suggests, 'Gower did not wish to give up the traditional spring morning scheme [of courtly love allegories], but ... was obliged to place the dream at night' to fit the tradition of exegetical dream-visions.[3] She adds that Gower 'manipulates historical account and allegorical interpretation in such a way that they never fully coincide ... The author leaps continuously from one manner of presentation to another.'[4] Kathryn Lynch mentions the *Vox* book I in her treatment of the medieval dream-vision only to say that the work shows Gower using

---

[1] A. C. Spearing, *Medieval Dream-Poetry* (Cambridge, 1976).
[2] Kathryn Lynch, *The High Medieval Dream-Vision: Poetry, Philosophy, and Literary Form* (Stanford, CA, 1988), p. 185.
[3] Maria Wickert, *Studies in John Gower*, trans. Robert J. Meindl (Washington DC, 1981), p. 29.
[4] Wickert, *Studies*, p. 46.

the dream-vision mode 'mainly as an authenticating device, to secure for himself the authority of prophecy'.[5] More recent views are generally even less appreciative. Steven Justice suggests that the *Vox* I's visionary pose is 'manifestly contrived', presenting this view as Pertelote's and thus Chaucer's judgment of Gower's *Vox* book I in *The Nuns' Priest's Tale*, but the opinion is also clearly Justice's own. Pertelote, thus Chaucer, thus Justice, all find that 'what Gower calls a prophetic revelation is just the familiar, willed fiction of the poetic dream-vision',[6] and Justice finds that the hypocrisy in this runs deep. The awkward formal features of the *Vox* I are symptoms, he argues, of Gower's bad-faith effort in seeking to reclaim authority as the representative of the 'common voice', an effort he made just after the Rising fundamentally challenged the right of a learned courtier or any other member of 'official England' to make such a claim. By decrying the utter monstrosity of the rebels in a visionary mode, Justice observes, Gower found a way to speak for everyone else. The event was 'a threat to Gower's project, but also an opportunity for it'.[7]

'Opportunity' expresses an old complaint about Gower's poetry in general, and the heavy claims to authority in the dream-vision tradition bring that issue to the fore. Yet is there any continuous development, any poetic and intellectual integrity, in Gower's uses of the dream-vision, or are those simply his most nakedly desperate bids for authority while he tacks – as usual – to changing political winds? Modern scholarship has subtle ways to make that old charge, and the most recent and stimulating ones (like Justice's) have, as it happens, focused on the dream-vision form as their barometer. Thus Frank Grady has argued that the whole tradition of topical dream-visions, which Grady finds epitomized by Gower's *Vox* I, collapsed with the advent of the Lancastrian regime. Contrasting *Vox* I, together with other topical English dream-vision poems (the others all in English), with topical but not 'visionary' poetry written shortly after the Lancastrian accession, including Gower's *Cronica Tripertita*, Grady argues that English writers abandoned the dream-vision form as a vehicle for contemporary social narratives after the deposition of Richard II because of the insecurities surrounding the ensconcing of Henry IV: a surreal mode was a particularly infelicitous way to affirm the new regime's wobbly authority, which narrowed the literary options of 'the generation of 1399'. 'The difficulties posed by the deposition', Grady suggests, 'were obstacles to thinking clearly and logically about political stability'; thus topical political narrative turned away from using dream-visions to employ 'the apparent fixity and unalterable archival persistence of legal documents, chronicles, and statutes'.[8] Thus if Justice finds Gower using the special authority of the dream-vision to make

---

[5] Lynch, *High Medieval Dream-Vision*, p. 165.
[6] Steven Justice, *Writing and Rebellion: England in 1381* (Berkeley, CA, 1994), p. 215.
[7] Ibid., p. 213.
[8] Frank Grady, 'The generation of 1399', in *The Letter of the Law: Legal Practice and Literary Production in Medieval England*, eds Emily Steiner and Candace Barrington (Ithaca, NY, 2002), pp. 222–3.

a transparently duplicitous bid for 'prophetic revelation' when his previous authority as the 'voice of the people' was undercut by the Rebellion, Grady sees Gower abandoning a genre that did not have enough authority to face down the uncertainties of political disruptions.[9]

Such politically grounded perspectives on literary history are stimulating, though their conclusions could be challenged against wider or narrower perspectives. In a wider European framework, for instance, it is not correct to say that *Vox* I was the end of the topical dream-vision. Rather, it was the front edge of a cluster of works using such a form by writers who were, like Gower, more or less independent secular writers committed to addressing the powerful members of secular culture on matters of general public importance. A number of these used the abstract and surreal resources of the dream-vision mode to present as well as analyze the forces behind the events of current history. One might consider, for instance, the huge prose French *Songe du Vieil Pelerin* by Philippe de Mézières, finished a few years later, around 1390, with its vision of the narrator's pilgrimage surrounded by allegorical virtues urging highly specific political and financial reforms for the nobles and king of France to ponder, including an elaborately significant allegory of the French ship of state 'Gracieuse' – just as Gower uses a conceit of a ship of state at the end of *Vox* I.[10] Or one might consider Honoré Bovet's Latin *Somnium super materia scismatis* (*Dream of the Matter of the Schism*) of 1394, or his French *Apparicion de maistre Jehan de Meun* of 1398, both of which use dream imagery in similarly advisory ways. Or one might note Christine de Pizan's surreal French version of a Boethian political dream-vision allegory, the *Avision* of 1405–6, which offers a highly peculiar allegorical analysis of her career and France's political history.[11] In the other historical direction, political argument and analysis had long been framed as 'prophecy', reaching back – as Gower was well aware – to the book of Daniel; in England, the mode can be found at least as early as Gerald of Wales' twelfth-century account of a Lincolnshire knight who told Henry II that he had been told by St Peter and the Archangel Gabriel in a vision that the king would soon die if he did not carry out a list of social reforms; those in fact summarize the main points later found in Magna Carta.[12] Nor was Gower's strange uses of visionary authority unparalleled in his own time

---

[9] But compare Eve Salisbury's point that *Vox* I's 'monstrous' poetic mode, whose textual pastiche or 'cento' she links to ideas about monstrous births, suits the social disorders it portrays: 'Remembering origins: Gower's monstrous body politic', in *Re-Visioning Gower*, ed. R. F. Yeager (Asheville, NC, 1998), 159–84.

[10] Philippe de Mézières, *Le Songe du Vieil Pelerin of Philippe de Mézières, Chancellor Cyprus*, ed. G. W. Coopland, 2 vols (Cambridge, 1969). The 'Gracieuse' appears in book II (de Mézières, *Le Songe du Vieil Pelerin*, vol. i, summary at pp. 427–41, text at pp. 537–636).

[11] Honorat Bovet, *Medieval Muslims, Christians, and Jews in Dialogue: The 'Apparicion Maistre Jehan de Meun'*, ed. and trans. Michael Hanley (Tempe, 2005); Honorat Bovet, *L'Apparicion Maistre Jehan de Meun et le Somnium super materia scismatis*, ed. Ivor Arnold (Paris, 1926); Christine de Pizan, *Lavision-Cristine*, ed. Sister Mary Louis Towner (Washington DC, 1932). See Renate Blumenfeld-Kosinski, *Poets, Saints, and Visionaries of the Great Schism, 1378–1417* (University Park, PA, 2006).

[12] W. L. Warren, *King John* (Berkeley, CA, 1961), p. 179.

and place, when appeared not only the English works that Grady mentions – *Winner and Waster* and *Piers Plowman* – but also John Ergome's highly topical political Latin commentary on 'John of Bridlington's' cryptic Latin verses the *Vaticinium*, whose glosses, at least, elucidating the political warnings, analysis and judgments of the surreal verses themselves, were written for Humphrey, ninth earl of Gloucester, in the 1370s.[13] Gower's *Vox* I certainly presents some similarity to those earlier works in England, but charts the new directions taken by the subsequent works in Latin and French written on the Continent in his period and later. In this wider view both before and after, his work stands as the first of a number of dream-visions built in an intellectually elite literary mode but claiming quasi-visionary authority, and not simply unfolding political and social judgments but also using allegory to account for the forces by which secular culture was shaped and changed. Gower was the first, not the last, of this 'generation', not to mention a harbinger of more overtly self-authorizing visionary authors to follow in England, from Spenser to Milton to Blake and beyond.

But Grady is right that this combination of features is only thinly presented in dream-visions in England after 1399, or rather, and I think more fairly, after Gower. From the fifteenth century only two English poems with political dream-vision sequences have come down to us: *Mum and the Sothsegger* and *The Crowned King*, both probably before 1415 but both found only in much later single manuscripts. Both are explicitly dependent on *Piers Plowman* and sharpen that work's topical capabilities, but neither develops the visionary form extensively as a means to do so. *Mum*'s single acephalic copy offers an elaborate allegory of truth-telling over favour-currying at court, but includes an explicit dream-vision for only a 412-line stretch of the fragment's 1752 lines and in terms that seem to ignore the rest of the poem's theme of speaking truth to power (the narrator's dream of an old gardener explaining the nature of an ethical polity in terms of busy bees who drive out lazy drones once they see how those deplete the 'comune profit'). The very brief *Crowned King* presents blandly direct advice from a 'clerk' to a king, like an expansion of the 'clergial' Lunatic in *Piers Plowman* B (Prol., lines 123–7), now asking the king to attend to his humbler subject's needs, especially those of the poor, rather than those who sway him with lavish gifts.[14]

In contrast, Chaucer's non-topical or only very obliquely topical dream-visions set the terms for dream-visions in the fifteenth century, and there seems no direct reception of any of Gower's dream-visions then.[15] Indeed, we have to look hard even for his own continuous development of the form. Yet his several distinct dream-visions – *Vox* I, the opening and closing dreams

---

[13] For references and discussion of Ergome, see Andrew Galloway, 'The rhetoric of riddling in late-medieval England: the "Oxford" riddles, the *Secretum philosophorum*, and the riddles in *Piers Plowman*', *Speculum*, 70 (1995), 78–9.

[14] Both in Helen Barr, ed., *The Piers Plowman Tradition* (London, 1993).

[15] See the convenient anthology, Dana Symons, ed., *Chaucerian Dream Visions and Complaints* (Kalamazoo, MI, 2004).

in the *Confessio* and Alceone's dream of Ceix in the centre of the *Confessio*, all preceded by one other, little-noticed instance in the *Mirour* – appear, when put together, bright focal points of his broader literary developments. Those developments are not simply varying strategies for advancing his own authority, although that topic is certainly a continuous consideration and point of examination.[16] It can be granted that *Vox* I strains under the inconsistent principles and weight of its several kinds of bids for authority, but we should also credit Gower at least with elaborating his own writerly and intellectual calculation and artifice in opposition to what he presents as the monstrous appetites of the rebels in their metamorphoses. A key element of Gower's dream-visions, in fact, is their complex attention to the powers of appetite and need, shaping and distorting the body politic as much as the individual lover and even the rational mind. Linked to that focus is also an exploration of the fallibility of 'reason' especially when it reaches too high and claims too much power – an exploration that undermines his views of visionary authority in general – even, implicitly but perhaps not completely inadvertently, his own. These elements are stressed generally in his poetry, but most prominently, if least stably, in his dream-visions.

Both appetite and rationalization are profoundly this-worldly, humanist focuses. Indeed, a pervasive feature of Gower's dream-visions is, paradoxically, a skepticism, a disenchantment, about the supernatural forces that the dream-vision genre – traditionally that most enchanted of genres – brought to focus, both love-visions and religious revelation. As Wickert suggests, one reason for *Vox* I's formal instabilities is its combination of kinds of dream-visions, though we might add that this extends rather than thwarts its perspectives on need and desire. More destabilizing, however, is how Gower's interpretive efforts and calculated writerliness in all his dream-visions keep the writer's urge for power as visible as any other desire he surveys. Chaucer's *House of Fame* and *Parliament of Fowls* also explore how erotic desire merges with further socially consequential appetites, while wryly noting the writer's urges to classify dreams, seek 'tydynges', or keep reading. But Gower presents so earnest and unrelenting a competition between the writer's powers and the world he surveys that, even when not topical, the results seem more philosophical than fictive: a genuine debate about the role of reason in a world of urgent and competitive willfulness and appetites. Similarly, scholars have usually found the Latin glosses to the *Confessio* authorial but seen their authority as limited, even a staged debate about the authority of clerical, Latin guidance.[17] Gower's dream-visions are

---

[16] My own earlier treatment of *Vox* I can be indicted for over-stressing this, although it considers other issues as well: Andrew Galloway, 'Gower in his most learned role and the Peasants' Revolt of 1381', *Mediaevalia*, 16 (1993 for 1990), 329–47.

[17] See Derek Pearsall, 'Gower's Latin in the *Confessio Amantis*', in *Latin and Vernacular: Studies in Late Medieval Texts and Manuscripts*, ed. A. J. Minnis (Cambridge, 1989), 13–25; Siân Echard, 'With Carmen's help: Latin authorities in the *Confessio Amantis*', *SP*, 95 (1998), 1–40; A. Galloway, 'Gower's *Confessio Amantis*, the *Prick of Conscience*, and the history of the Latin gloss in early English literature', in *John Gower: Manuscripts, Readers, Contexts*, ed. Malte Urban (Turnhout, 2009), 39–70.

still more forcefully managed by explicators and explication; but in turn, his dream-visions stress more directly than usual how thought exhibits appetites as dangerous as the rebellious and other non-rational needs those describe. In this sense, his dream-visions epitomize his debates about the forces governing the social world.

What is almost certainly the earliest example we have in Gower of attention to the dream-vision form, in fact, displays it under the sign of self-serving manipulation and interpretation.[18] In the *Mirour de l'Omme*, perhaps from 1378, the figure 'Somnolence', under 'Accidie' (Sloth), is personified as a mendacious and self-indulgent dream-vision expositor:[19]

> Car lors se couche a lée chiere,
> Ne ja pour soun de la clochiere
> Au matin se descouchera;
> Ainz le labour de sa priere
> Laist sur la Nonne et sur le frere;
> Asses est q'il ent soungera.
>   Car Sompnolence ad joye grant
> Quant poet songer en son dormant,
> Et dist que ses avisiouns
> Vienont de dieu, dont en veillant
> Sicome luy plest vait divinant;
> Car solonc ses condiciouns
> En fait les exposiciouns,
> Et met y les addiciouns
> De sa mençonge en controevant;
> Mais a les premuniciouns,
> Qui son a ses perdiciouns,
> Ne vait du rien considerant. (*Mirour*, lines 5180–96)[20]

---

[18] It has been argued that the short allegorical French dream-vision titled *Le Songe Vert*, whose narrator is dressed in black to lament his dead beloved and then in a dream-vision of Venus is restored to hope for new life and love and green clothing, could also have been by Gower, and thus might present an earlier dream-vision poem by him. But there is no direct or, in my view, persuasively indirect evidence for this, other than Gower's facility with French and the probable fourteenth-century English origin of that poem. See Ethel Seaton, '*Le Songe Vert*: its occasion of writing and its author', *MÆ*, 19 (1950), 1–16. The poem is edited by Léopold Constans: '*Le Songe Vert*', *Romania*, 33 (1904), 490–539. Seaton, although offering the argument for Gower's authorship, notes the differences from Gower's other poetry in metre, theme and even presumed patron at the date when she thinks the poem could be written (Richard II, to commemmorate his marriage to Isabelle in 1395). One might add that, unlike the narrator in the *Songe Vert* but like Chaucer, Gower does not earnestly present himself as a noble lover in any poetry. The *Songe Vert*'s affinities seem instead to lie with Chaucer's *Book of the Duchess* and Froissart (who seems a plausible candidate for authorship). For a forceful argument that the *Songe Vert* should be seen as the work of a French poet from the Ile-de-France or Picardy and was influenced by (and 'seems almost a sequel of') Chaucer's *Book of the Duchess*, see James I. Wimsatt, *Chaucer and the French Love Poets: The Literary Background of the Book of the Duchess* (Chapel Hill, NC, 1968), pp. 137–46.

[19] On the *Mirour*'s genre, date and audience, see R. F. Yeager, 'Gower's French audience: the *Mirour de l'Omme*', *CR*, 41, 2 (2006), 11–37; and 'Politics and the French language in England during the Hundred Years' War: the case of John Gower', in *Inscribing the Hundred Years' War in French and English Cultures*, ed. Denise Baker (Albany, NY, 2000), pp. 127–57.

[20] Citations of Gower are from Macaulay; translations are mine.

('For he goes to bed with joyful face, and does not get up in the morning at the sound of the church-bells; he leaves the labour of his prayers to the nun and friar; it's enough for him to dream about it. For he takes great joy when he can dream while sleeping, and he says that his revelations come from God, such that when awake he begins prophesying as he wishes. For according to his circumstances he makes his expositions of them, elaborating them with his lying while contriving them. But he doesn't pay any attention to premonitions of his own downfall.')

Every one of the major formal features of dream-visions, courtly or religious, is present here, though subject to devastatingly sceptical scrutiny. If a dream-vision is supposed to be a disturbing revelation, here it is a comforting fraud. If it is traditionally brought on by a dreamer falling asleep in the lap of nature's bounty, here it is the result of a willed desire to remain in bed. If it customarily gives access to uncontrollable passions, erotic or spiritual, here it is an opportunity for deliberate self-gratification. Although this passage most overtly presents a hypocrite religious visionary, it serves also to satirize the erotic tradition of dream-visions like the *Roman de la Rose*. Like Gower's parodic visionary, the *Rose*'s visionary-narrator claims that all those who say dreams are *mençonges* are wrong, since everything he dreamed, 'which was very beautiful and pleased me very much', came true, just as Macrobius says when he described King Scipio's 'avision'.[21] Gower's portrait even echoes the *Rose* narrator's phrasing at the opening of his poem: 'et vi un songe en mon dormant' (*Roman de la Rose*, line 26; cp. *Mirour de l'Omme*, line 5186, 'quant poet songer en son dormant'). And of course the Lover of the *Rose*, like Somnolence, ignores Reason's advice about the ills that attend Fortune's love. Locating this portrait under Somnolence parallels how the Lover in the *Rose* is led into love's garden by Oiseuse, 'Leisure.' The prominence of Oiseuse in that courtly work may at least explain why Gower, rather ingeniously, located this issue here: I find no other instance of Somnolence or Sloth that embodies or treats dream-visions or their exposition.[22]

The underlying criticism of Somnolence's kind of dream-vision and dream-vision exposition is of course close to what Steven Justice says about Gower as dream-vision poet: fashioning authority that claims transcendent status but is actually based on self-serving purposes. Given Gower's keen awareness of this kind of hypocrisy, then, what led him to his emphatic claims in *Vox* I of prophetic authority for what can easily be seen to have already happened to the author? The potential for some criticism of his posture in *Vox* as human in inspiration after all, and humanly confected in presentation, might, however, have been tolerable there because *Vox* I

---

[21] Guillaume de Lorris and Jean de Meun, *Le Roman de la Rose*, ed. Félix Lecoy, 3 vols (Paris, 1965–70), I, lines 27–30. Translations, where needed, are Charles Dahlberg's: Guillaume de Lorris and Jean de Meun, *The Romance of the Rose*, 3rd edn (Princeton, NJ, 1995).

[22] Siegfried Wenzel, *The Sin of Sloth: Acedia in Medieval Thought and Literature* (Chapel Hill, NC, 1967), p. 127, remarks that 'there is nothing like an Ode to Accidie or a Sonnet on Sloth ... of great lyrical stature' in medieval culture: but it seems that from Gower's point of view, that is precisely what erotic, courtly dream-visions were, even the great *Rose*.

spends its efforts indicting those who allow their appetites rather than their reason to rule. The shift between what the narrator first claims to be simply 'memorable tokens of a certain occurrence' (line 17) and at the end calls 'the pattern of whatever the future holds' (line 2144) might even mark a point of pride in displaying himself as an author in control of his analysis and his medium, whose narrative includes his contemplating a future moment of his writing – e.g., 'Dum mea mens memor est, scribens memoranda notabit, / In specie sompni que vigilando quasi / Concepi pauidus …' ('while my mind is mindful it will note in writing the things to be remembered, which in the form of a dream I in horror conceived as if awake' [lines 2135–7]). Such hyperbolic gestures toward rational and expository control highlight his theme that the rebels' appetites unravel the 'natural' social order and change their obediently useful animal bodies into wilfully transformable and aggressively appetitive, not useful creatures.

Yet rationality and desire are not so easily kept apart in this narrative: for, to the rebels, thought was the first cause of their dangerous disruption. The rebels allowed appetite to take over, Gower says, because 'the mind's stupid meditation is inclined to want more things, | Which impede its wishes more than its desires can bear' ('Voluere plura solet animi meditacio stulta, | Que magis impediunt quam sua vota ferunt' [lines 213–14]). Once allowed, that thought knew no bounds to its appetite, and found expression in subsequent bodily transformations coextensive with their raving desires:

> Aprini dentes deformant ora canina,
> Est quorum morsus pestifer atque grauis:
> Quanto plus escas sumunt minus hii saturantur,
> Insaciata fames semper inheret eis. (*Vox*, I, lines 417–20)

> ('The teeth of a boar deformed the canine mouths, whose bite was poisonous and fierce; the more they took food the less they were satiated: an insatiable hunger was always within them.')

Developing this theme of 'appetite shaping nature' in a dream-vision, though, is fundamentally destabilizing in another way, because it engages and inverts the basic machinery of the genre. From Alan of Lille on, Nature's endlessly creative powers are central to the dream-vision tradition. Gower would have learned from Alan's *De planctu naturae* how human desires, especially for sodomy, seek to pervert the natural structure of things such as grammar, but he applies that point to its ultimate degree of overthrowing the power of Nature altogether, and moreover demonstrates it directly in Nature's own field of action.[23] In *Vox* I, an opening claim to Nature's central agency and fecund power (in the May morning scene) is violently displaced by a poetic mode that places human thinking and consequently human appetites at the centre of natural form. In turn, that decentring of Nature

---

[23] Indeed, allegorical dream-visions had long challenged nature's and even God's ultimate dominion: for an interesting claim about the writer's overthrowing of God's powers in the twelfth-century works of Bernardus Silvestris, see Linda Lomperis, 'From God's book to the play of the text in the *Cosmographia*', *Medievalia et Humanistica*, 16 (1988), pp. 51–71.

is carried further by the author's own continual signs of writerly control. Having made thought so central to how disruption occurs, the poem as a work of thought proceeds to enact that disruption by how the writer shapes Nature, abandoning any claims to mere representation of an 'external' experience or revelation. The result is an unsettling analogy between the rebels' deforming appetite and the writer's literary manipulation. The poem – and writer – completes the rebels' usurpation of nature's agency, with strange consequences in the work's modes of allusion and narrative consistency. Gower's poetic persona mutates, for instance, into a register that, as Wickert observed, creates 'a striking mixture of heathen and Christian motifs that makes interpretation difficult'.[24] To be sure, classical posturing and pseudonyms are common in the medieval Latin tradition, from Alcuin through the letters of Gower's near-contemporary Petrarch – and here, too, perhaps a late medieval continental context fits Gower better than an English one. But in Gower's *Vox* I the mixture of Christian and pagan roles makes the everyday Christian identity of the speaker seem postured too. By the middle of the poem the dream narrator speaks of the events themselves on Corpus Christi Thursday and Friday in bizarrely classically personified terms:

> Si prius ira Iouis nocuit violenta, sequenter
> Mota Venus duplo facta furoris agit. (*Vox*, I, lines 955–6)
>
> ('If the prior violent wrath of Jove had been harmful, Venus subsequently carried out deeds stirred by double the fury.')

Calcas, Antenor, Thersites, Diomedes, Ulysses all populate an abruptly classicized London, and the narrator sums up all this sense of a humanly constructable and unconstructable world in describing London's own 'denaturing nature':

> O denaturans vrbis natura prioris,
> Que vulgi furias arma mouere sinis! (*Vox*, I, lines 979–80)
>
> ('O denaturing nature of the former city, who allow the furies of the mob to take up arms!')

Shortly thereafter the narrative passes through a series of further metaphors that may serve to display rhetorical virtuosity, but also thwart with increasing energy any 'natural' narrative frameworks such as the sudden presentation of the Tower of London as a ship (of state). The entire narrative explicitly furthers the process of 'denaturing' expected forms and limits, including those of the dream-vision form. The rebels' sins are made the writer's powers, and the latter's authority thus stands darkly collusive with what he indicts.

The narrative ends with a claim that all this is a *waking* sleep, 'vigiles sompni', suggesting not only that the topical events are more 'real' than

---

[24] Wickert, *Studies*, p. 52.

dream, but also that we have inhabited a fully confected world over which the writer intends to exert still more control:

> O vigiles sompni, per quos michi visio nulla
> Sompniferi generis set vigilantis erat!
> O vigiles sompni, qui sompnia vera tulistis,
> In quibus exemplum quisque futurus habet!
> O vigiles sompni, quorum sentencia scriptis
> Ammodo difficilis est recitanda meis! (*Vox*, I, lines 2141–6)

> ('O waking sleep, through which my vision was not of the sleep-inducing sort, but of wakefulness! O waking sleep, you bring true dreams, in which is the pattern of whatever the future holds! O waking sleep, whose hard meaning must be recited in my writings!')

The oxymoronic notion of 'waking sleep' probably derives from Guillaume de Machaut's *Fontainne Amoreuse* (1360), the widely copied fourteenth-century dream-vision poem in which the narrator lies anxiously in a 'waking-sleep,' a 'dorveille' (line 63), while he overhears the knight lamenting his lady's unawareness of his love and his imminent departure.[25] This half-conscious state seems designed to cast mystery on whatever is experienced, leaving its value and interpretation, its grip on reality of one kind or another, a matter for the reader to puzzle out. Machaut's use probably also influenced John Clanvowe's *Book of Cupid*, whose narrator is 'Not al on slepe, ne fully wakyng' (line 88); so, too, Philippe de Mézières frames his political 'dream of the old pilgrim' (finished in 1390) as occurring while he was 'moitie dormant moitie veillant' (1.89).[26] The trope flickers on into Shakespeare's *Midsummer Night's Dream*, when, after the enchantments have been removed from the four lovers, Lysander can recount the recent events 'amazedly', 'Half sleep, half waking' (IV.i.147); the play closes with Puck wryly suggesting that if the play has not pleased the audience, they should think that they 'have but slumb'red here / While these visions did appear' (V.i.425–6).[27]

---

[25] Guillaume de Machaut, *The Fountain of Love ('La fonteinne amoureuse'), and Two Other Love Vision Poems*, ed and trans. R. Barton Palmer (New York, 1993).

[26] See John Clanvowe, *The Works of Sir John Clanvowe*, ed. V. J. Scattergood (Cambridge, 1975); Philippe de Mézières, *Le livre de la vertu du sacrement de marriage*, ed. Joan B. Williamson (Washington DC, 1993); Thomas Hill, focusing on a Marian lyric with the phrase, usefully collects some early Patristic instances of the notion of the 'sleep of sin': '"Half-waking, half-sleeping": a tropological motif in a Middle English lyric and its European context', *RES*, n.s. 29 (1978), 50–56. Hill, however, does not consider Machaut's use of the phrase in a love-vision, however, or Gower's or Philippe de Mézières' subsequent uses of it in political visions.

[27] From William Shakespeare, *The Riverside Shakespeare*, ed. G. Blakemore Evans *et al.* (Boston, 1974). The effect and implications of a half-dreaming state have repeatedly been discussed in Shakespeare criticism, and sometimes *Midsummer Night's Dream* has been generally linked to Chaucer's dream-visions (e.g., by Charlotte Porter and Helen Clarke in their 1903 edition, excerpted in *Shakespeare, The Critical Tradition: A Midsummer Night's Dream*, ed. Judith Kennedy and Richard Kennedy (London, 1999), pp. 346–7). The specific medieval tradition

All these works speak to a sense of displacement from received dream-vision forms and traditions – both religious and erotic – that has settled over dream-visions as they move toward wider social and political perspectives and self-consciousness in the later fourteenth century. These strategies recognize in varying ways human responsibility or half-responsibility for conditions that have traditionally seemed beyond human control. For Gower, this 'waking sleep' epitomizes his difficult balance between a writer's own desires and those of the disruptive social world that he is analyzing, and between a self-conscious emphasis on control and a claim to transcendent inspiration. One might think that the far end of such tapping of dangerous powers and potentially dangerous pride are later figures like Marlowe's Faustus or Milton's Satan.

This is a deeper and more sustained issue in Gower's work than the usual charges of opportunism can accommodate. But politics do shape literary and intellectual history at deep levels. There is evidence suggesting that 1381 and, especially, its aftermath made these problems timely and brought these themes to the fore. On 8 March 1382 parliament and king, 'citing the treasonable hostile rising of divers evildoers in congregations and conventicles throughout the realm and their perpetration of treasons, homicides, arsons, etc.', commissioned posses of local higher nobility and clergy to persecute 'any who incite to rebellion, to suppress their meetings, arrest their goods, or take security as they think fit'. If the posse should uncover any meetings that are 'suspicious or excessive in number' they are to 'do justice upon them without delay'.[28] As Steven Justice stresses, the Rising 'blindsided' official England, but it also seems that a hypervigilance took hold afterward. This might be seen as crystallizing what H. Marshall Leicester has called the period's general 'disenchantment': the tendency for contemporaries to see in many institutions human rather than divine agency.[29] But disenchantment comes to different social groups in different ways and at different paces. For the rebels, 1381 marked the explosion of decades of cynicism about just how little royal tax officials and monastic landlords had their interests at heart.[30] For the higher estates and 'official England', the rudest awakening probably did not arrive until the Rising itself, when members of those social worlds were made exceedingly aware at a blow of how fragile the interlocking unity of the social world was.

Gower was well positioned to fasten on and speak to the mood of this aftermath. Among those commissioned on 8 March 1382 to ride through

---

behind that half-dreaming state, however, has apparently not been noted by Shakespeare scholars.

[28] *Calendar of the Patent Rolls Preserved in the Public Record Office: Richard II, 1381–1385* (London, 1897), vol. II, p. 138.

[29] H. Marshall Leicester, Jr, *The Disenchanted Self: Representing the Subject in the Canterbury Tales* (Berkeley, CA, 1990), pp. 26–8.

[30] See Rosamund Faith, 'The "great rumour" of 1377 and peasant ideology', in *The English Rising of 1381*, eds R. H. Hilton and T. H. Aston (Cambridge, 1984), pp. 43–74; Andrew Galloway, 'Making history legal: *Piers Plowman* and the rebels of fourteenth-century England', in *William Langland's Piers Plowman: A Book of Essays*, ed. Kathleen Hewett-Smith (New York, 2001), pp. 7–39.

and scrutinize Kent – hotbed of the Rising – was Sir Arnald Savage, later speaker of the Commons. Gower was to make Sir Arnald executor of his will, and Malcolm Parkes suggests that Savage was one of those responsible for compiling and distributing the post-mortem versions of Gower's Latin poetry.[31] With Sir Arnald on the commission was Sir William de Septvanz, who early in life had owed Gower a considerable amount of money, which he had repaid by selling Gower some valuable property cheaply in 1364. This sale involved Gower in a widely notorious parliamentary trial the following year, since William turned out to be underage,[32] but Gower managed to keep the property. He went on to sell most of it in 1373 to Sir John Cobham, third baron Cobham, also a Kent landowner, and thus also commissioned to join the 1382 Kent inquiry.[33]

The Kent commission provides an opportunity to see in action and close association a core group of Gower's social and perhaps literary contacts and patrons among the higher estates. From this group emerged other literary responses than Gower's to the Rising, for on the Kent commission too was Thomas Brinton, bishop of Rochester, famous for his learned and well-crafted sermons. Two of Brinton's sermons from this period recall Gower's *Vox Clamantis*, particularly its dream-vision of the Rising in book 1. On 16 March, just nine days after receiving the parliamentary commission with the other men of substance from Kent, Brinton preached a sermon on *Erumpe et clama* (Galatians 4:27) – 'Burst forth and cry out' – in which he says that preachers should declare the right way to all levels of society – yet magnates, 'middling' and 'popular' people are all now ignoring such voices. He himself, he says, should be a *vox clamantis in deserto* by declaring that the traditions should be properly maintained concerning who can be confessed, who absolved. We should not, he emphasises, let the blood of Archbishop Simon Sudbury (killed by the rebels in London), crying out for vengeance like Abel's blood from the ground, go unheard. Excommunications of anyone directly and without coercion involved in such actions must stand without any absolution by local clergy: *clamitat pro vindicta*.[34]

At a minimum, this shows that after 1381 the theme of a *vox clamantis* sounding the alarm was not Gower's unique theme. It is even possible that Brinton's sermon was written with some knowledge of Gower's *Vox* I; or perhaps Brinton had some knowledge of Gower's first version of the entire

---

[31] M. B. Parkes, 'Patterns of scribal activity and revisions of the text in early copies of works by John Gower', in *New Science Out of Old Books: Studies in Manuscripts and Early Printed Books in Honour of A. I. Doyle*, eds Richard Beadle and A. J. Piper (Aldershot, 1995), pp. 81–121.

[32] The details are in John Fisher, *John Gower: Moral Philosopher and Friend of Chaucer* (London, 1965), pp. 51–4 and 313–18; see also Mathew Giancarlo, *Parliament and Literature in Late Medieval England* (Cambridge, 2007), pp. 90–128 and Elliot Kendall, *Lordship and Literature: John Gower and the Politics of the Great Household* (Oxford, 2008), 38–41. None mentions Septvauns' connection to the 1382 Kent inquiry.

[33] On Cobham's career and his possible architectural and inscriptional response to the Rising, see Cristina Cervone, 'John de Cobham and Cooling Castle's charter poem', *Speculum*, 83 (2008), 884–916, and the essay by Carlson in this volume.

[34] Thomas Brinton, *The Sermons of Thomas Brinton, Bishop of Rochester (1373–1389)*, ed. Sister Mary Aquinas Devlin, 2 vols, continuous pag. (London, 1954), sermon 99, vol. II, p. 457.

Vox Clamantis, completed earlier and starting with what is now book II, Gower then fashioning a new opening to his work that capitalised on Brinton's bringing of the Rising into the same frame of reference; or some further combination of these interactions.[35] In any case, Brinton preached another sermon two months later, in May 1382, with the approaching summer probably stirring memories of the rebellion from the June before.[36] This sermon is still more suggestive of the atmosphere and themes of Gower's dream-vision of the Rising. Focused on the text *Vigilate*, 'Awake!' (I Peter 5), the sermon stresses that we should not be resting quiet but should instead be constantly alert to sin. Those who murdered Archbishop Sudbury or destroyed church property, Brinton stresses again, may not be absolved by priests or confessors; only the pope may absolve them. Just as the devil makes everyone who drinks the world's stupifying pleasures senselessly asleep in sin ('insensibilis et dormiunt in peccatis'), so we ought to awaken from such sins. Brinton then shifts to a non-allegorical Aristotelean expansion of his theme of sleep and wakefulness. Proper sleep, he says, regulates and restrains the body, allowing a good countenance, joyous face, sensible words, prudent counsel and graciousness. And just as the devil deceives many souls into sin by too much sleeping (or dreaming: the word *sompnia* can mean either), so excessive waking produces many other sins. Those excessively waking as well as those 'spending their nights in dreams' (or 'sleep'), Brinton concludes, are livid in color, fetid in smell, rash in their words and ungracious in their deeds.

The 'sleeping' of the English lords before the Rising is mentioned by at least one other contemporary: Thomas Walsingham, monk of St Albans, who, in his long account of the Rising, declares at one point that '[the peasants'] masters had not woken up to the need to oppose these evil acts, but like men who were fast asleep, remained quiet and inactive at home, that is, until the men of Kent and Essex met and joined forces, producing an army of about 100,000 common people and peasants.'[37] But Brinton, like Gower, plays this theme far more elaborately, and almost as bizarrely. For the shift in Brinton's sermon to what we would separate as a medical discourse of oversleeping and insomnia seems strange in the allegorical context of clergy being 'alert' to their duties, though no stranger than Gower's mixed registers in his dream-vision. As vigilance becomes the unlikely centre to Gower's dream-vision, so the need for more sleep becomes the odd coda to Brinton's sermon on *Vigilate*. For both, a mixture of kinds of argument about interpreting or controlling sinful appetite seems to respond to a sense of appetite unleashed by either the somnolence or the over-stimulation of reason. For both, this issue helped explain the problems of the social world:

---

[35] For the conclusive evidence of a pre-1381 version of the *Vox* lacking book 1, see Fisher, *John Gower*, pp. 101–9.

[36] Brinton, *The Sermons*, ed. Devlin, sermon 100, vol. II, pp. 458–62. Devlin's headnote gives 18 May 1381 for the sermon, an error for 1382.

[37] *The St Albans Chronicle: The 'Chronica maiora' of Thomas Walsingham, vol. 1, 1376–94*, eds and trans John Taylor, Wendy R. Childs and Leslie Watkiss (Oxford, 2003), pp. 414–15.

both Gower and Brinton suggest that those who rebelled were filled with new wakeful energy; both use the theme and the form of dreams and sleep to ponder the implications. Like Gower's, Brinton's focus is on the power of conscious human choice to transform human bodies and minds, directly or indirectly, and for better or worse.

It should be clear, however, that Gower's use of dreams and dream-expositions to focus on the unstable relation between ideas and appetites and their joint power over the social and natural world did not begin or end with the Rising. Just as he portrays self-deceptive and manipulative dream-vision narrators under 'somnolence' in the *Mirour*, so under into the category of 'somnolence' in the *Confessio Amantis* from the 1390s appears a yet more complicated instance of dreams and dream-exposition. The instance now is the transparent plea of Amans, the narrator of Gower's long English poem, to manipulate reality to fit his wish-fulfilment dreams. This is followed by Genius's retelling of the story from Ovid of Ceix and Alceone, also found, like the topic of 'half-sleeping', in Guillaume de Machaut's *Fonteinne Amoreuse*.

In the *Confessio* the Lover's remarks about his own dreams of being with his beloved seem at first innocent forms of self-gratification, suppressing (like Somnolence in the *Mirour*) any sense of destructive consequences or 'perdicioun'. But as the Lover's views unfold he reveals his desire to retreat into his dream forever, with more sinister implications:

> Bot after, whanne I hiede take,
> And schal arise upon the morwe,
> Thanne is al torned into sorwe,
> Noght for the cause I schal arise,
> Bot for I mette in such a wise,
> And ate last I am bethoght
> That al is vein and helpeth noght.
> Bot yit me thenketh be my wille
> I wolde have leie and slepe stille,
> To meten evere of such a swevene,
> For thanne I hadde a slepi hevene. (*Confessio*, IV, lines 2906–16)

Ultimately, this moment looks back to the *Roman de la Rose* where the God of Love tells the Lover that he will sometimes ecstatically dream that he is holding his lover 'entre tes braz trestote nue' but will then awake and lament that he does not really have her, enduring more pain than ever: 'God! Shall I ever see the day when I may actually be in the situation that I imagine? I would want it even with the condition that I should die straightway' (lines 2427–50). In Gower, however, the glance at death becomes more direct, and the effect of such a reaction to cold reality disturbingly parallels Alceone's response to her nightmare of seeing her husband Ceix dead, which Genius goes on to describe:

> Upon the morwe and up sche sterte,
> And to the see, wher that sche mette
> The bodi lay, withoute lette
> Sche drowh, and whan that sche cam ny,

> Stark ded, hise armes sprad, sche syh
> Hire lord flietende upon the wawe.
> Wherof hire wittes ben withdrawe,
> And sche, which tok of deth no kepe,
> Anon forth lepte into the depe ... (*Confessio*, IV, lines 3078–86)

Juxtaposing Alceone's visions with the Lover's certainly deflates any pretentions by the latter to visionary authority. But the juxtaposition has further effects as well. The Lover's sadness at awakening and 'thinking by my will' – a phrase that, significantly, describes intellection driven by appetite – is shown to hold the potential for a wish to die, just as Alceone attempts suicide after finding her husband dead. So, too, the Lover's willed escapism in turn offers a lens for seeing Alceone's and Ceix's half-hidden responsibility for the horrible outcome of their story. Ceix flees Alceone in a distracted haste to help his brother, ignoring her wrenching pleas and his own immediate second thoughts, which return to his mind as he drowns. She in turn is drowned, figurally and (almost) literally, by her sorrow. The story presents human need as oceanic in power, but also as generated by choice and thought, and as subject to equally powerful external consequences. As the tale of Ceix and Alceone unfolds, the Lover's self-indulgent desire to keep sleeping thus acquires a long shadow. Human beings may be far more responsible for fortune than they think, as Gower insists throughout his poetry: 'That we fortune clepe so | Out of the man himself it groweth' (*Confessio*, Prol., lines 548–9). His dream-visions show with particular emphasis that such responsibility derives from a mixture of appetites and rational interpretations that keeps even reason from having transcendent authority.

This is not a perspective that either courtly or religious dream-vision poets could easily continue. Gower's reassessments of the dream-vision form throughout his career progressively and caustically dissolve its claims to revealing suprahuman powers, while using the form to explore the connections between human thought and interpretation and human needs and appetites. To trace the reception of Gower's reassessments of dream-visions in English literature we must look outside the dream-vision tradition. Indeed, perhaps in part because of the stresses to which Gower and others subjected it, that tradition ceases as a prestigious literary vehicle of any kind by the end of the fifteenth century.[38] The pathetically mixed motives of Gower's insatiable Lover who uses dreams to 'think by his will' that he should remain asleep, and perhaps die, can, however, be seen behind other works. I have already mentioned Marlowe and Milton, but there may be more proximate responses to Gower's concerns with human manipulations

---

[38] For a wider view of that history see Andrew Galloway, 'Visions and visionaries', in *The Oxford Handbook of Medieval Literature*, eds Elaine Treharne and Greg Walker (Oxford, forthcoming 2010). Outside the continuation of a prestigious literary genre, prophetic claims about dreams continued to emerge at least into the seventeenth century, especially in periods of general political instability such as the Commonwealth: see Keith Thomas, *Religion and the Decline of Magic* (New York, 1971), pp. 128–32.

of and responses to visions. In a famous sonnet in Samuel Daniel's sonnet sequence *Delia*, of 1592, the narrator shows a similar pairing of dream-wishes and dream-interpretation that is now overtly death-embracing:

> Care-charmer sleepe, sonne of the Sable night,
> Brother to death, in silent darknes borne:
> Relieue my languish, and restore the light,
> With darke forgetting of my cares returne.
>   And let the day be time enough to morne,
> The shipwrack of my ill-aduentred youth:
> Let waking eyes suffice to wayle theyr scorne,
> Without the torment of the nights vntruth.
>   Cease dreames, th'ymagery of our day desires,
> To modell foorth the passions of the morrow:
> Neuer let rysing Sunne approue you lyers,
> To adde more griefe to aggrauat my sorrow.
>   Still let me sleepe, imbracing clowdes in vaine;
>   And neuer wake, to feel the dayes disdayne.[39]

Gower remade the dream-vision genre into a new tool of subjective as well as social analysis of need and rationalization, and his disenchanted refashioning of it to those ends established crucial foundations for later poets and many other thinkers, allowing those too to reassess shadowy appetites and their consequences with eyes half-open.

---

[39] From the 1592 text, in Samuel Daniel, *Samuel Daniel: Poems, and A Defence of Ryme*, ed. Arthur Colby Sprague (Cambridge, MA, 1930), p. 33.

Chapter 24

John Gower's French and His Readers

R. F. YEAGER

The collected works of the English poet John Gower, who died in 1408, run to about 30,000 lines divided into Latin, Middle English and some form of French, at roughly a third each. Linguistically speaking he deserves to be called, as he often is, a bit of a fence-sitter, or a bet-hedger, but there is of course another way to look at Gower's three languages. Indeed, he suggests it himself (for I am quite convinced that the words are his own) in a Latin poem supposedly penned by 'a certain philosopher' and known, from its first two words, as 'Eneidos, Bucolis'.[1] In it, Gower is found superior to Virgil, whose 'justly famous' three works the *Aeneid*, the *Bucolics* and the *Georgics* are all nonetheless only in Latin, while Gower 'wrote [...] three poems in three languages, | So that broader schooling might be given to men' ('Te tua set trinis tria scribere carmina linguis | Constat, ut inde viris sit scola lata magis'). Now, if indeed Gower, 'fingens se auctor esse Philosophorem', wrote that about himself, we have reason to take a somewhat greater account than we have yet of differences in the kinds of work he produced in each of his three languages.[2]

Clearly, Gower the writer of French who ought to stand outlined visibly before us had different ambitions for each of the poems he wrote. Because of his evident trilingual fluency, he could make choices – and must have – about the use to which he put each language.[3] Although he never says specifically, in a theoretical way, what he is up to, Gower does come pretty close in the Prologue of the *Confessio Amantis* when he states that:

---

[1] For a full text and translation, see my own *John Gower: The Minor Latin Works* (Kalamazoo, MI, 2005), pp. 84–6. See also Macaulay, iv, 361 (Latin text only). Unless otherwise specified, all subsequent references to the works of Gower are from Macaulay.

[2] See the Latin commentary Gower wrote for his own *Confessio Amantis*, book I, line 60: 'Hic quasi in persona aliorum, quos amor alligat, fingens se auctor esse Amantem, varias eorum passiones variis huius libri distinccionibus per singula scribere proponit' ('Here, as if in the guise of others whom love constrains, the author, feigning himself to be the Lover, proposes to write one by one about their different passions, in the various sections of this book').

[3] An interesting recent take on what French may have meant to Gower's unconscious is Jane Gilbert, 'Men behaving badly: linguistic purity and sexual perversity in Derrida's *Le Monolinguisme de l'autre* and Gower's *Traitié pour essampler les amantz marietz*', *Romance Studies*, 24 (2006), 77–89. Gilbert's argument has class and political implications: see esp. pp. 85, 87.

>   ... for that fewe men endite
>   In oure englissh, I thenke make
>   A bok for Engelondes sake (*Confessio*, Prol, lines 22–*24)

– or 'king Richardes sake', depending on the version. And Gower is, I think, making a similar statement, albeit not in so many words, when at the end of his life he seems greatly to prefer writing in Latin.[4]

Given that my present concern is the nature of Gower's French and his audience, it is relevant to observe that this apparent preference for using Latin and English in serious works written after 1399 – along with their relative percentages: one poem in English to a dozen in Latin to zero in French – is transparently political.[5] John Fisher and others have made much of Henry V's commitment to English in government documents and personal letters, but, like Richard II, Henry IV also approved of and promoted English.[6] (Henry IV, for example, left the first royal will in English; his son, whose will is in English too, might thus be thought of as merely following paternal precedent).[7] Thus when Gower selects English to write pointedly to Henry IV in an attempt to temper policy, as he does in 'In Praise of Peace', we need to note the politics of its language. We may say the same of the Latin pieces: Gower also addresses Henry, seemingly directly, in briefer poems 'Rex celi deus', 'O recolende' and 'H. aquile pullus' in particular, all of which reflect upon his rulership; and the substantial *Cronica Tripertita*, as the dedicatory epistle to Archbishop Arundel that prefaces the All Souls manuscript so obsequiously testifies, was composed to please an intensely partisan, Lancastrian readership as well.[8]

If, following the now fully enshrined theoretical principle that 'absence is presence', there does not seem to be a scrap of serious writing in French

---

[4] With the lone exception of the poem 'To King Henry IV/In Praise of Peace' in Middle English, and one other exception discussed below.

[5] See Derek Pearsall, 'Gower's Latin in the *Confessio Amantis*', in *Latin and Vernacular: Studies in Late-Medieval Texts and Manuscripts*, ed. A. J. Minnis (Cambridge, 1989), pp. 13–25; Siân Echard, 'Gower's books of Latin: language, politics and poetry', *SAC*, 25 (2003), 123–56; and further my own 'Politics and the French language in England during the Hundred Years' War: the case of John Gower', in *Inscribing the Hundred Years' War in French and English Cultures*, ed. Denise Baker (Albany, NY, 2000), pp. 127–57.

[6] J. H. Fisher, 'A language policy for Lancastrian England', *PMLA*, 107 (1992), 1168–80; on Richard II's promotion of English, see 'Did Richard encourage the English language?', in T. Jones, R. F. Yeager, T. Dolan, A. Fletcher and J. Dor, *Who Murdered Chaucer? A Medieval Mystery* (London, 2003), pp. 35–9.

[7] For the wills of Henry IV and Henry V, see J. Nichols, ed., *A Collection of All the Wills, now known to be extant, of the Kings and Queens of England, Princes and Princesses of Wales, and Every Branch of the Royal Blood, from the reign of William the Conqueror to that of Henry the Seventh, exclusive; with explanatory notes and a glossary* (London, 1780), pp., respectively, 203–6, 236–42. English seems to have run in the blood of the direct Lancastrian line: Henry VI's will is also in English (pp. 291–319); those of Richard II and Edward IV, however, are in Latin (respectively, pp. 191–202, 345–8).

[8] For the full text and translation of 'Rex celi deus', 'O recolende' and 'H. aquile pullus' see my own *Minor Latin Works*, pp. 43–5, 46–7; also Macaulay, iv, 343–5. For the epistle to Arundel, see Macaulay iv, 1–2 (Latin only); John Gower, *The Major Latin Works of John Gower*, trans. Eric Stockton (Seattle, WA, 1962), pp. 47–8. See also Lynn Staley, 'Gower, Richard II, Henry of Derby, and the business of making culture', *Speculum*, 75 (2000), 68–96.

extant which we can attribute indisputably to Gower's latter years (save one, and that a compromised example, as I shall point out shortly), then that dearth must be political too, in one way or another. At the very least, it logically reflects what Gower thought could be done with, and in, French, and for whom – all decisions political in the broad sense, in other words. And this leads us, via an unwavering line, directly to identifying Gower's readership – which, for purposes of discussion, we may divide into two lots: those for whom he probably wrote intentionally, targeting their interests and hopeful of striking the bull's eye, and those who read his work unbeknownst to him, picking up a copy from, say, the collection of a friend.

This latter group, although no less interesting than the former – indeed, in several ways the more interesting – can be addressed here in shorter space. There is, after all, very little evidence one can muster regarding who, around 600 or so years ago, borrowed a manuscript or read over a friend's shoulder, or heard that friend reading poetry aloud across a crowded room. Nonetheless, we have been gifted with one solid case which is worth discussing for more reasons than its singularity alone. There exists in the British Library a manuscript – London, BL MS Stowe 951 – which contains three pieces: an English translation of John of Hildesheim's *Historia Trium Regum* (better known as *The Three Kings of Cologne*); a Middle English poem *Speculum Vitae* (*The Mirror of Life*), thought by many the work of William of Nassington; and something called there 'Exhortacio Contra Vicium Adulterii'. This proves to be a Yorkshire-dialect translation of the eighteen French balades that make up Gower's *Traitié Pour Essampler les Amantz Marietz*, to which has been added a prefatory stanza, or prologue, and a nineteenth balade by way of a summing-up. Both are claimed by the translator, who identifies himself (one supposes) as 'Quixley' in the prologue stanza. Henry Noble MacCracken, who edited the *Traitié* translation for the *Yorkshire Archaeological Journal* in 1909, identified the translator/poet Quixley as one John Quixley of Quixley Hall, a minor landholder whose daughter Alice was married in September 1402.[9] MacCracken posited that the careful *pater* John Quixley gave his translation to young Alice as a wedding present.

Well, perhaps. Who knows what the Quixley *pere et fille* were like at home? But, in general, balade sequences fulminating against adultery are not the sort of thing most fathers think of as wedding gifts for daughters, and so conceivably we ought to look beyond MacCracken's suggestions for other explanations. Nonetheless, it is important to take up his notion of authorship here, because if he was correct about who and what Quixley was it suggests some important things about Gower's audience. So does the date. Gower was still alive in 1402, and could have been aware of Quixley – perhaps even supplying him with a copy of the *Traitié*. MacCracken, noting that Quixley Hall was only a few miles away from Stittenham, where lived a family of Gowers, supposed that they, as proud relations of the famous London poet, shared their manuscript with their neighbour. But how close John Gower

---

[9] H. N. MacCracken, 'Quixley's Ballades Royal (?1402)', *YAJ*, 20 (1909), 33–50; for his argument regarding authorship, see pp. 37–9.

might have been to the Gowers of Stittenham remains unclear – and in any case, what is most intriguing about MacCracken's Quixley candidate, apart from the date, is his social class.[10] If someone like John Quixley were reading John Gower's *Traitié* in its original language in 1402 it means that at the beginning of the fifteenth century we might infer the poet's French audience to include literate regional gentry like the Knevet family of Norfolk or, in slightly different guise, a Robert Thornton or a Sir John Paston – or even a rural John Carpenter, whose library was easily old-fashioned enough to have included Gower.[11] And, in that event, we ought to be pondering potential lines of distribution and dissemination among readers of this class from Southwark to points north, and potentially elsewhere.[12]

But of course, nothing we know of any of these readers' collections indicates that they possessed a jot of Gower's in French. And, in any case, MacCracken quite probably mistook 'Quixley' by a couple of decades and more than that number of leagues. A likelier candidate is one Robert de Quixley, who became prior of Nostell Priory and prebend of Bramham in 1393, maintaining both posts until his death in 1427.[13] Both priory and prebend lie within the honour of Pontefract, the great Lancastrian strong-

---

[10] J. Hurt Fisher seems fairly to have settled the question of John Gower's origins in Kent, with small likelihood of any connection with the Gowers of Stittenham, a 'family prominent after the 16th century': see *John Gower, Moral Philosopher and Friend of Chaucer* (New York, 1964), p. 41.

[11] On such readers, see, generally, A. I. Doyle, 'English books in and out of court from Edward III to Henry VII', in *English Court Culture in the Later Middle Ages*, eds V. J. Scattergood and J. W. Sherborne (London, 1983), pp. 163–81. On the Knevets, see F. Wormald and C. E. Wright, eds, *The English Library before 1700: Studies in Its History* (London, 1958), p. 158; on Thornton, see J. J. Thompson, *Robert Thornton and His Book-Producing Activities: Aspects of the Transmission of Certain Medieval Texts in the Light of Their Present Context in Thornton's Manuscripts* (York, 1983); on Paston, see *Paston Letters and Papers of the Fifteenth Century*, ed. N. Davis (Oxford, 1971), vol. I, pp. 516–18, 574–5; on Carpenter, see T. Brewer, *Memoir of the Life and Times of John Carpenter* (London, 1836; rpt 1856).

[12] The idea is important to consider, nevertheless: as Jocelyn Wogan-Brown has reminded me in a private communication, 'the first burst of Francophone pastoralia is northern', northern links with France were significant via well-placed ports and 'however un-*Anglo-Normanisant* and Paris-centered Gower's French might be, that doesn't mean the north couldn't have an active French reception context and connections from north to south along which it sought works such as the *Traitié*.'

[13] York Archiepis, Reg. Arundel, fol. 43; W. Dugdale, *Monasticon Anglicanum: A History of the Abbies and Other Monasteries, Hospitals, Friaries, and Cathedral and Collegiate Churches, with their dependencies, in England and Wales; also of all such Scotch, Irish, and French Monasteries as were in any manner connected with religious houses in England...*, rev. edn, eds J. Caley, H. Ellis and B. Bandinel, 6 vols in 9, vol. 6 in 3 pts (London, 1830), 6, 1, p. 91, also prints a chronology of the Nostell priors. A third possibility has been raised obliquely by Ralph Hanna, who notes, 'Quixley is a name derived from a place, modern Whixley, six miles east of Knaresborough. Three later Ripon chaplains share the name and presumably came from there, John, Robert and William'; see 'Some North Yorkshire scribes and their context', in *Medieval Texts in Context*, eds G. D. Caie and D. Renevey (London, 2008), pp. 167–91 (p. 173). This John Quixley, suggested by Hanna, flourished *c.*1478, his Robert and William *c.*1501. Taking the name of one's place of origin was commonplace for those in orders – and is evident in the form of Prior Robert de Quixley's name. Like the three suggested by Hanna, Prior Robert had connections with the village of Quixley, near Ripon. On the language of BL MS Stowe 951, see *LALME*, iii, p. 646 (linguistic profile 526), although NB: the entry analyses only *Speculum Vitae*, locating its origin near Liverpool; *Historia Trium Regum* and 'Quixley's' translation, however, are noted simply as 'not NM'.

hold; Bramham, indeed, being triangularly but about fourteen miles from there, and from York, and in the ducal gift. Nostell Priory, of which nothing now remains, stood a bit further to the south-west. Notably, Nostell was an Austin priory, as was St Mary Overey in Southwark where Gower lived, doubtless as a corrodian, from the late 1370s until his death in 1408. There are several reasons to suspect an Augustinian origin for 'Quixley's' translation, and this Austin connection of Southwark and Nostell thus opens yet another possible conduit for the dissemination and transport of Gower's balades northward.[14] From 1215, Augustinian abbots and priors were required to gather every three years at Chapter for several days of deliberation, in venues that on occasion included Nostell and London.[15] Books are known to have passed for copying from one Austin house to another; certainly the triennials provide a plausible means, as might too the regular site-by-site visitation of three overseeing canons, selected at the triennial Chapters from different houses in rotation.[16] Finally, among the few facts as yet brought to light regarding Robert de Quixley are one or two suggestive of his cast of mind, and therefore intriguing. The longest tenured of its priors, he seems to have laboured successfully to restore not just Nostell's fiscal footing but its moral balance also – and to have been a believer in the power of books to effect the process.[17] Either under his direction or (more

---

[14] William of Nassington, possibly the poet of the *Speculum Vitae*, may have been an Augustinian; certainly John Waldeby was, for whom prayers are solicited in two manuscripts of the *Speculum*. (On Waldeby, see especially M. J. Morrin, *John Waldeby, OSA, c.1315–c.1372: English Augustinian Preacher and Writer: With a Critical Edition of His Tract on the 'Ave Maria'* (Rome, 1972–4). Potentially more indicative is 'Quixley's' use of Augustine's *Confessions* and *De nuptiis et concupiscentia* in the balade he wrote himself (XIX) as an addendum to the *Traitié*. See my full discussion in the introduction to my edition/translation, *John Gower: Cinkante Balades and Traitié Pour les Amantz Marietz* (Kalamazoo, MI, forthcoming 2010).

[15] *Chapters of the Augustinian Canons*, ed. H. E. Salter (London, 1922), pp. ix–x.

[16] Extant Chapter Acts are incomplete, especially for those held in the south, but Acts from Chapters hosted by northern houses have Nostell several times a gathering-place. While no known record survives of St Mary Overey as host, the Acts of the Chapter at Newstead in 1371 have the priors of Southwark and Nostell both present; at the Northampton Chapter in 1404 Southwark is unlisted, but Nostell is in attendance alongside the priors of Twynham and Southwick, two closely related houses from the see of Winchester, which also included Southwark. See *Chapters*, ed. Salter, pp. 69, 80. On the passing of manuscripts between Austin houses, see A. Lawrence, 'A northern English school? Patterns of production and collection of manuscripts in the Augustinian houses of Yorkshire in the twelfth and thirteenth centuries', in *Yorkshire Monasticism: Archaeology, Art and Architecture, from the 7th to the 16th Centuries*, ed. L. R. Hoey (Leeds, 1995), pp. 145–53; and, further, the discussion of Jean-Pascal Pouzet in this volume.

[17] Not that many Austin priors would have thought otherwise: the Augustinian Rule predicates the availability of books, for liturgy, reading aloud at meals and individual devotions as well. See, e.g., *The Bridlington Dialogue*: 'Proinde quoniam oratio et lectio potiora sunt quam quelibet exterior actio, ipsa quoque lectio sagina quedam est orationis, potioribus propensiorem curam modo clam, modo palam impendamus. Cum enim oramus, cum Deo loquitur. Cum autem legimus, nobiscum Deus loquitur' ('Further, since prayer and reading are to be preferred to any outward activity, and reading is, moreover, the sustenance of prayer, we should devote ourselves more earnestly to those more desirable pursuits, sometimes in private, and sometimes in public. For when we pray, we speak to God; and when we read, God speaks to us'). Text from Robert of Bridlington, *The Bridlington Dialogue: An Exposition of the Rule of St Augustine for the Life of the Clergy*, trans. A Religious of C. S. M. V [R. P. Lawson] (London, 1960), 162, 163a. It was a lasting position in the order: 'Codices',

probably) from his own hand, an Act Book of Nostell's priors was written 'by way of example for the servants of God' ('ad exemplum servorum dei').[18] Such a man would have known how to employ Gower's *Traitié* had it fallen into his hands via one route or another.

But, whoever he was, 'Quixley' represents our first category of reader, the serendipitous reader, whose presence one infers but can seldom – as apparently in this case – identify with certainty. For we can be sure that neither John nor Robert de Quixley was in Gower's sights when he wrote the *Traitié*. What about our second audience, then – those for whom Gower thought he was writing in French? Paradoxically enough, Robert de Quixley, Prior of Nostell, is in one important sense very probably just the reader – or at least, just the *kind* of reader – Gower had in mind. BL MS Stowe 951 looks like a compendium-in-process for priory use. Certainly it is easier to imagine Yorkshire canons reading Gower's *Traitié* with appreciation than it is a Yorkshire bride – or a Flemish immigrant bride, for that matter. Macaulay's long-held assumption – seconded by John Fisher, along with nearly everyone else who has seen fit to comment – that Gower wrote the *Traitié* as a wedding present for his own bride, Agnes Groundolf, on the occasion of their marriage in 1398 is unjustified, too, and smacks of nineteenth-century masculinist supposition.[19] Subject matter aside, the formal structure of the eighteen *Traitié* balades, all but the last lacking envoys, suggests strongly an earlier moment of composition c.1385–90 – during the period, in other words, following the death in 1377 of Machaut, champion and model of the envoy-less balade, and the subsequently successful dominance of Deschamps's envoyed balades, a style he developed, he tells us in his *L'Art de Dictier*, deliberately to break free from his old master.[20]

This formal distinction – balade with or without envoy, Machauldian or Deschampian – lends perspective on Gower's other sequence, the so-called *Cinkante Balades* ('so-called' because there are actually fifty-three. In the sole extant manuscript copy, London, BL Additional MS 59495, formerly and more memorably known as Trentham, two balades have been numbered 'IIII' and two dedicatory balades to Henry IV appended). As I have suggested elsewhere, that the *Cinkante Balades* have envoys indicates Gower's probable familiarity with the most famous collection of late-fourteenth-century balades, the *Livre de Cent Ballades*, begun by Jean de Saint-Pierre, seneschal d'Eu, c.1386.[21] The *Livre de Cent Ballades* is a love debate, the first fifty being a dialogue between an old knight and a young about the proper ways to wage

---

stated Robert Richardson (c.1530), 'sunt religiosorum armature, contra diaboli tentationem' ('Books are the armour of the religious against the temptation of the devil'); see Robertus Richardinus, *Commentary on the Rule of St Augustine by Robertus Richardinus*, ed. G. G. Coulton (Edinburgh, 1935), p. 146.

[18] *De gestis et actibus priorum monasterii sancti Oswaldi*, from the prologue; Leeds, District Archives MS NP/c1, fol. 84. On Robert de Quixley's probable authorship, see my discussion in *John Gower: Cinkante Balades and Traitié Pour les Amantz Marietz* (pp. 85–6).

[19] Fisher, *John Gower*, pp. 85–6.

[20] For a suggested date of composition even earlier, see Hume in this volume.

[21] That is, in 'John Gower's audience: the Ballades', *CR*, 40 (2005), 81–105.

war and love. An impasse being reached, the opinion of others is solicited, provoking responses by the *crème de la crème* of French chivalric society: Philippe d'Artois, count of Eu, the younger Bouccicaut, Jean de Cresécque, Regnaut de Trie, later the Admiral of France, Jean de Chambrillac, seneschal of Périgord, the dukes of Orléans and Berry, and – quite interestingly for our purposes – Guillaume de Trignonville, friend of Deschamps, Christine de Pizan, and François d'Auberchicourt, whose father Eustace fought with the Black Prince in Spain, and whose relation Jean, a long-time Lancastrian retainer and confidant of John of Gaunt, was probably known to both Chaucer and Gower. Oton de Granson, from whose work Chaucer borrows, composed his own balade responses to *Le Livre c.*1390–91, when the sequence was all the rage in Paris.

So Gower probably had a target as well as a model when he wrote his *Cinkante Balades*. The title is a clue – as are the two dedicatory balades (the second of which is fragmentary, alas!) to Henry IV addressed as 'gentils Rois'. These two dedicatory balades together constitute the anomalous example I mentioned earlier of Gower's post-usurpation French work. They have misled some of the few readers his balades have attracted over the years into the belief that Gower may have written the entire *Cinkante Balades* sequence for Henry, but this is clearly impossible – there simply were not sufficient hours in the day after 1399, when Gower had so much else in hand, including the *Cronica Tripertita*, revisions to the *Vox Clamantis*, at least three shorter Latin poems and the Middle English 'In Praise of Peace'. Besides, such stuff had passed its moment. Whether one views the reign of Henry IV as heady times – at least at the beginning – or bloody, the balade sequence concerned with love had no market at the flint-eyed opening of the fifteenth century.

No market, that is, except as a propitiatory gift to Henry, who, as a participant in the great tournament held at St Inglevert in 1390 had jousted and feasted with the poets of the *Livre de Cent Ballades* even as that collection circulated for the first time. It must have been a shrewd guess on Gower's part that Henry would have known what he was getting in the *Cinkante Balades*, and appreciated it as the only effort by one of his countrymen to emulate, if not overtop, his continental friends and poets-in-arms. Oddly enough, Henry's gladness at such a present might have been especially high just after taking power, because we have evidence that at this time the usurper believed that poets singing a prince's praises and competing with each other around the palace were a necessary (for which read, 'legitimating') pendant to power – an idea he acquired, one thinks, from spending time in 1398 with Gian Galeazzo Visconti, overlord of Milan, who had a less pressing but nonetheless related problem justifying his own right to rule. Not coincidentally, perhaps, both Visconti and Henry attempted to recruit Christine de Pizan to join their retinues as writer-in-residence in 1401–2.[22] Thus it is important, in thinking about Gower's French audience, to recognize

---

[22] Christine tells the story herself: see Christine de Pizan, *Christine de Pizan: Le Livre de l'Advision Christine*, eds C. Reno and L. Dulac (Paris, 2001), pp. 112–13.

Henry as an example of a reader of the second kind – not, that is, someone like Prior Robert de Quixley, whose essentially serendipitous contact with the *Traitié* Gower undoubtedly never engineered, but rather someone whom Gower knew and specifically intended to read his French poems.

Yet (paradoxically again), for all their categorical differences, in another very instructive way Henry and Robert de Quixley are indeed alike as readers. The two dedicatory balades excepted, Gower did not write any of the *Cinkante Balades* for Henry the man. He clearly did, however, assemble his sequence as an answer of his own to the challenge of French *chevalier* poets of Henry's *type*, his *class*. In the same way, the needs of Quixley the Austin prior of Nostell – not those of the individual Robert de Quixley, the particular Yorkshireman who penned the translation – were likely, as a type or class, to have influenced Gower's design and execution of the *Traitié*. Both of these claims have implications worth considering – but before doing so, it is necessary to say something about Gower's largest French project, the *Mirour de l'Omme*. Whom might Gower have had in mind as his readership for that?

I have left the *Mirour* untouched until now because in many ways it is both his most difficult work to peg as to audience, and also the simplest. The *Mirour*'s sources and formal inspiration are theological and confessional (i.e., the plea to the Virgin at the end) to a degree that Gower never attempts elsewhere. It is also – at least the bulk of it, up to the Marian prayer – the earliest work of his we have. Moreover, Gower probably shifted his target audience during the *Mirour*'s writing from a circle of pious *chevaliers* exemplified by Henry of Grosmont, first duke of Lancaster and author of the Anglo-French *Livre de Seyntz Medicines* (d. 1361) to the Austin canons of St Mary Overey, among whom he took up residence about 1378, and for whose library and use I believe he finally finished the poem, following a number of years' hiatus.[23] The *Mirour* itself thus reflects in a single work something of the two different, but yet similar, audiences I have projected for the *Cinkante Balades* and the *Traitié*: aristocratic Lancastrians and men of the cloth.

What, then, can we learn from such observable confluences in Gower's French poems? Well, first and foremost, perhaps, that there is much more work to do before we fill in lines of understanding currently being laid down. More specifically – and by way of suggesting directions such work might take – I will conclude with four points.

First, Gower's French vocabulary. As Brian Merrilees has demonstrated, Gower's French is closer to that of France than to the usage of his English predecessors and contemporaries.[24] This clearly reflects Gower's identifiable reading. While true Anglo-Norman works like Thomas of Kent's *Roman de Toute Chevalerie* are represented in the works from which he borrows, none-

---

[23] I make this argument at some length in 'Gower's French audience: the *Mirour de l'Omme*', *CR*, 41 (2006), 111–37.

[24] See B. Merrilees and H. Pagan, 'John Barton, John Gower and Others: Variation in Late Anglo-French', in *Language and Culture in Medieval Britain: The French of England 1100–1500*, ed. Jocelyn Wogan-Browne et al. (York, 2009), 118–34.

theless French books written by Frenchmen in France greatly outnumber them.[25] These latter being Gower's models – and especially given his centonic poetic proclivities – it is unsurprising that a significant measure of his lexicon is Central French.[26] What will, I suspect, prove more intriguing with further research is the influence of his intended readership on his product. In the process of editing and translating Gower's two balade sequences for publication I am becoming aware of vocabulary found in the balades but not in the *Mirour*. Ruling out such obvious site-specific words as 'benefice' and 'circumcision' (in the *Mirour*, not in the balades), or 'Cupide' (the reverse), one finds, alone in the balades, examples such as 'gai' (*Balades*, 36, lines 2, 10) and 'enmaladis' (*Balades*, 14, lines 3, 19); both are Central French forms. Intriguing also is a word such as 'chois' – another Central French form which Gower uses three times, one each in the *Mirour*, *Cinkante Balades* and *Traitié*, but only in a 'fin amour' context; and similarly 'cristal/cristall', once in the *Mirour* and three times in *Cinkante Balades*, always conjoined to ladies' eyes. Gower, it is plain, recognized the dialect – in every sense of that term – that his courtly readers employed to converse amongst themselves, and 'Frenchified' his own Anglo-Norman (as well as tailoring his poetic forms) to claim his legitimacy as an equal participant in the discourse. His balades, then, should be deemed an ambitious enterprise in more ways than one.

The second point regards what the appearance of the *Traitié* in the hands of the prior of Nostell (assuming my identification of Robert de Quixley as the Yorkshire translator is correct), and the use he found for it, indicates about communication between Austin canonical houses – and Austin canons, *inter se* – under the Lancastrians. Very probably this should prove more revelatory about the 'unintended' category of Gower's readers, but perhaps not altogether, since, as I remarked earlier, Gower must have written the *Traitié* in expectation of readers at St Mary Overey. As readers, one Austin canon may have been, for him, as good as another. But, beyond this, the demonstrable presence of a *Traitié* in two Austin priories many miles, if only a decade or two, apart could be another significant clue to transmission of French books between confraternal libraries, and hence of late medieval reading patterns as well. And so, *ipso facto*, can the 'Quixley' translation itself. Assuming, as I think probable, that Gower's *Traitié* was translated as part of a programme of Robert de Quixley's to introduce morally redemptive reading into his canons' reach, what does it mean about the state of French fluency in Yorkshire in the 1420s that in BL MS Stowe 951 'Quixley' retains all Gower's original Latin commentaries to the *Traitié* balades, and even writes one of his own (albeit rather clumsily) to accompany Balade 19, even as he turns Gower's French into English? Again, the testimony of the Chapter Acts may shed some light here: at the triennial at Northampton in

---

[25] Particularly helpful on this point are Ardis Butterfield, '*Confessio Amantis* and the French tradition', in *Companion*, pp. 165–80, and Peter Nicholson, *Love and Ethics in Gower's 'Confessio Amantis'* (Ann Arbor, MI, 2005).

[26] On Gower's use of cento, see my 'Did Gower write Cento?', in *John Gower: Recent Readings*, ed. R. F. Yeager (Kalamazoo, MI, 1989), pp. 113–32.

1325 a statute was passed enjoining canons needing to speak during the hours of silence to use only Latin or French; but by 1443 sermons were delivered at the Osney Chapter only in English and Latin.[27] Such evidence requires thoughtful investigation.

The third point regards the politics of Gower's lexical self-consciousness, and the aesthetics. I have already noted the political nature of Gower's election of English, Latin or French for each particular project. Clearly, even the single-word lexical decisions of dialect such as those I have just mentioned, although *in parvo,* are precisely the same in political terms as the larger choice of one tongue or another rendered with an eye toward swaying an audience. Hence to say that the *Mirour de l'Omme* was written in French because Henry of Grosmont (and Edward III) read and wrote that language is a complex statement, freighted with intelligence no less about Gower's allegiances than about his art. It would be fruitful, I think, to look for lexical correlations of the vocabulary of Grosmont's *Livre de Seyntz Medicines* with the earlier portions of the *Mirour* – and not simply by way of establishing a more accurate date for the writing of the poem. In this regard, the Lancastrian presence and the proximity and appointive power of Pontefract may be multiplicitously revealing of language, as well.[28]

And, finally, on politics and art again. Dedicatory poem number one to Henry IV, prefacing the *Cinkante Balades* in the Trentham manuscript, is followed there by Latin verses, also addressed to Henry. They contain, I think, two significant unveilings of Gower's uncommon linguistic self-awareness being applied to his readership – of Gower caught in the act, to steal a line from Yeats, of being 'the Political Man' – both *in macro* (that is, how, for reasons of national politics, as well as for personal advancement, he sized up and appealed to a *known* reader – i.e., category two) and *in micro* (that is, of the poet pulling the cover off his decision-making process regarding work of what kind to express in what language). In the third stanza of the dedicatory (French) balade, Gower describes the poem he writes, in rather lovely fashion, as a locus (rendered literally) 'where the songs flower' ('u sont les ditz floriz'). This, very clearly, is intended to contrast with the Latin verses following. As he tells us in the following stanza (what is, technically, in a Deschampian balade, the envoy, although here, in all probability, the appended Latin was intended to serve that function as well): 'Here following is flawless language, | Because in Latin I have written my message' ('Ci ensuant ert de perfit langage, | Dont en latin ma sentence ai compris').[29]

---

[27] *Chapters*, ed. Salter, pp. 14, pp. xxxi–xxxii.
[28] On the *Livre* of Henry of Grosmont and Gower's *Mirour*, see my 'Gower's French audience: the *Mirour*'.
[29] Gower's fourth stanza is 'O gentils Rois, ce que je vous escris | Ci ensuant ert de perfit langage, | Dont en latin ma sentence ai compris: | Q'en dieu se fie, il ad bel avantage.' ('O gentle King, this which I write for you – | What follows here uses polished language, | Whose message I have written in Latin: | Whoso trusts in God, he has the best of it'). Text in Macaulay, i.336; translation my own.

The Latin following consists of the first eight lines (out of twenty-nine) of Gower's poem 'O Recolende', written without a doubt for the occasion of Henry's coronation on 13 October 1399, amalgamated with the four-line prophecy poem 'H. Aquile Pullus', also composed in 1399, either for the coronation or to celebrate the elevation of the future Henry V to Prince of Wales on 15th of October and to duke of Aquitaine on 23rd of October, and a two-sentence prayer, in prose, for Henry's prosperity and preservation.[30] What Gower is about here is almost overwhelmingly interesting in many ways. For present purposes, however, let it suffice to note Gower's description, in the French envoy, of the Latin verse immediately following as 'perfit langage', implying, apparently, its superiority over the French of the *Cinkante Balades*. Since this opinion seems of a piece with his practice – his concentration on Latin and English after 1398 (and 'Quixley's' too, for that matter) – we should probably take his expression of preference here seriously, as an indicative frame for future discussions of Gower's French at the end of his life, and perhaps of his later readership as well.*

---

[30] On dating the composition of these poems, see my *Minor Latin Works*, pp. 7, 75, 77–8; and further David R. Carlson, 'A rhyme distribution chronology of John Gower's Latin poetry', *SP*, 104 (2007), 15–55, 38–40.

* A version of this essay first appeared in *Language and Culture in Medieval Britain: The French of England c. 1100–1500*, ed. Jocelyn Wogan-Browne et al. (York, 2009) and is reprinted here by kind permission of the editor and York Medieval Press.

Chapter 25

Conjuring Gower in *Pericles*

MARTHA DRIVER

Though John Gower's poetry is now rarely regarded as central to medieval studies, his work was popularly read and very well known in the early modern period. The figure of the poet Gower 'that first garnisshed our Englysshe rude' is mentioned five times in John Skelton's *Garland of Laurel*, and Gower is cited or appears subsequently as an emblem of a great poet in early modern works by Robert Greene, Ben Jonson and John Webster.[1] The poet Gower further appears as the central player in William Shakespeare's *Pericles, Prince of Tyre*, in which he is given sustained dramatic life well beyond the limited mention Shakespeare makes directly to another medieval poet, Geoffrey Chaucer. Helen Cooper points out that 'Shakespeare's return to Gower is a measure of the high value he was prepared to place on the native English traditions of poetry.'[2] This essay expands upon Cooper's assertion to explore the poet's early modern reputation as specifically seen in Shakespeare's representation of Gower, and then briefly examines aspects of Gower's resurrection in modern stage productions of Shakespeare's play.

As is well known, *Pericles* does not appear in the First Folio; its text was first published in the later Quarto of 1609. The play was entered on 20 May 1608 in the Stationers' Register. It is often described as flawed and badly written; some scholars believe it was a memorial reconstruction by some of the actors similar to the 'bad quarto' of *Hamlet*.[3] Others say Shakespeare picked up a dramatic project begun by George Wilkins, author of a related novel, *The Painfull Adventures of Pericles Prince of Tyre*, published in 1608. Wilkins gave evidence along with Shakespeare in a lawsuit in 1613, and Katherine Duncan-Jones has proposed that Shakespeare may have dined

---

[1] John Skelton, 'Garlande or Chapelet of Laurell', in John Skelton, *The Complete English Poems*, ed. V. J. Scattergood (New York, 1983), pp. 312–58 (p. 323). Gower's early modern appearances in Greene, Jonson and Webster are discussed in Helen Cooper, '"This worthy olde writer": *Pericles* and other Gowers, 1592–1640', in *Companion*, pp. 99–113 (pp. 99–104). Text citations to *Pericles, Prince of Tyre* are taken from William Shakespeare and George Wilkins, *Pericles*, ed. Suzanne Gossett, 3rd edn (London, 2004; rpt 2006), subsequently cited as Gossett. The author thanks Elisabeth Dutton and Robert F. Yeager for their help with references.

[2] Cooper, '"This worthy olde writer"', p. 106.

[3] Gary Taylor, 'The transmission of Pericles', *Publications of the Bibliographical Society of America*, 80 (1986), 193–217. Cited in Gossett, p. 25.

in Wilkins's house (Wilkins was also a victualler) between 1604 and 1608.[4] Earlier critics believed the play was a product of Shakespeare's youth, among them John Dryden, who wrote 'Shakespeare's own muse her *Pericles* first bore', while Edmund Malone, in his Shakespeare editions of the 1780s, asserted that *'Pericles* was the entire work of Shakespeare, and one of his earliest compositions.' This idea was repeated by Henry Norman Hudson, who, in his 1901 introduction to the Aldus Shakespeare *Pericles*, described the play as 'some exercise of the "prentice hand"'.[5]

More recently, some scholars have tended once again to assign the entire play to Shakespeare, arguing rather convincingly that it is the first of the four great romances written late in Shakespeare's life (the others are *Cymbeline*, *Winter's Tale* and *The Tempest*) and that it represents a first experiment in the dramatic genre that comes to be called romance.[6] In the words of Barbara Everett:

> *Pericles* is often bad, and bad in a special way; it is archaic. Gower's first words in the play say this, and say it touchingly. [...] the effect of badness comes from Shakespeare teaching himself to write like a botched and patchworked old script.[7]

The play retells the story of Apollonius, known from the classical period, and draws mainly on Gower's version of the story in the *Confessio Amantis*, along with other sources. Pericles, Prince of Tyre, is pursued by King Antiochus because through solving a riddle he has uncovered the king's incest

---

[4] Katherine Duncan-Jones, *Ungentle Shakespeare: Scenes from his Life* (London, 2001), pp. 205–8. Cited in Gossett, p. 56. One source thought to have been consulted by Shakespeare is Lawrence Twyne's novel, *The Patterne of Painefull Adventures* (London, 1594; rpt 1607), STC 709, 709.5, 710. No copy of the first edition is extant. For a concise summary of arguments that Shakespeare collaborated with Wilkins, see Brian Vickers, *Shakespeare Co-Author: A Historical Study of Five Collaborative Plays* (Oxford, 2002), pp. 291–332, who further suggests that Wilkins's novel was in fact based on Shakespeare's (and his?) play (p. 304).

[5] John Dryden, who was born fifteen years after Shakespeare's death and lived 'near enough the author's time to have learned the stage tradition from contemporaries', is discussed in *Shakespeare's History of Pericles, Prince of Tyre*, ed. William J. Rolfe (New York, 1898), p. 14. Edmund Malone, in his Shakespeare editions of the 1780s, asserted that 'Pericles was the entire work of Shakespeare, and one of his earliest compositions' (Rolfe, *Shakespeare's History of Pericles*, p. 15). William Shakespeare and George Wilkins, *Pericles, Prince of Tyre*, ed. Henry Norman Hudson (New York, 1901), p. xiv.

[6] For definitions of medieval romance see Carol Fewster, *Traditionality and Genre in Middle English Romance* (Cambridge, 1987), pp. 18, 21. Helen Cooper describes Shakespeare's development of romance out of medieval stories in *The English Romance in Time: Transforming Motifs from Geoffrey of Monmouth to the Death of Shakespeare* (Oxford, 2004), pp. 13–14, 31, 72, 97–8, 261, 264–8, 412–16. For suggestions that *Pericles* is wholly Shakespeare's, see Barbara Everett, '"By the rough seas reft": how the "badness" of the *Pericles* Quarto may be of Shakespeare's making', *TLS* (11 August 2006), 13–16, available at http: tls.timesonline.co.uk (accessed Aug. 18, 2007), and R. F. Yeager, 'Shakespeare as medievalist: what it means for performing Pericles', in *Shakespeare and the Middle Ages*, eds Martha W. Driver and Sid Ray (Jefferson, NC, 2009), pp. 215–31, 215–16, 224, n. 2, 224–5, n. 3, 225, n. 4, and esp. 225, n. 6, citing William Shakespeare and George Wilkins, *Pericles, Prince of Tyre*, eds Doreen DelVecchio and Antony Hammond (Cambridge, 1998), p. 15, who comment, 'We as editors don't really care who wrote *Pericles* (though we do believe it to be the product of a single creative imagination): [...] it is "a masterpiece"'.

[7] Everett, '"By the rough seas reft"', p. 8.

with his daughter. Pericles then sails from place to place, marries Thaisa, who apparently dies in childbirth aboard ship, and places their child, Marina, with friends to be raised. Marina is kidnapped by pirates and sold into a brothel before Thaisa is found alive and the family is reunited. Including Gower, 'an actual medieval poet and moralist[,] among its cast members', allows Shakespeare to engage with Gower's medieval points of view, making the play 'one of the most moralistic and least psychologically complex plays in the canon'.[8] Why would Shakespeare, nearing the end of his career, create a medieval poet-narrator and employ in his play some of the dramatic elements of an earlier time? F. David Hoeniger suggests:

> that the very idea of reviving the medieval poet on the stage and having him present his own ancient story was meant to appeal to an audience that had developed a liking for things old-fashioned and antiquarian. It was the time of [William] Camden and the Society of Antiquaries.[9]

In Shakespeare's day historical works like John Stow's *Survey of London* and Stow's *Summary*, in which Gower appears, along with Stow's literary editions of Chaucer and Skelton and William Camden's *Britannia*, represented important cultural landmarks and were widely read. *Pericles*, too, looks backward to an earlier age and an earlier style of drama, including pageantry and dumb shows, even as it represents Shakespeare's fledgling attempt at writing in a new genre.

Shakespeare knew Gower through several media: the *Confessio Amantis* was available to him in manuscript and in William Caxton's or, more probably, Thomas Berthelette's printed editions.[10] The poet's effigy, his head resting on his three major works, was readily seen in St Saviour's, Southwark Cathedral, the parish that served those associated with the playhouses along with those employed in local brothels (the brothel and Marina's escape from it also figure in *Pericles*, 4.2, 4.5).[11] St Saviour's, a short walk from the Bankside theatres, was the church where Shakespeare paid twenty shillings to have his brother 'Edmond Shakespeare a player … buried in the Church with a forenoone knell of the great bell' on 31 January 1607, a year when it seems likely that Shakespeare was also at work on *Pericles*.[12] Shakespeare's resurrection of Gower 'From ashes' (*Pericles* 1.0.2) not only reflects the play-

---

[8] Dakin Matthews, 'Foreword: "the skeleton in the mirror", an interview with Dakin Matthews by Michael Almereyda', in *Shakespeare and the Middle Ages*, eds Martha W. Driver and Sid Ray (Jefferson, NC, 2009), p. 2. For background on Apollonius of Tyre, see Elizabeth Archibald, *Apollonius of Tyre: Medieval and Renaissance Themes and Variations* (Cambridge, 1991).

[9] F. David Hoeniger, 'Gower and Shakespeare in *Pericles*', *SQ*, 33, 4 (Winter, 1982), 461–79 (p. 464).

[10] A good case for this is made in Yeager, 'Shakespeare as medievalist', pp. 216–17, n. 13 (p. 225, n.15, pp. 225–6). STC 12142, 12143, 12144.

[11] For more on the Southwark brothels in the sixteenth century see M. Carlin, *Medieval Southwark* (London, 1996), pp. 209–29 (pp. 223–9); Henry Ansgar Kelly, 'Bishop, prioress, and bawd in the stews of Southwark', *Speculum*, 75, 2 (2000), 342–88 (pp. 367–80).

[12] Florence Higham, *Southwark Story* (London, 1955), p. 14; *Southwark Cathedral: The Authorised Guide* (London, 2006), p. 19.

wright's wish to look backward to an earlier age but also seems to evoke England's Roman Catholic past.

Richard Hillman remarks upon the choric role of Gower in *Pericles*, which he aptly terms 'the most sustained literary allusion to be found in Shakespeare'.[13] In *Pericles*, Gower is bodied forth and given 'A local habitation and a name';[14] he is a fully developed walking metaphor. Geoffrey Chaucer, whose reputation has surpassed Gower's, among modern readers at least, is mentioned only briefly in another late play, the John Fletcher–Shakespeare collaboration *The Two Noble Kinsmen*, the plot of which is drawn from Chaucer's 'Knight's Tale':

> [Our play] has a noble breeder and a pure,
> A learned, and a poet never went
> More famous yet 'twixt Po and silver Trent.
> Chaucer, of all admired, the story gives;
> There, constant to eternity, it lives.[15]

In performance Chaucer can be signified only symbolically, as he was in one memorable production of *The Two Noble Kinsmen* at the Berkeley Shakespeare Festival of 1985. The Prologue was spoken by the play's director, Julian López-Morillas, 'who, starting up from the middle of the audience, dressed in everyday clothes and carrying a copy of F. N. Robinson's Chaucer under his arm, slowly made his way down to the stage as he spoke'.[16] Chaucer's texts supplied rich materials for Shakespeare's drama, but Chaucer himself appears only as a footnote.

In *Pericles*, however, Gower is the main character and speaks eight monologues, the first and last of which serve as bookends to open and close the dramatic action. Shakespeare gives no other medieval poet this attention. Furthermore, although Shakespeare draws plots from Chaucer, most notably for *A Midsummer Night's Dream, Troilus and Cressida* and *The Two Noble Kinsmen*, the scant number of direct references, phrases or lines from Chaucer's verse is often explained by citing the antiquity of Chaucer's language, which Shakespeare is said not to have fully understood.[17] But, curiously, the poetry of Gower's *Confessio Amantis*, which is equally

---

[13] Richard Hillman, 'Shakespeare's Gower and Gower's Shakespeare: the larger debt of *Pericles*', *SQ*, 36, 4 (Winter 1985), 427–37 (p. 428).

[14] William Shakespeare, *A Midsummer Night's Dream*, ed. Harold F. Brooks (London, 1979; rpt 1983), p. 104, 5.1.15–17.

[15] William Shakespeare and John Fletcher, *The Two Noble Kinsmen*, ed. Lois Potter (Walton-on-Thames, 1997), pp. 137–8, 1, Prologue, 10–14.

[16] Phyllis Brooks, 'Berkeley Shakespeare Festival: summer 1985', *SQ*, 37, 3 (1986), 393–9 (p. 396). Director Nagle Jackson set the 1994 Oregon Festival production of *The Two Noble Kinsmen* at Ashland 'in the time of Chaucer, whose portrait hung above the stage throughout'. The actors occasionally gestured toward or spoke their lines to this portrait. For further description, see Lois Potter, 'Shakespeare Performed: *The Two Noble Kinsmen* in 1993–94', *SQ*, 47 (1996), 197–203 (p. 200).

[17] Ann Thompson, *Shakespeare's Chaucer: A Study in Literary Origins* (Liverpool, 1978), pp. 4–5, 10, 216–19.

antiquated, seems to have posed no such barriers.[18] And as Gower's central role in *Pericles* seems to indicate, the comparative reputations of Chaucer and Gower were seen somewhat differently in Shakespeare's day from the way they are now.

Both Chaucer and Shakespeare were claimed as Protestant poets from the early modern period, though their religious allegiances are perhaps not quite so clearly delineated in modern scholarship.[19] Gower, however, seems resolutely and consistently affiliated with Roman Catholicism, the old religion, and is thus an interesting poet for Shakespeare to choose as the narrator and prime mover of the action of *Pericles*. In Gower's day St Saviour's, Southwark, was known more familiarly as St Mary's Overey ('over the river'), and Gower contributed to the restoration of the church, spent his last years as a tenant in the precinct, directed the erection of his tomb there and, in his will,

> made careful provision for the welfare of his own soul, for special prayers to be said daily in the chantry with a yearly obit on the Friday after the feast of St Gregory; he even obtained an indulgence of 1,500 days for all who knelt to pray beside his tomb.[20]

Much of this history of what is now Southwark Cathedral was known in Shakespeare's day; how much to Shakespeare himself is open to surmise.

Could his choice of Gower over Chaucer perhaps suggest that Shakespeare was himself leaning toward Roman Catholicism as he neared the end of his life? There have been scholarly arguments put forth about the Catholicism of Shakespeare's father, his daughter, his schoolteachers and his associates; the Arden family of his mother, Mary, was decidedly Catholic.[21] Gary

---

[18] Geoffrey Bullough provides a close comparison of passages from the *Confessio Amantis* and *Pericles* in *Narrative and Dramatic Sources of Shakespeare* (New York, 1966), vi, pp. 359–69, 375–423. For Shakespeare's deliberate archaizing of Gower speeches in *Pericles*, see Yeager, 'Shakespeare as medievalist', pp. 220–22, 228 n. 40, n. 43.

[19] For more on Gower's early modern reputation, see Neil Gilroy-Scott, 'John Gower's reputation: literary allusions from the early fifteenth century to the time of "Pericles" ', *YoES*, 1 (1971), 30–47. For the Protestantism of Chaucer, see Alice S. Miskimin, *The Renaissance Chaucer* (New Haven, CT, 1975), pp. 255–61; Alexandra Gillespie, *Print Culture and the Medieval Author: Chaucer, Lydgate, and Their Books, 1473–1557* (Oxford, 2006), 187–228; Martha Driver, 'A false imprint in Chaucer's Workes: protestant printers in London (and Zurich?)', in *Sources, Exemplars, and Copy-Texts: Influence and Transmission, Essays from the Lampeter Conference of the Early Book Society*, ed. William Marx (Lampeter, 1999), pp. 131–54; James Simpson, *Reform and Cultural Revolution: The Oxford English Literary History, Volume II, 1350–1547* (Oxford, 2002), pp. 40–42. Shakespeare is generally assumed to have been Protestant – except when he is not (see note 21 below).

[20] Higham, *Southwark Story*, p. 75.

[21] Robert Miola, 'Shakespeare's religion', *First Things* (May 2008), available at http://www.firstthings.com/article.php3?id_article=6202 (accessed December 2009), provides a clear overview of recent scholarship. Arguments for 'Catholic Shakespeare' have been put forth in E. A. J. Honigmann, *Shakespeare: The 'Lost Years'* (Manchester, 1998); Peter Millward, *Shakespeare's Religious Background* (Chicago, MI, 1973); Richard Wilson, *Secret Shakespeare: Studies in Theatre, Religion and Resistance* (Manchester, 2004); and perhaps more tentatively in Stephen Greenblatt, *Will in the World: How Shakespeare Became Shakespeare* (New York, 2004), pp. 100–4, 108–9, 113–16, 149, 161–2, 317–21, 387–8. David N. Beauregard, *Catholic Theology in Shakespeare's Plays* (Newark, NJ, 2008), p. 15, among other scholars, notes that the family of Mary Arden, Shakespeare's mother, was resolutely Roman Catholic; see also Eamon Duffy, 'Was Shakespeare a Catholic?', *The Tablet* (27 April 1996), 536–8; and David

Taylor has noted elements of Catholic belief especially in Shakespeare's last plays: 'ceremony, ritual, intercession ... hallowing music' that appear 'in pagan robes in these plays'.[22] Examples from *Pericles* may be seen in the saintly Marina, the nun-like Thaisa and Diana, the virgin goddess, who can be read as a figure for the Virgin Mary (among many other associations). Diana is attended by the divine 'music of the spheres' (*P*, 5.1.218) and, like Mary, is a proponent of virginity and chaste wedded love.

While Shakespeare's plays are plastic in terms of the evidence they provide and may be read in many ways, it is known that soon after its composition *Pericles* was performed by recusant actors the Cholmley Players, also known as the Simpsons of Egton Bridge, in the North Riding of Yorkshire during the Christmas season of 1609/10. Suzanne Gossett points out that Yorkshire audiences may have noticed that 'Pericles's greeting to his daughter, "thou that beget'st him that did thee beget", approximates Marian theology'.[23] Some critics have also seen Thaisa's separation from Pericles after giving birth to Marina as analogous to 'the month-long lying-in period of early modern newly delivered mothers' which concluded with a ritual called 'the churching of women', originally a Jewish ritual of purification that was later practised in Roman Catholicism, then appropriated by the Anglican Church and retained in the prayer book to this day.[24] And this example illustrates precisely the problem with reading Roman Catholicism too deeply into the fiction of *Pericles*. Discerning Protestant practice from Catholic ritual cannot

---

Bevington, *Shakespeare's Ideas: More Things in Heaven and Earth* (Oxford, 2008), p. 111, who comments that 'Members of his mother's Warwickshire family in particular seem to have remained loyal to the old faith.'

[22] Gary Taylor citation appears in Miola, 'Shakespeare's religion', online see n. 21.

[23] Gossett, p. 87, citing *Pericles* 5.1.185.

[24] 'Churching' as an early Christian practice derived from Jewish tradition is succinctly discussed in Bonnie W. Anderson and Judith P. Zinsser, *A History of Their Own: Women in Europe from Prehistory to the Present* (New York, 1988), vol. 1, pp. 80–81. Nicholas Orme, *Medieval Children* (New Haven, CT, 2003), pp. 27, 33, provides a good description of the practice in the Middle Ages. Eamon Duffy, *The Stripping of the Altars: Traditional Religion in England 1400–1580* (New Haven, CT, 1992), pp. 583–4, describes women during the northern rising of 1569 (under the reign of Elizabeth) who 'seem[ed] often to have sought Catholic churching from the priests'. The language of *The First Prayer-Book of Edward VI* (Oxford and London, 1877 [1522]), describes 'The Churching of Women', also called 'The Thanks-giving of Women after child birth', and uses much the same language as *The Book of Common Prayer ... According to the Use of The Protestant Episcopal Church of 1945* (New York, 1945), pp. 305–7, which also includes 'The Thanksgiving of Women After Child-birth', with the instruction that 'The Woman, at the usual time after her delivery, shall come into the Church decently apparelled, and there shall kneel down in some convenient place' (p. 305). The subject heading of the 1979 edition, *The Book of Common Prayer ... According to the Use of The Episcopal Church* (New York, 1979), has more broadly become 'A Thanksgiving for the Birth or Adoption of a Child' (pp. 439–45). In this case, both 'parents, with other members of the family, should come to the church'. The ritual in the Middle Ages was connected with Marian cults, specifically the Purification of the Virgin Mary. Interestingly, in the fourteenth century, John Wycliffe 'suggested that the statues of the Virgin so dear to English women were no better than Diana of the Ephesians'; see Margaret Aston, *Faith and Fire: Popular and Unpopular Religion, 1350–1600* (London, 1993), p. 223. For further references to churching of women, see Caroline Bicks, 'Backsliding at Ephesus: Shakespeare's Diana and the churching of women', in *Pericles: Critical Essays*, ed. David Skeele (New York, 2000), pp. 205–27; David Cressy, 'Purification, thanksgiving, and the purification of women in post-Reformation England', *Past and Present*, 141 (November 1993), 106–46.

always be definitive. On the other hand, the choice of Gower over Chaucer as main character seems suggestive, whether of Shakespeare's own religious leanings or of Gower's reputation as an important moral force in the early modern period. For example, Gower is the central character in another early modern work, Robert Greene's 1592 *Greenes Vision*, in which 'ancient', moral Gower bests Chaucer in a story-telling contest. Cooper describes Gower's story as 'little more than a framework for its abundance of *sententiae*', but Greene's dream vision sets as a moral teacher Gower, who represents one kind of literature, above Chaucer, who represents another.[25]

For *Pericles* Shakespeare draws on book VIII of the *Confessio Amantis*, which describes the adventures of Apollonius of Tyre, and also very probably on book II, which includes the tale of Constance, who is 'twice consigned to the sea' and twice survives 'to bring others to virtue through her own goodness'. Constance is eventually 'miraculously reunited with her husband and father'.[26] This plot is used as well by Chaucer's Man of Law (who further refers to the story of 'Tyro Appollonius' and 'the cursed King Antiochus'), and is reshaped by Shakespeare in *Pericles*.[27] On the one hand, the tale of Constance mirrors the adventures of Pericles's wife, Thaisa, and, on the other, Constance's benign agency in bringing others to virtue is seen in Pericles's daughter Marina. Hillman argues that Shakespeare is not just reading book VIII of the *Confessio* but drawing on Gower's entire work and that Gower provides the precedent for 'Shakespeare's use of love themes as a means of exploring larger issues of human spirituality and self-realization'.[28]

In the play's opening Prologue, Gower describes himself as resurrected 'From ashes'. Onstage he lives again:

> To sing a song that old was sung,
> From ashes ancient Gower is come;
> Assuming man's infirmities,
> To glad your ear, and please your eyes. (*Pericles*, 1.0.1–4)

Gower then guides the audience through multiple scene changes and a tangled narrative that spans decades. Gower's monologues explain the action of the several dumb shows ('What's dumb in show I'll plain with speech' (*Pericles*, 3.0.14)). At several points Gower urges viewers to engage with the action onstage, as, for example, in Act 3, when the audience is asked to imagine 'This stage the ship, upon whose deck | The sea-tossed Pericles appears to speak' (*Pericles*, 3.0.59–60), and he often asks for the viewers' forbearance ('Only I carry winged time, | Post on the lame feet

---

[25] *Greenes Vision* is discussed in Cooper, '"This worthy olde writer"', pp. 101–5; Cooper, *English Romance in Time*, pp. 276, 293–4, 300; Kelly Jones, '"The quick and the dead": performing the poet Gower in *Pericles*', in *Shakespeare and the Middle Ages*, ed. Martha Driver and Sid Ray (Jefferson, NC, 2009), p. 206; Yeager, 'Shakespeare as medievalist', p. 217; Louise M. Bishop, 'A touch of Chaucer in *The Winter's Tale*', in *Shakespeare and the Middle Ages*, eds Martha Driver and Sid Ray (Jefferson, NC, 2009), pp. 237–9.
[26] Thompson, *Shakespeare's Chaucer*, pp. 83–4.
[27] *Ibid.*, p. 84.
[28] Hillman, 'Shakespeare's Gower', pp. 427–537 (p. 428).

of my rhyme; | Which never could I so convey, | Unless your thoughts went on my way' (*Pericles*, 4.0.47–50)). Gower's purpose is to clarify the action, instruct the audience and moralize the tale. As Everett remarks, 'Gower so guides us through the ensuing shows and spectacles, the hazy texture of styles and images, as to seem like some psychopomp leading us through new and buried depths of feeling.'[29] The description of Gower as a 'psychopomp', literally a conductor of souls to the afterlife, is apt, given the opening context Shakespeare supplies for him. In his role as 'authorial presenter', Gower seems to control the presentation of the whole play;[30] he is the learned literary authority who asks us to suspend our disbelief and look beyond the action to understand its meaning:

> We commit no crime
> To use one language in each several clime
> Where our scenes seem to live. I do beseech you
> To learn of me, who stand in the gap to teach you
> The stages of our story. (*Pericles*, 4.4.5–9)

It is as a teacher, in fact, or as 'a didactic expositor', in the language of Walter F. Eggers, that Gower is mainly played in modern production.[31]

Kelly Jones describes Gower as 'the living agent of the play's performance [who] exhibits a playful concern with the unstable, vulnerable, and unreservedly performative nature of authorship itself'.[32] In modern theatrical production Shakespeare's representation of Gower as a moral teacher, a reputation inherited from a number of earlier writers, is retained even as the medieval foundations for Gower's character are sometimes lost; Gower is protean, taking many shapes, from Scottish bard to calypso singer.[33] He is shown mainly as moral teacher who tells stories to illustrate his points, and this is the way modern audiences and reviewers remember him.[34]

One of the most powerful characterizations of Shakespeare's Gower that I have seen was represented by Brenda Wehle, who played Gower in

---

[29] Everett, '"By the rough seas reft"', p. 3.
[30] Hoeniger, 'Gower and Shakespeare in *Pericles*', pp. 463–4.
[31] Walter F. Eggers, 'Shakespeare's Gower and the role of the authorial presenter', *PQ*, 54 (1975), 434–43, 436.
[32] Jones, '"The quick and the dead"', p. 203.
[33] *Ibid.*, pp. 208–9; Yeager, 'Shakespeare as medievalist', pp. 223–4; Gossett, pp. 91–106.
[34] The only filmed version of *Pericles*, a BBC Time-Life production, stars a bearded, grey-haired Edward Petherbridge in the Gower role; the production remains very close to the script and is quite effective. A review of the 1998 *Pericles* stage production at the Public Theatre in New York says that the actor Philip Goodwin, who played Gower, 'declaims with all the emotional commitment of a substitute teacher', at least capturing some of the instructional aspects of the role; Peter Marks, 'Theatre review: high jinks on the high seas, and a little Shakespeare, too', *New York Times* (10 November 1998), available online at http://query.nytimes.com (accessed 29 December 2009). Bette Bourne, best known for his role as Quentin Crisp on the New York and London stages, has also played Juliet's Nurse in *Romeo and Juliet* and Lady Bracknell in Oscar Wilde's *Importance of Being Earnest*. In the 2003 production of *Pericles* at the Lyric Theatre, Bourne played the role of Gower 'straight': 'as a sceptical schoolmaster. [...] Wearing an overall, and employing a blackboard and chalk the better to instruct his bemused class'; Paul Bailey, 'Insecure units', *London Times* (10 October, 2003), available at http://tls.timesonline.co.uk (accessed 29 December 2009).

Pericles at the Brooklyn Academy of Music in 2004.[35] For her performance as Gower, the tall and stately Wehle was costumed in a simple medieval tunic. Her visible enjoyment of the outrageous turns of plot was evident, and her lines were spoken boldly forth in an exuberant style found in the best of academic lectures. Michael Basile, reviewing this production for the *Shakespeare Bulletin*, likewise noted Wehle's 'avuncular bemusement over the story's incredible resolution'.[36]

Casting a woman actor to play Gower might be seen as a gimmick or as simply a modern inversion of the practice of having men play women on Shakespeare's stage. In this case, however, Wehle's appearance as Gower intently focused the attention of the audience on the agency of the female characters in the story. In this version, tying Gower to the feminine linked his character to the positive and generative aspects of the play, causing focus to shift from its hero, Pericles, to the actions and positioning of the female characters.

For example, in Act 4, Marina buys off the pander Bolt and provides her curriculum vitae to escape the bawdy house: 'I can sing, weave, sew and dance, | [...] And I will undertake all these to teach. | I doubt not but this populous city will | Yield many scholars' (*Pericles*, 4.6.186–90). This scene re-enacts the account given earlier by Gower of Marina's education in the Prologue to Act 4, where he describes Marina as an adept poet and writer: 'She would with rich and constant pen | Vail to [praise] her mistress Dian' (*Pericles*, 4.0.28–9). Gower here further describes Marina as gaining 'Of education all the grace | Which makes her both the heart and place | Of general wonder' (*Pericles*, 4.0.10–11). Her learning is re-emphasized by Gower in the Prologue to Act 5, where he extols Marina's gifts at singing, dancing and embroidery – 'pupils lacks she none of noble race, | Who pour their bounty on her' (*Pericles*, 5.0.9–10) – as well as her intellectual gifts – 'Deep clerks she dumbs' (*Pericles* 5.0.5), a line that Elizabeth Archibald has considered at some length, commenting somewhat dryly, 'Half a line for her brains, and three and a half for her sewing'.[37]

When Gower is played by a woman, however, the lines of the Prologues seem naturally and directly to commend Marina for her range of talents,

---

[35] Wehle has taken other 'trouser roles'. She played the dual parts of the Queen and Belarius in *Cymbeline* at San Diego's Old Globe Theatre in 1999, and she is particularly known for her role as Demophon in Peter Sellars's production of Euripides' *The Children of Herakles*, which originated at the Loeb Drama Center in Cambridge, MA, and had two European tours. (In this version of *The Heracleidae*, however, the character of Demophon, King of Athens, in Euripides' original was updated to 'daughter of Theseus and President of Athens'.)

[36] Michael Basile, '*Pericles*: theatre review', *Shakespeare Bulletin*, 22 (Autumn 2004), 110. Peter Nicholson recently forwarded a brief note on a 2008 production of *Pericles* in Hawaii with Eden-Lee Murray as Gower (shown in a long grey wig with a shell garland and her arms festooned with bracelets) in the *Star Bulletin* available at http://www.starbulletin.com/multimedia/photo_galleries/viewer/?galID=51007327. Compare this with a very glamorous picture of the same actress in the *Star Bulletin*, 13, no. 227 (14 August 2008), available at http://archives.starbulletin.com/2008/08/14/news/berger.html (accessed 29 December 2009).

[37] Elizabeth Archibald, '"Deep clerks she dumbs": the learned heroine in *Apollonius of Tyre* and *Pericles*', *Comparative Drama*, 22, 4 (1988–9), 289–303 (pp. 295–6).

both those traditionally associated with women, such as needlework and textile work, and those less so, such as teaching, writing and surpassing the knowledge of clerks. Marina's liberation speech to Bolt (also liberating on other levels) is set up and then reaffirmed by Gower in the Prologues, which commend his heroine as a fellow teacher of 'many scholars' and also as a reflection of himself.

Women characters are crucial to the several themes that *Pericles* enacts – among them, the transcendence of human suffering and the healing power of patience and love. Through the intelligent intervention and agency of the women characters, especially Marina, happy resolution – the restoration of Pericles' identity and the reuniting of his family – is achieved. If you have endured even a 'thousandth part' of my experience, Pericles tells Marina, 'thou art a man, and I | have suffered like a girl. Yet thou dost look | like Patience, gazing on kings' graves and smiling | extremity out of act' (*Pericles*, 5.1.127–30). While the actor who plays Gower is usually stable in the sense that he or she plays only the one role (in a play in which doubling and even trebling roles for actors has been customary since the early modern productions), the casting of Wehle as Gower, who is the controlling element, reflects modern ideas about gender, pointing the attention of the audience away from Pericles to the actions of the female characters in the play.

Active female characters can be found as well in Gower's *Confessio*, which in some sixty-five stories celebrates women's strength, power, patience under adversity and in some cases their resistance to culturally constructed gender roles.[38] And, as Helen Cooper so movingly observes,

> Shakespeare's own dramatization of the old tale – his dramatization, indeed, of the telling of an old tale, since the storyteller himself, in the shape of Gower, acts as its presenter – is rather a recuperation of romance itself. And with romance comes his most generous recuperation of female sexuality; of active female sexual choice as the well-directed and faithful will for good, and women's desire as desirable both to their earthly lovers and to the divine order.[39]

Knowingly or not, some modern productions of *Pericles* seem to provide a glimpse of this Gower by showing him as a wise instructor from whom audiences still can learn.

While Shakespeare does not afford Chaucer so much as a walk-on part in any of the plays, he places Gower in the central role in *Pericles*. Gower, like Prospero in *The Tempest*, is the prime mover of the action. He is the narrator of the dumb shows. He is the benevolent guardian of Marina, Thaisa and Pericles through their tests and trials. Because of their moral and steadfast love Gower brings them at last to 'their desired haven', reuniting the

---

[38] For Gower's emphasis on women's agency in the *Confessio Amantis* and the interpretation of later artists, see Martha Driver, 'Women readers and Pierpont Morgan MS M. 126', in *John Gower: Manuscripts, Readers, Contexts, Disputatio*, ed. Malte Urban (Turnhout, forthcoming 2010), pp. 67–91. Also see Martha Dana Rust, *Imaginary Worlds in Medieval Books: Exploring the Manuscript Matrix* (New York, 2007), pp. 143–9, 154–62.

[39] Cooper, *English Romance in Time*, p. 268.

family, 'Virtue preserved from fell destruction's blast, | Led on by heaven and crowned with joy at last' (*Pericles*, Epilogue, 5–6).[40] And in so doing Shakespeare's Gower reaffirms the moral message at the end of book VIII of the *Confessio Amantis*, teaching 'What is to love in good manere' (line 2010).

Productions (briefly) discussed

1984 *Pericles: Prince of Tyre*, d. David Jones, with Mike Gwilym, Edward Petherbridge, Amanda Redman, John Woodvine, Annette Crosbie and Juliet Stevenson. UK, US: BBC and Time-Life Films (videotape)

1996 *Pericles, Prince of Tyre*, d. James Roose-Evans, with Justin Butcher and Ben Okafor. Riverside Studios.

1998 *Pericles, Prince of Tyre*, d. Brian Kulick, with Sam Tsoutsouvas. Joseph Papp Public Theater, New York Shakespeare Festival.

2002 *Pericles, Prince of Tyre*, d. Adrian Noble, with Ray Fearon. Royal Shakespeare Company, Roundhouse.

2004 *Pericles, Prince of Tyre*, d. Bartlett Sher, with Brenda Wehle. Theatre for a New Audience, Brooklyn Academy of Music.

2004 *Pericles, Prince of Tyre*, d. Neil Bartlett, with Bette Bourne. Lyric Theatre, Hammersmith.

---

[40] The safe port for sailors who survive stormy seas to be brought into 'their desired haven' is described in Psalm 107:25–31, King James Version, and seems particularly pertinent to the resolution of *Pericles* as the tale of a faithful servant and just man who travels the sea and is happily reunited with his virtuous wife and child.

Bibliography

Primary texts

Manuscripts

Cambridge, St John's College, MS A. 7
Cambridge, St John's College, MS N. 11 (524)
Cambridge, Trinity College, MS O. 2. 30 (1134)
Canterbury Cathedral, Dean and Chapter Library, MS Lit. E. 10 (101)
Leeds, District Archives MS NP/C1
London, British Library, MS Additional 63592
London, British Library, MS Cotton Faustina A. viii
London, British Library, MS Cotton Tiberius C. vii
London, British Library, MS Egerton 272
London, British Library, MS Harley 3490
London, British Library, MS Harley 7333
London, British Library, MS Royal 7. A
London, British Library, MS Royal 7. A. I
London, British Library, MS Royal 7. A. IX
London, British Library, MS Royal 10. B. VII
London, British Library, MS Stowe 951
London, The National Archives, Public Record Office E101/411/9
London, Society of Antiquaries, MS 134
Oxford, Bodleian Library, MS Ashmole 1285
Oxford, Bodleian Library, MS Bodley 822
Oxford, Bodleian Library, MS Bodley 294
Oxford, Bodleian Library, MS Digby 138
Oxford, Bodleian Library, MS Fairfax 3
Oxford, Bodleian Library, MS Hatton 92
Oxford, Bodleian Library, MS Rawlinson B. 177
Oxford, Merton College, MS 325
Oxford, Trinity College, MS 31
Oxford, Trinity College, MS D 29
Paris, Bibliothèque de la Sorbonne, MS 153
York, Borthwick Insitute, MS Register 14

Reference works and catalogues

Alford, John A., ed., *Piers Plowman: A Glossary of Legal Diction* (Cambridge, 1988).
Baker, J. H., *Manual of Law French*, 2nd edn (Aldershot, 1990).
Baker, J. H. and S. F. C. Milsom, *Sources of English Legal History: Private Law to 1750* (Guildford, 1986).
Bullough, Geoffrey, *Narrative and Dramatic Sources of Shakespeare* (New York, 1966).
Calendar of the Patent Rolls Preserved in the Public Record Office: Richard II, 1381–1385 (London, 1897).

BIBLIOGRAPHY

Catalogue of the Stowe Manuscripts in the British Museum, 2 vols (London, 1895, 1986).
Chapters of the Augustinian Canons, ed H. E. Salter (London, 1922).
Coulson, F. T. and B. Roy, *Incipitarium Ovidianum: A Finding Guide for Texts in Latin Related to the Study of Ovid in the Middle Ages and Renaissance* (Turnhout, 2000).
Dugdale, W., *Monasticon Anglicanum: A History of the Abbies and Other Monasteries, Hospitals, Friaries, and Cathedral and Collegiate Churches, with their dependencies, in England and Wales; also of all such Scotch, Irish, and French Monasteries as were in any manner connected with religious houses in England...*, rev. edn, eds J. Caley, H. Ellis and B. Bandinel, 6 vols (London, 1830).
Emden, A. B., *A Biographical Register of the University of Oxford to A.D. 1500*, 3 vols (Oxford, 1957; rpt 1989).
Gullick, M. and T. Webber, 'The binding descriptions in the library catalogue from Leicester Abbey', in *Leicester Abbey: Medieval History, Archaeology and Manuscript Studies*, eds J. Story et al. (Leicester, 2006), pp. 147–72.
——, 'Summary catalogue of surviving manuscripts from Leicester Abbey', in *Leicester Abbey: Medieval History, Archaeology and Manuscript Studies*, eds J. Story et al. (Leicester, 2006), pp. 173–92.
Hammond, Eleanor Prescott, *Chaucer: A Bibliographical Manual* (New York, 1908; rpt 1933).
Ker, N. R., *Medieval Libraries of Great Britain*, 2nd edn (London, 1964).
——, *Medieval Manuscripts in British Libraries* (Oxford, 1969–92).
Madan, F., H. H. E. Craster and N. Denholm-Young, *A Summary Catalogue of Western Manuscripts in the Bodleian Library at Oxford*, 7 vols (Oxford, 1895–1937).
Nichols, J., ed., *A Collection of All the Wills, now Known to be Extant, of the Kings and Queen of England, Princes and Princesses of Wales, and Every Branch of the Royal Blood, from the Reign of William the Conqueror to that of Henry the Seventh, Exclusive; With Explanatory Notes and a Glossary* (London, 1780).
Pickles, J. D. and J. L. Dawson, *A Concordance to John Gower's 'Confessio Amantis'* (Wolfeboro, NH, 1987).
Sharpe, Richard, *A Handlist of the Latin Writers of Great Britain and Ireland before 1540* (Turnhout, 1997).
Singer, Dorothy Waley, with Annie Anderson, *Catalogue of Latin and Alchemical Manuscripts in Great Britain and Ireland Dating From Before the XVI Century*, 3 vols (Brussels, 1928–31).
Southwark Cathedral: The Authorised Guide (London, 2006).
Thorndike, Lynn and Pearl Kibre, *A Catalogue of Incipits of Medieval Scientific Writings in Latin* (Cambridge, MA, 1937).
Victoria History of the Counties of England, III: A History of the County of York, East Riding, ed. J. K. Allison (London, 1976).
Walther, Hans, *Proverbia Sententiaeque Latinitatis Medii Aevi: Lateinische Sprichwörter und Sentenzen des Mittelalters in alphabetischer Anordnung*, 6 vols (Göttingen, 1963–9).
Watson, A. G., *A Descriptive Catalogue of the Medieval Manuscripts of All Souls College Oxford* (Oxford, 1997).
——, *Medieval Libraries of Great Britain. Supplement to the Second Edition* (London, 1987).
West's Encyclopedia of American Law, 2nd edn (Detroit, 2008).
Woodruff, C. E., *Catalogue of the Manuscript Books in the Library of Christ Church, Canterbury* (Canterbury, 1911).

Printed primary texts

Agrippa, Henry Cornelius, *De occulta philosophia*, ed. Karl A. Nowotny (Graz, Austria, 1967).
Albertus Magnus, *De mineralibus*, in *Opera Omnium*, ed. August Borgnet (Paris, 1890).
Aquinas, St Thomas, *Summa Theologiae*, trans. Fathers of the English Dominican Province (Allen, TX, 1981).
——, *Summa Theologiae*, ed. John Fearon, O. P. (Cambridge, 2006).
Aristotle, *Ethica Nicomachea*, VI.iv, trans. Grosseteste, *In decem libros ethicorum Aristotelis ad Nicomachum expositio* (Rome, 1949).
Ashby, George, *George Ashby's Poems*, ed. Mary Bateson, EETS e.s. 76 (London, 1899).
Aubrey, John, *Remains of Gentilisme and Judaisme*, ed. James Britten (London, 1881).
Augustine, *The City of God Against the Pagans*, trans. R. W. Dyson (Cambridge, 1998).
——, *De civitate dei*, eds B. Dombart and A. Kalb, 2 vols (Turnholt, 1955).
——, *Confessions*, ed. J. J. O'Donnell (Oxford, 1992).
Barr, Helen, ed., *The Piers Plowman Tradition* (London, 1993).
Benvenuto da Imola, *Comentum super Dantis Aldigherij Comoediam*; cited from *Divine Comedy*, ed. and trans. C. S. Singleton (Princeton, NJ, 1970–75).
Biblia Sacra Iuxta Vulgatam Versionem, ed. Robert Weber, 4th edn (Stuttgart, 1994).
Boni, Pietro Antonio, *The New Pearl of Great Price; a Treatise Concerning the Treasure and Most Precious Stone of the Philosophers. Or the Method and Procedure of This Divine Art; with Observations Drawn from the Works of Arnoldus, Raymondus, Rhasis, Albertus, and Michael Scotus*, trans. Arthur Edward Waite (London, 1963).
The Book of Common Prayer ... According to the Use of The Episcopal Church (New York, 1979)
The Book of Common Prayer [...] According to the Use of The Protestant Episcopal Church of 1945 (New York, 1945).
Bovet, Honorat, *L'Apparicion Maistre Jehan de Meun et le Somnium super materia scismatis*, ed. Ivor Arnold (Paris, 1926).
——, *Medieval Muslims, Christians, and Jews in Dialogue: The Apparicion Maistre Jehan de Meun of Honorat Bovet*, ed. and trans. Michael Hanley (Tempe, 2005).
Brewer, T., *Memoir of the Life and Times of John Carpenter* (London, 1836; rpt 1856).
Brinton, Thomas, *The Sermons of Thomas Brinton, Bishop of Rochester (1373–1389)*, ed. Sister Mary Aquinas Devlin, 2 vols (London, 1954).
Brunetto Latini, *Li Livres dou Tresor*, eds and trans Paul Barrette and Spurgeon Baldwin (New York, 1993).
Cassian, John, *Iohannis Cassiani Conlationes xxiiii*, ed. Michael Petschenig (Vienna: Gerold, 1886).
Chastellain, Georges, *Oeuvres de Georges Chastellain, 5: Chronique*, ed. Kervyn de Lettenhove (Brussels, 1864).
Chaucer, Geoffrey, *Chaucer's Major Poetry*, ed. Albert C. Baugh (New York, 1963).
——, *Chaucer's Poetry: An Anthology for the Modern Reader*, ed. E. T. Donaldson (New York, 1958).
——, *The Complete Poetry and Prose of Geoffrey Chaucer*, ed. John H. Fisher (New York, 1977).
——, *The Complete Works of Geoffrey Chaucer*, ed. W. W. Skeat, 6 vols (Oxford, 1894).
——, *The Riverside Chaucer*, gen. ed. Larry D. Benson, 3rd edn (Boston, 1987).
——, *The Poetical Works of Chaucer*, ed. F. N. Robinson (Boston, 1933).
——, *The Works of Geoffrey Chaucer*, ed. F. N. Robinson, 2nd edn (Boston, 1957).
Chrimes, S. B. and A. L. Brown, *Select Documents of English Constitutional History 1307–1485* (London, 1961).

BIBLIOGRAPHY

Christine de Pizan, *Christine de Pizan: Le Livre de l'Advision Christine*, eds C. Reno and L. Dulac (Paris, 2001).
——, *Le Livre des trois vertus*, eds Charity Cannon Willard and Eric Hicks (Paris, 1989).
The Chronicle of Adam Usk 1377–1421, ed. and trans. Chris Given-Wilson (Oxford, 1997).
The Chronicles of London, ed. C. L. Kingsford (Oxford, 1905).
Chronicon Adae de Usk, 1377–1421, ed. Sir E. M. Thompson, 2nd edn (Oxford, 1904).
Chronicon Angliae, ed. Edward Maunde Thompson (London, 1874).
Cicero, Marcus Publius, *Speech on Behalf of Publius Sestius*, trans. Robert A. Kaster (Oxford, 2006).
Clanvowe, John, *The Works of Sir John Clanvowe*, ed. V. J. Scattergood (Cambridge, 1975).
Cola di Rienzo, 'Letter 49' (to Charles IV, 1350), in *Vom Mittelalter zur Reformation*, ed. K. Burdach (Berlin, 1912).
——, *The Life of Cola di Rienzo*, ed. and trans. John Wright (Toronto, 1975).
Daniel, Samuel, *Samuel Daniel: Poems, and A Defence of Ryme*, ed. Arthur Colby Sprague (Cambridge, MA, 1930).
Dante, Alighieri, *The Divine Comedy*, ed. and trans. C. S. Singleton (Princeton, NJ, 1970–75).
——, *The Divine Comedy*, trans. Kenneth MacKenzie (London, 1979).
Defoe, Daniel (attrib.), *Street-robberies, consider'd* (London, 1728).
Edmund of Abingdon, *'Speculum Religiosorum' and 'Speculum Ecclesie'*, ed. H. P. Forshaw (London, 1973).
Edward, Second Duke of York, *The Master of Game*, eds William A. Baillie-Grohman and F. N. Baillie-Grohman, intro. Theodore Roosevelt (London, 1904).
English Historical Documents: 1327–1485, ed. A. R. Myers (New York, 1969).
Ficino, Marsilio, *De vita triplici, libri tres*, ed. Martin Plessner (Hildesheim, Germany, 1978).
The First Prayer-Book of Edward VI: compared with the successive revisions of The Book of Common Prayer / also a concordance to the rubricks in the several editions (Oxford, 1877).
[Geiler, John, of Kayserberg] (attrib.), *Scomata*, in *Margarita Facetiarum* (Strasburg, 1508).
Geoffroi de Charny, *A Knight's Own Book of Chivalry*, intro. Richard Kaeuper, trans. Elspeth Kennedy (Philadelphia, PA, 2005).
The Good Wife Taught Her Daughter, ed. Tauno F. Mustanoja, Annales Academiæ Scientiarum Fennicæ, BLXI, 2 (Helsinki, 1948).
The Governance of Kings and Princes: John Trevisa's Middle English Translation of the De Regimine Principum of Aegidius Romanus, eds David C. Fowler, Charles F. Briggs and Paul G. Remley (New York and London, 1997).
Gower, John, *The Complete Works of John Gower IV. The Latin Works*, ed. G. C. Macaulay (Oxford, 1902).
——, *Confessio Amantis*, ed. Russell A. Peck with Latin translations by Andrew Galloway, 3 vols (Kalamazoo, MI, 2000–2004).
——, *The English Works of John Gower*, ed. G. C. Macaulay, 2 vols, EETS e.s. 81–82 (London, 1900–1901; rpt 1979).
——, *The Latin Verses in the 'Confessio Amantis': An Annotated Translation*, eds Siân Echard and Claire Fanger, with A. G. Rigg (East Lansing, MI, 1991).
——, *The Major Latin Works of John Gower*, trans. Eric Stockton (Seattle, WA, 1962).

——, *John Gower: The Minor Latin Works (with* 'In Praise of Peace' *Edited by M. Livingston),* ed. and trans. R. F. Yeager (Kalamazoo, MI, 2005).

——, *Mirour de l'Omme (The Mirror of Mankind),* trans. William Burton Wilson, rev. Nancy Wilson Van Baak (East Lansing, MI, 1992).

Gregory the Great, *Moralia in Job: Sancti Gregorii Moralia in Job,* ed. Marcus Adriaen, 2 vols. (Turnholt: Brepols, 1979).

Guillaume de Lorris and Jean de Meun, *Le Roman de la Rose,* ed. Félix Lecoy, 3 vols (Paris, 1965–70).

——, *Le Roman de la Rose,* ed. Daniel Poiron (Paris, 1974).

——, *The Romance of the Rose,* trans. Charles Dahlberg, 3rd edn (Princeton, NJ, 1995).

Havelok the Dane, Four Romances of England, eds Ronald B. Herzman, Graham Drake and Eve Salisbury (Kalamazoo, MI, 1999).

Hetoum the Armenian, *Hetoum: A Lytell Cronycle: Richard Pynson's Translation (c.1520) of La Fleur des histoires de la terre d'Orient (c.1307),* ed. Glenn Burger (Toronto, 1988).

The Holy Bible: Douay Version translated from the Latin Vulgate (Douay, 1609; Rheims 1582). (London: Catholic Truth Society, 1956).

How the Wise Man Taught His Son, in *Codex Ashmole 61: A Compilation of Popular Middle English Verse,* ed. George Shuffleton (Kalamazoo, MI, 2008).

Joachim of Fiore, *Il Libro delle Figure,* eds L. Tondelli, M. Reeves and B. Hirsch-Reich (Turin, 1953).

Johannis de Trokelowe, et Henrici de Blaneforde, monachorum S. Albani, necnon quorundam anonymorum Chronica et Annales, Rolls Series 28, ed. Henry Thomas Riley, 3 vols (London, 1866).

The King of Tars, ed. Judith Perryman (Heidelberg, 1980).

Langland, William, *Piers Plowman: The B Text,* eds George Kane and E. Talbot Donaldson (London, 1975).

Livy, *The Early History of Rome,* trans. Aubrey de Selincourt (Harmondsworth, 1960).

——, *History of Rome,* trans. B. O. Foster, 4 vols (Cambridge, 1952).

Lydgate, John, *A Critical Edition of John Lydgate's 'Life of Our Lady',* eds R. A. Klinefelter and V. F. Gallagher (Louvain, 1961).

——, *Fall of Princes,* ed. Henry Bergen, EETS e.s. 121–124 (Oxford, 1924–7).

——, *The Minor Poems of John Lydgate,* ed. Henry Noble McCracken, EETS e.s. 107 (1911); EETS o.s. 192 (Oxford, 1934).

de Machaut, Guillaume, *'The Fountain of Love' ('La fonteinne amoureuse') and Two Other Love Vision Poems,* ed. and trans. R. Burton Palmer (New York, 1993).

Maidstone, Richard, *Concordia (The Reconciliation of Richard II with London),* ed. David Carlson, trans. A. G. Rigg (Kalamazoo, MI, 2003).

Manningham, John, *The Diary of John Manningham of the Middle Temple, 1602–1603,* ed. Robert Parker Sorlien (Hanover, NH, 1976).

Le Menagier de Paris, eds Georgine E. Brereton and Janet M. Ferrier (Oxford, 1981).

de Mézières, Philippe, *Le livre de la vertu du sacrement de marriage,* ed. Joan B. Williamson (Washington DC, 1993).

——, *Le Songe du Vieil Pelerin of Philippe de Mézières, Chancellor Cyprus,* ed. G. W. Coopland, 2 vols (Cambridge, 1969).

The Middle English Breton Lays, eds Anne Laskaya and Eve Salisbury (Kalamazoo, MI, 1995).

Minot, Laurence, *The Poems of Laurence Minot 1333–1352,* ed. Richard H. Osberg (Kalamazoo, MI, 1996).

Mirk's Festial: A Collection of Homilies by Johannes Mirkus, ed. Theodore Erbe, EETS e.s. 96 (London, 1905).

de Montaigne, Michel, *Oeuvres complètes*, eds Albert Thibaudet and Maurice Rat (Paris, 1962).

Morrin, M. J., *John Waldeby, OSA, c.1315–c.1372: English Augustinian Preacher and Writer: With a Critical Edition of His Tract on the 'Ave Maria'* (Rome, 1972–4).

Mum and the Sothsegger Edited from the Manuscripts Camb. Univ. Ll. iv. 14 and Brit. Mus. Add. 41666, eds Mabel Day and Robert Steele, EETS o.s. 199. (Oxford, 1936).

A Myrour to Lewde Men and Wymmen: A Prose Version of the Speculum Vitae, ed. from BL MS Harley 45, ed. Venetia Nelson (Heidelberg, 1981).

Neckam, Alexander, *Alexandri Neckam De naturis rerum libri duo: with the poem of the same author, 'De laudibus divinæ sapientiæ'*, ed. Thomas Wright (Oxford, 1863).

Nicolaus Eymericus, *Directorium inquisitorum* (Rome, 1585).

Otto of Freising, *The Two Cities: A Chronicle of Universal History to the Year 1146 A.D.*, trans. C. C. Mierow (New York, 1928).

Ovid, *Fasti*, ed. James George Frazer (Cambridge, 1967).

——, *Metamorphoses*, ed. G. P. Goold, 2 vols (Cambridge, MA, 1984).

Papon, Jean, *Recueil d'arrests notables des cours souveraines de france* (Paris, 1601).

The Parliament Rolls of Medieval England, eds C. Given-Wilson, P. Brand, A. Curry, R. E. Horrox, G. Martin, W. M. Ormrod and J. R. S. Phillips (Leicester and Woodbridge, 2005).

Paston Letters and Papers of the Fifteenth Century, vol. I, ed. N. Davis (Oxford, 1971).

Pearl, Poems of the Pearl Manuscript: Pearl, Cleanness, Patience, Sir Gawain and the Green Knight, eds Malcolm Andrew and Ronald Waldron, 5th edn (Exeter, 2007).

Petrarch, *Petrarch's Lyric Poems: The Rime Sparse and Other Lyrics*, ed. and trans. Robert M. Durling (Cambridge, MA, 1976).

Ptolemy, *Almagest*, trans. G. J. Toomer (London, 1984).

Receuil d'arts de seconde rhétorique, ed. E. Langlois (Paris, 1902).

The Record and Process of the Renunciation and Deposition of Richard II (1399) and Related Writings (Toronto, 2007).

Riga, Peter, *Aurora: Petri Rigae Biblia Versificata. A Verse Commentary on the Bible*, ed. Peter E. Beichner, 2 vols (Notre Dame, 1965).

Robert of Bridlington, *The Bridlington Dialogue: An Exposition of the Rule of St Augustine for the Life of the Clergy*, trans. A Religious of C. S. M. V. [R. P. Lawson] (London, 1960).

Robertus Richardinus, *Commentary on the Rule of St. Augustine*, ed. G. G. Coulton (Edinburgh, 1935).

Roger of Howden, *Chronica*, ed. William Stubbs, 4 vols, Rolls Ser. 51 (London 1868–71).

The Romans of Partenay or of Lusignen: Otherwise Known as The Tale of Melusine, ed. Rev. W. W. Skeat, EETS o.s. 22 (London, 1866).

Rotuli parliamentorum: ut et petitiones, et placita in parliamento, eds Richard Blyke, John Strachey *et al.*, 8 vols (London, 1780–1832).

Rupert of Deutz, *De sancta trinitate et operibus eius*, ed. Hrabanus Haacte, 4 vols. (Turnholt: Brepols, 1971–2).

Rymer, Thomas, *Foedera, conventiones, literae, et cujuscunque generis acta publica, inter reges Angliae*, 3rd edn (The Hague, 1739–1945).

The St Albans Chronicle: The 'Chronica maiora' of Thomas Walsingham, vol. 1, 1376–94, eds and trans John Taylor, Wendy R. Childs and Leslie Watkiss (Oxford, 2003).

Scot, Reginald, *Reginald Scot's the Discoverie of Witchcraft*, ed. Montague Summers (London, 1930).

Secretum Secretorum, ed. Robert Steele (Oxford, 1920).

Sedulius, *Sedulii Scotti Collectaneum in apostolum*, ed. Hermann Josef Frede and Herbert Stanjek, 2 vols. (Freiburg: Herder, 1996–7).

Shakespeare, William, *A Midsummer Night's Dream*, ed. Harold F. Brooks (London, 1979; rpt 1983).
——, *The Riverside Shakespeare*, ed. G. Blakemore Evans (Boston, 1997).
—— and John Fletcher, *The Two Noble Kinsmen*, ed. Lois Potter (Walton-on-Thames, 1997).
—— and George Wilkins, *Pericles, Prince of Tyre*, ed. Henry Norman Hudson (New York, 1901).
—— and George Wilkins, *Pericles, Prince of Tyre*, eds Doreen DelVecchio and Antony Hammond (Cambridge, 1998).
—— and George Wilkins, *Pericles*, ed. Suzanne Gossett, 3rd edn (London, 2004; rpt 2006).
——, *Shakespeare's History of Pericles, Prince of Tyre*, ed. William J. Rolfe (New York, 1898).
Sir Tristrem, *Lancelot of the Laik and Sir Tristrem*, ed. Alan Lupack (Kalamazoo, MI, 1994).
Skelton, John, *The Complete English Poems*, ed. V. J. Scattergood (New York, 1983).
'Le Songe Vert', ed. Léopold Constans, *Romania*, 33 (1904), 490–539.
Speculum Vitae: A Reading Edition, ed. Ralph Hanna III, 2 vols, EETS o.s. 331–332 (Oxford, 2008).
Statius, *Achilleid*, ed. and trans. D. R. Shackleton Bailey (Cambridge, MA, 2004).
The Statutes of the Realm, eds J. Caley *et al.*, 11 vols in 12 (London, 1810–28).
The Statues of the Realm, ed. T. E. Tomlins (London, 1816).
Thābit ibn Qurrah al-Harrānī, *De imaginibus*, in *The Astronomical Works of Thabit b. Qurra*, ed. Francis J. Carmody (Berkeley, CA, 1960).
——, *Historia Anglicana*, ed. Henry Thomas Riley, 2 vols (London, 1869).
The Three Kings of Cologne: An Early English Translation of the 'Historia Trium Regum' by John of Hildesheim, ed. C. Horstmann, EETS o.s. 85 (London, 1886).
The Three Kings of Cologne, Edited from London, Lambeth Palace MS 491, ed. Frank Schaer (Heidelberg, 2000).
The Tragedy of Master Arden of Faversham, ed. M. L. Wine (London, 1973).
Twyne, Lawrence, *The Patterne of Painefull Adventures* (London, 1594; rpt 1607).
Valerius Maximus, *Memorable Doings and Sayings*, ed. and trans. D. R. Shackleton Bailey (Cambridge, MA, 2006).
Walsingham, Thomas, *The Chronica Maiora of Thomas Walsingham (1376–1422)*, eds and trans D. Preest with J. G. Clark (Woodbridge, 2005).
The Westminster Chronicle, 1381–1394, eds L. C. Hector and B. F. Harvey (Oxford, 1982).

Secondary texts

Agamben, Giorgio, *Homo Sacer: Sovereign Power and Bare Life*, trans. Daniel Heller-Roazen (Stanford, CA, 1995).
——, *State of Exception*, trans. Kevin Attell (Chicago, MI, and London, 2005).
Akbari, Suzanne Conklin, 'Alexander in the Orient: bodies and boundaries', in *Postcolonial Approaches to the European Middle Ages*, eds Ananya Jahanara Kabir and Deanne Williams (Cambridge, 2005) pp. 105–26.
Allen, Elizabeth, *False Fables and Exemplary Truth in Later Middle English Literature* (New York, 2005).
Allen, R. S., 'John Gower and Southwark: the paradox of the social self', in *London*

and Europe in the Later Middle Ages, eds J. Boffey and P. King (London, 1995), pp. 111–47.

Amsler, Mark, 'The Wife of Bath and women's power', *Assays*, 4 (1986), 67–83.

Amsterdam, Anthony G. and Jerome Bruner, *Minding the Law* (Cambridge, 2000).

Anderson, Bonnie W. and Judith P. Zinsser, *A History of Their Own: Women in Europe from Prehistory to the Present*, 2 vols (New York, 1988).

André, Bernard, 'De sancta Katharina carmen "Cum Maxentius imperator" and De Sancto Andrea Apostolo "Si meritis dignas" (c.1509–1517)', *Sacris Erudiri*, 46 (2007), 440–50.

Archibald, Elizabeth, *Apollonius of Tyre: Medieval and Renaissance Themes and Variations* (Cambridge, 1991).

——, *Incest and the Medieval Imagination* (Oxford, 2001).

——, '"Deep clerks she dumbs": the learned heroine in *Apollonius of Tyre* and *Pericles*', *Comparative Drama*, 22, 4 (1988–9), 289–303.

Aston, Margaret, *Faith and Fire: Popular and Unpopular Religion, 1350–1600* (London, 1993).

Bacon, Marion, ed., *Life at Vassar: Seventy-five Years in Pictures* (Poughkeepsie, 1940).

Bailey, Paul, 'Insecure units', *London Times* (10 October 2003).

Baker, J. H., *An Introduction to English Legal History*, 4th edn (London, 2002).

Barron, Caroline M., 'The quarrel of Richard II with London, 1392–7', in *The Reign of Richard II: Essays in Honour of May McKisack*, eds F. R. H. Du Boulay and Caroline M. Barron (London, 1971), pp. 173–201.

——, 'William Langland: a London poet', in *Chaucer's England: Literature in Historical Context*, ed. Barbara Hanawalt (Minneapolis, MN, 1992).

Barsella, Susanna, 'Boccaccio, Petrarch, and Peter Damian: two models of the Humanist intellectual', *MLN*, 121, 1 (2006), 16–48.

Basile, Michael, '*Pericles*: theater review', *Shakespeare Bulletin*, 22 (Autumn 2004), 110.

Bately, Janet, '"Here comes the judge": a small contribution to the study of French input into the vocabulary of the law in Middle English', in *Placing Middle English in Context*, eds Irma Taavitsainen et al. (Berlin, 2000), pp. 255–75.

Baudrillard, Jean, *Seduction*, trans. Brian Singer (New York, 1990).

Baugh, A. C. and Thomas Cable, *A History of the English Language*, 5th edn (London, 2002).

Beauregard, David N., *Catholic Theology in Shakespeare's Plays* (Newark, NJ, 2008).

Beichner, P. E., 'Gower's use of *Aurora* in *Vox Clamantis*', *Speculum*, 30 (1955), 582–95.

Beidler, Peter G., 'Transformations in Gower's *Tale of Florent* and Chaucer's *Wife of Bath's Tale*', in *Chaucer and Gower: Difference, Mutuality, Exchange*, ed. R. F. Yeager (Victoria, B.C., 1991), pp. 100–114.

——, ed., *John Gower's Literary Transformations in the Confessio Amantis* (Washington DC, 1982).

Bellamy, J. G., *The Law of Treason in England in the Later Middle Ages* (Cambridge, 1970).

Bennett, J. A. W., 'Gower's "Honeste Love"', in *Patterns of Love and Courtesy: Essays in Memory of C. S. Lewis*, ed. John Lawlor (London, 1966), pp. 107–21.

Bennett, Michael J., 'The court of Richard II and the promotion of literature', in *Chaucer's England: Literature in Historical Context*, ed. Barbara Hanawalt (Minneapolis, MN, 1992), pp. 3–20.

——, 'The historical background', in *A Companion to the "Gawain"-Poet*, eds Derek Brewer and Jonathan Gibson (Cambridge, 1997), pp. 71–90.

——, '*Sir Gawain and the Green Knight* and the literary achievement of the northwest midlands: the historical background', *JMH*, 5 (1979), 63–88.

Bevington, David, *Shakespeare's Ideas: More Things in Heaven and Earth* (Oxford, 2008).

Bicks, Caroline, 'Backsliding at Ephesus: Shakespeare's Diana and the churching of women', in *Pericles: Critical Essays*, ed. David Skeele (New York, 2000), pp. 205–27.

Bishop, Louise M., 'A touch of Chaucer in *The Winter's Tale*', in *Shakespeare and the Middle Ages*, eds Martha Driver and Sid Ray (Jefferson, NC, 2009), pp. 237–9.

Blamires, Alcuin G., 'The Wife of Bath and Lollardy', *MÆ*, 58 (1989), 224–42.

Bloom, Harold, *The Anxiety of Influence* (Oxford and New York, 1973).

Bloomfield, Morton W., *The Seven Deadly Sins* (East Lansing, MI, 1952).

Blumenfeld-Kosinski, Renate, *Poets, Saints, and Visionaries of the Great Schism, 1378–1417* (University Park, PA, 2006).

Boffey, Julia, '"Cy ensuent trois chaunceons": groups and sequences of Middle English lyrics', in *Medieval Texts in Context*, eds Graham D. Caie and Denis Renevey (London, 2008), pp. 85–95.

Bollard, J. K., 'Sovereignty and the Loathly Lady in English, Welsh and Irish', *LSE*, n.s. 17 (1986), 41–59.

Bolte, Johannes, 'Begnadigung zum Stricktagen oder zur Heirat', *Zeitschrift des Vereins für Volkskunde*, 27 (PLACE, 1917).

Bourdieu, Pierre, *The Field of Cultural Production*, ed. and trans. Randal Johnson (New York, 1993).

——, *Outline of a Theory of Practice*, trans. Richard Nice (Cambridge, 1977).

Bowers, John M., *The Politics of 'Pearl': Court Poetry in the Age of Richard II* (Cambridge, 2001).

——, *Chaucer and Langland: The Antagonistic Tradition* (Notre Dame, IN, 2007).

——, '"Beautiful as Troilus": Richard II, Chaucer's Troilus, and figures of (un)masculinity', in *Men and Masculinity in Chaucer's 'Troilus and Criseyde'*, eds Tison Pugh and Marcia Smith Marzec (Cambridge, 2008), pp. 9–27.

——, 'Chaucer after Retters: the wartime origins of English literature', in *Inscribing the Hundred Years' War in French and English Cultures*, ed. Denise N. Baker (Albany, NY, 2000), pp. 91–125.

——, 'Latinity, colonialism, and resistance', in *Chaucer: Contemporary Approaches*, eds Susanna Fein and David Raybin (University Park, PA, 2009).

——, '*Pearl* in its royal setting: Ricardian poetry revisited', *SAC*, 17 (1995), 115–19.

——, 'Three readings of *The Knight's Tale*: Sir John Clanvowe, Geoffrey Chaucer, and James I of Scotland', *JMEMS*, 34 (2004), 279–307.

——, 'Two professional readers of Chaucer and Langland: Scribe D and the HM 114 Scribe', *SAC*, 26 (2004), 113–46.

Braeger, Peter C., 'The illustrations in New College MS. 266 for Gower's conversion tales', in *John Gower: Recent Readings*, ed. R. F. Yeager (Kalamazoo, MI, 1989), pp. 275–310.

Brand, Paul, 'The languages of the law in later medieval England', in *Multilingualism in Later Medieval Britain*, ed. D. A. Trotter (Cambridge, 2000), pp. 63–76.

Brewer, Derek, 'Chaucer's anti-Ricardian poetry', in *The Living Middle Ages: Studies in Mediaeval English Literature and Its Traditions*, eds Uwe Böker, Manfred Markus and Rainer Schöwerling (Stuttgart, 1989), pp. 115–28.

ten Brink, Bernhard, *Chaucer: Studien zur Geschichte seiner Entwicklung und zur Chronologie seiner Schriften* (Münster, 1870).

Brooks, Phyllis, 'Berkeley Shakespeare Festival: summer 1985', *SQ*, 37, 3 (1986), 393–9.

Brundage, James A., 'Rape and seduction in the medieval canon law', in *Sexual Practices and the Medieval Church*, eds Vern Bullough and James Brundage (Amherst, NY, 1994), pp. 141–8.

Buidler, Peter, 'New terminology for sources and analogues: or, let's forget the lost French source for *The Miller's Tale*', *SAC*, 28 (2006), 225–30.

Bullón-Fernandez, Maria, *Fathers and Daughters in Gower's 'Confessio Amantis'* (Cambridge, 2000).

Burnley, J. D., 'Chaucer, Usk, and Geoffrey of Vinsauf', *Neophilologus*, 69 (1985), 284–93.

Burrow, John A., 'Gower's poetic styles', in *Companion*, pp. 239–50.

Burrows, T. N., 'The foundation of Nostell Priory', *YAJ*, 53 (1981), 31–5.

——, 'The geography of monastic property in medieval England: a case study of Nostell and Bridlington Priories (Yorkshire)', *YAJ*, 57 (1985), 79–86.

Burton, Janet, *The Monastic Order in Yorkshire, 1069–1215* (Cambridge, 1999).

Butterfield, Ardis, '*Confessio Amantis* and the French tradition', in *Companion*, pp. 165–80.

Bynum, Caroline Walker, *Holy Feast and Holy Fast: The Religious Significance of Food to Medieval Women* (Berkeley, CA, 1987).

Calin, William, *The French Tradition and the Literature of Medieval England* (Toronto, 1994).

Calkin, Siobbahn Bly, *Saracens and the Making of English Identity: the Auchinleck Manuscript* (New York, 2005).

Carey, Hilary M., *Courting Disaster: Astrology at the English Court and University in the Later Middle Ages* (New York, 1992).

Carlin, M., *Medieval Southwark* (London and Rio Grande, 1996).

Carlson, David R., 'English poetry, July–October 1399, and Lancastrian crime', *SAC*, 29 (2007), 374–418.

——, 'Gower on Henry IV's rule: the endings of the *Cronica Tripertita* and its texts', *Traditio*, 62 (2007), 207–36.

——, 'Gower *pia vota bibit* and Henry IV in 1399 November', *ES*, 89 (2008), 377–84.

——, 'Gower's early Latin poetry: text-genetic hypotheses of an *Epistola ad regem* (ca. 1377–1380) from the evidence of John Bale', *MSt*, 65 (2003), 293–317.

——, 'A rhyme distribution chronology of John Gower's Latin poetry', *SP*, 104 (2007), 15–55.

Carlson, Marvin, *Performance: A Critical Introduction* (New York, 1996).

Carpenter, Christine, *Locality and Polity: A Study of Warwickshire Landed Society, 1401–1499* (Cambridge, 1992).

——, 'Law, justice, and landowners in late medieval England', *Law and History Review* 1, 2 (1983), 205–37.

Carpenter, Humphrey, *J. R. R. Tolkien: A Biography* (Boston, 2000).

de Certeau, Michel, *The Practice of Everyday Life*, trans. Steven Rendall (Berkeley, CA, 1984).

Cervone, Cristina, 'John de Cobham and Cooling Castle's charter poem', *Speculum*, 83 (2008), 884–916.

Cherniss, Michael D., *Boethian Apocalypse: Studies in Middle English Vision Poetry* (Norman, OK, 1987), 116–18.why page range?

Chism, Christine, *Alliterative Revivals* (Philadelphia, PA, 2002).

Chrimes, S. B., 'Richard II's questions to the judges, 1387', *Law Quarterly Review*, 72 (1956), 376–81.

Clanchy, Michael, 'Law and love in the Middle Ages', in *Disputes and Settlements: Law and Human Relations in the West*, ed. John Bossy (Cambridge, 1983), pp. 47–67.

Clementi, D., 'Richard II's ninth question to the judges', *EHR*, 86 (1971), 96–113.

Coffman, G. R., 'John Gower in his most significant role', *University of Colorado Studies* Series B, no. 2, 4 (1945), 52–61.

Cohen, Jeffrey Jerome, ed., *The Postcolonial Middle Ages* (New York, 2000).
Cohn, Norman, *The Pursuit of the Millenium: Revolutionary Millenarians and Mystical Anarchists of the Middle Ages* (London, 1957; rpt 1970).
Coleman, Janet, *English Literature in History, 1350–1400* (London, 1981).
Coleman, Joyce, 'Lay readers and hard Latin: how Gower may have intended the *Confessio Amantis* to be read', *SAC*, 24 (2002), 209–35.
——, 'Philippa of Lancaster, queen of Portugal – and patron of the Gower translation?', in *England and Iberia in the Middle Ages*, ed. María Bullón-Fernández (New York, 2007), pp. 135–65.
Collette, Carolyn P., *Performing Polity: Women and Agency in the Anglo-French Tradition, 1395–1620* (Turnhout, 2006).
—— and Vincent DiMarco, 'The matter of Armenia in the age of Chaucer', *SAC*, 23 (2001), 317–58.
Connolly, M., *John Shirley: Book Production and the Noble Household in Fifteenth-Century England* (Aldershot, 1998).
Cooper, Helen, *The English Romance in Time: Transforming Motifs from Geoffrey of Monmouth to the Death of Shakespeare* (Oxford, 2004).
——, 'Chaucerian representation', in *New Readings of Chaucer's Poetry*, eds Robert G. Benson and Susan J. Ridyard, intro. Derek Brewer (Cambridge, 2003), pp. 7–29.
——, 'The four last things in Dante and Chaucer: Ugolino in the House of Rumour', *NML*, 3 (1999), 39–66.
——, '"Peised Evene in the Balance": a thematic and rhetorical topos in the *Confessio Amantis*', *Mediaevalia*, 16 (1993), 113–39.
——, '"Welcome to the *House of Fame*: 600 years dead: Chaucer's deserved reputation as 'the father of English poetry'", *TLS*, 5091 (27 October 2000), 3–4.
——, '"This worthy olde writer": *Pericles* and other Gowers, 1592–1640', in *Companion*, pp. 99–113.
Copeland, Rita, *Rhetoric, Hermeneutics, and Translation in the Middle Ages* (Cambridge, 1991).
Crane, Susan, *The Performance of Self: Ritual, Clothing, and Identity During the Hundred Years War* (Philadelphia, PA, 2002).
Craun, Edwin T., *Lies, Slander, and Obscenity in Medieval English Literature: Pastoral Rhetoric and the Deviant Speaker* (Cambridge, 1997).
Cressman, Russell Ralph, 'Gower's *Cinkante Balade's* and French court lyrics' (unpublished doctoral dissertation, University of North Carolina at Chapel Hill, 1983).
Cressy, David, 'Purification, thanksgiving, and the purification of women in post-Reformation England', *Past and Present*, 141 (November 1993), 106–46.
Creswell, Julia, 'The tales of Acteon and Narcissus in the *Confessio Amantis*', *Reading Medieval Studies*, 7 (1981), 32–40.
Culler, Jonathan, *On Puns* (New York, 1988).
Davies, R. R., 'Richard II and the Principality of Chester 1397–9', in *The Reign of Richard II: Essays in Honour of May McKisack*, eds F. R. H. Du Boulay and Caroline M. Barron (London, 1971), pp. 267–70.
Dempster, Germaine, *Dramatic Irony in Chaucer* (Stanford, CA, 1932).
Dickinson, J. C., *The Origins of the Austin Canons and Their Introduction into England* (London, 1950).
Dimmick, Jeremy, '"Redinge of Romance" in Gower's *Confessio Amantis*', in *Tradition and Transformation in Medieval Romance*, ed. Rosalind Field (Cambridge, 1999), pp. 125–37.
Dinshaw, Carolyn, *Chaucer's Sexual Poetics* (Madison, WI, 1989).

——, 'Rivalry, rape and manhood: Gower and Chaucer', in *Violence Against Women in Medieval Texts*, ed. Anna Roberts (Gainesville, FL, 1998), pp. 137–60.

Doyle, A. I., 'English books in and out of court from Edward III to Henry VII', in *English Court Culture in the Later Middle Ages*, eds V. J. Scattergood and J. W. Sherborne (London, 1983), pp. 163–81.

—— and M. B. Parkes, 'The production of copies of the *Canterbury Tales* and the *Confessio Amantis* in the early fifteenth century', in *Medieval Scribes, Manuscripts and Libraries: Essays Presented to N. R. Ker*, eds M. B. Parkes and A. G. Watson (London, 1978), pp. 163–210.

Driver, Martha, 'A false imprint in Chaucer's Workes: protestant printers in London (and Zurich?)', in *Sources, Exemplars, and Copy-Texts: Influence and Transmission, Essays from the Lampeter Conference of the Early Book Society*, ed. William Marx (Lampeter, 1999), pp. 131–54.

——, 'Printing the *Confessio Amantis*: Caxton's edition in context', in *Re-Visioning Gower*, ed. R. F. Yeager (Asheville, NC 1998).

——, 'Women readers and Pierpont Morgan MS M. 126', in *John Gower: Manuscripts, Readers, Contexts, Disputatio*, ed. Malte Urban (Turnhout, forthcoming 2010), pp. 67–91.

Du Boulay, F. R. H and Caroline M. Barron, eds, *The Reign of Richard II: Essays in Honour of May McKisack* (London, 1971).

Duffy, Eamon, *The Stripping of the Altars: Traditional Religion in England 1400–1580* (New Haven, CT, 1992).

——, 'Was Shakespeare a Catholic?', *The Tablet* (27 April 1996), 536–8.

Düll, Siegrid, Anthony Luttrell and Maurice Keen, 'Faithful unto death: the tomb slab of Sir William Neville and Sir John Clanvowe, Constantinople 1391', *Antiquaries Journal*, 71 (1991), 174–90.

Duncan, E. H., 'The literature of alchemy and Chaucer's Canon's Yeoman's Tale: framework, theme, and characters', *Speculum*, 43 (1968), 633–4.

Duncan-Jones, Katherine, *Ungentle Shakespeare: Scenes from his Life* (London, 2001).

Dyer, Christopher, *Making a Living in the Middle Ages: The People of Britain 850–1520* (London, 2003).

Eberle, Patricia, 'Miniatures as evidence of reading in a manuscript of the *Confessio Amantis* (Pierpont Morgan MS M.126)', in *John Gower: Recent Readings*, ed. R. F. Yeager (Kalamazoo, MI, 1989), pp. 311–64.

Echard, Siân, ed., *A Companion to Gower* (Cambridge, 2004).

——, 'Gower's books of Latin: language, politics and poetry', *SAC*, 25 (2003), 123–56.

Eggers, Walter F., 'Shakespeare's Gower and the role of the authorial presenter', *PQ*, 54 (1975), 434–43.

Eisner, Sigmund, *A Tale of Wonder: A Source Study of The Wife of Bath's Tale* (New York, 1957).

Emmerson, Richard K., 'The prophetic, the apocalyptic, and the study of medieval literature', in *Poetic Prophecy in Western Literature*, eds Jan Wojick and Raymond-Jean Frontain (Madison, NJ, 1984), pp. 40–54.

——, 'Reading Gower in a manuscript culture: Latin and English in illustrated manuscripts of the *Confessio Amantis*', *SAC*, 21 (1999), 143–86.

Epstein, Robert, 'London, Southwark, Westminster: Gower's urban contexts', in *Companion*, pp. 43–60.

Equiano, Olaudah, *The Interesting Narrative and Other Writings*, ed. Vincent Caretta (New York, 2003).

Esch, Arno, 'John Gower's Erzahlkunst', in *Chaucer und seine Zeit: Symposion für Walter F. Schirmer*, ed. Arno Esch (Tübingen, 1968), pp. 207–39; and trans. Linda

Barney Burke, 'John Gower's narrative art', in *Gower's Confessio Amantis: A Critical Anthology*, ed. Peter Nicholson (Cambridge, 1991), pp. 81–108.

Evans, Joan, *Magical Jewels of the Middle Ages and the Renaissance Particularly in England* (Oxford, 1922).

Evans, Ruth, Andrew Taylor, Nicholas Watson and Jocelyn Wogan-Browne, 'The notion of vernacular theory', in *The Idea of the Vernacular: An Anthology of Middle English Literary Theory 1280–1520*, eds Jocelyn Wogan-Browne *et al.* (Exeter, 1999), pp. 314–30.

Everett, Barbara, '"By the rough seas reft": how the "badness" of the *Pericles* Quarto may be of Shakespeare's making', *TLS* (11 August 2006), 13–16.

Faith, Rosamund, 'The "great rumour" of 1377 and peasant ideology', in *The English Rising of 1381*, eds R. H. Hilton and T. H. Aston (Cambridge, 1984), pp. 43–74.

Fellows, Jennifer and Ivana Djordjevi, eds, *Sir Bevis of Hamtoun in Literary Tradition* (Cambridge, 2008).

Fenster, Thelma and Daniel Lord Smail, eds, *Fama: The Politics of Talk and Reputation in Medieval Europe* (Cornell, 2003).

Ferster, Judith, *Fictions of Advice: The Literature and Politics of Counsel in Late Medieval England* (Philadelphia, PA, 1996).

Fewster, Carol, *Traditionality and Genre in Middle English Romance* (Cambridge, 1987).

Field, Rosalind, 'The heavenly Jerusalem in *Pearl*', *MLR*, 81 (1986), 7–17.

Fienberg, Nona, 'Thematics of value in *The Book of Margery Kempe*', *MP*, 87, 2 (1989), 132–41.

Finke, Laurie, '"All is for to selle": breeding capital in the Wife of Bath's Prologue and Tale', in *Geoffrey Chaucer: The Wife of Bath: Complete, Authoritative Text with Biographical and Historical Contexts, Critical History, and Essays from Five Contemporary Critical Perspectives*, ed. Peter G. Biedler (New York, 1995), pp. 171–87.

Finlayson, John, 'Definitions of Middle English romance', *CR*, 15, 1/2 (1980–81), 44–62, 168–81.

Fish, Stanley, *There Is No Such Thing as Free Speech, and It's a Good Thing, Too* (Oxford and New York, 1993).

Fisher, John Hurt, *The Emergence of Standard English* (Lexington, KY, 1996).

——, *John Gower: Moral Philosopher and Friend of Chaucer* (New York, 1964; London, 1965).

——, 'A language policy for Lancastrian England', *PMLA*, 107 (1992), 1168–80.

——, 'The revision of the Prologue to the *Legend of Good Women*: an occasional explanation', *South Atlantic Bulletin*, 43 (1978), 75–84.

Fléchier, Esprit, *Mémoirs de Fléchier sur les Grands-Jours d'Auvergne*, ed. Yves-Marie Bercé (Paris, 1984).

Fletcher, Angus, *The Prophetic Moment: An Essay on Spenser* (Chicago, MI, 1971).

Fletcher, Christopher, *Richard II: Manhood, Youth, and Politics, 1377–99* (Oxford, 2008).

Foucault, Michel, *The History of Sexuality*, trans. Robert Hurley, 3 vols (London, 1979–88).

Fox, George Gillespie, *The Mediaeval Sciences in the Works of John Gower* (New York, 1966).

Frank, Robert W. Jr, *Chaucer and 'The Legend of Good Women'* (Cambridge, MA, 1972).

Fried, Debra, 'Rhyme puns', in *On Puns*, ed. Jonathan Culler (New York, 1988) pp. 83–99.

Froide, Amy M., 'Marital status as a category in early modern England', in *Singlewomen in the European Past 1250–1800*, eds Judith M. Bennett and Amy M. Froide (Philadelphia, PA, 1999), pp. 236–69.

Galbraith, V. H., 'John Seward and his circle', *Mediaeval and Renaissance Studies*, 1 (1941–3), 85–104.

Gallacher, Patrick J., *Love, the Word, and Mercury: A Reading of John Gower's 'Confessio Amantis'* (Albuquerque, NM, 1975).

Galloway, Andrew, 'Gower in his most learned role and the Peasants' Revolt of 1381', *Mediaevalia*, 16 (1993 for 1990), 329–47.

——, 'Gower's *Confessio Amantis*, the *Prick of Conscience*, and the history of the Latin gloss in early English literature', in *John Gower: Manuscripts, Readers, Contexts*, ed. Malte Urban (Turnhout, forthcoming 2010).

——, 'The literature of 1388 and the politics of pity in Gower's *Confessio Amantis*', in *The Letter of the Law: Legal Practice and Literary Production in Medieval England*, eds Emily Steiner and Candace Barrington (Ithaca, NY, and London, 2002), pp. 67–104.

——, 'Making history legal: *Piers Plowman* and the rebels of fourteenth-century England', *William Langland's Piers Plowman: A Book of Essays*, ed. Kathleen Hewett-Smith (New York, 2001), pp. 7–39.

——, 'The making of a social ethic in late-medieval England: from "Gratitudo" to "Kyndenesse"', *Journal of the History of Ideas*, 55 (1994), 365–83.

——, 'The rhetoric of riddling in late-medieval England: the "Oxford" riddles, the *Secretum philosophorum*, and the riddles in *Piers Plowman*', *Speculum*, 70 (1995), 78–9.

——, 'Visions and visionaries', in *The Oxford Handbook of Medieval Literature*, eds Elaine Treharne and Greg Walker (Oxford, forthcoming 2010).

Ganim, John M., 'Chaucer, Boccaccio, confession and subjectivity', in *The Decameron and the Canterbury Tales: New Essays on an Old Question*, eds Leonard Michael Koff and Brenda Deen Schildgen (London, 2000).

Ganzenmüller, Wilhelm, *Die Alchemie im Mittelalter* (Hildesheim, 1967).

Gastle, Brian, '"As if she were single": working wives and the late medieval English femme sole', in *The Middle Ages at Work: Practicing Labor in Late Medieval England*, eds Kellie Robertson and Michael Uebel (New York, 2004), pp. 41–64.

Genette, Gérard, *Narrative Discourse: An Essay in Method*, trans. Jane E. Lewin (Ithaca, NY, 1980).

Gessler, Jean, 'Le marriage sous la potence', *Le Folklore Brabançon*, 7, 37/38 (1927–8), 115–35.

Giancarlo, Matthew, *Parliament and Literature in Late Medieval England* (Cambridge, 2007).

——, 'Murder, lies, and storytelling: the manipulation of justice(s) in the parliaments of 1397 and 1399', *Speculum*, 77 (2002), 76–112.

Gilbert, Jane, 'Men behaving badly: linguistic purity and sexual perversity in Derrida's *Le Monolinguisme de l'autre* and Gower's *Traitié pour essampler les amantz marietz*', *Romance Studies*, 24 (2006), 77–89.

Gillespie, Alexandra, *Print Culture and the Medieval Author: Chaucer, Lydgate, and Their Books, 1473–1557* (Oxford, 2006).

Gillespie, James L., 'Richard II's archers of the crown', *Journal of British Studies*, 18 (1979), 14–29.

——, 'Thomas Mortimer and Thomas Molineux: Radcot Bridge and the appeal of 1397', *Albion*, 7 (1975), 161–73.

Gilroy-Scott, Neil, 'John Gower's reputation: literary allusions from the early fifteenth century to the time of *Pericles*', *YoES*, 1 (1971), 30–47.

Given-Wilson, Chris, *Chronicles of the Revolution 1397–1400: The Reign of Richard II* (Manchester, 1993).

—, *The Royal Household and the King's Affinity, 1360–1413* (New Haven, CT, 1986).
—, 'Perrers [married name Windsor], Alice (d. 1400/01)', *ODNB*.
— and Alice Curteis, *The Royal Bastards of Medieval England* (London, 1984).
Goodman, Anthony, *John of Gaunt: The Exercise of Princely Power in Fourteenth-Century Europe* (Harlow, 1992).
Goodrich, Peter, 'Literacy and the languages of the early common law', *Journal of Law and Society*, 14, 4 (1987), 433–6.
Goodwin, Amy W., 'The Griselda Game', *CR*, 39, 1 (2004), 41–69.
Grady, Frank, 'The generation of 1399', in *The Letter of the Law: Legal Practice and Literary Production in Medieval England*, eds Emily Steiner and Candace Barrington (Ithaca, NY, 2002), pp. 202–29.
—, 'Gower's boat, Richard's barge, and the true story of the *Confessio Amantis*: text and gloss', *Texas Studies in Literature and Language*, 44 (2002), 1–15.
—, 'The Lancastrian Gower and the limits of exemplarity', *Speculum*, 70 (1995), 552–75.
Grand, Roger, 'Justice criminelle: procédure et peins dans les villes aux XIIIe et XIVe siècles', *Bibliothèques de l'école des chartes*, 102 (1941), 51–108.
Green, Richard Firth, *A Crisis of Truth: Literature and Law in Ricardian England* (Philadelphia, PA, 1999).
Greenblatt, Stephen, *Will in the World: How Shakespeare Became Shakespeare* (New York, 2004).
Griffiths, Jeremy, '*Confessio Amantis*: the poem and its pictures', in *Gower's Confessio Amantis: Responses and Reassessments*, ed. A. J. Minnis (Cambridge, 1983), pp. 163–78.
Grinnell, Natalie, 'Medea's humanity and John Gower's romance', *Medieval Perspectives*, 14 (1999), pp. 70–83.
Hagman, Lynn Wells, 'A study of Gower's *Cinkante Balades*' (unpublished doctoral dissertation, University of Detroit, 1968).
Hamilton, George L., 'Some sources of the seventh book of Gower's *Confessio Amantis*', *MP*, 9 (1912), 323–46.
—, 'Studies in the sources of Gower', *JEGP*, 26 (1927), 491–520.
Hanawalt, Barbara, ed., *Chaucer's England: Literature in Historical Context* (Minneapolis, MN, 1992).
Hanna, Ralph III, *Pursuing History: Middle English Manuscripts and their Texts* (Stanford, CA, 1996).
—, 'Augustinian canons and Middle English literature', in *The English Medieval Book: Studies in Memory of Jeremy Griffiths*, eds A. S. G. Edwards *et al.* (London, 2000), pp. 27–42.
—, 'Some North Yorkshire scribes and their context', in *Medieval Texts in Context*, eds G. D. Caie and D. Renevey (London, 2008), pp. 167–91.
—, 'The Yorkshire circulation of *Speculum Vitae*', in *Design and Distribution of Late Medieval Manuscripts in England*, eds Margaret Connolly and Linne R. Mooney (York, 2008), 279–91.
Harding, Alan, *A Social History of English Law* (Gloucester, MA, 1963; rpt 1973).
Harris, Kate, 'John Gower's *Confessio Amantis*: the virtues of bad texts', in *Manuscripts and Readers in Fifteenth-Century England: The Literary Implications of Manuscript Study*, ed. Derek Pearsall (Cambridge, 1983), pp. 27–40.
—, 'The Longleat House extracted manuscript of Gower's *Confessio Amantis*', in *Middle English Poetry: Texts and Traditions, Essays in Honour of Derek Pearsall*, ed. A. J. Minnis (York, 2001), pp. 77–90.

BIBLIOGRAPHY

——, 'Unnoticed extracts from Chaucer and Hoccleve: Huntington MS HM 144, Trinity College, Oxford MS D 29 and *The Canterbury Tales*', *SAC*, 20 (1998), 167–99.

Hatton, Thomas, 'John Gower's use of Ovid in Book III of the *Confessio Amantis*', *Mediaevalia*, 13 (1989), 257–74.

——, 'The role of Venus and Genius in John Gower's *Confessio Amantis*: a reconsideration', *Greyfriar*, 16 (1975), 29–40.

Heal, Felicity, *Hospitality in Early Modern England* (Oxford, 1990).

Heather, P. J., 'Precious stones in the Middle-English verse of the fourteenth century', *Folklore*, 42 (1931), 217–64.

Heng, Geraldine, *Empire of Magic: Medieval Romance and the Politics of Cultural Fantasy* (New York, 2003).

Higham, Florence, *Southwark Story* (London, 1955).

Hill, Betty, 'Alexanderromance: the Egyptian connection', *LSE*, n.s. 12 (1981), 185–94.

Hill, Thomas D., '"Half-waking, half-sleeping": a tropological motif in a Middle English Lyric and its European context', *RES*, n.s. 29 (1978), 50–56.

——, '*Stet Verbum Regis*: why Henryson's husbandman is not a king', *ES*, 86, 2 (April 2005), 127–32 (p. 129).

Hillman, Richard, 'Shakespeare's Gower and Gower's Shakespeare: the larger debt of *Pericles*', *SQ*, 36, 4 (Winter 1985), 427–37.

Hines, John, Nathalie Cohen and Simon Roffey, '*Iohannes Gower, Armiger, Poeta*: records and memorials of his life and death', in *Companion*, pp. 23–41.

Hiscoe, David W., 'Heavenly sign and comic design in Gower's *Confessio Amantis*', in *Sign, Sentence, Discourse: Language in Medieval Thought and Literature*, eds Julian N. Wasserman and Lois Roney (Syracuse, NY, 1989), 228–44.

——, 'The Ovidian comic strategy of Gower's *Confessio Amantis*', *Mediaevalia*, 13 (1987), 257–74.

Horobin, Simon, 'A manuscript found in the library of Abbotsford House and the lost legendary of Osbern Bokenham', *English Manuscript Studies, 1100–1700*, 14 (2007), 132–64.

Hoeniger, F. David, 'Gower and Shakespeare in *Pericles*', *SQ*, 33, 4 (Winter 1982), 461–79.

Holdsworth, W. S., *A History of English Law* (London, 1903–9).

Holmyard, E. M., *Alchemy* (New York, 1957).

Honigmann, E. A. J., *Shakespeare: The 'Lost Years'* (Manchester, 1998).

Hope, Emily Allen, 'The *Speculum Vitae*: addendum', *PMLA*, 32 (1917), 133–62.

Hornstein, Lillian Herlands, 'The historical background of *The King of Tars*', *Speculum*, 16 (1941), 404–14.

Houk, Deborah Lyn, 'The Politics of Seduction: Comparing Balzac and Sand' (unpublished PhD dissertation, Univ. of Pennsylvania, Philadelphia, 1997).

Hunt, Tony, *Miraculous Rhymes: The Writing of Gautier de Coinci* (Cambridge, 2007).

Ito, Masayoshi, *John Gower, The Medieval Poet* (Tokyo, 1976).

Jones, Kelly, '"The quick and the dead": performing the poet Gower in *Pericles*', in *Shakespeare and the Middle Ages*, eds Martha Driver and Sid Ray (Jefferson, NC, 2009).

Jones, R., *The Royal Policy of Richard II: Absolutism in the Late Middle Ages* (Oxford, 1968).

Jones, T., 'Richard II: royal villain or victim of spin', *The Times* (4 October 2008).

——, 'Was Richard II a tyrant? Richard's use of the books of rules for princes', in *Fourteenth Century England, V*, ed. N. E. Saul (Woodbridge, 2008), pp. 130–60.

——, R. F. Yeager, T. Dolan, A. Fletcher and J. Dor, *Who Murdered Chaucer? A Medieval Mystery* (London, 2003).

Justice, Steven, *Writing and Rebellion: England in 1381* (Berkeley, CA, 1994).

——, 'Lollardy at court', in *Cambridge History of Medieval English Literature*, ed. David Wallace (Cambridge, 1999), pp. 670–73.

Kaluza, Max, *Chaucer und der Rosenroman: Eine Litterargeschichtliche Studie* (Berlin, 1893).

Kane, George, 'Outstanding problems of Middle English scholarship', in *Chaucer and Langland: Historical and Textual Approaches* (Berkeley, CA, 1989; rpt 1977), pp. 228–41.

Kaye, Joel, *Economy and Nature in the Fourteenth Century: Money, Market Exchange, and the Emergence of Scientific Thought* (Cambridge, 1998).

Kelly, Henry Ansgar, *Love and Marriage in the Age of Chaucer* (Ithaca, NY, and London, 1975).

——, 'Bishop, prioress, and bawd in the stews of Southwark', *Speculum*, 75, 2 (2000), 342–88.

Kendall, Elliot, *Lordship and Literature: John Gower and the Politics of the Great Household* (Oxford, 2008).

Kennedy, E. D., 'Gower, Chaucer, and French prose Arthurian romance', *Mediaevalia*, 16 (1993), 55–90.

Kerby-Fulton, Kathryn, *Reformist Apocalypticism and Piers Plowman* (Cambridge, 1990).

—— and Steven Justice, 'Scribe D and the marketing of Ricardian literature', in *The Medieval Professional Reader at Work*, eds Kathryn Kerby-Fulton and Maidie Hilmo (Victoria, B.C., 2001), pp. 217–32.

Kermode, Frank, *The Sense of an Ending: Studies in the Theory of Fiction* (New York, 1967).

Kiser, Lisa, *Telling Classical Tales: Chaucer and the 'Legend of Good Women'* (Ithaca, NY, 1983).

Kittredge, G. L., 'TITLE', *The Nation*, 71 (27 September 1900), pp. 254–6.

Knapp, Peggy A., 'The work of alchemy', *JMEMS*, 30 (2000), 575–99.

Knight, Stephen Thomas, *Rhyming Craftily: Meaning in Chaucer's Poetry* (Sydney, 1973).

Knowles, D. and R. N. Hadcock, *Medieval Religious Houses: England and Wales*, 2nd edn (London, 1971).

——, et al., eds, *The Heads of Religious Houses: England and Wales, I. 940–1216*, 2nd edn (Cambridge, 2001).

Kobayashi, Yoshiko, '*Principis Umbra*: kingship, justice and pity in John Gower's poetry', in *On John Gower: Essays at the Millenium*, ed. R. F. Yeager (Kalamazoo, MI, 2007), pp. 71–103.

Kolve, V. A., 'From Cleopatra to Alceste: an iconographic study of *The Legend of Good Women*', in *Signs and Symbols in Chaucer's Poetry*, eds John P. Hermann and John J. Burke (University AL, 1981), pp. 130–78.

Laidlaw, J. C., 'Christine de Pizan, the Earl of Salisbury and Henry IV', *French Studies*, 36 (1982), 129–43.

Landes, Richard, 'The fear of an apocalyptic year 1000: Augustinian historiography, medieval and modern', *Speculum*, 75 (2000), 97–145.

Lawless, George, *Augustine of Hippo and His Monastic Rule* (Oxford, 1987).

Lawrence, A., 'A northern English school? Patterns of production and collection of manuscripts in the Augustinian houses of Yorkshire in the twelfth and thirteenth centuries', in *Yorkshire Monsticism: Archaeology, Art and Architecture, from the 7th to the 16th Centuries*, ed. L. R. Hoey (Leeds, 1995), pp. 145–53.

Leicester, H. Marshall, Jr, *The Disenchanted Self: Representing the Subject in the Canterbury Tales* (Berkeley, CA, 1990), 26–8.
Lerner, Robert E., *The Powers of Prophecy: The Cedars of Lebanon Vision from the Mongol Onslaught to the Dawn of the Enlightenment* (Berkeley, CA, 1983).
——, 'The Black Death and Western European eschatological mentalities', *American Historical Review*, 86 (1981), 533–52.
——, 'Medieval prophecy and religious dissent', *Past and Present*, 72 (1976), 3–24.
——, 'Refreshment of the saints: the time after antichrist as a station for earthly progress in medieval thought', *Traditio*, 32 (1976), 97–144.
Lewis, C. S., *The Allegory of Love* (Oxford, 1939).
——, 'Gower', in *Gower's Confessio Amantis: A Critical Anthology*, ed. Peter Nicholson (Cambridge, 1991), pp. 15–39.
Lightbown, Ronald W., *Mediaeval European Jewellery, with a Catalogue of the Collection in the Victoria and Albert Museum* (Hong Kong, 1992).
Lindeboom, W., 'Rethinking the recensions of the *Confessio Amantis*', *Viator*, 40 (2009), 319–48.
Linden, Stanton J., *Darke Hierogliphicks: Alchemy in English Literature from Chaucer to the Restoration* (Lexington, KY, 1996).
Lipton, Emma, *The Politics of Sacramental Marriage in Late Medieval English Literature* (Notre Dame, IN, 2007).
Little, Katherine, 'Chaucer's parson and the specter of Wycliffism', *SAC*, 23 (2001), 225–53.
Lomperis, Linda, 'From God's book to the play of the text in the *Cosmographia*', *Medievalia et Humanistica*, 16 (1988), 51–71.
Loomis, Roger S., *Arthurian Literature in the Middle Ages: A Collaborative History* (Oxford, 1959).
de Lubac, Henri, *Exégèse médiévale: Les quatre sens de l'écriture*, 4 vols (Paris, 1959–64).
Lynch, Kathryn L., *The High Medieval Dream-Vision: Poetry, Philosophy, and Literary Form* (Stanford, CA, 1988).
——, 'Dating Chaucer', *CR*, 42 (2007), 1–22.
Macaulay, G. C., 'John Gower 6. The English *Confessio Amantis*', in *The Cambridge History of English and American Literature*, eds A. W. Ward, A. R. Waller, W. P. Trent, J. Erskine, S. P. Sherman and C. Van Doren, 18 vols (Cambridge, 1907–21), vol. 2, *The End of the Middle Ages*, eds A. W. Ward and A. R. Waller (Cambridge, 1908), pp. 153–78.
McCarthy, Connor, *Marriage in Medieval England* (Cambridge, 2004).
MacCracken, H. N., 'Quixley's Ballades Royal (?1402)', *YAJ*, 20 (1908), 33–50.
McFarlane, K. B., *Lancastrian Kings and Lollard Knights* (Oxford, 1972)
——, *The Nobility of Later Medieval England* (Oxford, 1973).
McGinn, Bernard, *The Calabrian Abbot: Joachim of Fiore in the History of Western Thought* (New York, 1985).
——, 'The abbot and the doctors: scholastic reactions to the radical eschatology of Joachim of Fiore', *Church History*, 40 (1971), 30–47.
——, 'Apocalypticism in the Middle Ages: an historiographical sketch', *MSt*, 37 (1975), 252–86.
——, *Visions of the End: Apocalyptic Traditions in the Middle Ages* (New York, rev. edn, 1998).
McGovern, William M., 'Contract in medieval England: the necessity for quid pro quo and a sum certain', *The American Journal of Legal History*, 13, 3 (1969), 173–201.
Machan, Tim William, *English in the Middle Ages* (Oxford, 2003).
——, 'Medieval multilingualism and Gower's literary practice', *SP*, 103 (2006), 1–25.

McKelvey, John Jay, *Principles of Common-Law Pleading*, 2nd edn, revd (New York, 1894; rpt 1917).

McKinley, Kathryn, 'Lessons for a king from John Gower's *Confessio Amantis*', in *Metamorphosis: The Changing Face of Ovid in Medieval and Early Modern Europe*, eds Alison Keith and Stephen Rupp (Toronto, 2007), pp. 107–28.

Mahoney, Dhira B., 'Gower's two Prologues to *Confessio Amantis*', in *Re-visioning Gower*, ed. R. F. Yeager (Asheville, NC, 1998), pp. 17–37.

Malina, Bruce J., *The Social World of Jesus and the Gospels* (New York, 1996).

Manzalaoui, M. A., '"Noght in the Registre of Venus": Gower's English mirror for princes', in *Medieval Studies for J. A. W. Bennett*, ed. P. L. Heyworth (Oxford, 1981).

Marks, Peter, 'Theater review: high jinks on the high seas, and a little Shakespeare, too', *New York Times* (10 November 1998).

Markus, Robert A., *Saeculum: History and Society in the Theology of St Augustine*, rev. edn (Cambridge, 1989).

Martin, G. H., 'Henry Knighton's *Chronicle* and Leicester Abbey', in *Leicester Abbey: Medieval History, Archaeology and Manuscript Studies*, eds J. Story et al. (Leicester, 2006), pp. 119–25.

Masciandaro, Nicola, *The Voice of the Hammer* (Notre Dame, IN, 2007).

Matter, E. Ann, review: 'Gilbert Dahan, *L'éxégèse chrétienne de la Bible en Occident médiévale: XIIe–XIVe siècle*', rev. E. Ann Matter, *Speculum*, 77 (2002), 1272–4.

Matthews, Dakin, 'Foreword: "the skeleton in the mirror", an interview with Dakin Matthews by Michael Almereyda', in *Shakespeare and the Middle Ages*, eds Martha W. Driver and Sid Ray (Jefferson, NC, 2009).

Meecham-Jones, Simon, 'Questioning romance: Amadas and Ydoine in Gower's *Confessio Amantis*', *Parergon*, 17, 2 (2000), 35–49.

Mehl, Dieter, *The Middle English Romances of the Thirteenth and Fourteenth Centuries* (New York, 1969).

Mellinkoff, David, *The Language of the Law* (Boston, 1963).

Metlitzki, Dorothee, *The Matter of Araby in Medieval England* (New Haven, CT, 1977).

Meyer-Lee, Robert, *Poets and Power From Chaucer to Wyatt* (Cambridge, 2007).

——, 'Thomas Hoccleve and the apprehension of money', *Exemplaria*, 13 (2001), 173–214.

Middleton, Anne, 'The idea of public poetry in the reign of Richard II', *Speculum*, 53 (1978), 94–114.

Millward, Peter, *Shakespeare's Religious Background* (Chicago, MI, 1973).

Minet-Mahy, Virginie, *Esthétique et pouvoir de l'oeuvre allégorique à l'époque de Charles VI: Imaginaires et discours* (Paris, 2005).

Minnis, Alastair, *Chaucer and Pagan Antiquity* (Cambridge, 1982).

——, *Medieval Theory of Authorship: Scholastic Literary Attitudes in the Later Middle Ages*, 2nd edn (Aldershot, 1988).

——, 'Fifteenth-century versions of Thomistic literalism: Girolamo Savonarola and Alfonso de Madrigal', in *Neue Richtungen in der hoch- und spätmittelalterlichen Bibelexegese*, eds Robert E. Lerner and Elisabeth Müller-Luckner (Munich, 1996), pp. 163–80.

——, 'John Gower, *sapiens* in ethics and politics', *MÆ*, 49 (1980), 207–29.

—— and Ian Johnson, eds, *The Cambridge History of Literary Criticism*, vol. 2, *The Middle Ages* (Cambridge, 2005).

Miola, Robert, 'Shakespeare's religion', *First Things* (May 2008), http://www.firstthings.com/article/2008/04/002-shakespeares-religion-43 (accessed December 2009).

Miskimin, Alice S., *The Renaissance Chaucer* (New Haven, CT, 1975).

Mitchell, J. Allan, *Ethics and Exemplary Narrative in Chaucer and Gower* (Cambridge, 2004).
——, 'Gower for example: *Confessio Amantis* and the ethics of exemplarity', *Exemplaria*, 16 (2004), 203–34.
Mooney, Linne R. 'Chaucer's scribe', *Speculum*, 81 (2006), 97–138.
——, 'John Shirley's heirs', *YoES*, 33 (2003), 182–98.
Morawski, Lech, 'Law, fact and legal language', *Law and Philosophy*, 18 (1999), 461–73.
Morris, T. M., 'The Augustinian use of Oseney Abbey: a study of the Oseney Ordinal, Processional and Tonal' (unpublished doctoral thesis, University of Oxford, 1999).
Muscatine, Charles, *Chaucer and the French Tradition* (Berkeley, CA, 1957).
Musson, Anthony and W. M. Ormrod, *The Evolution of English Justice: Law, Politics and Society in the Fourteenth Century* (Houndmills, 1999).
Nicholson, Peter, *Gower's Confessio Amantis: A Critical Anthology* (Cambridge, 1991).
——, *Love and Ethics in Gower's 'Confessio Amantis'* (Ann Arbor, MI, 2005).
——, 'Chaucer borrows from Gower: the sources of the *Man of Law's Tale*', in *Chaucer and Gower: Difference, Mutuality, Exchange*, ed. R. F. Yeager (Victoria, B.C., 1991), pp. 85–99.
——, 'The dedications of Gower's *Confessio Amantis*', *Mediaevalia*, 10 (1984), 160–80.
——, 'Gower's revisions in the *Confessio Amantis*', *CR*, 19 (1984), 123–43.
——, review: 'David Carlson, "Gower on Henry IV's rule"', *JGN*, 28, 1 (2009), 7–8.
Nolan, Barbara, *The Gothic Visionary Perspective* (Princeton, NJ, 1977).
Nowlin, Steele, 'Narratives of incest and incestuous narratives: memory, process, and the *Confessio Amantis*'s "Middel Weie"', *JMEMS*, 35 (2005), 217–44.
Ogrinc, Will H. L., 'Western society and alchemy from 1200 to 1500', *JMH*, 6 (1980), 103–32.
Olsen, Alexandra Hennessey, *'Betwene Ernest and Game': The Literary Artistry of the 'Confessio Amantis'* (New York, 1990).
Olsson, Kurt, *John Gower and the Structures of Conversion: A Reading of the 'Confessio Amantis'* (Cambridge, 1992).
——, 'John Gower's *Vox Clamantis* and the medieval idea of place', *SP*, 84 (1987), 134–58.
Orme, Nicholas, *Medieval Children* (New Haven, CT, 2003).
Ormrod, W. M., 'Finance and trade under Richard II', in *Richard II: The Art of Kingship*, ed. Anthony Goodman and James Gillespie (Oxford, 1999), pp. 155–86.
——, 'The uses of English: language, law, and political culture in fourteenth-century England', *Speculum*, 78, 3 (2003), 773–8.
——, 'Who was Alice Perrers?', *CR*, 40, 3 (2006), 219–29.
Owen, Charles A. Jr, 'Notes on Gower's Prosody', *CR*, 28, 4 (1994), 405–13.
Palmer, J. N. N., *England, France and Christendom 1377–99* (Chapel Hill, NC, 1972).
——, 'The parliament of 1385 and the constitutional crisis of 1386', *Speculum*, 46 (1971), 477–90.
Parker, David, *The Commonplace Book in Tudor London* (Lanham, MD, 1998).
Parkes, M. B., *English Cursive Book Hands 1250–1500*, 2nd edn (London, 1979).
——, *Their Hands Before Our Eyes: A Closer Look at Scribes* (Aldershot, 2008).
——, 'Patterns of scribal activity and revisions of the text in early copies of works by John Gower', in *New Science Out of Old Books: Studies in Manuscripts and Early Printed Books in Honour of A. I. Doyle*, eds R. Beadle and A. J. Piper (Aldershot and Brookfield, 1995), pp. 81–121.
—— and A. I. Doyle, 'The production of copies of the *Canterbury Tales* and the *Confessio Amantis* in the early fifteenth century', in *Medieval Scribes, Manuscripts*

and Libraries: Essays Presented to N. R. Ker, eds M. B. Parkes and A. G. Watson (London, 1978), pp. 163–210.

Partington, J. R., 'Albertus Magnus on alchemy', *Ambix*, 1 (1937), 15–16.

Patterson, Lee, *Chaucer and the Subject of History* (Madison, WI, and London, 1991).

——, 'Perpetual motion: alchemy and the technology of the self', *SAC*, 15 (1993), 25–57.

Pearsall, Derek, *The Canterbury Tales* (London, 1985; rpt 1993).

——, *The Life of Geoffrey Chaucer* (Oxford, 1992).

——, *Old English and Middle English Poetry* (London, 1977).

——, 'The development of Middle English romance', *MSt*, 27 (1965), 91–116.

——, 'The Gower tradition', in *Confessio Amantis: Responses and Reassessments*, ed. A. J. Minnis (Cambridge, 1983), pp. 179–97.

——, 'Gower's Latin in the *Confessio Amantis*', in *Latin and Vernacular: Studies in Late-Medieval Texts and Manuscripts*, ed. A. J. Minnis (Cambridge, 1989), pp. 13–25.

——, 'Gower's narrative art', *PMLA*, 81 (1966), 475–84.

——, 'Langland's London', in *Written Work: Langland, Labor, and Authorship*, eds Steven Justice and Kathryn Kerby-Fulton (Philadelphia, PA, 1997), pp. 185–207.

——, 'Manuscripts and illustrations', in *Companion*, pp. 61–97.

——, 'The Rede (Boarstall) Gower: British Library, MS Harley 3490', in *The English Medieval Book: Studies in Memory of Jeremy Griffiths*, eds A. S. G. Edwards *et al.* (London, 2000), pp. 87–99, and his revised description in *JGN*, 28, 1 (2009), 20–34.

Peck, Russell A., *Kingship and Common Profit in Gower's 'Confessio Amantis'* (Carbondale, IL, 1978).

——, 'Folklore and powerful women in Gower's "Tale of Florent"', in *The English 'Loathly Lady' Tales: Boundaries, Traditions, Motifs*, eds S. Elizabeth Passmore and Susan Carter (Kalamazoo, MI, 2008), pp. 100–145.

——, 'John Gower and the Book of Daniel', in *John Gower: Recent Readings*, ed. R. F. Yeager (Kalamazoo, MI, 1989) pp. 159–87.

——, 'The politics and psychology of governance in Gower: ideas of kingship and real kings', in *Companion*, pp. 215–38.

——, 'The problematics of irony in Gower's *Confessio Amantis*', *Mediaevalia*, 15 (1993), 207–29.

Perloff, Marjorie, 'The sound of poetry/the poetry of sound: the 2006 MLA Presidential Forum', *PMLA*, 123, 3 (May 2008), 749–61.

Perry, Ben Edwin, *The Ancient Romances: A Literary–Historical Account of Their Origins* (Berkeley, CA, 1967).

Peterson, Ingrid J., *William of Nassington: Canon, Mystic, and Poet of the Speculum Vitae* (New York, 1986).

Pfaff, R. W., *The Liturgy in Medieval England* (Cambridge, 2009).

Plucknett, Theodore F. T., *Early English Legal Literature* (Cambridge, 1958).

Pohl, Christine D., *Making Room: Recovering Hospitality as a Christian Tradition* (Cambridge, 1999).

Pollock, Frederick and Frederic W. Maitland, *The History of English Law*, 2nd edn (Cambridge, 1968).

Pope, M. K., *From Latin to Modern French with Especial Consideration of Anglo-Norman* (place, 1934; rev. edn, 1952).

Porter, Elizabeth, 'Gower's ethical microcosm and political macrocosm', in *Gower's 'Confessio Amantis': Responses and Reassessments*, ed. A. J. Minnis (Cambridge, 1983), pp. 135–62.

Potter, Lois, 'Shakespeare performed: *The Two Noble Kinsmen* in 1993–94', *SQ*, 47 (1996), 197–203.

Pouzet, Jean-Pascal, 'Augustinian canons and their insular French books in medieval England: towards an assessment', in *Language and Culture in Medieval Britain: The French of England c.1100–c.1500*, eds J. Wogan-Browne *et al.* (York, 2009), pp. 266–77.

——, 'Book production outside commercial contexts', *The Production of Books in England 1350–1530*, eds A. Gillespie and D. Wakelin (Cambridge, forthcoming).

Pugh, Tison, *Queering Medieval Genres* (New York, 2004).

Raybin, David, '"And pave it al of silver and of gold": the humane artistry of *The Canon's Yeoman's Tale*, in *Rebels and Rivals: The Contestive Spirit in The Canterbury Tales*, eds Susanna Greer Fein, David Raybin and Peter C. Braeger (Kalamazoo, MI, 1991), pp. 189–212.

Read, J. and F. H. Sawyer, *Prelude to Chemistry: An Outline of Alchemy, Its Literature and Relationships* (New York, 1937).

Reeves, Marjorie, *The Influence of Prophecy in the Later Middle Ages: A Study in Joachimism* (Oxford, 1969).

——, *Joachim of Fiore and the Prophetic Future* (London, 1976).

——, 'The development of apocalyptic thought: medieval attitudes', in *The Apocalypse in English Renaissance Thought and Literature*, eds C. A. Patrides and Joseph Wittreich (Manchester, 1984), pp. 40–73.

——, 'History and prophecy in medieval thought', *Medievalia et Humanistica*, n.s. 5 (1974), 51–75.

——, 'The originality and influence of Joachim of Fiore', *Traditio*, 36 (1980), 269–316.

Richardson, H. G., 'Year books and plea rolls as sources of historical information', *TRHS*, ser. 4, 5 (1922), 38–40.

Rigg, A. G., *A History of Anglo-Latin Literature 1066–1422* (Cambridge, 1992).

Rigg, A. G. and Edward S. Moore, 'The Latin works: politics, lament and praise', in *Companion*, pp. 153–64.

Roberts, Jane, 'A Lancashire lease', in *People and Texts: Relationships in Medieval Literature*, eds Thea Summerfield and Keith Busby (Amsterdam, 2007), pp. 161–74.

Robins, William, 'Romance, *exemplum*, and the subject of the *Confessio Amantis*', *SAC*, 19 (1997), 157–81.

Rothwell, William, 'Aspects of lexical and morphosyntactical mixing in the languages of medieval England', in *Multilingualism in Later Medieval Britain*, ed. D. A. Trotter (Woodbridge, 2000), pp. 213–33.

——, 'English and French in England after 1362', *ES*, 6 (2001), 539–99.

——, 'The trilingual England of Geoffrey Chaucer', *SAC*, 16 (1994), 45–67.

Runacres, Charles, 'Art and ethics in the "exempla" of *Confessio Amantis*', in *Gower's 'Confessio Amantis': Responses and Reassessments*, ed. A. J. Minnis (Cambridge, 1983), pp. 106–34.

Rust, Martha Dana, *Imaginary Worlds in Medieval Books: Exploring the Manuscript Matrix* (New York, 2007).

Ryan, James D., 'Toleration denied: Armenia between east and west in the era of the crusades', in *Tolerance and Intolerance: Social Conflict in the Age of the Crusades*, eds Michael Gervers and James M. Powell (Syracuse, NY, 2001), pp. 55–64.

Sadlek, Gregory M., *Idleness Working: The Discourse of Love's Labor from Ovid through Chaucer and Gower* (Washington DC, 2004).

Said, Edward, *Orientalism* (London, 1978).

Salisbury, E., 'Violence and the sacrificial poet: Gower, the *vox*, and the critics', in *On John Gower: Essays at the Millenium*, ed. R. F. Yeager (Kalamazoo, MI, 2007), pp. 124–43.

Salter, Elizabeth and Derek Pearsall, 'Pictorial illustration of late medieval poetic texts: the role of the frontispiece or prefatory picture', in *Medieval Iconography and Narrative: A Symposium*, eds Flemming G. Andersen *et al.* (Odense, 1980), pp. 100–123.

Saul, N. E., *Richard II* (New Haven, CT, and London, 1997).

Scanlon, Larry, *Narrative, Authority, and Power: The Medieval Exemplum and the Chaucerian Tradition* (Cambridge and New York, 1994).

——, 'The riddle of incest: John Gower and the problem of medieval sexuality', in *Re-visioning Gower*, ed. R. F. Yeager (Charlotte, NC, 1998), pp. 93–127.

Schieberle, Misty, '"Thing which a man mai noght areche": women and counsel in Gower's *Confessio Amantis*', *CR*, 42 (2007), 91–109.

Schmitz, Götz, 'Gower, Chaucer and the classics: back to the textual evidence', in *John Gower: Recent Readings*, ed. Robert Yeager (Kalamazoo, MI, 1989), pp. 209–23.

——, 'The priesthood of genius: a study of the medieval tradition', *Gower's Confessio Amantis: A Critical Anthology*, ed. Peter Nicholson (Cambridge, 1991), pp. 117–42.

Schnell, Rüdiger, 'The discourse on marriage in the Middle Ages', *Speculum*, 73 (1998), 771–86.

Seaton, Ethel, '*Le Songe Vert*: its occasion of writing and its author', *MÆ*, 19 (1950), 1–16.

Sherborne, James W., 'Perjury and the Lancastrian Revolution of 1399', *Welsh History Review*, 14 (1988), 217–41.

Shoaf, R. A., *Dante, Chaucer, and the Currency of the World* (Norman, OK, 1983).

Simpson, James, *Reform and Cultural Revolution: The Oxford English Literary History, Volume II, 1350–1547* (Oxford, 2002).

——, *Sciences and the Self in Medieval Poetry: Alan of Lille's Anticlaudianus and John Gower's Confessio Amantis* (Cambridge and New York, 1995).

Skeat, W. W., *The Chaucer Canon* (Oxford, 1900).

Southern, R. W., 'Aspects of the European tradition of historical writing 2: Hugh of St Victor and the idea of historical development', *TRHS*, 5th ser. 21 (1971), 159–79.

Spargo, John W., 'The Canon's Yeoman's Prologue and Tale', in *Sources and Analogues of Chaucer's Canterbury Tales*, eds W. F. Bryan and Germaine Dempster (Chicago, MI, 1941), pp. 691–2.

Spearing, A. C., *Medieval Dream-Poetry* (Cambridge, 1976).

Staley, Lynn, *Languages of Power in the Age of Richard II* (University Park, PA, 2005).

——, *Margery Kempe's Dissenting Fictions* (University Park, PA, 1994).

——, 'Gower, Richard II, Henry of Derby, and the business of making culture', *Speculum*, 75 (2000), 68–96.

Stanbury, Sarah, *Seeing the Gawain-poet: Description and the Act of Perception* (Philadelphia, PA, 1991).

Steiner, Emily, *Documentary Culture and the Making of Medieval English Literature* (Cambridge, 2003).

Stevens, Martin, 'The royal stanza in early English literature', *PMLA*, 94 (1979), 62–76.

Stillwell, Gardner, 'John Gower and the last years of Edward III', *SP*, 45 (1948), 454–71.

Stow, George B., 'Richard II in Jean Froissart's *Chroniques*', *JMH*, 11 (1985), 333–45.

——, 'Richard II in John Gower's *Confessio Amantis*: some historical perspectives', *Medievalia*, 16 (1993), 3–31.

Strohm, Paul, *Hochon's Arrow: The Social Imagination of Fourteenth-Century Texts* (Princeton, NJ, 1992).

——, 'Chaucer's Lollard joke: history and the textual unconscious', *SAC*, 17 (1995), 23–42.

——, 'The origin and meaning of Middle English *romance*', *Genre*, 10 (1977), 1–28.

BIBLIOGRAPHY

——, 'Queens as intercessors', in *Hochon's Arrow: The Social Imagination of Fourteenth-Century Texts* (Princeton, NJ, 1992), pp. 95–119.

——, 'Saving the appearances: Chaucer's *Purse* and the fabrication of the Lancastrian claim', in *Chaucer's England: Literature in Historical Context*, ed. Barbara A. Hanawalt (Minneapolis, MN, and London, 1992), pp. 21–40.

——, '*Storie, spelle, geste, romaunce, tragedie*: generic distinctions in the Middle English Troy narratives', *Speculum*, 46, 2 (1971), 348–59.

Symons, Dana, ed., *Chaucerian Dream Visions and Complaints* (Kalamazoo, MI, 2004).

Tatlock, John S. P., *The Development and Chronology of Chaucer's Works* (London, 1907).

Taylor, F. Sherwood, *The Alchemists: Founders of Modern Science* (London, 1962).

Taylor, Gary, 'The transmission of Pericles', *Publications of the Bibliographical Society of America*, 80 (1986), 193–217.

Tester, Jim, *A History of Western Astrology* (Suffolk, 1987).

Thomas, Keith, *Religion and the Decline of Magic* (New York, 1971).

Thompson, Ann, *Shakespeare's Chaucer: A Study in Literary Origins* (Liverpool, 1978).

Thompson, J. J., *Robert Thornton and His Book-Producing Activities: Aspects of the Transmission of Certain Medieval Texts in the Light of Their Present Context in Thornton's Manuscripts* (York, 1983).

Thomson, Patricia, 'The "*Canticus Troili*": Chaucer and Petrarch', *Comparative Literature*, 11 (1959), 313–28.

Thorndike, Lynn, *A History of Magic and Experimental Science During the First Thirteen Centuries of Our Era*, 4 vols, 2nd edn (New York, 1923).

Thrupp, Sylvia, *The Merchant Class in Medieval London, 1300–1500* (Ann Arbor, MI, 1948; rpt 1989).

Tinkle, Teresa, *Medieval Venuses and Cupids: Sexuality, Hermeneutics, and English Poetry* (Stanford, CA, 1996).

Tolkien, J. R. R., '*Sir Gawain and the Green Knight*' (1953), in *The Monsters and the Critics and Other Essays*, ed. Christopher Tolkien (London, 2006), pp. 72–108.

Toste, Marco, 'Virtue and the city: the virtues of the ruler and the citizen in the medieval reception of Aristotle's *Politics*', in *Princely Virtues in the Middle Ages: 1200–1500*, eds I. P. Bejczy and C. J. Nederman (Turnhout, 2007), pp. 73–98.

Toulmin-Smith, L., ed., *Expeditions to Prussia and the Holy Land made by Henry, Earl of Derby* (London, 1894).

Trotter, D. A., ed., *Multilingualism in Later Medieval Britain* (Cambridge, 2000).

Tubbs, J. W., *The Common Law Mind: Medieval and Early Modern Conceptions* (Baltimore, MD, 2000).

Tuck, Anthony, *Richard II and the English Nobility* (New York, 1974).

Tyerman, Christopher, *England and the Crusades 1095–1588* (Chicago, MI, 1988).

Van Es, F. and Charles Didies, 'Encore le mariage sous la potence', *Folklore Brabançon*, 7, 42 (1928), 340–43.

Vauchez, André, *La Sainteté en Occident aux derniers siècles du moyen âge d'aprés les procés de canonisation et les documents hagiographiques* (Rome, 1981).

Vickers, Brian, *Shakespeare Co-Author: A Historical Study of Five Collaborative Plays* (Oxford, 2002).

——, 'On the function of analogy in the occult', in *Hermeticism and the Renaissance: Intellectual History and the Occult in Early Modern Europe*, eds Ingrid Mekel and Allen G. Debus (Washington DC and London, 1988), pp. 265–92.

Waithe, Marcus, *William Morris's Utopia of Strangers: Victorian Medievalism and the Ideal of Hospitality* (Cambridge, 2006).

Walker, Simon, *The Lancastrian Affinity, 1361–1399* (Oxford, 1990).

——, 'John, duke of Aquitaine and duke of Lancaster, styled king of Castile and León (1340–1399)', *ODNB*.
Wallace, David, *Chaucerian Polity: Absolutist Lineages and Associational Forms in England and Italy* (Stanford, CA, 1997).
——, *Premodern Places: Calais to Surinam, Chaucer to Aphra Behn* (Oxford, 2004).
Walter, D. P., *Spiritual and Demonic Magic from Ficino to Campanella* (London, 1958).
Warren, W. L., *King John* (Berkeley, CA, 1961).
Warton, Thomas, *The History of English Poetry from the Close of the Eleventh to the Commencement of the Eighteenth Century*, 4 vols (London, 1778).
Watson, Nicholas, 'The politics of Middle English writing', in *The Idea of the Vernacular: An Anthology of Middle English Literary Theory 1280–1520*, eds Jocelyn Wogan-Browne *et al.* (Exeter, 1999), pp. 331–52.
Watt, Diane, *Amoral Gower: Language, Sex and Politics* (Minneapolis, MN, 2003).
——, 'Literary genealogy, virile rhetoric, and John Gower's *Confessio Amantis*', *PQ*, 79 (1999), 389–415.
Webber, T. and A. G. Watson, eds, *The Libraries of the Augustinian Canons* (London, 1998).
Wenzel, Siegfried, *The Sin of Sloth: Acedia in Medieval Thought and Literature* (Chapel Hill, NC, 1967).
Wetherbee, W., 'Classical and Boethian tradition in the *Confessio Amantis*', in *Companion*, pp. 181–96.
——, 'Genius and interpretation in the *Confessio Amantis*', in *Magister Regis: Studies in Honor of Robert Earl Kaske*, ed. Arthur Groos (New York, 1986), pp. 241–60.
——, 'Latin structure and vernacular space: Gower, Chaucer and the Boethian tradition', in *Chaucer and Gower: Difference, Mutuality, Exchange*, ed. R. F. Yeager (Victoria, B.C., 1991), pp. 7–35.
——, 'Rome, Troy and culture in the *Confessio Amantis*', in *On John Gower: Essays at the Millennium*, ed. R. F. Yeager (Kalamazoo, MI, 2007), pp. 20–42.
Whitaker, Muriel A., '*Pearl* and some illustrated apocalypse manuscripts', *Viator*, 12 (1981), 183–96.
White, Hugh, *Nature, Sex, and Goodness in a Medieval Literary Tradition* (Oxford, 2000).
——, 'Division and failure in Gower's *Confessio Amantis*', *Neophilologus*, 72 (1988), 605–7, 613–15.
——, 'Nature and the good in Gower's *Confessio Amantis*', in *John Gower: Recent Readings*, ed. R. F. Yeager (Kalamazoo, MI, 1989), pp. 1–20.
Wickert, Maria, *Studies in John Gower*, trans. Robert J. Meindl (Washington DC, 1981).
Wilkins, Ernest H., '*Cantus Troili*', *ELH*, 16 (1949), 167–73.
Willard, James Field, 'Inland transportation in England during the fourteenth century', *Speculum*, 1, 4 (1926), 361–74.
Wilson, Richard, *Secret Shakespeare: Studies in Theatre, Religion and Resistance* (Manchester, 2004).
Wimsatt, James I., *Chaucer and His French Contemporaries: Natural Music in the Fourteenth Century* (Toronto, 1991).
——, *Chaucer and the French Love Poets: The Literary Background of the Book of the Duchess* (Chapel Hill, NC, 1968).
——, *Chaucer and the Poems of 'Ch' in University of Pennsylvania MS French 15* (Cambridge, 1982).
Wogan-Browne, Jocelyn, *et al.*, eds, *Language and Culture in Medieval Britain: The French of England c.1100–c.1500* (York, 2009).
—— with Nicholas Watson, 'The French of England: the *Compileison*, *Ancrene Wisse*, and the idea of Anglo-Norman', in *Cultural Traffic in the Medieval Romance World*,

eds Simon Gaunt and Julian Weiss, *Journal of Romance Studies*, 4, 3 (Winter 2004), pp. 35–58.

——, et al., eds, *The Idea of the Vernacular: An Anthology of Middle English Literary Theory 1280–1520* (Exeter, 1999).

Woodruff, C. E., *Catalogue of the Manuscript Books in the Library of Christ Church, Canterbury* (Canterbury, 1911).

Woolgar, C. M., 'Group diets in late medieval England', in *Food in Medieval England*, eds C. M. Woolgar, D. Serjeantson and T. Waldron (New York, 2006).

Wormald, F. and C. E. Wright, eds, *The English Library before 1700: Studies in Its History* (London, 1958).

Wright, L. C., 'Trade between England and the Low Countries: evidence from historical linguistics', in *England and the Low Countries in the Late Middle Ages*, eds Caroline Barron and Nigel Saul (Stroud, 1995), pp. 169–79.

Yeager, R. F., ed., *Chaucer and Gower: Difference, Mutuality, Exchange* (Victoria, B.C., 1991).

——, *John Gower: Cinkante Balades and Traitié Pour les Amantz Marietz* (Kalamazoo, MI, forthcoming 2010).

——, *John Gower's Poetic: The Search for a New Arion* (Cambridge, 1990).

——, ed. and trans., *John Gower: The French Balades* (Kalamazoo, MI, forthcoming 2010).

——, 'Did Gower write *Cento*?', in *John Gower: Recent Readings*, ed. R. F. Yeager (Kalamazoo, MI, 1989), pp. 113–32.

——, 'Gower's French audience: the *Mirour de l'Omme*', *CR*, 41, 2 (2006), 111–37.

——, 'Gower's Lancastrian affinity: the Iberian connection', *Viator*, 35 (2004), 483–515.

——, 'John Gower and the *exemplum* form: tale models in the *Confessio Amantis*', *Mediaevalia*, 8 (1982), 307–35.

——, 'John Gower's audience: the Ballades', *CR*, 40 (2005), 81–105.

——, 'John Gower's French', in *Companion*, pp. 137–51.

——, 'John Gower's images: "The Tale of Constance" and "The Man of Law's Tale"', in *Speaking Images: Essays in Honour of V. A. Kolve*, ed. R. F. Yeager and Charlotte Morse (Asheville, NC, 2001), pp. 525–57.

——, 'Learning to speak in tongues: writing poetry for a trilingual culture', in *Chaucer and Gower: Difference, Mutuality, Exchange*, ed. R. F. Yeager (Victoria, B.C., 1991), pp. 115–29.

——, 'Politics and the French language in England during the Hundred Years' War: the case of John Gower', in *Inscribing the Hundred Years' War in French and English Cultures*, ed. Denise Baker (Albany, NY, 2000), pp. 127–57.

——, 'Shakespeare as medievalist: what it means for performing Pericles', in *Shakespeare and the Middle Ages*, eds Martha W. Driver and Sid Ray (Jefferson, NC, 2009) , pp. 215–31.

Zeeman, Nicolette, '"Studying" in the Middle Ages – and in *Piers Plowman*', *NML*, 3 (1999), 185–212.

Index

Agrippa, Heinrich Cornelius 142, 144–5
Alain de Lille 205, 214, 288, 295
Albertus Magnus 142
alchemy 27, 30, 157–68, 169–81
Alexander (the Great) 32–4, 69, 71–2, 140, 143–4, 147–9, 155, 176, 184, 211, 266
Amans 54–5, 64, 76–7, 80–1, 130, 143, 145, 147, 152–3, 159, 165–6, 175, 194, 199, 206, 212–16, 217–26, 228–9, 240–3, 248, 301–2
Anne of Bohemia (Queen Anne) 280–1
Appellant Lords 86, 100–8, 129, 137
apocalypse 46–58
Aquinas, Thomas 61, 137, 203
Arabic (language) 172
Arion 46–58, 151–3, 251
Aristotle 34, 82, 140, 143, 147, 176, 197–8, 204, 211, 300
Armenia 35–45
Arnold of Villanova 158
Arnulf of Orléans 20
Arundel, Earl of (Richard Fitzalan) 101, 103, 105
Arundel, Thomas, Archbishop of Canterbury 94, 97, 101–2, 107n.12, 110, 305
astrology/astronomy 15, 33, 37, 82–3, 139–56
Augustinian movement 11–24, 49, 308
Avicenna 173

Bartholomaeus Anglicus 155
Beves of Hamtoun 37–8
Boccaccio 155, 276
Boethius 15, 18, 29, 244, 290
  see also Chaucer, *Boece*
Bible 14, 16–17, 47, 61, 68–70, 80, 82, 265
— I Corinthians 69
— Daniel 47–9, 69, 290
— Galatians 299
— Genesis 68, 200
— Gospels 47, 50, 55–6, 128, 201
— Isaiah 50, 51

— Psalms, Book of 51, 325n.40
— Romans 200
— I Thessalonians 200
— II Thessalonians 50
Black Death, the 93
Bonus, Petrus 162–3, 166
Bovet, Honoré 290
Brinton, Thomas, Bishop of Rochester 299–301
Brunetto Latini 34, 140, 186

Chaucer, Geoffrey 1, 17, 36, 45, 73, 79–81, 85, 175n.25, 188–90, 207, 279–85, 287, 291, 310, 315, 317–18, 321
— *Anelida and Arcite* 42, 44, 252
— *Boece* 198
— *Book of the Duchess*, the 240–2, 248, 252, 278
— *Canterbury Tales*, the 38, 78, 83, 115, 131, 164–5n.14, 172–4, 181, 183, 185–6, 189–94, 207–10, 240–2, 245–7, 250, 252–3, 254, 258–9, 276, 278, 279–84, 286–7, 289, 321
— *House of Fame*, the 253, 278
— *Legend of Good Women*, the 276–87
— *Parliament of Fowls*, the 281
— *Romance of the Rose*, the 252–3
— *Troilus and Criseyde* 207–10, 228, 240, 245–6, 250, 252–3, 278, 281, 285–6
Chrétien de Troyes 78, 255
Christianity 34, 41, 44, 50–3, 67, 72, 116–17, 120, 133, 196–7, 203, 213, 216, 218, 244, 263–4, 296
Christine de Pizan 155, 286, 290, 310
Church, the
  see Christianity
Cicero 42
Clanvowe, Sir John 281–2, 297
Cobham, John 101–3, 299
Cola di Rienzo 53
Comestor, Peter 14
Courtenay, William, Archbishop of Canterbury 95

crime
  see law
Crowned King, The 291
crusade 26, 38, 42, 81, 116

Daniel, Samuel 303
Dante 144, 157, 170, 278
David, King 57, 68, 268–9
Denne, William 89
Deschamps, Eustache 231, 309–10, 313
dream-vision 281, 288–303
Dunbar, William 217

economics 26, 28–30, 57–8, 157, 159, 164–6, 182–95, 198, 243, 290
Edmund of Abingdon 18, 24
Edward III 272–5, 313
Edward, Duke of York 282, 284
Egypt 26–34, 39, 43, 140, 283
English (language) 3–4, 114–16, 127, 155, 158, 163, 167, 172, 181, 189, 284–5, 287, 302, 304–5, 313–14, 318–19
Ergome, John 291

Ficino, Marsilio 142, 144
Fletcher, John 318
Fortescue, Sir John 118
French (language) 1, 3–4, 99, 114–17, 155–61, 219, 264, 273–5, 281, 284–5, 287, 290, 291, 304–14
Froissart, Jean 223, 231, 281

Genius 61, 64, 71, 74–5, 77–8, 80–1, 130, 143, 145, 147, 159, 161, 165–6, 176, 179, 194, 196–205, 206, 211, 212–13, 215–16, 217–21, 223–6, 228–9, 233n.8, 239–41, 243, 301
genre 74–84, 167–8, 186, 191, 194, 219, 236, 281
Giles of Rome 92, 94, 96
Gloucester, Duke of (Thomas of Woodstock) 101, 103, 105
Gloucester, 9th Earl of (Humphrey) 287, 291
Gower, John, biography 1–3, 263, 276, 279, 308, 319
—, works
  Carmen super Multiplici Viciorum Pestilencia 14, 87
  Cinkante Balades 214, 230–8, 272, 286, 309–14

Confessio Amantis 2, 3, 4–5, 14, 15, 17, 18, 25, 26–34, 35–45, 46–9, 56–8, 59–63, 67, 69–70, 74–84, 85, 87–90, 91, 96, 126–38, 139–56, 157–68, 169–70, 173–80, 182–8, 196–200, 205, 206–16, 217–29, 233n.8, 239–43, 263, 265–7, 276–87, 288, 301–2, 325
— Prologue 36, 46, 49–58, 62–3, 73, 80, 139–40, 167, 175, 180, 182, 183, 184, 187–8, 194–5, 197, 302, 304–5
— tales (Book):
  Achilles and Deidama (V), 127, 129–32, 136–7
  Acis and Galatea (II) 222
  Adrian and Bardus (V) 71–2, 159–60, 244–5, 251, 252
  Agamemnon and Clytemnestra, see Orestes (below)
  Alboin and Rosamund (I) 65–6, 210, 220
  Alexander and the pirate (III) 71
  Apollonius of Tyre (VIII) 63, 78, 211, 220, 227, 246–8, 252, 282, 316–17, 321
  Athemus and Demophon (III) 73
  Barlaam and Josaphat, see The gods of the nations (below)
  Boniface (II) 252
  Canace and Machaire (III) 220, 227, 282
  Capaneus (I) 210
  Ceix and Alceone (IV) 292, 301
  Constance (II) 153–4, 211, 321
  Crassus, see Virgil's mirror (below)
  Demephon and Phyllis (IV) 220, 283
  Diogenes and Aristippus (VII) 164–5
  Dives and Lazarus (VI) 81
  Eneas and Dido (IV) 153–4, 220, 283
  False bachelor, the (II) 72, 211, 220
  Florent (I) 63, 78, 183, 189–94, 215, 254–62, 276
  Foolish virgins, the (IV) 210
  Grosseteste (IV) 210
  Hercules and Achelons (IV) 75–6, 78, 80
  Hercules and Deianira (II) 266
  Jason and Medea (V) 96, 127, 132–4, 136–7, 145, 215, 220, 266, 283
  Jephthah's daughter (IV) 41–2

INDEX

Lucrece, Rape of (VII) 64, 72, 131, 170, 176–80, 248, 252, 266, 283
Lycurgus and his laws (VII) 64, 252
Midas (V) 27–30, 209
Mundus and Paulina (I) 210–11, 220, 266
Narcissus (I) 209–10
Nauplus and Ulysses (IV) 153
Nebuchadnezzar (I) 69, 210
Nectanabus (VI) 27, 32–4, 69, 143, 146–9, 155, 211, 220, 248, 266
Nero (VI) 72–3, 211
Orestes (III) 266
Paris and Helen (V) 211, 221, 266
Phrixus and Helle (V) 127, 135–7
Pompey and the king of Armenia (VII) 42–4
Pygmaleon (IV) 210
Pyramus and Thisbe (III) 283
Rosiphelee (IV) 40–2, 64–5, 78–9, 218–19, 244, 252
Saul and the witch (VI) 146
Solomon (VII) 252
Tereus (V) 96, 215, 219–20, 244, 248, 252, 266, 283
Theseus and Ariadne (V) 244, 248–9, 252, 283
Three questions, the (II) 70–1, 248–51, 252
Trojan horse, the (I) 79, 211
Trump of Death (I) 63–4
Two beggars, the (V), 243, 245, 249, 252
Two coffers, the (V) 243, 245
Ulysses and Penelope (IV) 220, 252
Ulysses and Telegonus (VI) 64, 145–6, 211, 266
Ulysses' dream (VI) 64
Valentinian (V) 266
Virgil's mirror (V) 210
Zoroaster (VI) 146
— The gods of the nations (Book V) 31–2
Cronica Tripertita 14, 18, 19–20, 68n.29, 69, 85, 87–9, 98–111, 274, 286, 289, 305, 310
'Eneidos, Bucolis' 304
'H. aquile pullus' 305, 314
'In Praise of Peace' 112–25, 272, 305, 310

Mirour de l'Omme (Speculum Meditantis) 3, 13, 14, 15, 57, 67, 69, 91–2, 137, 217, 222–3, 225–7, 242, 265, 268–72, 275, 284, 292–4, 301, 311–13
'O deus immense' 89
'O recolende' 305, 313–14
'Rex celi deus' 305
Traitié pour Essampler les Amantz Marietz 84, 214, 263–75, 306–7, 309, 312
Vox Clamantis 3, 11, 14, 16, 19, 20–21, 46, 48–9, 54–5, 66–9, 83, 86–9, 92–6, 109, 180, 196–205, 284, 288–92, 294–7, 299–300, 310
de Grandson [Granson], Otto [Oton] 231, 310
Greene, Robert 315, 321
Grosmont, Henry, Duke of Lancaster 311, 313
Groundolf, Agnes 263, 309
Guillaume de Machaut 223, 231, 297, 301, 309

Havelok 79–80, 83
Henry IV (Henry Bolingbroke, Earl of Derby, Duke of Lancaster) 2, 85–97, 99–100, 102, 107, 112–14, 117–18, 120–5, 135, 156, 169, 171, 186–7, 195, 272, 285–6, 289, 305, 309–11, 313–14
see also Lancastrian party
Henry de Bracton 192–3
Higden, Ranulf 33
Hoccleve, Thomas 17, 18, 80
Holcot, Robert 33

Islam 37, 39, 52, 116–17

Jean de Meun
see *Roman de la Rose*
Joachim of Fiore 51–2
John of Garland 20
John of Gaunt 88, 95, 274–5, 278, 286, 310
Jonson, Ben 315
Justinian 77

Kempe, Margery 191n.24
King Horn 83
King of Tars, The 37, 39
kingship 30–1, 37–8, 42–4, 47, 57–8,

355

INDEX

63–4, 72–3, 82, 91–7, 99, 113–14, 117, 120–1, 126–38, 139–40, 147, 155, 160, 176, 179–80, 185–6, 268–72
Knighton, Henry 19

Lancastrian party 85–97, 100–2, 110–11, 112, 118, 120, 122–3, 286–7, 289, 305, 307–8, 311–12
Langland, William 73, 83, 87, 172, 199, 279, 282, 284, 291
Latin (language) 1, 3–4, 14, 16, 19, 26, 82, 98, 109–10, 114–15, 118, 127–8, 158, 163, 172–3, 184, 219, 264, 266, 275, 284–5, 287, 291, 296, 304–5, 312–14
law 2, 3, 57–8, 179, 183, 191–2, 200, 203, 256, 258, 276
Livre de Cent Ballades 309–10
Lollardy 181, 280
London 68, 82, 96, 107–8, 182–3, 187–8, 190, 195, 261, 279–81, 284–5, 296
love 40–2, 57–8, 67, 70, 74, 91, 139, 145, 155–6, 166, 184, 205, 208, 212–16, 217–29, 231–8, 243, 254, 263, 266, 280, 288, 292, 294, 297–8, 312, 324
Lydgate, John 18, 80–1, 155

Maidstone, Richard 280–1
Mandeville's *Travels* 37, 39, 44
manuscript illustration 47, 147–56, 182
manuscripts 11–25, 184–5, 263, 265, 280, 286–7, 306
  Cambridge, St John's College, MS A.7 96n.23
  Cambridge, St John's College, MS N.11 (524) 14, 23
  Cambridge, Trinity College, MS O. 2. 30 23
  Canterbury Cathedral, Dean and Chapter Library, MS Lit. E.10 23
  Glasgow, Hunterian Library, MS T. 2.17 88
  London, BL, MS Additional 59495 ('Trentham') 230n.1, 309, 313
  London, BL, MS Additional 63592 23
  London, BL, MS Cotton Faustina A.viii 13, 23
  London, BL, MS Cotton Tiberius C.vii 19
  London, BL, MS Egerton 272 13–14, 23

London, BL, MS Harley 1612 141
London, BL, MS Harley 3490 18–19
London, BL, MS Harley 6291 89
London, BL, MS Harley 7333 17
London, BL, MS Harley 7334 286
London, BL, MS Royal 7. A. I 19, 23
London, BL, MS Royal 7. A. IX 24
London, BL, MS Royal 10. B. VII 24
London, BL, MS Sloane 3847 156
London, BL, MS Stowe 951 16, 306, 309, 312
London, Society of Antiquaries, MS 134 18
Longleat House MS 174 156
New York, Pierpont Morgan Library, MS M 126 47n.5, 48n.6, 48n.7, 147–56
Oxford, All Souls College, MS 98 89, 305
Oxford, Bodleian Library, MS Ashmole 1285 15–16, 21, 24, 25
Oxford, Bodleian Library, MS Ashmole 1471 141
Oxford, Bodleian Library, MS Bodley 294 36, 287
Oxford, Bodleian Library, MS Bodley 822 15
Oxford, Bodleian Library, MS Bodley 924 24
Oxford, Bodleian Library, MS Digby 138 21–2
Oxford, Bodleian Library, MS Fairfax 3 15, 47–8n.6
Oxford, Bodleian Library, MS Hatton 92 20, 22
Oxford, Bodleian Library, MS e Museo 52 141
Oxford, Bodleian Library, MS Rawlinson B.177 24
Oxford, Christ Church, MS 148 287
Oxford, Corpus Christi College, MS 198 286
Oxford, Merton College, MS 325 16
Oxford, New College, MS 266 47n.5, 147
Oxford, Trinity College, MS D 29 17
Oxford, Trinity College, MS 31 24
Paris, Bibliothèque de la Sorbonne, BS MS 153 14, 24
Princeton, Princeton University Library, MS 5 47–8n.6

356

INDEX

San Marino CA, MS EL 26.C.9 (the 'Ellesmere Chaucer') 287
marriage 39, 71, 133–4, 177, 185, 190–3, 204, 251, 254–62, 263–75, 306
Melusine 37, 39–40
Menagier de Paris 254
Merciless Parliament
  see Appellant Lords
Mum and the Sothsegger 291

Nebuchadnezzar 57
  see also Gower–works–*Confessio Amantis*–tales–Nebuchadnezzar
Neckam (Nequam), Alexander 17, 185
Nostell Priory 307, 309, 311–12

Old English (language)
  see English (language)
Ovid 17, 20, 27–31, 51, 59, 67, 75, 77, 82–3, 179, 220, 234, 301

papacy 37, 121, 170–1, 300
Partenay 39–40
Peasants' revolt, the 93–4, 96, 180, 288–90, 295–6, 298–300
Pearl 281, 286
Perrers, Alice 272–3
Petrarch 52–3, 185, 276, 278, 296
Philippe de Mézières 37, 40, 43–4, 290, 297
Pierce the Plowman's Creed 284
Piers Plowman
  see Langland, William
Pinkhurst, Adam 286
Pliny 185–6
politics 40, 46, 50, 54–8, 59, 66–7, 72–3, 82, 85–97, 128, 136–8, 174–6, 183, 187–9, 197–8, 205, 290–1, 298, 305–6, 313
Prussia 41

Quixley, John or Robert de 306–9, 311–12, 314

Radcot Bridge, Battle of 108
religion 31–4, 135, 162, 296, 298, 302
  see also Christianity, Islam
rhetoric 61, 173, 235, 296
rhyme royal 264, 278
Richard II 2, 36, 40, 44, 85–97, 98–111, 121, 123–4, 128–9, 137–8, 156, 169, 171, 184, 186–8, 217, 277, 279, 280–2, 284–5, 287, 289, 305
Riga, Peter [of] 16–17, 68n.30
rime riche 239–53
Roman de la Rose 196, 201–3, 205, 214, 223, 226, 288, 290, 294, 301
Rome 26, 44

St Mary Overey, see Southwark
Saracens
  see Islam
Savage, Sir Arnald 89, 298–9
Scribe D 286–7
Secretum Secretorum 92, 140
de Septvauns, Sir William 299
Seven Sages of Rome, The 83
Seward, John 20
Shakespeare, William 297, 315–25
  I Henry IV 169, 171
  Pericles 315–25
Shirley, John 17
sin 203, 216, 217–29, 270, 300
—, particular sins and vices
  adultery 227, 264–75, 306
  avarice 27, 80, 214, 224–5, 265
  covetousness 126, 217, 224
  cupidity 132–4
  delicacy 225–6
  detraction 222–3
  disobedience 219
  drunkenness 225–6, 266
  envy 214, 217, 222–4
  falssemblant 223
  flattery 138, 164–5
  foldelit 217, 227
  fornication 227
  gluttony 16, 72, 80, 145, 201, 217, 224–5
  hypocrisy 218, 289
  idleness 218
  incest 32, 220, 227, 282
  jealousy 225
  lechery 139, 217, 226–7, 265, 271
  lust 72
  pride 131, 134, 214, 217, 222, 224
  sacrilege 221
  sloth 40–2, 74, 157, 184, 188, 214, 217, 220, 241, 293–4, 300–1
  sodomy 295
  strife 224
  stupre 227

357

supplantation 223
usury 225
wrath 214, 217, 220, 222, 224
Sir Degarré 79
Sir Gawain and the Green Knight 225, 279, 284
Sir Isumbras 78
Sir Orfeo 79
Sir Tristrem 80
Skelton, John 315, 317
society 54–8, 59, 62–3, 92–7, 124, 129, 160, 169, 180–1, 183, 185–8, 191, 193, 291, 298, 300–1
Songe vert, Le 293n.18
Southwark 3, 11–24, 82, 91, 182–3, 279, 307–8, 311–12, 317, 319
Statius 130n.22
Sudbury, Simon, Archbishop of Canterbury 299–300
style 62, 66, 74–84, 98–111, 197, 239–53

Thābit ibn Qurrah al-Harrānī 142
The Good Wife Taught Her Daughter 264–5
theology 15, 69, 140, 170, 183, 198, 228, 292, 320
Thomas of Kent 311
'Toledo Letter', the 52–3

Tragedy of Master Arden of Faversham, The 259–60
translation 1–2, 18–19, 26
Trevisa, John 82
Troy 26, 73, 130, 153, 182, 208, 278, 286

Usk, Adam 107n.12, 110

Valerius Maximus 42–3
de Vere, Robert 108–9, 286
Vincent of Beauvais 33, 173, 283
Virgil 109–10, 304
Virgin Mary 231, 238, 311, 320

Walle, Roger 21–2
Walsingham, Thomas 110, 272–3, 286, 300
Warwick, Earl of (Thomas Beauchamp) 101, 103, 105
Webster, John 315
Wilkins, George 315–16
Winner and Waster 291
women 41, 65, 126–7, 189–92, 199–204, 230–8, 245–51, 265, 268, 271–2, 323–4
Woodville, Elizabeth 151
Wyclif, John 14, 24